Leadership and Management for Nurses

Core Competencies for Quality Care

Third Edition

Anita Finkelman, MSN, RN
Visiting Lecturer, Faculties of the Health Sciences, Nursing Department
Ben-Gurion University of the Negev, Beersheba, Israel

PEARSON

Boston   Columbus   Indianapolis   New York   San Francisco
Amsterdam   Cape Town   Dubai   London   Madrid   Milan   Munich   Paris   Montréal   Toronto
Delhi   Mexico City   São Paulo   Sydney   Hong Kong   Seoul   Singapore   Taipei   Tokyo

Publisher: Julie Levin Alexander
Publisher's Assistant: Sarah Henrich
Executive Editor: Pamela Fuller
Development Editor: Elisabeth Garofalo
Editorial Assistant: Erin Sullivan
Project Manager: Cathy O'Connell
Program Manager: Erin Rafferty
Director, Product Management Services: Etain O'Dea
Team Lead, Program Management: Melissa Bashe
Team Lead, Project Management: Cynthia Zonneveld
Full-Service Project Manager: Kelly Ricci, iEnergizer Aptara®, Ltd.
Manufacturing Buyer: Maura Zaldivar-Garcia
Art Director: Maria Guglielmo
Interior Design: Studio Montage
Cover Design: Beth Paquin
Vice President of Sales & Marketing: David Gesell
Vice President, Director of Marketing: Margaret Waples
Senior Product Marketing Manager: Phoenix Harvey
Field Marketing Manager: Debi Doyle
Marketing Specialist: Michael Sirinides
Marketing Assistant: Amy Pfund
Media Project Manager: Lisa Rinaldi
Composition: iEnergizer Aptara®, Ltd.
Printer/Binder: RR Donnelley/Roanoke
Cover Printer: Phoenix Color/Hagerstown
Cover Image: Firsik/Shutterstock

Credits and acknowledgments borrowed from other sources and reproduced, with permission, in this textbook appear on the appropriate page within text or on page 499.

Notice: Care has been taken to confirm the accuracy of information presented in this book. The authors, editors, and the publisher, however, cannot accept any responsibility for errors or omissions or for consequences from application of the information in this book and make no warranty, express or implied, with respect to its contents.

The authors and publisher have exerted every effort to ensure that drug selections and dosages set forth in this text are in accord with current recommendations and practice at time of publication. However, in view of ongoing research, changes in government regulations, and the constant flow of information relating to drug therapy and drug reactions, the reader is urged to check the package inserts of all drugs for any change in indications of dosage and for added warnings and precautions. This is particularly important when the recommended agent is a new and/or infrequently employed drug.

Library of Congress Cataloging-in-Publication Data
Finkelman, Anita Ward, author.
Leadership and management for nurses : core competencies for quality care / Anita Finkelman.—Third edition.
  p. ; cm.
Includes bibliographical references and index.
ISBN 978-0-13-405698-2
I. Title.
[DNLM: 1. Leadership. 2. Nurse Administrators. 3. Interprofessional Relations. 4. Nursing, Supervisory.
5. Quality of Health Care—standards. WY 105]
RT89
362.17'3068—dc23
2015018620

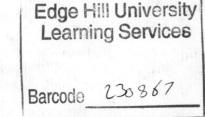

ISBN 13: 978-0-13-405698-2
ISBN 10:   0-13-405698-1

To Fred, Shoshannah, and Deborah, my family.
Nothing happens without their support and guidance.

About the Author

Anita Finkelman, MSN, RN is a visiting lecturer for the Faculties of Health Sciences, Nursing Department, Ben-Gurion University of the Negev in Beersheba, Israel. Recently she was visiting faculty at Northeastern University Bouvé College of Health Sciences School of Nursing for 4 years. She was the chair of the School of Nursing Accreditation Task Force. Her past positions include assistant professor of nursing at University of Oklahoma College of Nursing, where she taught undergraduate and graduate nursing research online and was course coordinator for undergraduate nursing research. She was awarded a VANA Program grant to develop an undergraduate long-term experience at the VA Medical Center in Oklahoma City, developing a summer internship and a postgraduate nurse residency program. At the University of Cincinnati, she was associate professor, clinical nursing, and also director of the Undergraduate Program. She received a BSN from TCU, Fort Worth, Texas, and a master's degree in psychiatric/mental health nursing, clinical nurse specialist, from Yale University, completing postmaster's graduate work in healthcare policy and administration at George Washington University. Additional health policy work was completed as a fellow of the Health Policy Institute, George Mason University. She has forty years of nursing experience, including clinical, educational, and administrative positions, and considerable experience developing distance learning programs, curriculum review and revision, and development of other online products related to simulation learning and distance education for publishers and healthcare organizations. Anita Finkelman served as director of staff education for two acute care hospitals and director of a large continuing education program at the University of Cincinnati. Consulting projects have focused on distance education, curriculum, teaching practices, nursing education accreditation, healthcare interprofessional education, health policy, and healthcare administration. She has authored many books, chapters, and journal articles; served on editorial boards; and currently is on the editorial board for *Home Health Care Nurse*. She has lectured on administration, healthcare education, health policy, continuing education, and psychiatric/mental health nursing, both nationally and internationally, particularly in Israel for Ben Gurion University of the Negev, where she served as guest faculty. In addition to this text, her other recent books are *Professional Nursing Concepts* (3rd ed.) (2016) from Jones & Bartlett Learning, *Teaching IOM: The Implications of the Institute of Medicine Reports for Nursing Education* (Vol. I and II) (3rd ed.) (2012) from American Nurses Association, and *Case Management for Nurses* (2011) from Pearson Education. The IOM book and the *Professional Concepts* book have won publishing awards. She has presented workshops across the country and internationally for nurse educators and staff educators focused on her IOM book and presented at major healthcare conferences, such as the American Association of Colleges of Nursing BSN annual meeting and the Deans' annual meeting as an invited speaker.

Reviewers

Carla Boyd, MSN, RNP
Nursing Faculty
Northwest Arkansas Community
College
Bentonville, Arkansas

Mary Jo Clark, PhD, RN, PHN
Professor
University of San Diego
San Diego, California

**Candi Constantine-Castillo, MBA,
MSN, FACHE, CEN, CPHQ, CPHRM,
CENP, NEA-BC, CSHA, HACP**
Clinical Faculty
Nursing University of Texas at Arlington
Arlington, Texas

**Jennifer L. Embree, DNP, RN,
NE-BC, CCNS**
Clinical Nurse Specialist
MSN Nursing Leadership & Health
Systems Track Coordinator
Clinical Assistant Professor
Department of Community and Health
Systems (CHS) Systems Track
Coordinator
Indiana University
Indianapolis, Indiana

Marcelline Harris, PhD, RN
Associate Professor
University of Michigan
Ann Arbor, Michigan

**Faith L. Johnson, BA, BSN, MA,
RN, CNE**
Faculty
Ridgewater College
Willmar, Minnesota

Mona P. Klose, MS, RN, CPHQ
Director of Quality Management
Assistant Professor of Nursing
University of Jamestown
Jamestown, North Dakota

Lisa Thuerauf, RN, MSN
Assistant Professor of Nursing
Upper Iowa University
Fayette, Iowa

Foreword

One might ask if there is a necessity for a book that discusses leadership and management for nurses as opposed to leadership and management for any other discipline. Anita Finkelman, in this important text, proves that such a book is essential. She has organized a powerful narrative that evolves from a conceptual base for leadership, reviewing theories and styles of the same, then leads us through the key elements of decision making, change in organizations, and the essentials of effective care delivery; then she lays out the core competencies that are absolutely necessary to be an effective leader in today's complex healthcare environment. She provides a powerful narrative of the essentials related to patient centeredness, which will be increasingly important as we move even further into the world of the accountable care organizations within the context of the Affordable Care Act. Core competencies are described and roles and responsibilities are provided in a way that gives essential guidance to any nurse leading effective teams, motivating staff, working on collaborative projects, and communicating complex content on an hour-to-hour basis. This text will be an important addition to any bookshelf for nurse leaders who are committed to better health and better health care for their patients.

Terry Fulmer, PhD, RN, FAAN
President, John A. Hartford Foundation
New York, NY

Preface

Health care is undergoing major changes, and the nursing profession should assume a major role in healthcare delivery. An important reason for these changes is the Institute of Medicine (IOM) initiatives to examine and recommend solutions focused on improving care.

The Institute of Medicine (IOM), established in 1970 and located in Washington, D.C., is an independent, nonprofit organization (Institute of Medicine, 2014). In April 2015 the IOM annual membership meeting voted to change the name of the IOM to the National Academy of Medicine (NAM). NAM has also just announced the launch of its new website, which provides information about elected members, initiatives, awards, and other NAM activities and access to its reports. Throughout this text, the National Academy of Medicine will be used, and all referenced material prior to this name change will appear from the Institute of Medicine. Many of the IOM reports are discussed throughout this text as they offer significant contributions to knowledge about health and healthcare delivery.

This third edition uses the IOM quality initiative as its framework, particularly the IOM five core competencies for healthcare professions. Nurse leaders and managers need to meet the competencies of:

- Provide patient-centered care.
- Work in interdisciplinary/interprofessional teams.
- Employ evidence-based practice.
- Apply quality improvement.
- Utilize informatics.

There is a great need to improve care in all types of healthcare settings, and this should be an integral part of nursing leadership and management as well as practice.

Leadership and management are content areas included in all nursing programs for undergraduate and graduate programs. There is a great need to develop nurses who are knowledgeable about these topics and able to apply the knowledge to their practice wherever it might be. This text provides opportunities for students to examine critical issues in healthcare delivery today. Typically nurses do not serve in management positions until they have some clinical experience; however, every nurse serves as a leader in practice as they provide and coordinate patient care, communicate and collaborate with staff and the interprofessional team, and solve problems and make decisions to ensure that patients receive quality, safe care. Nurses are involved in healthcare delivery processes on an organizational level such as serving on committees, task forces, and other teams that plan and make decisions for the healthcare organization as a whole. They also serve in leadership positions in professional nursing organizations. Every nurse who strives to provide quality, safe care; advocates for patients and their families; and endeavors to be recognized as a critical member of the healthcare team needs to demonstrate leadership.

See What's New in This Edition!

- **New Chapter:** *Public/Community Health: Expansion and Need for Leadership* provides content on nursing leadership in public/community health, Institute of Medicine public health reports, government initiatives, *Healthy People* and *Healthy Communities*, population health, core functions and services, disaster preparedness, and the National Health Security Strategy.
- **New Chapter:** *Staff Education to Meet Healthcare Professions Core Competencies and Improve Care* provides content about the organization and operations for staff education service within a healthcare organization, the American Nurses Association Standards: *Nursing Professional Development: Scope and Standards of Practice*, nurse residency programs, interprofessional education, and development of nurse managers.

- More emphasis on the Affordable Care Act and its impact on nursing practice, nursing leadership, and quality improvement.
- Greater focus on *The Future of Nursing: Leading Change, Advancing Health* report and earlier Institute of Medicine report on nursing and the implications for nursing leadership.
- Expansion of content on quality improvement such as quality improvement initiatives, measurement, and health informatics.
- Expansion of end-of-chapter student features: Applying Leadership and Management
  - BSN and Master's Essentials: Application to Content
  - Applying American Organization of Nurse Executive (AONE) Competencies
  - Engaging in the Content: Critical Thinking and Clinical Reasoning and Judgment with expansion of discussion questions and application exercises options identified for courses that are offered online

Organization of This Textbook

This textbook is divided into two sections that focus on leadership and management concepts and on the IOM core competencies for healthcare professions. All of the content is based on the need for leadership and improvement of care.

SECTION I: BASIC LEADERSHIP AND MANAGEMENT CONCEPTS Section I of this textbook lays the foundation for effective leadership and management. These concepts are the theoretical base, including change, leaders and managers, and competencies; healthcare policy; legal issues and ethics; change and decision making; organizational structure and effective care delivery; healthcare economics; and staff recruitment and retention. Organization and management within acute care healthcare organizations and within public/community health organizations are discussed as settings requiring effective nurse leadership and management. This content sets the stage for the second section, which focuses on critical healthcare professions core competencies.

SECTION II: HEALTHCARE PROFESSIONS CORE COMPETENCIES This section focuses on the Institute of Medicine core competencies for healthcare professions. The competencies are as follows:

- Provide patient-centered care.
- Work in interprofessional teams.
- Employ evidence-based practice.
- Apply quality improvement.
- Utilize informatics.

The 12 chapters in this section emphasize these core competencies and include content related to managing patient-centered care, consumers, diversity and disparities, building interprofessional teams, improving teamwork through collaboration, coordination, and conflict resolution, effective communication, evidence-based practice and management, and healthcare informatics. Two chapters focus on healthcare quality and policy issues with the second chapter examining implementation of quality improvement. The last chapter addresses staff education, a critical need in all healthcare organizations to assist in maintaining staff competencies and improvement of care. These core competencies relate to practice in all settings, but they also are important aspects of effective leadership and management.

Textbook Features

The textbook features provide students with additional methods to explore and apply leadership and management content.

Learning Outcomes—Directs your reading and approach to each chapter.

Key Terms—Identifies the terms that are important in the content.

What's Ahead—Introduces the chapter's content.

Applying Evidence-Based Practice: Evidence for Effective Leadership and Management—Found within each chapter is an example of evidence that focuses on leadership and management. This includes a summary of a published article or report, a citation, and questions to consider. You may want to locate the article or report and read it. Evidence-based practice and evidence-based management are very important in health care today.

Case Study—Within the chapter content is a case, which provides a brief scenario and questions.

Applying Leadership and Management—This feature is found at the end of each chapter and allows you to examine and apply the content by using the following methods:

BSN and Master's Essentials: Application to Content—Essentials from the American Association of Colleges of Nursing *BSN Essentials* and *Master's Essentials* are identified per chapter content.

My Hospital Unit: An Evolving Case Experience—Before you begin this book and related course, you need to take the first step to engage yourself in this topic. You need to create your own virtual clinical unit. What type of unit would you create as a nurse manager? Within this unit, you will reflect on content in each chapter as you build your knowledge of leadership and management in nursing and apply that knowledge as you apply the five core competencies for healthcare professions. You will be the nurse manager on the unit. Once you create the framework for your unit, you cannot make changes in the information that describes your unit unless you are doing so in response to a specific learning activity. You have to work within this description just as you would if you were nurse manager on a real unit.

How do you create your own virtual unit? First, you need to put your description in writing. Respond to the following questions as you describe your unit. Keep a record of the description and your responses per chapter as you manage your unit.

- Name your unit.
- What services are provided in the unit? It can be acute care or ambulatory care, for example, medical (may be subspecialty such as respiratory), surgical (may be a subspecialty such as orthopedics), OR, ER, ICU, obstetrics, pediatrics, behavioral health, and so on.
- What is the size of the unit (number of beds)? What is the size of the hospital (fewer than 100, 100–200, 200–300, more than 300 beds)?
- Is it an urban or rural hospital? Academic-teaching hospital, private, or government owned?
- How long have you been the nurse manager?
- What types of shifts do you have currently on the unit (8-, 10-, or 12-hour shifts; mix)?
- What hours/days do you typically work?
- Briefly describe at least four registered nurses (RNs) and four unlicensed assistive personnel (UAP). Decide if you have licensed practical/vocational nurses (LPN/LVN); if so, describe several. In the description, give first names, descriptions of their personalities, and current performance.
- You have a unit secretary. Name the unit secretary, and briefly describe personality and current performance.
- You have nursing and medical students on your unit.
- Create a floor plan for your unit. Indicate if rooms are single or double and location of work areas.

You are now ready to get into textbook content. At the end of each chapter, you will be asked to go to your unit and engage in interactive questions related to changes or problems that may be occurring in your unit or in your hospital. This learning activity will help you apply the content and examine issues as if you were a nurse manager.

Applying American Organization of Nurse Executives (AONE) Competencies—You are asked to consider which AONE competencies apply to chapter content. The competencies are found in Appendix A.

Engaging in the Content: Critical Thinking and Clinical Reasoning and Judgment—Provides discussion questions and application exercises. Options that may be used in an online course are identified.

References—Lists the chapter references.

Appendixes—Appendix A describes the American Organization of Nurse Executives (AONE) competencies. Appendix B provides an overview information about the Affordable Care Act of 2010.

Acknowledgments

Projects such as this one take time and certainly require support. My family deserves much of the credit for putting up with my endless writing projects. Elizabeth Karle assisted me with the first edition, helping to set a standard for this text. Lisa Gaw assisted with new graphics for the second edition. Elisabeth Garofalo has served as my incredible developmental editor for this text. She is a pleasure to work with, and her expertise has added to this text. Pam Fuller, Executive Editor at Pearson, has provided oversight and guidance throughout this project and many others. I thank all of these great experts for their assistance. My students and the faculty and staff I have worked with always provide me with issues to think about and to consider in a project such as this one.

Contents

Dedication   v

About the Author   vi

Reviewers   vii

Foreword   viii

Preface   ix

Acknowledgments   xii

SECTION I
Basic Leadership and Management Concepts   1

CHAPTER 1
Conceptual Base for Leadership and Management   2

The Institute of Medicine Report: *The Future of Nursing: Leading Change, Advancing Health*   4

Change in the Healthcare Delivery System: Implications for Nursing Leadership   6

Leadership and Management Theories and Styles   7

Leaders and Managers: A Comparison   15

Preparation and Development of Nurse Leaders and Managers   18

Nursing Professional Organizations' View of Nurse Leaders and Managers   20

The Image of Nursing and the Presence of Nursing Leadership   21

Making a Difference: Increasing Nurse Leaders   22

CHAPTER 2
Healthcare Policy, Legal Issues, and Ethics in Healthcare Delivery   28

Healthcare Policy   29

Patient Protection and Affordable Care Act of 2010 (ACA): Major Legislation   42

Legal Issues and Nursing Ethics: Impact on Decision Making in Management and Practice   46

Ethics: Impact on Decision Making in Management and Practice   52

CHAPTER 3
Operational and Strategic Planning: Change, Innovation, and Decision Making   65

Leading During Change and Change Management   66

The Five "Rs": Change and Decision Making in Action   66

The Concept of Change   70

A Decision: A Response to Change   79

Planning: Strategic, Operational, and Project   91

CHAPTER 4
Organizational Structure for Effective Care Delivery   95

Organizational Theories: Emphasis on Structure and Process   96

Healthcare Organizations   101

Professional Nursing Practice Within Nursing Care Models   110

CHAPTER 5
Healthcare Economics   119

Healthcare Financial Issues: Macrolevel   120

Government Health Benefit Programs   129

Insurer Reimbursement and Service Strategies to Control Cost and Quality   140

Reimbursement Issues: Impact on Nurses and Nursing Care   144

Healthcare Financial Issues: Microlevel   145

CHAPTER 6
Acute Care Organizations: An Example of a Healthcare Organization   155

Development of U.S. Hospitals   156

Framework for Effective Care   163

Acute Healthcare Delivery: Examples of Changes   172

Moving Forward to Leadership in Acute Care: Guidance from the Nurse Manager Engagement Project   177

A Conclusion and the Future   180

CHAPTER 7
Public/Community Health: Expansion and Need for Leadership   184

Institute of Medicine: *The Future of the Public's Health in the 21st Century*   185

Government Initiatives Supporting Community-Based Care: Federal, State, and Local   187

Population Health Versus Medical Model   190

Health Promotion and Prevention   191

Public/Community Health Services   193

Disaster Preparedness   195

Global Health Care: Critical Concerns Today   198

Nursing Leadership in the Community   199

CHAPTER 8
Recruitment and Retention: Meeting Staffing
   Requirements   206
Human Resources   207
Recruitment   212
Retention: Why Is It Important?   220
Performance Appraisal   223
Stress on the Job   229
Staffing and Variable Shortage: Critical Issues   232

SECTION II
Healthcare Professions Core
   Competencies   243

CHAPTER 9
Managing Patient-Centered Care   244
The Core Competency: Patient-Centered Care   245
Chronic Illness: A Key Healthcare Concern   249
Examples of Tools to Manage Patient-Centered
   Care   251
Current Approaches to Patient-Centered Care   262

CHAPTER 10
Diversity and Disparities in Health
   Care   267
Healthcare Diversity and Disparities   267
A Diverse Patient Population   270
Healthcare Literacy   272
Culture and Climate: Building Organizational Cultural
   Competency   274
Workforce Diversity   277
Strategies Facilitating Cultural Diversity in Healthcare
   Organizations   280

CHAPTER 11
Consumers and Nurses   287
The Consumer and Health Care   288
Public Policy and the Healthcare Consumer   289
Special Reports and Initiatives: Implications for Healthcare
   Consumers   291
Information Resources and the Consumer   292
Patient Satisfaction and Quality   293
The Nurse as Patient Advocate   295

CHAPTER 12
Developing Interprofessional and
   Intraprofessional Teams   298
Teams in Today's Healthcare Environment   299
The Team Leader   301
Team Structure and Process   304
Effective Teams   305
The Charge Nurse or Shift Manager and the
   Team   310
TeamSTEPPS®: An Organized Approach to
   Teams   312

CHAPTER 13
Improving Teamwork: Collaboration,
   Coordination, and Conflict Resolution   317
Collaboration   317
Coordination   320
Negotiation and Conflict Resolution   323

CHAPTER 14
Effective Staff Communication and Working
   Relationships   337
Communication: What Is It?   338
The Communication Process   340
Assessment of Communication Effectiveness   343
Communication Methods   348
Resolving Communication Problems and Improving
   Communication   353

CHAPTER 15
Delegation for Effective Outcomes   357
Delegation: What Is It?   357
Legal Issues Related to Delegation   358
The Delegation Process and the NCSBN Guidelines   364
Effective Delegation   365

CHAPTER 16
Evidence-Based Practice and Management   372
Research   372
Evidence-Based Practice   376
Evidence-Based Management   384
Research, Evidence-Based Practice, and Quality
   Improvement   387

CHAPTER 17
Healthcare Quality: A Critical Health Policy
   Issue   390
The Influence of the Institute of Medicine Healthcare Quality
   Reports   391
The Current Status on the Changing View of Quality   401
Examples of Other Indicators of Increased Interest in
   Healthcare Quality   402
Quality Improvement: A Growing Complex Process   407
The National Quality Strategy   412

CHAPTER 18
Implementing Healthcare Quality
   Improvement   419
Science of Improvement   420
Critical Healthcare Quality Issues   421
Workplace Safety   424
Quality Care: Measurement and Improvement   424
The Accreditation Process   434
Examples of Nursing Quality Initiatives   437
Collaborative Initiatives: A Great Need   438
Program Evaluation   439
Nursing Leadership in Continuous Quality Improvement   440

CHAPTER 19
Healthcare Informatics and Technology   447
Importance of Information and Clinical Technology   447
Informatics and Medical Technology: Implications on
    Healthcare Delivery   454
Improvement in Health Informatics   463

CHAPTER 20
Staff Education to Meet Health Professions Core
    Competencies and Improve Care   467
Importance of Staff Preparation and Quality Care   467
Description of Staff Development   468
The Staff Education Process: Development, Implementation,
    and Evaluation of Staff Education Learning Activities   474
Orientation   478
Continuing Education   479

Interprofessional Education   480
Nurse Residency Programs   482

APPENDIX A
Nurse Executive Competencies   487
I. Communication and Relationship-Building   487
II. Knowledge of the Health Care Environment   488
III. Leadership   490
IV. Professionalism   490
V. Business Skills   491

APPENDIX B
Health Care Reform Legislation 2010   493

PHOTO CREDITS   499

INDEX   500

SECTION I

BASIC LEADERSHIP AND MANAGEMENT CONCEPTS

Section I of this textbook lays the foundation for effective leadership and management. These concepts are the conceptual base including change, leaders and managers, and competencies; healthcare policy, legal issues and ethics; change and decision making; organizational structure and effective care delivery; healthcare economics; and staff recruitment and retention. Organization and management within acute care healthcare organizations and within public/community healthcare organizations are discussed as settings requiring effective nurse leadership and management. This content sets the stage for the second section, which focuses on critical core competencies for healthcare professions.

1

Conceptual Base for Leadership and Management

KEY TERMS

- accountability
- autocratic
- bureaucratic
- empowerment
- influence
- leadership
- management
- management functions
- mission statement
- Peter Principle
- power
- transformational leadership
- values
- vision

⬤ LEARNING OUTCOMES

Before you begin, take a moment to familiarize yourself with the learning outcomes for this chapter.

> Examine *The Future of Nursing* report and its relevance to nursing leadership.
> Interpret the implications of change in the healthcare delivery system on nurse leadership.
> Analyze the key modern leadership theories compared to older theories and implications for nursing leadership and management.
> Explain the importance of transformational leadership today and the relationship to the Institute of Medicine recommendations.
> Compare and contrast characteristics, roles, and responsibilities of leaders and managers.
> Compare and contrast the leadership and management competencies described by AONE, ANA, and AACN.
> Discuss the implications of the image of nurses on the nursing profession.
> Analyze the need for more nursing leaders.

WHAT'S AHEAD

In the changing healthcare environment, nursing needs effective leaders who can understand change and take on opportunities as they arise. Nurses need to recognize that every nurse needs to be a leader—even nurses providing direct care. Sternweiler (1998) presents some interesting ideas that can be applied to success in today's healthcare environment. Her motto is "be a willow tree." This unusual motto has relevance to many situations in which nurses find themselves today. Sternweiler's comments focus on clinical nurse specialists, but they also apply to all nurses in the current changing healthcare environment. The first point she makes is that willow trees have many branches, and many branches are required to extend into all the different areas in which nurses practice and serve as leaders and managers today. As nurses begin to consider where they want to begin their practice, they are soon confronted with many wonderful choices. Several of these opportunities are clearly defined, while others are not, and some have yet to be created. Willow trees also bend gracefully in the wind. This is an effective image of what nurses must do during change, which is a critical element of effective leadership. Flexibility leads to more success than rigidity; the branch that refuses to bend often breaks. Willow trees have wide-reaching but shallow root systems. It is much more painful to uproot deep, entrenched roots than it is to deal with an intricate but shallow root system. Again, flexibility is the key to success during such a period. Each day brings a new piece of information, a new perspective, a new change, and a new challenge. All this requires nurses who are able to move thoughtfully with the changes, recognizing them as opportunities. This image of nursing demonstrates that it is an exciting and ever-changing career. Nurse leaders, both formal and informal, need to set the stage for a positive approach to change and act as role models for staff; however, all nurses need to participate in making changes that improve care and the practice of nursing. Some of the key issues facing nurses are the following:

- The need to work together as a team, in both nursing teams and interprofessional teams, which is challenging due to differences in age, cultures, and other aspects, though these factors enrich the workforce
- Healthcare environments in which blame and punishment are practiced, even as those practices are disavowed on the surface, increasing the need to develop workplaces that commit to a culture of safety (Institute of Medicine, 1999)
- Increased pressure for results and less tolerance for mistakes; burnout, anger, and other negative emotions still have a stronghold in many healthcare settings
- Need for greater creativity and innovation, collaboration, and learning, coupled with requirements for managers to do more with less
- Increased occupational stress and violence in the workplace
- Need to develop effective methods for effective recruitment, retention, and staff engagement
- Need for greater nursing leadership at all levels within healthcare organizations (HCOs) and within the healthcare system and healthcare policy

As leadership and management are explored in this chapter and throughout the text, many perspectives are presented. Professional nurses need to open themselves up to a variety of ideas to arrive at a perspective of health care that enhances care delivery and the practice of nursing. This chapter discusses a variety of leadership and management theories and styles, nurse leadership, effectiveness, and managers. As nurses move through their careers, some nurses will always provide direct care, while still needing to demonstrate leadership. Some will decide to move into management positions or other professional roles within the HCO environment, requiring effective leadership competencies, while others may move back and forth between direct care and management positions. Being a nurse today requires leadership. "The term 'dispersed leader' has been described as the leadership of the future. This holds that there is not *a* leader, but that there are *many* leaders dispersing the responsibilities of leadership across the organization. Gone are the up/down, top/bottom, superior/subordinate relationships. We must be developing leaders at every level" (Shaw, 2007, p. 26). Shaw notes that the following are important aspects of nursing leadership that are current today. These aspects of leadership are emphasized in this chapter and across the textbook:

- Nurse leaders must have an understanding of the broader health and social system within which nursing functions.
- Nurse leaders must have good external awareness.
- Nurse leaders must be able to use the benefits of technology.
- Nurse leaders must have the ability to contribute to and help influence health and public policy.
- Nurse leaders must be able to motivate and encourage others to take positive action.
- Nurse leaders and nursing must be well informed and strategic in their thinking and action.
- Nurse leaders must be able to work with others to achieve common goals.
- Nurse leaders must be able to assess and develop new opportunities for nursing.
- Nurse leaders must be able to adapt and develop new roles and new skills as health systems change (2007, pp. 13–18).

The Affordable Care Act (ACA) passed in 2010 is having an impact on the nursing profession and provides new opportunities for nursing. There is greater emphasis on teams, quality, efficiency, care coordination, and evidence-based practice (EBP). Leadership is needed to lay the groundwork, support changes, provide guidance to staff, and engage staff in the improvement processes at all levels of the healthcare delivery system, working actively with other healthcare professionals. With this changing healthcare environment and the immediate need to improve care and the healthcare delivery system, there is greater need for education and preparation of nursing leaders and particularly unit-level managers. This chapter discusses management and leadership, as does the entire textbook. There is some discussion focused on distinguishing between management and leadership, but in reality there is need for managers who are leaders and leaders need to demonstrate management competencies.

THE INSTITUTE OF MEDICINE REPORT: *THE FUTURE OF NURSING: LEADING CHANGE, ADVANCING HEALTH*

The Institute of Medicine (IOM), established in 1970 and located in Washington, DC, is an independent, nonprofit organization (Institute of Medicine, 2014). In April 2015 the IOM annual membership meeting voted to change the organization's name to National Academies of Science, Engineering, and Medicine (NASEM) of the National Academy of Medicine (NAM). Throughout this text, the National Academy of Medicine will be used, and all referenced material prior to this name change will appear from the Institute of Medicine. The NAM is not a government agency, but it does provide external authoritative advice to policy makers and the public. The NAM cannot make laws, but it can influence others through its thorough review of problems and issues, which is done by selected expert panels, and published reports about this work that help others make informed decisions. The NAM website provides extensive information for healthcare professionals, policy makers, and consumers. Its reports are free through its website. Many of the IOM/NAM reports are discussed throughout this text as they offer significant contributions to knowledge about health and healthcare delivery.

In addition to the extensive work done by the NAM examining problems, it is also an honorific organization that selects more than 70 leaders to join its ranks each year. This membership provides the volunteer hours needed to complete the major work of the NAM. Nurse leaders are also members; for example, in 2013 four nurses were asked to join. Although nurses have been included in the NAM membership, there is need for more invitations for nurses to join the NAM. From 2005 to 2010, none of the nurse members served as chair or cochair for an IOM report. In a study that examined nurse participation in the IOM, the results indicated that as of 2011, 75% of nurse members did not participate in any type of IOM report, indicating a need to increase not only nurse membership but also active membership (Grey, Holzemer, & Larson, 2012). An NAM nurse member who has contributed to IOM initiatives over several years wrote the foreword for this text. NAM nurse members are leaders in nursing education, practice, and administration. Nurses often think of nursing leadership as something that happens in nursing professional organizations or in HCOs, for example, serving as the chief nurse executive or as nurse managers; however, there is great need to increase nursing leadership in all organizations and groups that may have an impact on health and healthcare delivery, such as the NAM.

In 2011 the Institute of Medicine published a report focused on nursing, *The Future of Nursing: Leading Change, Advancing Health*. This is a highly significant report, but before discussing its relevance and content, it is important to step back to 2004 and the publication of *Keeping Patients Safe: Transforming the Work Environment of Nurses* (Institute of Medicine, 2004). This report did not get the same level of attention that the 2011 report received, yet it was not a minor report. The report indicated that nurses have the potential to have significant roles in improving health care; however, they have not assumed leadership as they should and in many cases are not prepared to do so due to lack of leadership competency and lack of knowledge about quality improvement (QI). The report examined nurses' work environment and how the environment impacts QI. Content covers work environment design from the perspective of physical layout and evaluation of workspace; nursing shortage, which in early 2000 was rising; healthcare errors and the blame culture; patient safety risk factors and the nurse's role in prevention of errors and improving the quality of care; and work environment threats to quality care. The report identified the following healthcare delivery concerns and discussed implications for nurses and health care:

- Monitoring of patient status or surveillance
- Physiologic therapy
- Helping patients compensate for loss of function
- Emotional support
- Education for patients and families
- Integration and coordination of care (2004, pp. 91–100)

Even though this list is from a 2004 report, all of these concerns continue to be relevant today. At the time the report was completed, the IOM had published its initial major QI reports that began a long process and many more reports focused on QI (Institute of Medicine, 1999; 2001). The IOM identified the five healthcare profession core competencies that should be applied to all healthcare professions (Institute of Medicine, 2003a) and are used as a framework for this text. These competencies were also used as the basis for the development of the Quality and Safety Education for Nurses Institute (QSEN) and its core competencies for nurses (2014). The IOM 2004 report uses a different approach than its 2011 report. The first report focuses on nurses practicing acute care, primarily staff nurses who are the front line of defense against errors and act to improve care. The 2011 report does not focus so much on acute care but rather looks to the future, noting that nurses will move out of acute care. Although it is clear that nurses will always be needed in acute care, the report does not focus on this. The recommendations from the 2004 IOM report include:

- Adopt transformational leadership and evidence-based management.
- Maximize the capability of the workforce.
- Understand the work processes so they can be improved.
- Create and sustain cultures of safety.

All of these recommendations are discussed in this text, and the work to meet these recommendations is not yet completed. Leadership at all levels of nursing and in all segments of the profession (education, practice, and research) is required to accomplish these recommendations.

The Future of Nursing report focuses on expanding nurses' roles in a redesigned healthcare system. As noted by the IOM (2001), the healthcare system has been described as dysfunctional. This text provides examples of this dysfunction, but one could just go back and look at the nation's initial response in 2014 to Ebola cases in the United States: lack of a national plan that is implemented at national, state, and local levels; miscommunication; healthcare professionals not providing appropriate care; poor healthcare team communication; lack of clear patient education and guidance regarding isolation and so on; and lack of consistent policies and procedures. All of these factors led to a system that is not functioning well. The content in this text is designed to provide nurses with more knowledge about the healthcare system and particularly the need to improve it. Recommendations from the 2011 report, *The Future of Nursing*, include the following (2011, pp. S-8–S-12):

1. Remove scope-of-practice barriers. (Discussed further in Chapters 6 and 7.)
2. Expand opportunities for nurses to lead and diffuse collaborative improvement efforts. (Discussed further in Chapters 13, 17, and 18.)
3. Implement nurse residency programs. (Discussed further in Chapter 20.)
4. Increase the proportion of nurses with baccalaureate degrees to 80% by 2020. (Discussed further in Chapter 8.)
5. Double the number of nurses with doctorates by 2020. (Discussed further in Chapter 20.)
6. Ensure that nurses engage in lifelong learning. (Discussed further in Chapter 20.)
7. Prepare and enable nurses to lead change to advance health. (Discussed further in Chapter 3.)
8. Build an infrastructure for the collection and analysis of interprofessional healthcare workforce data. (Discussed further in Chapter 8.)

In comparing these eight recommendations with the concerns of the 2004 IOM report on nursing, it is easy to see that the later 2011 report focuses more education and advanced practice with concerns about scope of practice.

The Future of Nursing report identifies areas for nursing research priorities that are related to its recommendations: (1) Transforming Nursing Practice: Scope of Practice, Residencies, Teamwork, Technology, Value; (2) Transforming Nursing Education; and (3) Transforming Nursing Leadership. The third priority is relevant to this chapter. Research priorities noted in the report to transform nursing leadership require the following. (Comments related to this chapter and the text are provided in italics below.)

- Identification of personal and professional characteristics most critical to leadership of HCOs such as accountable care organizations/healthcare homes/medical homes/clinics. *As discussed in this chapter, leadership characteristics are important. The report seems to call out specific types of HCOs but includes few comments about the acute-care system and nurses. The focus of the report is mostly directed at primary care, when the U.S. healthcare system provides services in multiple types of settings—acute care, primary care, long-term care, home care—and the quality of care in the system is weak. Nursing leadership is required in all of these settings, not just in non-acute care such as primary care.*

- Identification of the skills and knowledge most critical to leaders of HCOs such as accountable care organizations/healthcare homes/medical homes/clinics. *The same comments about the previous priority can be made here. This text, such as in this chapter and in Chapter 20, includes content on this issue.*
- Identification of the personal and professional characteristics most important to leaders of QI initiatives in hospitals and other settings. *This is a critical need as was also noted in the 2004 IOM report, and is discussed in many chapters in this text, including Chapters 17 and 18. Much more needs to be done to increase QI content and learning experiences in undergraduate and graduate nursing programs as well as in staff education.*
- Identification of mentors that have been (or could be) most successful in recruiting and training diverse nurses and nurse faculty. *This is important but the ability of a good mentoring program to retain staff should not be overlooked. Turnover of new graduates is high as discussed in Chapter 8, and there is great need to implement effective strategies to engage new graduates and retain them.*
- Identification of the influence of nursing on important healthcare decisions at all levels. *Nurses need to be active in healthcare delivery at all levels, including health policy, as discussed in Chapter 2 as well as other chapters.*
- Identification of the unique contributions nurses make in healthcare committees or boards. *This is a role that is not commonly considered, but it is important for nurses to have an impact on the healthcare delivery system. We expect nurses to lead in both public/community HCOs and in acute care HCOs as noted in Chapters 6 and 7* (Institute of Medicine, 2011, p. 7-6).

In response to *The Future Report,* the Robert Wood Johnson Foundation (RWJF) and the American Association of Retired Persons (AARP) partnered to establish *The Future of Nursing: Campaign for Action.* The Center to Champion Nursing in America analyzes established data sets to evaluate the status of the work that has been done to meet the IOM 2011 report's recommendations to transform health care for the 21st century. The center also publishes updates on its website. This collaboration includes more than 80 health care, nursing, business, and consumer organizations, as described on its website. The collaboration's vision is: "Everyone in America can live a healthier life, supported by a system in which nurses are essential partners in providing care and promoting health" (Center to Champion Nursing in America, 2014). The result should be seamless, accessible, quality care for every American. The ACA of 2010 is part of the strategy to achieve this goal.

CHANGE IN THE HEALTHCARE DELIVERY SYSTEM: IMPLICATIONS FOR NURSING LEADERSHIP

As new nurses enter the healthcare system, they find an environment that seems to be constantly changing. It is easy to become frustrated with this because it is much easier to work when change is limited; one knows what to expect and when. However, the reality is HCOs and the nurses who work in them must adapt and cope with changes, and nurses need to be active participants in the change process. What is meant by these changes that seem so important? Consider the examples of changes found in Box 1-1. Most students, however, have observed many of these changes before they graduate.

This text includes content about these topics, as they are important in understanding the nurse's role, as well as leadership and management. Chapter 3 specifically focuses on change and decision making. Porter-O'Grady, a nursing leader, closes his discussion on healthcare change by suggesting that, "Without engaging and embracing the issues around a new emerging foundation for nursing practice in the 21st century, it is quite possible that nurses will fail to find a meaningful place in the 21st century health service" (Porter-O'Grady, 2001, p. 186). This could be interpreted as a pessimistic viewpoint, but it can also be seen as a challenge to all nurses to lead. These challenges continue to be emphasized, such as in the IOM/NAM reports. To be

BOX 1-1	A RAPIDLY CHANGING HEALTHCARE ENVIRONMENT

- New medical knowledge and technology
- Greater use of information technology
- Complex reimbursement system
- Greater use of a variety of settings where care is provided outside of acute care hospitals
- Increase in the uninsured and underinsured
- Greater diversity in patients and healthcare workforce
- Need to increase use of evidence-based practice
- Role changes in many healthcare providers and implications for nursing roles and functions
- Use of advanced practice nurses, clinical nurse specialists, clinical nurse leaders, physician assistants, and hospitalists/intensivists
- Need for greater collaboration and interprofessional education and practice to prepare nurses and other healthcare professionals to work on interprofessional teams
- Greater importance of the consumer, the patient, and the patient's family—patient-centered care
- Lack of healthcare policy or limited policy development in many areas, such as mental health, the uninsured, prescriptions for the elderly, chronic illness, and changing population demographics
- Emphasis on the National Academy of Medicine reports on healthcare quality and need for significant improvement
- Passage of the Accountable Care Act of 2010 and all its implications

successful in today's healthcare delivery system, a leader needs to actively pursue collaboration with peers and other healthcare professionals as well as reach outside of health care (for example, to consumers, local businesses, and local governmental agencies). Collaboration, as described by the American Nurses Association (ANA), requires understanding of the importance of expertise from within the profession and from other healthcare professionals (2010a). This is the common view of the collaborative relationship, requiring nurses to work across professional boundaries, which has been difficult for some nurses. They need to function with physicians, social workers, pharmacists, physical therapists, admission staff, and many more. The meaning of collaboration implies the ability to be flexible, listen to and include others, share information and ideas, work toward the best solution to a problem, and most of all to be comfortable in the collaborative environment. Nurses encounter many opportunities to collaborate every day. As leadership and management theories and styles are discussed and applied in this chapter's content, it is important to remember that collaboration is a key characteristic of effective leaders and managers. Teamwork and collaboration are discussed later in this text. Interprofessional teamwork and related collaboration are part of the NAM healthcare professions core competencies, and today there is even greater emphasis on teamwork. A nurse leader or nurse manager will not be effective today and in the future if he or she does not have the competencies needed to work with others collaboratively, to reach out to others—even in other healthcare professions—to communicate and engage others, and to recognize that effective work and quality care will not be reached without teamwork. Nurses have long worked together in teams, though not always effectively, and some have reached across to other healthcare professions, but now it is necessary. Collaboration, coordination, and conflict management are discussed in more detail in Chapter 13.

LEADERSHIP AND MANAGEMENT THEORIES AND STYLES

This section discusses modern **leadership** and **management** theories and styles, which affect healthcare leaders and nurse leaders who work in all types of healthcare settings. One should not get the impression that only those who hold the highest nursing management position or other high management positions in HCOs such as nurse executives are necessarily nurse leaders. Nurse leaders do not even have to be in formal "management positions" with management titles. There are many more nurses who are in lower-level management positions (for example, nurse managers, charge nurses, team leaders, and others), and if they demonstrate leadership competencies, they are considered formal nurse leaders. Both formal and informal nurse leaders are important to the profession and to healthcare delivery. In the end, leadership competencies are something that

BOX 1-2	REVIEW OF THE STAGES OF LEADERSHIP THEORY DEVELOPMENT

STAGE I *LEADER TRAITS*

Emphasized up to the late 1940s. These theories tried to determine personal qualities and characteristics demonstrated by leaders. An important assumption with this approach was the belief that leaders were born rather than made. Many qualities and characteristics were examined during this time, and the conclusions served as the basis for other theories.

STAGE II *LEADERSHIP STYLES*

Late 1940s through late 1960s. The emphasis was on training leaders, which was different from the earlier stage in which the emphasis was on the selection of leaders who innately had the required qualities. A critical concern was how to determine if someone was a leader prior to putting the person into a leadership position.

STAGE III FOCUSED ON *CONTINGENCY APPROACH*

Late 1960s through early 1980s. This approach examined all the situational factors surrounding leadership that might determine the effectiveness of different leadership approaches. What is happening in the environment and organization that might affect the leader?

STAGE IV *NEW LEADERSHIP APPROACHES*

Early 1980s through today. This stage is the focus in this text. Transformational leadership, as well as other approaches, has become more and more acceptable. There is greater emphasis on engagement of staff, teams, communication and collaboration, and the work environment and organizational culture. Change is embraced and seen as opportunity.

every nurse should strive to reach. To accomplish this, nurses need to have an understanding of relevant leadership and management theories and styles.

A Historical Perspective of Leadership Theories and Styles

There are many leadership theories and styles that have affected management and care delivery in HCOs. However, it is important to understand some aspects of the history of leadership and the effects some of the past theories and styles have had on modern theories. Typically the theories of the past emphasized control, competition, and getting the job done. Creativity was not considered important. Leadership theories and styles have changed over time, some still valid, some not, and some adapted to become part of modern theories. A historical review of the stages of leadership theory development indicates that there are four stages, which are highlighted in Box 1-2.

It is still possible to find leaders in HCOs that use the theories that were developed in the first three stages; for example, there are still organizations that use the **autocratic** and **bureaucratic** approaches to leadership and management as described in Box 1-3, though these theories are not considered to be as effective in the current healthcare delivery system.

The modern or current leadership theories and styles have their bases in earlier theories, but they have been developed as the needs of organizations changed, requiring different types of leaders and managers. Box 1-4 highlights the key theories' and styles' effects on organizational culture.

DEMING'S THEORY   This approach to management focuses on management and staff interaction. It is through this interaction and relationship building that trust is developed. Group work or teamwork and team ownership of work are the focus in this theory. Despite the fact that Deming's approach has been successful in some U.S. businesses, it has had less of an immediate impact on HCOs. Some HCOs still feature much centralized control, with upper management making many of the decisions rather than relying on staff participation. There are, however, an increasing number of leadership and management theories and HCOs that now recognize the value of staff participation.

DRUCKER'S THEORY   Peter Drucker is considered to be the father of modern management. His view of management stimulated the shift toward the realization of the importance of participatory organizations, which is similar to Deming's approach (Drucker, 1994). Drucker felt that staff should participate in as much of the planning and establishment of goals and decision making as

BOX 1-3	WHAT ARE AUTOCRATIC, BUREAUCRATIC, AND LAISSEZ-FAIRE LEADERSHIP?

AUTOCRATIC (AUTHORITARIAN, DIRECTIVE)

The leader makes decisions for the group, typically by issuing orders or directions. The leader assumes people are externally motivated and incapable of independent decision making. External motivators might be salary and benefits or job security. Today this style is most effective in emergencies (e.g., a fire on the unit or a cardiac arrest), when clear direction is required from one person. It is not as effective for long-term use.

BUREAUCRATIC (STRUCTURE, CONTROL)

The bureaucratic style is directly related to the autocratic style as the leader also presumes the group is externally motivated. The leader relies on organizational rules and policies, takes an inflexible approach, and gives directions, expecting them to be followed.

LAISSEZ-FAIRE (NONDIRECTIVE, PERMISSIVE, ULTRALIBERAL)

The leader assumes the group is internally motivated by recognition, achievement, increased responsibility, and so on and needs autonomy and self-regulation. The leader uses a hands-off approach. This leadership style is directly opposite of autocratic and bureaucratic leadership as the leader allows staff to do as they please rather than giving implicit instructions. Sometimes this style can be too detached, resulting in no leadership and floundering staff. When staff on a patient care unit feel there is no real leadership or guidance, the nurse manager is probably using laissez-faire leadership, though the manager may not actually realize this is the approach he or she is using.

possible. Individual autonomy is a critical part of this theory of management. Drucker believed that when staff participated in the core functions of management, the organization would be more effective. For example, staff nurses should provide input into planning and changes that might be necessary on the unit, and nurse managers should seek out staff members' ideas and ask them to assist with planning. Drucker's theory includes the assumption that leadership can be learned. Leaders are not born, but rather staff can be nurtured to gain greater leadership competency. This approach offers more opportunity to develop leaders and is important to nursing. Including leadership and management content in undergraduate education indicates that the nursing profession values leadership and recognizes the need to develop leadership and management competencies in students, as discussed later in this chapter.

BOX 1-4	SELECT MODERN LEADERSHIP THEORIES AND STYLES

- *Deming's Theory*
  Groups and teams
- *Drucker's Theory*
  Modern management; participatory management; leadership learned
- *Contingency Theory*
  Situation changes affect leadership
- *Management Grid Theory*
  Five styles ranging from little interest in production and people to maximum interest in production and people
- *Connective Leadership Theory*
  Caring, interconnectedness, collaboration
- *Emotional Intelligence Theory*
  Feelings and self-awareness; emotional competence
- *Knowledge Management Theory*
  Importance of knowledge; knowledge worker asset to organizations
- Leadership 2.0
  Integrates elements of several theories/styles; recognizes that leadership is difficult to describe; identifies core and adaptive skills
- *Servant Leadership, Collaborative Leadership, and Complexity Leadership*
  Three current theories/styles that are very similar to transformational leadership
- *Transformational Leadership Theory*
  Motivating followers; participatory leadership; moral agency; high recognition of staff

CONTINGENCY THEORY   In 1967 Fiedler developed the Contingency Theory by focusing on the situational variables that affect the leader-member relationship, task structure, and position power (Fiedler, 1967).

1. The leader-member relationship variable describes the type and quality of the leader's personal relationships with the followers. This variable is affected by the amount of confidence and loyalty followers have in their leader.
2. The task structure, the number of correct solutions to a given situational dilemma, focuses on the level of structure found in the group's task.
3. Position power, which addresses the power or amount of organizational support the leader receives from the organization, is critical to success.

Using these three major variables, Fiedler arrived at a number of variable combinations and identified which combinations were advantageous and which were disadvantageous to the organization and its leadership. He concluded that the best type of situation occurs when there are positive leader-member relations, high task structure, and high position power. Groups change, which then changes the situational variables. Leadership, which is contingent on these variables, then must also change. This might also be called *situational leadership*. With the leader taking into account the changes in the situation, this is not a static approach to leadership.

MANAGEMENT GRID MODEL   Another approach to understanding leadership is the Management Grid Model (Blake & McCanse, 1991). This model identifies five styles of leadership that are still relevant today.

1. *Impoverished leadership.* In this style the leader has limited interest in production or people. Work requirements are established at a minimum level.
2. *Country club leadership.* This type of leader has an interest in people, and staff describes the leader as friendly and outgoing. Productivity, however, is not a major concern.
3. *Authority-obedience leadership.* This leader focuses on efficiency and getting the job done. This includes providing a work environment in which staff can be productive, but the leader has less concern for staff members as people.
4. *Organizational "man."* This style of leadership focuses on balancing the necessity to accomplish the task while maintaining morale.
5. *Team leadership.* This type of leader is very concerned about productivity and about the impact of staff morale and satisfaction.

CONNECTIVE LEADERSHIP THEORY   Connective leadership theory focuses on caring. Interconnectedness is a key element in health care today with the increasing emphasis on the continuum of services to meet the needs of patients and communities across the age span and different delivery settings. In this particular approach to leadership, the leader needs to promote collaboration and teamwork within the HCO and among other organizations in the community. It recognizes that many groups exist within and outside an organization that can affect leadership style. Connecting to others—individuals, teams and groups, and organizations—leads to greater success. This viewpoint of leadership is incorporated in many of the current modern theories.

EMOTIONAL INTELLIGENCE THEORY   As leadership theory has moved toward considering the leader-follower relationship, theories have focused more and more on feelings and self-awareness, such as Goleman's theory of emotional intelligence (EI). Emotional competence is "a learning capability based on emotional intelligence that results in outstanding performance at work" (Bradberry & Greaves, 2003; Goleman, 1998, p. 24). Emotional competencies are learning abilities or job skills that can be learned. A person has the potential to develop the necessary skills or required competencies (Goleman, 2001). This relates back to other theories that have been discussed that assume people can learn to be more effective leaders. Goleman identifies domains or dimensions that are important to emotional intelligence, which he calls *clusters*; within each cluster, there are identified competencies.

- *Self-Management Cluster:* Focuses on managing internal emotions, impulses, and resources. *Competencies*: Emotional self-control, trustworthiness, conscientiousness, adaptability, achievement drive, and initiative.

- *Social-Awareness Cluster:* Focuses on reading people and teams and groups accurately. *Competencies*: Empathy, service orientation, organizational awareness.
- *Relationship-Management Cluster:* Focuses on inducing desirable responses. *Competencies*: Developing others, influence, communication, conflict management, visionary leadership, change catalyst, building bonds, and collaboration and teamwork.

It might seem that all of these competencies stand alone; however, Goleman notes that they occur in groups, which is why they are described as clusters. Each competency is on a continuum in that an individual may perform the competency at different levels. Nurses may demonstrate leadership and management competencies anywhere on the continuum. It takes time and support to learn about leadership. An individual competency may reach what is referred to as a "tipping point": when the individual excels in the competency. For example, a team leader seems to have it all together: the team is functioning well; the leader routinely gives feedback to team members; team members are very active in planning and are able to speak up when they have concerns; team members support one another and feel the team leader will support the team; communication is clear, the work seems to flow, and outcomes are met.

How does emotional intelligence leadership affect the organization's performance? This is an important question as there is no reason to continue with a leadership approach if it is not having a positive effect on the organization's staff and work. This theory supports the need for leadership to develop a work environment that supports and encourages staff to perform at an optimum level. All of this impacts organization effectiveness and improved performance. Applying EI to leadership style requires that the leader demonstrate the EI competencies of self-confidence, empathy, change catalyst, and visionary leadership. EI is more important than technical competencies. How smart a nurse is will not be as important as whether or not the nurse has, or is able to develop, critical EI competencies as a leader. New nurses typically need to develop at least some of the social and emotional competencies needed for effective performance in today's healthcare environment. A number of new nurses demonstrate some of these competencies at the time of graduation. It has not been proven that EI is a strong predictor of leadership success; however, it does have an impact. There is no doubt that nursing is a people-oriented profession in which emotional issues and responses are critical. It is also important for nurses to understand and manage their own emotions in an effective way—not only to provide effective care but also for self-care and to prevent staff burnout. In the work that the American Organization of Nurse Executives (AONE) has completed on nurse executive competencies, it has been noted that leaders not only need competencies that one would normally think of, such as planning effectively, coordinating, and decision making, but they must also possess "people skills," such as the ability to talk with others, develop trust, be transparent, and engage staff in the process. Those who support EI recognize that emotionally intelligent nurse leaders will bring the following to HCOs: improve performance, motivate staff, develop innovative ideas, effectively manage the work, and support others who provide **management functions**. The outcome should be more satisfied patients, nurses, physicians, families, and a work environment that provides the best for all concerned—quality care, safe care, effective work environment, staff retention and engagement, and maintaining an environment of improvement.

KNOWLEDGE MANAGEMENT THEORY   This leadership theory recognizes the importance of the knowledge worker, knowledge-intense organizations, interprofessional collaboration, and **accountability** found in the Information Age. Knowledge work is a combination of routine and non-routine knowledge-based work. Routine work (e.g., providing immunizations or other routine interventions or procedures) may require specialized knowledge that includes some level of predictability with anticipated probable outcomes. Non-routine knowledge work is full of exceptions, lacks predictability, requires interpretation and judgment, and may not be fully understood (e.g., altering care based on assessment data). Learning is an important component of knowledge work. Drucker (1993, 1994) first used the term *knowledge worker* when he described a person who works with his or her hands and with theoretical knowledge. HCOs are knowledge-intense organizations. In this type of organization, staff are the organization's knowledge assets or intellectual capital. As will be discussed in later chapters, critical thinking, clinical reasoning and judgment, and evidence-based practice and management are important in today's organizations, focusing on the need for knowledge that can be applied to improve care. This new age of knowledge growth requires workers who use information to produce knowledge, solve problems, and meet organizational goals. Nurses should be viewed as knowledge workers, not laborers. Today a person's title is *not* the most important element; rather, it is the person's expertise and knowledge that are the critical elements. Staff may have expertise and knowledge yet lack the insight that allows them to appreciate the impact of their behavior on other individuals. The latter represents a lack of a sense of fair play, commitment to collaboration, willingness to share the limelight, and a growing sense of self that considers one's strengths and weaknesses, all critical for effective leadership and team effectiveness. It may not always be easy to clearly predict what may be the result of a decision, which means that a person or team must be willing to take calculated risks. When a manager or a staff member takes risks during decision making, there is a chance of loss or lack of success. Given this chance, it is important to continually work to understand and reduce risk. It is, however, not always possible to have time to assess a situation to its fullest, nor is it always possible to recognize all viable solutions to a problem and identify all risks. These factors can make risk taking difficult, but this limitation should not eliminate the need for taking risks in some situations.

What does the manager in a knowledge-work environment do when he or she is no longer always expected to tell staff what to do? This new manager brings together people with different knowledge bases to reach the most effective performance. This is done through effective individual performance but also by using teamwork and engaging staff in planning and the work processes. Knowledge-based managers must be facilitators and integrators. They support diverse team members who work toward reaching a common goal. No single staff member can know everything that is required for practice today; therefore, the interprofessional team becomes the focus. In addition, this is emphasized by the NAM core competencies for healthcare professions. An important goal in nursing today is the development of staff to maximize team member efficiency. Team members should be viewed as assets; they are valuable to the team and the organization. It is important to decrease the time that team members spend doing functions and tasks that are not as important or, if they are professionals, functions that are not critical professional tasks. Examples of these are (a) RNs transporting patients, (b) RNs completing paperwork that does not require professional competencies, and (c) RNs searching for equipment or needed supplies.

The NAM strongly supports the need for a knowledge-based and learning healthcare system. This system should provide clear standards for patient care and reflect EBP and evidence-based management (EBM). (See Chapter 16 for more information.) The system should focus on feedback and improvement. "A learning healthcare system is one that maintains a constant force on the health and economic value returned by care delivered and continuously improves in its performance. To provide this iterative cycle of delivery, measurement, and improvement, leaders must be engaged and maintain ownership of the process. Through effective change leadership or management, leaders are empowered and equipped with tangible skills to make the case for change and ensure that the future state vision is clearly and consistently communicated" (Gocski & Barton, 2014, p. 83). Leaders recognize the need for this type of system and provide the infrastructure for an effective healthcare system with checks and balances to maintain continuous assessment and improve performance.

LEADERSHIP 2.0 This is an example of a current view of leadership that integrates many of the aspects of the previously described leadership styles (Bradberry & Greaves, 2012). It recognizes that leadership is difficult to clearly describe. Most people know when they have worked with a leader and when they have not, but explaining this perspective is not always easy. Leadership 2.0 examines what is required for people to get into leadership positions and the skills required to be a great leader or at least more effective than other leaders. Core leadership focuses on the first issue, describing required skills as (1) strategy, which includes vision, acumen, planning, and courage to lead; (2) action, which includes decision making, communication, and mobilizing others; and (3) results, which includes risk taking, results focus, and agility. These skills will not make a leader great, but every great leader needs these core skills. Adaptive leadership skills move a leader into a higher level of leadership effectiveness. These skills are (1) emotional intelligence, which includes self-awareness, self-management, social awareness, and relationship management; (2) organizational justice, which includes decision fairness, information sharing, and outcome concern; (3) character, which includes integrity, credibility, and values differences; and (4) development, which includes lifelong learning and developing others.

CASE STUDY

Leadership Style: How Do You Decide?

After six years on the orthopedic unit, a nurse has been chosen for the nurse manager position on the unit. She wanted the position, but she is now concerned about how she will handle it. A nurse manager from another unit will mentor her in the nurse manager role. As the orientation takes place, the new nurse manager begins to assess the different leadership styles that are used. What she notices most is that the nurse manager she is shadowing usually tells staff what to do and that there are morale issues on her unit. The nurse manager who is in orientation hears staff talking behind the back of her mentor about how they do not trust her and they hold back information. They receive very little feedback, and when it is given, it is usually negative. A staff nurse comments, "We never know what is going on." Over lunch with her mentor, the new nurse manager asks how she should approach this new position. The response is, "Just do what comes naturally." The new nurse manager is dissatisfied with this approach.

Questions:

1. Do you think the new nurse manager's response is normal or abnormal? Why?
2. Based on the information that is provided, what leadership style is the mentor using? If you were the mentor, how would you have responded to the new nurse manager?
3. If you were the new nurse manager, select the leadership style you would use, describe it and its related leadership theory, and why you chose it.
4. How does trust impact the nurse manager–staff relationship?

SERVANT LEADERSHIP, COLLABORATIVE LEADERSHIP, AND COMPLEXITY LEADERSHIP These current models of leadership are related and also integrate earlier theories and styles, particularly transformational leadership (Fallon, Begun, & Riley, 2013). Servant leadership focuses on the leader's need to serve. This leader delegates authority to engage staff, praises and celebrates staff successes, focuses on staff not self, provides opportunities for staff development and learning, and is committed to the organization. Collaborative leadership focuses on working together, which is a key NAM core competency (interprofessional teamwork). This leader is less concerned with hierarchy, though recognizes that there are times when the leader must assume active direction, such as during emergencies. Complexity leadership recognizes that the work environment and processes are complex, requiring collaboration, direction, and commitment. Adaptation is needed and learning and diversity are critical elements in the complex environment. This leader demonstrates tolerance for uncertainty.

EFFECTIVE LEADERSHIP: TRANSFORMATIONAL LEADERSHIP AND INNOVATION **Transformational leadership** is viewed as an effective style for today's dynamic healthcare system. This style actually combines many of the elements of the more current theories and styles discussed in this chapter. It is also recognized as the most effective style in the IOM report on leadership (2003b). This type of leader recognizes that staff are critical to success and actions taken by this leader support the need for effective staff engagement.

1. *What is transformational leadership?* Transformational leadership is a theory or style that focuses on the need for leaders who are willing to embrace change, reward staff, guide staff members in understanding their roles within the organization and the importance of the organization or a positive work environment, and work toward developing a self-aware staff that is able to take risks to improve. This does not mean that the transformational leader is not concerned with the critical organizational functions that are required to get the work done and are emphasized in other current leadership theories and styles; however, the transformational leader begins with a **vision**, a view of the organization in the future. What could the organization be? A **mission statement**, supporting the vision, describes the organization's purpose and the current position of the organization. Why is it so important to have a vision? The vision allows the organization, its leaders or managers and staff, to look into the future, based on reasonable facts and experience, and to use this vision to become involved in opportunities to improve.

2. **Why did transformational leadership develop?** When the healthcare system began to experience extreme and frequent change, the current leadership styles were not effective in the chaotic changing atmosphere. Organizations needed the skills and knowledge of a greater number of the staff to cope. The leader also needed to be ahead of the change as much as possible. This required vision, creativity, and new leadership styles that empower staff. Transformational leadership is the leadership style recommended by the IOM in its report *Leadership by Example* (2003b) and mentioned in other IOM reports (2004; 2011). This style is focused on change and how the leader adopts change as opportunity for improvement. Rather than seeing change as a barrier, the transformational leader is engaged in the change process and draws staff into the process. Change can lead to opportunities.

3. **What are the qualities or characteristics of a transformational leader?** Qualities and characteristics that have been identified in transformational leaders are self-confidence, self-direction, honesty, energy, loyalty, commitment, and the ability to develop and implement a vision. **Empowerment** is an important component of transformational leadership. This does not mean that the leader gives away all power, and in fact, when staff are empowered, they typically are more productive, which reflects positively on the leader. The transformational leader who has these qualities can lead staff during times of creative development but also can ensure that operational issues are handled, making sure the work is done effectively, even during times of stress and crisis.

It is not easy to describe effective leadership; there is certainly no magic formula. As noted in the previous discussion of leadership theories and styles, effective leaders need vision, influence, and power. The vision of the future guides the leader in making day-to-day decisions. Leaders use **influence**, which is the informal strategy of cooperation combined with formal authority of a position to develop trust. The leader needs to be persuasive and use productive communication. **Power** enables the leader to influence others, and by doing this, the leader can change staff attitudes and behavior, preferably moving toward meeting expected outcomes. **Values**, the importance that is attached to something that guides action, are more important today in understanding effective leadership. An example of the impact of values is found in HCOs that focus on the bottom line, cutting costs with little concern about the effect on quality of care. This communicates a particular value to staff, patients, and the community. Healthcare organizations, however, that communicate the importance of a caring environment and support the highest quality care to individual patients, while still maintaining concern about economic views, are communicating different values. Leaders of these two types of organizations are actively involved in communicating critical values, albeit very different ones. The leader in the first type of organization focuses more on financial issues and is less willing

APPLYING EVIDENCE-BASED PRACTICE

Evidence for Effective Leadership and Management

CITATION: Rolfe, P. (2011). Transformational leadership theory: What every leader needs to know. *Nurse Leaders,* 54–56. Retrieved from http://www.sciencedirect.com/science/article/pii/S1541461211000164

OVERVIEW: Transformational leadership is an effective leadership style. This author describes her personal experience in applying transformational leadership and developed this style so she can be an effective leader.

APPLICATION: Applying transformational leadership can improve organizations and their outcomes. Key attributes of transformational leaders are self-knowledge, expertise, authenticity, flexibility, vision, charisma, shared leadership, and the ability to inspire and motivate followers (Ward, 2002). Understanding what these mean and how to develop them is critical for nurse leaders in today's healthcare environment.

Questions:

1. Describe the framework that is illustrated in the figure within this article. How does this framework relate to your view of nursing and to leadership and management?
2. What strategies does the author suggest to new nurse leaders?
3. What do healthy environments support?

to listen to staff concerns about the quality of care unless it has a major impact on costs. The leader in the second type of organization is more willing to look at the total care picture, listen to staff, and look for opportunities to improve care but does not forget the need to consistently monitor operations and costs. Understanding a leader's values is critical to understanding how that leader might function in an organization and how the organization's values might mesh or collide with the leader's values. Nurse leaders/managers who are working in organizations in which they disagree with the organization's values may experience stress and an inability to go along with the organization's strategies. Ultimately these nurse leader/managers may leave the organization.

LEADERS AND MANAGERS: A COMPARISON

Leadership and management are not the same, although they are interconnected. It is important to understand how these roles compare and recognize that the goal is to have managers who are also leaders. Effective leaders need to demonstrate some management competencies.

Changes in Nurse Leader Positions in Healthcare Organizations

To develop a fuller understanding of nurse leadership and the need to "step outside the box," it is important to have an appreciation of the following:

1. Where nursing leadership came from
2. Where nursing leadership is today
3. How leadership and management theories and styles affect nursing leadership

The manager's job is to accomplish the work of the organization. This is true regardless of the type of organization such as acute care hospital, home care agency, long-term care organization, clinic, and so on. Manager roles and functions vary with the type of organization and the level of management. Typically management is viewed from three levels: first-level, middle-level, and upper-level managers.

First-level managers manage the work of non-managerial staff and the day-to-day activities of a specific work team or group. Examples of first-level managers are unit managers and charge nurses. Middle-level managers typically supervise several first-level managers. An example of a middle-level manager is a director of surgical services or women's health. These managers also serve as liaisons between first-level managers and upper-level managers. The upper-level managers are responsible for establishing goals and strategic plans for the organization. They are the organization's executives and top administrators. Examples of upper-level managers are a chief nurse executive (CNE), vice president of patient services, chief executive officer (CEO), chief operating officer (COO), and medical director. Not all organizations have all three levels, and titles may vary. There are also nurses who hold positions that are not usually considered to be managers yet require effective leadership competencies to meet their required functions. Examples are clinical nurse specialist (CNS); advanced practice registered nurse (APRN), who may work in any setting including acute care; clinical nurse leader (CNL); and doctor of nursing practice (DNP). These positions will be discussed later in this text.

What is the historical development of the "nurse leader" in HCOs? The nurse leader in acute care settings was first called the director of nursing (DON). The DON focused on nursing care in hospitals and had limited interaction with hospital administration or involvement in overall HCO planning. The DON typically had little idea about or interest in the budget. These positions often were held for many years, and turnover rates were low. In addition, few of these nurses had advanced degrees. In the late 1970s and early 1980s and as the DON's power began to increase, some hospitals changed the DON title to vice president of nursing. In these cases more of these nurses had advanced degrees. Slowly this nurse leader began to interact more with hospital administration and to assume more responsibility for the nursing department's planning and budget. The next step in title changes and expansion of roles was the move to vice president of patient services, which in some organizations is referred to as chief nursing officer (CNO). (A vice president for patient services is not found in every acute care setting, but it is increasing.) This was a significant change as it recognized that the nurse leader

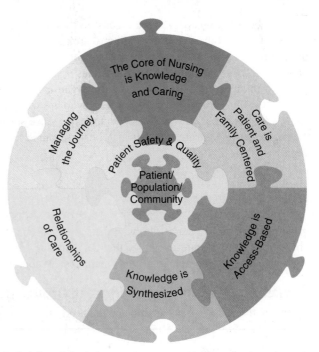

Figure 1-1 AONE Guiding Principles

Source: From *AONE Guiding Principles*, copyright 2010, by the American Organization of Nurse Executives (AONE). All rights reserved.

had the ability to have an impact on broader patient care issues, not just nursing issues. This nurse leader is responsible for nursing care, other clinical delivery services, and sometimes provides oversight of support services such as medical records. Healthcare organizations continue to vary in their views of the nurse leader. In addition, more nurses are now moving into overall administration positions in healthcare settings such as acute care hospitals, home care, long-term care, and ambulatory care. When nurses hold the positions of chief executive officer (CEO) or chief operating officer (COO), they have reached the point where they oversee the entire HCO. How did this happen? Some nurse leaders have clearly demonstrated to HCOs that they can handle these responsibilities. In addition, many of the values that are important to nursing have become more important in health care in general (e.g., caring, respect for the patient, and identification and evaluation of outcomes). When nurses move into these higher positions, they bring these values with them; however, to be successful, these nurses also need to be competent in all of the administrative tasks that are involved in these high-level positions. Appendix A describes the AONE competencies illustrating how this position requires leadership and management competencies. Figure 1-1 provides an overview of the AONE guiding principles (2010).

Differences and Similarities Between Managers and Leaders

The key difference between managers and leaders is that managers typically focus on managing or maintaining equilibrium and daily operations, whereas leaders are focused more on change and often have broader views of organizations and strategies. Most people think of management as a particular position in an organization, and this is true. Leadership, however, does not require a specific position. Nursing requires management, but nursing also needs leadership. What are some examples of the differences between a leader and a manager? What does it mean for a person to inspire others as a leader? The leader communicates to staff the importance of their contributions and recognizes their successes. In doing so, the staff member is motivated to continue to improve and be effective. Leaders are also persuasive in that they are able to convince others to make changes and to improve. Through the leader's influence, care can be improved and the work situation can become more productive. Leaders ask questions, take risks, and are challenged by change. In contrast, managers may be less able to handle unstable or non-routine situations and may be focused on what works now. Managers who develop leadership competencies are more effective and handle non-routine situations better while focusing on the management functions. Managers must be competent in these key management functions:

- Planning
- Organizing
- Leading
- Controlling

Leaders gain their authority from their ability to influence others to get the work done. A manager's authority comes from the manager's position in the organization, such as a team leader, nurse manager for a unit or service, assistant director of nursing, or vice president of nursing/nurse executive. There is no doubt that managers are different in not only what they do but also in how they do their work and the authority they hold.

Successful leaders commit to lifelong learning and improvement. They also encourage staff members to pursue lifelong learning goals and serve as coaches and mentors, helping to reach the goal of improving care. Flexibility is a key factor in leadership. This is demonstrated when leaders must plan and respond to problems using a solid knowledge base and work with others to achieve goals. This does not mean that a nurse manager is not also involved in planning, but many are not or do not do this effectively. More effort needs to be made to prepare nurse managers to be more effective leaders. Consider the following leader roles.

1. *Expert.* An expert has an in-depth understanding of a particular topic or function. An expert will strive toward the best performance.
2. *Administrator.* The leader needs to ensure that the organization, unit, or service operates effectively. In this role, the leader looks for ways to improve efficiency and provides the framework for practice, such as policies and procedures, guidelines, values, systems, and other necessary rules to get the job done. The administrator is the most closely aligned role to nurse manager functions.
3. *People person.* In this role the leader ensures that the staff has the training and education to meet the performance requirements. In addition, the leader strives to provide a work environment in which the staff feel comfortable to share information and opinions and work as a team.
4. *Strategist or planner for the future.* The leader also takes on the role of change agent and facilitator. In this role the leader strives to make the most of change to improve the organization, even taking risks to accomplish effective change, engaging staff in the process.

If one rereads these descriptions of the roles, "manager" could be substituted for "leader" *if* the manager demonstrates leadership qualities and characteristics. An overlap of management and leadership roles is found in the need for broad-perspective decision making, communication, and understanding of the motivation of followers.

There are several common myths about leadership. It is easy to assume that leaders can do it all. This is a myth. There are other myths about leadership, such as anyone who is appointed an administrator or a manager must be a leader. This is not always the case. Ideally, nurse manager selection should be based on the best person for the position and should be someone who has demonstrated potential to function in a management role in which one is also a leader; however, this does not always happen. The **Peter Principle** (Peter & Hull, 1969) describes a major leadership and management problem in bureaucratic organizations. The problem occurs when staff members are promoted for doing a good job with their assigned tasks, such as direct patient care, but as they climb up the hierarchical ladder, they eventually are promoted to a position for which they are not competent. One such example would be a staff nurse who provides quality care and is considered to be an expert clinician by coworkers and management who is then promoted to a management position but has limited management competency. It is assumed that because the nurse is an expert clinician, she or he will be an effective manager and leader. This is not necessarily the case, and even if the nurse has the potential to be an effective leader, he or she would still need to develop additional leadership and management competencies. The danger of this type of promotion is that demotion is not something that is done very easily. Typically the staff member stays in the position, though he or she may be incompetent as a manager and a leader. The reward system in nursing has in general been to reward good clinical staff with a management position rather than within clinical practice, which has led to problems. Nursing needs to reward clinical expertise in a manner that retains nurses in direct care positions. Even though the Peter Principle was identified many years ago, it is still operative in HCOs and applies to nursing.

Nursing education focuses on preparing nurses to manage patient care, which does not fully develop managers who have to deal with many problems not directly related to patient care. This education includes some content about the four major manager functions; however, much more needs to be done. The term "management" is used frequently in nursing and typically brings to mind the idea of "control." In health care, however, it is difficult to "control" all factors that might impact care and decisions. Some managers do focus primarily on control as their management style, which may lead to ineffective leadership. The first step in moving from a nurse manager to a nurse leader is to give up some of this control and recognize the value of full staff engagement. This is not always easy for new nurse managers to do, and many experienced nurse managers also have problems giving up control and allowing staff to participate more in decision making and planning. This approach is contradictory to transformational leadership.

PREPARATION AND DEVELOPMENT OF NURSE LEADERS AND MANAGERS

Leadership development is even more important today as noted in the recommendations of the *Future of Nursing* report (Institute of Medicine, 2011). The report emphasizes the need for greater leadership, which means there must be support for development of leadership competencies. Some nurse leaders learn on the job; some attend training programs; and some pursue higher degrees, such as master's or doctoral degrees. "No matter the pathway or desired role, nurses who seek greater professional involvement develop a deeper sense of their own authority and of the leadership they can provide throughout the course of their careers. It's not just a matter of whether a nurse is a leader, but whether a nurse develops and exercises leadership skills" (Hassmiller & Truelove, 2014, p. 61). This preparation must be based on the nurse manager role and the need for leadership competencies, including the four management functions.

Nurse managers are directly responsible for maintaining standards of care, managing fiscal resources, and developing staff. Some of the titles for this middle-management position include nurse manager, head nurse, nursing unit manager, and nursing or nurse coordinator. Nurse manager responsibilities vary from organization to organization, but the most effective nurse managers recognize the importance of engagement at the direct care level and application of the four major management functions. Some positions focus more on management and others more on clinical care, but most commonly it is a combination. Many nurse managers need to be prepared to effectively respond to staff stress, low morale, staff uncertainty, staff turnover, inadequate quality care outcomes, productivity concerns, and decreasing budget, all of which are common problems today. Critical competencies to accomplish these activities, which are related to the major management functions, include the following:

- Communication
- Team management and team building
- Understanding of staff needs and ability to assess staff mood and morale
- Self-confidence
- Assessment of productivity and performance of individuals, teams, and units
- Innovation
- Ability to engage and influence others
- Ability to cope with stress and conflict and manage so as to support others and prevent negative responses
- Critical thinking using active methods to analyze and respond to problems
- Ability to guide staff in using clinical reasoning and judgment
- Networking
- Managing resources (e.g., budgeting, staffing)
- Enhancing employee performance (e.g., mentoring)
- Evaluating effectiveness and efficiency: Quality improvement
- Delegation
- Clinical and organizational expertise
- Flexibility

- Collaboration (interprofessional)
- Coordination
- Outcome oriented: patient-centered care
- Problem solving and decision making
- Evaluation and analysis
- Managing change
- Operational and strategic planning

Figure 1-2 identifies some core leader competencies and supporting behaviors that are relevant to nursing leadership.

New managers and leaders do not just need to have management competencies. They also need to be more aware of their inner selves and plan their careers—where they want to go and how they will get there (McBride, 2010). These skills and competencies are important for every nurse, and this is one reason this content is important for all nursing students. It is easy to say, "I am not going to be a manager," but many management skills and competencies as well as what is required to be a leader are related to the daily practice of every nurse.

The Work Environment: Caring and Trust

Managers who are leaders need to care for their staff. What does this mean? The manager should listen to staff, recognize when staff need special support and guidance, and take time to respond to the staff. There are times when staff lack confidence, and the nurse manager needs to help increase staff confidence. To accomplish this, the manager may provide positive feedback and guidance or additional educational opportunities to develop new competencies. A key job of a manager is to make sure that the staff understand instructions and that those instructions are carried out effectively. In doing so, the manager is exercising authority but also building staff confidence to do their jobs. The manager establishes an environment in which the staff recognize that it is acceptable to identify problems and to speak out when performance has not been as effective or when they have concerns or problems. Staff members should not fear that they will be reprimanded and should feel they can trust their manager rather than be concerned about negative outcomes (Institute of Medicine, 1999). When errors occur, a manager who is also a leader does not punish staff but rather uses the error as an opportunity for improvement and assesses the

	Leads Others	Extends Influence Beyond the Chain of Command	Leads by Example	Communicates
Leads	• Provide purpose, motivation, inspiration. • Enforce standards. • Balance mission and welfare of Soldiers.	• Build trust outside lines of authority. • Understand sphere, means, and limits of influence. • Negotiate, build consensus, resolve conflict.	• Display character. • Lead with confidence in adverse conditions. • Demonstrate competence.	• Listen actively. • State goals for action. • Ensure shared understanding.
	Creates a Positive Environment	Prepares Self	Develops Leaders	
Develops	• Set the conditions for positive climate. • Build teamwork and cohesion. • Encourage initiative. • Demonstrate care for people.	• Be prepared for expected and unexpected challenges. • Expand knowledge. • Maintain self-awareness.	• Assess developmental needs. Develop on the job. • Support professional and personal growth. • Help people learn. • Counsel, coach, and mentor. • Build team skills and processes.	
	Gets Results			
Achieves	• Provide direction, guidance, and priorities. • Develop and execute plans. • Accomplish tasks consistently.			

Figure 1-2 Eight Core Leader Competencies and Supporting Behaviors
This figure is used by the U.S. Army for leadership training. The content relates to nursing leadership.

Source: U.S. Army. (2006). *Army leadership: Competent, confident, and agile.* Retrieved from www.us.army.mil

impact of the system on the error. This approach is discussed further in quality improvement content found in Chapters 17 and 18. Managers need to recognize staff members with a kind word and comment; to respond in a personal manner. Managers need to be able to admit failure themselves, and in doing so, act as role models for staff by demonstrating that managers need to improve. The effective manager will be seen as a leader who inspires excellence and motivates others to excellence, all of which relate to earlier theories discussed such as emotional intelligence, connective leadership, transformational leadership, and so on.

There are four critical qualities that are important in developing trust: competence, congruity, constancy, and caring. In today's healthcare environment, the complex work environment may be tense, staff may be tired, morale may be low, and work requirements may have increased. Leaders must constantly foster trust by demonstrating loyalty and supporting staff. How does a manager develop trust? First, the manager needs to have competence, preferably leadership competencies. How do staff recognize when a person is a leader? Usually staff members will have a feeling that the manager is able to accomplish what needs to be done. It can be difficult to describe this feeling, but the staff describe the manager as a person of integrity. Staff members want their manager to be on their side and do not want to be left alone when things get difficult. This is particularly important when there is conflict. Managers who make promises to staff need to keep the promises. If the manager cannot keep a promise, staff should be given a timely, clear explanation. In addition, managers need to demonstrate to their staff that they trust that staff performance will be effective. Most people have likely experienced relationships in which trust was not present. Typically these relationships involve situations where the person's actions and words did not mesh. If this becomes a pattern, then trust never develops or it is destroyed. It is then very difficult to regain trust. Managers must be honest and play fair with their staff. Consistency is critical in any leadership position and is also related to caring and trust. When authority is exercised, it must be consistent to develop staff respect for the manager. When managers "play favorites" and criticize other staff, often for no reason, distrust results. In these situations staff will not respect the manager, and this will affect work outcomes and patient care. Effective managers work every day to engage staff and build trust, providing an effective, caring work environment.

NURSING PROFESSIONAL ORGANIZATIONS' VIEW OF NURSE LEADERS AND MANAGERS

Nursing professional organizations typically provide support and resources to develop nursing leadership. The following organizations are particularly involved in advocating and developing nursing leadership, but from different perspectives based on their purposes and constituencies. The American Nurses Association (ANA) has a broad membership and is considered to be the major nursing organization. Although its membership does not represent the majority of nurses, its primary focus is nurses in practice. The American Association of Colleges of Nursing (AACN) membership concentrates on academic nursing programs, as does the National League for Nursing (NLN). The American Organization of Nurse Executives (AONE) membership is focused on nurse executives and managers. Specialty nursing organizations may also provide resources for nursing leadership development, and all of them support the need for nursing leadership.

- American Nurses Association: The ANA standards include elements related to leadership and management competencies, particularly found in the *Scope and Standards of Professional Nursing Practice* (2010a), *Guide to the Code of Ethics for Nurses* (2010b), and *Nursing Administration: Scope and Standards of Practice* (2009).
- American Academy of Nursing (AAN): The AAN is an important nursing organization that recognizes nursing leaders, who become fellows (FAAN). The organization and its fellows are actively involved in health policy, quality care concerns, health promotion, and strengthening healthcare delivery nationally and internationally.
- American Association of Colleges of Nursing (AACN): *The Essentials of Baccalaureate Education for Professional Nursing Practice* (2008) and *The Essentials of Master's Education in Nursing* (2011) include leadership as necessary components of baccalaureate and master's degree programs. Many of these essentials are applied in the end-of-chapter activities of this text.

- National League for Nursing (NLN): This is an organization for faculty and leaders. Leadership is included in NLN recommendations and resources for faculty. NLN also established the Centers of Excellence Program to recognize nursing programs that provide strong leadership in nursing education and the Academy of Nursing Education that recognizes individual nurses for their excellent leadership in education. The NLN also provides a program for certification of nurse educators.
- American Organization of Nurse Executives (AONE): The AONE has identified key competencies for nurse executives and managers, which are identified in Appendix A, where students are asked to apply these competencies to the content in this text (American Organization of Nurse Executives, 2005). The AONE recommends that these competencies be included in graduate nurse leader education programs. Nurse leaders should be minimally prepared at the baccalaureate or master's in nursing level. Nurse leaders may provide leadership and management for units, departments, services or at the system level and may also hold other healthcare leader positions in a variety of non-governmental and governmental organizations/agencies/departments. For many of these positions, the minimum educational preparation should be a master's degree, and nurses holding positions at system or organization levels should have a doctoral preparation (American Organization of Nurse Executives, 2014).

All of these activities and development of standards demonstrate that leadership is important and needs to be supported and developed in all nurses, beginning with pre-licensure nursing programs and graduate programs.

Based on current data about the nursing workforce and significant reports on health care such as those from the IOM, the AACN identifies "hallmarks of the professional nursing practice environment":

1. Manifest a philosophy of clinical care emphasizing quality, safety, interdisciplinary [interprofessional] collaboration.
2. Recognize contributions of nurses' knowledge and expertise to clinical care quality and patient outcomes continuity of care, and professional accountability.
3. Promote executive level nursing leadership.
4. Empower nurses' participation in clinical decision-making and organization of clinical care systems.
5. Maintain clinical advancement programs based on education, certification, and advanced preparation.
6. Demonstrate professional development support for nurses.
7. Create collaborative relationships among members of the healthcare provider team.
8. Utilize technological advances in clinical care and information systems (American Association of Colleges of Nursing, 2014, pp. 5–6).

All of these hallmarks are discussed throughout this text. Furthermore, they are correlated with the NAM core competencies for healthcare professions, and all require leadership.

THE IMAGE OF NURSING AND THE PRESENCE OF NURSING LEADERSHIP

The results from a Robert Wood Johnson Foundation poll "Nursing Leadership from Bedside to Boardroom: Opinion Leaders' Perceptions" noted that:

- Opinion leaders feel that nurses' primary areas of influence are reducing medical errors (51%), improving quality of care (50%), and coordinating patient care in the healthcare system (40%).
- Large majorities of opinion leaders said they would like to see nurses have more influence in a large number of areas, including reducing medical errors and improving patient safety (90%); improving quality of care (89%); promoting wellness and expanding preventive care (86%); improving healthcare efficiency and reducing costs (84%); coordinating care through the healthcare system (83%); helping the healthcare system adapt to an aging population (83%); and increasing access to health care (74%).
- Seventy-five percent of opinion leaders say government officials will have a great deal of influence in health reform in the next five to ten years, compared to 56% for insurance

executives, 46% for pharmaceutical executives, 46% for healthcare executives, 37% for doctors, 20% for patients and 14% for nurses.
- Opinion leaders identified the top barriers to nurses' increased influence and leadership as not being perceived as important decision makers (69%) or revenue generators (68%) compared with doctors; nurses' focus on primary rather than preventive care (62%); and nursing not having a single voice in speaking on national issues (56%).
- Opinion leaders rank nurses behind six other stakeholders when it comes to health reform over the next five to ten years (Robert Wood Johnson Foundation, 2010, p. 5-3).

This poll provides a snapshot of public and professional views of nursing. The survey focused on leadership, and it does not provide a positive view of nursing leadership, despite the fact that nurses are trusted. It identifies where improvement is needed, such as lack of influence and areas where nurses could add more but do not, and reveals that nurses need to know how to influence others. Notably one of these is in QI, which is supported by the comments and recommendations from the IOM reports. Nurses need to know more about access to care and primary care and how to participate actively in this process. They need to know more about healthcare economics and the innovation process to participate in the development of new services. Continuing education will help nurses to be effective decision makers. There exists a need for greater professional organization, which currently is diluted due to multiple nursing organizations, without one clear organization representing nursing. The bottom line is nurses need to assume more leadership, both in HCOs and in nursing professional organizations.

A 2013 Gallup Poll indicated that nurses continue to rank high or very high in the public's view of professions for their honesty and ethics (Swift, 2013). Often consumers do not really have a complete or accurate view of the roles nurses hold throughout the healthcare system. The view of the nurse as a helping person, the "angel" perspective, is very common; however, there is much more to nursing that needs to be communicated to the public.

Nursing continues to contend with the fact that it is primarily a women's profession; however, the number of men in nursing is increasing, albeit slowly. In 2011 there were about 3.2 million women RNs and 333,000 men RNs (U.S. Census Bureau, 2013, p. 2). For comparison, in 1970 2.7% of RNs were men, and in 2011 there were 9.6% men. Men are represented more among nurse anesthetists at 41%. The American Assembly for Men in Nursing (AAMN) is a professional organization that advocates for more men in nursing and supports their professional roles in nursing. Its website provides information about its activities.

There have been many media stories about how difficult the profession of nursing can be; how the work environment is stressful; and in some cases, how staff shortages affect care and workload. These data impact recruitment of potential students. More needs to be done to ensure that there is a more consistent message. Johnson & Johnson partnered with the nursing profession to develop a series of excellent television ads and other marketing methods that demonstrate the positive qualities of nursing as a career choice (Gordon & Nelson, 2005). The first series emphasized the caring aspects of nursing, and the second, a broader view of the profession. It is important to make sure that nurses see their choice of nursing as a lifetime commitment to a career and that nurses have a sense of pride in their profession. This message needs to be communicated to the public, especially to groups who might consider pursuing nursing. The message needs to be clear and accurate to be really effective. "There have been recommendations made to move away from the 'virtue script' toward a knowledge-based identity for nurses" (Gordon & Nelson, 2005, p. 62). Nurse leaders need to assume a role in marketing efforts. The profession must emphasize that nurses can be, and in many cases are, leaders in the healthcare environment. Leadership is a critical component of the profession.

MAKING A DIFFERENCE: INCREASING NURSE LEADERS

How do nurses become leaders? Nursing leaders need to be developed. This process begins during academic preparation and should continue throughout a nurse's career. Nursing education should take advantage of leadership opportunities in clinical settings and for students within the education institution. The first step is to make a commitment to lifelong learning, as will be discussed in

Chapter 20. As students enter clinical practice and their careers, they will be confronted with change. Leaders use change as opportunities for learning. Becoming involved in professional organizations is also an important part of developing leadership. This may begin with participation in the National Student Nurses Association (NSNA) and Sigma Theta Tau International (STTI), which is the nursing honor society with an invitation membership based on scholastic and leadership criteria. Invitations are offered to undergraduate and graduate students and to nurse leaders in the community who may have not joined during their academic years. The NSNA Leadership University provides opportunities for student recognition of leadership and management skills they develop in NSNA activities. The NSNA website provides leadership resources and other information for students.

Mentoring is also part of leadership. Some nursing programs facilitate mentoring so students can help one another. Networking, which can be helpful, can begin as a student. It is important to remember that faculty, peers, and nurses in clinical settings, as well as nurses who are met outside of school or clinical practice, may at some point be important individuals in a nurse's career. There are not enough nurses to fill all of the nurse leadership positions available today. Some nurses will eventually move into formal management positions, and others will apply leadership skills in non-management positions and in professional activities such as professional nursing organizations.

The nursing profession must find a way to increase the pool of potential nurse leaders. HCOs use career ladders, nurse residency programs (see Chapter 20), ongoing staff education on leadership and management, and input from potential managers in planning how they might move into management positions, recognizing the responsibility of preparing replacements for managers and leaders who will retire or leave their positions. Typically a new nurse enters the organization at the lowest level (staff nurse) and must meet specific criteria and competencies to move "up the career ladder" to different clinical levels. Leadership is included in the criteria and competencies (e.g., membership on committees, chair of committees, development of unit-based materials such as patient education or a change in a policy or procedure, mentoring new nurses, serving as preceptor for nursing students, implementing EBP, or developing/participating in research). The major nursing organization for nurse executives and managers is the AONE. AONE is a subsidiary of the American Hospital Association and "provides leadership, professional development, advocacy and research to advance nursing practice and patient care, promote nursing leadership excellence and shape public policy for healthcare nationwide" (American Organization of Nurse Executives, 2014). As organizations and the nursing profession consider the best methods for leadership development, there are guidelines that should not be forgotten, as discussed earlier in this chapter.

The majority of nurses will never be in a formal management position. So why is there all of this interest in leadership and management? It is important to recognize that leadership competencies are not required only for high positions in nursing. Staff nurses need to know how to function effectively in complex organizations and apply many leadership competencies such as leading teams and providing guidance to other staff to ensure that patient outcomes are met. In May of 2003, the AACN published a white paper, *The Role of the Clinical Nurse Leader* (CNL) (2003). The position of the AACN is that leadership is very important in nursing. This position is supported in recent Institute of Medicine reports related to healthcare quality in which nurses are described as leaders and important in making a difference in the quality of health care (Finkelman & Kenner, 2012). However, there needs to be greater recognition that leadership is required for all nursing positions, not just special positions such as CNL, advanced practice nurses, or nurses with a DNP.

The AACN recognizes the need to incorporate more leadership development in undergraduate and graduate programs. This decision is based on 10 assumptions about the healthcare delivery system and nursing.

1. Practice is at the systems level. Nurses must practice in all types of settings and are accountable for care outcomes of clinical populations (e.g., working mothers, patients in a clinic, children in a community).
2. Population-level care outcomes are the measure of quality practice. Performance will be measured by clinical and cost outcomes.
3. Practice guidelines are based on evidence.

4. Client-centered practice is intra- and interprofessional.
5. Information will maximize self-care and client decision making.
6. Nursing assessment is the basis for theory and knowledge development.
7. Good fiscal stewardship is a condition of quality care.
8. Social justice is an essential nursing value.
9. Communication technology will facilitate the continuity and comprehensiveness of care.
10. The CNL must assume guardianship for the nursing profession.

These assumptions are related to current leadership and management theories and styles that have been discussed in this chapter and will be emphasized throughout the text. The role of nurse leader is critical for patients, their families, and the delivery system as a whole. Nurses have really been in this role for a very long time. Some were more prepared than others for it, and now it is important to recognize that every nurse needs to develop leadership qualities and competencies, whether or not they are in a formal management position.

As nursing leadership expands during a time of healthcare reform, more attention needs to be given to entrepreneurial and intrapreneural nursing initiatives (Wilson, Whitaker, & Whitford, 2012). This requires that nurses be seen as equal partners, which is currently not the case. The future will bring many new roles, but nurses need to be up front and create innovation to improve health and healthcare services. People with entrepreneurial spirit do not wait for others to direct them or to create new ideas; they do it themselves. The intrapreneural person (employee) works within an organization to develop new approaches, whereas the entrepreneur functions outside an employer-employee situation. Entrepreneurial nurses have their own businesses, such as a home health agency, clinic, or consulting firm. They might be authors, legal nurse experts, creators of medical equipment, developers of digital products, or any number of other activities. These examples of self-employment involve risk for the nurse, but typically these nurses are strongly committed to what they do. Additional examples are schools of nursing that develop healthcare services such as clinics or operate mobile vans to provide care within their communities; faculty and students work in these settings. Innovation is emphasized in *The Future of Nursing* report, recognizing the need for new models and processes to improve performance (Institute of Medicine, 2011; Porter-O'Grady, 2001). Stepping outside the box to envision new ways of doing things, trying them out, and evaluating outcomes are now critical in the expanding and changing healthcare system. Nurses will also need to assume more leadership in policy development and implementation, as will be discussed in Chapter 2.

In addition to developing nurse leaders, it is also important to consider what can be done to keep nurse managers from leaving their positions. The Nurse Manager Engagement Project (NMEP), a two-year study funded by the Robert Wood Johnson Foundation (RWJF), examined this question at six major U.S. medical centers and included interviews with 30 nurse managers (Mackoff, 2011). Why is it important to pay attention to maintaining a consistent nurse manager pool? Staff nurses indicate that they are more satisfied when there is consistent management—managers with whom they can form a relationship. The implementation of middle managers impacts development of nurse leaders at all levels. As is true with any staff who leave a position, it is costly for the organization: the expense of developing the manager who then leaves and the subsequent cost of orienting and developing a new manager. At the time this study began, nurse manager satisfaction was low compared to past nurse manager satisfaction. This study preferred to use the term of "engagement" rather than "retention," viewing the latter as restricting. This opinion was supported by the interviews. Understanding nurse manager retention is based on nurse manager engagement, which was described as exceptional work and longevity. Instead of focusing the question on why nurse managers leave, the study focused on a positive question: Why do nurse managers stay? The examination included nurse manager behaviors, capabilities and attributes, and the nature of the culture in which they worked. The conclusions emphasize the importance of the line of sight or the manager's understanding of his or her daily work and its relationship to the overall vision and mission of the organization. This leads to greater ability to understand one's impact on patient care—connecting management tasks with patient outcomes. The NMEP concludes that the line of sight can be developed; it is not necessarily innate, which is supported by current leadership theory. Managers also need to cope with emotional situations that come with the position (e.g., to effectively use self-reflection and self-regulation and set reasonable boundaries). Socialization and sustainment are also important parts of engagement.

Cultures may need to be transformed to support engagement. The use of the term "cultures" can be described in the following ways: culture of excellence, culture of learning, and culture of generativity (nurturing the next generation of leaders/managers), culture of meaning (clear vision and mission), and culture of regard (responsiveness to others and their ideas).

A systematic review was conducted to examine leadership practices of healthcare managers and their impact on HCOs, providers, and patients (Cummings et al., 2008). More knowledge is needed to better understand the factors that influence nursing leadership and how these factors may impact recruitment and development of nurse leaders. The systematic review included multidisciplinary literature that examined the factors that contribute to nursing leadership and the effectiveness of educational interventions in developing leadership behaviors among nurses. The studies reviewed focused on one or more of the following: leadership behaviors and practices; leadership traits and characteristics; influence of context; and leadership styles, skills, and roles. "As healthcare faces a looming shortage of nursing leaders and nurses, understanding the factors that contribute to enhancing nursing leadership can help organizations create strategies to develop leaders and enhance succession planning and staff retention. The findings of this systematic review suggest that leadership qualities can be developed through specific and dedicated educational activities. Characteristics such as transformational, high relationship styles and previous leadership experience are identified as contributing to leadership qualities" (Cummings et al., 2008, p. 247). This systematic review noted that many of the studies had weak designs, and thus the value of these results was limited as evidence. More effective research is needed to provide nursing with solid results that will provide support for interventions to develop and promote viable nursing leadership for the future. Better nursing leadership is needed "to achieve the goal of developing healthy work environments for healthcare providers and optimizing quality care for patients" (Cummings et al., 2008, p. 247). This will be necessary as the profession works to meet the recommendations from *The Future Report* (Institute of Medicine, 2011) and other demands in the rapidly changing healthcare delivery system. In Chapter 16 EBP is discussed, but also there is emphasis on the need for more EBM to further develop research about leadership and management. *The Future Report* includes a list of priorities for research as noted in this text.

Today, nurse leaders are challenged to be the best leader they can be. To improve means learning must be active. "Nurses who seek greater professional involvement develop a deeper sense of their own authority and of the leadership they can provide throughout the course of their careers" (Hassmiller & Truelove, 2014, p. 61). Chapter 20 focuses on staff education, which includes education and development of leadership at all levels. Development of leadership and management competencies frequently occurs on the job; however, academic programs, continuing education, leadership fellowships, and many other development opportunities need to be part of career development. This chapter begins the process for each student—to consider the important elements of leadership and management in health care and for the nursing profession.

APPLYING LEADERSHIP AND MANAGEMENT

My Hospital Unit: An Evolving Case Experience

In the text introduction, you were asked to create a description of your own hospital unit. You will be the virtual nurse manager for this unit. You will revisit your unit at the end of each chapter. Decisions you make in each chapter need to be considered when you make subsequent management decisions in later chapters. For this chapter you enter your unit and consider the following. As the nurse manager of this unit, what type of leadership do you want to use? Why did you select this style? How will you demonstrate your leadership style in day-to-day activities on your unit? Write a description for your position as nurse manager that reflects your philosophy of leadership and management. How will you develop staff leadership?

BSN and Master's Essentials: Application to Content

(All *Essentials* apply to this chapter content, but more critical *Essentials* are identified.)

BSN Essentials (American Association of Colleges of Nursing, 2008) as Applied to this Chapter:

II. Basic Organizational and Systems Leadership for Quality Care and Patient Safety

VIII. Professionalism and Professional Values

Master's Essentials (American Association of Colleges of Nursing, 2011) as Applied to this Chapter:

II. Organizational and Systems Leadership

Applying AONE Competencies

Identify which of the AONE competencies found in Appendix A apply to the content of this chapter.

Engaging in the Content: Critical Thinking and Clinical Reasoning and Judgment

Discussion Questions

1. Compare and contrast the leadership theories and styles discussed in this chapter. Select one that interests you the most, and explain your choice.
2. How are the more current leadership theories/styles (servant, collaborative, complexity, and transformational) related to one another? What has been the impact of the older theories/styles on the current theories/styles?
3. In your own words, compare and contrast the role of the nurse executive and the nurse manager. How is the role of the nurse team leader different?
4. Select a time when you assumed a leadership role (does not have to be in health care). This could be a current role or one from the past. Consider the content in this chapter, and analyze how you thought you demonstrated leadership or could have improved your leadership.
5. Why is the image of nursing important?

Application Exercises

1. In teams, compare and contrast the two major IOM reports on nursing (*Keeping Patients Safe* and *The Future of Nursing: Leading Change, Advancing Health*). How are they similar and how are they different? What are the pros and cons to the two approaches taken in the reports? How does each report support nursing and what segments of the profession? Teams can present their analyses to the entire class and discuss. The full reports are available at the National Academy of Medicine website. [(Online Application Option)]
2. Select a nurse manager in one of your clinical sites. Ask the nurse manager the following questions: (1) Why did you want to become a nurse manager? (2) What are the key management skills/competencies you use? (3) What style of leadership do you use and why? (4) Ask the nurse manager to compare and contrast the differences between a nurse manager and a nurse leader. Share your data with your classmates, and compare and contrast with their data.
3. As you gain more clinical experience in school and after graduation, observe how others lead and manage. Make a conscious effort each week in clinical settings to observe leadership and management. Begin a blog with your classmates in this course to share your observations. Do not include staff names, patient names, or names of organizations for privacy reasons. Explore issues or questions that intrigue you.
4. In team discussion, identify leader and manager characteristics and competencies described in this chapter. Are they reasonable? Why or why not? Are there others you would add and why?
5. Ask several nurses in practice about their experiences with change in health care. Discuss results in class team discussion and compare.

References

American Association of Colleges of Nursing. (2003). Excerpt from *White Paper on the Education and Role of the Clinical Nurse Leader*™. Washington, DC: American Association Colleges of Nursing.

American Association of Colleges of Nursing. (2008). *The essentials of baccalaureate education for professional nursing practice*. Washington, DC: Author.

American Association of Colleges of Nursing. (2011). *The essentials of master's education in nursing*. Washington, DC: Author.

American Association of Colleges of Nursing. (2014). *Hallmarks of professional nursing practice environments*. Retrieved from http://www.aacn.nche.edu/publications/white-papers/hallmarks-practice-environment

American Nurses Association. (2009). *Nursing administration: Scope and standards of practice*. Silver Spring, MD: Author.

American Nurses Association. (2010a). *Scope and standards of professional nursing practice.* Silver Spring, MD: Author.

American Nurses Association. (2010b). *Guide to the code of ethics for nurses.* Silver Spring, MD: Author.

American Organization of Nurse Executives. (2005). AONE nurse executive competencies. Chicago, IL: Author.

American Organization of Nurse Executives. (2010). AONE guiding principles. Retrieved from http://www.aone.org/resources/principles.shtml

American Organization of Nurse Executives. (2014). About AONE. Retrieved from http://www.aone.org/membership/about/welcome.shtml

Blake, R., & McCanse, A. (1991). *Leadership dilemmas—Grid solutions.* Houston, TX: Gulf Publishing.

Bradberry, T., & Greaves, J. (2003). *The emotional intelligence quickbook: Everything you need to know.* San Diego, CA: TalentSmart.

Bradberry, T., & Greaves, J. (2012). *Leadership 2.0.* San Diego, CA: TalentSmart.

Center to Champion Nursing in America. (2014). Campaign for Action—Overview. Retrieved from http://campaignforaction.org/CFA-overview

Cummings, G., How, L., MacGregor, T., Davey, M., Wong, C., Paul, L., & Stafford, E. (2008). Factors contributing to nursing leadership: A systematic review. *Journal of Health Services Research & Policy, 13*(4), 240–248.

Drucker, P. (1993). *Post-capitalistic society.* New York, NY: Harper Business Publications.

Drucker, P. (1994). The age of social transformation. *Atlantic Monthly, 274*(5), 53–80.

Fallon, L., Begun, J., & Riley, W. (2013). *Managing health organizations for quality and performance.* Burlington, MA: Jones & Bartlett Learning.

Fiedler, F. (1967). *A theory of leadership effectiveness.* New York, NY: McGraw-Hill.

Finkelman, A., & Kenner, C. (2012). *Teaching IOM: Implications of the Institute of Medicine reports for nursing education* (3rd ed.). Silver Spring, MD: American Nurses Association.

Gocski, T., & Barton, A. (2014). Why clinical change leadership is essential for project success. *Clinical Nurse Specialist*, March/April, 83–85.

Goleman, D. (1998). *Working with emotional intelligence.* New York, NY: Bantam Books.

Goleman, D. (2001). An EI theory of performance. In C. Cherniss & D. Goleman (Eds.), *The emotionally intelligent workplace* (pp. 27–44). San Francisco, CA: Jossey-Bass.

Gordon, S., & Nelson, S. (2005). An end to angels. *AJN, 105*(5), 62–69.

Grey, M., Holzemer, W., & Larson, E. (2012). Nurse IOM members' contributions to the Institute of Medicine. *Nursing Outlook, 60*(4), 208–212.

Hassmiller, S., & Truelove, J. (2014). Are you the best leader you can be? *American Journal of Nursing, 114*(1), 61–67.

Institute of Medicine. (1999). *To err is human.* Washington, DC: National Academies Press.

Institute of Medicine. (2001). *Crossing the quality chasm.* Washington, DC: National Academies Press.

Institute of Medicine. (2003a). *Health professions education.* Washington, DC: National Academies Press.

Institute of Medicine. (2003b). *Leadership by example.* Washington, DC: National Academies Press.

Institute of Medicine. (2004). *Keeping patients safe: Transforming the work environment of nurses.* Washington, DC: National Academies Press.

Institute of Medicine. (2011). Excerpt from *The Future Of Nursing, Leading Change, Advancing Health.* National Academy of Sciences.

Institute of Medicine. (2014). About the IOM. Retrieved from http://www.iom.edu/About-IOM.aspx

Mackoff, B. (2011). *Nurse manager engagement. Strategies for excellence and commitment.* Burlington, MA: Jones & Bartlett Learning.

McBride, A. (2010). *The growth and development of nurse leaders.* New York, NY: Springer Publishing Company, Inc.

Peter, L., & Hull, R. (1969). *The Peter principle: Why things go wrong.* New York, NY: William Morrow.

Porter-O'Grady, T. (2001). Profound change: 21st century nursing. *Nursing Outlook, 49*(4), 182–186.

Quality and Safety Education for Nurses Institute. (2014). QSEN. Retrieved from http://qsen.org

Robert Wood Johnson Foundation. (2010). *Nursing leadership from bedside to boardroom: Opinion leaders' perceptions.* Retrieved from http://www.rwjf.org/en/library/research/2010/01/nursing-leadership-from-bedside-to-boardroom.html

Rolfe, P. (2011). Transformational leadership theory: What every leader needs to know. *Nurse Leaders,* 54–56. Retrieved from http://www.sciencedirect.com/science/article/pii/S1541461211000164

Shaw, S. (2007). *Nursing leadership.* Oxford, England: International Council of Nurses; Blackwell Publishing.

Sternweiler, V. (1998). Career journeys: How to be a successful clinical nurse specialist—be a willow tree. *Advanced Practice Nursing, 3*(4), 31–33.

Swift, A. (2013). Honesty and ethics rating of clergy slides to new low. Nurses again top list; lobbyists are worse. Retrieved from http://www.gallup.com/poll/166298/honesty-ethics-rating-clergy-slides-new-low.aspx

U.S. Census Bureau. (2013). Men in nursing occupations. Retrieved from http://www.census.gov/people/io/files/Men_in_Nursing_Occupations.pdf

Ward, K. (2002). A vision for tomorrow: Transformational nursing leaders. *Nursing Outlook, 50,* 121–126.

Wilson, A., Whitaker, N., & Whitford, D. (2012). Rising to the challenge of healthcare reform with entrepreneurial and intrapreneurial nursing initiatives. *The Online Journal of Issues in Nursing, 17*(2). Retrieved from http://www.nursingworld.org/MainMenuCategories/ANAMarketplace/ANAPeriodicals/OJIN/TableofContents/Vol-17-2012/No2-May-2012/Rising-to-the-Challenge-of-Reform.html

2

Healthcare Policy, Legal Issues, and Ethics in Healthcare Delivery

KEY TERMS

- allow-natural-death (AND) directive
- assault
- autonomy
- battery
- beneficence
- civil law
- common law
- consent emergency exception
- consent implied by law
- cost-benefit analysis
- criminal law
- disparity
- doctrine of *res ipsa loquitor*
- do-not-resuscitate (DNR) directive
- durable power of attorney (medical power of attorney)
- ethics
- implied consent
- informed consent
- justice
- law
- living wills
- lobbyists

● LEARNING OUTCOMES

Before you begin, take a moment to familiarize yourself with the learning outcomes for this chapter.

> Explain why nurses should be involved in healthcare policy and the political process.
> Examine examples of key healthcare policy issues.
> Compare and contrast private and public policy.
> Apply the policy-making process including implications of the political process.
> Discuss how nurses can be involved in the policy-making process.
> Explain how federal and state laws can affect health care.
> Critique the Patient Protection and Affordable Care Act of 2010 and the provisions relevant to nursing.
> Explain how malpractice and negligence relate to nursing practice.
> Discuss the implications of scope of practice.
> Apply ethical decision making to management situations.
> Analyze the impact of healthcare fraud on the healthcare system.
> Examine how nurses can become involved in reducing healthcare fraud and abuse and cope with ethical dilemmas presented by fraud.

WHAT'S AHEAD

Nurses in one medical center who recognized the need for change and the roles of nurses in the change process made the following statement: "To preserve the quality of care while becoming cost competitive, and to strengthen nurses as integral players in this evolving market, we must become a part of the solution—for our patients, ourselves, and the institutions in which we practice. Our goal is to improve the quality of care provided by nurses, increase both job and patient satisfaction, and strengthen our institution's position in a highly competitive market" (Nokleby Elder et al., 1998, p. 34). This viewpoint continues to be critical today and is even supported more by the Institute of Medicine (IOM) *Quality Chasm* series of reports on health care. When nurses assume a leadership role in policy development, this better ensures that both nurses' and patients' needs are included in critical healthcare policies, legislation, and regulation, all of which are directly connected to ethical decision making in the healthcare environment. This chapter presents content about healthcare policy and legal and ethical issues, which are all interrelated. Policy has both ethical and legal ramifications. Nurses need to understand policy development, ethics, and legal concerns while they provide care and when they are in leadership roles.

HEALTHCARE POLICY

Why is healthcare policy relevant to nurses? Given the current status of health care as demonstrated in the IOM reports on quality and recent significant legislation to reform health care, nurses should actively participate in health policy. It has considerable impact on nursing. An isolationist approach is never helpful, and for nursing it may actually be a destructive approach. Nurses practice in the healthcare environment, which includes health policy and its effects on healthcare services and the profession. Health policy impacts nursing practice, education, staffing, roles, and responsibilities. Legislation and regulation on the state and federal levels affect nursing practice daily. To become active participants in the healthcare environment and be prepared for the changes that are inevitable, nurses as leaders must become involved in policy development at the local, state, and national levels. Healthcare policy is critical because it determines what services are provided, who provides and who can receive the services, reimbursement, improvements in health care, healthcare organization (HCO) changes, and standards. Nurses have always been concerned about consumers. This concern for and understanding of consumers and their needs is an important component of successful policy development. As patient advocates, this is an ideal time to take a leadership position to protect patient rights, ensure that patient needs are met, and ensure that the nursing profession retains its strength. Figure 2-1 provides a view of the importance of health policy to nurses.

This section of the chapter focuses on healthcare policy: how it is developed to provide background for the specific policy issues that are discussed. The scope of this text will not allow for all of the possibilities, but will try to address some of the more important ones. Legislation is also discussed in this section because it has an impact on health policy. Box 2-1 provides a list of the critical issues found in the rapidly changing healthcare environment that relate to health policies, legal, and/or ethical concerns.

Key Healthcare Policy Issues

This text discusses many important healthcare concepts, including increasing cost of health care, disparity in healthcare delivery, commercialization of health care, and consumers. Policies typically address these concepts. The most significant health policy change in the past few decades is the health policy reform legislation passed in 2010: the Patient Protection and Affordable Care Act (P.L. 11-148) and Health Care and Education Reconciliation Act (P.L. 111-152), discussed later in this chapter and throughout the text. Both laws are typically referred to as the Affordable Care Act, or ACA.

- malpractice
- medical-industrial complex
- negligence
- nonmalfeasance
- policy
- policy-making process
- political process
- private policy
- public policy
- resource allocation
- *respondeat superior*
- veracity
- vicarious liability
- whistle-blowers

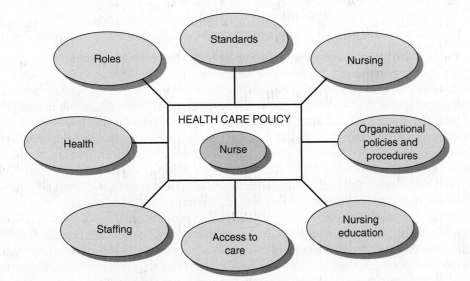

Figure 2-1 Why is health care policy relevant to nurses?

BOX 2-1	CRITICAL ISSUES RELATED TO HEALTHCARE POLICY, LEGAL, AND/OR ETHICAL ISSUES

- Changing practice patterns and the physician
- Cultural diversity and healthcare disparities
- Federal and state governments
- Growth of advanced practice nursing
- Healthcare consumerism
- Healthcare profession role changes
- Health profession education
- Immigration
- Legislation
- Aging
- Healthcare economics

- Medical-industrial complex: Privatization and corporate health care
- Interprofessional teams
- Health literacy
- Move from acute care to greater use of primary care
- Quality care
- Reimbursement
- Restructuring and reengineering
- Uninsured and underinsured
- Patient rights and confidentiality
- Healthcare informatics

INCREASING COST OF HEALTH CARE OVER TIME Since the 1990s, the United States has been descending into a more and more expensive healthcare system. In 1997 the system was described as "a healthcare system that is unique among nations. It is the most expensive of systems, outstripping by over half the healthcare expenditures of any other country. By many technical standards, U.S. medical care is the best in the world, but leaders in the field declared in 1997 at a national round table that there is an 'urgent need to improve healthcare quality'" (Broder, 1997, p. 1). In 2008 Senator Tom Daschle took this perspective a step further and stated, "We like to boast that we have the highest standard of living in the world, and yet at the dawn of the twenty-first century we are the only industrialized nation that does not guarantee necessary healthcare to all of its citizens" (p. 3). This view was further supported by the IOM reports describing the U.S. healthcare system (1999, 2001, 2003):

- The American healthcare delivery system is in need of fundamental change (p. 1).
- Healthcare today harms too frequently and routinely fails to deliver its potential benefits (p. 1).
- The performance of the healthcare delivery system varies considerably (p. 3).
- The healthcare system as currently structured does not, as a whole, make the best use of its resources (p. 3).
- What is perhaps most disturbing is the absence of real progress toward restructuring healthcare systems to address both quality and cost concerns or toward applying advances in information technology to improve administrative and clinical processes (p. 3).
- Healthcare today is plagued by a serious quality gap (p. 35) (Institute of Medicine, 2001).

The U.S. and global economic problems of 2008–2010 increased the healthcare system and insurance coverage problems. In a survey of Americans conducted February 2009, the news was not positive (Henry J. Kaiser Family Foundation, 2009). More than half of the Americans surveyed (slightly more than 53%) indicated that they limited their medical care due to cost in the past year. The results indicated that there was grave concern about affordability and accessibility of health care when needed. Many people were relying more on over-the-counter drugs rather than visiting a physician (35%), and 34% were not keeping dental appointments. Twenty-one percent were not filling prescriptions, and 15% were cutting pills in half or skipping doses. Nineteen percent experienced major financial problems due to medical care that could not be put off. The survey also addressed the respondents' view of healthcare reform. The Obama administration seemed to focus more on providing some citizens with help to cover healthcare costs and getting coverage for those without rather than taking steps to improve the quality of care. Given that there has been considerable concern about the quality of care as noted in recent IOM reports, it is important to keep this part of the equation in mind. A dysfunctional healthcare system costs more money than a functional system that provides quality care with fewer errors and complications.

By 2015, this view has not really changed. Chapters 17 and 18 discuss more information on the quality concerns in the healthcare system. The United States still battles the contradiction of having a very expensive healthcare system that is not providing high-quality services and outcomes. In 2012 the president of the IOM commented that "the system is neither as successful as it should be nor as sustainable as it must be" (Fineberg, 2012, p. 1020). He pointed out the expense compared to other countries as well as the life expectancy data indicated the United States was still behind; even the countries that had shorter life expectancies had managed to improve. Inefficiency and need to improve quality of care were key concerns.

Health care is a large, complex industry whose financing is influenced by many factors, particularly social expectation, technological developments, political factors, and economic trends, the last of which, in the past few years, has been the most critical factor. For example, losing one's job usually means also losing health insurance coverage. Financial issues affect all aspects of the provision of care, settings, and services, such as inpatient care, ambulatory care, home care, primary care, long-term care, public health, pharmaceuticals, medical supplies, medical transportation, medical technology, medical research, and so on. Compared with other countries, the United States has the most expensive healthcare system, though it has the highest standard of living and economic status. Rising medical costs have driven many of the changes in health care in the past few decades. As insurance coverage expanded, it became available to more people. There was little incentive not to use health insurance coverage when the patient was required to pay limited out-of-pocket expenses. This, however, changed as employers and insurers recognized that this system led to overuse and eventually to the expansion of managed care. In the past, healthcare professionals often paid limited attention to the costs of care (e.g., ordering tests and procedures, using supplies, extending hospital stays) and were not concerned about the relationship of treatment appropriateness, outcomes, and costs. Technological advancement has had both positive and negative impacts. Clearly these advancements have led to more effective diagnostic approaches and treatment; however, advancements also increase costs. The development of new equipment, procedures, and drugs is expensive, and these costs are passed on to the customer (the medical facility) or the employer and the consumer (the patient). The increasing use of prescription drugs and their costs are also difficult problems for insurers, healthcare providers, and patients. New drugs usually mean improved treatment, but there is a cost. Whether or not it is a reasonable cost is a critical question. Defensive medicine, which is making medical decisions to protect oneself from lawsuits (e.g., ordering diagnostic tests to make sure nothing is missed), also affects healthcare costs.

Cost-containment and cost-effectiveness efforts have been tried for many years, some with more success than others. This will undoubtedly continue, and it is important for nurses to understand the problems and possible solutions so they can participate actively in resolving cost issues. For example advanced practice registered nurses have to tackle the same challenges as physicians when dealing with reimbursement and all its requirements, many of which are aimed at controlling practice. The increasing costs and limited access to health care have led to major problems with the number of uninsured and underinsured in this country, estimated in 2013 to be 41 million (Henry J. Kaiser Family Foundation, 2014). By April 2014, when ACA plan enrollment started, an estimated 8–11 million were enrolled in an insurance plan, reducing the number of uninsured. More are expected to enroll by 2015, though the total number of uninsured is projected to remain at about 30 million in the coming years (Sanger-Katz, 2014). Chapter 5 discusses reimbursement related to ACA in more detail. Universal health coverage is still not a reality for this country. While the ACA has had an impact on the number of uninsured, it does not offer universal healthcare coverage. Everyone is required to have insurance or pay a fee for not having coverage. In an effort to lessen the number of uninsured, Medicaid eligibility expanded, thereby increasing its enrollment.

In conclusion, the IOM noted, "Needed new infrastructures will challenge today's healthcare leaders—both clinical leaders and management. The necessary environmental changes will require the interest and commitment of payers, health plans, government officials, and regulatory bodies. New skills will require new approaches by professional educators. The 21st-century healthcare system envisioned by the committee—providing care that is evidence-based, patient-centered, and systems-oriented—also implies new roles and responsibilities for patients and families" (Institute of Medicine, 2001, p. 20). Chapters 17 and 18 include more content about these critical reports.

DISPARITY IN HEALTHCARE DELIVERY   **Disparity** in healthcare delivery is certainly related to the number of uninsured and underinsured, but it is also more than this. The Institute of Medicine report *Unequal Treatment: Confronting Racial and Ethnic Disparities in Health Care* (2002) addressed factors that might cause disparities in health care. The report indicates that bias, prejudice, and stereotyping on the part of healthcare providers might be major factors in explaining differences in care. In addition, the report identified clinical uncertainty as an important factor.

> This was described as any degree of uncertainty a physician may have relative to the patient's condition, which leads the physician to depend on inferences. The doctor can therefore be viewed as operating with prior beliefs about the likelihood of patients' conditions, 'priors' that will be different according to age, gender, socioeconomic status, and race or ethnicity. When these 'priors' are considered alongside information gathered in a clinical encounter, both influence medical decisions. (Institute of Medicine, 2002, p. 3)

Disparities were particularly found in cancer, cardiovascular disease, HIV/AIDS, diabetes, and mental illness.

What can be done to improve the problem? Healthcare reform legislation of 2010 requires greater monitoring of health disparities with analysis of trends and strategies. This has partially been addressed by the earlier IOM recommendation for a national annual review, the National Healthcare Disparities Report (NHDR) published by the Agency for Healthcare Research and Quality (AHRQ). (See Chapters 17 and 18 for more information.) However, there also needs to be more cross-cultural education for healthcare professionals to improve awareness of how cultural and social factors affect health care, which should focus on attitudes, knowledge, and skills. Nursing education has included additional content and learning experiences related to cross-cultural issues. There also needs to be greater standardization of data collection to gain more understanding of the problem. Nurses need to be leaders in providing direction for this data collection as these are data that affect their practice. A third strategy that needs consideration is the development of policies that look at the entire healthcare system to decrease fragmentation in delivery and the education of healthcare professionals. Fragmented delivery affects nursing care. (For example, patients may be more acutely ill when admitted to a hospital or when they come to a clinic because previous care was not coordinated effectively.) Chapter 10 includes additional content on culture, diversity, and disparities in health care.

COMMERCIALIZATION OF HEALTH CARE   Since 1994, the United States has struggled to determine the best way to "achieve reasonably equitable distribution of healthcare, without losing control of total spending on healthcare, and without suffocating the delivery system with controls and regulations that inhibit technical progress" (Reinhardt, 1994, p. 106). This struggle continues today. Most industrialized countries have chosen to focus on equitable distribution of health care by providing universal coverage; however, the United States continues to vacillate between equity and innovative dynamism while maintaining a primarily employer-based reimbursement system. The result has been one of limited success on both sides. A definite result of this struggle has been the development of the **medical-industrial complex**. Health care has changed from a social good to a product. Healthcare delivery has become commercialized, and healthcare professionals, such as hospitals and physicians, have turned more toward business techniques, using multiple methods such as advertising and tighter control of costs to survive. The rapid growth in hospitals and other types of healthcare facilities has at times put pressure on all providers to find patients. This pressure leads to economic problems with increasing costs, and also to new healthcare delivery approaches. Not all of these factors have been negative, as some changes have resulted in improvement with better management and increased focus on community care. In most communities competition is high among all types of HCOs. After the Clinton administration effort to reform health care failed, most of the major changes occurred in the private sector. These changes nevertheless were modest and did not address the growing number of uninsured. It is, however, the private sector focus that set the stage for the rapid growth of managed care and the tremendous change experienced by the healthcare delivery system. As managed care expanded, it experienced more criticism. Inevitably blame became an issue. Many questions arose as managed care became more complex. Who started managed care? Who wanted it? Was it the employers, who experienced accelerating healthcare costs for their employees? Was it the government, which also experienced this cost acceleration? Was it the consumer, who wanted better access to care and also decreased personal costs? What did the provider want? What were these groups willing to give up? What was managed care supposed to be? These questions have not been easy to answer as the healthcare system turned more to business methods and managed care. The fact is that the healthcare delivery system is very complex, with many players, and there is no easy solution for the problem of increasing healthcare costs. The United States now moves into the era of ACA. Since this is new legislation and its provisions are activated over time, its impact on the healthcare industry is as yet unclear. However, it is apparent more people now have insurance coverage, which has implications across the healthcare delivery system. (See Appendix B.)

CONSUMERS   There is no doubt that consumers (patients) have been greatly troubled by many of the changes that have occurred in the healthcare delivery system. Of particular concern to consumers are:

- increasing access problems.
- increasing costs.
- decreasing quality.
- confusion over the role of third-party payers.
- caregiver competence and ethics.
- impersonal care.
- decreased communication.

Consumers can no longer rely on having the same physician to care for them over time. Communities are finding that their local hospitals are merging, disappearing, or being purchased by large for-profit healthcare corporations. With these changes hospitals often lose their communities. Many consumers lost their trust in the healthcare system and its providers, physicians, nurses, and the like. During these changes, managed care was very influential. The past few years have revealed a backlash against managed care with anti-managed care legislation, which was targeted to reduce managed care control over healthcare processes and decisions. The media played an important role in getting the word out about managed care and consumer concerns. Congress focused on issues of healthcare consumer rights, and cases related to managed care found their way to the U.S. Supreme Court. Employers even felt the backlash from their employees, who requested more healthcare plan options and insisted on their right to choose their own healthcare providers. This does not mean that managed care was eliminated, but rather that it has changed over the years. It has also had an impact on all types of healthcare insurers that have adopted many of the managed care approaches to healthcare coverage. Recent legislative activity has finally addressed the growing concern of prescription coverage for seniors, yet even before the legislation was passed, there were criticisms about the proposed coverage (e.g., the amount of out-of-pocket costs seniors would still have to pay). It is clear that consumers are assuming a greater role in healthcare policy and that this will continue. Chapter 5 describes healthcare economics in more detail, and Chapter 11 discusses healthcare consumerism. Nurses need to be more aware of consumerism as they often assume the role of patient advocate.

Public and Private Policy

Despite the active involvement of healthcare professional organizations and others in the United States, the federal government is the major influence on the financing, structure, and delivery of healthcare services. The United States does not have universal healthcare coverage nor does it have a national system of health care, even with the strong federal government influence. One might conclude that because of the federal government's major role, the United States would have an overall healthcare policy. This, however, is not the case. The lack of a coordinated federal and state view of healthcare delivery often results in different, sometimes conflictual, approaches to health problems. Some policies are poorly written and designed. Others are purposely vague so many groups can feel they are represented by the policy. Not everyone will be a winner with every policy. This is particularly important to understand with healthcare policy. Some groups are represented and receive the services they need, and in the same policy, others are denied services due to lack of funds, resources, and the like.

Box 2-2 identifies some of the key federal government departments and agencies that participate actively in developing public policy. Figure 2-2 describes the U.S. Department of Health and Human Services.

BOX 2-2	IMPORTANT FEDERAL GOVERNMENT DEPARTMENTS AND AGENCIES

- Agency for Healthcare Quality and Research (AHQR)
- Center for Medicare & Medicaid Services (CMS)
- Centers for Disease Control and Prevention (CDC)
- Consumer Product Safety Commission (CPSC)
- Department of Health and Human Services (HHS)
- Food and Drug Administration (FDA)
- National Institute for Occupational Safety and Health (NIOSH)
- National Institutes of Health (NIH)
- Occupational Safety and Health Administration (OSHA)
- Veteran's Administration (VA)

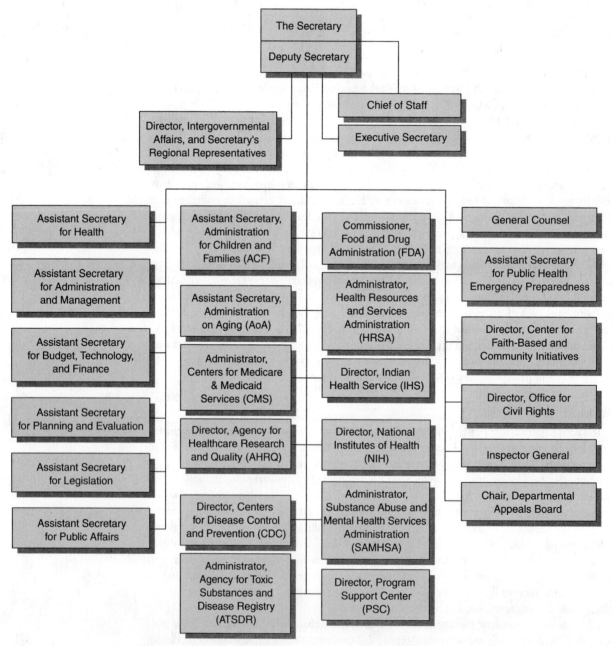

Figure 2-2 U.S. Department of Health and Human Services

BOX 2-3	EXAMPLES OF ORGANIZATIONS IMPORTANT TO THE HEALTHCARE DELIVERY SYSTEM THAT INFLUENCE HEALTHCARE POLICIES

- National Association of Children's Hospitals and Related Institutions (NACHRI)
- American Academy of Hospice and Palliative Medicine (AAHPM)
- American Association of Homes and Services for the Aging (AAHSA)
- American Association of Retired Persons (AARP)
- American Home Care Association (AHCA)
- American Hospital Association (AHA)
- American Nurses Association (ANA)
- American Organization of Nurse Executives (AONE)
- Nursing specialty organizations
- American Public Health Association (APHA)
- Disease-focused organizations (e.g., Arthritis Foundation [AF], American Diabetes Association [ADA])
- The Joint Commission
- National Association of Private Psychiatric Hospitals (NAPPH)
- National Association of Public Hospitals (NAPH)
- National Committee for Quality Assurance (NCQA)
- National Health Council (NHC)

There are two major categories of policies: private and public. **Private policy** is healthcare policy that is developed by either HCOs or a profession, such as nursing. Some examples of organizations that participate in healthcare policy development are identified in Box 2-3.

Public policy should reflect the needs of the public, but politics influence and shape many policies, sometimes to the detriment of the policy. This is when political conflict can occur and has occurred in healthcare policy issues. Should those who have good healthcare insurance coverage give up something so those who do not have coverage can get it? One can find disagreement on the answer to this question. Public policies are categorized as (1) regulatory policies (e.g., registered nurse [RN] licensure that regulates practice) and (2) allocative policies, which involve money distribution. The second type of policy provides benefits for some at the expense of others to ensure that certain public objectives are met (Finkelman & Kenner, 2016). It is difficult to develop public policy because there are often potential conflicts that must be considered. It is also impossible to meet all needs for all people. This means that choices, deals, and compromises will be made, and this is where politics have an effect. **Cost-benefit analysis** is used to determine the pros and cons of the various alternatives, which should lead to the best choice. Figure 2-3 describes several types of public policies that are relevant to healthcare policy.

The Policy-Making Process

A **policy** is a course of action that affects a large number of people, and it is stimulated by a need. Policies may include a mixture of laws, regulations, interpretations, court decisions, and other information relevant to the policy content. What is the purpose of healthcare policy? It can answer questions such as the following:

- What healthcare services are reimbursed?
- What is the reimbursement for a particular healthcare service?
- Who can obtain reimbursement for a service?
- How are healthcare resources allocated?
- Who is eligible for specific healthcare services?
- Who may provide a service?
- What are the educational requirements and competencies required for specific healthcare professionals?
- Who pays for healthcare services?

These are all critical questions in today's healthcare environment, and they demonstrate the impact that policy has on healthcare delivery. Why are these questions important for nurses? Input from healthcare professionals is important during the policy-making process. Healthcare

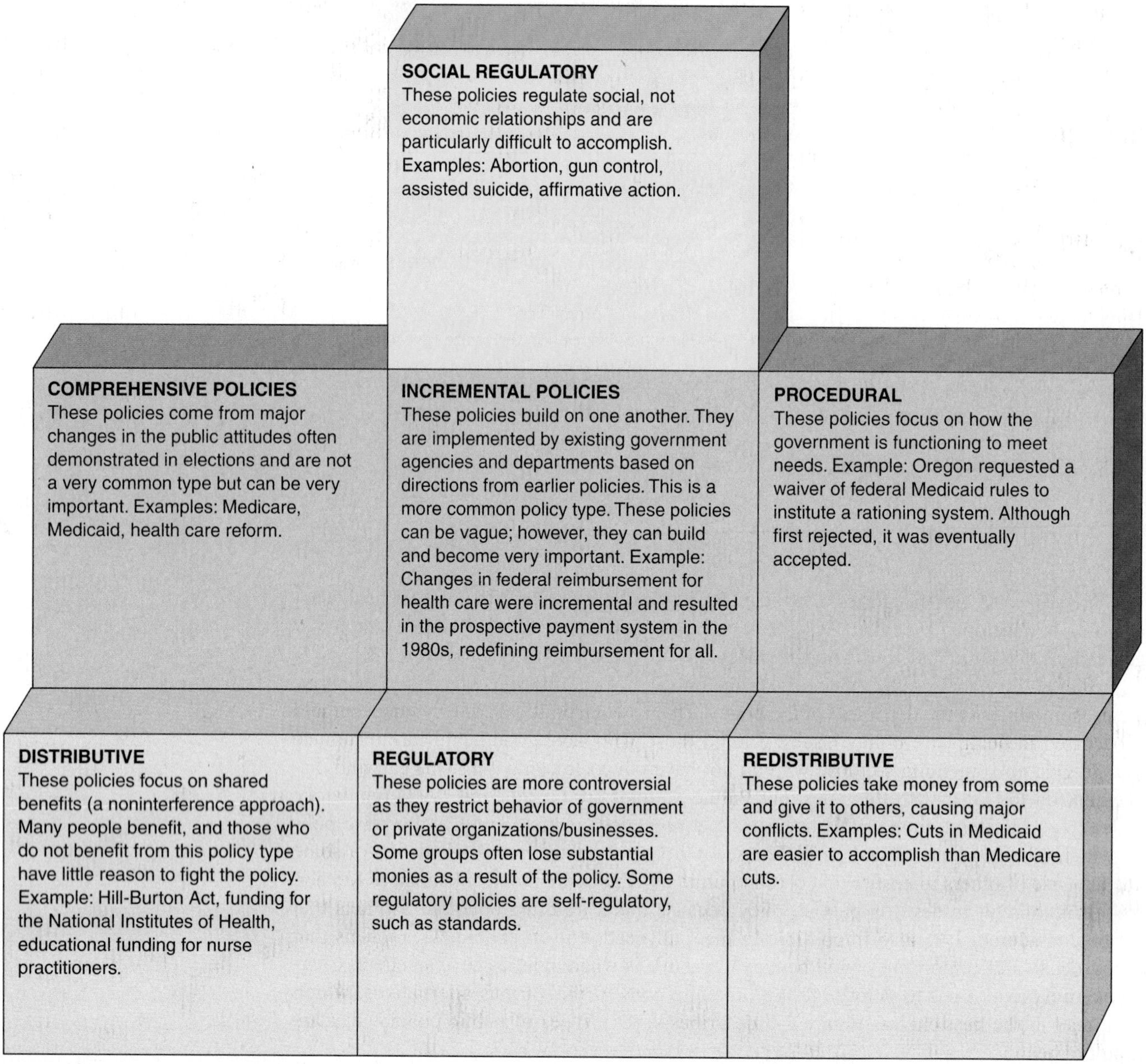

SOCIAL REGULATORY
These policies regulate social, not economic relationships and are particularly difficult to accomplish. Examples: Abortion, gun control, assisted suicide, affirmative action.

COMPREHENSIVE POLICIES
These policies come from major changes in the public attitudes often demonstrated in elections and are not a very common type but can be very important. Examples: Medicare, Medicaid, health care reform.

INCREMENTAL POLICIES
These policies build on one another. They are implemented by existing government agencies and departments based on directions from earlier policies. This is a more common policy type. These policies can be vague; however, they can build and become very important. Example: Changes in federal reimbursement for health care were incremental and resulted in the prospective payment system in the 1980s, redefining reimbursement for all.

PROCEDURAL
These policies focus on how the government is functioning to meet needs. Example: Oregon requested a waiver of federal Medicaid rules to institute a rationing system. Although first rejected, it was eventually accepted.

DISTRIBUTIVE
These policies focus on shared benefits (a noninterference approach). Many people benefit, and those who do not benefit from this policy type have little reason to fight the policy. Example: Hill-Burton Act, funding for the National Institutes of Health, educational funding for nurse practitioners.

REGULATORY
These policies are more controversial as they restrict behavior of government or private organizations/businesses. Some groups often lose substantial monies as a result of the policy. Some regulatory policies are self-regulatory, such as standards.

REDISTRIBUTIVE
These policies take money from some and give it to others, causing major conflicts. Examples: Cuts in Medicaid are easier to accomplish than Medicare cuts.

Figure 2-3 Types of public policy

professionals have expertise that may affect policy outcome, and nursing practice is often directly affected by healthcare policy. The **policy-making process** should be very familiar to nurses because it is a problem-solving process, similar to the nursing process. The policy-making process steps are described in Figure 2-4.

To arrive at the best solution, it is critical to begin by assessing the problems. The assessment recognizes that policies impact every aspect of life depending on the specific policy. For example, healthcare policies impact such concerns as quality of care, services provided, who can provide care, reimbursement, and much more. Each policy will have its own criteria, identified during the policy-making process. Today, however, typical criteria used in the development of healthcare policy include the following:

- Cost-benefit analysis
- Efficiency
- Equity

Generally people think of policy as providing the greatest good for the greatest number of people, but not all policies do this. Political feasibility must be considered when policies are

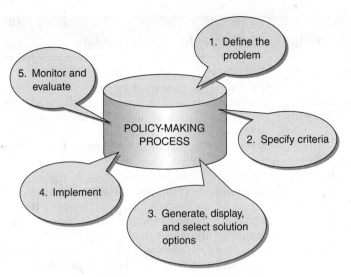

Figure 2-4 The policy-making process

developed because it can make the difference between a successful policy and a failed one. If a policy is developed and legislation is proposed that supports the policy but there is limited political support for it, the policy and its legislation will never be accepted. Outcomes have become a more important consideration in policy development. Outcome delivery analysis allows for more informed decision making. Outcome data are used to assist in the development of healthcare policy by either improving, deleting, or creating new policies. With the increasing concern about the quality of care, outcomes are even more important to better understand current care delivery (Institute of Medicine, 2001).

The Political Process, Health Policy, and the Nurse

Since most health policy comes through the legislative process, politics cannot be ignored. There are many stakeholders who want to influence the legislative process, and most are not elected officials. Nurses should be no exception. Nurses can get involved in the **political process**, often at the local and state levels, and provide input in the direction that health policy will take, how it will be implemented, and how best to evaluate the results. Nurses need to understand the process and the system so they can influence these decisions. More nurses have assumed leadership roles in policy making by holding elected public offices in state legislatures and Congress and positions in many government agencies. This gives nursing more voice in policy making at all levels. Lobbying is another important tool. Coalition building helps nurses join with other groups that have similar interests. This increases opportunity to demonstrate strength in numbers and better clarify nursing perspectives about health care and about the nursing profession. Networking and collaboration require some compromises. The result should be as effective as possible. All of this is related to leadership and the skills of communication, planning, decision making, collaboration, responding to change effectively, and encouraging participation of nurses at all levels. Political factors need to be considered in the review of possible solutions to policy issues. Selecting a solution that does not have a chance of succeeding due to politics is not helpful and only leads to frustration. When legislation is enacted, the next step is to develop rules or regulations that guide implementation of the law or the policy. As policy is implemented, it should be monitored, which may lead to additional changes. This entire process is cyclical in that evaluation data lead to other policies or reshaping of current policy. The process is dynamic as it is affected by many factors. Table 2-1 describes this process.

Healthcare Policy and Nursing

As changes occur in the healthcare environment—policy, legislation, regulation, and ethics—it is important for nurses to understand and participate in the legislative process and consider how policy may affect ethical decision making. Active involvement of nurses in all of these areas must occur at the local, state, and federal levels.

Table 2-1	APPLYING THE POLICY DEVELOPMENT PROCESS	
Policy Process	**Applied to Legislative Process**	**Example**
Policy issue develops	Senator learns about consumer concern about a health issue and has staff work on the problem.	Staffing levels in acute care hospitals are affecting the quality and safety of care. Various hospitals provide examples of errors and lack of quality that have led to patient deaths and complications that have extended the need for treatment.
Gather data about issue	Legislative staff gather data about the issue; some data may come from federal departments or agencies, which act as resources for legislative activity. Criteria are developed to evaluate the data (e.g., cost, efficiency, equity, and political feasibility).	Experts, patients, insurers, hospitals, nurses, physicians, and so on provide testimony. Data related to errors, quality, and access will be used to further understand the problem. Data about enrollment and graduation rates in nursing schools would be important to obtain. Costs related to lack of staff, including costs for the hospitals, insurers, employers, and patients (consumers), should be reviewed.
Coalition building	Senator will form coalitions to back the legislation with other senators, representatives, and other stakeholders such as healthcare professional organizations.	Examples of stakeholders who would be interested in this problem and solution would be healthcare professionals (nurses, physicians) and their organizations, American Hospital Association, insurers, employers, consumer groups, nurse educators, and others. Building a coalition from these groups would help to get the bill passed.
Identify possible solutions	Apply cost-benefit analysis of data to determine possible solutions; consider testimony from experts, lobbyists' input and pressure; arrive at list of possible solutions.	Cost data would be used to help assess cost-benefit for each of the possible solutions. Some examples of solutions might be do nothing, require every hospital to have a specific number of staff, require hospitals to use a patient classification system or require that every hospital use the same system, require minimum staffing ratios, and many others.
Select a solution	Federal (or state) written law will probably repeat some of the activities described as part of "identify possible solutions" to gather more data or clarify. Coalition building also continues throughout the process.	For this example, requiring a minimum ratio is selected as the solution. (This does not indicate that it is the best solution but is used as an example in this scenario.) A law is drafted by the senator based on information gathered during the first phases of the process. The senator will need to gain additional support in the Senate and in the House of Representatives to get the law passed. The law will wind its way through the legislative process.
Implement policy	Rules and regulations are developed; staff receive feedback on rules and regulations and implement rules and regulations to apply the law.	HHS develops draft of rules and regulations that will be used to implement the law. Professional organizations respond to them by providing feedback. The AHA submits criticisms. Rules and regulations are revised and may be posted for additional comments. By a specific date, rules and regulations are effective and required by law. Hospitals will have to get this information and make appropriate changes to meet requirements (e.g., increase staffing or alter ratios, recruit more staff, and so on).
Monitor outcomes: Evaluation	Federal department or agency responsible for implementation develops evaluation plan and monitors outcomes. The department may have to report to Congress at specific times and may recommend and implement changes as long as they are within the framework of the law. Otherwise, the department will need to recommend legislative changes (new law or amendments to the law).	Outcomes analysis is ongoing. What are the outcomes of the plan to establish a minimum staffing ratio? Are hospitals able to meet the requirement deadlines? If not, what are the barriers? Can the barriers be addressed and how?

ROLE OF NURSING   What are some examples of issues that have affected nursing?

1. An example of a policy issue that offers nursing many opportunities and substantial risks is the development of managed care in healthcare reimbursement. Nurses recognize that there are aspects of managed care that demonstrate positive changes in healthcare delivery, such as preventive services and a greater emphasis on the continuum of care rather than episodic care. Nurses have also had to cope with staffing shortages, shortened hospital stays, increasing patient acuity both in the hospital and in the community, fewer staff, and a complex reimbursement system. These changes have made it difficult for nurses and other healthcare professionals to deliver what they believe is quality care.

2. Understanding health policy and its implications for leadership and management is a journey through the healthcare delivery system, its players, successes, limitations, and future. If there is acceptance that the healthcare environment is dynamic and changing, one must consider what the role of the nurse will be in this process and what the end product will be. The new healthcare environment demands that providers take responsibility for whole populations. The focus is not just on curing patients but also preventing illness and providing care across the healthcare continuum. All types of settings and all providers need to focus on providing high-quality care, and it must be cost effective. Healthcare professionals need to develop new skills, competencies, and attitudes toward their work to reinvent their professional culture. Nursing has recognized this change by including more content about public/community health in education. (See Chapter 7.)

3. The increase in direct reimbursement for care provided by advanced practice registered nurses is an excellent example of the impact of legislation and government on registered nursing practice. Over time, this reimbursement has expanded. As more advanced practice registered nurses practice in primary care settings, they will need to meet the same reimbursement requirements as physicians along with insurer performance evaluation.

4. The federal government continues to provide additional funding for nursing education, something that is a major concern each year as the federal budget is developed. State legislation has also had a major impact on nursing practice. Healthcare legislation often offers opportunities to pilot new programs in education and delivery. For example, the Health Resources and Services Administration (HRSA) offers funding for grants to try new education and practice approaches such as academic-clinical partnerships, nurse residency programs, programs to increase diversity in the nursing profession, and scholarship and loan opportunities.

5. An example of a health policy change that has had a major impact on healthcare delivery in California was the passage of legislation that requires California hospitals to meet fixed nurse-to-patient ratios. This is affecting health policy in other states and on the federal level, as similar legislation is considered. Staffing is discussed further in Chapter 8.

Healthcare issues that are affected by nursing—and few are not—require nursing input if nursing is to remain a viable healthcare profession. How do nurses participate in healthcare policy development? Active participation in nursing organizations gives every nurse a voice as nursing organizations are often represented on committees that develop healthcare policy or provide input (e.g., the President's Advisory Commission on Consumer Protection and Quality in the Health Care Industry, 1996–1998, and the recent Institute of Medicine reports on quality health care). Chapters 17 and 18 include additional information on these topics. Nursing organizations use **lobbyists** to make regular contact with elected officials, at both state and federal levels, to influence policy development. In fact, some of these lobbyists are nurses. Each year, the American Nurses Association (ANA) identifies key issues that it will focus on as it lobbies Congress. Typical issues include nurse staffing plans and ratios, mandatory overtime, nurse education incentives and funding, needlestick protection, advanced practice Medicaid reimbursement and scope of practice, care coordination, whistle-blower protection, ergonomics, nursing workforce data, latex allergies, continued competence, unlicensed assistive personnel, workplace violence, nurse immigration, and the nursing workforce. These issues have a direct impact on practice. Individual nurses are encouraged to contact their own elected representatives and provide them with important information about nursing and healthcare needs in their communities. Nursing expertise has been beneficial to policy makers, but if nurses do not speak out, they will not be recognized for their expertise.

Nursing expertise can be used to assist policy development through testimony at local, state, and federal legislative levels. Understanding consumer needs and acting as the patient's advocate have been important elements of nursing for a long time. Nurses can help consumers understand healthcare policy, legislation, regulation, and their effect on healthcare delivery. There should be no doubt that every nurse has a role to play. It may be in writing a letter to a member of Congress, calling a senator, attending a nursing organization meeting, providing expert testimony, serving on a local or state healthcare planning committee, or participating in other types of activities to influence policy development.

IMPORTANCE OF COLLABORATION IN HEALTHCARE POLICY   Concern over healthcare changes, policy, and reimbursement has even brought nurses and physicians closer as they work collaboratively for a common goal: better-quality care. Nurses and physicians need to do much more of this to solve problems such as staff cutbacks, error rates, patients' rights, and ethical concerns.

An example of collaboration between nursing and other organizations is ANA's project with Johnson & Johnson to develop several media campaigns to address the need for more nurses. Nurses recognize the need to further develop the image of nursing and that combining communication skills, consumer education, and media expertise will help to improve the image. Sometimes this will mean collaborating with others such as physicians and other healthcare professionals to initiate a broader media impact that affects the profession's image as a member of the interprofessional team, and at other times, it will mean focusing just on nursing and what nurses can do. Collaboration is required as healthcare professionals participate in healthcare changes. New ways to support collaboration need to be created (Finkelman & Kenner, 2016; Institute of Medicine, 2003).

Legislation: Impact on Healthcare Delivery and Policy

What is important healthcare legislation, both federal and state, and how has this legislation affected healthcare delivery? Legislation is a part of health policy and has a direct impact on legal and ethical issues in healthcare delivery. Legislation occurs at all three government levels: federal, state, and local. Most healthcare legislation is found at the federal and state levels, so these will be the focus in this chapter. Nurses should, however, be aware of relevant local legislation that might be passed by cities or counties.

FEDERAL LEVEL   The federal legislative process is clearly defined. The ANA website includes a description of the process that can be used by nurses as they become involved in policy development. The political action component of the ANA is very active in influencing health policy and monitoring legislation. Other nursing organizations, such as the American Organization of Nurse Executives (AONE), the National League for Nursing (NLN), the American Association of Colleges of Nursing (AACN), and nursing specialty organizations, are also involved.

When legislation is signed into law, the work is not done. Most legislation establishes or modifies federal or state programs. When this occurs, the administrative responsibility of the law becomes the responsibility of a government agency, program, or department. For example, in the Department of Health and Human Services (HHS), the Center for Medicare and Medicaid Services (CMS) is responsible for implementation of Medicare and Medicaid laws. Before a law is put into practice, regulations that describe how it will be implemented are developed. The regulations can make a difference in the law's success. In the federal arena, draft regulations are published in the *Federal Register*, which makes the regulations available for public comment. In some cases, public hearings are held to discuss the regulations. When healthcare legislation and its regulations are important to nurses, representatives from nursing organizations often comment on regulation drafts. In addition, nurses may have participated earlier in the healthcare policy development, such as by providing expert testimony to Congressional committees, lobbying efforts, and so forth. Regulations can affect staffing, HCO policies and procedures, access to care, and other delivery issues. All comments about regulations are considered, and the agency, program, or department releases the final regulations. This occurs at least 30 days prior to the effective date of application. After that date, the law and its regulations are in effect.

Understanding the history of critical healthcare legislation, relationships between laws, and their effect on the delivery system is very important for all healthcare professionals who hope to participate in future healthcare policy development and implementation. There is no doubt that remaining current with federal legislation can be a time-consuming activity, which is why nursing organizations have lobbyists who follow legislation and provide input as well as political action committees (PACs) to influence the policy-making and election processes. The ANA website includes information about its PAC. As nurses enter practice, laws relevant to their practice should be understood. With access to the Internet, it is easier to keep current with healthcare legislation.

What are the critical federal legislation and regulation actions related to healthcare delivery in the United States? The two pieces of legislation and their amendments that have had the most impact on the health and welfare system in the United States are the Social Security Act of 1935 and the Public Health Act of 1944. The changes and additions to these laws demonstrate the long-term effect laws can have on society. Passing legislation should not be taken lightly because it may not be easy to reverse and has a major impact on citizens and consumers. Accountability and responsibility are critical components of the legislative process.

STATE LEVEL   States are active in healthcare policy, legislation, and regulation. Generally they are involved in financing, delivery of services, and oversight of insurance. The latter has become very important when managed care developed and had an impact on all types of healthcare insurance. There are five typical healthcare areas in which the states have major input:

1. *Public health and safety.* States are responsible for protecting public welfare, including services related to such areas as prevention and treatment of communicable diseases, monitoring of environmental health conditions, harm from violence, and workplace accidents.
2. *Provision of indigent care.* Most state constitutions require that the state, either alone or with local governments, provide health care to those who cannot pay for it. This is usually done through state or local government-run facilities and the Medicaid program, which is a state and federal government program. This care adjusts as healthcare policy, delivery, and reimbursement change.
3. *Purchase care.* Many states have been changing from providers of health care to purchasers of care. This is particularly relevant for the Medicaid program and for state public employees for whom the state provides insurance coverage. This requires that states monitor the care (performance and outcomes) they purchase.
4. *Regulation.* States are responsible for licensing and/or credentialing facilities and professionals to ensure quality and for regulating insurers. Through this process, states get involved in regulation of healthcare services issues such as quality improvement, use review, solvency, benefits, marketing, access to services, provider contracting, rating, grievances and appeals, organizational structure, reporting, consumer concerns, and confidentiality. These activities demonstrate the major role that states have in the regulation of insurers.
5. *Resource allocation.* Historically states have not been responsible for funding of medical and nursing education because this has been in federal hands; however, some states have become more involved in funding issues for nursing education due to the increasing concern in some states about short-term and long-term nursing shortages. States are involved in identifying state healthcare delivery needs (e.g., number of healthcare professional graduates a state needs to meet healthcare requirements). Some states still assist in funding public healthcare facilities. Due to the California legislation in 2002 that directed the California state health department to develop staffing guidelines, many other states have considered doing something similar, which means state governments will be more involved in health **resource allocation**. This is a good example of how legislation passed in one state can impact other states and what they might consider legislative issues.

States have their own processes for developing, passing, and implementing their laws and procedures related to their regulation processes, although they are usually similar to the federal process. Nurses need to understand their state processes and participate when content is relevant to nursing. Nurses are usually even more involved in the process at the state level than at the federal level. The state nurses' association is often the major player. State activities are more accessible to nurses for lobbying, support of candidates, involvement in committees, and personal contact with legislators. Often nurses feel less intimidated by the state level than the federal level. As noted earlier, Table 2-1, provides a description of the relationship between the policy process and the legislative process.

PATIENT PROTECTION AND AFFORDABLE CARE ACT OF 2010 (ACA): MAJOR LEGISLATION

Early in the Obama administration, significant steps were taken to begin to address the crisis in health care:

- President Obama signed the Children's Health Insurance Reauthorization Act on February 4, 2009, which provides quality health care to 11 million children—4 million of whom were previously uninsured.
- The American Recovery and Reinvestment Act protects health coverage for 7 million Americans who lose their jobs through a 65 percent COBRA subsidy to make coverage affordable.
- The Recovery Act also invests $19 billion in computerized medical records that will help to reduce costs and improve quality while ensuring patients' privacy.
- The Recovery Act also provides:
  - funding in the amount of $1 billion for prevention and wellness to improve America's health and help to reduce healthcare costs.
  - funding in the amount of $1.1 billion for comparative effectiveness research that will give doctors objective information about which treatments work and which do not.
  - funding in the amount of $500 million for health workforce to help train the next generation of doctors and nurses (The White House, 2009).

The Obama administration's 2009 healthcare reform approach initiative goals included the following:

- Reduce long-term growth of healthcare costs for businesses and government
- Protect families from bankruptcy or debt because of healthcare costs
- Guarantee choice of doctors and health plans
- Invest in prevention and wellness
- Improve patient safety and quality of care
- Ensure affordable, quality health coverage for all Americans
- Maintain coverage when you change or lose your job
- End barriers to coverage for people with preexisting medical conditions (The White House, 2009)

The Patient Protection and Affordable Care Act became law on March 23, 2010 (P.L. 111-148), and the Health Care and Education Reconciliation Act of 2010 followed on March 30, 2010 (P.L. 111-152) (*Washington Post*, 2010). The latter law reconciled some concerns with the Senate version, which became P.L. 111-148. Public Law 111-148 has numerous provisions covering a broad range of issues from health reimbursement, delivery, research, delivery models, and practice. This is significant legislation; however, there is always the potential that over time the law will be changed; this is part of the political process. The law will be implemented over a number of years with some provisions not implemented until 2018, as described in Appendix B. The following are some of the provisions that may or may not be related to reimbursement in the law that relate to nursing:

- Increase nursing student loans to expand the profession
- Increase geriatric education
- Increase funding for advanced nursing education
- Provide grants for nurse-managed health centers
- Establish accountable care organizations (ACOs)
- Increase nursing faculty loans
- Arrange for workforce diversity grants
- Provide and expand prevention programs
- Improve public health education and services
- Expand primary care
- Establish Patient-Centered Outcomes Research Institute (PCORI)
- Promote changes in home health services

Box 2-4 describes the "Key Provisions of the Affordable Care Act by Year".

BOX 2-4	KEY FEATURES OF THE AFFORDABLE CARE ACT BY YEAR

On March 23, 2010, President Obama signed the Affordable Care Act. The law puts in place comprehensive health insurance reforms that will roll out over four years and beyond.

Overview of the Healthcare Law

2010: A new Patient's Bill of Rights goes into effect, protecting consumers from the worst abuses of the insurance industry. Cost-free preventive services begin for many Americans.

2011: People with Medicare can get key preventive services for free, and also receive a 50% discount on brand-name drugs in the Medicare "doughnut hole."

2012: Accountable care organizations and other programs help doctors and healthcare providers work together to deliver better care.

2013: Open enrollment in the Health Insurance Marketplace begins on October 1.

2014: All Americans will have access to affordable health insurance options. The Marketplace allows individuals and small businesses to compare health plans on a level playing field. Middle- and low-income families will get tax credits that cover a significant portion of the cost of coverage. And the Medicaid program will be expanded to cover more low-income Americans. All together, these reforms mean that millions of people who were previously uninsured will gain coverage, thanks to the Affordable Care Act.

2010

New Consumer Protections

- **Putting Information for Consumers Online.** The law provides a place where consumers can compare health insurance coverage options and pick the coverage that works for them.
- **Prohibiting Denying Coverage of Children Based on Preexisting Conditions.** The healthcare law includes new rules to prevent insurance companies from denying coverage to children under the age of 19 due to a preexisting condition.
- **Prohibiting Insurance Companies from Rescinding Coverage.** In the past, insurance companies could search for an error or other technical mistake on a customer's application and use this error to deny payment for services when he or she got sick. The healthcare law makes this illegal. After media reports cited incidents of breast cancer patients losing coverage, insurance companies agreed to end this practice immediately.
- **Eliminating Lifetime Limits on Insurance Coverage.** Under the law, insurance companies will be prohibited from imposing lifetime dollar limits on essential benefits, such as hospital stays.
- **Regulating Annual Limits on Insurance Coverage.** Under the law, insurance companies' use of annual dollar limits on the amount of insurance coverage a patient may receive will be restricted for new plans in the individual market and all group plans. In 2014 the use of annual dollar limits on essential benefits such as hospital stays will be banned for new plans in the individual market and all group plans.
- **Appealing Insurance Company Decisions.** The law provides consumers with a way to appeal coverage determinations or claims to their insurance company and establishes an external review process.

- **Establishing Consumer Assistance Programs in the States.** Under the law, states that apply receive federal grants to help set up or expand independent offices to help consumers navigate the private health insurance system. These programs help consumers file complaints and appeals, enroll in health coverage, and get educated about their rights and responsibilities in group health plans or individual health insurance policies. The programs will also collect data on the types of problems consumers have, and file reports with the U.S. Department of Health and Human Services to identify trouble spots that need further oversight.

Improving Quality and Lowering Costs

- **Providing Small Business Health Insurance Tax Credits.** Up to 4 million small businesses are eligible for tax credits to help them provide insurance benefits to their workers. The first phase of this provision provides a credit worth up to 35% of the employer's contribution to the employees' health insurance. Small non-profit organizations may receive up to a 25% credit.
- **Offering Relief for 4 Million Seniors Who Hit the Medicare Prescription Drug "Doughnut Hole."** An estimated 4 million seniors will reach the gap in Medicare prescription drug coverage known as the "doughnut hole" this year. Each eligible senior will receive a one-time, tax-free $250 rebate check. *First checks mailed in June 2010 and will continue monthly throughout 2010 as seniors hit the coverage gap.*
- **Providing Free Preventive Care.** All new plans must cover certain preventive services such as mammograms and colonoscopies without charging a deductible, copay, or coinsurance.
- **Preventing Disease and Illness.** A new $15 billion Prevention and Public Health Fund will invest in proven prevention and public health programs that can help keep Americans healthy—from smoking cessation to combating obesity. *Funding begins in 2010.*
- **Cracking Down on Healthcare Fraud.** Current efforts to fight fraud have returned more than $2.5 billion to the Medicare Trust Fund in fiscal year 2009 alone. The new law invests new resources and requires new screening procedures for healthcare providers to boost these efforts and reduce fraud and waste in Medicare, Medicaid, and CHIP.

Increasing Access to Affordable Care

- **Providing Access to Insurance for Uninsured Americans with Preexisting Conditions.** The Preexisting Condition provision provides new coverage options to individuals who have been uninsured for at least six months because of a preexisting condition. States have the option of running this program in their state. If a state chooses not to do so, a plan will be established by the Department of Health and Human Services in that state.
- **Extending Coverage for Young Adults.** Under the law, young adults will be allowed to stay on their parents' plan until they turn 26 years old (in the case of existing group health plans, this right does not apply if the young adult is offered insurance at work). Check with your insurance company or employer to see if you qualify.

(continued)

BOX 2-4	KEY FEATURES OF THE AFFORDABLE CARE ACT BY YEAR (CONTINUED)

- **Expanding Coverage for Early Retirees.** Too often, Americans who retire without employer-sponsored insurance and before they are eligible for Medicare see their life savings disappear because of high rates in the individual market. To preserve employer coverage for early retirees until more affordable coverage is available through the new Exchanges by 2014, the new law creates a $5 billion program to provide needed financial help for employment-based plans to continue to provide valuable coverage to people who retire between the ages of 55 and 65, as well as their spouses and dependents.

- **Rebuilding the Primary Care Workforce.** To strengthen the availability of primary care, there are new incentives in the law to expand the number of primary care doctors, nurses, and physician assistants. These include funding for scholarships and loan repayments for primary care doctors and nurses working in underserved areas. Doctors and nurses receiving payments made under any state loan repayment or loan forgiveness program intended to increase the availability of healthcare services in underserved or health professional shortage areas will not have to pay taxes on those payments.

- **Holding Insurance Companies Accountable for Unreasonable Rate Hikes.** The law allows states that have or plan to implement measures that require insurance companies to justify their premium increases will be eligible for $250 million in new grants. Insurance companies with excessive or unjustified premium exchanges may not be able to participate in the new health insurance Exchanges in 2014.

- **Allowing States to Cover More People on Medicaid.** States will be able to receive federal matching funds for covering some additional low-income individuals and families under Medicaid for whom federal funds were not previously available. This will make it easier for states that choose to do so to cover more of their residents.

- **Increasing Payments for Rural Healthcare Providers.** Today 68% of medically underserved communities across the nation are in rural areas. These communities often have trouble attracting and retaining medical professionals. The law provides increased payment to rural healthcare providers to help them continue to serve their communities.

- **Strengthening Community Health Centers.** The law includes new funding to support the construction of and expand services at community health centers, allowing these centers to serve some 20 million new patients across the country.

2011

Improving Quality and Lowering Costs

- **Offering Prescription Drug Discounts.** Seniors who reach the coverage gap will receive a 50% discount when buying Medicare Part D–covered brand-name prescription drugs. Over the next 10 years, seniors will receive additional savings on brand-name and generic drugs until the coverage gap is closed in 2020.

- **Providing Free Preventive Care for Seniors.** The law provides certain free preventive services, such as annual wellness visits and personalized prevention plans for seniors on Medicare.

- **Improving Healthcare Quality and Efficiency.** The law establishes a new Center for Medicare & Medicaid Innovation that will begin testing new ways of delivering care to patients. These methods are expected to improve the quality of care and reduce the rate of growth in healthcare costs for Medicare, Medicaid, and the Children's Health Insurance Program (CHIP). In addition, by January 1, 2011, HHS will submit a national strategy for quality improvement in health care. Learn more about the Center for Medicare & Medicaid Innovation from its website.

- **Improving Care for Seniors After They Leave the Hospital.** The Community Care Transitions Program will help high-risk Medicare beneficiaries who are hospitalized avoid unnecessary readmissions by coordinating care and connecting patients to services in their communities.

- **Introducing New Innovations to Bring Down Costs.** The Independent Payment Advisory Board will begin operations to develop and submit proposals to Congress and the president aimed at extending the life of the Medicare Trust Fund. The board is expected to focus on ways to target waste in the system and recommend ways to reduce costs, improve health outcomes for patients, and expand access to high-quality care.

Increasing Access to Affordable Care

- **Increasing Access to Services at Home and in the Community.** The Community First Choice Option allows states to offer home- and community-based services to disabled individuals through Medicaid rather than institutional care in nursing homes.

Holding Insurance Companies Accountable

- **Bringing Down Healthcare Premiums.** To ensure premium dollars are spent primarily on health care, the law generally requires that at least 85% of all premium dollars collected by insurance companies for large employer plans are spent on healthcare services and healthcare quality improvement. For plans sold to individuals and small employers, at least 80% of the premium must be spent on benefits and quality improvement. If insurance companies do not meet these goals because their administrative costs or profits are too high, they must provide rebates to consumers.

- **Addressing Overpayments to Big Insurance Companies and Strengthening Medicare Advantage.** Today Medicare pays Medicare Advantage insurance companies more than $1,000 more per person on average than is spent per person in Traditional Medicare. This results in increased premiums for all Medicare beneficiaries, including the 77% of beneficiaries who are not currently enrolled in a Medicare Advantage plan. The law levels the playing field by gradually eliminating this discrepancy. People enrolled in a Medicare Advantage plan will still receive all guaranteed Medicare benefits, and the law provides bonus payments to Medicare Advantage plans that provide high-quality care.

2012

Improving Quality and Lowering Costs

- **Linking Payment to Quality Outcomes.** The law establishes a hospital Value-Based Purchasing (VBP) program in Traditional

BOX 2-4 (CONTINUED)

Medicare. This program offers financial incentives to hospitals to improve the quality of care. Hospital performance is required to be publicly reported, beginning with measures relating to heart attacks, heart failure, pneumonia, surgical care, healthcare associated infections, and patients' perception of care.

- **Encouraging Integrated Health Systems.** The new law provides incentives for physicians to join together to form "accountable care organizations." These groups allow doctors to better coordinate patient care and improve the quality, help prevent disease and illness, and reduce unnecessary hospital admissions. If accountable care organizations provide high-quality care and reduce costs to the healthcare system, they can keep some of the money they have helped save.
- **Reducing Paperwork and Administrative Costs.** Health care remains one of the few industries that relies on paper records. The new law will institute a series of changes to standardize billing and requires health plans to begin adopting and implementing rules for the secure, confidential, electronic exchange of health information. Using electronic health records will reduce paperwork and administrative burdens; cut costs; reduce medical errors; and most important, improve the quality of care.
- **Understanding and Fighting Health Disparities.** To help understand and reduce persistent health disparities, the law requires any ongoing or new federal health program to collect and report racial, ethnic, and language data. The Secretary of Health and Human Services will use this data to help identify and reduce disparities.

Increasing Access to Affordable Care

- **Providing New, Voluntary Options for Long-Term Care Insurance.** The law creates a voluntary long-term care insurance program—called CLASS—to provide cash benefits to adults who become disabled. **Note: On October 14, 2011, Secretary Sebelius transmitted a report and letter to Congress stating that the department does not see a viable path forward for CLASS implementation at this time.**

2013

Improving Quality and Lowering Costs

- **Improving Preventive Health Coverage.** To expand the number of Americans receiving preventive care, the law provides new funding to state Medicaid programs that choose to cover preventive services for patients at little or no cost.
- **Expanding Authority to Bundle Payments.** The law establishes a national pilot program to encourage hospitals, doctors, and other providers to work together to improve the coordination and quality of patient care. Under payment "bundling," hospitals, doctors, and providers are paid a flat rate for an episode of care rather than the current fragmented system where each service or test or bundles of items or services are billed separately to Medicare. For example, instead of a surgical procedure generating multiple claims from multiple providers, the entire team is compensated with a "bundled" payment that provides incentives to deliver healthcare services more efficiently while maintaining or

improving quality of care. It aligns the incentives of those delivering care, and savings are shared between providers and the Medicare program.

Increasing Access to Affordable Care

- **Increasing Medicaid Payments for Primary Care Doctors.** As Medicaid programs and providers prepare to cover more patients in 2014, the act requires states to pay primary care physicians no less than 100% of Medicare payment rates in 2013 and 2014 for primary care services. The increase is fully funded by the federal government.
- **Open Enrollment in the Health Insurance Marketplace Begins.** Individuals and small businesses can buy affordable and qualified health benefit plans in this new transparent and competitive insurance marketplace.

2014

New Consumer Protections

- **Prohibiting Discrimination Due to Preexisting Conditions or Gender.** The law implements strong reforms that prohibit insurance companies from refusing to sell coverage or renew policies because of an individual's preexisting conditions. Also, in the individual and small-group market, the law eliminates the ability of insurance companies to charge higher rates due to sex or health status.
- **Eliminating Annual Limits on Insurance Coverage.** The law prohibits new plans and existing group plans from imposing annual dollar limits on the amount of coverage an individual may receive.
- **Ensuring Coverage for Individuals Participating in Clinical Trials.** Insurers will be prohibited from dropping or limiting coverage because an individual chooses to participate in a clinical trial. Applies to all clinical trials that treat cancer or other life-threatening diseases.

Improving Quality and Lowering Costs

- **Making Care More Affordable.** Tax credits to make it easier for the middle class to afford insurance will become available for people with income between 100% and 400% of the poverty line who are not eligible for other affordable coverage. (In 2010 400% of the poverty line comes out to about $43,000 for an individual or $88,000 for a family of four.) The tax credit is advanceable, so it can lower your premium payments each month, rather than making you wait for tax time. It's also refundable, so even moderate-income families can receive the full benefit of the credit. These individuals may also qualify for reduced cost-sharing (co-payments, co-insurance, and deductibles).
- **Establishing the Health Insurance Marketplace.** Starting in 2014 if your employer doesn't offer insurance, you will be able to buy it directly in the Health Insurance Marketplace. Individuals and small businesses can buy affordable and qualified health benefit plans in this new transparent and competitive insurance marketplace. The Marketplace will offer you a choice of health plans that meet certain benefits and cost standards. Starting in 2014, members of Congress will be getting their

(continued)

BOX 2-4 | **KEY FEATURES OF THE AFFORDABLE CARE ACT BY YEAR (CONTINUED)**

healthcare insurance through the Marketplace, and you will be able to buy your insurance through the Marketplace too.

- **Increasing the Small Business Tax Credit.** The law implements the second phase of the small business tax credit for qualified small businesses and small non-profit organizations. In this phase, the credit is up to 50% of the employer's contribution to provide health insurance for employees. There is also up to a 35% credit for small non-profit organizations.

Increasing Access to Affordable Care

- **Increasing Access to Medicaid.** Americans who earn less than 133% of the poverty level (approximately $14,000 for an individual and $29,000 for a family of four) will be eligible to enroll in Medicaid. States will receive 100% federal funding for the first three years to support this expanded coverage, phasing to 90% federal funding in subsequent years.
- **Promoting Individual Responsibility.** Under the law, most individuals who can afford it will be required to obtain basic health insurance coverage or pay a fee to help offset the

costs of caring for uninsured Americans. If affordable coverage is not available to an individual, he or she will be eligible for an exemption.

2015

Improving Quality and Lowering Costs

Paying Physicians Based on Value, Not Volume. A new provision will tie physician payments to the quality of care they provide. Physicians will see their payments modified so those who provide higher-value care will receive higher payments than those who provide lower-quality care.

HHS will not enforce these rules against issuers of stand-alone retiree-only plans in the private health insurance market.

Source: U.S. Department of Health and Human Services. (2014c). Key Features of the Affordable Care Act by Year. Retrieved from http://www.hhs.gov/healthcare/facts/timeline/timeline-text.html

---

Due to the ACA, changes in the structure of the health system have already occurred. ACOs are groups of providers that come together to provide coordinated services (e.g., for Medicare patients). Providers may be eligible for bonuses if they provide effective care. The medical home model is another approach to changes in the delivery system. This model provides interprofessional primary care services that are planned and coordinated. Nurse-managed health centers (NMHCs) are also increasing. These centers are advanced practice registered nurse (APRN) practices providing primary care and/or wellness services to underserved or vulnerable populations. The centers are associated with a nursing education program such as a college of nursing. The ACO, medical home model, and NMHC all focus on coordinated care for patients. Retail clinics are also expanding, typically with APRNs providing services. These are located in shopping areas such as drugstores, supermarkets, and so on.

These examples in Box 2-4 focus on nursing and delivery of care; however, the main focus of ACA is reimbursement. Any provision that requires funding calls for allocation of funds, which may or may not occur, which means some of the provisions listed above may not receive implementation funding. Additional content about reimbursement is found in Chapter 5, though many chapters include comments about this new law and its impact on healthcare delivery.

When the ACA became law, the ANA issued a press release that stated, "'ANA strongly believes that this law is a significant victory for the patients we serve. They'll have greater protection against losing or being denied health insurance coverage, and they'll have better access to primary care and the wellness and prevention programs that will keep them healthier,' said ANA President Rebecca M. Patton, MSN, RN, CNOR. 'However, we recognize that the debate over reform is not over. We are committed to helping nurses and the public understand how this change affects their lives, and will continue our work to build an affordable healthcare system that meets the needs of everyone'" (American Nurses Association, 2010, p. 1). The nursing profession has continued to support the ACA implementation. *The Future of Nursing* report discusses implications of the law and changes, as discussed throughout this text (Institute of Medicine, 2011).

LEGAL ISSUES AND NURSING ETHICS: IMPACT ON DECISION MAKING IN MANAGEMENT AND PRACTICE

Each nurse confronts legal issues daily in practice, although often it may not be obvious. Administering medication, restraining patients, protecting patients from falls, or observing a patient on suicide precautions all have legal components. Documentation is critical to any legal issue that may

APPLYING EVIDENCE-BASED PRACTICE

Evidence for Effective Leadership and Management

CITATION: U.S. Senate. (2010). The Patient Protection and Affordable Care Act. Retrieved from http://www.dpc.senate.gov/healthreformbill/healthbill04.pdf

OVERVIEW: *The following is a summary of the key content areas found in the Patient Protection and Affordable Care Act of 2010.*

The Patient Protection and Affordable Care Act (ACA) will ensure that all Americans have access to quality, affordable health care and will create the transformation within the healthcare system necessary to contain costs. The Congressional Budget Office (CBO) has determined that the ACA is fully paid for, ensures that more than 94 percent of Americans have health insurance, bends the healthcare cost curve, and reduces the deficit by $118 billion over the next 10 years and even more in the following decade.

Title I. Quality, Affordable Health Care for All Americans

The ACA will accomplish a fundamental transformation of health insurance in the United States through shared responsibility. Systemic insurance market reform will eliminate discriminatory practices by health insurers such as preexisting condition exclusions. Achieving these reforms without increasing health insurance premiums will mean that all Americans must have coverage. Tax credits for individuals, families, and small businesses will ensure that insurance is affordable for everyone. These three elements are the essential links to achieving meaningful reform.

Title II. The Role of Public Programs

The ACA expands eligibility for Medicaid to lower-income persons and assumes federal responsibility for much of the cost of this expansion. It provides enhanced federal support for the Children's Health Insurance Program, simplifies Medicaid and CHIP enrollment, improves Medicaid services, provides new options for long-term services and supports, improves coordination for dual-eligibles, and improves Medicaid quality for patients and providers.

Title III. Improving the Quality and Efficiency of Health Care

The ACA will improve the quality and efficiency of U.S. medical care services for everyone, and especially for those enrolled in Medicare and Medicaid. Payment for services will be linked to better-quality outcomes, and the ACA will make substantial investments to improve the quality and delivery of care and support research to inform consumers about patient outcomes resulting from different approaches to treatment and care delivery. New patient care models will be created and disseminated, rural patients and providers will see meaningful improvements, and payment accuracy will improve. The Medicare Part D prescription drug benefit will be enhanced, and the coverage gap, or doughnut hole, will be reduced. An Independent Payment Advisory Board will develop recommendations to ensure long-term fiscal stability.

Title IV. Prevention of Chronic Disease and Improving Public Health

To better orient the nation's healthcare system toward health promotion and disease prevention, a set of initiatives will provide the impetus and the infrastructure. A new interagency prevention council will be supported by a new Prevention and Public Health Investment Fund. Barriers to accessing clinical preventive services will be removed. Developing healthy communities will be a priority, and a 21st-century public health infrastructure will support this goal.

Title V. Healthcare Workforce

To ensure a vibrant, diverse, and competent workforce, the ACA will encourage innovations in healthcare workforce training, recruitment, and retention and will establish a new workforce commission. Provisions will help to increase the supply of healthcare workers. These workers will be supported by a new workforce training and education infrastructure.

Title VI. Transparency and Program Integrity

To ensure the integrity of federally financed and sponsored health programs, this title creates new requirements to provide information to the public on the health system and promotes a newly invigorated set of requirements to combat fraud and abuse in public and private programs.

Title VII. Improving Access to Innovative Medical Therapies

Biologics Price Competition and Innovation. The ACA establishes a process under which FDA will license a biological product that is shown to be biosimilar or interchangeable with a licensed biological product, commonly referred to as a reference product. No approval of an application as either biosimilar or interchangeable is allowed until 12 years from the date on which the reference product is first approved. If FDA approves a biological product on the grounds that it is interchangeable to a reference product, HHS cannot make a determination that a second or subsequent biological product is interchangeable to that same reference product until one year after the first commercial marketing of the first interchangeable product.

Title VIII. Community Living Assistance Services and Supports

Establishment of national voluntary insurance program for purchasing community living assistance services and support (CLASS program). The ACA establishes a new, voluntary, self-funded long-term care insurance program, the CLASS Independence Benefit Plan, for the purchase of community living assistance services and supports by individuals with functional limitations. The HHS secretary will develop an actuarially sound benefit plan that ensures solvency for 75 years, allows for a five-year vesting period for eligibility of benefits, creates benefit triggers that allow for the determination of functional limitation, and provides a cash benefit that is not less than an average of $50 per day. No taxpayer funds will be used to pay benefits under this provision.

(continued)

APPLYING EVIDENCE-BASED PRACTICE (CONTINUED)

Title IX. Revenue Provisions

Excise Tax on High-Cost Employer-Sponsored Health Coverage. The ACA levies a new excise tax of 40 percent on insurance companies or plan administrators for any health coverage plan with an annual premium that is above the threshold of $8,500 for single coverage and $23,000 for family coverage. The tax applies to self-insured plans and plans sold in the group market, and not to plans sold in the individual market (except for coverage eligible for the deduction for self-employed individuals). The tax applies to the amount of the premium in excess of the threshold. A transition rule increases the threshold for the 17 highest-cost states for the first three years. An additional threshold amount of $1,350 for singles and $3,000 for families is available for retired individuals age 55 and older and for plans that cover employees engaged in high-risk professions.

Title X. Strengthening Quality, Affordable Care

Title X made many improvements to the preceding nine titles, and descriptions of those changes are included above.

Questions:

1. Do you think this law has left out any critical healthcare policy issues? If so, what has been left out?
2. Review each of the titles (topical issues found in the legislation). Select three that interest you, and examine them in more detail. How do they relate to nurses and nursing care?
3. If you had to select which title was the most important, what would you select and why?

arise in the clinical setting. The statement "if it isn't documented, it didn't happen" is highly relevant to any malpractice suit. What do nurses need to know about the legal issues? Nurses do not have to be attorneys, but should seek the advice of an attorney whenever they are involved in a serious legal issue. Some issues, however, bear some review so nurses have a basic understanding of the critical issues. Prior to reviewing these issues, it is important to distinguish the difference between law and ethics. **Law** is the formal organization of societal values that are demonstrated through laws that are passed then implemented on the local, state, and federal levels, and in some cases, even internationally. **Ethics** focuses on what ought to be done in relation to what is done. Understanding legal issues is important for any nurse in practice and for nurses who are leaders.

Basic Legal Terminology

Laws are developed and implemented through organizations within society. State legislatures or Congress, as well as state and local governments, develop these laws. They are then implemented by state and federal law enforcement agencies or other agencies such as the state board of nursing. There are several types of laws.

1. **Common laws** are rules and principles that were derived from past legal decisions that were developed in England then brought to the United States.
2. **Criminal law** concerns offenses against the general public, and response is directed at deterrence, punishment, and/or rehabilitation of the person who committed the crime. Examples of behavior or actions that relate to this law would be murder, robbery, and rape. Criminal law can also apply to healthcare situations as it covers assault and battery, which can occur in the healthcare setting.
3. **Civil law** concerns the rights of individuals, and remedies typically involve payment of money or some other type of compensation. An area of civil law that most concerns nurses is tort law as it includes negligence, personal injury, and medical malpractice.

The following provides information about basic legal terms that are important for the nurse to understand.

1. *Negligence* and *malpractice* are terms that are not uncommon for nurses to hear. What is the difference between negligence and malpractice?
   - "**Negligence** is failure to exercise reasonable care, or the degree of care that a reasonably prudent person would exercise under the same or similar circumstances . . . **Malpractice** is a more specific term . . . professional negligence committed by a person in his or her professionally licensed capacity" (Westrick, 2014, p. 369).
   - The standard in negligence is average level of care. A variety of sources for standards exist (for example, expert witness testimony, accreditation requirements, publications by experts, clinical practice guidelines or pathways, statutes and regulations, advertising for

BOX 2-5	**ELEMENTS OF NEGLIGENCE**

1. There was a duty owed to the patient.
2. There was a breach of duty or standard by the healthcare professional.
3. There was harm caused by the breach of duty or standard.
4. The person (plaintiff) experienced damages or injuries.

services, contracts, and professional standards). To prove negligence, there are four elements that must be met, which are described in Box 2-5.

- Damages or injuries may be physical, emotional, loss of job, loss of present and/or future earnings, disfigurement, disability, pain and suffering, loss of enjoyment of life, and so on.

- Negligence can be unintentional (when no harm was intended) or intentional (for example, invasion of privacy or false imprisonment are examples of intentional acts, although these are rare in health care). Both types of negligence can occur in health care when a patient's privacy is not maintained or when a patient is held against his or her wishes without legitimate medical reasons.

- The elements that must be met for malpractice are the same as those for negligence with the emphasis on what would be expected from a professional. Some of the examples of potential risks for nurses are failure to adequately assess, monitor, and communicate; failure to act as the patient's advocate (for example, not providing patient education to a patient who has diabetes); or failure to protect a patient when the patient is suicidal or at risk for falls. Every nurse needs to consider these risks when care is provided or when holding management positions.

- As noted earlier, there are certain elements that must be proved by the plaintiff; however, there is an exception, which is called the **doctrine of *res ipsa loquitor***, which means that the "thing speaks for itself" (Westrick, 2014). This rule of evidence indicates that although one may not be able to prove that an individual did something to cause harm or injury, because there is harm or injury, the negligence can be inferred.

- A question that often comes up with nurses is who is responsible for negligence: the nurse or the nurse's employer? ***Respondeat superior*** is the doctrine that the employer may also be responsible if the nurse was functioning in the employee role at the time of the negligence in a situation where the employer controlled the nurse (Westrick, 2014). This means that both the HCO and the nurse could be sued. This is also referred to as **vicarious liability**.

- Other terms of interest are assault and battery, although many nurses may not see how these apply to nursing care. **Assault** does not require physical contact, only that the patient fears harmful contact may occur. There has to be some consideration given to timing and the fear that results, as one could not call a threat that happens several days earlier assault. **Battery** requires actual physical contact. Both of these are considered intentional torts. They are good reasons for obtaining informed consent from patients before procedures are performed, which could be considered assault or battery if the patient does not consent.

2. Consumer rights issues have become more and more important in health care. Consent, living wills, durable powers of attorney, and assisted suicide are some of these issues. The Patient Self-Determination Act of 1990 was initiated to address issues about patient decisions (Westrick, 2014). Healthcare providers must now ask patients if they have living wills, durable powers of attorney, or advance directives. The goal of this law is to make individuals more aware of their rights and the importance of making informed decisions while, it is hoped, giving some consideration to the costs of care. Nurses must follow their organization's policies and procedures related to any of these issues.

- **Informed consent** may be either oral consent that occurs when the patient agrees verbally after receiving information or in written form. **Implied consent** can be as simple as, after the nurse explains, the patient allows the nurse to proceed with the care, and in this case, there is no risk of battery. Noninvasive procedures do not require informed consent.

- **Consent emergency exception** is consent that may occur in emergency situations when, even though the patient may not be able to provide consent for emergency treatment, such treatment can be given. The following elements must be met to be **consent implied by law**: (1) reasonable belief that delay would lead to serious bodily injury or death, (2) the patient is incapable of giving or denying consent (unconscious), (3) there is no one available to act as the patient's guardian, or (4) there is no reason to believe that consent would not be given if the patient were capable of such (Westrick, 2014, pp. 93–94).

- Informed consent mandates that the physician or independent healthcare practitioner provide the patient with information, patient's consent is voluntary with no pressure, and the patient is competent (communicate choices, understand information, and understand the situation). It is an interactive process in that the healthcare provider is required to tell the patient who will perform the procedure or treatment, discuss available alternatives to the recommended treatment, and identify possible harm in language the patient can understand. Patients must be informed that they have the right to refuse treatment. If there is no informed consent, the practitioner is at risk for negligence. Informed consent can be given orally or in writing, and it can also be implied by the patient's behavior or, as noted earlier, in emergency situations it can be presumed. The physician or the independent practitioner is accountable for obtaining informed consent. So where does this leave the nurse who is not an APRN functioning as an independent practitioner? The nurse is not accountable for obtaining the consent for every risky or invasive nursing action, as most routine nursing interventions are implied or there is oral consent (for example, the patient agrees to take the medication). Whenever the patient refuses treatment of any kind, the patient's refusal must be respected. A nurse is not required to obtain informed consent for medical procedures for which the nurse is not the primary provider. For example, the best approach is for the nurse to wait until the patient's physician explains the procedure and obtains informed consent to begin patient teaching. Some hospitals and other types of HCOs may prohibit nurses from obtaining written consent for specific procedures that are offered by other providers. It is important for each nurse to know about these prohibitions and to follow them. Physicians may legally delegate getting informed consent to a nurse; however, if a problem occurs, the physician is still at risk. In this situation the nurse is also at risk. The nurse may not be delegated to get informed consent for procedures performed by a physician (Westrick, 2014).

- Informed consent for human research is very important. Many nurses participate in research in a variety of settings such as hospitals, clinics, and research institutes. This consent needs to provide the potential research subjects/participants with enough information so the study is understood and benefits and risks and subject/ participant responsibilities are identified. They need to be informed about discomforts, confidentiality, compensation if harm occurs, and right to leave the study (Polit & Beck, 2014).

- **Living wills** are supported by the Patient Self-Determination Act of 1990. HCOs must advise patients of their rights, including the right to have written advance directives such as a living will. This document describes what a competent adult directs healthcare providers to do related to life-sustaining medical care in situations where the person may become terminally ill or unconscious (Westrick, 2014). Pain measures and comfort care are not denied in these advance directives; however, resuscitation is a matter of whether the patient chooses a do-not-resuscitate (DNR) or not. Nutrition and hydration may or may not be provided depending on the living will. If a person is competent, a living will serves no purpose as the person can speak for himself. Several important points about living wills should be noted. Living wills are usually not very specific. When healthcare providers do not follow a living will, this may lead to legal actions against the physician. Many HCOs require that for changes to be made in how a living will is implemented that two physicians agree; however, there is no legal protection for the healthcare provider against civil or criminal liability. Nurses should never act as witnesses to living will documents and should not be surrogates for a patient unless he or she is a blood relative.

- The **durable power of attorney (medical power of attorney)** is another method or type of advance directive that an individual can use to communicate the type of care desired. A competent person may appoint a surrogate (often several are identified in priority order) to make healthcare decisions for that person when the person is not able to do so. This addresses some of the limitations with the living will since it identifies a person who is actually making the decisions for the patient. Typically individuals select someone they trust will carry out their directives, which are discussed while the individual is competent to do so. The surrogate does not have to be a family member, although it is highly advisable that persons inform their families about these documents and decisions prior to needing them. The surrogate may not act unless the patient is unable to do so.

- A **do-not-resuscitate (DNR) directive** or **allow-natural-death (AND) directive** is another form of advance directive that patients may request when they receive care. The physician may be implementing advance directives when writing a DNR order, but DNR orders can be written without an advance directive. Family members should also be consulted to prevent increasing family stress and possible legal actions. Healthcare organizations have policies and procedures to follow when patients request a DNR, and these should be followed. If the patient is able, there should be some discussion between the physician and patient about the decision. If the patient agrees, families are included in the discussion. There are specific intervals designated for reevaluation of the decisions. With all of these issues related to treatment, it is critical that nurses contribute by assessing the patient and communicating effectively with the patient, family, and physician. End-of-life decisions are not easy to discuss. The nurse is often in a position to discuss these critical issues; however, the physician should also be involved in the process. What happens if a patient's preferences are disregarded? The nurse should contact the organization's ethics committee, which many HCOs have. In doing this, the nurse acts as the patient's advocate. The nurse, of course, needs to be aware of state laws and requirements related to these serious decisions. If there is no ethics committee or procedure, then the nurse should contact nursing management, though nursing management should also be contacted if there is a referral to the ethics committee.

- Assisted suicide is another patient rights issue that has become more important; however, this one is much more complex. States typically have laws governing this. The ANA opposes any nursing participation in assisted suicide, as this would violate the ANA *Code for Nurses* (American Nurses Association, 2015). Any concerns about potential assisted suicide should be reported to management staff and to the organization's ethics committee. Participation in assisted suicide may lead to legal charges.

In conclusion, nurses are obligated to follow the law and the profession's code of ethics. How can lawsuits be prevented as many occur even when quality care was provided? Why do patients sue healthcare providers? Many patients who sue are typically angry with one or more of their healthcare providers, perhaps about not being told what they needed to know, lack of respect, lack of privacy, or suspected substandard care. It is very important to understand the patient's perception as this helps explain why a lawsuit has been filed. Effective communication must be part of the relationship. Effective leadership is also critical—understanding and applying legal principles while providing care and guiding others as they provide care such as unlicensed assistive personnel (UAPs), licensed practical nurses (LPNs), licensed vocational nurses (LVNs), or other team members. The red flag areas to watch are the following:

- Inadequate assessment of the patient
- Medication errors
- Inadequate training for an assignment
- Faulty equipment
- Inadequate communication
- Failure to follow proper policy and procedures, apply standard of care, or act as patient advocate (Westrick, 2014, p. 30)

Nurse managers should support nurses to avoid malpractice claims by (1) keeping current with the state's Nurse Practice Act, (2) being familiar with the HCO's policies and procedures, (3) understanding the appropriate standards of nursing care, and (4) documenting all nursing care accurately and thoroughly (Westrick, 2014, p. 30).

Patient Privacy: The Law Expands

"It has been foundational, at least since Hippocrates, that patients have a right to have personal medical information kept private. . . . The chief public-policy rationale is that patients are unlikely to disclose intimate details that are necessary for their proper medical care to their physicians unless they trust their physicians to keep that information secret" (Annas, 2003, p. 1486). Regulations about patient privacy were added to the Health Insurance Portability and Accountability Act of 1996 (HIPAA) and went into effect in April 2003, representing the first comprehensive standards to protect patient privacy. Each nurse needs to be aware of and follow the policies and procedures related to oral, written, or electronic patient identifiable data set up by the HCO regarding issues where the nurse practices. There are some key areas, however, that are affected by these new privacy regulations:

- Patients must be informed of their privacy rights.
- Patients must be informed as to who will see their records and for what purpose.
- Patients have the right to inspect and obtain a copy of their medical records. (There are some exceptions to this that each organization should make clear to staff.)
- Valid authorization to release health information must contain certain information, such as a copy of the signed authorization given to the patient, in understandable language, and how the patient may revoke authorization.
- Although information may be used for research purposes to assess outbreak of a disease, all individual identifiable data must be removed.
- Personal data may not be used for marketing (for example, pharmacies may not share this information with others for this purpose).

These privacy standards are complex and require HCOs to make changes in how they manage information. They also require that staff are trained and updated about the changes. The standards give patients more control while at the same time making providers more accountable for keeping information private. This is federal law, but if a state has more rigorous privacy requirements, then the state requirements would have to be followed.

Scope of Practice and Its Implications

State Nurse Practice Acts include provisions about registered nurse (RN), LPNs/LVNs, and advanced practice registered nurses (APRNs) describing what the specific healthcare provider can do in their role, under their licensure (Westrick, 2014). The scope of practice provides guidance and boundaries. For example, APRN scope of practice typically includes diagnosing and medication prescriptions, and some states require collaboration with physicians. Some states include mandatory continuing education requirements to ensure continued RN competency. The IOM *The Future of Nursing: Leading Change, Advancing Health* report's first recommendation is to remove scope-of-practice barriers. "APRNs should be able to practice to the full extent of their education and training" (2011, p. S-8). As has been discussed, scope-of-practice is tied to legal concerns in the state Nurse Practice Act, and each state has its own practice act. There are similarities, but there is no requirement that the laws be identical. States must protect their citizens, and this includes their health and safety. Figure 2-5 describes the ANA's Model of Professional Nursing Practice Regulation.

ETHICS: IMPACT ON DECISION MAKING IN MANAGEMENT AND PRACTICE

Ethics is interwoven throughout healthcare policy development, implementation, and legal issues that arise during the delivery of health care. Nurses cannot avoid ethical issues and need to understand ethical decision making. Leadership competencies are related to ethics; for example, decision making often includes ethical issues. Implementing health policies may require consideration of ethics. "Ethics refers to a standardized code or guide to behaviors. Morals are learned through growth and development, whereas ethics typically is learned through a more organized system, such as a standardized ethics code developed by a professional group" (Finkelman & Kenner, 2016, p. 174) such as the *Guide to the Code of Ethics for Nurses with Interpretive Statements* (American Nurses Association, 2015).

Figure 2-5 Model of Professional Nursing Practice Regulation

Source: From *Specialization and Credentialing in Nursing Revisited: Understanding the Issues, Advancing the Profession* by Margretta Madden Styles, Mary Jean Schumann, Carol J. Bickford, Kathleen White. Copyright © 2008 by American Nurses Association. Reprinted with permission. All rights reserved.

Ethical Decision Making

Healthcare providers encounter many ethical dilemmas in their practice and/or if they serve in leadership positions. An ethical dilemma occurs when a person is forced to choose between two or more alternatives when neither of them is perfect and the situation surrounding the choice is complex, emotional, related to values, and controversial. Healthcare organizations need to integrate an ethical framework into their daily operations and require leaders to lead by example. Individual nurses and other healthcare providers must also deal with these critical questions when confronted with ethical issues. Four primary principles, as described in Figure 2-6, are used to make ethical decisions: autonomy, beneficence, justice, and veracity (Westrick, 2014).

1. **Autonomy** is a principle that has always been important to nurses. Patients have the right to determine their own rights.
2. The second ethical principle is **beneficence**, or doing something good. Nurses are to inflict no harm and to safeguard the patient.

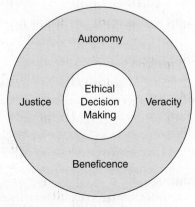

Figure 2-6 Ethical decision making

3. Patients should also be treated fairly or with **justice**. This, of course, is a problem when decisions are made that determine which patients will receive treatment.
4. The fourth primary principle is **veracity**. Truth telling is critical for effective patient communication and developing trust with the patient. Informed consent is one example of a potential ethical problem that may be affected by veracity. If incomplete information is not shared with a patient, then veracity has not been met.

Professional Ethics

As has been discussed, professional organizations play an important role in policy making and legislation at the local, state, and federal levels, but they are also important in defining professional standards and ethics. The ANA's *Code of Ethics for Nurses with Interpretive Statements* (2015) is the primary resource for nursing ethical guidance for the nursing profession, and the code is based on the profession's values and need for professional integrity (American Nurses Association, 2015). All provisions in the *Code* are described in Box 2-6.

Professional ethics applies to both nursing management and clinical issues. Several studies have been conducted about nursing ethics. A study conducted in 1994 but still relevant today asked nurse administrators to identify decisions that had represented ethical dilemmas

---

BOX 2-6	CODE OF ETHICS FOR NURSES

Provision 1

1.1 Respect for Human Dignity

1.2 Relationships with Patients

1.3 The Nature of Health

1.4 The Right to Self-Determination

1.5 Relationships with Colleagues and Others

Provision 2

2.1 Primacy of the Patient's Interests

2.2 Conflict of Interest for Nurses

2.3 Collaboration

2.4 Professional Boundaries

Provision 3

3.1 Protection of the Rights of Privacy and Confidentiality

3.2 Protection of Human Participants in Research

3.3 Performance Standards and Review Mechanisms

3.4 Professional Responsibility in Promoting a Culture of Safety

3.5 Protection of Patient Health and Safety by Acting on Questionable Practice

3.6 Patient Protection and Impaired Practice

Provision 4

4.1 Authority, Accountability, and Responsibility

4.2 Accountability for Nursing Judgments, Decisions, and Actions

4.3 Responsibility for Nursing Judgments, Decisions, and Actions

4.4 Assignment and Delegation of Nursing Activities or Tasks

Provision 5

5.1 Duties to Self and Others

5.2 Promotion of Personal Health, Safety, and Well-Being

5.3 Preservation of Wholeness of Character

5.4 Preservation of Integrity

5.5 Maintenance of Competence and Continuation of Professional Growth

5.6 Continuation of Personal Growth

Provision 6

6.1 The Environment and Moral Virtue

6.2 The Environment and Ethical Obligation

6.3 Responsibility for the Healthcare Environment

Provision 7

7.1 Contributions Through Research and Scholarly Inquiry

7.2 Contributions Through Developing, Maintaining, and Implementing Professional Practice Standards

7.3 Contributions Through Nursing and Health Policy Development

Provision 8

8.1 Health Is a Universal Right

8.2 Collaboration for Health, Human Rights, and Health Diplomacy

8.3 Obligation to Advance Health and Human Rights and Reduce Disparities

8.4 Collaboration for Human Rights in Complex, Extreme, or Extraordinary Practice Settings

Provision 9

9.1 Articulation and Assertion of Values

9.2 Integrity of the Profession

9.3 Integrating Social Justice

9.4 Social Justice in Nursing and Health Policy

for them. The following were considered important in rank order, with the first decision occurring most frequently:

1. Staffing levels and mix of staff types
2. Developing/maintaining standards of care
3. Allocating/rationing of scarce resources
4. Incompetent physicians
5. Demotion/termination of employees
6. Employee relations
7. Incompetent nurses
8. Selection/hiring of employees
9. Treatment versus non-treatment
10. Promotion of employees
11. Diversification of services
12. Downsizing services
13. Access to care for the indigent
14. Marketing/advertising services
15. Labor negotiations with nurses (Borawski, 1995, p. 61)

These issues indicate that nurses struggle with many situations that place them in ethical dilemmas (e.g., what to do and how to do it right). Today these issues continue to present ethical dilemmas for nurses as practitioners and leaders.

Making Complaints to the Board of Nursing

Each state board of nursing has the responsibility to protect the public health in its state. Nurses who are licensed in a state can and should make complaints to the board when they are concerned about patient health and safety. In the late 1980s and early 1990s, Texas experienced major psychiatric healthcare fraud and abuse problems in some for-profit psychiatric hospitals, which is discussed in more detail later in this section. Some psychiatric nurses said they contacted their board and did not receive assistance (Mohr, 1996, 1997). Boards of nursing must be responsive, or they will find that nurses will not bother to contact them.

Leadership is required of all nurses, even those on boards of nursing. A leader is able to confront difficult issues and take risks, which is what the nurses who reported problems did in the example described above. All nurses should be knowledgeable about their state's practice act and use this law and its related rules and regulations as a guide in making decisions about issues and complaints to the board. If nurses have any concerns about legal issues and personal professional liability, consulting an attorney is also recommended. Boards of nursing have a specific process for reviewing complaints and deadlines that must be met. During the investigation period, boards do not reveal the source of a complaint. State boards of nursing should be contacted for information about each state's reporting process.

Healthcare Reimbursement and Ethics

The medical industry struggles with medical and business ethical issues daily, and nurses are also confronting more and more ethical dilemmas due to these struggles. Managed care has had a major impact on healthcare delivery and reimbursement, with HCOs and providers facing conflicts between financial incentives and the insurer's mission (or potential ethical duty) to provide appropriate care. It is recognized that some insurers are better than others, and this must imply that some type of standard has been used to compare one with the other to arrive at this conclusion. Are there standards? Can conflicts between business ethics and medical ethics within the same organization be resolved? Healthcare professionals want to apply medical ethics to insurers, though most insurers are not involved in providing direct care. An example of an exception to this is health maintenance organizations (HMOs), which are a form of managed care reimbursement but also are engaged in providing care. Many people view medical care as being a different product from other business "products." Do the same ethical obligations that apply to healthcare professionals also apply to insurers? Business ethics that promote fair competition— people are free to make voluntary choices to buy or sell goods or services—do not fully apply to the healthcare insurance business. Patients are not always free to choose their insurance or their provider, or they may have limits placed on these decisions by their employers. Investor-owned

CASE STUDY

Risky Staff Performance and Ineffective Management

As nurse manager of a behavioral health unit in an acute care hospital, you are responsible for the overall management and quality of care provided on a 30-bed inpatient unit with an average length of stay of four days. Staffing is short and you have four new nurses with limited or no mental health experience. Last night a patient was injured during a restraint procedure. You are reviewing the incident report in your office and decide to review restraint data for the past three months. You are shocked when you see that restraints have increased by 15% and that one nurse, who has been there only four months, has been involved in 75% of these restraints regardless of the shift she worked. You then review the medical records for these patients and find that documentation of the incidents is not complete, there is little reevaluation of the patient as required, and basic patient needs were not met effectively. You then talk to several staff members who have worked with the nurse during the shifts when the restraints occurred. They describe the nurse as "difficult" and "demanding" with "limited tolerance for negative patient behavior." She does not include staff in decision making such as whether to restrain a patient. This all concerns you, so next you look at her personnel file. The nurse had six months of previous mental health experience and two years of acute care medical nursing experience. You notice that she should have had two to three completed reference checks, but only one is in the file and that one is vague. You are overwhelmed with what you have uncovered.

Questions:

1. What do you think about this nurse manager and how she has handled quality improvement issues, personnel issues, and overall decision making on her unit?
2. What are the legal and ethical issues related to the care this staff nurse has provided?
3. How should the nurse manager respond to this nurse and to her multiple problems?
4. Following this experience, what does the nurse manager need to do long term to improve her own management competencies?

(for-profit) insurers have a very important relationship with their stockholders, who expect a financial return on their investment in the insurance business. The same is true of investor-owned healthcare provider organizations (e.g., hospitals, clinics, home care agencies, long-term care facilities). These organizations will always experience conflicts between their business needs to control costs to meet their budgetary requirements and their contractual obligations to provide healthcare services to the purchasers of their services, typically the employer who contracts for employee health benefits and their stockholders.

The relationship between the insurer and the patient/enrollee is a contractual one. The insurer is responsible only for meeting the requirements of the health plan contract, and there is no requirement that all contracts must be the same. There is inequality in insurer contracts and benefits, and this is not considered to be an ethical problem. However, the ACA is addressing some aspects of insurance policy inequality, for example, by eliminating the preexisting illness limitation, providing coverage for adults up to age 26 on their parent's plan, and offering free screening for some diseases.

Lack of choice, such as provider choice, is a red flag for consumers. For example, when the ACA went into effect, some consumers were forced to change providers. Some plans are trying to incentivize enrollees to use certain providers by offering reduced co-pays for certain provider use. This has caused problems. Choice is part of the enrollee's decision to join a health plan, and even that is limited by the employer's selection of plans. Patients rarely have complete information about the plan when they join, and many do not really become interested in these details until they need services. The ideal would be the patient/enrollee who reviews each health plan option, including all of the details related to benefits, providers, outcome data, and the like, and decides on the best plan based on the individual's and his or her dependents' health status and needs.

If one could identify ethical standards for insurers, these standards would include insurer accountability for the scope and quality of the patient care delivered, fairness, honesty, truthfulness, respect for persons, and justice. These standards, however, may be difficult to meet. For example, allocation of resources may conflict with many of these standards. If an insurer must ensure that all of its enrollees receive care, there will be decisions made that will be unfair or unjust for some enrollees but fair and just for others. Patient satisfaction is directly affected by decisions the insurer makes, and sometimes insurers make decisions that dissatisfy enrollees but meet the insurer's financial goals. The insurer makes a choice and decides what will bring it the most benefit; however, this is a delicate decision because patient satisfaction is also very important to insurer survival. Too much patient dissatisfaction can lead to the loss of employer health contracts. Additional content on reimbursement is found in Chapter 5.

Healthcare Rationing

Healthcare rationing does occur in the U.S. healthcare delivery system, though it is not a formalized rationing system. Actually there was a time when rationing was more the norm, but the patient played a critical role. Prior to health insurance, patients served as their own gatekeepers. As patients were financially responsible for their own care, they rationed services for themselves and their families, aided by a physician with whom they shared strong community and often personal ties. These physicians realized that any care provided beyond the financial means of the patient was, and would probably remain, uncompensated care (Randall, 1994). An example of current rationing is the organ donation programs that allocate organs to patients based on identified criteria. Another example was Oregon's rationing system for Medicaid patients. This system prioritized diagnoses that would receive healthcare reimbursement; however, the system experienced problems. No other state has developed a rationing system similar to that of Oregon.

Resource allocation is a more acceptable term than *rationing*. Resource allocation is necessary and inevitable in some form due to excessive healthcare costs and limited resources. The key question is how it should be done. A type of rationing occurs at the bedside or in the clinic when the individual physician declines to administer beneficial treatments because of costs that will be incurred by the insurer, services the insurer will not cover, or services the provider knows will have a negative impact on the provider's performance evaluation. Preferably decisions to not provide treatment are done in consultation with the patient and the patient's family, but this is not always the case. Is this preferable to having a rationing or resource allocation system that is centralized and bureaucratic with many rules? Is this more equitable, impartial, visible, and predictable? These are difficult questions for which there is no perfect answer. When this is applied to insurers, the view changes because third-party reimbursement typically focuses on the needs of the insurer's population/members, which is different than the traditional fee-for-service insurance plans. Insurers are generally not concerned with the greater good of the entire community, but only with decisions that affect their members and their business needs. This is a major ethical dilemma that will continue in the healthcare system.

Healthcare Fraud and Abuse

Over the past two decades, health care has experienced major problems with fraud and abuse, and these have implications for nursing. Healthcare fraud and abuse include legal and ethical elements that need to be considered. Nurses have also been involved in these fraud and abuse cases. It is important that nurses are aware of these situations and their outcomes and that they consider implications for individual nurses and the profession as a whole.

In the mid-1990s, as HCOs changed to corporate models, it was noted that "the transformation of our healthcare system is having several perverse effects. It is producing corporate conglomerates with billions of dollars in assets that compensate their executives as grandly as basketball players. These conglomerates are battling to control physicians in many locations and because they have cash and monopolistic power, they often succeed" (Kassirer, 1995, p. 50). At a U.S. Congressional committee meeting in 1994, the healthcare fraud problem was described in the following manner: "An effective antifraud program will be crucial to curing the healthcare crisis. Fraud is a cancer, spreading rapidly throughout our healthcare system. Unless we do something about fraud, and waste, and abuse we will never, never get healthcare costs under control. The General Accounting Office (GAO) estimates that 10% of our total healthcare expenditures, both public and private, are lost to fraud and abuse" (U.S. House of Representatives, 1994, p. 1). Healthcare fraud has been defined by the National Health Care Anti-Fraud Association (NHCAA) as "the intentional deception or misrepresentation that an individual or entity makes when the misrepresentation could result in some unauthorized benefit to the individual, or the entity or to some other third party" (Coppola, 1997, p. 46). The Health Insurance Portability and Accountability Act of 1996 (HIPAA) established a program to identify and prosecute healthcare fraud. This program is called Health Care Fraud and Abuse Control Program (HCFAC). Healthcare fraud and abuse have been particularly problematic in psychiatric care, large healthcare corporations, and more recently in long-term care and home care, particularly related to Medicare reimbursement.

What is the current status of healthcare fraud in the United States? In 2013 the federal government recovered more than $4.2 billion from fraud-associated federal healthcare programs. From 2009 to 2013, the amount recovered was $19.2 billion (U.S. Department of Health and Human Services and Department of Justice Health Care Fraud and Abuse Control Program, 2013). This represents a lot of money. If one considers what could have been done with the money to improve care, it is a major loss. There clearly have been more organized methods to recover the money as demonstrated by these amounts. The Federal Bureau of Investigation (FBI) is responsible for this work. More information about its efforts can be found on the FBI website. This demonstrates a serious problem with healthcare professionals and HCOs that are participating in activities to take money for their own, and in some cases, have led to legal actions and convictions. Conducting this effort also costs money. The ACA legislation recognizes healthcare fraud as a major problem and thus provides provisions to increase monitoring and enforcement of laws to prevent fraud (U.S. Department of Health and Human Services, 2014a). The Centers for Medicare & Medicaid Services (CMS) is a focus of a lot of healthcare fraud. To address this problem, in March 2011 the CMS initiated a project to revalidate all 1.5 million Medicare-enrolled providers and suppliers to meet the new Affordable Care Act screening requirements. What have been the results? By September 2013, more than 535,000 providers were screened, and more than 225,000 lost the ability to bill Medicare due to the ACA requirements and other proactive initiatives. Other providers were removed because they had felony convictions, were not operational at the address CMS had on file, or were not in compliance with CMS rules (U.S. Department of Health and Human Services, 2014b). The common CMS fraud activities are (U.S. Department of Health and Human Services, 2014b):

- billing for "phantom patients."
- billing for medical goods or services that were not provided.
- billing for more hours than there are in a day.
- paying a "kickback" in exchange for a referral for medical goods or services.
- concealing ownership in a related company.
- using false credentials.
- double-billing for healthcare goods or services not provided.

Given such a bleak picture of healthcare fraud, what is the view of future activities? The Department of Justice indicates that national healthcare expenditures are estimated to exceed $3 trillion in 2014, and this provides opportunity for healthcare fraud schemes to increase. In 2009 the attorney general (Department of Justice) and HHS formed a collaboration to directly attack healthcare fraud: the Healthcare Fraud Prevention and Enforcement Action Team (HEAT). Part of this initiative includes assigning 40 prosecutors to the Medicare Fraud Strike Force. All of these actions demonstrate the seriousness of this problem and the expectation that it will increase (U.S. Department of Justice, 2015).

WHISTLE-BLOWING   The False Claims Act (FCA) was passed during the Civil War to reward citizens who exposed fraud against the government; however, it became a more useful law after it was amended in 1982. This is the federal law that protects whistle-blowers—those who expose federal fraud. Healthcare fraud, as is true of most fraud, is very difficult to prove. Having people on the inside of the organization who are willing to share information is often critical to successfully prove fraud. If a nurse decides to file a suit and report fraud and the government decides to intervene in the nurse's case, the nurse is entitled to a percentage of the government's ultimate recovery. If the government does not intervene in the nurse's case and the nurse continues with the case, the nurse is entitled to larger percentage of the recovery. Needless to say, this is quite an incentive; however, it is not easy to report an employer. Employees have concerns about retaliation, and there is no doubt that this is a highly stressful, long, drawn-out process. There are protections for employees who act as **whistle-blowers**, for example if the employee is fired, demoted, or discriminated against for these actions, he or she can bring a claim against the employer for unlawful retaliation. The employee would be entitled to both job reinstatement and twice the amount of lost back pay. The FCA, however, applies only to federal cases. When an employee reports fraud, the employee must be the original source of the knowledge. An employee cannot obtain the information from a publicly disclosed source, such as a newspaper or government report, and then report it.

In 2010 a major whistle-blowing case occurred that involved two nurses in Texas (Lowes, 2010); however, there was a dispute about whether this was whistle-blowing or employees just doing their job. This term may no longer be relevant when staff report concerns about quality, which should be an expectation. In this particular case in Texas, two nurses at a hospital reported a physician to the medical board. They were concerned about safe practice. The advantage to whistle-blowing is it legally shields someone who reports, but in this case, the nurses were charged with misuse of information. The sheriff in the town was a close friend of the physician. One of the charges against one nurse was dropped, and the second went to trial, receiving a not-guilty verdict. The fact that this occurred when the nurses were doing what is expected from a licensed healthcare professional—to advocate for patient safety—is disturbing. As is discussed in more detail in Chapters 17 and 18, HCOs need a culture of safety where the staff feel safe reporting quality concerns. There is no need for more of blame culture, where fear rather than patient advocacy drives decisions.

Not all who are accused of fraud and abuse are guilty. The complex, ever-changing regulations make it very difficult for HCOs and their staff to keep current; consequently, it is easy to make an honest error. This is not fraud because fraud requires intention to do wrong. Calling this fraud can be a serious problem. A fraud accusation affects an HCO's and its providers' reputations, and it is often difficult to erase this when an honest error is finally recognized. The number of fraud and abuse cases has increased in the past few years, and much of this increase is due to greater efforts to discover fraud and abuse, with Congress allocating more funds to combat healthcare fraud and abuse.

EXAMPLE: HEALTHCARE FRAUD AND ABUSE IN PSYCHIATRIC HOSPITALS   The psychiatric healthcare fraud and abuse of the 1980s and 1990s provides a view of what can happen when a system confronts the dilemma of care versus the bottom line and chooses the bottom line (Mohr, 1996, 1997). During this time period, healthcare corporations, particularly investor-owned chains that provided psychiatric services, increased throughout the country. New hospitals were built, and hospitals were rapidly bought and sold. What happened in these hospitals? Patients were charged for care they did not receive. Patient records indicated that inappropriate care was provided, such as a large number of medications that could not have been administered in one day without causing detrimental effects, which indicated that the medications had not actually been administered. Patients, however, were charged for multiple doses that never were administered. Fraudulent submissions of insurance claims were common. Patient abuse occurred when:

- patients were admitted when they did not need to be hospitalized.
- parents were told their children were seriously ill when they were not.
- patients were given medications they did not need.
- teenagers were abducted and admitted to the hospital.
- patients were restrained unnecessarily and for long periods of time.
- patients were denied their rights.
- patients experienced verbal abuse.

These are only a few of the many abuses and examples of fraud from this scandal. The FBI conducted raids on hospitals to confiscate records and shut down computers to prevent purging of records (Rundle, 1993). After reviewing congressional testimony, it is easy to wonder if the examples are from the late 19th century rather than the end of the 20th century (U.S. House of Representatives, 1992, 1994; U.S. Senate, 1992). Texas State Senator Michael J. Moncrief stated in one of these meetings, "In Texas, we have uncovered some of the most elaborate, aggressive, creative, deceptive, immoral, and illegal schemes being used to fill empty hospital beds with insured and paying patients" (U.S. House of Representatives, 1992, p. 7). Clearly these HCOs were focusing on business, using questionable business ethics, and had little concern for patients or healthcare professional ethics such as the *Code for Nurses* and physician ethics.

What happened to healthcare professionals in these hospitals? Some staff members spoke out, including nurses and physicians, but it was not uncommon for them to be threatened with job loss or to actually lose their jobs. There were threats of blacklisting and reports of false claims against employees, such as use of illegal drugs, to licensing boards; verbal abuse and ostracism; and other types of threats to prevent employees from reporting fraud and abuse (Mohr, 1996, 1997).

Why would someone continue to work in this environment? In some cases reporting problems to the board of nursing or state agencies did not get timely responses. Others experienced extreme stress, fear, and emotional and physical problems. In other situations nurses felt that if they stayed and worked in the situation, they might be able to help the patients who were abused, even though this typically did not happen. There were some nurses who did speak out but found it extremely stressful and painful. This example of psychiatric fraud and abuse demonstrates how easy it is for some HCOs and individual professionals to cross the line and ignore ethical behavior. This is certainly not a positive example of what can happen when ethics are left behind, but much can be learned from it.

EXAMPLE: OPERATION RESTORE TRUST   In the late 1990s, other major healthcare corporations experienced major fraud and abuse problems (Eichenwald, 1997, 1998; U.S. Department of Health and Human Services and U.S. Department of Justice, 2009). Federal investigations found widespread fraud, overcharges, and substandard care. The elderly are a vulnerable group in the United States, as are those with mental illness. Naturally the vulnerable are most prone to experience the impact of fraud and abuse. When Medicare fraud and abuse occurs, the federal government can become involved because Medicare is a federal program. The psychiatric problems were exposed when patients who received Civilian Health and Medical Program of the Uniform Services (CHAMPUS) coverage, the federal program for military dependents, were abused or experienced fraud. The federal government could then become involved and use all of its related agencies such as the FBI and the General Accounting Office in the investigation. The home care Medicare fraud led to the development of a program to monitor and correct these problems called Operation Restore Trust. This program has been a burden for many home care agencies, particularly for those who have not committed fraud but made honest mistakes; however, the government is determined to correct healthcare fraud and abuse. This abuse continues with estimates that $60 billion is lost annually. The CMS website provides current information about healthcare fraud and abuse for healthcare providers and patients.

EXAMPLE: VETERANS HEALTH ADMINISTRATION   In 2014 information was released about the Veterans Health Administration. Patients had been put on waiting lists that were not active lists and never received appointments. This alone is unethical and impacted patient healthcare outcomes, but in addition, administrators and other staff changed documentation, which is a legal document. This is fraud. Administrators had been given incentives for meeting certain outcomes, such as short waiting lists, and incentivizing some leaders/managers to step outside the bounds of professional, ethical, and legal behavior. The goal of improvement is critical, but if it leads some to take actions that are not acceptable or appropriate, then a problem exists.

Organizational Ethics

Many HCOs have followed other types of businesses in creating processes to address ethical concerns. Why all this interest in corporate ethics? Certainly one could cite the increasing examples of healthcare fraud as previously discussed as one reason, but probably even more important was the creation of new federal sentencing guidelines in 1991. Fines were reduced for white-collar crimes if a business could demonstrate that it had a comprehensive ethics program. A corporate compliance model has been implemented in HCOs and is required for all providers who offer services to Medicare and Medicaid beneficiaries as part of the CMS conditions of participation. The Office of Inspector General (OIG) of the HHS is responsible for enforcing these rules. Since few if any hospitals do not receive these government reimbursements, most hospitals must comply. Due to these changes, healthcare corporate compliance committees are now more common. The quality and commitment of compliance ethics programs must, however, be monitored. Monitoring can easily be another paper process that might look good in theory but does not truly reflect the organization's culture and the behavior of its employees. Organizations must ensure that behaviors change. Some of these organizations also have ethics officers. What is their authority, and how can they really effect change? These are critical questions that organizations should ask. It is not easy to change organizational culture, and it takes time. Is there a true commitment to improve, or is this being done to put the organization in a better legal position in case there are problems? What are some of the activities of these compliance programs? The high-risk areas vary from one organization to another. Examples are licensure and credentialing with current and appropriate licensure, scope of practice that is consistent with the state nurse practice act and practice acts as they relate to other healthcare professionals, compliance with hospital policies and procedures, and documentation.

Employee education is an important activity that affects compliance outcomes. Topics that might be covered include the organization's mission and values, code of conduct, compliance plan, roles and responsibilities of the compliance officer, compliance with laws and regulations, conflicts of interests, financial and accounting records, fraud and abuse, professional standards and codes of ethics, confidentiality of patient information and organization information, physician relations, patient rights, respect and concern for others, and anti-trust issues. Some of these topics are not applicable to all staff. For example, not all staff need an understanding of financial and accounting records. All staff, however, need to know the procedure for reporting their concerns about ethical issues in a manner that protects them from employer retaliation. Staff may see the compliance program as just another "change" that will have little impact on the organization, culture, or staff behaviors. This staff attitude needs to be addressed by the HCO if the organization plans to truly change its organizational culture and commit itself to a more ethical work environment. Organizational leaders must be role models for all of the staff, and they need to know what is right or wrong and do the right thing. It is not uncommon for managers to deal with several ethical issues at one time, all of which affect decision making.

Nurses Coping With Ethical Dilemmas

Nurses have responsibilities related to ethics, including maintaining knowledge of the professional *Code for Nurses* (2015), recognition of personal values, understanding of the decision-making process and its application to nursing practice, recognition and understanding of the importance of policy and legal issues, and the ability to be assertive.

The goal is to reach a balance between the extremes, and this is not easy to accomplish. Decision making in the healthcare environment requires recognition of different viewpoints and compromises. Strategies that are used by some HCOs to cope with ethical dilemmas are ethics committees and nursing ethics groups. Ethics committees provide opportunities for interprofessional staff to discuss ethical dilemmas that staff experience in the organization. The committee is advisory. As is true with all discussions of ethics, there is no perfect answer. Typical issues that are discussed by these committees include do-not-resuscitate policies, patient self-determination, brain-death protocols, informed consent, euthanasia, and patient competency. Issues related to managed care and reimbursement and clinical decision making have also become more common topics. Ethical dilemmas such as these can lead to staff frustration and do affect the delivery of patient care.

Nursing ethics groups provide forums for discussion about nursing ethics. It is not always easy for staff to report or discuss ethical concerns. Nurses who participate in nursing ethics committees gain knowledge and skills that are required for ethical decision making. These nurses are then better prepared to participate in interprofessional ethics committees and to make their own ethical decisions.

Political ethical conflicts occur within HCOs. This is demonstrated daily today in health care as nurse managers and other staff confront conflicts between financial issues and care. What is best for patients and what is best for the HCO are not always the same. These can be tough choices. An HCO has a political component to its environment, and leaders need to be aware of the political environment. Nurse managers and staff must consider beneficence or the obligation to benefit one's employer/organization and the patients. However, should the team agree with the HCO without thought of what this agreement means and the ethics involved? Ethical principles are important. Nurses must consider **nonmalfeasance**, to do no harm to the institution or those it serves. This obligation also relates to the employees. Respect for persons, another key principle, is also important when the staff makes decisions that affect patients but also when managers make decisions that affect staff. Managers have to ensure that procedures are followed; however, this needs to be done respectfully (for example, when staff is told that mistakes have been made). Justice, or treating others fairly and impartially, is a frequent dilemma for managers. Staff need to be approached in an impartial manner with fairness. Truth telling is the obligation to be truthful or honest in decisions and approaches to others. Utility, or trying to maximize the greatest good from a situation, is also important, though not easy to do. Nursing staff confront ethical issues daily, and they need support. The nursing leader and other leaders and managers within an HCO are key to how effective management, staff, and the HCO as a whole handle ethical dilemmas.

APPLYING LEADERSHIP AND MANAGEMENT

My Hospital Unit: An Evolving Case Experience

It is time to return to your unit. You may wonder how you would apply this content on health policy to your unit today. Search the literature and the Internet for information about current health policy issues. You might examine current healthcare issues that your state legislature is considering, search the Government Affairs section of the ANA website, and review newspapers and the Internet for current health policy issues. Select one topic and examine it. How would you apply this topic and the information to the work you do as a nurse manager on your unit? Be as specific as possible. Why is it important for you as a nurse manager to keep current with health policy issues?

BSN and Master's Essentials: Application to Content

BSN Essentials (**American Association of Colleges of Nursing, 2008**) **as Applied to this Chapter:**

I. Liberal Education for Baccalaureate Generalist Nursing Practice
V. Healthcare Policy, Finance, and Regulatory Environment
VIII. Professionalism and Professional Values

Master's Essentials (**American Association of Colleges of Nursing, 2011**) **as Applied to this Chapter:**

I. Background for Practice from Science to Humanities
VI. Health Policy and Advocacy

Applying AONE Competencies

Identify which of the AONE competencies found in Appendix A apply to the content of this chapter.

Engaging in the Content: Critical Thinking and Clinical Reasoning and Judgment

Discussion Questions

1. How would you support the statement "Nurses need to be aware of and involved in health policy development"? (Online Application Option)
2. Examine the issue of patient privacy and how it applies to management of a unit.
3. How are the ethical principles of beneficence and justice related to healthcare reimbursement policy? (Online Application Option)

4. Describe the requirements needed to prove malpractice.
5. What is scope of practice? What does your state's nurse practice act say about scope of practice in your state? Why is this important? How is this discussed in *The Future of Nursing* report? (Access the report through the National Academy of Medicine website.)

Application Exercises

1. Visit the American Nurses Association site on healthcare policy (Government Affairs). What are the current policy issues addressed? How might you apply them to nursing leadership and management? Discuss with your team in class. (Online Application Option)
2. Identify a potential ethical dilemma you have observed or experienced. Describe the situation and discuss its relationship to the ethical principles. (Online Application Option)

3. Review Appendix B, which describes some of the provisions of the healthcare reform law of 2010. In small teams discuss the law and its potential impact on healthcare delivery and nursing.
4. How does your school of nursing prepare students for HIPAA? Critique this preparation.
5. What do your state nursing organizations do to influence health policy in your state? Provide some examples. What has your state done to address healthcare abuse and fraud?

References

American Association of Colleges of Nursing. (2008). *The essentials of baccalaureate education for professional nursing practice*. Washington, DC: Author.

American Association of Colleges of Nursing. (2011). *The essentials of master's education in nursing*. Washington, DC: Author.

American Nurses Association. (2010). *Nursing: Scope and Standards of Practice*. Silver Spring, MD: Author.

American Nurses Association. (2015). *Guide to the code of ethics for nurses with interpretive statements*. Silver Spring, MD: Author.

Annas, G. (2003). HIPAA regulations—A new era of medical-record privacy? *The New England Journal of Medicine, 348*(15), 1486–1490.

Borawski, D. (1995). Excerpt from "Ethical Dilemmas for Nurse Administrators", *Journal of Nursing Administration, 25*(7/8), 60–62, Wolters Kluwer Health, Inc.

Broder, P. (1997, October 26). Health care: The problems persist. *Washington Post*, p. A1.

Coppola, M. (1997, March–April). Identifying and reducing health care fraud in managed care. *Group Practice Journal* (3), 46.

Eichenwald, K. (1997, November 4). Reshaping the culture at Columbia/HCA. *New York Times*, p. C2.

Eichenwald, K. (1998, February 14). Columbia/HCA fraud case may be widened, U.S. says. *New York Times*, p. B2.

Fineberg, H. (2012). A successful and sustainable health system—how to get there from here. *New England Journal of Medicine, 366*, 1020–1027.

Finkelman, A., & Kenner, C. (2016). *Professional nursing concepts. Competencies for quality leadership*. (3rd ed.). Boston, MA: Jones and Bartlett.

Finkelman, A., & Kenner, C. (2016). *Teaching IOM: Implications of the Institute of Medicine reports for nursing education* (3rd ed.). Silver Spring, MD: American Nurses Association.

Henry J. Kaiser Family Foundation. (2009). News Release. Retrieved from http://www.kff.org/kaiser-polls/posr022509pkg.cfm

Henry J. Kaiser Family Foundation. (2014). Key facts about the uninsured population. Retrieved from http://kff.org/uninsured/fact-sheet/key-facts-about-the-uninsured-population/

Institute of Medicine. (1999). *To err is human: Building a safer health system*. Washington, DC: National Academies Press.

Institute of Medicine. (2001). *Crossing the quality chasm*. Washington, DC: National Academies Press.

Institute of Medicine. (2002). *Unequal treatment: Confronting racial and ethnic disparities in health care*. Washington, DC: National Academies Press.

Institute of Medicine. (2003). *Health professions education*. Washington, DC: National Academies Press.

Institute of Medicine. (2011). *The future of nursing: Leading change, advancing health*. Washington, DC: National Academies Press.

Kassirer, J. (1995). Managed care and the morality of the marketplace. *New England Journal of Medicine, 333*(1), 50–52.

Lowes, R. (2010, March 3). Whistle-blowing nurses case highlights need for more open quality of care culture. *Medscape Medical News*. Retrieved from http://www.medscape.com

Mohr, W. (1996). Dirty hands: The underside of marketplace health care. *Advances in Nursing Science, 19*(1), 28–37.

Mohr, W. (1997). Outcomes of corporate greed. *Image: Journal of Nursing Scholarship, 29*(1), 39–45.

Nokleby Elder, K., O'Hara, N., Crutcher, T., Wells, N., Graham, C., Heflin, W. (1998). Managed care: The value you bring. *American Journal of Nursing, 98*(6), 34–39.

Polit, D., & Beck, C. (2014). *Essentials of nursing research. Appraising evidence for nursing practice*. (8th ed.). Philadelphia, PA: Lippincott Williams & Wilkins.

Randall, V. (1994). Impact of managed care on ethic answers and underserved populations. *Journal of Health Care for the Poor and Underserved, 5*(3), 224–236.

Reinhardt, E. (1994). Managed competition in health care reform: Just another American dream or the perfect solution. *Journal of Law, Medicine and Ethics, 22*(2), 106–120.

Rundle, R. (1993, August 27). National medical facilities raided by U.S. agents. *Wall Street Journal*, pp. A1, A4.

Sanger-Katz, M. (2014, October 26). Is the Affordable Care Act working? Retrieved from http://www.nytimes.com/interactive/2014/10/27/us/is-the-affordable-care-act-working.html?emc=eta1&_r=0#uninsured

U.S. Department of Health and Human Services. (2014a). Benefits of Affordable Care Act for Americans. Retrieved from http://www.hhs.gov/healthcare/facts/timeline/graphictextonly.html

U.S. Department of Health and Human Services. (2014b). Common Medicaid rip-offs and tips to prevent fraud. Retrieved from http://www.cms.gov/Medicare-Medicaid-Coordination/Fraud-Prevention/FraudAbuseforConsumers/Ripoffs_and_Tips.html

U.S. Department of Health and Human Services. (2014c). Key Features of the Affordable Care Act by Year. Retrieved from http://www.hhs.gov/healthcare/-facts/timeline/timeline-text.html

U.S. Department of Health and Human Services and Department of Justice Health Care Fraud and Abuse Control Program. (2013). Departments of Justice and Health and Human Services announce record-breaking recoveries resulting from joint efforts to combat health care fraud. Retrieved from http://www.hhs.gov/news/press/2013pres/02/20130211a.html

U.S. Department of Health and Human Services and U.S. Department of Justice. (2009). Stop Medicare Fraud. Retrieved from http://www.stopmedicarefraud.gov/

U.S. House of Representatives. (1992, April 28). *The profits of misery: How inpatient psychiatric treatment bilks the system and betrays our trust. Hearing before the Select Committee on Children, Youth and Families, One Hundred Second Congress, Second Session.* Washington, DC: U.S. Government Printing Office.

U.S. House of Representatives. (1994, July 19). *Deceit that sickens America: Health care fraud and its innocent victims. Hearings before the Subcommittee on Crime and Criminal Justice of the Committee on the Judiciary House of Representatives, One Hundred and Third Congress, Second Session.* Washington, DC: U.S. Government Printing Office.

U.S. Department of Justice. (2015). Healthcare fraud unit. Overview. Retrieved from http://www.justice.gov/criminal/fraud/hcf/

U.S. Senate. (1992, July 28). *Hearing before the Committee on the Judiciary United States Senate, Senate Bill 2652, One Hundred Second Congress, Second Session.* Washington, DC: U.S. Government Printing Office.

U.S. Senate. (2010). The Patient Protection and Affordable Care Act. Retrieved from http://www.dpc.senate.gov/healthreformbill/healthbill04.pdf

Washington Post. (2010). Landmark: The inside story of America's new health-care law and what it means for us all. Washington, DC: Author.

Westrick, Susan J., & McCormack Dempski, Katherine. (2008). Excerpt from *Essentials of Nursing Law and Ethics*. Boston, MA: Jones & Bartlett.

White House, The. (2009). Health reform. Retrieved from https://www.whitehouse.gov/healthreform

3 Operational and Strategic Planning: Change, Innovation, and Decision Making

⬤ LEARNING OUTCOMES

> Examine the implications of *The Future of Nursing: Leading Change, Advancing Health*.
> Discuss critical nursing issues related to reengineering, redesigning, reregulating, right-sizing, and restructuring.
> Explain why the concept of change is important in the healthcare environment and to nursing leadership and management.
> Assess the external trends and factors that impact nursing practice and healthcare organizations.
> Compare and contrast two key change theories.
> Apply eight key steps in the change process.
> Analyze the issue of resistance to change and strategies for overcoming this resistance.
> Develop strategies to improve responses to change.
> Apply the decision-making process.
> Compare and contrast successful strategic and operational planning.

WHAT'S AHEAD

The healthcare delivery system is not a static system as it experiences changes daily and in some cases hourly. Staff members tend to think that leaders and managers will save the day by helping them cope with the ever-changing healthcare environment, maybe making it disappear; however, nurse leaders and managers also struggle to cope with change and to help staff. What does this mean? Nurses at all levels must make a commitment to the change process and take active roles in it. Change that comes from and is totally managed by a manager will not be successful today. Staff members who pull back and wait for the manager to make the difference will also find that changes will continue to occur but without their input.

Understanding change and its potential landmines are important to be successful today, but we must also recognize the benefits of change, though we often complain about it. Change can invigorate us. If we had no change, there would be no need for critical thinking. After a time we would know all of the answers or approaches to expected problems. After a time we would also find this to be a rather boring environment in which to work, though for most of us it would initially be comfortable. Complacency and isolationism can be very destructive landmines. (Finkelman, 2001, p. 195)

"Engaged nurse managers do not cope with change but are energized by it and welcome it" (Mackoff, 2011, p. 44). This chapter focuses on change and decision making in organizations. What are the critical change and decision-making processes, and how does change impact staff,

KEY TERMS

- change
- clinical judgment
- clinical reasoning
- compacts
- critical thinking
- decision-making process
- deep dive process
- dichotomous thinking
- empathy
- empower/ empowerment
- facilitators
- force-field analysis model of change
- macrosystem
- mesosystem
- microsystem
- mutual recognition
- operational planning
- PDSA cycle
- planning
- project planning
- Quinn's theory of change
- readiness for change
- reciprocity
- redesigning

- reengineering
- regulations
- reregulating professional practice
- resistance
- restraining forces
- restructuring nursing education
- strategic planning
- SWOT analysis
- team decision making
- vision
- work redesign
- workaround

healthcare organizations (HCOs), and their decisions? It is difficult to separate change from decisions as responding to change requires that decisions be made, some minor, and some more important and complex. Nurses participate in the change process and make decisions wherever they practice.

LEADING DURING CHANGE AND CHANGE MANAGEMENT

The Future of Nursing: Leading Change, Advancing Health (Institute of Medicine, 2011) has stimulated a lot of change for the nursing profession and most likely will be doing so for some time. The recommendations from the report focus on change in practice and education and the need for greater nursing leadership and expansion of the healthcare workforce. The Robert Wood Johnson Foundation (RWJF) partnered with the Institute of Medicine (IOM) and formed the Initiative for the Future of Nursing (Robert Wood Johnson Foundation, 2014). In addition, the Center to Champion Nursing in America (CCNA) was established in partnership with the American Association of Retired Persons (AARP) and RWJF. The goal is to mobilize stakeholders to ensure that the *Future of Nursing* report recommendations are met and for nurses to assume more leadership in the change process to address healthcare challenges of access, quality, and cost (Center to Champion Nursing, 2014). The IOM report notes that the size of the nursing profession of more than 3 million registered nurses can make an important impact on the healthcare delivery system—there is opportunity for the profession and for change to improve. The report and follow-up activities are connected to the Affordable Care Act of 2010 (ACA). "The ACA represents the broadest changes in the healthcare system since the 1965 creation of the Medicare and Medicaid programs and is expected to provide insurance coverage for an additional 32 million previously uninsured Americans. Although the passage of the ACA is historic, realizing the vision outlined above [in the report] will require transformation of many aspects of the healthcare system" (Institute of Medicine, 2011, p. S-1). (See Appendix B.) To participate actively nurses need to develop leadership competencies, and a key competency is change management. To meet *The Future of Nursing* report's recommendations requires an understanding of change and the change process and the ability to effectively implement the change process as a leader or as a team member.

THE FIVE "Rs": CHANGE AND DECISION MAKING IN ACTION

The healthcare delivery system has been adjusting to changes in reimbursement, staff shortages, budget cuts, technology, role changes, and much more, all of which have had a major impact on nursing. Change has driven the need for the five "Rs," which particularly affect HCOs, nursing education, and nursing practice. The five "Rs" are as follows:

1. Reengineering/redesigning/restructuring the healthcare organization
2. Redesigning the workforce
3. Reregulating professional practice
4. Rightsizing the workforce
5. Restructuring nursing education.

Each one of the five Rs is about change and requires decision making and change management on the part of the HCO and its staff. Understanding the historical and in some cases current impact of the five Rs provides an introduction to the importance of change, decision making, and change management for nurses.

Reengineering/Redesigning/Restructuring the Healthcare Organization

Reengineering was used in many HCOs for a number of years, and though not used currently, it had an influence on the current status of many organizations. The IOM discusses the impact that reengineering has had on nursing in its report on nursing that was published prior to *The Future of*

Nursing report (Institute of Medicine, 2004, 2011). Other terms used to describe this process are restructuring and **redesigning**. This process represents more than a minor organizational change; it was a reinvention or recreation of processes, work, and systems. Often reengineering was not easy for nurses to accept as the process sometimes resulted in radical changes in how nursing was practiced, and thus nurses were reluctant to participate. To actively participate in reengineering, nurses needed to understand their own work and be willing to explore improving their practice.

Often reengineering focused mostly on reducing full-time equivalents (FTEs), primarily nursing, developing or reducing services, or decreasing length-of-stay. This was usually done with limited nursing input. Varied reengineering strategies were used. An important related issue today is the growing emphasis on patient-centered care, which requires a combination of reengineering and work redesign. The goals are to improve patient and customer satisfaction, quality of care, and cost reduction. The use of the term "patient-centered care" is important in the IOM reports on healthcare quality, and it is one of the five core competencies of healthcare professions. The idea of arranging work around the patient rather than specialized departments has great potential for providing an opportunity to deliver nursing care that meets patient needs; however, this has not been easy to accomplish. The IOM reports (2003, 2004) now consistently emphasize patient-centered care. Although the reports emphasize quality, the IOM reports also discuss the relevance of efficiency and design of work. It takes time and commitment and requires significant change in the organization to provide patient-centered care. Over many years, patient care has been delivered in hospitals with the number of departments increasing and more and more staff interacting with the patient. Specialization has led to problems of poor communication, complex processes, increased paperwork, poor collaboration, and error. How would a hospital become more patient centered? What redesign would be necessary? What role would nurses play? These are critical examples of decisions that must be made as planning is done to make major changes in HCOs. Whenever HCOs undergo major redesign, retrospective evaluation needs to occur to assess the outcomes, and nurses at all levels should be actively involved.

The new initiative Transforming Care at the Bedside (TCAB), which was influenced by the IOM report *Keeping Patients Safe* (2004) and the Institute for Health Improvement (IHI), has had an impact on organizations in which TCAB is used. This initiative is discussed further in Chapter 18. The focus is again on quality but also the design of work to improve quality care. TCAB uses the change approach called Deep Dive, which is discussed later in this chapter. This initiative focuses on small pilots in hospitals to make needed changes and actively use nurses in the process (Robert Wood Johnson Foundation, 2009; Institute for Health Improvement, 2015). TCAB is an example of current approaches to reengineering care, but it is important to understand the history of the use of reengineering as it had a major impact on how nurses practice today in hospitals.

Redesigning the Workforce

Demands that managed care placed on clinical settings to increase productivity and patient and customer satisfaction, and at the same time provide lower cost quality care, pressured nurse executives and managers to institute **work redesign**, which is part of reengineering. With the nursing shortage, the need for work redesign was even more important. Improved efficiency that results in more effective practice with less staff is critical, and since a major shortage is predicted for the future, this issue continues to be important. This has led to the development of, and changes in, inpatient care delivery models, such as the use of patient-centered care and changing staff mix, therefore, altering the number of RNs, unlicensed assistive personnel (UAP), and licensed practical nurses (LPNs/LVNs) and changing of responsibilities. The effectiveness of these changes varies. Traditional nursing roles and activities need to be assessed and may need to be rejected to change to more effective roles that allow for more innovative approaches. Nurses need to provide supportive data to demonstrate the impact that their own roles and activities have on efficiency, improved care, and patient outcomes. The problem, however, is that there are many perspectives on nursing work redesign. Determining the best way to design how staff work together to provide quality, safe care that includes patients is the key issue. Some hospitals have introduced the new role of the clinical nurse leader (CNL), which is discussed in Chapter 4; however, the introduction of a new role needs to be planned by an HCO so staff understand the role and implications on other roles. New roles impact current roles and cause problems if not thought through carefully.

When HCOs confront the need to make changes in responsibilities, functions, and tasks in the delivery system, the most common reasons have been due to concerns about costs, productivity, and outcomes. Work redesign is used to address these concerns; however, there are other factors that need to be considered. Nurses are responsible for ensuring a baseline level of performance. If UAP are used, nurses need to ensure that training and supervision are provided to UAP to ensure patient safety and quality care. (Content from Chapter 15 on delegation applies to this issue.) The nursing profession must also be careful about new delivery models or how staff are organized to provide care (for example, the use of teams), as discussed in Chapter 4. There needs to be more research to validate the outcomes of these models so evidence-based management (EBM) can be implemented more effectively. The bottom line is nursing needs data to support these delivery changes.

Are models effective? If not, why? What can be done to make them more effective? Should the model be used? Under what circumstances is the model effective or ineffective? Nurses should be asking these questions, not waiting for others to do so. Nurses should also be directly responsible for finding the answers, analyzing the results, and making decisions about needed changes.

Reregulating Professional Practice

Why is **reregulating professional practice** an important change issue today? Chapter 2 includes some information on regulation, for example the need for recognition of scope of practice with advanced practice registered nurses (APRNs) (Institute of Medicine, 2011). Nurses have discovered that many of the changes that are taking place in health care, such as the use of telehealth, workforce mobility, and mergers (or several HCOs forming one organization, which may then have parts of the organization in different states), are affecting licensure. Today many nurses are providing care across state lines and in situations in which the patient is in a different state from the one in which the nurse is licensed and located, particularly near state borders, which makes access easier. The use of telenursing is also growing, which allows for greater opportunities to provide nursing care over distances using telecommunication and other technologies. This type of care is considered to be within the practice of nursing, even if it is not "hands-on care" or direct care. In addition, restructuring of health care has led to an increase in multistate healthcare systems, which has affected how nurses are employed and where they work.

To understand the recent proposed changes in regulation, it is important to recognize how regulation is applied. The purpose of practice regulation is to ensure public safety. Boards of nursing regulate nursing practice. The right of states to regulate practice is based on the Tenth Amendment to the U.S. Constitution, the states' rights amendment. This amendment provides *each state* with the right to regulate nursing practice within its own state but not within other states. This is why nurses who move from one state to another to work must obtain licensure in the new state. **Reciprocity**, or one state's need to recognize a license issued by another state, is primarily based on national board scores; however, the nurse must still apply for an RN licensure in the state, meet individual state requirements such as continuing education, and pay state fees. Due to changes in health care, boards of nursing and nursing organizations have been discussing changes that need to be made nationwide in the regulation of nursing practice. The dilemma is that licensure remains state based yet state borders may no longer bind nursing practice. Various options were considered by the National Council of State Boards of Nursing (NCSBN) to resolve this dilemma, but thus far, the option selected to address this licensure problem is **mutual recognition**. The implementation of this type of licensure requires an interstate compact, which is an agreement between two or more states, entered into for the purpose of addressing a problem that transcends state borders. **Compacts** are created when two or more states enact identical statutes establishing and defining the compact and its role. The result is the creation of both state law and an enforceable contract with other states that adopt the compact. Not all states have made decisions to make this change and collaborate with adjacent states about RN licensure, but there is a trend in this direction. Information about current states participating in mutual recognition can be found on individual state boards of nursing websites and on the NCSBN website.

Rightsizing the Workforce

"Rightsizing" and "downsizing" are terms that cause nurses to shudder, as they suggest that the HCO might reduce staff. During times of downsizing, hospitals decrease their staff and beds, but then they have to reverse those decisions as needs rise. The number of applications to nursing programs has increased, but wait lists have grown at the same time. The economic crisis of 2009–2010 had a major impact on this problem, increasing the number applying. In addition, hospital acuity remains high, requiring greater numbers of competent staff. Chapter 8 discusses staffing issues in more detail.

Rightsizing focuses on how much staff is required to do the job, though this has never been easy to predict or accomplish. Budget plays a major role. Since education for healthcare professionals takes time, it is important to try to predict future needs. The goal is to determine how many healthcare professionals need to be educated to meet the future needs and ensure that there will be jobs for them when they complete their education and training. It is clear that there are not enough nurses now, and the predictions for the future indicate there will be greater need, particularly when the baby boomer nurses retire. The economic problems did slow down retirements, and many nurses returned to nursing or increased their hours. The shortage has undergone fluctuations: more nurses returned to practice during the economic crisis of 2009–2010 and there was an increase in the number of applicants to nursing programs. Some areas of the country found that they no longer had a severe shortage. As a result, new graduates had a difficult time getting positions due to the return of nurses who had not been in practice and the impact of nurses not taking early retirement because they needed more income. However, this does not eliminate the concern about the number of nurses who will be retiring soon and the need for replacement. Approaching the problem only from the point of view of getting the "right" number of nurses is not helpful. Since it will probably not be possible to get the number of nurses desired, other strategies will be needed to change how nursing care is provided to reduce the number of nurses required.

Restructuring Nursing Education

When **restructuring nursing education** is discussed, there are two critical focus areas. The first is academic education, and the second is continuing education for nurses who are practicing. Nursing education must make curriculum changes to prepare nurses to meet current and future healthcare needs and work more collaboratively with practice partners (Finkelman & Kenner, 2007). Several recent reports emphasize the need for change and improvement such as the IOM report *Health Professions Education* (2003) and the newest report on nursing education, *Educating Nurses: A Call for Radical Transformation* (Benner, Sutphen, Leonard, & Day, 2010). Beverly Malone, chief executive officer for the National League of Nursing, comments on this nursing report: "This book represents a call to arms, a call for nursing educators and programs to step up in our preparation of nurses. This book will incite controversy, wonderful debate, and dialogue among nurses and others" (Benner et al., 2010, back cover). The report is all about change: change in the delivery of health care and the practice of nursing that drives critical need for change in nursing education. The IOM report also emphasizes need for change and five core competencies that all healthcare professions should meet. These five core competencies are also emphasized in the newest edition of the *Essentials of Baccalaureate Education for Professional Nursing Practice* (American Association of Colleges of Nursing, 2008) and *The Essentials of Masters in Nursing* (2011).

The importance of the consumer as a significant player in the healthcare environment, emphasizing patient-centered care, must be part of this preparation. However, this is not new to nursing education; nursing has always emphasized the importance of the patient's role. Understanding the interplay of values, motivations, and incentives of the major players or stakeholders in health care, including insurers, providers, purchasers of health care, and consumers, helps nurses understand the healthcare culture in which they practice. Stakeholders sometimes have competing interests that affect decisions. Healthcare markets continue to change, which means nurses at all levels need to be aware of these changes and know how to react positively to change and, in many cases, even anticipate it. Understanding the reasons healthcare delivery has become more business oriented and knowing its effect on nursing practice is also important. Today there is a greater emphasis on service, innovation, cost effectiveness, and customer service. To be successful in the increasingly business-oriented healthcare environment, nurses need to be flexible. Nurses do need to have some understanding of the impact of costs on care and recognize that they have a fiscal responsibility. They should be active in trying to reduce costs whenever possible and to better explain the impact nursing care has on cost of care. Lack of understanding about this responsibility is no longer an acceptable reason for not participating in reducing costs. All nurses need to be prepared to be leaders as well as team members. In addition, education needs to provide more content and learning experiences that assist students in developing leadership competencies. All of these needs require a review of nursing curricula and nursing practice to better prepare nurses for practice.

The second area of concern about nursing education is the need for continuing education. All nurses need to be lifelong learners. Practice should be based on current knowledge. Not only is current information needed, but there also needs to be opportunities to understand and apply the knowledge. Staff education and continuing education is discussed in more detail in Chapter 20.

THE CONCEPT OF CHANGE

Change is something that occurs that makes a difference. Change has become the norm for all healthcare providers, but what is being changed? In general, everything; however, the important examples of change are related to an HCO's structure, roles and responsibilities, communication methods and systems, policies and standards, culture, leadership and management approaches, and competencies and attitudes. In fact, before one change is completed, there seems to be another one waiting in the wings to come on center stage. Some changes even come together, forcing staff and management to juggle multiple changes at one time.

Change disturbs the equilibrium, so there also needs to be an effort to learn how to work in an environment whose equilibrium is frequently out of balance. Every staff member and nurse manager needs to understand his or her own personal response to change, both effective and ineffective responses. One concern is there are healthcare providers or units in HCOs that feel stability and security are more important than looking forward to the opportunities and innovation that are offered by the change process. In these HCOs, staff feel frustration as they struggle with change that will inevitably occur while their leadership says, "We want things to stay the same."

So why bother with change if it causes so much stress and problems? Factors outside the HCO are a key driver in the need for change. Some changes are actually made so the organization can survive. Many HCOs today function from day to day, and in the long term, they may close or merge with other HCOs. Nurses work daily in environments where external factors have an impact on what they do and their ability to influence the healthcare delivery system. Each nurse has opportunities to be a change agent, but these opportunities are driven by and affected by many critical external factors. Nurse managers serve also as change agents and change coaches. Box 3-1 identifies examples of these external factors that may affect change in healthcare delivery.

BOX 3-1	EXTERNAL FACTORS THAT AFFECT CHANGE

- Local, state, and federal government: policy, laws, and regulations
- Technology
- Economics
- Reimbursement
- Competition
- Providers
- Managed care
- Providers of all types
- Medicare and Medicaid
- Demographics
- Nurse Practice Acts
- Health care professional organizations
- Health care professional standards
- Accreditation of HCOs
- Malpractice issues
- Community culture
- Nurse recruitment and retention
- Community support of HCOs
- Labor unions
- Research
- Local businesses
- Access to care
- Nursing education
- Reimbursement
- Marketing
- Uninsured and underinsured patients
- Pharmaceutical industry
- Consumers and consumer organizations
- Information technology
- Social service agencies
- Health status of the community
- Media and image
- Patient rights, privacy, and confidentiality
- Disasters and response

Examples of Change Theory

There are many theories about change, but only two theories are discussed in this chapter: Lewin's theory and Quinn's theory, a newer theory.

LEWIN'S FORCE-FIELD MODEL OF CHANGE AND FORCE-FIELD ANALYSIS   Lewin proposed a change theory that he called a **force-field model of change**, which includes three stages (Lewin, 1947).

1. *Unfreezing stage.* This stage focuses on developing problem awareness and decreasing forces that maintain the status quo. This includes the recognition of a problem and whether or not there is a feeling that the problem can be improved. Examples of methods that might be used to promote unfreezing are interview results, surveys, and quality improvement (QI) data or meetings in which there is an open discussion of relevant issues. The result should be a better understanding of the issue or problem.
2. *Moving stage.* In this stage the issue or problem is clearly identified, and goals and objectives/outcomes are developed. Strategies are developed and implemented. This is the working stage of the process where new values, attitudes, and behaviors are promoted.
3. *Refreezing stage.* This stage occurs when the change is incorporated into the work environment and its processes. This stage may take some time as it is easy to slip back to the way things were, so during this phase, the goal is to prevent a return to the past. In today's healthcare environment, organizations typically experience refreezing for one change while beginning another change. This is something that was not as critical when Lewin developed his theory.

The theory of force-field analysis is used to improve the change process. In this analysis the manager (change agent/coach) and staff identify the driving forces or factors that will help to move the situation in the direction of the anticipated change or the desired outcome. To be effective, this should be a collaborative process between the manager and staff. If the manager identifies these forces and analyzes them without staff input, the analysis may not be as effective. Frequently staff are able to identify factors that might make a strategy more effective. Examples of driving forces are increasing staff, increasing staff time to provide direct care, decreasing costs, or increasing availability of expertise. The focus should be on increasing acceptance of the change.

Restraining forces or forces that may keep the change from occurring should not, however, be ignored. What might be a restraining force? Examples include staffing concerns, increased safety risks, and decreasing quality. These factors may be anything that prevents change from moving forward. After the driving and restraining forces are identified, there are three possible approaches that might be used to cope with them, which are described in Figure 3-1:

1. Increase the number or strength of the driving forces
2. Decrease the number or strength of the restraining forces
3. A combination of both.

It is easy to apply these approaches in health care, but it does require information about the organization, staff, processes, and the change issue or problem. It is also important to include the informal processes such as the grapevine and informal leaders who may or may not be supportive. This information must be carefully analyzed using each of the approaches described in Lewin's theory.

Rogers' theory (2003) focused on change as being more complex than how Lewin described change. This led to the term "diffusion of innovations," meaning that when a new idea is adopted or an innovation occurs, there are consequences to consider.

QUINN'S THEORY OF CHANGE   When an organization experiences change, it usually faces a major dilemma of a "slow death" or "deep change" (Quinn, 1996, 2000). When does "slow death" occur? If an organization finds it is more comfortable accepting the status quo and not changing, "slow death" occurs. This is demonstrated when staff experience burnout, lack energy, or feel hopeless or trapped. Staff are seen as pulling back and running around, doing insignificant things. There is no vision or clear description of the future for the organization.

How do HCOs and their leaders typically cope with slow death? The first response is probably obvious: they resign themselves to the situation or may deny it is occurring. Another

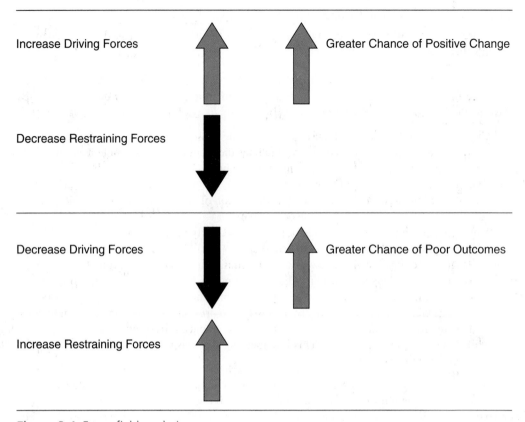

Figure 3-1 Force-field analysis

response is to try to find a way around the problem or a way out, hoping that the slow death will not cause a major problem. These two responses are not positive responses and usually make the situation worse as the HCO will not adapt when it is needed. The positive coping method is to engage in "deep change." This is the method that a transformational leader would take. Deep change requires that the need for change is understood and accepted and that adjustments are made in the organization to respond to the need, empowering others and making changes in the power structure. **Quinn's theory of change** is an approach that is easily applied with current leadership theories discussed in Chapter 1, such as transformational leadership and emotional intelligence.

The Process of Change and Shared Decision Making

The literature discusses many approaches to change. The following describes one example of an eight-step process for leading organizational change (Kotter International, 2014). When the eight steps of the change process are experienced, change can occur at all levels of the HCO (for example, within a unit or division, at one location such as a community clinic, or throughout the entire organization). Regardless of where or how much of the HCO is affected, **resistance** and acceptance will be experienced.

1. ***Create a sense of urgency.*** Applying unfreezing means that staff need to be motivated to make the changes, to feel a sense of urgency to change. Staff need to feel that change is required. This impacts motivation to make change successful. If, however, change occurs too fast, the organization and its staff may not be able to respond effectively, and this may affect other organizational functions.
2. ***Building guiding coalition.*** Clearly the change agent/coach is important during change. The change agent/coach (e.g., a nurse manager, team leader, staff nurse, or any member of the management team) is the person(s) who works to bring about the change. Focusing just on this role, however, is not enough. It is important to also have coalitions or staff teams that can help push the change forward. This means the change agent/coach seeks political support for the change—gaining staff support and agreement. Task forces often are used

and provide a place to develop a shared understanding. Many ideas will be discussed, and this is exciting. This process also helps bring staff "on board"—to recognize the need for the change. If, however, the discussion never gets to planning and gets stuck going over and over the problem, it then may act as a barrier or resister to change.

3. *Form strategic vision and initiatives.* The **vision** provides direction for the change. Staff need to know what that vision is and how it relates to them. After they agree on what the outcome should be—a view of the future—then specific objectives need to be identified to reach the outcome. Change agents/coaches need to keep the vision simple and real, and it needs to mean something to the staff so it engages them. Sharing the vision with staff members so they can understand and participate actively requires multiple methods, forums, and repetition to ensure that all staff members gain an understanding.

4. *Enlist volunteer army.* Major changes in an HCO require empowerment of staff members so they can actively participate in all phases. To **empower** or the act of **empowerment** is to enable to act. When staff feel empowered, they are then more committed to the change. This process involves an interrelationship of authority resources, timely and accurate information, and accountability. It is at this time that barriers, such as staff resistance, are dealt with to move the change process along.

5. *Enable action by removing barriers.* Leadership needs to identify barriers throughout the change process and initiate strategies to reduce or remove them. The initial plan for change should include an assessment of potential barriers with a plan to address.

6. *Generate short-term wins.* If a change process focuses on only the long-term results, management and staff will lose steam somewhere along the way. Change takes time, but people need to feel that they are moving forward. Identifying short-term, measureable outcomes and evaluating when they are met will help management and staff members feel they can make it to the end point. In addition, they can see that progress has been made. These short-term wins do much to build morale and a sense of success. They act as benchmarks that keep the change process on target.

7. *Sustain acceleration.* It is at this point that complacency can return. Staff may feel that things really are fine and nothing more needs to be done. When short-term goals or outcomes are met and recognized, this helps staff to see that there is movement, preferably positive movement, toward the goal. Staff members may need to be reminded that some changes take time. A typical problem that is encountered with change is how to keep it going. Many managers and staff seem to be able to recognize a need for change, plan for change, and even implement change with greater ease than maintaining the change. There is a greater risk of slowing down the change process at this point, almost as if all involved say, "OK. We did it. What's next?" If this occurs, then the final goal(s) will not be met. Stopping too soon often is the reason staff feel that the HCO never seems to make changes effectively; it never completes anything.

8. *Institute change.* Evaluation should not be ignored. The measurable goals or outcomes developed earlier in the process are now used to measure success. Were the goals met? Changes that HCOs and their staff undergo are not written in stone. As has been noted in this chapter, change is now constant, so getting too settled is not a good idea. Organizations not only have to be concerned with future change, but they also need to monitor each change process. Adjustment may be needed, and if so, it needs to take place as soon as possible. Staff will become very discouraged if this does not occur. The inability to adjust can do considerable damage to morale, recruitment and retention, productivity, and quality of care and can impact staff willingness to participate in other change experiences.

Change needs to be connected with the organizational culture and to other activities within the organization.

Shared values are important in every HCO. As change occurs, there may need to be changes in these values so there is a match between the change and the organizational culture. Examples of values are recognition of the importance of staff involvement in decisions, positive recognition of diversity, and management that respects the employee, leading to effective shared decision making. Changing values must be done carefully and only when absolutely necessary. This can cause stress as management and staff may feel insecure when values are challenged, but this can be worked through with recognition of new, shared values. For example, if an organization wants more staff input and uses this feedback, staff may be unsure about this change in values because this approach may not have been valued in the past. Some may wonder why managers are now interested in what they have to say. Some may doubt that the change will actually happen. Management needs to take the time to explain why they now value staff input, and then managers at all levels need to demonstrate that they mean it. It is important, however, to recognize that not all changes require changes in values.

READINESS FOR CHANGE   **Readiness for change** means that management and staff are willing to take on the challenge of change and to invest in the effort. At this time, they are ready to begin the work of change. Not all staff will be ready at the same time, and some will never be ready. Readiness is affected by trust, the relationship between staff and management, fear and concern about what might be lost, staff experience, seriousness of the change, history with both personal and work-related changes, effectiveness of communication, staff and management commitment to the organization, and the planning process or lack thereof. Even the U.S. Department of Health and Human Services (HHS) is interested in the change process; for example, it has developed an extensive module on readiness assessment for planning projects and change describing assessment of readiness for change as:

> A major factor of organizational QI program readiness involves commitment from key decision-makers. Your organization's staff should be highly motivated to improve quality and supportive of system wide efforts to expand patient care. Your organization will improve its QI program readiness by working to build employee morale and stressing the importance of quality improvement. It may also be valuable to identify leaders within your organization who can help promote QI aims and projects. Another factor of organizational readiness includes the financial investment and time commitment needed to support quality improvement. The readiness assessment will help your organization identify changes that need to be made to invest in its QI project, like reassigning responsibilities, shifting staff schedules and cutting back on costs. Resource readiness is also a critical factor since additional oversight and data collection tools will be needed to manage quality improvement. By evaluating existing resources and finances, your organization can ensure that adequate money, staff, information technology, and other resources are in place to support its QI project during implementation and throughout the entire process. The resource assessment will help your organization prioritize its QI goals and allocate resources for support. Lastly, your organization's QI efforts should coincide with its mission and overarching goals. QI projects that do not align with system wide goals may confuse employees and communicate disorganization (U.S. Department of Health and Human Services, Health Resources and Services Administration, 2014).

Facilitators, or champions for change, are committed change agents/coaches. These facilitators make it possible to make a change. Managers who use self-reflection to understand behavior and how the behaviors affect the organization's response to change are more effective facilitators of change, demonstrating that they can be change coaches. They are visible and accessible, and thus better able to lead the staff. The staff members can easily communicate with their manager to express their reactions and ideas. Getting teams involved in the change process facilitates change. Staff members who feel that they can participate in this process and have some freedom to act will improve the change process to reach a more effective outcome. Few situations are so clear that there is only one approach. Recognizing this acts as a facilitator. "Wiggle room" that allows for flexibility helps organizations to develop creative approaches to change. Innovation is a critical need and an important leadership competency.

Empathy is a critical key to readiness for change. It is related to effective communication and participation, which are always important. What is empathy? Empathy occurs when one is able to put oneself in the shoes of another person. It is empathy that helps in the understanding of acceptance, resistance, or a mixed reaction to change. With this information, concerns can be better addressed, and it is hoped, the change process will go more smoothly. If managers and staff take time to get to know one another, this will improve empathy. Then there will be some ability to anticipate how others might respond. This is more than just sending and receiving information. Staff need to understand the "why," "what," and "how" about the change. Change cannot really be successful without inclusion of some empathy and effective communication.

Participation from all staff involved also improves communication and the final outcomes. Participatory management/leadership sometimes is viewed as the miracle that will solve all problems. Just get the staff involved, and the task is accomplished. It does not work this way. Participation must be managed and used carefully. It also means staff must have responsibility and accountability. Timing and clear direction must also be part of the process. An important factor is how much management really believes that staff participation is critical to success. Lip-service acceptance of the need for staff participation will only be more destructive, leading to distrust between staff and management. Staff know when management is asking for participation because it is "the thing to do" rather than from a deep-seated belief that this is the best approach. Empathy clearly affects readiness for change since understanding, which is improved with empathy, is required for readiness.

RESISTANCE TO CHANGE   Most managers and staff have experienced forced change, change that appeared to be useless, as well as times when it would just be better to have things stay the way they were, protecting the status quo. Staff resistance to change places major roadblocks to success and progress. Why might staff or even managers be resistant to a change? Typically change means someone has to give up something or make some adaptation, which is stressful. Along with the stress, the person may not be able to see the benefits, and no one points the way to the positive aspects of the change. The person is concerned about:

1. *Fears and biases* due to lack of understanding.
2. *Perceptual issues* when the person cannot appreciate the situation around the change.
3. *Economic threat*, which may lead to job change, job loss, decreased salary, and lack of promotion.
4. *Social threat* when the social structure of the organization changes.

Many barriers and facilitators that affect the change process can be found in any HCO. Some of the typical barriers are inability to consider another point of view whether it is individuals, a group, or a specialty; lack of a clear plan that includes measurable goals or outcomes; hidden agendas and power struggles; fear of failure; too many changes; and the current status is better than another alternative.

Resistance to change is inevitable and can be experienced by managers, staff, the organization as a whole or parts of it, the community outside the organization, and consumers. Most people do not like disequilibrium because it makes them feel uncomfortable. Resistance to change is often the first response to disequilibrium. With the need for change occurring rapidly today, there is less time for adjustment, though staff do need time to do this. When there is little time for adjustment, resistance can be greater.

Though all of these are possible reasons for resistance, the most common reason for resistance is lack of staff input and participation. Sometimes it is difficult to identify the reasons for resistance; however, it is important to try to identify these reasons. If this can be done, strategies can then be taken to prevent them or decrease their impact, such as by applying Lewin's theory to decrease the barriers and increase the facilitators.

Loss plays a role in resistance to change and should be included in the assessment of resistance. Loss is a natural experience with change. What is loss? Examples of loss that staff may experience are old ways of doing things, current or past job responsibilities, loss of pay or of funding for a project, a manager or staff person who may leave his or her job, or loss of familiar structure. Security is important to staff. Changes in workplace or environment and changes in work team and familiar colleagues are threatening to staff members. Staff need to grieve these losses then move on. Some staff members do this with greater ease than others. Grieving requires (a) recognition of the loss, (b) letting go, and (c) moving on. Management and staff can experience any of these losses. These possible losses will be on staff minds as change occurs. It is natural for staff to want to protect what is valuable, and this can then become a resistance to change.

Is there value to this resistance to change? Yes, there can be value to resistance as it can force management or the change agent/coach to clarify the need for change and develop a plan with a clearer statement of purpose. Those who question change may be providing valuable information of flaws that can be solved before serious mistakes are made in planning. Resistance may indicate that the communication process has not worked in getting a clear message across, and this should not be ignored. Sometimes resistance is used against those who are resistant. Staff members who are resistant may be identified as not being team players. This approach can be very destructive, as it sets a tone of clamping down on those who offer a different point of view. Resistance should be viewed as a motivator to make the message clearer and to use input from others. Further assessment is then required to improve the plan and clearly state the outcomes. Managers who demonstrate leadership competence understand the need to respond in the following way: "I need to stop and listen."

A critical factor in coping with resistance to change is the long-term relationship that exists between management and staff. If this relationship has been positive, with trust and open communication, then resistance can usually be handled effectively. If this relationship does not exist, then coping with resistance will be more difficult. Managers must spend time on building and maintaining staff relationships, as this will be the key to success. Since some resistance should be expected, planning for resistance needs to be included whenever change is occurring. First, staff must understand why change is needed—the vision for change, advantages and disadvantages, how it might adversely affect staff, how change relates to competitive needs, and the financial benefits. Losses may occur, and this potential requires open discussion. Alliances need to be formed to gain political support for the change. What is political support? This is when one person supports another because that person feels a personal allegiance and will support the person's ideas. When leaders allow staff to openly discuss concerns without fear of punitive actions, resistance can be dealt with openly. Clearly data that can be provided to support the need and direction for change are very important. It may be necessary to stop doing what is being done and take a step back. Resistance needs to be viewed as an honest friend or a cue. Allowing others to tell their story or express their concerns will help make resistance a positive experience rather than a barrier to success. When children cross the street, they are taught to "Stop, look, and listen." This is what needs to be done when resistance occurs.

There are also internal and external key factors that influence how an organization responds to change (for example, a change in policy, regulations and accreditation, organization, or financial issues). Each of the following factors needs to be considered to effectively manage change.

1. *Internal and external policies.* It is important to understand how change affects and is affected by internal and external policies before actions are taken. Are there health policies such as state or federal laws that would affect a decision about the need for a change? External policies may seem to be disconnected but really provide required direction (for example, a state's nurse practice act describes what RNs may do). Internal policies are those that exist within an organization. Clearly internal policies might be changed, possibly more than once, to adapt to a situation; however, what is the policy's present status? An example is the increased use of UAP. If an HCO wants to increase the use of UAP in the organization, what does the HCO policy say about the UAP's present role, and how does this role relate to the change the hospital wants to make? What does the state board of nursing say about the UAP roles and responsibilities? Internal and external policies must be reviewed and met when changes are made. Changes in external policy require political advocacy.

2. *Regulations and accreditation.* **Regulations** are very important and describe how laws are to be implemented. They are developed by governmental agencies after legislative bodies pass laws, as in the previous example when boards of nursing develop regulations related to their state's nurse practice acts. Another example is the HHS, which develops regulations for specific laws passed by Congress (for example, when laws about Medicare are passed, there still need to be rules set up to address implementation of the law, which are much more detailed than the law itself). Standards and accreditation also have an impact on change (for example, nursing standards of care and the standards developed by the Joint Commission that are used when HCOs are evaluated for accreditation).

3. *Organization.* Organizational issues, such as the organization's vision statement (how it views itself in the future); structure (departments, who reports to whom); size, roles, and functions of staff and administration; communication; morale and culture; willingness to change; financial status; quality improvement; and the HCO's position and relationship with the community are all key to understanding the organization, how it will respond to change, and what needs to change. For example, if an HCO is experiencing low staff morale as well as having financial problems, it will have problems responding to a need to

change its documentation system. Staff will probably not be eager to make changes, and there may be limited funds to develop a new system to effectively train staff. In addition, planning change needs to consider the organizational structure: the microsystem, mesosystem, and macrosystem perspectives. The **microsystem** level looks at the organization from inside out, at the unit level where direct care work is done. The **mesosystem** level focuses on creating the conditions leading to organizational performance improvement: helping staff be successful, identifying and getting resources staff need, and developing measures to track improvement. The **macrosystem** views the organization from outside in, setting a vision for micro- and mesosytems, leadership and management support, and so on across the organization as a whole.

4. ***Financial issues.*** Costs can never be ignored, and during change, responses may be costly. Change may actually be driven by increased cost. For example, an HCO may decide to eliminate its obstetrical service because it is not getting enough admissions and is in competition with another HCO that has a large obstetrical service. In an uncertain healthcare industry, facts are important. First, regardless of the decision maker (government, insurers, businesses, HCOs), cost constraints will continue to tighten. Second, as data become more available and more reliable, it will increasingly be used in decision making. Data will drive how care is delivered by forcing improvement opportunities and determining how the HCO competes with other HCOs.

Along with the consideration of influences on the HCO, an organization needs to include continuous quality improvement in the change process. In doing so, the organization's leaders create a plan for excellence and ensure better implementation of the plan. Continuous quality improvement is discussed in more detail in Chapters 17 and 18.

WHERE TO BEGIN WHEN CONFRONTED WITH CHANGE   Strategies to respond to change are very important throughout the change process. Staff involved in change need to respond and think carefully, for example, the nurse listens to others and avoids snap judgments. This is an attitude of "yes and . . ." rather than "yes, but . . ." This nurse will ask others who are trusted for honest feedback, develop personal creativity, and will improve coping with change through these acts.

ACCEPTANCE OF CHANGE   After the discussion of resistance to change, it is easy to assume that all staff resist change, but this is not true. There is no doubt that when a situation is very bad, staff tend to welcome change, hoping it will improve a dysfunctional situation. What about the situations that are not so extreme? The key issue in acceptance is not what might be lost, but rather what will be gained. This is where the focus should be, though concerns about what might be lost should not be ignored. These gains are related to the loss factors, but they focus on the positive.

- Staff members feel they will be more secure in their jobs and more of their skills will be used. There may be an increase in money through salary, benefits, and other incentive changes.
- There may be an improved overall budget.
- Someone may receive a promotion or a new manager may be assigned who may give staff more authority.
- Status and prestige may improve with more space, special responsibilities, or a new location. Job responsibilities may change and improve.
- Better working conditions may be gained with new equipment, work schedule, or better workspace.
- Self-satisfaction in the job or the work environment may occur.
- Staff members may find themselves in work situations that provide them with better personal contacts or social relationships.
- The change may require less time and effort to get the job done because work will be more efficient.

In conclusion, there may also be some staff members who have mixed reactions to change—some resistance with some acceptance. How an individual identifies or predicts what will be gained and what will be lost are critical factors in directing the individual's response to change—whether it is resistance, acceptance, or somewhere in between.

THE NURSE MANAGER: THE CHANGE AGENT AND CHANGE COACH During the change process, the change agent, who may be a nurse executive, nurse manager, nurse team leader, staff nurse, and so on, understands the change, supports it, and works with staff to engage them in the change. There is no doubt that leadership is one of the most critical factors affecting change, particularly major changes, in an HCO. It can make a difference in whether or not the change process will be effective. Transformational leadership has a positive effect on the change process.

Like their staff, managers must cope with frequent changes. It is important for staff to understand the manager's response to change as it affects staff involvement. The major role of the manager is to implement change as directed from upper level administration or management. Some managers feel that they must respond positively to all requests even if they disagree with the need or the specific change. Why do they do this? They may be afraid about what might happen to them if they do not agree. They may want to be seen as a loyal manager. If the manager does disagree, the manager may decide to ask why this change is required. The manager may then need to explain reasons for the lack of support for the change and make recommendations for other approaches. There are certainly managers who have come to the point where they cannot agree with upper level management directives for change, and if they cannot influence the change process, they may then leave their positions. During these times, stress will be very high, and undoubtedly this will spill over onto the staff.

There are other roles that managers need to take. Change agents/coaches do not wait for change; they look for it and embrace it as an opportunity. In addition, a manager may implement some change independently from the total organization, without involvement from those above the manager. These changes usually pertain to the manager's unit or department and do not affect others outside that area. There are fewer and fewer situations that can meet this criterion as collaboration across areas is becoming more important in successful organizations. If the budget is involved, then the manager must carefully consider how to respond and how to involve upper management. It takes courage to initiate change as it involves risk taking, a higher risk than just implementing change that may be directed from above. Staff need to be involved and understand that risk taking includes them. The manager may risk altering staff morale, loss of staff, loss of quality care, loss of money from the budget, poor image, and so on. Participation from staff members means they become direct participants, adding their input to the plan. Changes that are

APPLYING EVIDENCE-BASED PRACTICE

Evidence for Effective Leadership and Management

CITATION: Kalisch, B., & Begeny, S. (2010). Preparation of nursing students for change and innovation. *Western Journal of Nursing Research, 32*(2), 157–167.

OVERVIEW: This critical question influenced this study: How do we prepare the next generation of nurses who will need to adapt and innovate in the changing healthcare delivery system? To respond to this question, the study examines "the information processing styles of nursing students in baccalaureate programs and also the extent to which the current nursing educational system promotes the development of creativity, an action orientation, and a willingness to change to prepare them for the demands of the health care system" (p. 158). The Organizational Engineering Model is used in this study. This model describes four information processing styles: reactive simulator, logical processor, hypothetical analyzer, and relational innovator. The sample included 271 freshman, sophomores, and seniors in two baccalaureate nursing programs. The study used a validated survey, I-Opt, to determine preference in task completion, change, and directions (performer, conservator, perfector, and changer). The study concludes that schools of nursing recruit students who use the *conservator information style*, which focuses on "outcome certainty

and deliberate response" (p. 157). In addition to frequently recruiting *conservator* students, schools of nursing are graduating students who are *conservators*, so the students have not changed their processing style by the time of program completion.

APPLICATION: Change is critical in clinical practice and in leadership and management. Understanding how nurses respond to change can help to determine if interventions are needed to improve change response. According to this study, though the sample is small and more research is required, nurses do have a problem with their change response. As noted in this study, the nursing education report (2010) by Benner et al. also identifies this as a major concern.

Questions:

1. How does your typical response to change relate to the styles described in this study?
2. Do you think you need to improve in how you respond to change? If so, why and how?
3. What recommendations would you give to your nursing program to help students better understand and respond to change? Provide specific examples.

implemented when there is a crisis carry with them an even higher risk for failure. At this time, careful planning may be put aside; the result is then often a haphazard response. Change agents/ coaches need to be very effective in initiating adaptive work (figuring out the best way to adapt how work is done while still meeting the work demands). Certainly change is stressful for everyone, yet this cannot be used as a barrier to improvement.

During the change process, it is also important to consider the impact of the organizational culture. How does the change agent/coach create and sustain the right culture? Change agents demonstrate the critical values through their words and actions. As managers manage the environment and work, they also provide a vision for the staff. This is a time when words and actions need to be consistent. It is not a time for conflict or inconsistency. For some changes, the culture also needs to change. This is not easy to do and requires a planned approach. During the change process, staff empowerment becomes important. Empowerment of staff is a critical part of effective change management. This helps to increase motivation. When staff members are empowered, they need to know their responsibilities and be given the authority required to get the job done. If training or further education is necessary, then staff need assistance in getting it. To move forward with change, staff need information, and standards must be clear. This engages all staff members in the decision-making process.

A DECISION: A RESPONSE TO CHANGE

This section of the chapter focuses on decision making and planning, which are functions that every nurse uses in the practice of nursing. Any response to change requires decisions, and many of these decisions require careful planning.

Decision making is a process that requires data/information, analysis, identification of choices, and a choice—the decision. Decision making is done to achieve a goal. When decisions are made, the goal is usually related to both tasks and relationships and can vary as to how much focus is placed on each of these. Those who make decisions must learn to cope with being right some of the time and also learn to live with imperfect solutions. To make a sound decision, which is what people desire to do, the most important consideration is the criteria that are used to guide the decision.

How is decision making related to planning? Nurses actively use decision making in a variety of situations, particularly during planning—patient care planning, planning the workday, and more involved planning for specific projects such as changing documentation or how the unit is organized. During all phases of the planning process, decisions are made. Each day a nurse makes multiple decisions that affect the nurse, the patient, other staff, the patient's family, and many others. Nursing practice is made up of a series of decisions. Decisions are required to resolve a discrepancy or a problem. Typically "decision making" and "problem solving" are used interchangeably, although decisions do not always focus on problems. Decisions, however, are made when problems are solved. Figure 3-2 describes some of the key reasons for planning.

Decision Styles

Why are creativity and innovation important in the decision-making process? Stepping "outside the box" is mentioned frequently today in all types of organizations. Decision making that routinely results in similar outcomes and does not consider innovative outcomes will not be as effective long term. Styles of decision making are affected by creativity and innovation. The common types of styles are unilateral, individual, and authoritarian decision making, all of which focus on one person making a decision with limited or no input from others. The opposite of this style is participative and consensus decision making (shared decision making). Here the emphasis is on including others in the decision making, even if an individual must make the final decision. The individual, however, using this style would pay close attention to feedback from others before making the final decision.

It is typical for managers to primarily use one style, though some managers use mixed styles or may switch styles depending on the situation. For example, as was discussed in Chapter 1 about contingency leadership theory, when a situation changes, different factors become more important and the manager may need to change styles. A nurse manager may encourage staff participation in decisions and allow time for this, but if the unit is suddenly short staffed, then the manager may need to step in and make decisions quickly.

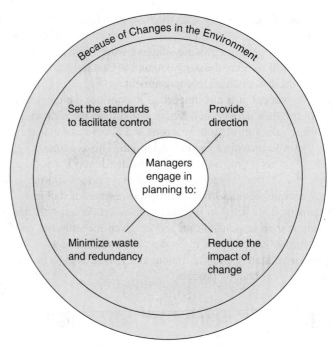

Figure 3-2 Reasons for planning

Systematic and intuitive decision styles are two other approaches to decision making. Systematic decision makers form their decisions more logically and use a structured approach, focusing more on planning and some of its tools. Intuitive decision makers are at the other end of the spectrum; here the focus is on a trial-and-error approach. They may ignore information and change their alternatives if it does not feel right. This is the "gut" approach. A staff member will say, "I just had a feeling about it." Again, the situation can make a difference. When a nurse has expertise in an area, decisions may appear to be more intuitive because the nurse may feel more confident and can rely more on a "gut feeling." In this case the decision is probably supported by experience. Ideally nurses should use both decision styles depending on the situation and their expertise, and most do use a combination.

Team decision making is another style that is used more today. It focuses on synergy, which is the combination of people's efforts that results in an output that is greater than the sum of the parts—shared decision making. Multiple ideas and experiences come together to form a decision. There are advantages and disadvantages to using team decision making. Advantages clearly focus on the fact that ideas from more than one person tend to improve other ideas and the final decision. As team members discuss an issue, ideas tend to bounce off each other, which stimulates further ideas. The major disadvantage of using this style is it takes longer to make a decision. Some issues or problems are made worse by team decision making (for example, during an emergency, when decisions must be made quickly and clearly so all can follow them). The need during a crisis is for someone to make a decision and move the process along. Staff members need to know that their ideas are important, though they cannot always be used. These ideas or suggestions can be considered after the potential crisis has passed then used to improve future decisions. When feedback is not recognized, those giving the feedback will feel left out and wonder why they wasted their time. Managers sometimes think that they use staff feedback and that this should be obvious, but often it is not so obvious to staff. Recognition goes a long way to improve morale, encourage staff to increase participation, and improve team decision making.

Team decision making allows for more points of view and develops more acceptance and commitment from those who participate. The result usually is greater effort to make the decision work during implementation. Why would there be disadvantages to team decision making? If the team process is ineffective, it may actually shorten or interfere with the decision-making process, which then affects the quality of the outcome. There may be greater pressure for consensus when members may not actually agree. Some teams experience dominance by one individual, diluting the effect of team input. Team members can believe so much in their own ideas that they are unable to openly consider other ideas. Team decisions can also take longer, which for some situations may be a disadvantage.

Teams can, of course, be quite successful in making decisions, but decision making does not just happen. There usually must be some guidance or facilitation. Brainstorming requires that all members are clear about what the issue is about and what it is not about. During brainstorming, the team leaders should set a reasonable time limit as this pushes staff to move toward a result. Ground rules should be established to keep the focus on the current topic or problem, use of constructive criticism, and listening to others. While the team develops ideas, recording them is important so they are not lost.

There are methods other than brainstorming that also facilitate team decision making, such as idea-generating questions (for example, "If we had enough staff, what would we do?" and "If we had the funding, how would we solve the problem?"). It is helpful to stimulate the team so the members consider how similar problems were solved in the past, and the team compares and contrasts the past with the present problem. Taking a different point of view than what would normally be taken may help the team understand the problem or issue from another perspective, which may lead to different alternatives, moving the decision making "out of the box."

Types of Decisions

Are there any major differences in the types of decisions? There are two major types that most staff encounter. The first is the need for programmed or structured decisions. These decisions are more repetitive and routine, take less time, and typically are related to a policy or procedure. For example, if a patient leaves the hospital against medical advice (AMA), there is a procedure for an AMA discharge, or if a nurse misses an order for a medication, there is a procedure to follow such as whom to notify, what to document, and so on. Most decisions are of this type, which is a good thing as these take less time. The second type, nonprogrammed decisions, is not so routine, and some may be crises. Situations that require this type of decision require more time, collection of data, critical thinking and analysis, and may require consultation with others. These decisions may be completely new experiences. They require more judgment.

Another view of the types of decisions considers the focus of the decision. One type is patient care decisions that nurses make in their practice that affect direct patient care, and this is the type of decision that most nurses do. The second type is decisions about the condition of work. This type affects the work environment, groups of patients, and how work is conducted. Though the nurse manager is involved in this type of decision making, as nurses become involved as leaders in the healthcare delivery system, they become more involved in the second type of decisions.

The Decision-Making Process

The **decision-making process** is dynamic. The most effective decisions are made in collaboration with others in the HCO. Collaboration between nurses and physicians also affects nurses' participation as it provides greater opportunities for nurses to participate. When collaboration is present, nurses and physicians share responsibility and, it is hoped, respect one another more. Knowledge, ideas, and skills are shared. This type of relationship can only improve decision making. The key steps in the decision-making process are identified in Figure 3-3.

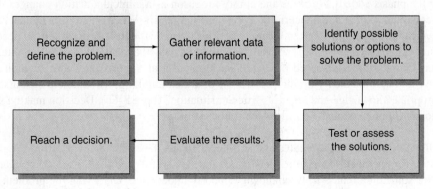

Figure 3-3 The decision-making process

BOX 3-2	CRITICAL THINKING SKILLS

- Knowledge, experience, judgment, and evaluation
- Interpretation
- Effective listening
- Application of moral reasoning and values
- Comprehension, application, analysis, and synthesis
- Awareness of self
- Mistakes happen and we learn from them

CRITICAL THINKING AND CLINICAL REASONING AND JUDGMENT: REACHING BEST DECISIONS

Nursing has become very complex with change occurring almost daily in nursing management and clinical practice. This complex, shifting environment often leads to stress for all levels of staff. Managers and team leaders need to actively use critical thinking and be particularly skilled in coping with stress and embrace opportunities to make change a positive experience for themselves, all staff, and the HCO. **Critical thinking** is a commitment to look for the best way to resolve a problem or respond to a request, preferably based on the most current research and practice findings (evidence-based practice [EBP] and evidence-based management [EBM]). For example, Alfaro-LeFevre (2011) discussed how critical thinking is involved in the thinking process:

- Reasoning
- Generates and examines questions and problems
- Intuition and feelings
- Weighs, clarifies, and evaluates evidence

Box 3-2 identifies some critical thinking skills. Nurses use critical thinking as they provide direct care, but they also use it as they coordinate care; advocate for the patient; work with other staff to resolve issues on the unit; ensure that quality, safe care is provided on the unit; and collaborate with others. Nurses who serve on committees and task forces use critical thinking in the work that must be done.

It is easy to slip into **dichotomous thinking** when you are in the process of decision making. This type of thinking should be avoided because when problems and situations are viewed in a polarized manner—things are seen as either "good" or "bad"—ineffective decision making results because it limits choices for patients and for other types of decisions that need to be made.

In response to change, critical thinking should be part of problem solving and decision making. It is important, however, to note that critical thinking is not the same as problem solving or decision making. Nurses who develop critical thinking skills will relieve their own stress, solve problems, and make more effective decisions.

In their report on nursing education, Benner et al. question whether nursing has focused too much on critical thinking, ignoring other aspects of practical reasoning (2010). The report discusses the need to know when to use critical thinking and when to not use it. Critical reflection is also needed so nurses can ask questions (about an event, patient, and so on) that lead to new interpretations. "Nurses need multiple ways of thinking, such as clinical reasoning and clinical imagination as well as critical, creative, scientific, and formal critical reasoning. By **clinical reasoning** [emphasis added], we mean the ability to reason as a clinical situation changes, taking into account the context and concerns of the patient and family. When nurses use clinical reasoning, they capture the patients' trends and trajectories" (p. 85). **Clinical judgment** is needed to determine if published research is relevant for a specific patient and situation and the value of the research. This is evidence-based practice. The Benner et al. report states that "cynicism and excessive doubt, often the by-product of overuse of critical thinking, will not help the nurse draw on appropriate knowledge and act in a particular situation" (pp. 85–86). Decision making should be a thoughtful process, and it involves the following steps.

IDENTIFY THE NEED FOR DECISION MAKING: WHAT IS THE PROBLEM?

After a review of related issues, the need to make a decision should be carefully defined. A solution cannot be found for something that is truly unknown or poorly understood. Clarifying the problem is not always easy. Staff may have different perspectives on the issue. For example, one staff member may think a problem about quality care might be due to low staffing, and another may attribute it to lack of appropriate training of unlicensed assistive personnel.

After the analysis of the problem, goals need to be established so all staff know the direction that is to be taken. Identifying goals is the only way to know if results are met. Who sets the goals? This can vary. The typical situation is that the manager sets the goals or in some instances, higher levels of managers may do this. As discussed throughout this text, however, the more staff are involved, the better the decision-making process. Setting goals is part of this process. Team leaders also set goals, and individual staff members set goals as they do their work. In the end, who sets the goals depends on the issue or problem that is being addressed. Goals/outcomes need to be clear, reasonable, and achievable.

Proactive planning helps to improve decision making and decrease stress about necessary decisions. This means there must be some anticipation of problems. Those who understand trends, history, risks, healthcare policy, and how problems are connected to one another, as well as identify signs that might indicate a need for a response, will be more able to anticipate and begin decision making early rather than later, when the problem may be more complicated.

DECISION-MAKING CONDITIONS   When discussing decision-making conditions, the first major issue is who is responsible for making the decision. Managers and staff can get themselves into further problems when they take on decisions that are not theirs to make or they do not make decisions they are responsible for making. How does one find out about who is responsible for a decision? Position descriptions should clarify some of this. The immediate supervisor is also an important resource to help clarify responsibility. During the hiring process and orientation, staff members need clear direction about their responsibilities. If they are confused or unclear about their decision-making responsibilities, they are responsible for asking about them to gain greater clarification. A staff member's comfort level with making decisions is also very important. Staff members who feel uncomfortable may avoid decisions, let others make the decisions, execute the decision-making process poorly, or arrive at poor decisions, which only makes them more uncomfortable. Those who work with this staff member will also feel uncomfortable about the decisions that are made, which affects morale, productivity, safety and quality, staff turnover, and the overall work environment.

What are the key reasons for staff discomfort with decision making? Risk is a concern along with lack of transparency. As mentioned earlier, staff are always concerned about loss—what will change and will it be better. Further data collection and analysis are important at this time. Some staff members are uncomfortable with the possible consequences of risk taking. When this occurs, the staff member might ask, "What is the worst thing that could happen?" It is important to consider impact and strategies to reduce risks. Maybe the person is focusing too much on the negative aspects. Others feel uncomfortable when the risk factors are unknown. Again, there needs to be more data collection, analysis, and talking to others who may help clarify the issue. Others find they are uncomfortable when certain types of decisions must be made, such as decisions related to budget, staffing, or termination of personnel. If this is the case, it is important to learn more about these areas and gain some expertise and confidence. Improving decision-making competency is important for all staff and managers. Increasing knowledge, researching to gain more information, and getting additional experience helps to improve decision making. Discussing concerns with colleagues is an important strategy for every nurse to use.

BARRIERS TO DECISION MAKING   Barriers to decision making may focus on a variety of factors, and they are similar to barriers to change. Whenever barriers are considered, it is critical to be clear about the barriers that exist within the HCO. Examples of typical barriers are dysfunction, poor communication, lack of staff participation, changing organization ownership or administration, inadequate staff, poorly prepared managers, inadequate budget, inadequate staffing levels, policies and procedures, and poor relationships with the community and consumers. There are other barriers that focus more on the individuals who make the decisions. Taking decision-making shortcuts (workarounds) can be an advantage, but this can also be a barrier to success when the shortcut limits data collection, analysis, and the quantity and quality of alternatives that are considered. If description of an issue or problem is really off track, this can act as a barrier. A frequent error in describing an issue or problem occurs when the person unconsciously considers some information to be more important when it is not. Another major barrier is an individual's psychological set, which is a rigid strategy or point of view. When a staff member enters the decision-making process with a rigid idea about possible cause(s) or strategies, there is an immediate block to success. Because barriers change, they need to be considered throughout the decision-making process.

DATA COLLECTION   Data that are collected are determined by the need and the outcomes. It is important first to complete the analysis of the issue or problem. What is the issue or problem? This will then direct data collection. It is easy to get carried away with data collection, which can lead to a situation of just collecting data for the sake of collecting it. The first consideration must be existing data. What data are already available, collected for another purpose, but could be used for this new purpose? When existing data are used, it is important to determine if the data meet the specific need.

Data are then analyzed to determine the cause, which requires objectivity. It is easy to assume something is the cause then unconsciously insert this assumption into the analysis of the data collected. Getting different perspectives of the data is also important rather than relying on just one individual or a few.

SELECTING ALTERNATIVES   For most problems, there are multiple alternative solutions that could be used to solve the problem or prevent a problem if that is the goal. It is best to have a number of alternatives from which to select. When the final alternative is selected, it needs to meet the critical criteria that were identified as important for success such as time limitation and resources including staff, space, expertise, and educational level of staff. Alternatives are usually evaluated according to three conditions:

1. *Certainty* indicates that there is considerable information about the issue or problem, which indicates a very high probability of meeting the outcome.
2. *Risk* indicates that some but not a lot of information is known.
3. *Uncertainty* indicates there is no knowledge of the probability of success.

The third type of alternative is the least secure approach. Most alternatives are selected based on the second type. Most staff can provide many examples of situations when problems were confronted with the thought that there was high probability that the alternative selected was going to achieve the goal desired, yet this did not occur.

Selecting alternatives also requires reflection on experience, which provides data about the probability of success as past mistakes can teach staff what not to do or which directions usually do not lead to success. In this selection, trading off or compromise often is required. Decision making is a dynamic process, so give-and-take is part of the process. Organizational and individual values will affect the alternatives selected, and thus it is difficult to avoid ethics when some decisions are made. For example, organ transplants involve a decision-making process, one that is highly structured, and this is certainly a decision process that involves ethical and legal issues.

When alternatives are selected, it is critical to ask if an alternative is practical. Some alternatives are not practical, and pursuing them will only increase frustration and cause more problems. Collaborating with others by asking them if they think it is practical and what might be some of the "real" concerns about the selection of the alternative usually improves decisions. There need to be realistic estimates of resource requirements (staff, supplies and equipment, and so on) during the planning. At this point, planning also includes an assessment of staff capabilities (not just staff numbers), and this information relates to the plan and its implementation. If additional capabilities are required, then this needs to be included in the plan (for example, a consultant or an expert to teach staff new computer skills so a new computerized physician order system can be implemented that will affect how nurses review orders). Timelines are identified for all of the activities in the plan so specific steps and accountabilities for staff can be identified. Throughout the process, it is important to be a step ahead. This can be done by frequently asking "what if" questions to identify situations that might arise to block the solution or make strategies or interventions ineffective.

IMPLEMENTING AND SELLING THE DECISION   Selling the decision focuses on decision acceptance. How committed to the decision are those who will be affected by it? This is a key question. Earlier in this chapter, resistance to change was discussed. This information applies to commitment to decisions and plans. Decisions that meet strong resistance will fail. Those who are needed to move the decision forward need to understand what is behind the decision.

Some decisions require a detailed action plan, but most do not. The key to implementation is timing. When to make the decision and when to implement it are frequently difficult to determine. Procrastination is common in decision making. Concern about lack of full information or clarity about the problem or directions given and who may need to be involved as well as agreement with identified outcomes can slow the process down. Each of these reasons has very clear solutions. All relate to getting more information, planning, and developing a clear viewpoint of the issue at hand. Another problem is making impulsive decisions. These decisions lead to more problems. If pressure is felt to make a decision now, then it is best to stop and consider why and what could be done to improve the decision making. It is rarely helpful to make decisions when emotions such as anger are strong. Those who want to jump in too soon should step back and take time to collaborate with others to work through the decision and to write plans down. Time taken to do this will decrease impulsiveness. The plan needs to include specific information as to actions and responsibilities.

EVALUATING RESULTS Evaluating results of decisions or plans is never easy. By the time one thinks this should be done, another change, decision, and plan are in process. However, neglecting evaluation has long-term consequences. The quality of a decision depends heavily on the goals selected and the strategies used to achieve them. Evaluation is thus intricately tied to the beginning, middle, and end of the decision-making process. This provides valuable data about when approaches need adjustment to prevent the situation from becoming too complex or not meeting the outcome.

Those who were involved in decision making should be involved in the evaluation. This requires objectivity. Staff who buy into a plan may be more reluctant to say it needs adjusting or has failed. For one reason, it probably means more change and stress; however, if this is not done, greater stress can also be expected.

AVOIDING WORKAROUNDS A **workaround** is "a rushed, improvised response to a breakdown in a work process, without pausing to analyze and correct the underlying problem" (Finkelman & Kenner, 2012, p. 208). How does this apply to change and decision making? Most HCOs are organized around functions with more ambiguity than clear responsibility. The system naturally breaks down as work is done. When this happens, the typical response is to just find a way to accomplish the task that needs to be done without stopping to analyze why there is a problem and solving the problem. In this situation, which is a workaround, frequently nothing is learned from the experience and thus improvement does not occur. The problem most likely will reoccur because no attempt has really been made to solve it. The following steps, with the change process embedded, may be used to avoid workarounds (Spear, 2005; Halbesleben, Savage, Wakefield, & Wakefield, 2010):

1. Work is designed as a series of ongoing experiments that immediately reveal problems.
2. Problems are addressed immediately through rapid experimentation.
3. Solutions are disseminated adaptively through collaborative experimentation.
4. People at all levels of the organization are taught to become experimentalists.

Decision-Making Processes, Tools, and Methods

There are many tools and methods used today to improve decision making and planning. Examples of some processes used are the following:

GAP ANALYSIS This is a method used to better understand where you are and where you want to go—what is the "gap." This then guides you in planning to reach your outcome. Gap analysis is a natural method used by most people who do not know that this is what the analysis is called.

COST-BENEFIT ANALYSIS This process is commonly used in health policy, but also many HCOs use it to clarify implications change has on cost. This analysis includes identification of the costs and the benefits, which may be more than financial such as changes in prestige, expertise, and staff morale, and so on. Then the two lists are "added up" and compared. This comparison helps in the decision-making process, but it should not be the only perspective used to make decisions.

PLAN-DO-STUDY-ACT (PDSA) CYCLE It is important to determine if a change will actually improve the work processes and/or environment and meet the intended goal(s). Too often this is neglected when a change really will have no positive impact or limited impact. The **PDSA cycle** is used to test a change (Institute for Health Improvement, 2014). During *Step One (Plan)*, the objective of the test is stated, predictions are made about what will happen and why, and a plan to test the change is developed. In *Step Two (Do)*, a small test is done with identification of problems encountered and first analysis of data. *Step Three (Study)* leads to more in-depth analysis of test data with comparison of predictions to data and summarization. During *Step Four (Act)*, the perspective of the change and intervention(s) may be revised based on what has been learned from the test. Other tests of the plan may be initiated.

DEEP DIVE PROCESS The **deep dive process** is used by the TCAB initiative (Institute for Health Improvement, 2015). The TCAB pilots use this process of an in-depth brainstorming session to arrive at methods to improve care at the bedside. The process, which can be applied to any type of change effort, includes the following:

- Clinical and nonclinical representatives from services and departments meet for a half-day session to focus on innovation related to a specific issue or theme. Management representatives also attend.
- This session encourages engagement in the issue and brainstorming. Time is needed to really get this involvement. After the deep dive, snorkels may occur on a regular basis. These are shorter brainstorming sessions.
- There should be agendas for the deep dive and snorkel sessions. Agendas should include time for storytelling. This allows time for individual members to discuss specific process-related work challenges. Asking, "What is your pet peeve?" or "What are you worried about the most?" can get to the critical concerns.
- Brainstorming should be directed toward identifying how things might be changed to improve.
- Post all ideas so all can see. Allow time for the ideas to be reviewed and expanded or changed.
- Vote on the changes to determine which ones will be tested, setting priorities.
- Describe how the tests will be conducted and evaluated.
- Identify who will lead the process, develop a timeline, and share this information with staff who need to know it.

Examples of Specific Methods and Tools

Box 3-3 provides examples of data collection methods. Figure 3-4 provides several examples of tools that can be used in collecting and analyzing data.

BOX 3-3	COMMON DATA COLLECTION METHODS

INTERVIEW
Interviews can be unstructured or structured. The unstructured interview provides opportunity to gain more detailed information with limited boundaries. Structured interviews, which use a standard form and/or format, are less flexible and collect standardized data. For both types of interviews, after the interviews are conducted, data must be summarized and analyzed, and this can take time.

OBSERVATION
Observation is often used when complex data are required. It might be used if a clinic needed data about the flow of work. Observation may be used to document what staff were doing, time factors, and impact of the physical layout. This type of observation would require a standard checklist or documentation form for the observers and clear guidelines as to what is to be observed and recorded.

QUESTIONNAIRE/SURVEY
This perhaps is the simplest method, and it is used frequently. It can be less expensive to administer. The questionnaire or survey may be used to collect information about facts such as how many staff are working at a particular time or how many patients were assigned particular staff members. Another type of data is procedure performance data. Evaluative data can also be obtained; for example, how does the staff feel about a change in the admission procedure or a change in documentation. Questions can be asked as to whether or not the procedure was followed or does staff feel prepared for the change.

Cause-and-effect diagram. This is a diagram that describes a specific process with its causal factors and their consequences. The focus is on improving understanding of possible causes. Another term for this diagram is a *fishbone diagram.*

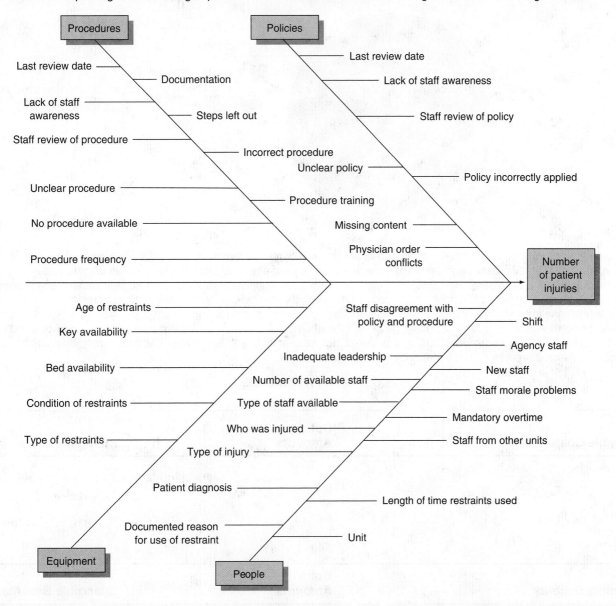

Pareto chart. This method may be used after a cause-and-effect diagram is developed in order to identify the causes of primary importance. Data are described according to the frequency of each cause and displayed according to the most frequent and least frequent. This will help to narrow the data so that the data can be used to determine the best action to take.

Figure 3-4 Making sense of data: Methods

Pie chart. This is another type of graph that provides a description of percentages of the whole. This is a common graph that most have seen.

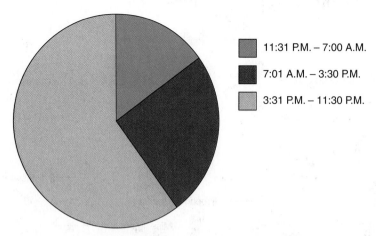

■	11:31 P.M. – 7:00 A.M.
■	7:01 A.M. – 3:30 P.M.
■	3:31 P.M. – 11:30 P.M.

Cost-benefit analysis. This is a method that is used to analyze two or more alternatives in order to determine which alternative will bring the greatest rewards or benefits compared with the costs. Cost-effectiveness is the focus. Both tangible and intangible benefits and costs are considered. Tangible costs might include funds, supplies, space, equipment, staff salaries and benefits, loss of staff, orientation costs, recruitment costs, and so on. Intangible costs might include downtime, staff resistance, decrease in morale, increase in errors, and changes in quality. Intangible benefits might include improved morale, improved level of staffing, increase in communication, and so on. Tangible benefits might include an increased number of patients seen or admitted, decrease in length-of-stay or complications, money saved, decrease in incidents, and so on. The cost benefit ratio can then be determined, which is represented by benefits divided by costs.

COST-BENEFIT ANALYSIS

Solution:

Tangible Costs	Dollar Amounts	Intangible Costs
✓	$	✓
✓	$	✓
✓	$	✓
✓	$	✓
		✓
Total Costs	$	

Tangible Benefits	Dollar Amounts	Intangible Benefits
✓	$	✓
✓	$	✓
✓	$	✓
✓	$	✓
		✓
Total Costs	$	

$$\text{Cost Benefit Ratio} = \frac{\text{Benefits (\qquad)}}{\text{Costs (\qquad)}} = \underline{\qquad}$$

Figure 3-4 Making sense of data: Methods (*continued*)

Graph. A graph is used to describe performance over a period of time in an attempt to identify trends. The line graph, used in this example, can describe one or more sets of data. This example describes two sets of data: the number of procedures and the clinical units. Then the data can be compared.

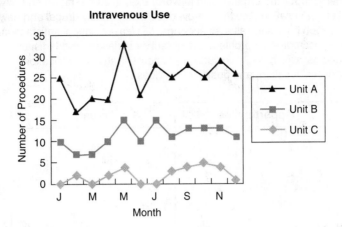

Flowchart. This is a type of chart that is helpful when there is a need to describe a decision-making process. The chart should be developed by a group or team who is involved in the process. The flowchart helps all focus on the process rather than just seeing one part or a part that relates to them as individuals. Typically these charts use common symbols, for example, (A) box represents a function, task, or department; (B) a diamond represents a decision; and (C) arrows indicate the flow of information. After the flowchart is developed, it is then easier to identify repetitive steps, unnecessary steps, or other steps that just do not make sense in the process.

Histogram. This is a bar graph, which illustrates the frequency distribution of a variable or variables in continuous data.

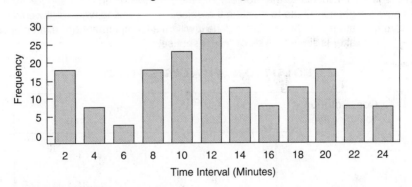

Figure 3-4 (*continued*)   (*continued*)

WOTS-up. This is a method that is used to analyze the weaknesses, opportunities, threats, and strengths of a particular situation. Weaknesses focus on internal factors such as lack of management development, qualifications of staff, level of staffing, staff expertise, financial status, marketing efforts, location, quality of services, and so on. Opportunities are the factors that are viewed as positive and have the potential to move the organization forward. Examples are nurse and physician recruitment levels, new programs or services, new markets, population growth, improved technology, new drugs, and new facilities. Threats are serious factors that might hold the organization back such as staff shortage, decreased patient satisfaction, decrease in insured patients, decrease in demand for services, accreditation problems, malpractice litigation, and legislative changes. The fourth category includes the organization's strengths, which might include management style, qualifications and expertise of staff, financial status, increased demand for services, location, and quality of services.

Weaknesses	Opportunities	Threats	Strengths

Solution analysis grid. This method first identifies the problem and the objective. Then each suggested alternative to resolve the problem is analyzed as to how it might contribute to meeting the objective by ranking whether it would have a high, medium, or low contribution; cost in dollars; timeframe or the amount of time it will take to implement (for example, short range, long range, or immediate); and feasibility. The latter is simply a "yes" or "no" response.

SOLUTION ANALYSIS FIELD

Alternative Solution	Cost Solution to Objectives	Cost $	Time	Feasibility

Figure 3-4 Making sense of data: Methods (*continued*)

CASE STUDY

Change: An Opportunity or a Disaster?

A home health agency is undergoing restructuring. This involves changes in staffing, roles and responsibilities, scheduling, and client assignments. As the director of nursing (DON) you are responsible for this change. You know it will be challenging. The staff is about 50/50 new and long-term employees. One of your supervisors has openly expressed his concern that these changes will not work. You know that the RNs will have to cover more clients, but you have some flexibility in home health aide assignments. You don't want to lose RNs, but the changes have to be made.

Questions:

1. How would you use the deep dive process to implement these required changes?
2. Apply the PDSA cycle to this change initiative. Include barriers and strategies to overcome.
3. Describe an evaluation plan that you will use at 3, 6, and 12 months.

PLANNING: STRATEGIC, OPERATIONAL, AND PROJECT

Overview

Why is it important to plan? If organizations or staff members operate without a plan or map, will they get to their goals or their destination? An analogy would be traveling to an unknown place without a map or directions. Getting lost increases stress, takes time, may increase expenses, and may interfere with reaching the destination, which is the goal. Most nurses have worked in situations where there were no goals, the goals were unclear, or goals were kept a secret. This is not a great way to work. What if patients were cared for without a plan? How would staff know if outcomes were met? How organized would the care be? How would staff know their responsibilities? Crisis management seems to be more the norm in HCOs. It is certainly important to learn how to deal with crises, but a better approach, whenever possible, is to plan, both short range (operational) and long range (strategic). Leaders do not have the luxury of saying, "I don't have time to plan." Organizations cannot afford not to.

When there is recognition that a change is needed, particularly one that is fairly major, the planning process goes into action. A plan is a picture of a future vision, ideally painted by a team, and planning needs to consider the HCO's vision, mission, and goals. **Planning** includes multiple decisions and is directly affected by change. Planning is the pivotal step in the process of getting there. There are three types of planning:

1. **Strategic planning** is what an organization does when it considers long-term issues and goals. It includes planning that is done by the organization's components, such as its departments or services. The organization looks at its vision and its organizational assessment data and asks, "Where are the gaps? What would it take to get there?" A typical result is the organization's plan for the next five years.
2. **Operational planning** focuses on a shorter range, and operational plans are part of strategic planning. Operational plans should not conflict with strategic plans and should provide steps to meeting strategic goals. This plan focuses on the day-to-day functions (operations) of an organization and its divisions/departments/units. For example, a medical unit would have an operational plan that is reviewed annually and managed throughout the year. The nurse manager and ideally the staff will identify key goals for the year that are in sync with the strategic plan for the nursing department and for the HCO. Specific steps are identified for reaching the goals and needed resources (financial, staffing, equipment and supplies, and so on) are identified. The feasibility of the goals is a critical question to consider. Content in this chapter on change and decision making relates to this process of planning. HCO higher management must approve operational plans. These plans also are more flexible than strategic plans, requiring frequent monitoring and adjustment as needs arise. For example, if admissions increase unexpectedly, needed resources are impacted. It may be

that more new graduates are hired to adjust for staffing needs, and then they need more orientation and mentoring, changing the operational plan by adding more unit orientation and staff development.

3. **Project planning** focuses on a specific project, which can be short or long term. Examples include a plan to change documentation such as introducing an electronic medical/health record (EMR/EHR), introducing a new admission procedure or new service, or changing staff roles. Project planning must take into account strategic plans so there is no conflict. Project plans should help the organization reach strategic goals. For example, if one of an organization's operational goals is to develop the use of interprofessional teams in all departments and units, a project plan that focuses on training staff would need to be developed by staff education. Content in this chapter is also applied to this type of planning.

SWOT Analysis

SWOT analysis is a structured method that examines (1) strengths, (2) weaknesses, (3) opportunities, and (4) threats so the planning team will have a better understanding of the status of the situation and the organization. SWOT is often used for strategic planning to assess their status as an organization or business. However, it can also be used for project planning. Each of the steps requires that questions are asked and honest answers given. The government, businesses, and HCOs use this analysis method. SWOT helps to focus collection of information and analysis of that information.

Team Approach

Team planning is the most effective type of planning. Individuals, particularly in management and leadership positions, plan all the time; however, strategic, operational, and project plans are best done by a team of stakeholders and experts. Chapters 12, 13, and 14 discuss teams—structure and function of teams, collaboration, coordination, conflict resolution, and communication. These all apply to effective team planning when the team implements the change and decision-making processes as planning is done, implemented, and evaluated.

Planning Concerns

Common errors made in planning are developing a plan that is too specific and does not allow for flexibility when unexpected need arises; not engaging the stakeholders; and failure to plan for risks. Projects include four major constraints that need to be included in the planning: (1) What will be done and who will do the work (scope of the project); (2) how long the project will take (timeline); (3) what materials and supplies are needed (resources) and how much will each phase cost; and (4) the level at which the project will be completed (outcomes/performance criteria) (Dearman & Davis, 2011, pp. 59–61).

Proactive Leadership

Proactive leadership is required to ensure effective change management. The steps for a leader or manager to manage planned change are (Fallon, Begun, & Riley, 2013, p. 321):

1. Engage in debate or dialogue about the need for change and the nature of the proposed solution.
2. Communicate consensus or decision to all stakeholders.
3. Form a coalition to manage the change process.
4. Develop a work plan and ways to measure progress (metrics: schedule, target goals, indicators).
5. Implement the proposed change by integrating it into organizational culture, structure, and strategy.
6. Listen and learn, adjusting the nature of the solution and the speed of the process as needed.

Throughout the planning process, the leader or manager needs to listen, learn, and adapt the planning as needed. This requires frequent collection of feedback. Resources have to be available, and not just at the beginning but throughout the project. A problem that can occur is funding changes during the project, sometimes requiring major changes in the project plan. Recommendations for effective change include: focus on the big picture, know the players, be realistic, do not run too lean (ensure you have the resources), expect the unexpected, set and check against milestones (Bradberry & Greaves, 2012, pp. 41–43).

APPLYING LEADERSHIP AND MANAGEMENT

My Hospital Unit: An Evolving Case Experience

As the nurse manager on your unit, you are confronted daily with new changes that come from above or within your unit. Sometimes you wonder if there will be "normalcy" when you do not have to deal with a new policy, form, new staff, change in budget, and so on. Today you are sitting at your desk after attending report, and you know that some changes need to be made. You may select any issue that is of interest to you that you might want to change as nurse manager. Describe the issue or problem and develop a detailed plan, applying the change and decision-making processes and content from this chapter to guide you. Ask a classmate to critique your plan for change, and critique your classmate's nurse manager plan. After you get the critique, revise the plan where you feel it needs revision, using the feedback you get. What have you learned from critiquing someone else's plan?

BSN and *Master's Essentials:* Application to Content

BSN Essentials (American Association of Colleges of Nursing, 2008) as Applied to this Chapter:

II. Basic Organizational and Systems Leadership for Quality Care and Patient Safety

Master's Essentials (American Association of Colleges of Nursing, 2011) as Applied to this Chapter:

I. Organizational and Systems Leadership
II. Quality Improvement and Safety

Applying AONE Competencies

Identify which of the AONE competencies found in Appendix A apply to the content of this chapter.

Engaging in the Content: Critical Thinking and Clinical Reasoning and Judgment

Discussion Questions

1. How do you feel about change? How do you react to change? What do you think you might improve so you might (a) be a more effective change agent and (b) better manage change made by others that impact you?
2. Several examples of methods that might be used to analyze data are described in Figure 3-4. Find examples of these methods in the literature or in your clinical setting. Do the methods help to provide a picture of the data? Why or why not? Share your examples. (Online Application Option)
3. Visit the Transforming Care at the Bedside (TCAB) website. Review the content, examples, PowerPoint presentations, and videos on the content. How does this content about TCAB relate to content in this chapter? (Online Application Option)
4. Describe the change process.
5. How is TCAB an example of the change process? Select one example from a TCAB pilot described on the TCAB website and apply it to this question.
6. What are some current healthcare changes that impact nursing?

Application Exercises

1. Team decision making is more and more common in health care today, particularly with the emphasis on interprofessional teamwork. There are many group/team techniques that can be used to improve team decision making. Nominal group/team technique (NGT) is one type of team decision making. Try using this technique in a small team. Follow these steps: (1) Individuals in the team first present their own ideas without interacting with the team by stating the viewpoint on a topic. (2) The team is then presented with a question related to the topic. (3) Each member writes down his or her own response to the question. (4) The responses are then presented one at a time for clarification. This phase is time limited. (5) Then all members rank the responses separately. The ratings are summarized and shared.
2. Divide into small teams. Change can be approached in a variety of ways; however, for this exercise, you are asked to use

Lewin's force-field model of change, described in this chapter. The team should identify something it would like to change in your nursing program, or it could be in your course. Select something that is not too complex. Now clearly state what you want to change and apply Lewin's model. Describe what you would do in each of the stages of the model. All teams should then share their proposed changes. (Online Application Option)

3. Each team should identify a problem that is of concern in a unit. The team should then develop a plan to resolve the problem.

4. Each team should discuss the relationship of *The Future of Nursing* report and change. The full report can be accessed on the National Academy of Medicine website. Also review the Robert Wood Johnson Foundation website on the Initiative on the Future of Nursing.

5. Interview a nurse manager or a team leader and ask about experience with change. Prepare three questions for the interview. Summarize and share results with your team in class. (Online Application Option)

References

Alfaro-LeFevre, R. (2011). *Critical thinking, clinical reasoning, and clinical judgment: A practical approach* (5th ed.). St. Louis, MO: Elsevier Saunders.

American Association of Colleges of Nursing. (2008). *Essentials of baccalaureate education for professional nursing practice*. Washington, DC: Author.

American Association of Colleges of Nursing. (2011). *The essentials of masters in nursing*. Washington, DC: Author.

Benner, P., Sutphen, M., Leonard, V., & Day, L. (2010). *Educating nurses: A call for radical transformation*. San Francisco, CA: Jossey-Bass.

Bradberry, T., & Greaves, J. (2012). *Leadership 2.0*. San Diego, CA: TalentSmart.

Center to Champion Nursing. (2014). The future of nursing. Retrieved from http://campaignforaction.org/

Dearman, C., & Davis, D. (2011). Planning a project for implementation. In J. Harris, L. Roussel, S. Walters, & C. Dearman (Eds.), *Project planning and management* (pp. 51–63). Sudbury, MA: Jones & Bartlett Learning.

Fallon, L., Begun, J., & Riley, W. (2013). *Managing health organizations for quality and performance*. Sudbury, MA: Jones & Bartlett Learning.

Finkelman, A. (2001). *Managed care: A nursing perspective*. Upper Saddle River, NJ: Prentice Hall.

Finkelman, A., & Kenner, C. (2007). Why should nurse leaders care about the status of nursing education? *Nurse Leader, 5*(6), 23–27.

Finkelman, A., & Kenner, C. (2012). *Teaching IOM: Implications of the Institute of Medicine reports for nursing education* (3rd ed.). Silver Spring, MD: American Nurses Association.

Halbesleben, J., Savage, G., Wakefield, D., & Wakefield, B. (2010). Rework and workarounds in nurse medication administration process: Implications for work processes and patient safety. *Healthcare Management Review, 35*, 124–133.

Institute for Health Improvement. (2014). Science of improvement: Testing changes. Retrieved from http://www.ihi.org/resources/Pages/HowtoImprove/ScienceofImprovementTestingChanges.aspx

Institute for Health Improvement. (2015). Transforming care at the bedside. Retrieved from http://www.ihi.org/Engage/Initiatives/Completed/TCAB/Pages/default.aspx

Institute of Medicine. (2003). *Health profession education*. Washington, DC: National Academies Press.

Institute of Medicine. (2004). *Keeping patients safe*. Washington, DC: National Academies Press.

Institute of Medicine. (2011). *The future of nursing: Leading change, advancing health*. Washington, DC: National Academies Press.

Kotter International. (2014). The 8-step process for leading change. Retrieved from http://www.kotterinternational.com/the-8-step-process-for-leading-change/

Lewin, K. (1947). Group and social change. In T. Newcomb and E. Hartely (Eds.), *Readings in social psychology*. New York, NY: Holt, Rinehart and Winston.

Mackoff, B. (2011). *Nurse manager engagement*. Boston, MA: Jones & Bartlett Publishers.

Quinn, R. (1996). *Deep change: Discovering the leader within*. San Francisco, CA: Jossey-Bass.

Quinn, R. (2000). *Change the world: How ordinary people can accomplish extraordinary results*. San Francisco, CA: Jossey-Bass.

Robert Wood Johnson Foundation. (2009). Review of the IDEO. Retrieved from http://www.rwjf.org/qualityequality/product.jsp?id=30070&parentid=30060&grparentid=30051

Robert Wood Johnson Foundation. (2014). Initiative on the future of nursing. Retrieved from http://the-futureofnursing.org/about

Rogers, E. (2003). *Diffusion of innovations* (5th ed.). New York, NY: Free Press.

Spear, S. (2005, September). Fixing healthcare from the inside, today. *Harvard Business Review*, 78–91.

U.S. Department of Health and Human Services, Health Resources and Services Administration. (2014). Readiness assessment and developing project aims. Retrieved from http://www.hrsa.gov/quality/toolbox/methodology/readinessassessment/part2.html

CHAPTER 4

Organizational Structure for Effective Care Delivery

LEARNING OUTCOMES

Before you begin, take a moment to familiarize yourself with the learning outcomes for this chapter.

> Compare and contrast the key organizational theories.
> Distinguish between structure and process.
> Explain the key differences between for-profit and not-for-profit healthcare organizations.
> Examine the use of marketing in healthcare delivery.
> Compare the key healthcare providers and their services.
> Apply the process for analyzing an organization.
> Compare and contrast the different nursing care models discussed in this chapter.
> Explain the key advantages of shared governance for nursing staff.

WHAT'S AHEAD

Healthcare organizations (HCOs) have a long history of being centralized, hierarchical-controlled organizations that focus on centralized staffing, policies and procedures, budget control, and daily variance reports with emphasis on punishment when goals are not met. Most find that control is easier to accomplish than using some of the newer leadership and management approaches. An atmosphere of control does not result in a staff environment of engagement and innovation, thus leading to HCOs that cannot adjust well to change. Changes in leadership approaches, as discussed in Chapter 1, have clearly affected organizational changes so the hierarchical type of organization is slowly fading away. This type of organization is not in sync with the more current leadership styles, such as transformational leadership. Over the years changes in reimbursement, such as the introduction of managed care, changes in patient deductibles and copayments, and now with the Affordable Care Act (ACA) changes such as elimination of preexisting conditions have had an impact on organization structure and function. The traditional approach to department-focused organizations is no longer as effective in this new environment of change. There is also greater need for healthcare provider accountability and for cost control due to reimbursement requirements focused on cost reductions and greater emphasis on outcomes. Another change is movement away from acute health care to wellness and more care provided in the community. Healthcare providers not only need to assist people to get better but also to keep them from getting sick. Healthcare organizations must now be change oriented if they want to survive and be effective. The Institute of Medicine (IOM) *Quality Chasm* series of reports emphasize that the current healthcare delivery system and its organizations are

KEY TERMS

- accountability
- adaptation
- authority
- bureaucracy
- centralization
- chain of command
- closed system
- cross-training
- decentralized
- departmentalization
- division of labor
- efficiency
- for-profit healthcare organization
- horizontal structure
- line authority
- macrosystem
- marketing
- matrix organization
- mesosystem
- microsystem
- mission statement
- not-for-profit organization
- nursing models
- open systems
- primary care
- primary nursing
- process

- **public/community health**
- **responsibility**
- **scalar chain**
- **secondary care**
- **service-line organization**
- **shared governance**
- **span of control**
- **structure**
- **SWOT**
- **systems theory**
- **tertiary care**
- **unity of direction or command**
- **vertical structure**
- **vision**

dysfunctional. This is a critical issue to consider as one examines HCOs. This chapter addresses theories about organizational structure and process by describing some theories and an overall view of HCOs. This content is connected with other content about leadership and management, change and decision making, collaboration, coordination, and coping with conflict. Chapter 5 extends this discussion by describing the financial element of HCOs. Chapter 6 examines one type of HCO, acute care hospitals, and Chapter 7 focuses on public/community health.

ORGANIZATIONAL THEORIES: EMPHASIS ON STRUCTURE AND PROCESS

There are many theories about organizations, and these theories have changed, many building on previous theories. The theories typically focus on structure, process, or both.

Organizational Theories and Governance

Many theories exist about organizational process and structure. Some of these theories include classical theory, bureaucratic organization, systems theory, microsystem/mesosystem/macrosystem, and service-line organization. Theories about organization really cannot be considered without relating them to leadership theories as they are interconnected.

CLASSICAL THEORY   Classical organization theory was described by Henri Fayol in 1916. His theory, though quite old, has had an effect on many theories that came after it. This theory includes principles that provide guidelines for organization. Some of these principles are important in understanding other theories. Box 4-1 highlights the key principles.

- The first principle is **division of labor**, which is a method for identifying an organization's specialized jobs. The tasks of the job are described in the position descriptions and are used to determine the division of labor. There is a clear delineation of the organization's rules that are found in its policies and procedures. The goal of this specialization is to increase productivity. It is also easier to identify where there is a breakdown in productivity and who is responsible for tasks.
- The second principle is **unity of direction or command**. Each staff member should report to only one supervisor.
- The third principle is **centralization**. This principle focuses on centralization with all decisions made by specific management levels. There should, however, be an optimum balance between centralization and decentralization, which is an organizational structure that pushes decision making and activities into the smaller components of the organization such as clinical units.
- **Authority** and **responsibility** form the fourth principle. The ideal is that there is equality between these two—responsibilities of the manager and the authority to do the job. In larger jobs authority is sometimes more difficult to identify.
- The last principle in the classical organizational theory recognizes that the **scalar chain** or the **chain of command** is important. This is a vertical chain of command for decisions and communication, from top to bottom or bottom to top, though the former is the most common. This is a pyramid structure in that higher up in the organizational structure, there are less management staff and ultimately one person is responsible.

Fayol's theory has been modified, and new theories have taken its place. The theory, however, did emphasize the need to understand an organization's structure, function, and process, which continue to be important (Mind Tools™, 2014).

BOX 4-1	CLASSICAL THEORY: KEY PRINCIPLES

- Division of labor
- Unity of direction or command
- Centralization
- Authority and responsibility
- Scalar chain or chain of command

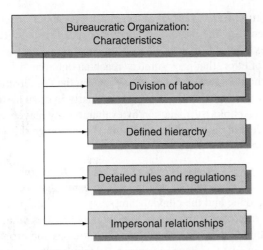

Figure 4-1 Bureaucratic organizations and characteristics

BUREAUCRATIC ORGANIZATION   This type of organization is highly structured. One organization that is most commonly referred to as bureaucratic is the government. This form of organization can be described as the most predictable but not necessarily the most effective. **Bureaucracy** is characterized by tight control, decreased uncertainty in the decision-making process, and very little individual staff choice. The goal is to ensure uniformity. Managers hold the authority, and staff are accountable to a manager. This type of organization appears impersonal, with decision making separated from the staff who do the work. Seniority is often used to gain promotion—based on the length of employment rather than skill or expertise. Positions are arranged in a hierarchy. Management, particularly top management, establishes the organization's vision or mission and its goals and objectives, making this centralized management. Control, however, is vested in top management. Figure 4-1 highlights the key characteristics. All of these characteristics are directly related to classical theory.

What type of leadership is found in this type of organization? Decision making is in the hands of the formal leader, and staff do not usually feel comfortable or free to express opinions. Staff members commonly lack confidence or trust in the leaders, and they are not encouraged to use creative problem solving. The expectation from management and staff is that the leader/manager will tell staff what to do. This type of organizational structure is found less and less frequently as it does not meet the demands of today's healthcare delivery system or approaches to leadership. However, some HCOs still use it, have remnants of it left in their organizations, or have leaders who wish that the organization were still bureaucratic and may continue to function in this way. Many HCOs have tried to flatten their structure and eliminate their multiple layers (decentralizing), as will be discussed further in this chapter. Some of these organizations have been more successful than others with this change effort.

SYSTEMS THEORY   **Systems theory** views organizations as one entity with multiple elements or components that interact interdependently. Feedback is a critical process in a system. Input, process, and output rely on feedback, which is the dynamic process in which an organism learns from experiences within the environment. Systems are viewed from the perspective of closed and opened systems (Siegrist, 2011). A **closed system** has limited or no interaction with its outside environment. It is isolated, and from a healthcare delivery perspective, this system/organization would not be in tune with the needs of its consumers. In this situation consumers would not be involved in the organization other than to receive its services. Most HCOs have discovered that this type of organization is ineffective and have turned more toward developing organizations with **open systems** in which interaction is easier and expected.

Within an HCO system, professional staff, administrative staff, equipment, supplies, and patients represent the system inputs. The process is the delivery of health care as patients work their way through the system to discharge. The outputs are the outcomes or results of that care, which are the critical concerns today in the push to improve care (Institute of Medicine, 2001). Adaptation, efficiency, and customer satisfaction are important in open systems, and criteria are used to determine system effectiveness. If an organization cannot adapt, it will cease to exist. **Adaptation** is the extent that the organization can and does respond to internal and external demands. Change drives the need for adaptation. **Efficiency**, which is the ratio of input to output, focuses on the amount of effort that is required to reach an outcome. Efficiency and productivity go hand in hand. Stakeholders (anyone who is affected by the organization's decisions and services, including employees) are very important, particularly in open systems. Thus, it is important to pay attention to stakeholder satisfaction by evaluating key player satisfaction. Who are the key players or stakeholders in the healthcare system? The customer, third-party payer, providers, and the consumer are the stakeholders.

MICROSYSTEM, MESOSYSTEM, AND MACROSYSTEM It is common for there to be two "camps" in HCOs—the management or administrative camp that focuses on governance, budgets, and getting the job done and the clinical camp that focuses on patient care. Typically each camp does not believe the other camp really understands or cares what is done. For example, administration does not understand the clinical side, its stresses and problems, and so on, which leads to dysfunction. Some experts have recommended focusing on a view of the HCO from the **microsystem**, **mesosystem**, and **macrosystem** perspective to address this concern. The key is to drill down to the smallest unit within the organization, the microsystem.

> A healthcare clinical microsystem is defined as the combination of a small team of people who work together on a regular basis—or as needed—to provide care, and the individuals who receive that care, who also can be recognized as a discrete subpopulation of patients. It has clinical and business aims, linked processes, a shared information environment and produces services and care which can be measured as performance outcomes. (ASHP Foundation, 2014)

Microsystems develop over time and typically are part of larger systems and organizations. The system cares for patients, meets staff needs, and maintains itself as a clinical unit. One view of a microsystem is that of a building block of the larger organization/system. The next level is the mesosystem, which supports the microsystems within an organization, providing resources required to meet the outcomes, thus connecting the microsystems to the HCO as a whole: the macrosystem. For HCOs that are part of a larger system, this network connects multiple macrosystems. Examples include a national healthcare delivery system of hospitals or a network that offers diverse service organizations across the continuum of care such as acute care, ambulatory care, home care, and so on. The goal is to make it possible for microsystems to provide high-quality, efficient service. If all of the microsystems are accomplishing this, it reflects positively on the mesosystem and the macrosystem.

SERVICE-LINE ORGANIZATION The **service-line organization** groups activities according to product or service, such as women's health, emergency and urgent care, behavioral health care, and health and wellness. Interprofessional planning is increasingly being used in organizations. The IOM reports (2003) recognize the importance of interprofessional planning because it enhances collaboration and identifies core healthcare providers that should be involved. For example, if planning occurs for behavioral health services, then behavioral health (psychiatric/mental health) nursing staff, psychiatrists, psychologists, social workers, and other mental health staff, would be involved in the process. Even though an organization is structured around services/products, there still need to be some standardized features that continue to apply to all services/products. Position descriptions would have some content that is standardized along with specific content related to the service/product. Another example might include documentation forms that apply across all service areas; however, the emergency department or mental health services may require specialized documentation. Administration in these HCOs cross specialties and functions and require greater collaboration.

It is clear that this structure can be confusing for staff who have worked in more traditional nursing departments. It is even difficult to describe. In this type of structure, management and staff need to learn more about the new structure and how it affects processes, staff, and management relationships. Staff should also be asked for input as the organization adapts to these changes. The service-line type of organization has become more common in health care due to greater emphasis on collaboration and coordination.

Organization Structure and Process

STRUCTURE   Typically a description of an organization includes information about its **structure** and **process**. Why is it important to understand this? As organizational theories developed, they tended to focus on one of these aspects of organization, although some focus on both. Why are an organization's structure (what the organization looks like) and its process (how things are done) important? For example, if a nurse does not understand to whom he or she reports, this can be a problem (structure). If the nurse does not understand the communication process for reporting an error (process), this can lead to problems. What are the aspects of structure and process that are important to understand?

First, how do staff find out about an HCO's structure? The best place to begin is with the organizational chart for the entire organization and the charts for its components, such as departments, divisions, and units. As discussed earlier, the microsystem and other systems need to be interrelated to be effective. The chart provides a visual of the chain of command, centralization/decentralization approach, departments, and span of control. It is important that this chart be updated as changes are made in the organizational structure. When assessing an organization's structure, it is important to remember that each organization has a formal and an informal aspect. How are these aspects demonstrated? The HCO's organizational chart describes the formal positions and hierarchy; however, this does not reflect the informal structure. Staff members who are leaders even if they do not hold formal titles in the hierarchy, would not be identified in the structure described in the organizational chart. Although all managers have the same formal authority due to their positions as managers, the organizational chart would not clarify who was more powerful. These are examples of how much can be described in an organizational chart. A traditional structure uses vertical relationships or the chain of command to identify positions and supervision or reporting direction. The view of organizational structure has been changing for many HCOs as they move to greater emphasis on horizontal organization. Elements of the structure that are important to consider are highlighted in Box 4-2 and discussed below:

- *Vertical structure.* A **vertical structure** establishes line authority, uses centralized decision making, and is found in bureaucratic organizations, with staff reporting "up the line" through the organization.
- *Horizontal structure.* A **horizontal structure** focuses on departmentalization related to functions and decentralized decision making.
- *Line authority or the chain of command.* A more traditional approach to authority in organizations, **line authority** or the chain of command identifies to whom each staff member reports. For example, in line authority a staff nurse would report to the nurse manager, the nurse manager to the director of the service, the director of the service to the nurse executive, and the nurse executive to the chief executive officer.
- *Staff authority.* Staff who function in an advisory capacity and cannot force other staff to do something must use influence, or staff authority, to make an impact. This can be a difficult position, but it has become more common. Staff authority is less clear because this relationship is advisory. An example is the director of nursing education or staff development in a hospital, who typically has no line authority over the nurse managers but has an informal relationship. The director can suggest and advise nurse managers to initiate certain educational programs but cannot direct nurse managers. Key skills for success in this type of position are effective communication, negotiation, building collaborative relationships, marketing, evidence-based practice, and leadership. Clinical nurse specialists (CNSs) and clinical nurse leaders (CNLs) usually hold staff authority positions.

BOX 4-2	ELEMENTS OF ORGANIZATIONAL STRUCTURE

- Vertical structure
- Horizontal structure
- Line authority or chain of command
- Staff authority
- Span of control
- Centralized or decentralized
- Departmentalization

- *Span of control.* **Span of control** is the number of people supervised by one person/ position. This is a critical concern in the classical theory of organizations, which emphasizes that there are limits to the number of staff a supervisor can effectively direct. Issues that affect the number of staff are (a) similarity and complexity of the jobs and functions, (b) geographic factors (for example, staff who are spread out in several clinics in a community as compared to staff who work on one unit in a hospital), (c) amount of direction and coordination required, and (d) amount of planning and time required to provide management. More efficient organizations usually have a shorter span of control for their managers.
- *Centralized and decentralized organizational structures.* A centralized structure is an approach focusing on centralized tasks and authority. A **decentralized** approach spreads tasks and authority out over components of the HCO. For example, how is staff education organized in a hospital? In a centralized approach, there is a staff development department that is responsible for staff orientation and education throughout the hospital, whereas a decentralized approach gives this responsibility to the divisions or units. In the latter case, there may still be centralized staff who provide some staff development services and also act as consultants to the units. In this case they typically are also responsible for overall hospital orientation and education/training that is required for all staff, and nurse managers are responsible for their own unit's staff development. In a decentralized organization, the nurse managers then have more independence in the management of their units in comparison to centralized organizations. (See Chapter 20.)
- *Departmentalization.* When an HCO divides or groups tasks, it is referred to as **departmentalization**. Functional departmentalization focuses on grouping related jobs, while territorial departmentalization focuses on grouping jobs according to location within the organization. An example of a functional departmentalization, which is common in HCOs, is the department of surgery, which might include the preoperative area, operating rooms, and postanesthesia care unit (PACU). Another example is the obstetrics department composed of labor and delivery, postpartum, nurseries, and the neonatal intensive care unit. In some HCOs the clinics for these specialty areas are also included in the department. This is very similar to a product/service-line approach. A different approach is to have all clinics, regardless of specialty, included in one ambulatory care department.
- *Matrix organization.* A **matrix organization** structure attempts to balance functional and service or product organizations. Staff belong to a functional department, such as a nursing department, and to a service or product department, such as women's health. Dual authority is part of this type of structure as staff report to two managerial systems.

The informal organization is also very important. This is what works behind the formal organization. Sometimes informal leaders are more powerful than formal leaders. They can have significant influence on the change process. Informal organization can be found at all levels of a formal organization, from the unit to the upper level. In the ideal situation, the formal and the informal organizations work together and not against each other.

PROCESS   Organizational process, the second critical descriptor of an organization, focuses on how the organization operates. Particularly important process factors are communication, decision making, policies and procedures, interprofessional teamwork, collaboration, organization performance and job performance, goal attainment and results, quality improvement, budget, marketing, and future plans. All of these factors are discussed in other chapters. Nurses participate in all of these aspects of organizational process whether they are staff nurses or managers.

The organization's vision, mission statement, and goals and objectives should be included in a review of an organization's process. The **vision** is important in describing the organization's beliefs and values. An organizational philosophy answers the question of "why" for an organization. Vision statements from HCO nursing departments or services should reflect the key values of nursing practice and the HCO as a whole. Patient-centered care is now a critical element of HCO visions and goals, supported by work done by the National Academy of Medicine (NAM) and identifying it as one of the five core competencies of healthcare professions.

Reimbursement changes have also had major impact on HCOs and present organizations and nurses with new challenges such as the current expansion of healthcare reimbursement

BOX 4-3	ELEMENTS OF ORGANIZATIONAL PROCESS

- Decision making
- Delegation
- Coordination
- Communication
- Evaluation

options due to the ACA. How organizations demonstrate this in their actions is difficult and not always easy to identify. How can HCOs continue to incorporate these key concepts such as caring in their changing organizations and also change their vision and goals to meet future changes? The nurse executive is responsible for ensuring that values expressed in an HCO's nursing vision are implemented. The mission statement clarifies the organization's purpose. It describes what the organization is, while the vision describes what the organization wants to be. Goals and objectives identify how the organization plans to meet its vision and mission. The **mission statement** provides a clear description of the organization's goals and objectives, which are influenced by the organization's core values and purpose. All of the staff needs to understand and be committed to the organization's vision, mission, and goals and objectives.

Vision and mission statements, as well as goals and objectives, all help to define the organizational process—how things work to get the job done. However, these are just words on paper if they do not become part of the everyday practice in an HCO. What are other important elements of process? Box 4-3 highlights the process elements.

- *Decision making.* Decisions are made frequently in all HCOs: decisions about patient care, how staff do their work, organization operations, and the future of the organization. Decision making is a critical element of organizational processes. (See Chapter 3.)
- *Delegation.* Decisions should be made as close to the task or activity as possible, which has made delegation even more important in today's healthcare organizations. It is important to remember that delegation does not relinquish the person who is delegating from the responsibility over the task. (See Chapter 14.)
- *Coordination.* Coordination is the process by which the parts of a process are synchronized or work together. The IOM (2003) describes the purpose of coordination as "to establish and support a continuous healing relationship, enabled by an integrated clinical environment and characterized by a proactive delivery of evidence-based care and follow-up" (p. 49). (See Chapter 13.)
- *Communication.* Communication is part of any HCO's processes. Without communication, nothing will get done in an organization; in fact, without communication, managers and staff would not know what to do. (See Chapter 14.)
- *Evaluation.* Evaluation of the organization's performance and that of individual staff performance assists the HCO in determining its needs in the planning process so goals and objectives can be met. All processes are evaluated in some form, whether it is a formal evaluation or staff concluding that some action was successful on an informal basis. (See Chapters 17 and 18.)

HEALTHCARE ORGANIZATIONS

This section discusses some key factors about the healthcare delivery system and its organizations. The healthcare system consists of all the agencies and professionals that are organized to provide health services. The three major purposes of the healthcare delivery system are to provide (a) health promotion and illness prevention, (b) diagnosis and treatment of illness and injury, and (c) rehabilitation and health restoration. Box 4-4 highlights these purposes.

There are three levels of healthcare services based on the complexity of the care required.

1. **Primary care** includes health promotion and education, preventive care, early detection, and environmental protection.
2. **Secondary care** focuses on diagnosis and treatment in the primary settings of acute care and emergency care.

BOX 4-4	HEALTHCARE DELIVERY SYSTEM PURPOSES

- Health promotion and illness prevention
- Diagnosis and treatment
- Rehabilitation and health restoration

3. **Tertiary care** focuses on long-term care, rehabilitation, and palliative care and care of the dying. Healthcare systems are varied in the level of services they provide, and some provide a combination of services (for example, a large medical center might provide acute care, ambulatory care, primary care, emergency services, a wellness center, home care, and also own a long-term care facility).

The second part of the healthcare delivery system is the public or population system, which provides care for the population or community. Both the personal systems, which focus on care for individuals, and the public systems provide a variety of services including health promotion, prevention and early detection of disease, diagnosis and treatment of disease with a focus on cure, rehabilitative/restorative care, and custodial care. Healthcare economics and reimbursement have had a major effect on both the personal and the public systems, as discussed in Chapter 5.

Healthcare settings can be described by a variety of characteristics, including the type of services offered, size, location (urban or rural), type of people served, and reimbursement methods. The following are examples of healthcare settings:

- **Public/community health** include government departments and agencies (federal, state, or local) funded primarily by taxes and administered by elected or appointed officials. Local health departments develop and carry out programs to meet the health needs of groups within the community and the community as a whole (See Chapter 7.)
- Physician practices/offices (or advanced practice registered nurses' [APRN] and certified nurse-midwives' [CNM] offices)
- Primary care
- Ambulatory care centers (one-day surgery centers, diagnostic centers)
- Clinics, which may be part of a hospital or external to hospitals, provide a variety of services (primary care, specialty care)
- Occupational health clinics, which provide health services at the worksite
- Community health centers
- School health services, some of which may be full-service clinics
- Emergency
- Urgent care
- Crisis intervention
- Hospitals (acute care) (See Chapter 6.)
- Behavioral health/psychiatric hospitals and community mental health centers
- Substance abuse treatment centers (inpatient and outpatient)
- Extended-care facilities, which include skilled nursing (intermediate care) and/or extended-care (long-term care) facilities and may be part of a hospital system or separate
- Retirement and assisted living centers
- Rehabilitation centers
- Home health agencies
- Hospice services, which may be provided in the home, in a hospital-based hospice unit, and/or in a separate facility

This list is not complete, but it does provide examples of the more common types of healthcare settings or organizations.

The U.S. healthcare system is complex, although it did not begin this way. In the past, care was primarily provided in the home and by visits to physician offices. This gradually developed into a more complex system as the role of hospitals grew. Today most care is still centered in the personal healthcare system rather than the public care system. Physician care was typically delivered in one of the following models:

1. The solo practice of a physician in an office, which continues to be present in some communities, although it is less and less common.
2. The single specialty group model, which consists of physicians in the same specialty who pool expenses, income, and offices.
3. Multispecialty group practice, which provides interaction across specialty areas.
4. The integrated health maintenance model that has prepaid multispecialty physicians.
5. Community health center—developed through federal monies in the 1960s (Finkelman, 2015, p. 187).

However, there have been other changes occurring in physician practice. Due to the increasing cost of running a practice, more physicians are giving up their private practices (Harris, 2010). In 2005 more than two thirds of the medical practices were physician owned, but three years later, the number decreased to below 50%. Approximately 50% of the practices are now owned by hospitals, and this percentage increases annually. Where did the physicians go? Some retired but most took salaried positions. This is leading to major changes in practice and physician-patient relationships. "The decline of private practices may put an end to the kind of enduring and intimate relationships between patients and doctors that have long defined medicine. A patient who chooses a doctor in a private practice is more likely to see that same doctor during each office visit than a patient who chooses a doctor employed by a health system" (Harris, 2010, p. B5). On the plus side, patients may benefit from higher quality care and better coordinated care in the new system—records can more easily be shared, specialists more easily accessible, and so on. There has also been an expansion of nurse-managed health centers and nurse practitioner practice settings. The newest IOM report on nursing (2011) emphasizes in its recommendations that nurses, particularly APRNs, need to be more active in providing primary care. The ACA is also driving changes such as more support for accountable care organizations, medical homes, and nurse-managed health centers, all emphasizing primary care.

Healthcare organizations are confronted with many factors that influence how they are structured and how they operate. The following factors have had an impact or continue to have an impact on HCO structure and processes:

- Problems with access to health care often resulting in disparity
- Increase in healthcare cost and cost containment to combat increased costs
- Hospital mergers and closings
- Growth of managed care and development of other reimbursement methods
- Shortage of healthcare providers (e.g., nurses, pharmacists, physicians)
- Increase in the number of uninsured and underinsured
- Improved clinical and informatic technologic advances (e.g., computers, organ transplants, extension of life, genetics, telehealth/telemedicine)
- Increased specialization, which may increase fragmentation of care
- Growing consumerism
- Changes in demographics (e.g., single-parent families, immigrant populations, lack of nearby extended family, aging)
- Increase in homeless populations and other vulnerable populations
- Increase in availability of drugs that are effective but may be expensive
- Lack of or limited coverage for prescriptions
- Uneven distribution of services (e.g., urban versus rural areas)
- Lack of clear health policies
- Unequal treatment for some health problems (e.g., mental health services)

For-Profit and Not-for-Profit Healthcare Delivery Systems

Two terms that are often used in health care, "for-profit" and "not-for-profit," can be confusing. They are nonetheless important terms as they identify an HCO's characteristics that impact many aspects of its structure and process. **For-profit healthcare organizations** have stockholders/shareholders who own stock in the business/organization. The organization is responsible to the stockholders, who expect to make a profit on their investment. If stockholders do not feel that they are making enough money on their investment, they may sell their stocks, and the organization will then have serious financial problems. Stockholders serve as an external control on decisions that are made by the organization. These HCOs receive the same type of reimbursement for care as not-for-profit delivery systems, which are called voluntary or public HCOs. In contrast, the **not-for-profit organization** does not have stockholders to whom it must report. Charitable institutions, governments, churches, and typical reimbursement sources fund not-for-profit HCOs. Both types of organizations, for-profit and not-for-profit, must still make a profit to survive today. The not-for-profit organization does not share this profit with shareholders as the for-profit organization does, but rather this type of organization reinvests its profit into its own organization to continue its services and maintain the organization. The for-profit organization, however, also does the same, but it must still share some profit with stockholders. Both financial approaches have direct effects on the HCO's vision, mission, goals, budget, management and decision making, use of resources, types of services, relationships with other organizations and the community, and how quickly the organization responds to change that can make a financial impact on the organization. Some for-profit organizations have experienced ethical and legal problems because of their need for financial success as discussed in Chapter 2. Nurses need to be aware of their employer's status related to profits. It can affect why and how decisions are made.

Marketing

Marketing is a new area for most nurses, and for many it may arouse negative reactions because nurses may see it as too "businesslike" and not ethical. Why is it important for nurses to be aware of healthcare marketing and understand some aspects of it? The **marketing** process drives major decisions in health care as HCOs compete with one another for patients and for third-party payer (insurer) contracts. Ineffective marketing may result in an HCO cutting staff and services if it cannot attract enough patients.

The marketing process includes three elements:

1. A determination of what is wanted and needed.
2. A method(s) for reaching what is wanted or needed.
3. An understanding of the patient, customer, or consumer and the service or need.

These elements should sound familiar because they are similar to those described in the nursing process. Like the nursing process, the marketing process is complex. It is dependent on data, interaction between people, problem solving, decision making, and evaluation of results. A market is an actual or potential consumer or customer who might need a product or service. For example, for a CNM, a market would be women in a specific community or geographic area who are of childbearing age. A more specific market would be women in that community or geographic area who might use the services of a CNM. This is referred to as segmenting. Factors that help identify segments of a market are age, sex, diagnosis, past medical treatment, geography, accessibility, insurance coverage, and economic status. Selling is often confused with marketing, but selling is only one part of the marketing process. Nurses can be very helpful in the marketing process with their consumer skills: the ability to talk with patients, understanding of patient needs, their emphasis on health promotion and disease and illness prevention, understanding of the healthcare delivery system and the community, and problem-solving skills.

Marketing goals are established by the HCO based on assessment data. The following are examples of goals that might be identified for a community clinic:

- To develop accessible patient services.
- To increase the number of patient visits per month by 5%.
- To provide health promotion and disease and illness prevention services to all pediatric patients.
- To increase active patient participation in their care (self-management).
- To develop patient education support groups focusing on chronic illness (e.g., asthma, arthritis, hypertension).

As illustrated by these examples of goals, marketing is connected to providing direct patient care services, quality improvement, risk management, administration, decision making and planning, performance appraisal, staff development, and community relationships.

BOX 4-5	THE FOUR Ps OF MARKETING

1. Product	3. Price
2. Promotion	4. Place

THE FOUR Ps OF MARKETING   The four Ps of marketing are product, promotion, price, and place. Box 4-5 highlights these principles.

- Products are the goods or services that meet the customer's needs. For a community clinic, this would include physical exams, patient education, immunizations, well-child care, and blood pressure screening.
- Promotion is what is often referred to as advertising. How does the community clinic get the word out about the services or products it provides? Informing local hospitals and other community agencies about its services to obtain referrals and advertising on the Internet or on radio is promotion.
- Pricing focuses on identifying the cost of a product or service. Much of this is in the hands of third-party payers and the government, which determine their own reimbursement levels; however, if reimbursement does not cover expenses and provide some profit, this is a major problem for the HCO.
- The fourth P is place, or getting the product or service to the consumer. This includes such factors as physical location, hours, wait time for appointments, type of location, accessibility to the facility, transportation, parking, handicap accessibility, and the type of setting, such as its "warmth," easy-to-locate offices, and so on.

THE MARKETING PLAN   The marketing plan is a written description of the organization and what it wants to be in the future. The plan includes a description of the organization (for example, a group of nurse practitioners, an interprofessional group of practitioners, a clinic, hospital, and so on), the environment in which the organization operates, its potential and actual consumers, its competitors, and its plans for the future. Change is inevitable so a marketing plan is never really complete. If the marketing plan does not change over time, it becomes just another piece of paper. A marketing plan contains five parts, as highlighted in Box 4-6:

1. Situational analysis is sometimes referred to as **SWOT**—the strengths, weaknesses, opportunities, and threats analysis of the organization. All of these elements are described with relevant data to support the ideas presented. Data from both internal and external environments are included in the analysis.
2. Marketing goals and objectives that are reasonable and specific to the organization are identified. A marketing goal might be to increase the number of patients from a specific geographic area by 20%. If this geographic area had a large number of professional women, single and married, a related objective might be to develop a special health promotion program for women ages 30 to 40. Decisions such as this need to be based on data.
3. Marketing strategy considers the marketing mix and the marketing budget. The marketing mix describes the specific combination of the four Ps, focusing on how the combination of product, promotion, price, and place influences consumers to use the organization's services. As the marketing budget is developed, resources are allocated to each service area. For example, the budget identifies the amount of resources (financial, staff, space) that will be allocated to market the health promotion program for women ages 30 to 40.
4. Action plans describe specifically how the marketing goals and objectives will be met. The written plan identifies actions to be taken, responsibilities and accountabilities, and time frames.
5. Evaluation is ongoing. It provides feedback as the plan is implemented and goals are achieved, as well as information that might indicate a need for a change in the plan. Any change must be carefully considered; however, no plan should be so sacred that it cannot be revised (Mind Tools™, 2010).

BOX 4-6	MARKETING PLAN

- Situational Analysis (SWOT)
- Goals and Objectives
- Marketing Mix and Budget
- Action Plans
- Evaluation

The ACA requires that nonprofit hospitals conduct a community needs assessment every three years and adopt an implementation plan based on this assessment.

Healthcare Providers: The Interprofessional Team

Healthcare providers can be classified as organizations such as a hospital or a clinic and as individual providers such as an individual nurse or physician. Both types provide care to individuals and groups of patients. There are many different types of healthcare provider organizations, as noted earlier in this chapter.

The factors discussed earlier that have affected organization structure and process frequently cause these organizations to change. The growth of managed care influenced the decrease in hospitalization and lengths of stay and the need for provider/physician performance. This led to growth in primary care. Due to the push to decrease hospitalization when patients are admitted to hospitals, they are often now much more acutely ill, requiring more care when admitted. At the same time, hospitals are encouraged to discharge patients as soon as possible. These patients then return home still sick and often require care from family members or a home health agency. Home health services and hospice services have also increased. This shifting has had a major impact on physician practices, clinics, hospitals, home health agencies, hospices, and long-term care facilities, and certainly on nursing practice in all of these organizations. At the same time, advanced practice nursing has grown, and APRNs are now found in many of these HCOs.

These changes have also had an influence on the use of hospitalists and intensivists (Society of Hospital Medicine, 2014). Physicians usually hold these positions, but some hospitals are using nurse practitioners and clinical nurse specialists in these roles. The hospitalist, a generalist, provides medical coverage for hospitalized patients instead of the patient's personal or primary care physician covering the patient. After discharge, the patient returns to his or her personal physician. Intensivists cover patients in the intensive care units and have considerable intensive care experience, something that most primary care physicians do not have. The major disadvantage is the patient does not have a relationship with the hospitalist or intensivist. A study examined the impact of hospitalist workload and quality and efficiency of care (Elliott, Young, Brice, Aguiar, & Kolm, 2014). This retrospective study of two years of admissions indicates that when workload increases, there is an association of clinically meaningful increases in length of stay and cost. As is true for many healthcare staff, increasing workload can have a negative impact.

The following provides a brief review of the major types of professional and nonprofessional members of the healthcare team:

- *Registered nurse (RN).* This appears to be a simple designation; however, there are different types of educational routes to obtain a license to practice nursing. These include diploma, associate degree, and baccalaureate degree. In addition, more nurses are obtaining master's degrees, though still only a small number get doctorates. These advanced degrees provide them with the opportunity to practice more independently, teach, or do research. Nurses practice in all types of health settings.
- *Clinical nurse leader (CNL).* This role requires a CNL master's degree. The American Association of Colleges of Nursing (AACN) states that the CNL is a "provider and manager of care at the point of care to individuals and cohorts. The CNL designs, implements, and evaluates patient care by coordinating, delegating and supervising the care provided by the healthcare team, including licensed nurses, technicians, and other health professionals" (2007, p. 6).
- *Advanced practice registered nurse (APRN) and clinical nurse specialist (CNS).* Both of these types of nurses obtain education beyond a baccalaureate degree with special content

related to either primary care or acute care. A nurse practitioner specializes in such areas as adult health, family health, pediatrics, neonatal, gerontology, anesthesia, and psychiatric/mental health/behavioral health nursing. Nurse practitioners may work in clinics, the community, private practice, the home, the hospital, or long-term care facilities—any setting where health care is provided. A CNS typically works in acute care settings. Some hospitals are using CNSs and APRNs as hospitalists.

- *Certified registered nurse anesthetist (CRNA).* This nurse has completed graduate specialty in nurse anesthesia. Typically this is a master's degree; however, these programs are transitioning to doctor of nursing practice (DNP) degrees. CRNAs work in both inpatient and ambulatory care settings that require anesthesia services.

- *Certified nurse-midwife (CNM).* This is a nurse who has completed an additional educational program that focuses on midwifery. Nurse midwives work in all types of settings in which women's health and obstetrical services are provided.

- *Doctor of nursing practice (DNP).* This is the newest nursing degree and is a practice-based doctoral program. The AACN comments about this degree: "Nurses prepared at the doctoral level with a blend of clinical, organization, economic, and leadership skills are most likely to be able to critique nursing and other clinical scientific findings and design programs of care delivery that are locally acceptable, economically feasible, and which significantly impact healthcare outcomes" (2004, p. 7). The goal is to transition APRNs, nurse anesthetists, and certified nurse-midwives to the DNP as the terminal degree.

- *Physician (MD).* A physician has a medical degree and typically specializes in a specific area of practice (e.g., internal medicine, surgery, pediatrics, gynecology, etc.). There is a growing physician shortage, just as there is a nursing shortage. In addition, physicians have gravitated to specialty services rather than to primary care, often due to financial concerns. Specialty care reimbursement is higher. With this shortage in primary care and also the expected growth in patient numbers due to the ACA, there is greater interest in increasing the number of APRNs and physician assistants (PAs) and need for more nurse anesthetists and certified nurse-midwives. APRNs and PAs would be more involved in primary care. There is also need to increase the number of physicians, and medical schools are increasing enrollment.

- *Licensed practical/vocational nurse (LPN/LVN).* Licensed practical/vocational nurses perform some specific nursing functions and play a critical role in providing direct patient care. They have high school degrees and additional training. They work in all types of settings under the direct supervision of a registered nurse. The use of LPN/LVNs varies from state to state.

- *Unlicensed assistive personnel (UAP).* The increased use of UAP on the healthcare team has caused some controversy in the past few years; however, UAP are critical members of the team. Aides and assistants have been in existence for a long time. Their responsibilities have changed over the years, and today they are providing more direct patient care. Registered nurses supervise UAPs and must ensure that they are able to provide safe care to the patient. The home health aide functions fairly independently in the home, usually seeing the patient more than the home care nurse, who supervises the home health aide and makes periodic home visits. The amount of UAP education and training is highly variable, and this has caused some of the concern about what they are able to do and the effect on the quality of care. Further information about UAP and delegation is found in Chapter 15.

- *Registered dietician (RD).* This healthcare professional assesses the patient's nutritional status related to health. A registered dietician may work in hospitals, long-term care facilities, clinics, community health areas, and in the home. Another similar healthcare provider is the nutritionist, who has knowledge about nutrition and food in the community setting and recommends healthful diets and provides nutrition counseling and education.

- *Social worker (SW).* Social workers assist patients and their families with problems related to reimbursement, access to care, housing, care in the home, transportation, and other social problems and sometimes mental health concerns. They may also hold specialized positions as discharge planners and as case managers, particularly in acute care facilities or hospitals; however, they work in all types of settings.

- *Occupational therapist (OT).* Occupational therapists assist patients with impaired functions to reach the patient's maximum level of physical and psychosocial independence. They work in all types of settings, including assessment of home needs and adaptation.

- *Speech-language pathologist.* Speech-language pathologists assist patients who need rehabilitative services related to speech and hearing. They work in all types of settings.
- *Physical therapist (PT).* Physical therapists focus on assisting patients who are experiencing musculoskeletal problems with rehabilitation and reaching maximum physical functioning. They work in all types of settings.
- *Pharmacist.* Pharmacists are concerned with ensuring that patients receive the appropriate medication by preparing and dispensing medications. Pharmacists have become much more involved in patient education about medications and in monitoring and evaluating the effects of medications. They work in all types of settings, including the local drug store, where they play a critical role in ensuring safe prescriptions and in providing consumer education.
- *Respiratory therapist (RT).* Respiratory therapists provide care to patients with respiratory illnesses. They use oxygen therapy, intermittent positive pressure respirators, artificial mechanical ventilators, and inhalation therapy.
- *Chiropractor.* Chiropractors are concerned with improving the function of the patient's musculoskeletal system with various treatment modalities (e.g., spinal manipulation, diet, exercise, and massage). Interest in using chiropractors has been increasing as the consumer has become more interested in nontraditional medical interventions.
- *Paramedical technologists.* Paramedical technologists work in various medical technology areas (e.g., radiology, nuclear medicine, and other laboratories) (Finkelman, 2015, pp. 193–194).

Other common providers are physician assistants (PAs), who diagnose and treat certain diseases and injuries under the direction of a physician, dentist, case manager, or spiritual support person (chaplain).

Nontraditional healthcare providers have become more important as consumers have increased their use of alternative or complementary therapies. There is great variation in how these services are accepted by healthcare professionals. In some communities some of these services can be found within traditional HCOs, and traditional healthcare providers are also incorporating the use of alternative therapies into their practice. In other communities there is less integration of these services. Reimbursement for these services is still highly variable. Some of these therapies include massage therapy, herbal therapy, healing touch, energetic healing, acupuncture, acupressure, and so on. Some of the problem areas with these therapies are limited research to support their effectiveness, limited or lack of formal training and licensure requirements for practitioners, lack of standards, and limited or no reimbursement. The National Institutes of Health (NIH) has established a center, the National Center for Complementary and Alternative Medicine (NCCAM), which focuses on alternative or complementary therapies and now funds research to determine the effectiveness of these therapies. These issues need to be addressed before these therapies and their practitioners will be fully accepted in the healthcare system.

Organizational Analysis

After reviewing some of the critical aspects related to organizations in this chapter, how would one go about analyzing an HCO to better understand or assess its functioning? The following might be included in this analysis:

- *Integration of vision and mission into organizational structure.* The vision and mission statements are the driving forces behind all decisions, or they should be. They provide critical information about the HCO's philosophy and values. It is also important to remember that many organizations have beautifully written vision and mission statements yet never really make them come alive. When an organization is analyzed, the important issue is whether or not the vision and mission match what the organization and its staff actually do.
- *Description of corporate culture, historical determinants.* The culture of an HCO and its history have a major impact on the way staff interact, communicate, work as teams, and feel rewarded and recognized or feel neglected. It also affects organization outcomes. The community in which the organization must survive also affects the organization's culture. (See Chapter 7.)
- *Structural design of the organization.* Organizational structure varies, and structure affects how organizations communicate, work together, and solve problems or do not solve prob-

lems, which represent the organization's process. The structure of HCOs is changing, and some of these efforts are resulting in positive outcomes.

- *Decision-making patterns.* How does the organization handle decision making? This can be highly variable from one organization to another and even within an organization. Some nursing leaders and other organizational leaders have greater skill in this area than other leaders. All organizations need improvement in decision making. Do staff feel that decisions are handled well? Is there staff input? Is shared governance used, and how effective is it? What is the response to accountability? How empowered are the staff?

- *Communication patterns.* Understanding communication within an organization provides an important perspective of how the HCO functions. How is communication conducted? Who communicates with whom? What are the formal and informal aspects? How successful is communication? How is technology used? Do staff members feel they are listened to when they speak up? How can this be improved? How are interprofessional, intradepartmental, and interdepartmental communication described? How do the communication patterns affect the change process? How does the HCO communicate with the community and with other HCOs? (See Chapter 14.)

- *Alignment of goals across subsystems.* Integrative systems and multiorganizations are more common organization structures today. Subsystems, whether they are subsystems of a multiorganization with multiple entities (one hospital in a system that has several hospitals) or the subsystems of one organization (departments and services), must be aligned. If goals of the subsystems are not in alignment with overall organizational goals, there will be conflicts, and it will be difficult to determine organization outcomes. This does not, however, mean that subsystems might not propose different goals; however, then subsystems must convince the overall organization that this change is appropriate.

- *Incorporation of quality and safety as a value.* There is no doubt that quality and safety are critical issues today in health care. All HCOs are involved in quality improvement; however, some are much more successful than others. In analyzing an organization, its quality improvement effort needs to be assessed. When an organization's quality and safety are assessed, much can be learned about the organization's vision and mission, goals and objectives, structure and process, communication, decision making, use of resources, and what is really important to the organization. Is the organization using evidence-based practice and evidence-based management? The key question to ask is this: What are its outcomes? (See Chapters 17 and 18.)

- *Use of human resources.* Clearly, use of human resources is critical today. Some organizations are just sitting around, worrying about the number of empty positions, but others are quite active in trying to find creative solutions. Understanding human resource needs and planning to meet them is a daily organizational concern. (See Chapter 8.)

- *Effective financial and information infrastructure planning.* As organizations are analyzed, consideration must be given to their financial status and effective financial planning. Outcomes are always tied to financial issues and cannot be ignored. All HCOs and providers are struggling with reimbursement issues and how these issues affect practice. (See Chapter 5.)

- *Information management.* A critical component within an HCO is how information is used (Institute of Medicine, 2003). What information is available? Who has it? How is it collected? Is it reliable and valid? How is the information used? How has technology impacted the collection and use of information? Is the organization in compliance with legal requirements (e.g., patient privacy and HIPAA)? Information management is a growing component of HCOs. (See Chapter 19.)

- *Organizational responsiveness to change.* Change is a running thread throughout all of the discussions in this text. Organizations that cannot change effectively will struggle, and many will disappear. Change cannot be avoided, so the best approach is to learn how to effectively adapt—making sound decisions based on sound evidence and data (evidence-based practice and evidence-based management). This also provides opportunities for expanding or adapting educational offerings for staff. Healthcare organizations are at different stages of development in how they respond to change. Analysis of an organization should include an assessment of the organization's response to change. Leaders have a major impact on the organization's ability to change effectively. (See Chapter 3.)

APPLYING EVIDENCE-BASED PRACTICE

Evidence for Effective Leadership and Management

CITATIONS: Catrambone, C., Johnson, M., Mion, L., & Minnick, A. (2009). The design of adult acute care units in U.S. hospitals. *Journal of Nursing Scholarship, 41*(1), 79–86.

Institute of Medicine. (2004). *Keeping patients safe: Transforming the work environment of nurses.* Washington, DC: National Academies Press.

OVERVIEW: This descriptive study examined the current state of hospital unit design characteristics recommended by the Agency for Healthcare Research and Quality (AHRQ) in 81 adult medical-surgical units and 56 intensive care units in six metropolitan areas. The AHRQ recommends that the following unit design characteristics positively impact patient outcomes: single rooms, work areas for staff that are not a long distance from the bedside, frequent staff hand hygiene stations, certain types of unit configuration, percentage of private rooms, and presence or absence of carpeting. The purpose of this study is to provide a benchmark and to assess nursing environments. Data were collected by observation, measurement, and interviews. The researchers conclude that few of the hospital units met the AHRQ recommendations. Further research is required to expand understanding of these design elements, their interaction, and impact on outcomes.

APPLICATION: Healthcare organizations are much more than a description of the organization. They are also physical buildings.

Several recommendations in the Institute of Medicine (IOM) report *Keeping Patients Safe: Transforming the Work Environment of Nurses* (2004) pertain to design of work and workspace to prevent and mitigate errors. This study on unit design elements relates to the IOM work, which is referenced in the study. There are many factors and elements that impact the quality of care, and design is one of them. Historically nurses typically have had limited input into design of units, but more hospitals are including nursing management and staff nurses in the decision-making process when facilities are renovated or new buildings are built. For a long time, nurses just had to work within the space they had even if the design did not consider nursing staff needs; however, more is known today about the impact of space and design on work processes and staff.

Questions:

1. Based on your clinical experience, why is unit structure important to staff and to patient outcomes? Present three examples to support your opinion.
2. Why do you think it would be important to have standards related to unit structure and environment?
3. If you were a patient, what type of unit would you want to be on? Describe it and explain why this is the type of unit you would prefer.

- *Organizational readiness for the multicultural world.* The United States and most of its communities are finding that they are now multicultural communities. Providers are caring for patients from many different cultures, and this affects their care. Staff who come from many different cultures are more common, and this impacts the organization's communication, staff relationships, problem solving, decision making, and morale. The United States must deal with many critical issues related to access of care and lack of insurance, and much of this has an impact on minority cultures—diversity and disparities in health care. (See Chapter 10.)
- *Effective leadership.* Effective leadership is critical to the success of any organization. As organizations are analyzed, their leaders should be identified and assessed. What is the leadership style? Does the leadership provide what is needed to help the organization succeed? Effective leadership means that staff need to be engaged in the organization. (See Chapter 1.)
- *Assessment of future organizational challenges and opportunities.* Future needs should be considered in the assessment of an organization. Is the organization preparing for the future? Does it have a strategic plan? What is included in the plan? Is the plan reasonable? What is the process the organization uses to cope with future organization challenges and opportunities? Are the challenges and opportunities identified? Change and planning are now part of daily work in HCOs. (See Chapter 3.)

PROFESSIONAL NURSING PRACTICE WITHIN NURSING CARE MODELS

The American Nurses Association (2010) defines nursing as "the protection, promotion, and optimization of health and abilities, prevention of illness and injury, alleviation of suffering through the diagnosis and treatment of human response, and advocacy in the care of individuals, families, communities, and populations" (p. 66). The American Organization of Nurse Executives (AONE) assumptions for future patient care delivery include the following:

- *Assumption 1:* The role of nurse leaders in future patient care delivery systems will continue to require a systems approach with all disciplines involved in the process and outcome models.
- *Assumption 2:* Accountable Care Organizations will emerge and expand as key defining and differentiating healthcare reform provisions that will impact differing care delivery venues.
- *Assumption 3:* Patient safety, experience improvement and quality outcomes will remain a public, payer and regulatory focus driving work flow process and care delivery system changes as demanded by the increasingly informed public.
- *Assumption 4:* Healthcare leaders will have knowledge of funding sources and will be able to strategically and operationally deploy those funds to achieve desired outcomes of improved quality, efficiency, and transparency.
- *Assumption 5:* The joint education of nurses, physicians, and other health professionals will become the norm in academia and practice promoting shared knowledge that enables safer patient care and enhancing the opportunity for pass-through dollars to apply to APRN residencies and/or related clinical education (2010, pp. 1–3).

The five NAM core competencies are interrelated with these assumptions. Also, all of these elements have been discussed in earlier chapters or will be discussed in later chapters, as they are critical aspects of leadership and management. Intertwined within these critical elements is the recognition of the importance of leadership, autonomy, responsibility, delegation, and accountability.

Autonomy, which focuses on an individual's ability to make decisions, requires competence and skills that focus on the nurse–patient relationship. It also means that there needs to be an organized assessment method to determine patient care needs and reassigning staff. Nurses also have the right to consult with others as professionals when they provide or manage care. Autonomy, control, and decision making are related, and state Nurse Practice Acts reflect on nurse autonomy. Nurses who feel that they have autonomy know that they have the right to make decisions in their daily practice and also actively participate in developing organizational policy and change. Staff autonomy, however, does not work in organizations in which leaders are authoritarian and when centralized decision making and control are key characteristics of the organization. This situation will quickly lead to conflict. In addition, the work environment must be conducive to collaboration with physicians and all relevant staff, as is discussed in Chapter 13. A nursing practice model that does not address responsibility will not be effective. Along with this is the need to clearly recognize the importance of delegation. Delegation is discussed in more detail in Chapter 15. **Accountability** is a term that is typically found in job descriptions and descriptions of organizational structure. "It is related to answerability and to responsibility—judgment and action on the part of the nurse for which the nurse is answerable to self and others for those judgments and actions" (Fowler, 2015, p. 44). "Responsibility refers to the specific accountability or liability associated with the performance of duties of a particular nursing role and may, at times, be shared in the sense that a portion of responsibility may be seen as belonging to another who was involved in the situation" (Fowler, 2015, p. 44). Nurses need to know that when they provide patient care, their work has relevance—it must reach outcomes.

Accountability, autonomy, and responsibility need to be considered when nursing practice models are assessed. Nursing models of care are developed to support or enhance professional practice, and by considering these elements and characteristics, the models will be more effective. Within an HCO, how do nurses provide nursing care? What is a model of care? Are these elements found in the model? Models might also be called nursing or patient care delivery systems. These models have undergone major changes over the past several decades. Nursing practice models have been used to implement resource-intensive strategies with the goal of decreasing expenses and using staff more effectively. **Nursing models** help to identify and describe nursing care. The NAM emphasis on the five core competencies could also be used for a model, and as newer models are discussed later, it is easy to see how these five competencies are the key elements of healthcare delivery.

Historical Perspective of Nursing Models

The following is a description of common models, some of which have undergone many changes over the years or are not used anymore, but they have had an impact on newer models.

TOTAL PATIENT CARE/CASE METHOD   In this model, which is the oldest, the registered nurse is responsible for all of the care provided to a patient for a shift. A major disadvantage of this model is the lack of consistency and coordinated care when care is provided in eight-hour segments. This type of care is rarely provided today, except among student nurses who are assigned to provide all of the care for a patient during the hours that they are in clinical. Even in this case, the students frequently do not provide all of the care as they may not be qualified to do this, and a staff nurse maintains overall responsibility for the care. Home health agencies use a form of this model when nurses are assigned patients and provide all the required home care; however, even this has been adapted as teams provide more home care. An RN may coordinate the care and provide professional nursing services, but a home care aide may provide most of the direct care, and other providers such as a physical therapist, dietician, and social worker may be required for specialty care.

FUNCTIONAL NURSING   The model of functional nursing is a task-oriented approach, focusing on jobs to be done. When it was more commonly used, it was thought to be more efficient. The nurse in charge assigned the tasks (e.g., one nurse may administer medications for all or some of the patients on a unit; an aide may take vital signs for all patients). A disadvantage of this model is the risk of fragmented care. In addition, this type of model also leads to greater staff dissatisfaction with staff feeling they are just grinding out tasks. When different staff members provide care without awareness of other needs and the care provided by others, individualized care may also be compromised. This model is not used much now. It can be found in some long-term care facilities and in some behavioral/psychiatric inpatient services, although in a modified form. In the latter situation, a registered nurse may be assigned the task of medication administration for the unit, and psychiatric support staff may be assigned such tasks as vital signs and safety checks of all patients. In this situation, RNs would still be assigned to individual patients to coordinate their care.

TEAM NURSING   This model was developed after World War II during a severe nursing shortage and other major changes in medical technology occurred. It replaced functional nursing. A nursing team consists of a registered nurse, licensed practical/vocational nurses, and UAP. This team of two or three staff provides total care for a group of patients during an 8- or 12-hour shift. The RN team leader coordinates this care. In this model the RN has a high level of autonomy and assumes the centralized decision-making authority. Although the past approach to team nursing was thought to use decentralized decision making with decisions made closer to the patient, there actually was limited team member collaboration. In addition, these teams tended to communicate only among themselves and not as well with physicians and other healthcare providers. The team concept or model also focused on tasks rather than patient care as a whole. More current versions of the team model are different from this earlier type. Currently the team model has been changed to meet shifts in organizations and leadership corresponding to the needs for better consistency and continuity of care as well as collaboration and coordination and patient-centered care.

PRIMARY NURSING   In the late 1970s, care became more complex, and nurses were dissatisfied with team nursing. In the **primary nursing** model, the primary nurse, who must be an RN, provides direct care for the patient and the family; an associate nurse provides care following the care plan developed by the primary nurse when the primary nurse is not working and assists when the primary nurse is working. The primary nurse needs to be knowledgeable about assigned patients and must maintain a high level of clinical autonomy. When primary nursing was first used, it was easier to substitute RNs for other healthcare providers as cost was not as much of a focus as it is today. Over time the nursing shortage changed and salaries increased. Implementing primary nursing then became more difficult, and healthcare cost moved to the top of the concerns. Primary nursing is often viewed as a model in which the primary nurse has to do everything, limiting collaborative or team efforts, although it does not have to be implemented in this way.

Second-generation primary nursing clarified some of the issues about this practice model. One of the critical problems with primary nursing was whether or not it required an all-RN staff, which was thought to increase staff costs. The second-generation view of primary nursing noted that the mix of staff was more important than having an all-RN staff. Another concern with primary nursing was a need to develop a clear definition of 24-hour accountability, which was interpreted by some as 24-hour availability. This, of course, is not a reasonable approach, and it really does not apply to primary nursing. When the primary nurse is not working, the associate nurse provides the care. Primary nursing is a responsibility relationship between the nurse and the patient. The primary nurse is not the only caregiver but does have responsibility for planning nursing care and ensuring that care outcomes are met. Only registered nurses can be primary nurses. This role and the model require RNs who are competent and possess leadership skills. Primary nursing is not used as much today.

CARE AND SERVICE TEAM MODELS   In the 1980s care and service team models began to replace primary nursing. These models are implemented differently in different hospitals, as is true of most of the models. Key elements of these models are empowered staff, interprofessional collaboration, skilled workers, and a case management approach to patient care—all elements related to the more current views of leadership and management (IOM, 2011). Care and service teams introduced the different categories of assistive personnel (e.g., multiskilled workers, nurse extenders, and UAP). There has been some disagreement as to whether these new staff member roles were complementary or involve the substitution of professional nursing care.

COMPLEMENTARY MODELS   Complementary models began in 1988 by using nurse extenders, such as a unit assistant, who would be responsible for environmental functions. The nurse would then have more time for direct patient care. Does this reduce costs? When nurse positions are changed to nurse extender positions, there is some cost reduction, but this change can impact all nursing staff. Complementary models are not used as much today and have been replaced by substitution models in HCOs. Substitution models tend to use multiskilled technicians to perform select nursing activities, and the RNs supervise these activities.

Another approach is **cross-training**. This involves training staff to work in different specialty areas or to perform different tasks. For example, a respiratory therapist may be trained not only to perform typical respiratory therapist tasks but also phlebotomy and basic nursing care. This offers much more flexibility in that staff can fulfill many different needs. They can then be used, as staffing adjustments are needed for changes in patient census or acuity. It is critical that this cross-training meet patient needs so staff will be able to deliver quality, safe care and not feel undue stress while delivering the care. It is also important that state practice act requirements are met, and this is not always easy to accomplish. It requires HCO education staff to provide support, ongoing educational training, and documentation of competencies, as well as management staff that understand which staff members are qualified to move from area to area. Hospitals and other HCOs have tried to find the best methods for using substitution without compromising quality and safety and yet control costs. As demands change, different models will be required, and nursing leadership to develop these models will be critical.

CASE MANAGEMENT MODEL   As with earlier team models, the RN must spend time coordinating care and the work. The focus of the team is on patient-centered care as opposed to the nurse–patient relationship. The case management model is based on the assumption that patients with complex health problems, catastrophic health situations, and high-cost medical conditions need assistance in using the healthcare system effectively, and a case manager can help patients with these needs (Finkelman, 2011). Case managers may also work with the teams to achieve outcomes, which increases shared accountability. Case management can be viewed as a nursing model when the case manager is a nurse; however, in some HCOs nurses are not used as case managers but rather other healthcare professionals such as social workers serve as case managers. Several healthcare professional organizations and experts have defined case management; however, there clearly is no universally accepted definition for case management. Case management is used in many different types of settings, and the setting also affects the definition.

Examples of Newer Nursing Models

INTERPROFESSIONAL PRACTICE MODEL   The interprofessional practice model is emphasized in the IOM reports on quality improvement by identifying the importance of all health professions meeting the interdisciplinary or interprofessional competency and emphasizing the need to work in interprofessional teams "to cooperate, collaborate, communicate, and integrate care in teams to ensure that care is continuous and reliable" (2003, p. 4). These teams include providers from different healthcare professions and occupations designed to meet the required patient needs. With increasing complex patient care needs, this model is better able to address needs and to effectively use a mix of expertise and knowledge to reach patient outcomes. Patient-centered care is the focus.

SYNERGY MODEL FOR PATIENT CARE™   This model of care was developed by the American Association of Critical-Care Nurses, but it has been applied in all types of nursing units. The model recognizes the need to match the nurse's competence with the patient's characteristics, needs, and the clinical unit (American Association of Critical-Care Nurses, 2014). Patient characteristics incorporated into this model are as follows (American Association of Critical-Care Nurses, 2014):

- *Resiliency:* the capacity to return to a restorative level of functioning using compensatory/ coping mechanisms; the ability to bounce back quickly after an insult
- *Vulnerability:* susceptibility to actual or potential stressors that may adversely affect patient outcomes
- *Stability:* the ability to maintain a steady-state equilibrium
- *Complexity:* the intricate entanglement of two or more systems (e.g., body, family, therapies)
- *Resource availability:* extent of resources (e.g., technical, fiscal, personal, psychological, and social) the patient/family/community brings to the situation
- *Participation in care:* extent to which patient/family engages in aspects of care
- *Participation in decision making:* extent to which patient/family engages in decision making
- *Predictability:* a characteristic that allows one to expect a certain course of events or course of illness

The Synergy model ties the above patient characteristics with the following nurse competencies (American Association of Critical-Care Nurses, 2014):

- *Clinical judgment:* clinical reasoning, which includes clinical decision making, critical thinking, and a global grasp of the situation, coupled with nursing skills acquired through a process of integrating formal and informal experiential knowledge and evidence-based guidelines.
- *Advocacy and moral agency:* working on another's behalf and representing the concerns of the patient/family and nursing staff; serving as a moral agent in identifying and helping to resolve ethical and clinical concerns within and outside the clinical setting.
- *Caring practices:* nursing activities that create a compassionate, supportive, and therapeutic environment for patients and staff, with the aim of promoting comfort and healing and preventing unnecessary suffering. Includes, but is not limited to, vigilance, engagement, and responsiveness of caregivers, including family and healthcare personnel.
- *Collaboration:* working with others (e.g., patients, families, healthcare providers) in a way that promotes/encourages each person's contributions toward achieving optimal/realistic patient/ family goals. Involves intra- and interprofessional work with colleagues and community.
- *Systems thinking:* body of knowledge and tools that allow the nurse to manage whatever environmental and system resources exist for the patient/family and staff, within or across healthcare and nonhealthcare systems.
- *Response to diversity:* the sensitivity to recognize, appreciate, and incorporate differences into the provision of care. Differences may include, but are not limited to, cultural differences, spiritual beliefs, gender, race, ethnicity, lifestyle, socioeconomic status, age, and values.
- *Facilitation of learning:* the ability to facilitate learning for patients/families, nursing staff, other members of the healthcare team, and community. Includes both formal and informal facilitation of learning.
- *Clinical inquiry (innovator/evaluator):* the ongoing process of questioning and evaluating practice and providing informed practice. Creating practice changes through research use and experiential learning.

PATIENT NAVIGATION   Patient navigation is a model that has primarily focused on patients with cancer who are at risk for poor cancer outcomes though other types of patient populations have also benefited from patient navigation (Wells et al., 2008). Clinical nurse leaders often hold the position of nurse navigator. Patient navigation focuses on decreasing barriers to better ensure that patients get the care they need when they need it (Finkelman, 2011). This model is "an intervention designed to reduce health disparities by addressing specific barriers to obtaining timely, quality healthcare" (Wells et al., 2008, p. 2010).

THE ACA AND NEW MODELS   *The Future of Nursing* (Institute of Medicine, 2011) includes content about transformational models of nursing across different care settings. The report notes there are some common themes from the examples reviewed. "In order to meet the challenges of the future, we must embrace technology, foster partnerships, encourage collaboration across disciplines and settings, ensure continuity of care and promote nurse-lead/nurse managed health care" (p. 402). The ANA has also commented on the ACA and its potential impact on nursing models of care. The ANA notes, as do other sources such as the NAM, that the healthcare system is dysfunctional and fragmented. A major goal of the ACA is to rebalance the healthcare system's resources by identifying several models of care, focusing on primary care, that might help to reach this goal (2010):

- Accountable Care Organization (ACO): Provides a collaborative model for primary care providers and specialists who work together to achieve quality care and control costs. ACOs that are successful receive financial incentives. ACOs are part of the Medicare Program. Providers may include MDs, APRNs, CNSs, and PAs.
- Medical/Health Homes: The focus in this model is on primary care providers coordinating patient care. Financial incentives as well as interprofessional teams may also be part of this model.
- Nurse-Managed Health Clinic (NMHC): This is a clinic that is managed by nurses that provides comprehensive primary care and wellness services and must be associated with a university/college/department of nursing, a federally qualified health center, or an independent nonprofit health or social services agency. This type of clinic is led by APRNs.

Shared Governance and Empowerment

Shared governance is an approach to management that engages staff at all levels in the decision-making process. This does not mean that there are inactive or ineffective leaders and managers, but rather they meet their management responsibilities by ensuring that staff are active in the processes, which increases each nurse's influence over the organization, empowering staff.

Shared governance can be viewed as a management philosophy, a professional practice model, and an accountability model that focuses on staff involvement in decision making, particularly in decisions that affect their practice. In doing this, the model provides staff with autonomy and control over implementation of their practice—legitimizing control over their own practice. Nurses in these organizations usually feel less powerless and are more efficient and accountable.

A critical factor in shared governance is that accountability and responsibility are found in the same person. Accountability should rest in the person who is most likely to be the most effective person to complete the function. For individual staff to be accountable and responsible for a function or task, staff must also have the authority to make sure that the right decisions are made.

Transformational leadership enhances shared governance. As was discussed in Chapter 1, an important element of leadership is self-awareness, and it is essential in shared governance. In this type of organizational arrangement, staff members feel committed to the HCO and view themselves

CASE STUDY

Does a Nursing Model Make a Difference?

You are the director of staff development in a large university hospital, and the chief nurse executive (CNE) has met with you to discuss orientation for student nurses and faculty. The CNE is concerned that students and faculty do not understand the hospital's new nursing model, Synergy Model for Patient Care™. She tells you it is your job to correct this problem. You leave the meeting overwhelmed. This seems like a big responsibility to you. The hospital has many nursing students from three schools of nursing that use its services for practicum. All have to attend a four-hour orientation to the hospital, which is already overburdened with content, and the faculty and students have limited time for orientation. The units have also been struggling with applying the model since it was initiated six months ago.

Questions:

1. Why is it important for the students and faculty to understand the model?
2. How does the nursing model relate to the organization's theory or approach?
3. How would you describe this model? Consider methods and examples.
4. Develop a plan that you will submit to the CNE explaining how you will address this problem. Whom might you include in developing the plan and in implementing it?

as partners in meeting the goals of the HCO. In shared governance nurse managers typically are not directly involved in daily direct patient care, although there are some managers who are still involved in direct care. The typical responsibilities of the nurse manager are staffing, program evaluation, personnel evaluation, coordination, allocation of resources, financial activities, and planning, as discussed in Chapter 1. If patient care outcomes are not met, it is the responsibility of the nurse providing the care to address this issue. The nurse manager may become involved, but it is the direct care provider who should take the lead. In other words, clinical practice is the responsibility of the practitioners. When clinical problems occur, the nurse who provides direct care must be the one to solve these problems, working with the care team. The main factor in shared governance is that decision making is spread over a larger number of staff and is decentralized. Nurses are accountable for not only their management activities but also their practice. Healthcare organizations that use shared governance must have clear communication processes, or the organization will encounter problems and confusion in the decision-making process. The key components of shared governance are practice, quality, education, and peer process/governance. How are these accomplished? As with any such change, some organizations actually change and others merely *appear* to change to this model, but in the latter situation, very little has really changed in the decision-making process or in actual practice. Shared governance is associated with collaboration, horizontal relationships, and investment, and these need to be demonstrated in the organization. The change has to be real, and typically when it is, staff are more satisfied.

Organizations that use this model require some type of structure that relates to the shared accountability, such as councils, cabinets, committees, or a combination of these groups or teams that make the decisions. The chain of command is not the same as in traditional organizations. In the shared governance model, these groups make many of the decisions about policies, procedures, and other aspects of getting the work done. How might shared governance be implemented?

Healthcare organizations have been working for several years to create leaner and more effective organizations. It is important to recognize that to move toward a shared governance model, the organization must take a comprehensive change approach and not an incremental approach. All parts of the organization and all staff must be expected to change. This is very difficult to accomplish, but if shared governance is the goal, it is necessary.

Decentralized decision making is now found in many HCOs, and it is frequently associated with participative management strategies such as a shared governance model. This approach to organizational structure and process is associated with the economy, job satisfaction, and retention. For decentralization to be effective, staff must have autonomy to make decisions. All of this is intimately connected with shared governance. It requires staff members who are committed to the organization's values and goals and demonstrate this by working to meet the goals.

APPLYING LEADERSHIP AND MANAGEMENT

My Hospital Unit: An Evolving Case Experience

Return to your unit. The nursing department has decided that it needs to establish a nursing model. You are on the committee that will lead this initiative. The committee includes three other nurse managers, the chief nurse executive (CNE), and four staff nurses. Do some research of the nursing literature on nursing models and review content in this chapter to better understand the historical development of nursing models. Select one model that you like, and prepare a description and rationale that you would use to convince the committee that this is the best model. This model will be used on all patient units in your hospital, and now you need to decide how you will implement it on your unit. Develop a plan to implement the model. Remember to review content on change because this is a major change. You also need to focus on planning. How might this model impact your philosophy of leadership that you developed earlier? For each of the My Hospital Unit exercises, it is important to build on previous exercises; decisions you made in past chapters impact current decisions you make. You may find you need to make changes because previous decisions you made do not work well with newer decisions. This is what leadership and management is all about—review and assessment, research literature, reflection, analysis and change, and decisions.

BSN and *Master's Essentials:* Application to Content

BSN Essentials (American Association of Colleges of Nursing, 2008) as Applied to this Chapter:

II. Basic Organizational and Systems Leadership for Quality Care and Patient Safety

Master's Essentials (American Association of Colleges of Nursing, 2011) as Applied to this Chapter:

II. Organizational and Systems Leadership

Applying AONE Competencies

Identify which of the AONE competencies found in Appendix A apply to the content of this chapter.

Engaging in the Content: Critical Thinking and Clinical Reasoning and Judgment

Discussion Questions

1. Compare and contrast organizational structure and process. Provide examples.
2. Select an organizational theory you like, and explain why you chose it. (Online Application Option)
3. What is your opinion of healthcare organization marketing? (Online Application Option)
4. What is the difference between a for-profit and a not-for-profit healthcare organization?
5. What are the advantages and disadvantages of using shared governance?

Application Exercises

1. Visit the website for the American Association of Critical-Care Nurses to learn more about their Synergy Model for Patient Care™. What do you think about this model?
2. The structure of a healthcare organization can be highly variable. The chapter content describes some aspects of organization structure. How would you apply this content about the organizational structure? Select a healthcare organization of any type, although it will probably be easier if you have experience with the organization. Review the organizational chart. Compare and contrast with content in this chapter. What organizational theory applies? Write a brief description of your analysis. You might include information about the types and titles of positions and departments, interrelationships and reporting processes, clarity of the chart, and complexity of the organization. Critical aspects are the reporting process and how it is described. Consider vertical and horizontal structures, line of authority, staff authority, span of control, centralized versus decentralized, departmentalization, and matrix structure. How might the theories discussed in this chapter apply? Write a brief description of your analysis.
3. The processes of a healthcare organization can be highly variable. The chapter content describes some aspects of organization structure. How would you apply this content about the organizational processes? Using the same HCO you used in #2, compare and contrast with content in this chapter. Typical sources of information about an organization's processes are its vision and mission statements and its goals and objectives. You need to try to find information about decision making, delegation, coordination, communication, and evaluation in the organization. Use the same organization you used for #2 activity.
4. Describe the roles you have observed in nursing staff when in clinical. Discuss in a team, and compare and contrast different student views. (Online Application Option)
5. In a team discussion, describe the healthcare organizations you have been in for clinical organizational analysis. Consider physical factors, including accessibility; culture; staff response to consumers, patients, and families; organization function; and so on. Compare and contrast different student views of the same and different healthcare organizations. (Online Application Option)

References

American Association of Colleges of Nursing. (2004). *Position statement on the practice doctorate in nursing*. Retrieved from http://www.aacn.nche.edu/DNP/DNPpositionstatement.htm

American Association of Colleges of Nursing. (2007). *White paper on the education and role of the clinical nurse leader*. Washington, DC: Author.

American Association of Colleges of Nursing. (2008). *The essentials of baccalaureate education for professional nursing practice*. Washington, DC: Author.

American Association of Colleges of Nursing. (2011). *The essentials of master's education in nursing*. Washington, DC: Author.

American Association of Critical-Care Nurses. (2014). Synergy model for patient care™. Retrieved from http://www.aacn.org/wd/certifications/content/synmodel.pcms?menu=certification#Patient

American Nurses Association. (2010). *Scope and standards of practice.* Silver Spring, MD: Author.

American Organization of Nurse Executives. (2010). *AONE guiding principles for future patient care delivery.* Retrieved from AONE_GP_Future_Patient_Care_Delivery_2010-2.pdf

ASHP Foundation. (2014). Understanding high-performing clinical microsystems. Retrieved from http://www.ashpfoundation.org/lean/cms7.html

Elliott, D., Young, R., Brice, J., Aguiar, R., & Kolm, P. (2014). Effect of hospitalist workload on the quality and efficiency of care. *JAMA, 174*(5), 786–793.

Finkelman, A. (2011). *Case management for nurses.* Upper Saddle River, NJ: Pearson Education, Inc.

Finkelman, A. (2015). The healthcare system. In M. Nies & M. McEwen (Eds.), *Community/public health nursing* (6th ed.) (pp. 186–201). Philadelphia, PA: Elsevier W.B. Saunders Company.

Fowler, R. (2015, reissue). *Guide to the code of ethics for nurses: Interpretation and application.* Silver Spring, MD: American Nurses Association.

Harris, G. (2010, March 26). More doctors giving up private clinics. *New York Times*, pp. B1, B5.

Institute of Medicine. (2001). *Crossing the quality chasm.* Washington, DC: The National Academies Press.

Institute of Medicine. (2003). *Healthcare professions education.* Washington, DC: The National Academies Press.

Institute of Medicine. (2011). *The future of nursing: Leading change, advancing health.* Washington, DC: The National Academies Press.

Mind Tools™. (2010). SWOT analysis. Retrieved May 23, 2010, from http://www.mindtools.com/pages/article/newTMC_05.htm

Mind Tools™. (2014). Henry Fayol's principles of management. Retrieved from http://www.mindtools.com/pages/article/henri-fayol.htm

Siegrist, B. (2011). Family health. In M. Nies & M. McEwen (Eds.), *Community/public health nursing* (5th ed.) (pp. 379–402). Philadelphia, PA: Elsevier W.B. Saunders Company.

Society of Hospital Medicine. (2014). Definition of a hospitalist and hospital medicine. Retrieved from http://www.hospitalmedicine.org/Web/About_SHM/Industry/Hospital_Medicine_Hospital_Definition.aspx

Wells, K., Battaglia, T., Dudley, D., Garcia, R., Greene, A., Calhoun, E., . . . Raich, P. (2008). Patient navigation: State of the art or is it science? *CANCER, 113*(8), 1999–2010.

5 Healthcare Economics

LEARNING OUTCOMES

Before you begin, take a moment to familiarize yourself with the learning outcomes for this chapter.

> Distinguish between the macrolevel and microlevel views of healthcare economics.
> Discuss critical issues related to current national healthcare expenditures.
> Analyze the role of the third-party payer.
> Explain how healthcare insurance is financed and by whom.
> Discuss the importance of the various government benefit programs.
> Examine healthcare reimbursement changes found in the Affordable Care Act of 2010.
> Explain service and reimbursement strategies used by insurers to control costs and improve quality and their association to managed care.
> Examine the impact of reimbursement on nursing.
> Analyze healthcare finances at the microlevel, including budgeting process, productivity, cost containment, and impact on nursing.

WHAT'S AHEAD

An understanding of healthcare financial issues is important for nurses as they practice in the healthcare environment and if they assume leadership roles. Financial issues can be viewed from a macro or micro perspective. The macro perspective concerns broad healthcare expenditures from a national view and reimbursement for healthcare services, providing a perspective of national healthcare economics. The micro perspective focuses on the financial issues related to individual healthcare organizations (HCOs) (for example, budgeting). This chapter focuses more on the macro perspective because this perspective must come first, and it is the perspective that most directly affects budgets and all nurses, regardless of their positions. This is not to say that the micro perspective is not important or will not be discussed. The basics of micro issues will be discussed; however, extensive details about budgeting and healthcare organization financing is content that is more appropriate to nurses who are entering management positions where these skills are absolutely critical. The critical need for new nurses is to understand who pays for health care, how this payment is made, and how reimbursement affects healthcare delivery, which is the macro perspective, and some essential basics related to budgeting in HCOs, nurses' roles in the process, and how budgets impact nursing care.

KEY TERMS

- annual limits
- benefit plan
- budget
- capital budget
- capitation
- copayment/coinsurance
- cost containment
- customer
- deductible
- diagnosis-related groups (DRGs)
- discounted fee-for-service
- exclusions
- formulary
- full-time equivalent (FTE)
- operational budget
- per diem rate
- premium rate setting
- productivity
- prospective payment
- prospective payment system (PPS)
- provider panel
- retrospective payment
- salary and wage budget
- third-party payer

HEALTHCARE FINANCIAL ISSUES: MACROLEVEL

During nursing's long history, for most of that time, nurses showed little interest in financial issues. Nurses were typically unprepared to participate in financial decision making, and healthcare administrators often did not encourage or support nurse managers/leaders to participate in the financial side of health care. The inclusion of content related to health economics, finance, and business management into nursing curricula evolved slowly, which was a serious limitation as it prevented active nursing involvement in healthcare finance. This important content continues to require further development in graduate nursing programs. Gradually nurse administrators developed an increased interest in budgeting; however, they have had to contend with hospital administrators who did not feel that nurse administrators needed to be involved in the budget.

In 1978 the National League for Nursing (NLN) published conference papers from a meeting of nurse executives who represented acute care, long-term care, community health, and university settings (1978). The conference focused on raising nurse executives' awareness of the need to be involved in budget preparation. An important impetus for this recognition was the development of prospective payment that was to be used by Medicare to control costs. Chief nurse executives (typically called directors of nursing at this time) and the managers needed to have a better understanding of healthcare finances. One administrator stated, "The 1980s will find us even more concerned with belt tightening and intensifying voluntary efforts to contain healthcare costs. The future is in our hands" (National League for Nursing, 1978, p. 5). The belt tightening that was predicted for the 1980s occurred, and it continues today. Nurse administrators began to realize that they needed to assume a more active role in budget development to meet their goals for nursing services, and this also requires understanding of healthcare reimbursement. Why is it important for nurses to understand reimbursement?

- Reimbursement affects patient care delivery: types of treatment, choice of provider, and length of treatment.
- Reimbursement has an impact on provider performance and patient outcomes.
- Reimbursement affects financial resources that are available for HCOs (for example, staffing, equipment and supplies, renovation and expansion, and so on).

This early recognition of the need for involvement, however, focused only on the nursing management level: nurse executives and nurse managers. Staff nurses were, in most cases, still out of the loop; however, nursing can no longer afford to isolate staff nurses from financial issues. All nurses need a greater understanding of how financial decisions are made, by whom, why, and how these decisions make a difference in the care a patient receives; number of staff available to provide that care; access to services, supplies, and equipment; and so on. Expanding nursing leadership in healthcare delivery requires an understanding of critical healthcare economic concerns and processes.

The Institute of Medicine Addresses the Cost of Care:
Best Care at Lower Costs

The Institute of Medicine (IOM) in its series of reports on healthcare quality also addressed the issue of costs and their relationship to quality (2012). This report focuses on the need to continue to work toward quality care while reducing costs, noting that this requires commitment to incentives, culture, and leadership focusing on continuous learning to accomplish this goal. There are three major imperatives for change: (1) the rising complexity of modern health care, (2) unsustainable cost increases, and (3) outcomes below the system's potential. The National Academy of Medicine (NAM) recommends and recognizes that today there are more tools and approaches to address this complex problem of increasing costs with poor outcomes, for example, team-based care, computing power, connectivity, and systems engineering. Many stakeholders need to be involved to resolve the ongoing healthcare cost problem.

National Healthcare Expenditures

The healthcare industry is an extremely large one whose financing is influenced by many factors, particularly social expectation, economic trends, technological developments, government policies, and political factors. And in the past few years, the U.S. economy has been the most critical factor. Financial issues affect all aspects of the provision of care, settings, and services, such as inpatient care, ambulatory care, home care, primary care, long-term care, public health, pharmaceuticals, medical supplies, medical transportation, medical technology, medical research, and so on. Compared with other countries, the United States has the most expensive healthcare system with the highest living standard and economic status. Despite this, the United States has a large number of people without insurance coverage. In 2013, prior to changes in enrollment options due to the Affordable Care Act (ACA) 41 million people were uninsured and in mid April 2014, after the first enrollment period, 8 million people enrolled in plans, lowering the number of uninsured (Henry J. Kaiser Family Foundation, 2014). Data from ObamaCare fluctuates, and it will take several years for the full impact to be made clear (ObamaCare Facts, 2015):

- Eight million enrolled during the 2014 open enrollment (October 2013–April 2014).
- An estimated 11.7 million enrolled during 2015 (November 2014–February 2015) open enrollment. This includes 4.5 million who re-enrolled from 2014.
- As of March 2015, a total of 16.4 million received coverage due to the Marketplace options, Medicaid expansion, young adults staying on their parents' plan, and other ACA provisions. This translates to an uninsured rate of 11.9%, down from 18% in 2013.

Enrollment will increase and change, allowing for factors such as nonpayment toward premiums, dropout rates, or first-time enrollment (ObamaCare Facts, 2015). This increase in enrollment will have more impact on reducing the number of uninsured. It is important to note that the majority of Americans who have been receiving health insurance through their employers are not directly involved in the changes initiated by the ACA other than implications for benefits and, in some cases, coverage of adult children. The employer-based insurance approach has not changed in the United States.

Despite the fact that there is a decreasing length-of-stay rate and increasing use of nonhospital services, hospital costs are higher than any other type of healthcare organization/provider. Healthcare expenditures are expected to continue to increase. An understanding of healthcare expenditures includes an appreciation of how the nation's health dollar is spent and also who pays for health care or the healthcare funding sources as described in Figure 5-1. It is also important to recognize that healthcare expenditures change annually, and data analysis and report of results is rarely current to the present year.

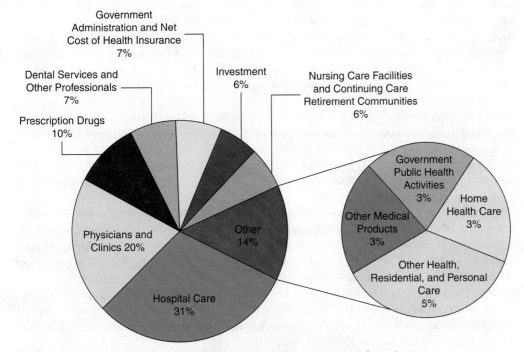

Figure 5-1 The Nation's Health Dollar, Calendar Year 2011, Where it Went

Source: Centers for Medicare & Medicaid Services, Office of the Actuary, National Health Statistics Group. Retrieved from http://www.cms.gov/Research-Statistics-Data-and-Systems/Statistics-Trends-and-Reports/NationalHealthExpendData/Downloads/PieChartSourcesExpenditures2011.pdf

"As a result of more rapid growth in public spending, the public share of total healthcare spending is expected to rise from 47 percent in 2008, exceed 50 percent by 2012, and then reach nearly 52 percent by 2019" (Centers for Medicare & Medicaid Services, 2010). How do recent data regarding healthcare spending impact current approaches to controlling healthcare costs and healthcare policy? Many experts believe that all of the "fat" has been removed from budgets, or rather the easier, more obvious methods to reduce costs have been used. To decrease costs further or even to just maintain the cost level so it does not increase will require more serious, difficult decision making. The ACA will have an impact on these financial projections, with the intention of decreasing costs, but its impact will really not be known for some time. However, some aspects of cost are known at this time. During initial enrollment in 2013, premiums varied, and some who enrolled in the new ACA options experienced increases. In the fall of 2014, enrollment period premiums also varied. People who do not get their insurance coverage through their employers and get it through the Insurance Exchanges set up by the U.S. Department of Health and Human Services (HHS) to meet ACA provisions need to "shop" annually to get the best deals as changes in cost occur. Those who pay lower premiums have higher copays and deductibles, and this increases costs if they need services.

Decreasing hospitalization has been greatly influenced by the need to decrease costs; however, new advances in health care and new methods for providing health care have made it easier to lower hospitalization stays and costs. Factors that have helped to decrease hospitalization costs are:

- early ambulation of patients so they can be discharged sooner.
- outpatient prep time before admittance to hospital for surgery.
- greater use of ambulatory surgery with less use of inpatient surgery and stay.
- better use of medications such as antibiotics to prevent infections before they occur.
- greater use of home care and skilled nursing care.
- more effective management of care within the hospital treatment period to reduce risk of readmission.

Prescription costs have risen due to an increase in the cost of drugs, greater use of many new drugs that are effective but expensive, and broader health insurance coverage for prescriptions. Another aspect of decreasing hospitalization costs is decreasing length of stay. Both of these changes have influenced patient acuity levels. Patients are admitted later and thus are sicker, and they leave quickly, which limits amount of time available to get patients and families ready for discharge. The patients then enter community services such as home care sicker, requiring more acute care than was true in the past. Home healthcare agencies now look for nurses who have had critical care experience to help with more complex care needs as home health needs increase. The largest portion of healthcare expenditures continues to be found in the hospital industry, despite decreasing lengths of stay and increasing use of nonhospital services. In 2010 the organization American Health Insurance Plans (AHIP) noted the continuing rising costs, with healthcare spending representing more than one sixth of the U.S. economy, an estimated $2.7 trillion spent annually (2014). AHIP identifies some of the causes of this excessive cost as: (1) higher prices for medical services, (2) paying for volume over value, (3) defensive medicine, (4) use of technologies and treatments without considering effectiveness, and (5) a lack of transparency of information on prices and quality.

Healthcare use and expenditures data are used to evaluate cost control outcomes. There is, however, another perspective of healthcare expenditures that is more complex than these data may indicate. Is spending more on medical care worth it in terms of its impact on the length and quality of life? Third-party payers must view healthcare expenditures from many perspectives using cost-benefit analysis. Nurses and nursing care do have an impact on these costs.

Two factors are important and will have long-term impact on healthcare coverage and expenditures. The economy is slowly improving, and if this continues, this will have a positive impact on health care. The ACA is now in effect, though it is still unsure what the final result will be, but it is clear more citizens have health insurance coverage.

Experts agree that our healthcare system has many inefficiencies, excessive administrative expenses, inflated prices, poor management, inappropriate care, waste, and fraud. All of these problems significantly increase the cost of medical care and health insurance for employers and workers and affect the security of families. With the growing economic crisis in 2008–2009, a greater

CHAPTER 5 • HEALTHCARE ECONOMICS **123**

number of families were affected. However, growth of healthcare spending has dropped over time but still is high. ACA is having some impact, but long-term effect is only a projection at this time. The consumer's major concern in choosing a health plan today continues to be personal cost.

The concern about the uninsured has increased over the years. "The uninsured refers to persons without any form of public or private coverage for hospital and outpatient care, for any given length of time" (Institute of Medicine, 2004a, p. 21). Along with this concern is the underinsured, an area that sometimes is ignored. The underinsured are "individuals or families whose health insurance policy or benefit plan offers less than adequate coverage" (Institute of Medicine, 2004a, p. 21). When this happens, these individuals and families are left with debt because they cannot pay uncovered care or they avoid getting care when they need it because their benefits do not cover required care. The U.S. safety net, which is represented by the HCOs that disproportionately serve the needy and uninsured, has been stretched as the number of uninsured and underinsured increases (Institute of Medicine, 2004a). However, increasing the safety net services will not solve the entire problem of the uninsured and underinsured. This approach may help some, but it is not enough to solve the problem. Both of these problems are major issues in the current healthcare reform debate. The ACA addresses some of the issues related to the uninsured, the safety net, and increasing costs of care. When full implementation of the law occurs in 2019, the goal is to provide an additional 32 million people with healthcare coverage. (See Appendix B.)

Reimbursement for Healthcare Delivery Services

You enter a patient's room, and he is speaking on the telephone. You overhear him say, "I don't care how much this hospitalization is costing. My insurance pays for it." You nod and agree. This example almost seems as if it came from another world, certainly not the real one, and both the patient and you, the nurse, need to enter the real one. Is it this simple?

Healthcare reimbursement in the United States is a pluralistic payment system with multiple payers from both the public and private sectors. It is complex, with many players, motivations, and a long history of change. U.S. insurance began in Boston in 1847. By the end of the 1860s, there were 60 health insurance companies. In 1911 Montgomery Ward and Company offered a plan that provided benefits to its employees who were unable to work due to illness or injury (Health Insurance Association of America, 1998). Employers began to offer health insurance coverage instead of increasing wages. Over time businesses offered employees insurance to get the tax benefit because employers' contributions for insurance benefits are exempt from federal and state taxes, which is a very important savings for employers. This led to an employer-based healthcare reimbursement system that still dominates today.

From 1987 to 1997, the U.S. experienced the first major indication that healthcare costs would continue to have a critical impact on the economy when health insurance premiums increased 90%, which was an incredible increase for those earning low wages (Cooper & Schone, 1997), and since this time, costs have continued to increase. With the increase in premiums as well as the increase in other out-of-pocket expenses, people began to make choices about insurance. Some decided to not enroll in a health insurance plan, and others limited their use of services to cut down on their personal costs. Employees who choose not to purchase coverage decide to take the risk and gamble that they will not need healthcare services. This has grown to be a major problem, and it is hoped the ACA will reduce this problem.

Today cost consciousness in the face of limited healthcare dollars has reached a level that crosses all care settings and patient populations to a much greater extent than in the past. Healthcare purchasers, typically employers and governments, are in a very influential position because the purchaser makes the major decisions (e.g., approval of reimbursable services, provider choice, length of stay, length of treatment, cost and quality relationship). All nurses require a greater knowledge of reimbursement to understand how reimbursement affects care provided, denial of care, and numerous factors related to the nursing practice within all types of HCOs. In the past, nurses did not discuss healthcare reimbursement with their patients. The business office typically is called to come and talk with a patient when questions arise. This is not an inappropriate intervention when a patient has billing questions; however, it has fostered a climate of separation. Nurses provide care, and "someone" pays. Patients, however, expect that nurses have some knowledge about reimbursement. The growth of managed care and other reimbursement changes made this knowledge even more important. Nursing standards identify financial resource management as an important nursing responsibility.

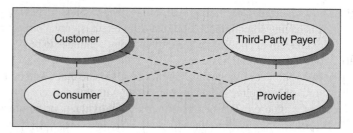

Figure 5-2   Key players in the health care environment

KEY PLAYERS IN THE REIMBURSEMENT PROCESS   The key players in reimbursement strategies are the insurer (third-party payer), the customer, the consumer, and the provider. These players are identified in Figure 5-2.

1. *Third-party payer/managed care organization/insurer.* With the development of managed care, the insurer, or **third-party payer**, no longer carries all of the financial risk for health care. Reimbursement strategies used by insurers are primarily aimed at reducing insurer financial risk; however, these strategies are often difficult to separate from service strategies that are used to improve service and thus thought to decrease costs. The insurer may use any of the managed care models and may be a national or regional insurer. With the advent of managed care, the insurer gained more power to influence care, and third-party payers have been more successful in decreasing their financial risk by using reimbursement and service strategies.
2. *Customer.* The **customer** is the person who contracts with the insurer. In most cases this is an employer or government through its insurance programs. The U.S. reimbursement system is employer based. The employer looks for the most cost-effective plans to meet the needs of its employees.
3. *Consumer/patient/enrollee/beneficiary.* The patient or enrollee is a key player in the healthcare system. If patients did not exist, there would be no need for insurers or providers. When a person chooses a health insurance plan, the person is referred to as a plan member or enrollee.
4. *Provider.* Who is the provider? Provider is a generic term. Depending on the health insurance plan, any of the following may be considered a provider: physician, advanced practice registered nurse (APRN), certified nurse-midwife (CNM), registered nurse, physician's assistant, certified registered nurse anesthetist (CRNA), pharmacist, dentist, optometrist, chiropractor, podiatrist, hospital, home health agency, hospice, long-term care facility, psychiatric hospital, skilled nursing home, infusion therapy agency, and so on. In short, a provider is any person or organization that provides health care.

WHAT IS HEALTH INSURANCE?   An insurer or third-party payer is the organization, private or public, that pays or underwrites coverage for health care for another entity, such as a business or individual. The third-party payer provides either group coverage or individual coverage. Most people who have insurance coverage receive it as an employee benefit or through membership in an organization, which is group coverage (e.g., a healthcare professional organization might offer health plans to its members). Most group insurers are commercial or for-profit insurers. Individual or personal insurance that is not part of employment is much more expensive for the purchaser or the enrollee. Sometimes individuals purchase personal insurance to cover gaps in their employment insurance. Others who are self-employed may have to purchase individual coverage plans. ACA now offers additional options to buy insurance through the ACA Insurance Exchanges (Marketplaces). The third-party payer (the insurer) actually pays the bills; however, the process is not simple. As insurance has grown, there has been an increase in insurer financial risk. The insurer could lose the money it invests, or it could miscalculate the amount of money it needs to cover all of its expenses, expected and unexpected. This could happen if too many of the health plan members require more health care than was estimated. The ACA addresses this issue by trying to get younger, and thus healthier enrollees in health insurance plans. This is a group that has not been enrolling in plans. If the insurer is a for-profit organization, it must also yield profits to pay its stockholders. Insurer administrative costs (e.g., staff, facilities, supplies, information systems, and other similar activities and functions) can also be very high.

How does the insurance process actually work to yield payment for healthcare services?

1. An individual experiences uncertainty about healthcare needs and treatment costs. Without this consumer uncertainty, there would be less need for insurance and less financial risk associated with health care. Given this uncertainty, there is a need to share the financial risk with other consumers to decrease individual risk.
2. When individuals decide to join an insurance plan, they put a specific amount of money into the pool or the insurance fund. The pool consists of the group of people that the insurer is covering for healthcare services.
3. The insurer assumes the role of managing or administering the pool of money. Plan members really do not want to do this for themselves.

For example, a large manufacturing company offers several healthcare coverage options to its employees. This company does not want to use its own resources to administer employee healthcare coverage, so it contracts with insurers to provide this service. The insurer will be better served, as will the purchaser of the healthcare plan (the employer) and the enrollees, if there are a large number of members/enrollees. This decreases the financial risk and the administrative costs and usually means there is greater diversification in the health statuses of members, with some healthier than others. The amount that is then paid to obtain the coverage, the premiums, is usually lower. There also will be a greater chance of a pool of members who will have different healthcare needs: some requiring no care, others needing limited care, and some with major medical care and long-term needs. The worst scenario for the insurer is to have a group of unhealthy members.

PROSPECTIVE VERSUS RETROSPECTIVE PAYMENT   Typically, when a customer considers purchasing a product, such as a car, the price is known before the purchase. The seller sets the price, and the purchaser decides to buy or not to buy the product, usually considering need, price, quality, and the like. This is **prospective payment**. The healthcare industry has had a different experience with setting prices. In the past, third-party purchasers of healthcare services devised a **retrospective payment** system. In this system the provider spent money while providing the care, requested payment for these expenses, then was paid. Providers liked this because they knew they would be paid for their services when they submitted their bills. This payment method was known as fee-for-service or billed charges for healthcare services. The provider established the fee-for-service, and the patient paid, usually through a third-party payer. For a long time, this was the major form of payment for health care. Fee-for-service payment typically did not put many limitations on the provider, and the insurer accepted the charges identified by the provider, so the provider made most, if not all, of the treatment decisions with the patient. As a consequence, there was little incentive to be cost effective when the provider knew that the requested charge would be paid in full.

Third-party payers thought that retrospective payment or using a fee-for-service method was a good approach, but after a time, this became an expensive way to do business. Then third-party payers began to put some limits on what they would reimburse, eliminating an automatic acceptance of all charges. The federal government, via its Medicare and Medicaid programs, was the first purchaser or third-party payer to develop a comprehensive **prospective payment system (PPS)**. The purpose of changing to this payment system, called the diagnosis-related group or DRG, was to decrease hospital costs. This system is not based on actual charges but rather on estimated, predetermined prices made by the payer, not the provider. The provider knows before the care is provided what the payer will pay for a particular service. Usually additional resources such as specialty care that may be used are not figured into this amount. In changing to prospective payment, the healthcare industry moved to the approach used by most sellers of products—here is the price; you either buy it or do not buy it. Now, it is quite clear that health care is a much more complex product. Just consider: Do consumers (patients) usually have a choice when they need care? Getting sick is different from deciding to buy a book, chair, dress, or car.

COMPENSATION FOR HEALTH SERVICES   Since the product, healthcare services, is not as simple as other types of products, a number of different approaches are used to pay for these services. Compensation for health services has an impact on nurses and nursing care. It has a trickle-down effect (for example, amount of available funds for hiring staff, buying supplies, paying for overtime, and so on). The typical types of reimbursement methods are discounted fee-for-service, per diem rates, diagnosis-related groups, and capitation. Home health care usually is reimbursed on a per-hour or per-visit basis. Insurers may use one of several of these methods or others in their reimbursement of healthcare services.

Discounted fee-for-service In the mid-1970s, early forms of managed care reimbursement methods began to use discounts. **Discounted fee-for-service** is a payment method that offers to pay the provider a specific percentage of the provider's usual charge or a reduced rate. The percentage can be a straight one, in which only a certain percentage is taken off the charge, or it can be a sliding scale, with the percentage changing based on specified criteria. Discounted services are part of a contractual arrangement with a third-party payer. An insurer may contract with a healthcare facility or any other type of provider to receive a discount for services provided. For example, an insurer's enrollees who receive care at that facility receive a 20% discount or rather are charged only 80% of the usual charge for the services. Clearly this is an advantage for the insurer. Sliding scales, another type of discount, are reflective of the volume of services provided. If the insurer requires a specific level of service, the fee scale will be adjusted or decreased. Most healthcare facilities, such as hospitals, have many contracts with insurers that have different discounts. If not all care is reimbursed at 100% of the costs, this leaves the healthcare provider with expenses that are not covered. This can have serious ramifications for the provider over the long term if the provider cannot cover these unpaid expenses. Providers, such as hospitals, outpatient clinics, physician practices, and home care agencies, must be very careful about the amount of care that is discounted and consider how the unpaid portion will be covered. This insurer advantage can become a healthcare provider disaster. If a provider's expenses are not fully covered by reimbursement, then the provider (for example, a hospital) may have to decrease its operating costs (e.g., decrease staffing, postpone renovation or purchase of new equipment, decrease amount of educational programs provided to staff, and so on).

Per diem rates A **per diem rate** is reimbursement that is fixed, based on each day in a healthcare facility (e.g., $600 per day). Services that may be covered, as well as expected length of stay and intensity of services, may be included in the agreed-upon per diem rate. This rate may also be discounted by the contract between the third-party payer and the provider. The per diem rate is an estimate of what the charges would be; however, this prospectively determined rate is all that is paid, even if the actual expenses are greater. Usually per diem rates vary for specialty areas; for example, daily rates for critical care, behavioral/psychiatric care, medical care, surgical care, or obstetrical care would not be the same (e.g., intensive care per diem would be higher than medical care per diem due to the staffing level, equipment, supplies, and so on). Per diem reimbursement is the negotiated rate per day times the number of days of care (e.g., $600 per day times the number of days in the hospital—three days would equal $1,800 per diem reimbursement).

Capitation The growth of managed care methods introduced one of the major changes in healthcare reimbursement—**capitation**. Capitation is a prepayment to a provider to deliver healthcare services to enrollees of a health plan. This is usually a monthly payment, but it can also be paid on an annual basis. The provider agrees to provide all care for the enrollee's healthcare needs that the provider is qualified to provide. If the enrollee requires no services in the allotted time period, the provider is still paid. If the enrollee's care incurs additional expenses, the provider receives no extra payment. The capitation method is dependent on a contract between the provider and a third-party payer. The focus is on covered lives, or the number of persons who are enrolled in a health plan, rather than individuals. For example, costs are typically described as inpatient days per 1,000, visits per 1,000, or cost per life. In doing this, the third-party payer no longer carries the full financial risk for the employer because much of it is shifted to the provider to keep costs down when decisions are made about care.

Employee contributions to coverage The employee pays some parts of the insurance coverage with the employer paying another part. The amount an employee pays, the premium, varies depending on the amount paid by the employer, the insurer's contract, and the amount of healthcare services used and how they are used. **Premium rate setting** is one of the most important decisions that a third-party payer can make and also an important decision for consumers. Rating is pricing. The third-party payer determines the premiums (price or rate) for its products or services. Premiums are usually calculated as an amount per member per month (PMPM). If the third-party payer miscalculates, it can mean that the insurer loses money and may become financially unstable because the third-party payer will then not have enough funds to pay for the healthcare services that its members require and to cover administrative expenses that are needed to manage the insurance plan.

Employee/member plan costs continue to increase, but early implementation ACA provisions have had variable impact on reducing these costs, depending on the plan chosen. The employee contribution to medical coverage usually includes some form of a deductible, copayment/coinsurance, and annual limits. Insurance plans are highly variable; these methods may not be included in all plans and can vary in how they are applied. Deductibles and copayments/coinsurance represent the employee's out-of-pocket healthcare expenses and are used by the insurer to control its costs. When the insurer increases the out-of-pocket expenses, the insurer pays less and the enrollee or member pays more. The ACA caps annual out-of-pocket medical and drug expenses. This is a major change and improvement.

1. *Deductibles.* A **deductible** is the amount the employee must pay before the third-party payer will begin to pay for healthcare services. The deductible may be handled one of two ways. Some plans require that the employee pay a single deductible for the employee and also for family members, which is applied to all services in the plan. The deductible for family members often is higher. The second method is the use of separate deductibles for categories of services, such as hospitalization, ambulatory care, and so on. Usually when employers and employees pay high premiums, the employee pays a lower deductible. Deductibles are usually not used by health maintenance organizations (HMOs).

   The deductible keeps the cost of the plan down because the enrollee is accepting responsibility for the initial, most frequent charges, those under the deductible limit. After the deductible is paid, the enrollee shares the expenses by paying the copayment or coinsurance. Typically this is shared with the insurer on an 80/20 basis. For example, each dollar above the deductible is paid in this manner: insurer pays 80 cents and enrollee pays 20 cents. If the medical bill is large, 20% can still be a sizable amount. A patient example illustrating how this is implemented is found in Box 5-1.

2. *Copayments/coinsurance.* A **copayment/coinsurance** is the fixed payment that the employee must pay per physician visit, procedure/treatment, or prescription. This is payment sharing between the insurer and the enrollee/patient. The payment typically is required at the time of the service and usually is an established amount, such as $10, or it can be a percentage. Copayments may be found in all types of coverage.

Annual limits   **Annual limits** have been very important, particularly for employees and their families who experience major medical expenses in a year. All plans had some type of limit on the amount that the employee is required to pay annually. However, the ACA legislation now prohibits the use of restrictive annual limits or lifetime limits on coverage for care.

BOX 5-1	DEDUCTIBLES AND COPAYMENTS: A PATIENT EXAMPLE

Hospital bill	$20,000
Patient deductible	−$ 200
	$19,800 **Medical charges after deductible paid**
Medical charges after deductible paid	$19,800
Patient share/copayment	× .20
	$ 3,960 **Amount of medical expenses to be paid by patient/copayment**

Deductible must be paid before the insurer will pay its portion. Patient must pay deductible and copayment.

Deductible	$ 200
Copayment	+$ 3,960
	$ 4,160 **Total amount to be paid by patient**

Despite insurance coverage, the patient must still pay $4,160, which is not a small amount.

When an employee joins a health plan or when an individual purchases insurance, the person becomes an enrollee/member/beneficiary/subscriber in the plan. The enrollee's family is not usually referred to as the enrollee. When they are included in the plan's coverage, they are called dependents, if that is an option available to the enrollee. The contract or covered services plan describes the eligibility criteria, benefits, and payments. These criteria identify when the enrollee and dependents are eligible for the services as well as when they are not eligible. For instance, a dependent child typically was not covered after a specific age or when he or she is no longer considered a dependent; however, the ACA changed this as adult children may be covered until age 26 if this is the choice of the parents and the adult child.

Coverage renewability is particularly important with individual health insurance policies and long-term care contracts. The ACA now restricts insurers from refusing to sell or renew policies because of an individual's health status, nor can individuals be excluded for preexisting conditions. This provision went into effect in 2014.

COVERED SERVICES AND ENROLLEE BENEFITS The written **benefit plan** describes the benefits that are provided to the enrollee and the financial coverage for those benefits or the covered services. Before covered services can be described, it is important to understand the relationship between the enrollee and eligibility for the covered services. Federal law requires that all employees who are eligible for an employer's plan be offered enrollment at the same price.

Benefits are a very important part of any healthcare plan. Important factors are the covered services, exclusions (services not covered), and limitations, which are impacted by healthcare reform legislation. Great variability has existed among plans in their benefit description and what is included or excluded. As an employee makes decisions about coverage, benefits can be a critical issue to consider, depending on the health and financial needs of the employee and the employee's family. In some cases, when there are major or chronic health problems, paying higher premiums to obtain maximum benefits may be the wisest choice. Plan benefits are also important to the provider because medical decisions are often based on the benefits that will be covered, which may not necessarily be what the patient needs.

Covered services are the healthcare services that the plan will cover or reimburse; however, the care or services must be medically necessary. What are the criteria used to determine if care is medically necessary? The insurer determines medical necessity with input from the provider. Clearly this is an area that creates conflict because the insurer, not the patient's healthcare provider, may become the major decision maker. Typical benefits included in healthcare plans supported by ACA provisions are the following:

- Hospital room and board
- Outpatient and inpatient surgery
- Office and inpatient physician visits
- Prescription drugs
- Nursing services
- Diagnostic and radiological laboratory tests
- Ambulance services
- Medical equipment, such as might be used in the home

Plans may include more specialized care, such as home health care, extended care, hospice care, inpatient and outpatient mental health care, and alcohol and substance abuse treatment. When plans cover these services, specific descriptions are included in the covered services document or plan. Typically home health care is used when skilled nursing care is required at home and usually covers required supplies and equipment. When hospice care is provided, it is usually covered for terminally ill patients who have six months or less to live, though some insurers are more flexible. Many healthcare providers do not support this approach and find it difficult to determine a specific time frame for the patient. Extended care may be covered for patients who need less intensive care than hospital care and require skilled nursing care, rehabilitation, and/or convalescent services. Mental health services and alcohol and substance abuse treatment services usually have more stringent limitations. The insurer identifies not only the benefits that are offered but often who may provide these services, a requirement that must be met for the insurer to cover or pay for the healthcare service. Special healthcare needs are always a concern for the insurer because they increase costs. Dental and vision coverage are services that receive special attention. In addition, the use of medical technology has become an increased concern for insurers and for consumers. The development of new medical technologies such as new treatment methods (e.g., robotics) and drugs is a positive step forward for healthcare delivery, but they cost money to develop and use. Insurers must evaluate new technologies carefully before agreeing to cover these new therapies that are often more expensive than other options, and in some cases there may be less evidence supporting their use.

Health promotion and disease prevention have become more important to insurers. In the past, traditional health insurance plans usually did not cover or provided only limited coverage for these services. Examples of preventive care that might now be included are annual physical exams, childhood immunizations, and mammograms, usually within a specified age range. Health promotion examples are health education classes, wellness centers, and smoking cessation groups. The ACA includes many provisions related to health promotion, prevention, and wellness, requiring insurers to provide more screening services.

Exclusions are the services that will not be covered by a healthcare plan. Excluded conditions can vary from plan to plan. Some examples of services that may not be covered are cosmetic surgery, orthodontic treatment, experimental treatment, and artificial insemination.

In summary: There are now more consumer protections. Whether you buy coverage on your own or get it through your job, the ACA's protections help make coverage more secure, so it is available when needed (American Association of Retired Persons, 2014).

- Your health plan can't drop your coverage just because you get sick and can't deny you services for health problems you had before your insurance started (known as preexisting conditions).
- Your health plan can't charge you more because of your gender or if you get very sick.
- Your health plan can't put dollar limits on how much it will pay for covered services you receive in a year (annual dollar limit) or over the life of the plan (lifetime dollar limit).
- Your health plan must cover certain recommended preventive care at no cost to you.
- There are limits on what your health plan can make you pay toward your deductible, coinsurance and copayments, but not your monthly payments (premiums).
- You can keep your children on your family plan through their 26th year—even if they don't live at home, are married, or attend school.

GOVERNMENT HEALTH BENEFIT PROGRAMS

The federal government is the major player in the healthcare arena because it covers a large percentage of the population through its various insurance programs such as Medicare and Medicaid. The passage of the ACA in 2010 increased the federal role in healthcare reimbursement and other aspects of healthcare delivery. The federal government benefit plans are Medicare, Medicaid, the Federal Employees Health Benefit (FEHB) Program, TRICARE, formerly the Civilian Health and Medical Program of the Uniformed Services (CHAMPUS). Health care is the major item in the federal budget each year. Nurses are involved in the care of all of these groups of patients, civilian and military, and many of the changes made in government reimbursement eventually impact all reimbursement.

An Overview of Medicare and Medicaid

Medicare is the federal healthcare insurance program that was established in 1965 by Title XVIII, Health Insurance for the Aged, as an amendment to the Social Security Act of 1935. Medicare is funded by the Medicare Trust Fund, which includes payroll tax contributions, and is the largest single payer in the United States. For many years, Medicare has played a major role in healthcare delivery despite the fact that it is a complex program that is difficult to understand. President Johnson signed the Medicare legislation in 1965, but earlier President Truman took the first steps toward this legislation. He envisioned this program as a critical step toward national health insurance (Daschle, 2008). Medicare has survived and changed over time. With the introduction of changes in Medicare reimbursement methods, such as DRGs, Medicare spending decreased. Interest in using managed care approaches to further decrease healthcare costs has increased over the years. Medicare spending, which is part of the federal budget, is expected to increase, making the need for further cost reduction very important. For example, in 2012 these expenditures increased 4.8%, while expenditures for private health insurance grew 3.2%. By 2023, health expenditures financed by federal, state, and local governments are projected to account for 48 percent of national health spending and to reach a total of $2.5 trillion; in 2012 such expenditures constituted 44% of national health spending and $1.2 trillion (Centers for Medicare & Medicaid Services, 2014g).

The elderly are living longer, requiring longer periods of healthcare services, and medical prices are going up. These factors have a major impact on the size of the trust fund that will be available long term for this federal program. There has been considerable concern about the growth of Medicare. The "baby boomers," people born between 1946 and 1964, are entering the Medicare beneficiary age range. This greatly increases the number of Medicare beneficiaries.

LEGISLATIVE AND REGULATORY ISSUES RELATED TO MEDICARE   The following discussion provides information about the legislation and regulations that have affected Medicare and its move toward managed care approaches to control costs.

- *Social Security Act of 1965 and Amendments.* The Social Security Act of 1965 with its subsequent amendments is the landmark legislation that established Medicare and also Medicaid and made the federal government the major player in health care. The creation of Medicare and Medicaid not only allowed many who could not afford care to receive care but also gave the federal government power to dictate standards, reimbursement methods, and influence other aspects of care. Few hospitals can avoid treating patients covered by these two programs, and when they do treat these patients, they must meet federal requirements and accept federal payment rates.
- *Tax Equity and Fiscal Responsibility Act of 1982.* The Tax Equity and Fiscal Responsibility Act of 1982 (TEFRA) established prospective reimbursement for Medicare acute care services using the DRG model. The law also introduced Medicare to managed care by promoting the use of HMOs with Medicare contracts. The ACA revisited the issue of Medicare managed care plans, and by 2018, the use of this type of plan for Medicare beneficiaries will be reduced.
- *Consolidated Omnibus Budget Reconciliation Act of 1985.* The Consolidated Omnibus Budget Reconciliation Act of 1985 (COBRA) affected most hospitals. It requires that all hospitals treating Medicare patients also treat all patients who request care in their emergency rooms to stabilize them, whether or not they are covered by Medicare or are able to pay. This law has had a major effect on emergency services, their inappropriate use, and escalating costs. Once a hospital receives federal funding, such as from Medicare, this federal law applies to the hospital's emergency services.
- *Medicare Catastrophic Coverage Act of 1988.* The Medicare Catastrophic Coverage Act was signed into law in 1988. This law recognized the economic disparity that existed among the elderly. The decision was made that elderly with greater personal funds should pay more for Medicare; however, this law did not last long. Two years later, it was repealed. This is an example of the power the consumer's voice, even a minority of the more affluent elderly, can have on legislation. This group of beneficiaries did not like paying higher premiums. In addition, the pharmaceutical companies were concerned about the drug benefit that was included, and they feared this would lead to greater price controls. They had a very strong, effective lobby in Congress.
- *Balanced Budget Act of 1997.* The Balanced Budget Act of 1997 (BBA) expanded the ability of Medicare to offer managed care options to its beneficiaries. This included Medicare beneficiaries who had enrolled in HMOs since 1985. The law increased the options to not only include Medicare HMOs but also Medicare preferred provider organizations (PPOs) and Medicare point-of-service plans (POS). Medicare contracts with nongovernmental insurers for these plans; however, over time use of these plans will change due to the ACA of 2010.
- *Medicare Prescription Drug Improvement and Modernization Act of 2003.* The Medicare Prescription Drug Improvement and Modernization Act of 2003 (MMA) created Medicare Part D, the newest Medicare benefit part. The focus of Part D is prescription coverage, a long-needed benefit for Medicare beneficiaries.
- *Patient Protection and Affordable Care Act of 2010 and Healthcare and Education Reconciliation Act of 2010.* Together, the Patient Protection and Affordable Care Act of 2010 and Health Care and Education Reconciliation Act of 2010 (ACA) are the most significant healthcare legislation in decades. The first has many provisions, while the second was used to reconcile differences between the Senate and House versions of this legislation. Additional information about the law is found in Chapter 2. Box 5-2 describes some of the reimbursement provisions including Medicare and Medicaid provisions found in the law.

BOX 5-2	EXAMPLES OF REIMBURSEMENT PROVISIONS IN HEALTH CARE AND PATIENT PROTECTION AND AFFORDABLE CARE ACT OF 2010

President Obama signed this legislation on March 30, 2010. This information represents only some examples of the provisions, not all of the law's provisions. The provisions are activated over several years.

EFFECTIVE 2010
Provisions

- Lifetime limits on benefits and restrictive annual limits will be prohibited.
- Seniors will get a $250 rebate to help fill the "doughnut hole" in Medicare prescription drug coverage, which falls between the $2,700 initial limit and when catastrophic coverage kicks in at $6,154.
- Insurers will be barred from imposing exclusions on children with preexisting conditions. Pools will cover those with preexisting health conditions until healthcare coverage exchanges are operational.
- New plans must provide coverage for preventive services without copays. All plans must comply by 2018.
- Young adults will be able to stay on their parents' insurance until their 27th birthday.
- Businesses with fewer than 50 employees will get tax credits covering 35% of their healthcare premiums, increasing to 50 percent by 2014.
- Improve care coordination for dual eligible's (Medicare and Medicaid) to improve access and quality.
- Medicaid to cover tobacco cessation programs for pregnant women.
- Qualified health plans must cover a minimum coverage without cost sharing for preventive services rated A or B by the U.S. Preventive Services Task Force, recommended immunizations and preventive care for infants, children, and adolescents, and additional preventive care and screenings for women. Refer to the USPSTF website for this information.
- Provide new options for home- and community-based services through Medicaid.
- Temporary funding ($5 billion) for national high-risk insurance pool for coverage of individuals with preexisting medical conditions who have been uninsured for at least six months.
- Insurance plans may not place lifetime limits on benefits and restrictive annual limits.
- Insurers may not rescind policies to avoid paying medical bills when a person becomes ill.
- People receiving coverage from large employers are not expected to experience major changes in premium costs or coverage.

EFFECTIVE 2011
Provisions

- A 50% discount will be provided on brand-name drugs for Prescription Drug Plan or Medicare Advantage enrollees. Additional discounts on brand-name and generic drugs will be phased in to completely close the "doughnut hole" by 2020.

- Cover only proven preventive services and eliminate cost sharing for preventive services in Medicare and Medicaid.
- The Medicare payroll tax will increase from 1.45% to 2.35% for individuals earning more than $200,000 and married filing jointly above $250,000.
- States can offer home- and community-based services to the disabled through Medicaid rather than institutional care beginning October 1.
- Medicare will provide free annual wellness visits and personalized prevention plans. New plans will be required to cover preventive services with no copay.
- Pharmaceutical companies will provide a 50% discount on brand-name prescription drugs for seniors; additional discounts phased in over the next 10 years.
- Community Living Assistance Services and Supports (CLASS), a voluntary long-term care program, will be created. When employees contribute to the program for five years, they would be entitled to a $50 per day cost benefit to pay for long-term care. CLASS does not cover all long-term care expenses. This is the first national government-run long-term care insurance program, primarily offered through employers.
- Develop a Medicaid plan option for enrollees with at least two chronic illnesses, one condition and risk of developing another, or at least one serious and persistent mental health condition to designate a provider as a health home.
- Provide access to comprehensive health risk assessment and a personalized prevention plan for Medicare beneficiaries. Health risk assessment model to be developed within 18 months after law's effective date.
- Provide incentives to Medicare and Medicaid beneficiaries to complete behavior modification programs (criteria need to be developed).
- Community First Choice Option for Medicaid beneficiaries with disabilities to receive community-based attendant services and supports rather than institutional care.
- Provides incentives to reduce Medicare readmissions due to infections or other preventable causes.

EFFECTIVE 2012
Provisions

- Create the Independence in Home demonstration program; providing primary care services in the home for high-need Medicare beneficiaries with the goal of reducing preventable hospitalization, reducing readmissions, improving health outcomes, improving efficiency of care, reducing costs, and achieving patient satisfaction.
- Required mental health parity, which means deductibles, copayments, and limits on the number of visits or days of coverage for mental health and substance abuse treatment, must be no more restrictive than for medical and surgical needs.
- Establish more training for behavioral health professionals.
- Develop nongovernmental research centers to investigate effective treatment for mental illness.

(continued)

BOX 5-2	EXAMPLES OF REIMBURSEMENT PROVISIONS IN HEALTH CARE AND PATIENT PROTECTION AND AFFORDABLE CARE ACT OF 2010 (CONTINUED)

EFFECTIVE 2013
Provisions

- Health plans must implement uniform standards for electronic exchange of health information to reduce paperwork and administrative costs.
- Increase Medicaid payments for fee-for-service and managed care primary care services provided by primary care physicians (family medicine, general internal medicine, or pediatric medicine).

EFFECTIVE 2014
Provisions

- Citizens will be required to have acceptable coverage or pay a penalty of $95 in 2014, $325 in 2015, $695 (or up to 2.5% of income) in 2016. Families will pay half the amount for children, up to a cap of $2,250 per family. After 2016, penalties are indexed to Consumer Price Index.
- Companies with 50 or more employees must offer coverage to employees or pay a $2,000 penalty per employee after their first 30 if at least one of their employees receives a tax credit. Waiting periods before insurance takes effect is limited to 90 days. Employers who offer coverage but whose employees receive tax credits will pay $3,000 for each worker receiving a tax credit.

- Insurers can no longer refuse to sell or renew policies because of an individual's health status. Health plans can no longer exclude coverage for preexisting conditions. Insurers can't charge higher rates because of heath status, gender, or other factors.
- Health insurance exchanges will open in each state to individuals and small employers to comparison-shop for standardized health packages.
- Medicaid eligibility will increase to 133% of poverty for all nonelderly individuals to ensure that people obtain affordable health care in the most efficient and appropriate manner. States will receive increased federal funding to cover these new populations.

Sources: Summarized by author from content from the following resources: Health Care and Education Reconciliation Act of 2010 (P.L. 111-152); Health Reform http://www.healthreform.gov/; White House Health Reform http://www.whitehouse.gov/healthreform; The Henry J. Kaiser Family Foundation http://www.kff.org; Hossian, Farhana. (2010, March 24). How people will be affected by the overhaul. *New York Times*, p. A18; Wolf, R., & Young, A. (2010, March 23). Bill spreads the pain, benefits. *USA Today*, pp. 4A–3A; Span, P. (2010, March 30). Options expand for affordable long-term care. *New York Times*, p. D5; Bernard, T. (2010, March 21). For consumers, clarity on health care changes. *New York Times*. Retrieved from http://www.nytimes.com.

The Health Care Financing Administration (HCFA) is the agency within the HHS that administers the Medicare program and the federal portion of Medicaid. It develops regulations to implement relevant federal laws. HCFA also reviews and must approve managed care contracts for Medicare beneficiaries and evaluates and reports on managed care contract performance. Medicare is financed from four sources. The most important source is the mandatory contributions made by employees and employers to the Medicare trust fund, which is used to provide hospital care. Employees contribute to the fund during their employment years, as do employers; however, the money that they contribute is actually used to reimburse care for people who are currently covered by Medicare. It is not saved to cover care for the contributing employees in the future. This means that current Medicare beneficiaries are actually covered by current employer and employee contributions. The other fund sources are general tax revenues, premiums paid by beneficiaries, and Medicare deductibles and copayments.

Some initiatives that are used to decrease Medicare costs include efforts to reduce hospital, home health, and provider payments. In some cases these savings have exceeded expectations. There are, however, some results that are troubling, which have had a ripple effect throughout the healthcare system. Today patients are sicker when they receive care, and thus need more intensive care at a time when nursing staff levels are reduced. Families are also greatly affected when they are left with the burden of caring for seriously ill family members at home with limited or no healthcare support such as home care. The ACA includes some provisions to assist patients who need to receive care in their homes.

MS-DIAGNOSIS-RELATED GROUPS **Diagnosis-related groups (DRGs)** is a statistical system that classifies care into groups. These groups, which include inpatient care, are then used to identify payment rates. This is a per-stay reimbursement that focuses on a single episode of care related to a diagnosis and includes all predetermined services delivered for that episode. The DRG system is a prospective payment system that is used as the payment system for Medicare reimbursement. Some third-party payers also use it. Box 5-3 summarizes some information about DRGs.

BOX 5-3   DIAGNOSIS-RELATED GROUPS

WHAT ARE DRGs?

Diagnosis-related groups (DRGs) are the basis of payment to hospitals under the Medicare prospective payment system (PPS). Each DRG represents a group of patients who are similar, both clinically and by use of resources. There is a specific payment rate for each DRG that is calculated by a formula. DRGs are the fixed payment amounts for each Medicare inpatient, regardless of length of stay. The location of the hospital, urban or rural, and wage levels are factored into this fixed price. Exceptions are those patients who are outliers or those with exceptional expenses.

HOW ARE DRGs ASSIGNED?

The patient's physician documents the patient's principal diagnosis by using classifications and terminology found in the *International Classification of Diseases, 10th Revision (ICD-10), Clinical Modification (ICD-10-CM)*. In addition to the principal diagnosis, the following are documented:

- Up to four secondary diagnoses
- Principal procedure and additional procedures
- Patient's age, sex, and discharge status

This information is reported to the hospital's Medicare fiscal intermediary. The information is used to classify the patient into one of 25 major diagnostic categories (MDCs). The principal diagnosis is the condition that caused the hospitalization. The patient is then assigned a DRG from within the MDC. Most MDCs are divided into surgical DRGs and medical DRGs. These DRGs may also be categorized by age, sex, and the presence or absence of complications or comorbidities.

WHAT IS THE MAJOR COMPLAINT ABOUT DRGs?

Severity of illness is not adequately considered.

The DRG system considers the types of patients a hospital treats or its case mix and the costs for treatment. Resources used and length of stay or bed days are important aspects of the incurred costs. This system focuses not on the number of patients, but rather on the types of patients and the resources they use. The major diagnostic categories (MDCs) are based on anatomical or pathophysiological groups and/or their clinical management. Within each MDC, there are a number of DRGs. Each DRG has an assigned relative average value indicating the amount of resources required to care for the patients in the DRG compared to other DRGs. This is called the case mix index (CMI). The DRG rates are also affected by the following:

- Location of the hospital (rural or urban)
- Wage index, which affects hospital costs
- Teaching hospital status and house staff training
- Recognition of outliers

Outliers are patients with cost of care or length of stay that is outside the expected. If a patient's hospital stay is longer than expected or total costs are greater than expected for the patient's DRG, then the patient is considered an outlier. Hospitals are very concerned when they have outliers because they need to investigate the reasons to ensure that costs are controlled.

DRGs have had and continue to have an impact on care. Coordination of all aspects of care becomes critical to meet length-of-stay requirements for a specific DRG. Patients who stay longer incur more costs. Timely admissions and discharges are important components of cost-effective care. Decreasing the length of stay while maintaining quality care and meeting outcomes could lead to hospitals making a "profit" and not losing money. The nursing staff does most of the documentation, and it is this documentation that provides important information that is required to assign DRGs to actual patient services. The DRG is assigned after the patient is discharged, when it is too late to change the care or the documentation. The DRG system does consider outlier factors when determining payment. The hospital may need to consider changes in care and more effective coordination of care. The goal is to decrease the number of outliers, and thus decrease financial risk for the HCO and risk of additional payment denials.

There is no doubt that Medicare and DRGs have had a tremendous impact on health care. They have decreased lengths of stay in hospitals, but this has also increased the need for home health care, long-term care facilities, and ambulatory care. There is also great drive to decrease readmissions.

One important change under the ACA is in how Medicare's hospital payment system treats hospital readmissions, cases in which a patient returns to the hospital within 30 days of discharge. Nearly one in five Medicare patients experienced such a readmission as of 2010, and many of these readmissions are believed to result from low-quality care during the initial admission or poor planning for how the patient will obtain care after discharge. However, before the ACA, hospitals had no incentive to invest in activities aimed at reducing readmissions and could actually be made worse off by doing so since they would lose payment for the avoided readmissions. This misalignment of incentives likely both increased costs and reduced quality. The ACA corrects these incentives by penalizing hospitals with high readmission rates (among patients with a specified set of diagnoses). There is already a downward turn in the number of readmissions after the implementation of this provision. (Office of the President, 2013, p. 15)

Costs have shifted to other settings, ones that were thought to be more cost effective.

MEDICARE ELIGIBILITY   Eligibility requirements include the following (Center for Medicare and Medicaid Services, 2014f). A person can receive Part A benefits at age 65 without having to pay premiums if the person:

- is eligible to get Social Security or Railroad Retirement Board benefits but has not yet filed for them,
- already receives retirement benefits from Social Security or the Railroad Retirement Board, or
- has a spouse with Medicare-covered government employment.

If the person is under 65, the person can receive Part A benefits without having to pay premiums if the person:

- has received Social Security or Railroad Retirement Board disability benefits for 24 months.
- has end-stage renal disease and meets certain requirements.

Employers are prohibited from forcing employees who are between the ages of 65 and 69 to use Medicare instead of their employer's health coverage, which would be a financial benefit for employers. If employers could do this, then they would not have to provide coverage for older employees in this age group, reducing healthcare insurance costs for employers. There continue to be new proposals to change benefits, eligibility, and funding for the Medicare program.

MEDICARE BENEFITS   The Medicare program is composed of four parts: Parts A, B, C, and D (Center for Medicare & Medicaid Services, 2014f).

- *Medicare Part A* is the hospital insurance plan, paying for inpatient treatment, skilled nursing facilities (not custodial or long-term care), home health care, and hospice care. Premiums are not paid if the beneficiary or spouse paid Medicare taxes while working. A person may purchase this coverage if the person does not meet past tax payment requirements but must meet citizenship or residency requirements and be 65 or older.
- *Medicare Part B* is the supplementary medical insurance program, which includes coverage for physician services, outpatient treatment, laboratory testing, and some preventive services. This part is voluntary and requires that the enrollee or beneficiary meet the requirements to be entitled to Part A and is also willing to pay Part B premiums. The Medicare beneficiary must also pay deductibles and copayments, which are not high. If the person also qualifies for Medicaid by meeting the requirement of limited financial resources, Medicaid pays the Medicare deductibles and copayments.

    Medicare Part B is very different from Part A. Part B resembles typical insurance coverage and is supplemental medical insurance. Its benefits include physician services and outpatient hospital services, including emergency services, ambulatory surgery, diagnostic tests, laboratory services, durable equipment, and some preventive services. Though enrollment in Part B is voluntary, most beneficiaries enroll because it provides coverage at a reasonable cost. Part B benefits are funded by premiums paid by beneficiaries, annual deductibles, and copayments.
- *Medicare Part C* covers Medicare Parts A and B for all medically needed services, but it is covered by private insurance companies that are approved by Medicare—referred to as Medicare Advantage (MA). In many cases this is a cheaper plan than the original Medicare plan and also includes prescription drug coverage (Part D). The ACA makes changes to this part, but they will be implemented over time. Medicare beneficiaries choose to participate in Part C.
- *Medicare Part D* provides coverage for prescription drugs for Medicare beneficiaries. Coverage for prescriptions have improved since Part D was implemented, but there still are cost issues for beneficiaries, some of which are addressed in healthcare reform of 2010.

Medicaid Legislative and Regulatory Issues

The following examples of legislation have had an impact on the Medicaid Program.

- *Social Security Act of 1965, Title XIX.* The Social Security Act of 1965, Title XIX, established the jointly funded Medicaid program. Each state and the federal government share the costs associated with Medicaid. The federal government develops the federal guidelines for the program, with HCFA acting as the overall federal agency responsible for its implementation. This legislation was a major breakthrough in establishing a program to provide care for those who could not afford it. The regulations related to this program have grown more complex since 1965, and other laws have also affected the program, such as the ACA expanding health insurance enrollment.

- *Personal Responsibility and Work Opportunity Reconciliation Act of 1996.* In 1996 there were several attempts to make major changes in Medicaid, and most were not passed. However, the Personal Responsibility and Work Opportunity Reconciliation Act of 1996 (also known as the Welfare Reform Act) was signed into law (U.S. Department of Health and Human Services, 2004). While the law eliminated Aid to Families with Dependent Children (AFDC), families who were eligible for AFDC are usually eligible for Temporary Assistance for Needy Families (TANF) (low-income families with children, including those who meet eligibility for TANF). Prior to this law, Medicaid eligibility income thresholds were set by individual states, and thus there was great state variation in eligibility. Now poorer states receive a greater percentage of federal matching funds to provide greater parity in state programs. The goal of this legislation is to move people off of welfare and into jobs; however, many lose their health benefits when they take jobs that do not offer benefits. This law provides 6 to 12 months of Medicaid coverage during the transition to work. There has been improvement with more people employed; however, there are now more uninsured because of this change and other reasons such as the increased use of temporary staff who get no health coverage, increasing self-employment, and the economic crisis that increased unemployment in 2009–2010.

- *Children's Health Insurance Program (CHIP).* This law, or Title XXI of the Social Security Act, was signed into law in 1997, establishing a state-federal partnership that targets the growing number of children not covered by health insurance (Centers for Medicare & Medicaid Services, 2014b). It covers children from families whose incomes are too high to receive Medicaid but too low for private insurance. There is state variation in CHIP. These children may then get their coverage through Medicaid or through a separate state program. CHIP has been successful, though it has had a rocky history. President George W. Bush would not expand CHIP; however, President Obama signed legislation expanding CHIP as one of his first acts in 2009. CHIP covers inpatient services, outpatient services, physicians' medical and surgical services, laboratory and radiological services, and well-baby and immunization services.

Medicaid is not just a state program, but a program that is funded by the federal government and the states jointly. Each state has its own Medicaid program that provides funding for health care and long-term care or nursing home care. What is the role of the federal government? The federal matching funds are designed so poorer states receive a larger percentage of the federal Medicaid funds to ensure more equity among the state programs. The state programs must meet federal guidelines established by HCFA. Each state, however, determines its own benefits, its eligibility requirements, and provider fee schedules based on federal guidelines. This is where problems and inequality occur, though ACA will have impact on some of these issues. There is a difference in programs from state to state, particularly in eligibility requirements. All states by federal law, however, must include persons who qualify for AFDC, all needy children under the age of 21, persons who qualify for Old-Age Assistance, persons who qualify for Aid to the Blind, persons who are permanently and totally disabled, and the elderly over 65 years and on welfare. When states set eligibility standards above the federal poverty level, this can cause major problems for many people who need these healthcare services and cannot receive Medicaid reimbursement. Eligibility standards may have a major effect on providers who may provide care with no reimbursement to cover their costs.

The Medicaid program has also undergone many changes due to the need for cost containment and the increasing use of managed care options and strategies. Medicaid is a program that has been troubled with bureaucracy and inadequate funding. Because of these factors, many providers are not willing to care for Medicaid beneficiaries. Medicaid managed care options, however, has made it easier for some providers to participate in the program. Medicaid is a complex program with many regulations. As cost-containment strategies increase, there is concern that coverage for some people will be eliminated or reduced to a point that many Medicaid beneficiaries may not have their health needs met. This comes at a time when ACA may alleviate some of this concern. Advocacy for these patients is very important.

MEDICAID AND THE AFFORDABLE CARE ACT The ACA expands coverage for the poorest Americans by creating an opportunity for states to provide Medicaid eligibility, effective January 1, 2014, for individuals under 65 years of age with incomes up to 133% of the federal poverty level (FPL) (see Table 5-1 for 2014 FPL) (Centers for Medicare & Medicaid Services, 2014c). For the first time, states can provide Medicaid coverage for low-income adults without children and be guaranteed coverage through Medicaid in every state without need for a waiver. Medicaid and Children's Health Insurance Program eligibility and enrollment will be much simpler and will be coordinated with the newly created Affordable Insurance Exchanges (Centers for Medicare & Medicaid Services, 2014c). This new system enables individuals and families to apply for coverage using a single application and have their eligibility determined for all insurance affordability programs through one simple process. In order to achieve this goal, federal funding is provided through a variety of venues to help states improve their eligibility and enrollment systems. States must agree to participate, and some have not, which impacts the number of uninsured and also results in a system that is not consistent from state to state.

TABLE 5-1	2014 POVERTY GUIDELINES FOR THE 48 CONTIGUOUS STATES AND THE DISTRICT OF COLUMBIA
Persons in family/household	**Poverty guideline**
For families/households with more than 8 persons, add $4,060 for each additional person.	
1	$11,670
2	15,730
3	19,790
4	23,850
5	27,910
6	31,970
7	36,030
8	40,090
2014 Poverty Guidelines for Alaska	
For families/households with more than 8 persons, add $5,080 for each additional person.	
1	$14,580
2	19,660
3	24,740
4	29,820
5	34,900
6	39,980
7	45,060
8	50,140

TABLE 5-1	(CONTINUED)

2014 Poverty Guidelines for Hawaii	
Persons in family/household	**Poverty guideline**
For families/households with more than 8 persons, add $4,670 for each additional person.	
1	$13,420
2	18,090
3	22,760
4	27,430
5	32,100
6	36,770
7	41,440
8	46,110

The separate poverty guidelines for Alaska and Hawaii reflect Office of Economic Opportunity administrative practice beginning in the 1966–1970 period. Note that the poverty thresholds—the original version of the poverty measure—have never had separate figures for Alaska and Hawaii. The poverty guidelines are not defined for Puerto Rico, the U.S. Virgin Islands, American Samoa, Guam, the Republic of the Marshall Islands, the Federated States of Micronesia, the Commonwealth of the Northern Mariana Islands, and Palau. In cases in which a federal program using the poverty guidelines serves any of those jurisdictions, the federal office that administers the program is responsible for deciding whether to use the contiguous-states-and-DC guidelines for those jurisdictions or to follow some other procedure.

The poverty guidelines apply to both aged and nonaged units. The guidelines have never had an aged/nonaged distinction; only the Census Bureau (statistical) poverty thresholds have separate figures for aged and nonaged one-person and two-person units.

Programs using the guidelines (or percentage multiples of the guidelines—for instance, 125% or 185% of the guidelines) in determining eligibility include Head Start, the Supplemental Nutrition Assistance Program (SNAP), the National School Lunch Program, the Low-Income Home Energy Assistance Program, and the Children's Health Insurance Program. Note that in general, cash public assistance programs (Temporary Assistance for Needy Families and Supplemental Security Income) do NOT use the poverty guidelines in determining eligibility. The Earned Income Tax Credit program also does NOT use the poverty guidelines to determine eligibility.

The poverty guidelines (unlike the poverty thresholds) are designated by the year in which they are issued. For instance, the guidelines issued in January 2014 are designated the 2014 poverty guidelines. However, the 2014 HHS poverty guidelines only reflect price changes through calendar year 2013; accordingly, they are approximately equal to the Census Bureau poverty thresholds for calendar year 2013. (The 2013 thresholds are expected to be issued in final form in September 2014; a preliminary version of the 2013 thresholds is now available from the Census Bureau.)

The poverty guidelines may be formally referenced as "the poverty guidelines updated periodically in the *Federal Register* by the U.S. Department of Health and Human Services under the authority of 42 U.S.C. 9902(2)."

Source: U.S. Census Bureau, 2013

There are other nonfinancial eligibility criteria that are used in determining Medicaid eligibility. To be eligible for Medicaid, individuals need to satisfy federal and state requirements regarding residency, immigration status, and documentation of U.S. citizenship. States can apply to the Centers for Medicare & Medicaid Services (CMS) for waivers to provide Medicaid to populations beyond what traditionally can be covered under the state plan. Some states have additional state-only programs to provide medical assistance for certain low-income people who do not qualify for Medicaid. No federal funds are provided for state-only programs (Centers for Medicare & Medicaid Services, 2014d).

MEDICAID BENEFITS Due to the great variation in the types of Medicaid beneficiaries, Medicaid must provide services across the healthcare continuum, from preventive care to long-term care and across the lifespan (Centers for Medicare & Medicaid Services, 2014a). Medicaid required benefits are described in Box 5-4. ACA has also had an impact on Medicaid benefits. It establishes Benchmark Benefit Plans (Centers for Medicare & Medicaid Services, 2014f). This new approach includes:

- mental health services and prescription drugs.
- tobacco cessation services for pregnant women.
- family planning.
- hospice care for children.
- preventive and obesity-related services.
- states' option to provide health homes for enrollees with chronic conditions.

The number of people without insurance and unemployed has overtaxed the Medicaid program. This problem is only increasing and is also addressed in healthcare reform initiatives of 2010. Patients who use Medicaid often have complex medical and socioeconomic issues and could benefit from case management. Every state Medicaid program provides pharmaceutical

BOX 5-4	MEDICAID BENEFITS

Mandatory Benefits
- Inpatient hospital services
- Outpatient hospital services
- EPSDT: Early and Periodic Screening, Diagnostic, and Treatment Services
- Nursing facility services
- Home health services
- Physician services
- Rural health clinic services
- Federally qualified health center services
- Laboratory and X-ray services
- Family planning services
- Nurse-midwife services
- Certified pediatric and family nurse practitioner services
- Freestanding birth center services (when licensed or otherwise recognized by the state)
- Transportation to medical care
- Tobacco cessation counseling for pregnant women

Optional Benefits
- Prescription drugs
- Clinic services
- Physical therapy
- Occupational therapy
- Speech, hearing, and language disorder services
- Respiratory care services
- Other diagnostic, screening, preventive, and rehabilitative services
- Podiatry services
- Optometry services
- Dental services
- Dentures
- Prosthetics
- Eyeglasses
- Chiropractic services
- Other practitioner services
- Private duty nursing services
- Personal care
- Hospice
- Case management
- Services for individuals age 65 or older in an institution for mental disease (IMD)
- Services in an intermediate care facility for the mentally retarded
- State plan home and community-based services- 1915(i)
- Self-Directed Personal Assistance Services- 1915(j)
- Community first choice option- 1915(k)
- TB related services
- Inpatient psychiatric services for individuals under age 21
- Other services approved by the Secretary
- Health homes for enrollees with chronic conditions – Section 1945

Source: Centers for Medicare & Medicaid. (2014). Medicaid benefits. Retrieved from http://www.medicaid.gov/medicaid-chip-program-information/by-topics/benefits/medicaid-benefits.html

services, even though it is an optional service. It is provided to prevent the use of more costly services, such as surgery or extensive inpatient treatment. States try to control pharmaceutical use by requiring prior authorization, prescription caps, and prospective utilization review. Other services that may be provided are case management, transportation, hospice services, personal care services, inpatient psychiatric services, physical and occupational therapy for speech/language/hearing disorders, and respiratory services for children who are dependent on ventilators. Home and community services may also be provided if the state receives a waiver to do so.

SPECIAL CONSIDERATIONS FOR PEOPLE WITH CHRONIC OR DISABLING ILLNESSES   Medicaid managed care options must include care needs for people with chronic and disabling conditions even though these care needs are often not as important for other groups of Medicaid recipients. These needs are individualized care that usually is more complex than care required for other types of patients, comprehensive service systems, and care without cure. The latter is most important, as the need for treatment is typically long term. States have taken various approaches to meeting the needs of these patients by using Medicaid managed care approaches.

THE UNINSURED   The number of uninsured is a growing problem in the United States, as discussed in earlier chapters. There continues to be an increasing number of people without coverage, though over time, ACA options should reduce this number. Children are at greater risk of having no insurance coverage. Sick people approaching 65 have the greater number of medical problems and higher costs. The people who are most likely to have insurance are those who are over 65, which is due to Medicare coverage. Adults who work for hourly wages often do not have a choice of employer-based insurance. Young adults also may decide not to pay for insurance, feeling that they have no need for it. People without insurance avoid preventive care and wait to receive medical treatment until it is an emergency, and thus frequently the care costs more. With the premiums rising, the problem of the uninsured will only increase.

One reason for this growth is the number of people who have lost Medicaid eligibility and thus healthcare coverage. Some people leave welfare for low-wage jobs, though this is difficult during times of high unemployment. Low-wage jobs typically do not offer healthcare coverage. Another group is people who are hired for temporary or contract positions. Many of these people had health insurance coverage in their full-time positions, which may have even been in high-level or professional positions. As more companies outsource, they hire people to fulfill only specific needs temporarily. These positions come without any benefits.

Federal Employees Health Benefit Program (FEHBP)

The FEHBP is a special insurance in that the employer is the federal government providing healthcare insurance to federal employees, retirees, and their dependents in the same way that any other employer might provide coverage, though the federal government funds it along with plan members. Because of this, it is not technically a government plan but rather an employer plan. This coverage is mandated by law and administered by the federal government's Office of Personnel Management. Members or enrollees of the FEHBP choose from a wide variety of healthcare plans during the government's annual enrollment period. Minimum benefits are required for plans to contract with the FEHBP. The federal government pays part of the premium. The enrollee must pay other costs.

Military Health Care

Healthcare coverage for military personnel and their dependents is another major healthcare expenditure for the federal government. The military health services system is not just an insurer but also a provider through its healthcare facilities globally. It provides health benefits to all active-duty military personnel. Retirees, dependents, and survivors received coverage through the Civilian Health and Medical Program of the Uniformed Services (CHAMPUS), with beneficiaries changing to Medicare at age 65. CHAMPUS was a fee-for-service insurance program for dependents; however, due to its increasing costs, the federal government also began using managed care approaches such as HMOs, point-of-service, and preferred provider plans. When this occurred, CHAMPUS was renamed TRICARE. The Veterans Health Administration has also undergone changes (e.g., introducing primary care, regional centers and marketing, case management). This system provides ambulatory care, acute care, and in some cases long-term care, for military veterans.

State Insurance Programs

States also offer insurance to their state employees. Usually the state government is a state's largest employer and consequently largest insurer, and there is some degree of choice among plan options for state employees. The state or a contracted provider administrates these plans. State employees contribute to the payment of this coverage in the same way they would if they were employed in the private sector.

INSURER REIMBURSEMENT AND SERVICE STRATEGIES TO CONTROL COST AND QUALITY

Healthcare reimbursement is a complex process, and it has become more complex by the use of managed care approaches. Understanding how this process works and who the players are in the process helps healthcare providers advocate for their patients and intervene in the process to ensure that quality care is not compromised and that healthcare professionals' needs are considered. Today reimbursement and managed care options and strategies are inseparable.

Nurses are also employed by all types of health insurers. They work with enrollees, determine allocation of benefits, and act as case managers. If they work for an HMO, they may provide direct care. Some nurses hold management positions. Over time, managed care approaches have become less important. All insurers have become more interested in consumer issues and recognize the need to attract consumers. This is partially due to the influence of managed care. There was a consumer backlash to the controlling aspects of managed care, and this backlash emphasized the need to listen to consumers. Today there is less emphasis on managed care as the best approach and more a blending of approaches to healthcare reimbursement and strategies to control cost and maintain quality.

Managed Care and Its Impact on Health Insurers: Strategies to Control Cost and Improve Care

The HMO was the first managed care model. Consumers were not always happy with HMOs, and this led to the development of other models. The problem of increasing healthcare costs became a serious issue in the 1980s. Insurers, who were in competition with HMOs, began to develop new models for healthcare management, and employers were interested in these other options. Today healthcare professionals and consumers experience a variety of different insurance plans. Over time, it has become more difficult to distinguish among the managed care options as health insurers in general have adopted many of the managed care strategies to reduce cost and improve care.

The most important difference in the various insurer models is the relationship between the insurer and the participating providers, particularly physicians. The role of traditional indemnity insurance (typical third-party payer insurance) was to process and pay medical bills. This began to change when managed care was developed and began to increase, providing a more comprehensive approach that has affected how insurers are organized. Insurers continue to process and pay medical bills, but insurers have become more involved in the management of their members' health care, focusing on appropriate care, when it is needed, and illness and disease prevention and even more health promotion. The following content discusses the strategies that were often first developed by managed care organizations and in many cases now are integral strategies used by most third-party payers or insurers.

How do insurers cut healthcare expenses and yet still ensure quality care? Service and reimbursement strategies are used to manage the healthcare services and to reduce costs. Today many different types of third-party payers use several of these strategies. It is important for all healthcare providers, including nurses in all types of settings, to understand the strategies that are used and their purposes. Service strategies are methods used by insurers to manage delivery of care. The purpose of these strategies is to decrease cost and provide quality care. The insurer wants to find better, more cost-effective treatments; however, this is a strategy that has not been fully used. There is no doubt that healthcare delivery has been affected by managed care service strategies, but it is not always clear if costs have been better controlled with these strategies or if the quality of care has changed, positively or negatively. If one considers that healthcare quality continues to be a problem over the years since managed care entered the reimbursement and healthcare delivery system, it would be difficult to say that managed care has brought major improvement to healthcare delivery. Efficiency is a critical component of these strategies. The goal is to minimize costs and choose services with the maximum excess of benefits over costs. Just focusing cost-containment efforts on decreasing costs will not be enough in the long run. Achieving the desired outcome has become more important over the past few years.

PROVIDER PANELS   The **provider panel** is a key managed care concept that now is part of many health plans. It is a group of providers that are contracted to provide service to enrollees in the health plan (approved for payment of services). Examples of providers are physicians, APRNs, CNMs, hospitals, clinics, long-term care facilities, home health agencies, laboratories, durable equipment suppliers, pharmacies, and so on. Provider panels are selected and organized in a variety of ways. Providers are accepted or rejected based on the insurer criteria. Clearly this has serious consequences for providers, for example, physicians who may not be accepted for a provider panel, even causing providers to lose patients who have to select another provider when their insurer no longer includes their provider in its panel. If the person continues with the provider who is not in the panel, then the person must pay out of pocket for the care. The ACA also has had an impact. When some people signed up for plans through the Insurance Exchanges, they found that their regular provider was not covered by the plan they had chosen. This has led to criticism of ObamaCare interfering with patient choice, something that was a major consumer concern when managed care was strong.

Control is a major issue. Physician providers may be selected as individual physicians or as groups of physicians. Medical groups contract with an insurer as a group, but the insurer still evaluates individual provider performance within the group. A medical or practice group is typically two or more physicians that work together to provide medical services to patients. Nurse practitioners and nurse-midwives may be part of a medical group and in some cases form their own groups. Usually these provider groups share a single office or may have satellite offices to expand their geographic coverage. There is one medical record for each patient that is shared among all the providers in the medical group. This facilitates coordination of care for the practice and for the patient. The ACA encourages this type of approach through its recommendations to establish accountable care organizations, medical/health homes, and nurse-managed health clinics. (See Chapter 4.)

PROVIDER PERFORMANCE   Provider performance has never been more important. Today, when insurers contract with new providers to join their provider panels or renew contracts with providers, insurers base their provider selection on specific criteria. Why is this so important? The insurer wants providers who offer cost-effective, quality care that meets the insurer criteria. As managed care developed through the 1980s and 1990s, cost effectiveness became more important than quality; today quality issues are slowly becoming more important. The goal of performance-based reimbursement evaluation is to alter provider performance. How the insurer goes about reaching this goal can vary and can mean the difference between success and failure. Rewards work better than sanctions, but both may be used. The insurer may financially reward providers who meet the insurer's criteria for cost-effective care by offering bonuses, or in some cases when provider performance does not meet insurer outcomes, the insurer may close the provider off from receiving new enrollees. The goal, in the case of risk of reducing services, with a provider is to discourage the use of inappropriate and costly services. Insurers typically use data and feedback, practice guidelines, protocols, and education to encourage providers to change their behavior. Examples of indicators that are used to evaluate provider performance are the following:

- Member satisfaction data
- Member complaint and grievance rates
- Wait time for appointments
- Utilization rates
- Immunization rates
- Complication rates
- Overall medical costs or medical costs per member per month
- Hospital admission and readmission rates
- Health screening rates
- Number and types of procedures
- Length of stay
- Number and types of prescriptions
- Sentinel events and other errors

LENGTH-OF-STAY (LOS) MANAGEMENT   Hospital occupancy rates and LOS for all types of patients have been decreasing. Managing LOS is an important method in controlling costs. The initiative to reduce LOS has increased the use of ambulatory care services/primary care, home care, subacute services, and other types of services that replace inpatient treatment. Nursing has been concerned about the decrease as it has affected patient care and patients' needs. There is increased nursing resource consumption as LOS is reduced. The first hospitalization days have higher requirements for nursing hours, particularly the first two days. Nurses are now caring for more acute patients on admission because patients are kept out of the hospital until it is absolutely necessary to admit them. This has increased care needs. There is also increased pressure to provide rapid patient and family education, with little time to provide it. Is money actually saved when LOS is shortened? At what point does the decreased LOS actually increase nursing costs? These are critical questions that require further research. It is important for nursing to continue to pursue further understanding of the impact of LOS on care needs and outcomes.

FORMULARIES   Advances in pharmaceuticals have helped patients to live normal lives and have decreased healthcare costs, but at the same time these advances have increased medical costs. This may seem contradictory; however, both have occurred. For example, antibiotics prevent patients from becoming sick or sicker; however, some antibiotics are very expensive, and overuse of antibiotics can lead to patient problems when future antibiotics are needed. Careful cost-benefit analysis is required. The federal government is more concerned about the increasing costs of drugs. To cope with these increasing pharmaceutical costs, the use of formularies is a critical reimbursement strategy that is used to control the ever-increasing costs of drugs. The **formulary** is the insurer's list of drugs or classes of drugs that the insurer prefers that providers use. There are three types of formularies: open, incentive, and closed. An *open formulary* means that the enrollee pays extra fees for using nonformulary drugs. With the *incentive formulary*, the insurer reimburses for drugs outside the formulary, but the enrollee is responsible for additional copay. This type of formulary is designed to encourage the enrollee not to use nonformulary medications. When a *closed formulary* is used, there is no reimbursement for drugs that are not in the formulary.

How does an insurer determine which drugs to include in its formulary? Most insurers use safety, effectiveness, cost, and cost effectiveness as their criteria. No insurer formulary includes all of the drugs approved by the Food and Drug Administration (FDA). The formulary typically focuses on generic drugs because these tend to be less expensive than the brand-name products, though usually chemically equivalent. Many drugs are the same, but their therapeutic effect or their side effects may vary. For some patients, excluding drugs that they have found helpful may be a serious problem. This is particularly important for patients with chronic illnesses for whom a specific drug is more effective. When the insurer's formulary changes and the drug is not included or if the patient changes third-party payers and the new insurer formulary does not include the drug, the patient may suffer. Insurers must also consider the value of adding new drugs that are expensive, including biotechnology products. These drugs and products tend to be very expensive. Clearly an insurer must weigh the costs and benefits of using these therapies. It needs data that demonstrate significant clinical advantages, but these advantages still may not be enough to support the decision to cover their use. Insurer protocols and authorization procedures are established for these highly expensive drugs. Another treatment issue is that most of the new biotech treatments are injectable, and typically insurers do not cover injectables under the category of pharmacy but rather as medical expenses. As these drugs become more common, this medical expense classification will require reconsideration. The pharmacy coverage may be different from other benefits, often more limited, and thus there may be some advantage in reclassifying biotech drugs as pharmacy expenses.

Many factors have an impact on the use of drugs today. Providers are inundated with drug information via the mail, Internet, and the ever-growing pharmaceutical sales force. Drug companies are also marketing directly to the consumer/patient through all types of media, which has increased the number of patients going to providers and requesting specific medications. All of this increases drug costs and the pressure that providers feel to prescribe drugs and sometimes, specific drugs. The formulary presents other problems for the prescribing provider. Some providers have found that certain drugs work better than others or have fewer side effects, but the patient's insurer formulary does not reimburse for these drugs. This presents a conflict for the provider and the patient/enrollee. In addition, most providers have contracts with many insurers. Each one has a formulary, and some are quite different from others. The provider, who is already inundated with paperwork and administration, is confronted with more information and differences. Many providers will choose the path of least resistance and use the least restrictive formularies, but these formularies may offer limited drug options. Insurer authorization may also be required to receive reimbursement for nonformulary drugs.

READMISSION REDUCTION PROGRAM   The ACA added a section to the Social Security Act establishing the Hospital Readmissions Reduction Program, which requires the CMS to reduce payments to hospitals with excess readmissions, effective for discharges beginning on October 1, 2012 (Centers for Medicare & Medicaid Services, 2014h). A key requirement is defining readmission of a patient covered by CMS as an admission to a subsection hospital within 30 days of a discharge from the same or another subsection hospital. The CMS website provides updated information about this program. Hospitals are now monitoring their readmissions to avoid losing money when patients are readmitted meeting the CMS criteria. If the patient is readmitted, CMS will not pay for the services nor can the hospital charge the patient, creating potential for significant negative impact on a hospital's budget. Nursing care is directly related to this, and patients need preparation for discharge to better ensure they will not be readmitted within 30 days.

HOSPITAL-ACQUIRED COMPLICATIONS   Federal legislation required that CMS identify conditions that: (a) are high cost or high volume or both, (b) result in the assignment of a case to a DRG that has a higher payment when present as a secondary diagnosis, and (c) could reasonably have been prevented through the application of evidence-based guidelines (Centers for Medicare & Medicaid Services, 2014e). This is focused on cost reduction as well as improving care. The current list of hospital-acquired complications (HACs), (e.g., patient fall with injury, catheter-associated urinary tract infections, and others) is available on the CMS website. The list is changed periodically. Hospitals are very involved in preventing HACs so they will not lose payment. Nursing care is related to all of the HACs, and nursing management is very involved in monitoring, preventing, and responding to HACs. Nongovernmental insurers are now moving toward developing their own HAC list with similar results for hospitals. Figure 5-3 provides some data on HACs with current data provided on the CMS website.

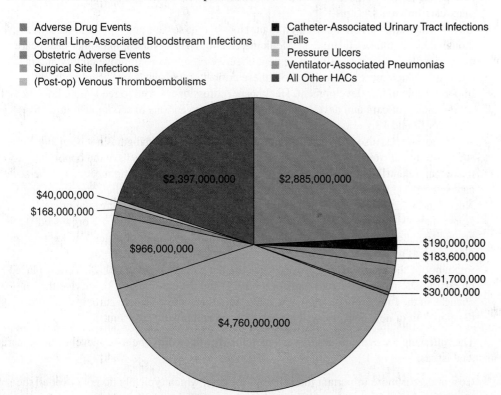

Figure 5-3 Estimated Cost Savings, by Hospital-Acquired Condition (HAC), 2010-2013

Source: U.S. Department of Health and Human Services. Agency for Healthcare Quality and Research. (2014). Hospital-acquired complications. Retrieved from http://www.ahrq.gov/professionals/quality-patient-safety/pfp/interimhacrate2013.html

REIMBURSEMENT ISSUES: IMPACT ON NURSES AND NURSING CARE

Reimbursement has a major impact on nurses and on nursing care. What are some ways this impact has been felt? Nurses are not expected to be reimbursement experts, but understanding how healthcare expenses are covered is helpful. It is particularly important if reimbursement affects which provider delivers care, to whom it is delivered, where and when it is delivered, what type of care can be provided, and when care might have to end. If one does not understand reimbursement and its role in healthcare delivery, one might think that these decisions have nothing to do with the payment of care and are only connected to the provider and the patient. This, however, is not true. Reimbursement is another layer of the complex healthcare delivery process and system that cannot be ignored. How have nursing and nurses been affected by reimbursement, and how can they affect reduction in costs? The following are some examples.

- Managing within fixed resources and decreasing costs by reducing waste and inefficiencies are more important to nursing today than they were in the past. Compared with other providers, nurses use the most resources, such as supplies and equipment, in the acute care setting, and through their usage, they can make a difference in reducing waste and inefficiencies. The early history of nursing was one of "you don't need to know the budget or what things cost." This attitude is no longer acceptable if the HCO expects to make a difference in reducing its costs.
- Nursing staff levels have also been affected by reimbursement as hospitals, and other HCOs have had to change staffing levels due to costs. This change requires nurses to assess how they deliver care and search for more efficient methods. In addition, nurses are speaking out more about staffing levels and their impact on patient care and quality and safety outcomes.
- Nursing has always been concerned with health promotion and prevention of illness and disease. Nursing education emphasizes this content even more today. Nurses have even entered the primary care area with the increased usage of APRNs, who may serve as primary care providers.
- Quality and outcomes are not foreign to nursing, but nurses are not experts in these areas, though they should be (Institute of Medicine, 2004b, 2011). Nurses, like other healthcare professionals, have yet to fully implement effective programs to improve quality and reach outcomes. Much must be learned about these critical processes. Nurses could play an important role in this development. Healthcare professionals need to reexamine how they assess quality of care and develop and implement interventions to accomplish this. (See Chapters 17 and 18.)
- Access to care has also been a concern of nursing, but again nursing has not been any more successful in this area than any other healthcare profession. Nurses have the opportunity to make major contributions when access to care is discussed in planning meetings in the acute care setting, and access issues are part of an important concern in public/community health. Nurses must participate actively in this planning, or they will be left out of the process.
- Nurses have been comfortable working in differentiated structures that are organized around specific diagnostic clusters (e.g., medicine, critical care, obstetrics, and support services such as nutritional or environmental services). More HCOs are recognizing that this might not be the most effective way to structure the work. Greater emphasis is now placed on coordination of work across parts of the HCO and the community. To survive the changes in the future and develop new roles, nurses need to be active participants in the development of new delivery systems and manage and practice in them.

The following are some issues that are particularly affected by the macrolevel of healthcare financial issues:

- Cost of care is more important than charges for care, which typically do not cover all the costs of care. This factor drives all decisions that are made, whether they are patient related or not. Operating costs have to be covered.
- Understanding healthcare reimbursement is critical, and not just by nurse leaders/managers, but by all nurses.

- The continuum of care has become more important and will continue to be so. What are its components? Are they easily accessible? What are the roles of nurses in helping the patient through the continuum and the roles of nurses within each component? Getting the appropriate care in the best setting from the most appropriate provider reduces costs.
- There is an increased emphasis on patient education and health promotion and prevention, which are aimed at improving quality but also decreasing costs.
- Caregivers (families, significant others) have assumed major roles in the healthcare delivery system, supporting and caring for family members. Are they prepared for this? Are they available for this? How does their usage affect healthcare costs?
- Provider performance evaluation is now the norm, even if it does cause stress. This includes performance data about hospitals, clinics, home care, long-term care, physicians, APRNs, and so on. Development of computer technology has helped move this along. These data are used to make reimbursement decisions. It is important to avoid focusing on blame and negative consequences.
- The hospital discharge process has become more important, for example, in reducing readmissions within 30 days of discharge. This affects the entire continuum of care, yet staff must often now care for sicker patients with less staff and time.
- Outcomes are constantly monitored. Paying for something that does not reach expected outcomes is costly. There can be negative consequences to this monitoring as noted in the Veteran's Administration example described in Chapter 2.
- Quality improvement and costs are interconnected in all types of healthcare settings.

HEALTHCARE FINANCIAL ISSUES: MICROLEVEL

The microlevel focuses on an individual HCO's financial issues. New nurses are typically not responsible for budgeting; however, a general understanding of the process as well as other related issues is important as they affect nurses and how they practice. More HCOs are asking for staff input during the budget process. For example, the nurse manager asks unit staff for input about needs and also about cost containment strategies.

Prior to entering a more detailed discussion, it is helpful to review that some organizations are classified as for profit and others as not for profit. It is not uncommon for staff to have only negative views of for-profit organizations. What do these two classifications really mean? In simplest terms, a for-profit organization must return some of its profits to its stockholders or owners. A not-for-profit organization does not have stockholders or owners who require returned profit; however, in this case the profit is reinvested in the organization. All organizations need to make a profit to stay in the "black" because, if this does not occur, debt will increase, the organization will be in the "red," and the organization over the long term will fail financially. This organization will be forced to reduce costs, which will impact care delivery and nurses. The key difference between these two types of organizations is how the profit is used. Even for-profit organizations need to use some of their profit on their organization; therefore, not all of it goes to stockholders or owners.

A second critical area in microlevel financing is the idea that budgeting is a very real description of the financial status of the organization. It is not something that is just described on paper. When the budget is prepared, it is just an educated guess; however, it needs to be based on a review of historical budget data and projected data and needs. This process requires data that are as accurate as they can be. Change is a frequent theme in this text, and this is certainly true of budgets. Changes in many factors that affect healthcare delivery can mean the provider or HCO must make budget adjustments. Examples of these factors are change in number of patients admitted, length-of-stay changes, decreasing amount of reimbursement, increased staffing costs or costs of staff benefits, change in the cost of supplies, need to renovate or expand space, expansion of computerized documentation, and need to repair or purchase new medical equipment.

The third critical issue is microlevel financial issues have a direct impact on the delivery of health care and on nursing. These finances directly affect decisions about staffing, supplies and equipment, renovation of facilities, types of services provided, quality of services, accessibility of services, employee education and training, and much more. So even if staff nurses do not prepare the budget, it directly affects them.

This section of the chapter discusses an overall review of the financial component of hospital/other types of HCOs, key financial management terminology, the budgeting process, productivity, and cost containment. Staff nurses typically are not directly involved in these functions, but nurses in management positions need to become more involved in budgeting and need to know much more about microlevel financial healthcare issues.

Hospitals and Other Types of Healthcare Organizations: Financial Activities

Each HCO has its own financial system; however, there are some common elements of these systems that are helpful for nurses to understand. They affect nursing staff and nursing care. The governing body of the organization such as the board of directors is ultimately responsible for the financial activities and stability of the organization. The board oversees the organization's budgetary process and approves the final budget.

- The budget is prepared and submitted by the organization's chief executive officer (CEO).
- The CEO may delegate the day-to-day financial operations to other staff such as the chief operating officer (COO) and the chief financial officer (CFO) or comptroller.
- The chief nurse executive (CNE), along with assistance from the CFO, is typically responsible for the nursing budget that is submitted to the COO then to the CEO.
- The key high-level management staff should collaborate in the development of the overall HCO budget. Department heads, which should include directors of nursing for services and nurse managers, participate by developing budgets for their services and units, and these budgets are passed up the line to become part of the overall budget.

This does not mean that all of these budgets are accepted as originally submitted. As the budgets go up the line, compromises need to be made; not all applicants will get what they request. The final product or organization budget is a compilation of all of these budget requests.

This process takes time. Data from past budgets are used in developing subsequent budgets. Staff may participate at the unit or service level as managers request staff input about budgetary needs for the coming year. Throughout the budget process, consideration should be given to the organization's vision; mission; goals; marketing plan; and in the case of departments or services, their visions, missions, and goals as well. For example, if an expansion of services is planned, then this would need to be included in the budget planning with consideration given to additional staffing, equipment and supplies, physical plant changes, marketing expenses, staff training, the impact expansion has on other services, and so on. If a unit needs to recruit more staff, this impacts the budget, adding recruitment and orientation costs. If there are new positions, then related pay and benefits are added. The budget process is really the same in all types of HCOs, but of course, the smaller and less complex organizations may not have as many levels in the process.

Key Financial Management Terminology

Financial management is highly complex and a specialty area in healthcare administration. The major goal is to obtain the funds necessary to meet the organization's goals. Nurses are not expected to be experts; however, they will hear some financial/budgetary terms and need to know what they are in order to participate as much as possible in this process. The organization needs accurate data to do the following: (a) guide operations of the organization, (b) make effective decisions about financial issues, and (c) monitor and control operations by using variance analysis.

The following are common budget terms:

- *Accounts receivable.* An amount owed to the HCO by a patient or customer for services. If these accounts are not paid in a timely manner, this does have an effect on the HCO's ability to pay its own bills.
- *Actual figures.* The exact amount of revenue and expenses the HCO experiences; these figures are not the amounts that were estimated or proposed for the budget, but rather the real numbers.
- *Asset.* An item owned by the HCO with value that can be identified objectively (for example, the value of equipment used in the operating room over a long period of time).

- *Bad debt.* An amount due to the HCO that will never be collected (for example, a patient who has no coverage for care and cannot pay the bill). Too much bad debt is a serious problem for an organization.
- *Balance sheet.* A financial statement identifying the HCO's assets and liabilities at a specific time. Assets are always found on the left of the balance sheet and liabilities on the right.
- *Budgeted figures.* The projected numbers the HCO expects in revenues and expenses that are identified in the budget.
- *Cost center.* The smallest functional unit that can be identified for cost control and accountability (for example, the cardiac care unit, the emergency department, pharmacy, etc.).
- *Cost per unit of service or unit cost.* The cost to produce a single unit of service (for example, provide a specific laboratory test, administer medications, prepare a meal, clean a room after discharge, or make a home visit).
- *Depreciation.* Allocation of cost of large capital assets by recognizing a portion of the cost for each year of its estimated life. If the HCO purchases equipment for the laboratory, it would estimate how long these machines typically last then determine how much of the cost to allocate to the budget each year. For example, if the equipment costs $10,000, and the equipment is expected to last for five years, the organization would allocate a certain amount of the $10,000 for each year. At the end of the five years, the equipment would not be an asset with value.
- *Direct costs.* Costs that are incurred in giving direct care, which is not simple to allocate or determine as it depends on the type of service the cost is covering. For example, direct cost for a nurse working in a neonatal unit would be costs of the nurse's time to provide an infant care or the supplies required to provide that care. Allocating supply costs is much easier than allocating staff time.
- *Expenditure.* A liability that is incurred from the acquisition of an asset (e.g., buying new equipment for the laboratory).
- *Expense.* A decrease in the HCO's equity due to operations (e.g., funds to purchase medical supplies, staff hours). Important expenses include supplies, which is an area where nurses can assist in controlling costs.
- *Fiscal year.* The identified time period for each budget cycle (July to July or January to January), which is then subdivided in a variety of ways—for example, biweekly, monthly, quarterly, semiannually.
- *Fixed costs.* The costs that do not increase or decrease as a result of changes in volume or patient days (for example, specific salary levels, minimum staffing required, electricity, depreciation, telephone, or computer).
- *Income statement.* A statement of revenues and expenses for a specific time period (see Box 5-5).
- *Indirect costs.* Costs that are indirectly related to patient care; for example, supplies needed to provide care would be direct costs while the unit secretary's time to order supplies would be indirect. However, despite the distinction noted in this definition and the definition of direct costs, the salaries for all involved in the examples (nurses, supervisor, and unit secretary) would be listed under direct costs in the budget.
- *Indirect overhead.* Costs that cannot be associated with a specific patient's care provided or support services. These costs are usually allocated to a department (for example, time spent completing unit data logs or ordering supplies).
- *Liabilities.* Money an organization owes to someone.
- *Overhead.* Any cost of doing business that is not a direct cost of service and cannot easily be allocated to individual patients and even to individual units or services (e.g., utility costs).
- *PD.* Patient day.
- *Per diem reimbursement.* Payment for a day of care regardless of the specific services provided each day.
- *Prospective reimbursement.* Payment schedules established prior to providing services.
- *Retrospective reimbursement.* Payment for services after they are provided (e.g., DRGs).
- *Total costs.* The combination of fixed and variable costs.
- *Unit of services.* The specific unit of healthcare service that a department or unit provides to its consumers (e.g., patient day, specific treatment or procedures, meals served, patient visits to a clinic, number of home visits).

- *Variable costs.* Costs that fluctuate with census or patient days, treatments, clinic visits, home visits, and so on. Costs that might be affected are number of meals, staffing levels, linen requirements, supplies, and so on.
- *Variance report.* A report describing the difference between the budgeted and actual figures.
- *Wage index.* The factor that is used to compare wages paid to specific categories of personnel in HCOs, such as hospitals, across the country (Finkler, Kovner, & Jones, 2012).

The Budgeting Process: An Overview

The budgetary process is long and cyclic. As soon as it is complete for the year, it begins again. Effective and realistic budgets require reliable data. What is a **budget**? It is a statement, usually annual, that describes the expected revenues or money that will be made by the HCO and expected expenses that will be required to provide the services. The budget should identify financial resources, who will use them, when, and the purpose of their use. Box 5-6 provides a sample departmental budget form.

Budgets must be live documents as they will need to be adjusted. Effective budgets are consistent with critical organizational qualifiers such as the vision, mission, goals, short-term and long-term strategic plans, and marketing plan. Budgets are composed of three parts:

1. **Salary and wage budget**, which is the largest part and includes salaries and wages, earned benefits (sick time, vacation time, health benefits, and so on), premium or overtime pay, and merit raises
2. **Operational budget**, which includes the estimate of the volume and mix of activities and services, and the resources required to provide them
3. **Capital budget**, which is the estimate of purchases of major capital items such as equipment, building, new furniture; it typically sets a cost amount to identify which items are to be included

BOX 5-5	SAMPLE INCOME STATEMENT FORM

Income Statement for Year Ended June 30, 2015

Patient Service Revenues	$_____
Less Allowances and Uncollectables	$_____
Net Patient Services Revenues	$_____
Other Operating Revenues	$_____
Total Operating Revenues	$_____
Less Operating Expenses:	$_____
Nursing Services	$_____
Other Professional Services	$_____
General Services	$_____
Administrative Services	$_____
Provision for Depreciation	$_____
Total Operating Expenses	$_____
Loss/Gain from Operations	$_____
Nonoperating Revenues	$_____
Unrestricted Gifts and Bequests	$_____
Unrestricted Income from Endowment Fund	$_____
Income and Gains from Board-Designated Assets	$_____
Total Nonoperating Revenues	$_____
Income for the Year	$_____

BOX 5-6	DEPARTMENT BUDGET

Department/Unit:_____ Fiscal Year:_____

Unit of Service/Patient Days	_____	Revenue	_____
Unit of Service/_____*	_____	Revenue	_____
Unit of Service/_____*	_____	Revenue	_____
		Total Revenue	_____

Expenses

Productive Salaries	_____
Nonproductive Salaries	_____
TOTAL SALARIES	_____
Employee Benefits	_____
Medical Supplies	_____
Dietary	_____
Minor Equipment	_____
Equipment Rental	_____
Audiovisual Supplies	_____
Recreational Supplies	_____
Copying	_____
Printing	_____
Books/Literature Staff	_____
Books/Literature Patients	_____
Maintenance	_____
Housekeeping	_____
Linens	_____
Total Expenses	_____
Profit	_____

*Unit of service (UOS) may include more than patient days and should be identified in option categories such as UOS/procedure, group session, patient visit.

Comments:

Nurse Manager Signature:_____ Date:_____

Management is responsible for three major budget functions:

1. Planning the budget, which is ongoing.
2. Management of ongoing activities and services in relationship to the budgeted items.
3. Control of spending, which requires careful identification of variances when the budget is not met and analysis of reasons for these variances. There has to be frequent review of the proposed budget and the actual budget. If there is a variance or difference between what was proposed in the budget and what was actually spent or money received, then this needs to be analyzed. For example, if the proposed annual budget allocated an amount for staff recruitment and the hospital finds that more staff than was expected have resigned, the hospital will need more funds for additional recruitment expenses. This may affect other aspects of the HCO if there is a need to cut other expenses to cover these other important needs. Patterns are then analyzed, and the reports provide the following:

- Describe the financial and statistical expression of the plans for the HCO.
- Describe how resources (staff, equipment, space, finances) are allocated.
- Provide a basis for measurement and evaluation of actual performance of the HCO's plan.
- Provide periodic reports that assist in management decision making.
- Create cost awareness throughout the HCO.
- Assist management in determining rates or prices.

If there are variances in the budget, then the manager should consider the following questions:

1. Why did the variance occur?
2. What effect does the variance have?
3. What can be done to prevent its reoccurrence?
4. What needs to be done to make the best of the situation?

Budgets are more than just the initial financial data described; otherwise, these goals could not be met. As the budget is applied over the year, performance data are monitored and analyzed. It is this performance that organizations use to guide budgetary decisions throughout the year. Is the organization making as much money (revenues) as it thought it would? If not, what impact does this have on expenses? If more money is made than was predicted in the budget, should the organization use that money or invest it? If expenses are higher than predicted in the budget, what steps need to be taken to ensure cost containment and funds to pay expenses? All of these questions have an impact on nurses and nursing care.

There are several benefits to developing and implementing a budget. First, of course, budgets force the organization to plan. Just as a family that has a certain income should plan how money will be spent, saved, and invested, an organization has these responsibilities. This encourages many levels of staff to participate in unit/service/department and overall planning. Cost containment is another major advantage of budgeting—forcing staff to consider how they use resources (allocation of services) and to consider how money needs to be conserved. The budgetary process provides opportunity for self-analysis, motivating staff, and the organization to improve performance.

There are also challenges to budgeting. There can be disagreement and competition among management staff about the budget, and consensus can be difficult to obtain. All levels of staff need to understand the process and its implications, which require education or training. Many organizations do not provide this to their staff. Budgeting does require flexibility as needs change, and sometimes making these changes is difficult. Another difficulty is some managers may focus too much on the budget without consideration of other organizational issues found in the vision, mission, goals, and strategic plans. Clearly, overbudgeting can lead to major problems, as can ignoring downturns and not adjusting the budget accordingly. The latter issues can lead to problems related to the survival for the organization as it might slip into "the red" and not be able to meet its financial demands.

As budgets are developed, the two main components of the budget are revenues and expenses. Revenues are projected based on past experiences and plans for the probable future. Types of data that are important to consider are number of patient days, procedures, treatments,

CASE STUDY

Staff Role in Budget Development

The nurse managers in a hospital have been asked to prepare budgets for their units. At the same time, the managers are told that the hospital's budget has serious problems with being over budget last year. This is the first year that nurse managers have been asked to participate in the budget development. At the nurse manager meeting, several nurse managers were angry now that the hospital had serious problems they were turning to the nurse managers. Maybe if they had been asked to participate in the budget process before there were problems, they might have been able to provide helpful strategies. Many nurse managers also felt they lacked the necessary skills to do the task. The nurse executive listened to their concerns at the meeting. After the meeting, the nurse manager from a medical unit returned to his unit and met with team leaders to ask their advice about the budget and the deficit.

Questions:

1. How should the nurse executive respond to the nurse managers' concern about their lack of skills to cope with this request?
2. How might macrolevel financial issues affect microlevel financial issues?
3. What might be the roles of staff nurses, team leaders, nurse managers, and nurse executives in budget development?
4. How might cost containment be used to address the deficit of the medical unit? Consider specific interventions or strategies that might be used.
5. How might this be viewed as an opportunity for nursing administration?

length of stay, number of clinic visits, number of home visits, types of patients, and so on. If the organization plans on adding new services, then data will have to be based on more speculation, considering what might be. Data about other HCOs might be used to project these revenues (for example, adding a new home care service and how this service might compete with other home care agencies). Strategic plans are also reviewed to identify possible revenues and expenses that might be affected by the plan. Probable expenses are carefully analyzed, again using past data. Examples of typical expense categories are as follows:

- Salary and wages
- Benefits
- Medical and other supplies
- Depreciation
- Administration costs
- Housekeeping
- Dietary
- Professional fees and other fees the HCO may be required to pay
- Capital equipment (medical and other)
- Furniture and furnishings
- Maintenance
- Pharmacy
- Orientation and education
- Printing
- Information technology
- Utilities
- Landscaping
- Legal fees
- Parking and security

Some of the expenses are fixed as they do not change due to activity and service levels, and some are variable. For example, costs for orientation increase when the numbers of new staff increase, number of deliveries increases costs for the obstetric department, and number of snow-storms increases the need for parking lot snow removal.

Productivity

Productivity must be considered during the budgetary process and also when changes occur in the healthcare arena. **Productivity** is the ratio of output (products and services) to input (resources consumed). The goal is to increase productivity or at the minimum not to decrease it. To do this, factors that affect both input and output need to be evaluated. Examples of factors affecting input are staff characteristics (mix, qualifications, experience, stability, length of shift, mandatory overtime), patients (number, ages, acuity, diagnoses, treatments), and organization (unit configuration, size, staffing, leadership and management, equipment, services, financial status). Examples of factors affecting output are number of emergency visits, deliveries, admissions, clinic visits, meals served, radiological procedures, total number of patient days, surgical procedures, and acuity.

How might productivity be assessed? Some examples are application of a patient acuity classification system, cost accounting, budget reports, position control, quality improvement monitoring, and **full-time equivalent (FTE)** analysis. An FTE is a full-time position that is equated to 40 hours of work per week, 80 hours per pay period, or 2,080 hours per year. It is not a person but a unit of time or time actually worked. Nonproductive time is included in the paid hours; productive time is actual time worked. The principal measure of input is worked hours, worked FTEs, or paid hours. However, it is also important to measure both "worked hours" productivity and paid hours productivity, which includes benefit allowances for sick time, vacation, and holidays.

Two critical productivity issues are efficiency and effectiveness. Efficiency is doing things right, while effectiveness is doing the right things. Both of these issues need to be assessed when productivity is analyzed. Cost containment and quality are related to productivity. Analyzing outcome variances is part of the process. Productivity is described in Box 5-7.

BOX 5-7	PRODUCTIVITY

Productivity = output ÷ by input

EXAMPLE:

Input: 24 hours of nursing care (one patient day). Inputs are predetermined budgeted nursing care hours per patient day based on the patient's acuity and required patient care activities.

Outputs: the outcomes; achieved patient goals.

Cost Containment

Cost containment must be part of the budgetary process, or the HCO may not survive. The problem with cost containment is it typically is viewed from a negative perspective, and this limits efforts to view it as a method to improve efficiency with limited negative impact. Quality and cost containment should be and are definitely connected. When decisions are made to control costs, there needs to be a balance. How does the cost of care affect quality? If costs are reduced, will quality of care be affected and in what way? These are critical questions that must be asked, and nurses who are involved in budgetary decisions should speak up and ask them. During this process, ethical issues may be brought up when difficult decisions are made. The typical cost-containment methods are as follows:

- Decrease overtime expenses.
- Decrease sick time expenses.
- Adjust staffing.
- Control empty positions/limiting filling positions.
- Prevent costly expenses for repair of equipment.
- Use supplies wisely.
- Decrease the inventory of supplies that are infrequently used or not used at all.
- Maintain productivity standards.
- Prevent employee accidents.
- Use methods to improve staffing decisions.

There often is a fear in organizations that only financial staff make cost-containment decisions, and this is a legitimate concern. These decisions should be made jointly with other management staff who appreciate the clinical implications of these decisions. There is no doubt

APPLYING EVIDENCE-BASED PRACTICE

Evidence for Effective Leadership and Practice

CITATION: Clarke, S. P., Raphael, C., & Disch, J. (2008). Challenges and directions for nursing in the pay-for-performance movement. *Policy, Politics, & Nursing Practice, 9*(2), 127–134. Retrieved from http://www.ncbi.nlm.nih.gov/pmc/articles/PMC2697611/?tool=pubmed

OVERVIEW: This article examines a current change in health care that focuses on the issue of pay-for-performance (P4P). This issue requires more input from nurse leaders as it will continue to expand, influencing nursing, healthcare budgets, and continuous quality improvement.

APPLICATION: This is a current issue in healthcare finances that has been important to nonnursing providers, but it should also have relevance to nurses. With the expansion of pay-for-performance,

multiple providers and healthcare organizations may experience its impact. This is a health policy and reimbursement issue but also includes performance and thus impacts quality care. Performance includes an evaluation of outcomes.

Questions:

1. What does pay-for-performance mean? How would it apply to nurses?
2. Why might it be important for nurses to pay more attention to P4P—benefits and risks for nursing?
3. What are the four ways that healthcare providers can prepare for P4P as suggested by this article? How do these strategies relate to nursing leadership and management?

today that budget cuts do occur, and many are necessary. Staff need to understand the reason for the cuts before the rumor mill about the cuts damages staff morale. Nursing management should seek out facts to respond to budget cuts and to plan accordingly. If nursing management approaches all budget cuts with a negative attitude, assuming that all cuts are nonproductive, nursing management will not be able to work collaboratively with the HCO's other management staff. Cost-containment efforts require an honest appraisal of the needs and approaches to resolve them. Nurse leaders need to be team players and willing to step back and objectively assess a problem. This does not mean that they do not advocate for nursing and for patient care delivery, but rather they do so in a professional manner. They need to discuss the problems and the cuts openly with other staff, providing explanations and support as needed. Staff members, too, need to be brought into the process as they may have some excellent ideas about how problems may be resolved. In the end, budget cuts need to be made carefully with consideration given to short-term and long-term effects. Nurse leaders must assume an active role in all phases of the process.

APPLYING LEADERSHIP AND MANAGEMENT

My Hospital Unit: An Evolving Case Experience

You have been told at the weekly nurse manager meeting that all units need to develop a cost-containment plan. You need to develop two cost-containment strategies for your unit. You begin by reviewing the content in this chapter. You might do some additional literature research on cost containment. Then you develop two strategies and describe them in a memo to the CNO. The memo should not be any longer than three double-spaced pages and should apply specifically to your unit. You need to then develop an implementation plan considering how you will inform and involve the staff. How will you know that your strategies have been effective? Remember that other decisions you may have made about your unit may have an impact on this activity.

BSN and *Master's Essentials:* Application to Content

BSN Essentials (American Association of Colleges of Nursing, 2008) as Applied to this Chapter:

  II. Basic Organizational and Systems Leadership for Quality Care and Patient Safety
  V. Healthcare Policy, Finance, and Regulatory Environments

Master's Essentials **(American Association of Colleges of Nursing, 2011) as Applied to this Chapter:**

  II. Organizational and Systems Leadership

Applying AONE Competencies

Identify which of the AONE competencies found in Appendix A apply to the content of this chapter.

Engaging in the Content: Critical Thinking and Clinical Reasoning and Judgment

Discussion Questions

1. How did managed care impact healthcare reimbursement and care delivery?
2. Compare and contrast the macrolevel and microlevel perspectives of healthcare financing. (Online Application Option)
3. Why should staff nurses, nurse team leaders, nurse managers, and executive nurse leaders participate in the HCO's financial planning? Describe ways in which each should participate. (Online Application Option)
4. What is the difference between the micro and macro levels of healthcare economics? (Online Application Option)
5. Describe the differences between Medicare and Medicaid.

Application Exercises

1. Ask a nurse manager to see a unit budget. Review the budget and identify the items in the budget. Ask the nurse manager about the budgetary process and his or her role.
2. Visit the Centers for Medicare & Medicaid Services (CMS) website. Review content on reimbursement, and consider how it might apply to a Medicare or to a Medicaid patient.
3. Discuss the provisions related to healthcare reimbursement in the Affordable Care Act, impact on the current reimbursement system, and your view of the provisions. Discuss in teams and present your conclusions to the class.
4. Discuss the current status of the uninsured and underinsured. Research the Internet government sources for current information. Include information on the impact of the Affordable Care Act. What are the current challenges? (Online Application Option)
5. Why is it important for nurses (management and direct provider levels) to be knowledgeable about healthcare economics and participate in financial decisions? Discuss in teams then present to the class. (Online Application Option)

References

American Association of Colleges of Nursing. (2008). *The essentials of baccalaureate education for professional nursing practice.* Washington, DC: Author.

American Association of Colleges of Nursing. (2011). *The essentials of master's education in nursing.* Washington, DC: Author.

American Association of Retired Persons. (2014). The healthcare law: More choices, more protections. Retrieved from http://healthlawanswers.aarp.org/en/facts/health-care-law-more-choices-more-protections

American Health Insurance Plans. (2014). Rising health care costs. Retrieved from http://www.ahip.org/Issues/Rising-Health-Care-Costs.aspx

Centers for Medicare & Medicaid Services. (2010). National health expenditure projections 2009–2019. Retrieved from https://www.cms.gov/Research-Statistics-Data-and-Systems/Statistics-Trends-and-Reports/NationalHealthExpendData/downloads/proj2009.pdf

Centers for Medicare & Medicaid Services. (2014a). Benefits. Retrieved from http://www.medicaid.gov/affordablecareact/provisions/benefits.html

Centers for Medicare & Medicaid Services. (2014b). About: About CHIP and Children's Medicaid. Retrieved from http://chipmedicaid.org/en/About

Centers for Medicare & Medicaid Services. (2014c). Coordination with affordable insurance exchanges. Retrieved from http://www.medicaid.gov/affordablecareact/provisions/coordination-with-affordable-insurance-exchanges.html

Centers for Medicare & Medicaid Services. (2014d). Eligibility (Medicaid). Retrieved from http://www.medicaid.gov/medicaid-chip-program-information/by-topics/eligibility/eligibility.html

Centers for Medicare & Medicaid Services. (2014e). Hospital-acquired conditions. Retrieved from http://www.cms.gov/Medicare/Medicare-Fee-for-Service-Payment/HospitalAcqCond/Hospital-Acquired_Conditions.html

Centers for Medicare & Medicaid Services. (2014f). Medicare and Medicaid Programs: Part A. Retrieved from http://www.medicare.gov/your-medicare-costs/part-a-costs/part-a-costs.html

Centers for Medicare & Medicaid Services. (2014g). National health expenditures fact sheet. Retrieved from http://www.cms.gov/Research-Statistics-Data-and-Systems/Statistics-Trends-and-Reports/NationalHealthExpendData/NHE-Fact-Sheet.html

Centers for Medicare & Medicaid Services. (2014h). Readmissions reduction program. Retrieved from http://www.cms.gov/Medicare/Medicare-Fee-for-Service-Payment/AcuteInpatientPPS/Readmissions-Reduction-Program.html

Cooper, P., & Schone, B. (1997). More offers, fewer takers for employment-based health insurance: 1987–1996. *Health Affairs, 16*(6), 142–149.

Daschle, T. (2008). *Critical. What we can do about the health-care crisis.* New York, NY: St. Martin's Press.

Finkler, S., Kovner, C., & Jones, C. (2012). *Financial management for nurse managers and executives* (4th ed.). Philadelphia, PA: W. B. Saunders Company.

Health Insurance Association of America. (1998). *Managed care: Integrating the delivery and financing of healthcare, Part A.* Washington, DC: Author.

Henry J. Kaiser Family Foundation. (2014). Key facts about the uninsured population. Retrieved from http://kff.org/uninsured/fact-sheet/key-facts-about-the-uninsured-population/

Institute of Medicine. (2004a). *Insuring America's health.* Washington, DC: The National Academies Press.

Institute of Medicine. (2004b). *Keeping patients safe. Transforming the work environment of nurses.* Washington, DC: The National Academies Press.

Institute of Medicine. (2011). *The future of nursing: Leading change, advancing health.* Washington, DC: The National Academies Press.

Institute of Medicine. (2012). *Best care at lower cost: The path to continuously learning healthcare in America.* Washington, DC: National Academies Press.

National League for Nursing. (1978). *Financial management of department of nursing services.* New York, NY: Author.

ObamaCare Facts. (2015). ObamaCare enrollment numbers. Retrieved from http://obamacarefacts.com/sign-ups/obamacare-enrollment-numbers/

Office of the President. (2013). *Trends in healthcare cost growth and the Affordable Care Act.* Washington, DC: Author.

U.S. Department of Health and Human Services. (2004). The Personal Responsibility and Work Opportunity Reconciliation Act of 1996. Retrieved from http://aspe.hhs.gov/hsp/abbrev/prwora96.htm

6 Acute Care Organizations: An Example of a Healthcare Organization

🔵 LEARNING OUTCOMES

Before you begin, take a moment to familiarize yourself with the learning outcomes for this chapter.

> Critique the development of U.S. hospitals and the role they play in the healthcare delivery system.
> Differentiate the key methods for classifying hospitals.
> Compare the key departments found in most hospitals.
> Apply the committee process.
> Analyze major changes that are occurring in hospitals and their impact on nursing.
> Discuss the implications of the Nurse Manager Engagement Project to healthcare delivery, nurse managers, and staff nurses in acute care.

WHAT'S AHEAD

There is greater emphasis on community-focused services today; however, since most new graduates begin their careers in hospitals, this is the appropriate place to begin to understand healthcare delivery settings. Hospital management is more complex than most businesses. As was discussed in Chapter 4, the hospital meets the criteria for an organization. It has a purpose and goals, people who work for it, and a systematic structure. Many hospitals continue to maintain a bureaucratic organization even if this is not the most effective type. Other hospitals, however, are undergoing restructuring and reengineering and thus changing into different types of organizations.

This text recognizes the critical need for nurses to understand some important elements related to hospital structure and functions to enable them to be more effective as care providers within this healthcare setting and to be effective leaders and managers. The first part of the chapter focuses on the typical hospital organization, and the second part discusses the Nurse Manager Engagement Project and its implications.

KEY TERMS

- continuum of care
- credentialing
- faith-based hospital
- for-profit (investor-owned or proprietary) healthcare organization
- government hospitals
- hospital
- hospital system
- length of stay (LOS)
- network
- not-for-profit healthcare organization
- privileging

DEVELOPMENT OF U.S. HOSPITALS

The acute care hospital has long been the major focus in the U.S. healthcare delivery system. What is a **hospital**? This might sound like a strange question; however, the definition contains important descriptive criteria. It is an organization whose primary purpose is to deliver patient care, both diagnostic and therapeutic, for certain medical conditions. These medical conditions may be focused on general acute care or highly specialized care, such as those found in psychiatric or rehabilitation hospitals. There is an organized medical staff, and continuous nursing services are provided under the supervision of registered nurses, which is a critical component of 24-hour care. All hospitals must follow certain laws and regulations: federal, state, and local. Accreditation, which is discussed in Chapter 18, is also a criterion used to describe a hospital. The following are various perspectives used to describe a hospital:

- Organization with purpose
- Medical and nursing care and professionals who must meet their own professional requirements and standards
- Standards established by laws, regulations, and accreditation
- A complex organization
- Importance of consumer role (See Chapter 11.)

The goals of the healthcare system include providing services that focus on (a) health promotion and illness prevention, (b) diagnosis and treatment, and (c) rehabilitation and health restoration and, if required, support during the dying process. To accomplish these goals, the system is organized by the complexity of the services required to meet each of the goals: primary, secondary, and tertiary care. Some hospitals focus on only one of these goals (for example, a rehabilitative hospital or a hospice focuses primarily on the third goal; however, others might meet all three). Hospital care is primarily secondary care, although other services related to primary care (such as clinic services and wellness programs) are also services hospitals might offer. Tertiary care may also be found in a hospital organization (for example, when a hospital offers a hospital-based hospice program or a rehabilitation unit). The U.S. healthcare system is a multiprovider system, as is illustrated by the number of different providers identified in Box 6-1. Hospitals can be described in many different ways and are constantly changing. A **hospital system** refers to a corporation that owns or manages health facilities, often using vertical integration, providing multiple services, not just acute care inpatient services. A **network** differs from a system in that it is a number of healthcare facilities that agree to deliver specific services, although each facility remains an independent organization.

As hospital organizations have changed, more mergers are occurring. A merger occurs when two or more organizations come together to form one organization. This is a challenge for

BOX 6-1	U.S. MULTIPROVIDER HEALTHCARE DELIVERY SYSTEM

- Acute care hospitals
- Specialty hospitals
- Physician offices: primary care and specialty
- Advanced practice nurses and nurse-midwives: practices
- Clinics: hospital and community
- Dental offices/clinics
- Urgent care centers
- Retail clinics
- Nurse-managed health clinics
- Accountable care organizations
- Medical/health homes
- Ambulatory care centers (e.g., one-day surgery centers, diagnostic centers)
- Industrial clinics as part of occupational health

- Extended care facilities, including skilled nursing (intermediate care) and extended care (long-term care)
- Retirement and assisted-living centers
- Rehabilitation centers
- Home health agencies
- Hospice services
- Psychiatric services and community mental health centers
- Substance abuse treatment centers (inpatient and outpatient)
- School health clinics
- Public health includes government agencies—federal, state, and local—funded primarily by taxes and administered by elected or appointed officials.

all of the organizations and their staff. Organizations have cultures and when a merger is created, the various organizational cultures merge to form one organization. Otherwise, the organizations and their staff continue to view themselves as separate organizations rather than one organization. (See Chapter 10 for more information on organization culture.) The community will also need to change its view of the healthcare organizations (HCOs), recognizing that individual organizations no longer exist and the merged organization is one organization. None of this is easy to accomplish, and some attempts at mergers have not been successful. Barriers to success are poor planning, lack of collaboration, territoriality, ineffective communication systems, lack of organization-wide leadership, and loss of control. All of this has a major impact on the organizations' nurses. In this situation, much work needs to be done to develop one organization. How this is accomplished and how much independence each organization in the merger may have is highly variable.

Acute Care Organization and Governance

Levels of management in acute care include top management, middle management, and first-line management. Every hospital has a board of trustees or board of directors, which acts as the governing body. This board is responsible for developing the organization's mission and goals, as well as setting the overall hospital policies. The board ensures that the hospital provides the services that it has designated. Typically these boards are made up of community and business leaders. Top management includes the chief executive officer (CEO) of the hospital, who reports to the board and is hired by the board, and other key management staff. The chief nurse executive (CNE), who may be called chief nursing officer (CNO), vice president of patient services, or the older title of director of nursing (DON). In some hospitals the CNE may also report to the board but more typically to the CEO and is also part of top management. The board has great influence over the functions and management of the hospital, and thus has a great impact on nurses and nursing care. It is important for the CNE to understand the board and develop strong communication mechanisms to get information to the board to ensure that patient care is of the highest quality and that the nursing staff are supported. The chief financial officer (CFO), another member of top management, is responsible for the organization's financial management. Other high-level administrative staff may also be considered top management, but this can vary from hospital to hospital. If a hospital has a CNE, the hospital may also have a director of nursing who may be included in middle or top management. In this case the CNE may be responsible for more than just nursing. For example, the CNE may also be responsible for medical records, social services, laboratory, and so on. The inclusion of other services or departments can vary from hospital to hospital. Supervisory staff are middle management, while nurse managers are examples of first-line managers. Coordinating the work of the three levels is key to an effective organization. Many organizations are flattening their administrative or management staff levels by eliminating levels. When this occurs, there may be fewer than the three levels described here.

The medical staff organization has great power in any hospital. This is a formal organization of the medical staff that provides services in the hospital, and it is part of the total hospital organization. These physicians may be on staff (paid by the hospital) or may have admitting privileges (which allows them to admit their patients and provide care within the hospital, although they are not paid directly by the hospital). To become a member of the medical staff, physicians have to complete a formal appointment process, which is described in the medical staff organization bylaws. References and credentials are checked as well as information about involvement in malpractice suits. **Credentialing** focuses on ensuring that practitioners meet certain qualifications. This is done by obtaining, verifying, and assessing qualifications such as licensure and certification to ensure that the person is qualified based on required position criteria. **Privileging** occurs when an HCO determines the scope of practice for a provider within the HCO. This is based on the provider's education, licensure, certification, and expertise. There would be a clear statement of what the physician is allowed to do within the hospital. For example, a physician who was not a qualified surgeon would not be allowed to perform surgery. The Joint Commission requires that independent licensed practitioners go through these two processes. Both processes represent strategies to better ensure quality provider performance. Advance practice registered nurses (APRNs), certified nurse-midwives (CNMs), and certified registered nurse anesthetists

APPLYING EVIDENCE-BASED PRACTICE

Evidence for Effective Leadership and Practice

CITATION: Hassmiller, S. (2009). Envisioning a future of nurse leaders in the boardroom. *NSNA Imprint*, November–December, pp. 28–30. Retrieved from http://campaignforaction.org/sites/default/files/Hassmiller-Envision-Future-Nurse-Leaders.pdf

OVERVIEW: Healthcare organization boards are the top-level decision-making body for healthcare organizations. Nurses have slowly developed as leaders in healthcare organizations starting with positions as director of nursing and moving to positions of leadership that are responsible for more than just nursing services. Are nurse leaders ready for next step?

APPLICATION: What do nurse leaders need to do to become more active on healthcare organization boards and to be stronger

participants? If one accepts that nurses need to be leaders in continuous quality improvement, then this should have an impact on all levels of healthcare organizations.

Questions:

1. What data describe the engagement of nurse leaders on healthcare organization boards?
2. Why is it important that nurse leaders serve on healthcare organization boards?
3. What does the author mean by the "bigger issues"? Why are they important?

(CRNAs) who want to admit and/or practice in a hospital must also go through this process. If the hospital is a university medical center, the medical school faculty also serves on the medical staff. House staff, interns, residents, and fellows can be found in all types of hospitals, not just university medical centers, but they provide care as "students," not as official members of the medical staff. They are paid by the hospital. Some hospitals have nurse residents, as described in Chapter 20, and they are paid by the hospital, often at reduced salary during the residency period as compared to nursing staff.

The medical staff committees typically include medical records, credentials, utilization review, infection control, and quality improvement committees. The committees focus on these areas to ensure that the patient care goals are met. A medical director or, in some hospitals, the chief of staff, is usually elected by the medical staff to serve as their leader. In some hospitals, however, the board of directors may select the medical director. Larger hospitals may also have service leaders or department heads for departments such as surgery, medicine, pediatrics, obstetrics/gynecology, psychiatry, emergency, pathology, and radiology. It is critical that the CNE and other nurse managers develop a strong, positive relationship with the medical staff organization and its leaders. Collaborating together supports greater, positive outcomes for patients and nursing staff.

Although the formal organization is very important in a hospital, so is the informal organization. Recognizing the informal organization and using it to the fullest to reach desired outcomes is a sign of an effective leader. Nurses at all levels can benefit from a greater understanding of "what makes the organization run" other than the formal structure. There are many times when it is the informal organization that actually gets the job done, as sometimes the formal organization interferes with or puts up barriers to effective functioning. Chapters 1 and 4 discussed leadership and organization in more detail, and this content is applicable to this chapter's content.

Classification of Hospitals

A number of factors are used to classify hospitals. The following describes these factors.

PUBLIC ACCESS Public access characteristics describe hospitals as community or noncommunity hospitals, determined by the amount of access that the public has to the hospital. Community hospitals are nonfederal, short-term, or other special hospitals, which the public may use. Noncommunity hospitals are characterized as federal, long-term, hospital units of institutions (prison hospitals, college infirmaries, psychiatric hospitals), hospitals for patients with chronic diseases (for persons with developmental disabilities or alcoholism and other chemical dependency problems), or psychiatric/mental health. Public access hospitals serve as a critical safety net resource for patients who either have no health insurance, have limited insurance, or are on Medicaid coverage—providing care for patients who have nowhere else to go. This part of the health system experiences great stress with complicated patients, limited funding, and often staff shortages. There are an increased number of patients requiring services from these hospitals, yet these are the hospitals with fewer resources to do the job.

OWNERSHIP   Identifying the owner of a hospital provides critical information about the organization—particularly who makes decisions and what is done with the profits. All hospitals need to make a profit to maintain financial stability and to maintain their physical plant and equipment. The following are different perspectives of ownership.

1. The **not-for-profit healthcare organization** is funded by reimbursement, just as all hospitals are, and also with donations and endowments. It is important to remember that this type of hospital must also make a profit. The key difference with investor-owned (for-profit) hospitals is that the not-for-profit hospital invests its profits back into the hospital, and none of the profit is given to others outside the organization.

2. The **for-profit (investor-owned or proprietary) healthcare organization** is owned and administered by corporations who have shareholders or stockholders who own stock in the corporation. The hospital is responsible to the shareholders, and the shareholders expect that the organization will make a profit so they can make money on their investment. As is true of hospitals in general, this type of organization also has a board of directors or trustees that reports to the shareholders. This is the fastest growing type of ownership. Typically the corporation is a large, national corporation. Examples are Hospital Corporation of America (HCA), Tenet Healthcare Corporation, and others. These healthcare corporations own hospitals and other types of healthcare provider settings throughout the country. Each of the components of the corporation is required to meet the corporate standards and to provide profit for the corporation.

3. **Faith-based hospitals** are owned and administered by a faith-based group such as Catholic hospitals, Jewish hospitals, and so on. They maintain not-for-profit status.

4. **Government hospitals** are owned by the government. Examples of these hospitals are military hospitals; state psychiatric hospitals; hospitals owned and operated by states, counties, or cities; Veteran's Administration hospitals; National Institutes of Health Clinical Center; and the Indian Health Services (federal agency in the U.S. Department of Health and Human Services), which provides health services for American Indian and Alaskan Natives. Government hospitals maintain not-for-profit status.

NUMBER OF BEDS   The number of beds is another hospital characteristic that is considered. The number of beds can vary, but common ranges are the following: 6–24, 25–29, 50–99, 100–199 (the greatest number are in this range), 200–299, 300–399, 400–499, and 599 or more (Dunn & Becker, 2013).

LENGTH OF STAY   **Length of stay (LOS)** is also used to classify hospitals. A hospital's average length of stay is used to determine if a hospital has a short-term (average LOS of less than 30 days) or long-term stay (average LOS of more than 30 days). Length of stay has been decreasing for acute care hospitals and specialty hospitals such as psychiatric hospitals. This has been affected by pressure from insurers, technological and scientific advancements, and more effective drugs and treatments, leading to more care provided in the community.

ACCREDITATION   Accreditation is another hospital characteristic, as hospitals are classified as accredited or nonaccredited. The Joint Commission, which is discussed in more detail in Chapter 18, is the voluntary accreditation organization that accredits hospitals and other HCOs. Hospital accreditation has been in existence for more than 60 years. An HCO uses its accreditation status in marketing and communicating to consumers that it provides quality care, though accreditation does not guarantee quality. Insurers want their plan members to receive care in accredited hospitals. Schools of nursing or medicine must use accredited hospitals for student clinical experiences.

LICENSURE   In addition to accreditation, licensure and certification are also important. HCO licensure of hospitals is done by states when the hospital meets certain state standards and requirements. Hospitals must be licensed through the state to provide services, though Joint

Commission accreditation is optional. However, hospitals that are not accredited may encounter reimbursement difficulties. For a hospital to receive Medicare and Medicaid reimbursement, it must be certified or given authority to provide this care by the Centers for Medicare & Medicaid Services (CMS), and it must be accredited. Accreditation, licensure, and certification all involve meeting specified standards and some type of routine inspection. This can consume much staff time and is costly, but it is important.

TEACHING   Hospitals are also classified as teaching or nonteaching. Teaching hospitals offer residency programs for physicians. These residency programs vary in size. Hospitals may be university affiliated (with a major connection to a university) or freestanding (not connected to a university but still maintaining a residency program). The latter might be a community hospital that has medical residents on their staff.

HOSPITAL SYSTEMS   A system is a newer characteristic that is used to classify hospitals. When large health systems or national health corporations first began, the emphasis was on horizontal integration or bringing together hospitals of like characteristics—similar size and purpose. After a time, these organizations have expanded, and diversification with more vertical integration providing multiple healthcare services, not just acute care, is desirable. This change has led to multihospital systems that include more than just hospitals; they often also include other types of provider organizations. For example, a corporation might include acute care hospitals, home health agencies, long-term care facilities, hospice care, and various ambulatory care provider organizations.

Typical Departments Found in an Acute Care Hospital

Hospitals are complex organizations with many departments and services. Some departments provide direct care services to patients, and others provide support services to facilitate the provision of care.

EXAMPLES OF DEPARTMENTS   The following are examples of typical departments and services:

- *Administration.* Administration may not be an official department but rather a description of administrative staff that supports the work of the organization—it provides direction. Typically administrative staff includes the CEO, CNE, CFO, and other high-level management staff. Titles can vary from hospital to hospital.
- *Admissions.* The admissions department ensures that patients are admitted in a timely and efficient manner. Reimbursement issues are resolved related to covered medical services during the admissions process. This department is involved in a great deal of paperwork and assigns patients to rooms and services. The department may be part of billing (financial) services or may work closely with these financial services.
- *Ambulatory care/outpatient services.* This department or service provides services to persons who generally do not need the level of care associated with the more structured environment of an inpatient or a residential program. Typically these services are organized by specialty (for example, medical, pediatrics, and orthopedics clinics). Usually these services are provided Monday through Friday during daytime hours, although there is now a greater recognition that consumers/patients need access to these services in more nontraditional hours due to work, child care, and other scheduling issues. Offering ambulatory care procedures and surgery has grown rapidly, and this has reduced the number of inpatient surgical procedures.
- *Clinical laboratory.* This department or service is equipped to examine material derived from the human body to provide information for use in the diagnosis, prevention, or treatment of disease; it is also called a medical laboratory. Some hospitals may contract out or outsource these services to a company that runs the laboratory tests then provides the hospital with the results. This may be more cost effective for the hospital, although it can lead to communication problems if there are no clear policies and procedures for this service and it is less in the control of the hospital. The hospital is still responsible for the quality of the services, but some or all of the staff who deliver the services are not hospital employees. More hospitals are considering it to be more cost effective to outsource these services.

- *Clinical respiratory services.* This department or service provides goal-directed, purposeful activity to patients with disorders of the cardiopulmonary system. Such services include diagnostic testing, therapeutics, monitoring education, and rehabilitation. Nurses are part of the staff.
- *Diagnostic procedures.* This department or service provides laboratory and other invasive, diagnostic, and imaging procedures. Nurses are part of the staff (e.g., endoscopy services).
- *Dietetic services.* This department or service delivers optimal nutrition and quality food services to individuals. This is a service that may be contracted out. Nurses need to work closely with dietetic staff to ensure that patients' needs are met.
- *Finance and budget.* This department ensures that there is a financial plan (budget) and financial analysis is routinely conducted to the organization's financial solvency.
- *Housekeeping/environmental service.* This department or service ensures the environment is clean. This is a service that may be outsourced, though the services themselves are provided within the organization.
- *Infection control program.* This department or service ensures there is an organization-wide program or process, including policies and procedures for the surveillance, prevention, and control of infection. Nursing is very involved in this area.
- *Infusion therapy services.* This department or service provides therapeutic agents or nutritional products to individuals by intravenous infusion for the purpose of improving or sustaining an individual's health condition. Nursing is very involved in this area.
- *Information management.* This department or service is responsible for ensuring that information can be collected and linked and is accurate and reliable. It monitors use of data and ensures that legal regulations are met and ethical issues such as confidentiality and providing secure systems are addressed. Computer equipment is a major concern. It needs to be appropriate to the needs of the organization, as well as efficient and effective. This department must work closely with nursing and medical services as well as other clinical departments who require access to information. It also must input data into the system and often train staff in their information management responsibilities such as inputting clinical data into the electronic medical/health record (EMR/EHR).
- *Material/resource management.* This department or service ensures the hospital has the needed supplies by selecting, purchasing, storing, distributing, and obtaining reimbursement for their use when appropriate. This is another service that may be outsourced. Nurses should be involved with this process because they need the correct supplies in a timely manner.
- *Medical equipment management.* Hospitals need to assess and control the clinical and physical risks of fixed and portable equipment used for the diagnosis, treatment, monitoring, and care of individuals. Medical equipment management provides this service. Nurses use equipment daily and need to be involved in monitoring safety issues and their application to the needs of patients.
- *Medical records.* This department or service ensures that the documentation process is maintained, develops relevant policies and procedures, and provides availability of data as required. This is a department that works closely with clinical departments and medical records as well as quality improvement. Nurses are the staff members who are responsible for most of the documentation, and they need to be very active in all aspects of medical records functions. This department should be involved in staff education about medical records.
- *Nursing service/patient care.* Nursing service is the key service in any acute care hospital as patients are admitted primarily for more intensive nursing care. This is not to say that patients do not receive other services that are important, but nursing care is critical to achieving patient coordination and reaching positive patient outcomes.
- *Occupational therapy services.* The department or service that provides goal-directed, purposeful activity to evaluate, assess or treat persons whose function is impaired by physical illness or injury, emotional disorder, congenital or developmental disability, or the aging process. Nurses assist in referring patients for these services and may collaborate in the delivery of the services.
- *Pharmacy/pharmaceutical care and services.* This is the department or service that is responsible for procuring, preparing, dispensing, and distributing pharmaceutical products

and the ongoing monitoring of the individual to identify, prevent, and resolve drug-related problems. Nurses administer most of the medications and thus need to work closely with this department.

- *Physical therapy services.* This department or service provides treatment with physical agents and methods such as massage, manipulation, therapeutic exercises, cold, heat, hydrotherapy, electric stimulation, and light to assist in rehabilitating individuals and in restoring normal function after an illness or injury. Nurses assist in referring patients for these services and may collaborate in the delivery of these services.
- *Radiology.* This department or service provides diagnostic services such as x-ray, magnetic resonance imaging (MRI), and computed tomography (CT) scans. Nurses prepare patients and may provide care during radiological procedures.
- *Respiratory care services.* This department or service delivers care to provide ventilatory support and associated services for individuals. Nurses monitor these services and assist.
- *Social work services.* This department or service assists individuals and their families in addressing social, emotional, and economic stresses associated with illness or injury. Nurses need to communicate, coordinate, and collaborate with social workers.
- *Staff development/education.* This department or service provides organized education designed to enhance skills of staff members or teach new skills relevant to their responsibilities and disciplines. This department is critical for maintaining nurses' competencies. (See Chapter 20.)
- *Quality improvement (QI).* This department ensures that the hospital meets standards (local, state, federal, and accrediting bodies) to ensure quality and safety of care. Risk management (RM) is typically part of this department. RM addresses prevention, monitoring, and control of areas of potential liability exposure and safety for patients, staff, and visitors. Chapters 17 and 18 focus on these critical topics. As discussed throughout this text, nurses need to assume major roles in QI, and this is strongly supported by the Institute of Medicine (IOM) quality reports and *The Future of Nursing* report (Institute of Medicine, 2011c).

This description of hospital departments and services is not complete; however, the descriptions identify some of the key departments commonly found in many hospitals.

ORGANIZATIONS AND COMMITTEES Committees are used by organizations for planning, obtaining staff input, and getting some of the organization's work completed. Including staff from various levels and areas of the HCO in committee membership offers greater opportunity for staff participation and commitment to required changes. Committees can also be very problematic—they can take time, can be unproductive and disorganized, and can lead to ineffective management. These problems need to be addressed so committees can be productive. Nurses do not like working on committees that are unproductive, as they do not have the time. To prevent some of these problems, the organization needs to consider the following:

- Establish clear committee purpose and goals.
- Identify appropriate committee membership.
- Develop effective communication processes.
- Provide support from management/administration.
- Collaborate and share committee results.
- Recognize that some problems are not appropriate for committee decision making.
- Ensure that appropriate data are available and used as needed.
- Schedule committee meetings so members can effectively participate.

Later in this chapter, the work that the policy and procedure committee does will be described as an example of a committee and its process. This is an example of a committee that is very important to nursing care. Acute care hospitals typically have many committees. These committees may be within a department or service, professional group such as physicians or nurses, or hospital wide. Committees are usually classified as standing or ad hoc.

A standing committee is one that meets regularly for a particular purpose and submits reports to designated management staff. Examples of standing committees might be policy and procedures, quality improvement, medical records, and infection control. Hospitals may have different titles for committees, but the titles given here represent typical titles or focus areas.

Ad hoc committees are established for a specific purpose with a specific time frame in mind. Some organizations may call these task forces. How long this type of committee exists can be highly variable and depends on the need and focus. Examples of this type of committee might be a committee that is formed to address a major change in the electronic medical/health record system.

Another characteristic of committees is they can be composed of members from one profession or be interprofessional. The latter type is best for any issue that crosses disciplines, which describes the majority of issues today. Committees have designated meeting times, maintain minutes, make decisions, and develop reports. Members need to prepare for meetings and attend regularly. There are two very common errors made with committees. The first error is having too many committees and too many meetings. When this occurs, staff members get tired of committee work and feel that they are just attending meetings. The second error is ineffective meetings. Both of these errors lead to problems—staff apathy, lack of effective results, loss of work time, lack of staff interest to participate, and so on.

NURSING ROLES ON COMMITTEES   Nurses need to be very active in the committee work in an acute care hospital and in any healthcare setting in which they work. Depending on how the hospital and its committee structure are set up, nurses may be selected or may volunteer for committee membership. Becoming involved in a committee provides a nurse with a different perspective of the hospital and its needs. Nurses have much to add when planning is done and decisions are made that affect patient care. The CNE needs to assume the leadership of ensuring a nursing presence on hospital committees.

FRAMEWORK FOR EFFECTIVE CARE

Chapters 17 and 18 discuss quality improvement in more detail. Quality improvement relies on standards as well as policies and procedures; however, the following provides information on these two topics as they relate to acute care hospitals and their operation and services.

Standards

Standards are used by hospitals to provide guidelines for care provided and professional responsibilities. They can have an impact on the quality of care, patient outcomes, and the workforce environment. The American Nurses Association (ANA) and specialty nursing organizations have developed many standards. These standards may be used within a hospital and other healthcare settings such as a home health agency, city health department, behavioral health hospital, or a hospital that may use the standards to provide guidance that is specifically developed by the hospital. Many hospitals use a combination of both approaches to develop their internal standards. A hospital typically has overall nursing standards and standards for specialty areas, for example psychiatry, ambulatory care, and obstetrics. These standards, however, should be consistent with the professional standards. Other sources of information about standards are local, state, and federal laws and regulations and accreditation organizations. Evidence-based practice (EBP) also emphasizes the use of standards and the development of standards based on what research demonstrates as effective care. Chapter 16 discusses the evidence-based approach as a tool that is used in health care.

There can be confusion about the different types of standards. A standard is an "authoritative statement defined and promoted by the profession by which the quality of practice, services, or education can be evaluated" (American Nurses Association, 2010, p. 67).

- *Standards of Professional Nursing Practice:* Authoritative statements of the duties that all registered nurses, regardless of role, population, or specialty, are expected to perform competently.
- *Standards of Professional Performance:* Describe a competent level of behavior in the professional role (American Nurses Association, 2010, p. 67).

Policies and Procedures

Policies and procedures are found in every hospital and other types of HCOs. Policies and procedures provide guidelines for staff when decisions are made or procedures are done. This section describes the policy and procedure development process in some detail and is an example of how an HCO develops its processes and how a committee might work.

DEFINITIONS OF POLICY AND PROCEDURE   Many definitions for policy and procedure are found in the literature, but one consistent comment is that the terms are different from and yet related to each other. How are policies and procedures different or similar?

- A policy is a statement that communicates to staff the expectations and vision/mission of the organization, department, and management. It provides a guideline for decision making. A policy may exist without a related procedure if staff require no further specific guidance. Because policies relate to the hospital's and the department's objectives and do not change very often, policies are revised less often than procedures. Review of a nursing department's policies should provide a total picture of the particular department's beliefs concerning its management and the nursing care it provides. Identifying a policy does not negate the need for individual judgment, nor does it negate the professional nurse's accountability for decision making.

- A procedure is a definite statement describing the step-by-step actions required for a specific outcome. It provides a recipe for reaching a specific goal, and that goal is often a completed treatment that is safe for the patient and efficient in the use of staff, time, supplies, and equipment. A procedure is more detailed than a policy, and changes in routine or treatment directly affect procedures, which then require revision. Written procedures support quality care and prevent errors that might be detrimental to the patient and to the department or hospital. Procedures and policies both help to maintain consistency and continuity; however, to do so, they need to be written in concise, easy-to-understand language and contain appropriate and up-to-date information. If policies and procedures are just words on paper, they will not be used by the staff, and all the effort, time, and money spent to develop them will therefore be wasted.

INFLUENCES ON POLICIES AND PROCEDURES   In addition to the general overriding concerns of quality care, risk management, and cost containment, each department within a hospital, including the nursing department, needs to consider eight factors that have an impact on policy and procedure development. When a hospital or department decides to develop or revise its policies and procedures, these factors should not be ignored. They are also important for most major changes that nursing might consider in an HCO. If a nursing department attempts to operate in isolation from other departments in the hospital, from the hospital organization itself or from the external environment, this leads to communication problems and work performance barriers. Because change is inherent, each of these factors requires frequent review to maintain relevant policies and procedures. (See Chapter 3.)

1. *Joint Commission.* The Joint Commission provides accreditation surveys for healthcare facilities and details the requirements for accreditation in its manuals and on its website. It is the first resource for any nursing department to use in policy and procedure development; however, the detailed content of policies and procedures needs to be individualized for the specific hospital. The Joint Commission did not write standards to be used as an individual hospital's or a nursing department's policy and procedure manual nor does it provide specific policies and procedures for hospitals, but rather it provides guidelines for content and direction. (See Chapter 18 for additional information about the Joint Commission and accreditation.)

2. *Professional standards.* As noted earlier, professional standards reflect a specific professional group's views on what is acceptable professional performance. Standards influence the types and content of policies and procedures.

3. *State and federal legislation.* State legislatures determine regulations that need to be monitored carefully, such as state nurse practice acts and related rules and regulations, reimbursement requirements, safety requirements, facility requirements, and staffing level regulations. In the federal arena, the most important issue is reimbursement. It is particularly critical for hospitals reimbursed by Medicare and/or Medicaid to understand current reimbursement legislation and regulations. For example, laws affect emergency department issues, and these legal requirements would have to be incorporated in policies and procedures about emergency admissions and transfers. As noted in this chapter and others, the

ACA is having a major impact on the healthcare system, but currently the final outcomes are unknown.

4. ***Court decisions.*** Court decisions have affected many areas of patient care, particularly when related to patient rights, length of stay, commitment, discharge planning, patient and staff protection, and informed consent. The hospital's legal counsel often provides guidance in this area. For example, groups that oppose the law have brought the ACA before several courts, including the Supreme Court, in attempts to reduce the law and even to determine its legality.

5. ***Reimbursement.*** Reimbursement governs or is a strong factor in many decisions made in hospitals, including decisions related to length of stay and type of treatment as well as discharge plans. In addition, staffing cuts and increased stress to patients and families caused by concern about the cost of care and the duration of care that is covered by their personal health insurance directly affect the healthcare environment. Hospitals have policies and procedures about checking health coverage, what is covered, and other aspects related to reimbursement.

6. ***Patient rights.*** Patient rights are part of both the Joint Commission standards and the ANA standards and are greatly impacted by the Health Insurance Portability and Accountability Act (HIPAA). These rights are identified in writing and shared with patients, families, and staff. In addition, the rights need to be incorporated into policies and procedures. For example, in a procedure that describes preoperative care, patient rights are supported through the informed consent process that identifies who should obtain informed consent, when, and how it is to be documented.

7. ***The community.*** The community in which the hospital is located must not be ignored. The hospital develops both a relationship with and an image in the community. Two areas of consideration are of particular importance. The type of support available to the patient and family in the community has a major effect on the hospital's ability to discharge patients and prevent complications and readmission. Examples of issues that need to be considered are availability of home health care, medical supplies and equipment, general support such as Meals on Wheels, social services, case management, and ambulatory care clinics. With the increasing movement to care in the community, hospitals need to develop more strategies for connecting their services with the community.

8. ***Evidence-based practice.*** The nursing department that is interested in maintaining an up-to-date department and providing quality nursing care uses research results and professional literature to develop and revise its policies and procedures, ensuring that they are evidence based. EBP needs to be integrated throughout the hospital and is a critical healthcare profession competency (Institute of Medicine, 2003, 2008, 2011a, 2011b, 2011c, 2011d). It is hoped that this external influence will also encourage the nursing department to support its own research and the development of literature for publication and thereby share its experiences with other nurses. The continuing progress of nursing care depends on nursing research conducted in the clinical setting. For these reasons, policies and procedures related to nursing research should be included. Evidence-based practice, as discussed in Chapter 16, stresses the need to collect and analyze data to support decisions. This includes management decisions such as the development of policies and procedures.

Figure 6-1 describes the key issues related to policy and procedure development.

FIRST STEPS IN THE POLICY AND PROCEDURE DEVELOPMENT PROCESS   After considering the major influences on policies and procedures, the policy development process has begun. Policy and procedure development is a complex process that ultimately affects both management of the nursing department and all of the care provided. The entire process takes place in the context of the critical concerns and influences previously described. It needs to involve all of the nursing staff. It is a process that flows from the chief nurse executive to the nursing management staff and to staff at all levels in the department. Policy and procedure development is typically the responsibility of a committee designated for this purpose. The following discussion describes the objectives, definitions, and format of policies and procedures as well as the development and implementation processes. This also provides an example of how committees function in HCOs. As each nursing department is different, this information serves only as guidelines. It should be noted that typically a hospital has an organization-wide committee on policies and procedures; however, in some hospitals the nursing department also has its own policy and procedure committee and coordinates

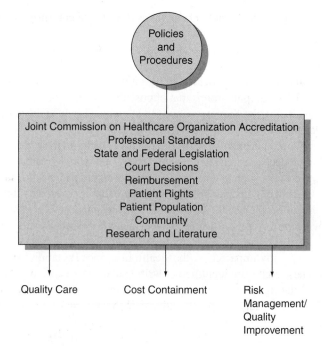

Figure 6-1 Key issues related to the development of policies and procedures

with the hospital-wide policy and procedure committee. Regardless of the type of structure, the process that is described applies to both types of committees.

The first step in developing policies and procedures for the nursing department is for nursing administration to identify the policy and procedure goals/objectives that will guide the overall policy and procedure development, implementation, and evaluation. If this is not the first step, policy and procedure development will be neither organized nor helpful to the nursing staff. Each hospital and its nursing service are different, and objectives can therefore vary. The following is a list of possible objectives that can serve as guidelines for individual nursing departments:

- To promote quality care and EBP
- To implement the hospital's and the nursing department's vision/mission and objectives
- To support effective implementation of the nursing care model
- To incorporate changes in health care into the hospital
- To increase the quality and quantity of work through consistent decision making and action
- To maintain cost containment through efficient use of staff, time, and supplies
- To meet accrediting agencies' requirements
- To maintain professional nursing standards
- To increase the quality of communication at all levels in the organization
- To promote a risk management program by preventing negligence and maintaining safety of patients, visitors, and staff
- To delineate lines of authority
- To increase interprofessional collaboration
- To assist in developing effective critical thinking and clinical reasoning and judgment
- To identify expectations for the staff and promote job security
- To promote the resolution of problems closer to the problem situation
- To act as a focus for discussion when differences occur and thus decrease the opportunity to personalize conflicts
- To decrease written communication regarding daily problems
- To decrease staff turnover due to poor communication and inadequate identification of expectations
- To assist with orientation for new, transferred, promoted, or temporary staff and for nursing faculty and students
- To assist with staff development for all nursing staff

Each policy and procedure should relate to at least one of the objectives.

POLICY AND PROCEDURE FORMATS   Formats for policies and procedures also vary greatly from hospital to hospital; however, certain elements always need to be included. These elements are the title, effective date, review date, purpose, and identification of the responsibility for final review. Boxes 6-2 and 6-3 describe examples of policy and procedure formats.

Most HCOs are now using digital forms for their policies and procedures, moving away from hard copies or manuals. This makes the information more accessible as long as staff can access a computer and get into the hospital intranet. It is also easier to update the policies and procedures, and changes can be quickly communicated to staff. As changes are made, it is easier to find related material that needs to be changed (for example, other policies and procedures) by searching for content.

POLICY AND PROCEDURE COMMITTEE   The policy and procedure committee is a very active committee and requires members who are willing to do work that at times may be tedious. As an advisory committee, the committee does not have the ultimate authority for the approval of a policy or a procedure. The final approval process and responsibility must be clearly defined. The best size

---

BOX 6-2	EXAMPLE OF A POLICY FORMAT

DEPARTMENT OF NURSING POLICY MANUAL
POLICY NUMBER

TITLE:
POLICY AREA:
EFFECTIVE DATE:
REVIEW SCHEDULE:
FINAL APPROVAL RESPONSIBILITY:
PRIMARY RESPONSIBILITY:

PURPOSE:

POLICY:

SUPPORTING EVIDENCE:

Approved by:

Date: _____   Review Dates: _____

BOX 6-3	EXAMPLE OF A PROCEDURE FORMAT

DEPARTMENT OF NURSING PROCEDURE MANUAL
PROCEDURE NUMBER

TITLE:
PROCEDURE AREA:
EFFECTIVE DATE:
REVIEW SCHEDULE:
FINAL APPROVAL RESPONSIBILITY:
WHO MAY PERFORM:
PURPOSE:

EQUIPMENT AND SUPPLIES:

ACTION:

SUPPORTING EVIDENCE:

for this committee is six to eight members with a chairperson. If the committee is too small, the members may feel burdened with work, and if it is too large, getting the members together efficiently becomes difficult. Establishing at least a two-year term of membership allows a reasonable time for the members to be productive on the committee. Since it is also important to get new ideas, committee membership should include both new and old members; therefore, there should be rotating changes in membership. This will ensure that there will be some experienced members on the committee at all times. The purpose of this committee is to develop the policies and procedures for the nursing department and to maintain a system for periodic review and revision of policies and procedures. This committee's work is never completed, and it thus requires active participation and an interest in this work from all members. With the increasing emphasis on EBP, it is important for all hospitals to ensure that current policies and procedures are evidence based.

ROLE OF NURSING ADMINISTRATION/MANAGEMENT   The CNE typically does not serve on the committee but has many responsibilities related to this committee. Examples of these responsibilities include the following:

- To clarify with hospital administration the nursing committee's relationship to the hospital policy and procedure committee and to provide written communication on this issue to the nursing committee.
- To appoint a chairperson (unless the chairperson is to be elected).
- To identify needs for policies and procedures.
- To communicate specific policy and procedure issues to the committee.
- To review and approve all new and revised policies and procedures.
- To communicate to nursing management and all nursing staff the importance of policies and procedures and encourage their input in the development process.
- To ensure that policies and procedures are implemented and evaluated.
- To review and respond to the committee's annual report.
- To provide resources to the committee such as secretarial assistance for the preparation of the policies and procedures.

Through the fulfillment of these responsibilities, the CNE communicates the importance of policies and procedures and coordinates the committee's work both within the department and with other departments, acting as a facilitator.

ROLE OF THE COMMITTEE CHAIRPERSON   The chairperson should be a nursing staff member who can organize well and work effectively with others. The committee is very busy, and consequently the chairperson should not have many responsibilities on other committees. The chairperson has the following responsibilities:

- Select committee members using the designated approval process.
- Establish a meeting schedule and attendance requirements.
- Establish a process for electing a committee secretary who will keep the minutes unless a staff secretary is provided to manage the minutes.
- Maintain contact with secretarial assistance provided by nursing administration/management.
- Ensure that all records are up to date (attendance, minutes, location of all policy and procedure manuals, annual reports, individual files on each policy and procedure, records of review dates for each policy and procedure).
- Ensure that the committee selects appropriate methods for identifying need and content of policies and procedures.
- Ensure that the committee develops the content for the policies and procedures and that the approval process is maintained.
- Establish a system for review of each policy and procedure.
- Select reviewers for policies and procedures, and maintain a list of the reviewers, the policies and procedures reviewed, the feedback, and deadlines.
- Participate in staff development related to policies and procedures.
- Prepare an annual report.

ROLE OF THE COMMITTEE MEMBERS   The policy and procedure committee's work will be more efficient and more responsive to actual needs if there is broad nursing representation on the committee. This representation allows for greater input and participation by nursing staff. Coming to the meeting prepared helps the committee do its work more efficiently and effectively. Committee members' responsibilities include the following:

- Attend meetings regularly.
- Complete designated work by deadlines.
- Assist in selecting appropriate methods for identifying need and content of policies and procedures.
- Collect data for policies and procedures.
- As needed, get feedback from staff about new policies and procedures or proposed changes.
- Review policies and procedures for committee approval before moving them through the committee approval process.
- Participate in staff development related to policies and procedures.

THE PROCESS OF POLICY AND PROCEDURE DEVELOPMENT It is important to remember that policies and procedures do not make robots out of the nursing staff. No two situations are exactly alike, and as a consequence, policies and procedures will be interpreted differently at different times. Professional nursing staff members are taught and encouraged to think through their decisions using the policies and procedures as guidelines. They are developed to help the staff, not to freeze creativity. This flexibility does not negate the importance of implementing policies and procedures but supports the idea that effective decision making requires more than just following a set of written rules.

1. ***Identification of need.*** After the committee structure is organized, the next step is to determine the policy and procedure needs of the nursing department. The best way to begin is to review existing policies and procedures. Policies and procedures may require no changes, require some changes, need to be eliminated, or need to be added. In addition, the major influences on policies discussed earlier in this section should be considered. A thoughtful evaluation of policies and procedures with input from nursing staff that uses them is very helpful in making these decisions.

   Many of the decisions in nursing departments are made in crisis situations. Health care is not static, and consequently, changes frequently occur suddenly and require immediate decisions. Decisions to develop a policy and procedure often are made during crises. However, responding to a crisis by saying, "We need a policy on this," is not always the best approach and can result in many infrequently used policies or procedures. Having too many policies and procedures can be just as harmful as having too few. Staff may begin to see all policies and procedures as "documents" with little substance. If nursing administration and the committee are aware of changes occurring in the department, the hospital, the community, and health care, then policies and procedures will more likely be developed in noncrisis periods with a less harried approach. The critical word in policy and procedure development is "change," a recurrent theme in this text. (See Chapter 3.) Changes may or may not affect policies and procedures, but they must always be considered. Changes in any of the following areas should be an indication for the committee to evaluate policies and procedures:
   - Hospital policies and procedures
   - Evidence—research and other types of evidence
   - Departmental organization
   - Vision/mission and objectives for the hospital and the department
   - Factors related to other departments that affect nursing
   - Patient population and needs
   - Medical procedures and treatment modalities
   - Nursing routines
   - Documentation
   - Quality improvement data and analysis
   - Electronic medical/health record system
   - Equipment changes
   - Staffing

- Position descriptions
- Incidents and consultations with attorney and HCO insurance carrier
- Reports from reviewing agencies and their criteria
- Reimbursement
- State and federal laws
- Current, relevant professional literature

There are many ways to obtain data that are useful in identifying policy and procedure needs. It is best to employ multiple methods and to evaluate these methods periodically to determine whether they provide relevant, timely data. Staff interviews and questionnaires are two methods; however, they both require time to develop, collect, and analyze. A poorly conducted interview or poorly written questionnaire will not result in helpful information, and consequently, the committee's time and effort will be wasted. Nursing staff members will also feel their time has been wasted. Surveys of other institutions may also be helpful, but again, surveys need to be well written and short. The response to a survey may not be great, so committees should not depend on this method for a major portion of the data.

Some data collection methods do not require as much preparation as interviews and questionnaires but do require thoughtful analysis after data collection. One of these methods is observation. One important reason for rounds by nursing management staff is to have the opportunity to observe, and committee members can also use this method. Not all that is observed is relevant to a policy or a procedure, so careful analysis of observations is important. Talking with nursing staff and physicians informally rather than using a structured interview can often reveal concerns and needs, but decisions cannot be made on what just a few people say. After informal discussion, further investigation will be necessary. Material that is already available, such as audits, incident reports, annual reports from nursing and other departments, requests for staff development on particular topics, and minutes from staff meetings, may reveal many needs for new policies and procedures or needs for change in existing ones. Another method that may provide data is interviewing new staff members after their orientation to find out what information was difficult for them to obtain and what problems they encountered in using the policies and procedures. Still another source is one that is often not considered: patients and their families, who frequently have concerns that relate to policies and procedures.

Need identification is a process. It does not happen just once, and it is never complete. Communicating the nature of need identification to the nursing staff helps to emphasize that their input into the process is always useful. Staff members should never put off communicating questions or concerns that they may have about policies and procedures. A committee or nursing management that does not listen to the nursing staff will soon encounter problems and will have ineffective policies and procedures.

2. ***Development of content.*** Before developing the content for a particular policy or procedure, the committee identifies the policy's or procedure's purpose. The committee asks, "What is the decision to be made?" and "Why make the decision?" At the same time, the committee identifies who will make the decision or perform the procedure. Policy and procedure content must support the vision, mission, and objectives of the department and the hospital, the state nurse practice act, and nursing standards. Content should be evidence based. The committee also needs to be alert to conflicts between policies and procedures. It is important to compare new or altered policies and procedures with others and determine if there is conflict or overlap or if the policy or procedure will cause problems with other departments. Department and overall HCO policies and procedures should not conflict or be repetitive.

In developing policies and procedures, there are several factors to keep in mind. First, terminology needs to be clear and concise. As lengthy, cumbersome statements do not communicate information quickly, short sentences are preferable. Abbreviations and acronyms may be used; however, when initially used, they need to be defined and should not conflict with the hospital's approved abbreviation/acronym list. Their meanings should be included for reference. So staff can make decisions efficiently, the information in a policy or procedure should be organized in logical steps. Committee members provide multiple checks of logical steps by asking questions such as the following: "Does this make sense? Can it be followed easily? Is it complete? Could it be stated more simply?"

3. ***Approval.*** After the content is developed, the approval phase begins. The approval process needs to be clearly designated. No policy or procedure should be implemented without written approval. This rule must be strictly enforced, particularly since there are probably copies of the draft that could be interpreted as official policy or procedure. All nursing staff should be told to check for the approval signature and date before applying a policy or procedure.

4. ***Implementation and communication.*** Implementation of a policy or a procedure requires planning and participation from the committee and nursing management. The goal of implementation is to ensure that all nursing staff are aware of the new or changed policy or procedure and to get them to apply it in appropriate situations. It is not always easy to get the nursing staff to use a policy or procedure. Management staff members become important in this effort, but they need a thorough understanding of the purpose and the content of the policy or procedure. All of this makes communication a very important part of the implementation process to assure that nursing staff know about the policy or procedure content, when it is in effect, who may make the decision or perform the procedure, and what the process is for providing feedback about a policy or procedure.

   A critical question about implementation that often arises is, "What keeps staff from using policies and procedures?" There are many answers to this question, and consideration of these answers will help to combat underuse and ineffective use of policies and procedures. Some of the most frequent reasons are staff members:

   - cannot find the policy and procedure when needed.
   - do not know what policies and procedures are available.
   - do not know how to access the computer, are unable to access a computer when needed, or are unable to find information on the computer. If hard copies only are used, they cannot easily access the documents.
   - do not understand how policies and procedures reflect the vision and goals of the department and the hospital.
   - do not feel the policies and procedures are practical or helpful.
   - do not like being told what to do and how to do it.
   - do not understand how the policies and procedures protect the patients and staff and support quality care.
   - feel that poor communication in the department results in a poor relationship between the staff and administration.
   - feel policies and procedures represent more paperwork.
   - do not have time to look for policies and procedures and review them so they can be applied.

   Staff may, however, have an appropriate reason for ignoring the policies and procedures. Each complaint needs to be discussed and, if necessary, resolved. It is, therefore, important to plan all steps of the development and implementation processes. Anticipation of some of the possible problems before they occur may provide a better chance of successfully implementing a policy or procedure.

   Staff development or education plays an important role in the implementation of policies and procedures. Staff development specialists frequently are directly involved in preparing staff for a new policy or procedure by providing programs about content related to a policy and procedure (for example, what happens during a code). (See Chapter 20.) As a consequence, staff development specialists need to be kept fully informed of changes. In fact, it can be helpful to have a staff education representative on the policy and procedure committee. Staff development nurses frequently are the first to recognize that a policy or procedure requires a change or that a new one is needed. When all of this information is filtered through appropriate channels, the result is a more comprehensive, useful policy and procedure process that then is used effectively on a daily basis when needed by the staff.

   Through staff education, nursing staff develop an understanding of why a policy or procedure exists and what the content means to their practice. It is clear that because the staff nurse cannot know everything, the nurse needs to know where to find information quickly. How can nurses be made to look for the policies and procedures? Reminding them whenever situations that require implementation of a policy or a procedure occur is one way; however, it is also necessary to have more structured methods such as written communications, inclusion of information in staff meetings, posters reminding staff of

BOX 6-4	POLICY AND PROCEDURE EVALUATION FORM

POLICY OR PROCEDURE NUMBER
TITLE:

What is/are the problem(s) you encountered with this policy or procedure?

What recommendations do you have for changes?

SIGNATURE:
UNIT:
DATE:

new policies and procedures, and staff development programs on these topics. Nurse managers and team leaders need to guide staff to policies and procedures and expect that they will be applied. Preceptors for new staff need to orient staff about policies and procedures, and nursing faculty and their students in the hospital for clinical should be expected to apply hospital policies and procedures.

5. *Evaluation and revision.* In most departments evaluation and revision is probably the weakest part of policy and procedure development. It is, however, critical to the success of implementation. An outdated policy or procedure can be just as detrimental to care and to the organization as no policy or procedure. Changes never come easily and usually involve some risk, but a system designed to ensure that every policy and procedure is evaluated regularly and that records are kept on this evaluation can ease change. Box 6-4 provides an example of an evaluation form that can be used to get feedback from staff who are using the policies and procedures.

Why has so much content been presented about policies and procedures and the development process? Policies and procedures provide guidelines or expectations to assist staff members as they make decisions and provide care. In addition, understanding one example that describes how an organization develops and provides direction to staff, such as through policies and procedures, helps in understanding project development. There is a problem and the organization goes about solving it. (See Chapter 3.)

ACUTE HEALTHCARE DELIVERY: EXAMPLES OF CHANGES

The acute care delivery system has experienced many major changes over the past decade. Examples include the change toward more community and primary care, emphasis on healthcare delivery and financial issues, changes in reimbursement, changes in HCO structures such as mergers or closings of hospitals, and expansion of large national healthcare systems. Other changes have led to problems for many communities (such as rural areas) when their hospitals close due to funding problems. Community members may then need to travel longer distances to get health services. The key factors that have affected healthcare delivery and the acute care hospital system are as follows:

- Problems with access (eligibility for government benefits such as Medicaid, transportation, hours of operation, number and type of providers, child care, cost of care)
- Reimbursement changes
- Increased number of the uninsured and underinsured

- Demographic changes (increasing age of population, single-parent families, immigrant growth, limited access to extended family members, diversity)
- Aging population with chronic illness and greater acuity and complications when hospitalized
- Improvement in technology that extends lifespan and increases costs
- Uneven distribution of healthcare services (for example, more services in urban areas as compared to rural areas)
- Increase in homeless population with limited healthcare access
- Increase in new drug therapies that are costly
- Increase in specialty usage, leading to fragmentation of care and increased cost

The IOM reports on quality identify that the system is dysfunctional (2001). The following is a discussion of examples of important changes affecting hospitals.

Emergency Services

Emergency services are not provided in only emergency departments (EDs) that are part of hospitals, but also in urgent care centers, which may be freestanding, separate from hospitals, or part of a hospital organization. In hospitals with trauma centers, the emergency services play a critical role in trauma services. The IOM has published several reports on emergency services. These services are described as "overburdened, underfunded, and highly fragmented" (2007b, p. 1). Frequently patients have to be sent to other hospitals due to overburdened ED units. Emergency care for children is also a problem (Institute of Medicine, 2007a). These patients have unique needs, and these services are not being provided at the required levels. Emergency medical services are described as "the initial stages of the emergency care continuum. It includes emergency calls to 9-1-1; dispatch of emergency personnel to the scene of an illness or trauma; and triage, treatment, and transport of patients by ambulance and air medical service. The speed and quality of emergency medical services are critical factors in a patient's ultimate outcome" (Institute of Medicine, 2006, p. 1). The 2006 report describes the system as having insufficient coordination, disparities in response time, uncertain quality of care, lack of readiness for disasters, divided professional identity, and limited evidence base.

Downsizing has also had a major impact on emergency services. This service is one of the areas of care that has received much media attention, primarily focused on reimbursement denial when insurers consider the care nonemergent. Health insurers may require preauthorization for emergency care in an attempt to control abuse of emergency services. Laypeople may consider many conditions an emergency, particularly when they are not sure what is happening to them. They go to the emergency room to have a healthcare professional diagnose their problem and need for treatment. Health plans, however, set their own standards for what constitutes an emergency; some plans do this more than others. There has been concern for a long time that an increasing number of patients are using emergency services as their primary care provider. This is especially true for the uninsured. This is not the best treatment for continuity or for most medical problems. It also increases the patient load in the emergency department and provides less staff to treat true emergencies. Emergency staff also become frustrated with these patients who should receive care elsewhere, and the frustration spills over onto the patients and their families.

Not only are emergency services experiencing an increase in the number of patients who do not need emergency services, but EDs hold patients in the ED even though the patient has been admitted to the inpatient service and should be transferred to appropriate inpatient units. With decreased staff working on the inpatient units and some beds closed, patients cannot be transferred out of the ED quickly. ED staff find this very frustrating, and these patients require staff time that should be used for patients who do need emergency services. Patients also become upset when they must wait for services or for inpatient admission. ED nurses need to be involved in recommending strategies for coping with these problems. This requires collaboration and an ability to assess these problems objectively. With the expertise that ED nurses have, they should participate in the development of solutions. A place to begin is to consider some of the following questions:

- Do local community providers need to extend their hours?
- Do patients know what care is available to them and how to access it?
- Could advanced practice registered nurses be used to assist with triaging patients or running urgent care clinics?
- Should the hospital develop an urgent care center, or is it best for the hospital to collaborate with existing urgent care providers?

There are many other possibilities, and with staff input, hospitals can resolve these critical problems. The ACA includes provisions about emergency and trauma services, recognizing the need for changes. A new trauma center program is to be established to increase emergency service capacity, fund research on emergency care, and develop demonstration programs to design, implement, and evaluate innovative care models in the emergency and trauma setting.

When decisions are made about emergency services' policies and procedures, their content must meet the requirements of the federal law, Emergency Medical Treatment and Active Labor Act of 1986 (EMTALA), or the hospital can be fined. In addition to the extension of coverage, EMTALA established a federal requirement that all hospitals with emergency services that participate in Medicare—and this is most hospitals—must treat all patients requiring emergency treatment or who are in labor. Inability to pay cannot be used as a reason to deny emergency treatment. This offers a major protection for the patient; however, the critical issue is the definition of an emergency and who defines it. Insurers are concerned about this use, but the patients for whom this law is addressed often have no insurance. How does this affect emergency service expenses? What is the hospital's moral obligation? Neither of these questions can be ignored, nor are they simple to answer. The following are aspects of this problem, which affect the ED, the entire hospital, and the whole healthcare delivery system in a community.

If patients are stable with little likelihood of deteriorating, they can be transferred. The patient must agree to the transfer; however, the patient must be legally competent to agree. Patients in this situation must realize that they can receive emergency treatment regardless of their ability to pay. As is always true, transferring patients from one unit to another (or in this case, to another facility) requires the nurse and/or physician give a report to staff in the receiving facility or unit and that the receiving facility or unit have the resources to provide the care the patient needs. The receiving admission office or the ED staff must be notified of the transfer and time of arrival of the new patient. Discharge against medical advice (DAMA or AMA) occurs when a patient decides to leave treatment when the physician or healthcare provider feels that treatment should continue.

Patient Access to Services

Patients have to get into and out of hospitals, and this process is one that can lead to problems for patients, their families, and the staff. As this content is discussed, consider how patients are admitted and discharged in local hospitals. What are the problems that occur? What can be done to improve the process for all concerned? It is not uncommon for staff who are responsible for the "paperwork" part of admission and discharge to be disconnected from the direct care providers, particularly nurses. This gap is where problems occur and frustration increases. This is when nursing staff are heard saying, "Don't they realize we don't have a clean room yet?" "How many more admissions can we handle this shift?" "This patient should have been sent to another unit because he does not meet our admission criteria." "Why is it taking so long to get those discharge papers?" "Where is the transport staff to take the patient down to his car?" The comments can go on and on. In the meantime, admissions staff members are also frustrated. They are saying, "Why can't they get those rooms cleaned up faster so we can move these patients out?" "We don't have the doctor's order for discharge." "This admission information is incomplete." "Where is the patient going after discharge?" "The nursing home will not accept his insurance." As was mentioned earlier in the content about committees, it is important to have interprofessional input for effective patient access services—admission and discharge. Transfers also cause problems, whether they are internal from unit to unit or external to other healthcare facilities. Transfers or handoffs are also times of increase in errors, which can lead to complications for the patient. Handoff errors are discussed further in Chapter 18. All of this can result in less cost-effective care. Admission and discharge problems take time, and this means additional costs to the organization. There is always the need to make sure the admission is appropriate to ensure that reimbursement for care is approved. These are major problems for hospitals.

Patient Education

For many years acute care settings have been required to provide patient education to meet accreditation requirements. Nursing education and the nursing profession also have a long history of emphasizing the role of nurses in providing patient education. Despite this emphasis on patient education, health care still has not been very successful in providing it. Insurers have begun to recognize the importance of patient education, believing that it will reduce costs and increase patient satisfaction. Patient education methods and evaluation of outcomes are still not fully understood. Providing patient education in acute care has become even more difficult with decreasing length of stay. Patients are sicker when admitted because efforts are first made to keep the patient out of the hospital, and if the patient is admitted, the stay is for only a short time. Patients are then often too sick to absorb patient education content, and when they begin to improve, they have less time to absorb the information because they are quickly discharged. Family members also have similar experiences; they are unable to focus on education when their family member is acutely ill, and when they can, it is time for discharge. Nurses are often tired, stressed, and have problems providing patient education with the rapid turnover of patients. Hospitals are turning more toward standardized patient education material, which they purchase. Nurses, however, need to assess these materials carefully and should participate in the development of these materials and their adaptation to meet individual patient needs. Standardized educational materials can be excellent resources if they meet the needs of the hospital and patients/families. These resources can also reduce staff preparation time and increase content consistency, which are both important factors in today's busy acute care hospitals. Rapid discharge also means that hospital nurses must develop effective communication and collaborative relationships with agencies and other providers who will care for patients after discharge. Patient education needs to continue, and hospital nurses must share what educational content has been provided and the response of the patient/family to ensure that additional patient education meets the needs of the patient/family.

Ambulatory Surgery and Procedures

There are many changes in acute care services occurring almost daily, and due to the increasing use of outpatient/ambulatory surgery, surgical services have experienced major changes. Hospitals are increasing the size of their outpatient or ambulatory surgery departments and adjusting to the need of moving patients into and out of the surgical service in one day or even a few hours. This has affected many departments, particularly preadmission testing, admissions, nursing, clinical laboratories, pathology, radiology, pharmacy, anesthesiology, postanesthesia recovery, and patient transportation. In some hospitals nurses call surgical patients at home prior to surgery to begin the nursing assessment and to give the patients brief preoperative education. Some patients come in several days prior to surgery for their preadmission testing on an outpatient basis then arrive at the hospital a few hours before their surgery for admission, which for some may be in the very early morning hours. Nursing staff may call patients a few days after surgery to assess their status. Surgical inpatient units are finding that their census has dropped because patients do not stay very long in the hospital after their surgeries, and the patients who do have inpatient surgeries have more complex procedures. Nurses have had to make adjustments in patient education that is typically provided after surgery because patients are now going home nauseated, barely recovered from anesthesia, and in pain. In these cases family members must provide postoperative care in the home, unless the patient requires professional home health services.

Discharges and Impact on Care Delivery

Hospitals are discharging patients earlier and sicker, and they are very concerned about readmission rates as this can have a negative financial impact on the hospital. (See Chapter 5.) Due to these new pressures, hospitals are developing methods to support patients and their families postdischarge, such as assessment for home care visits, which may be only a few or longer term (Study, 2011). This type of approach allows for flexibility depending on the patient's needs.

Advanced Practice Registered Nurses, Clinical Nurse Specialists, Clinical Nurse Leaders, Certified Nurse-Midwives, and Certified Registered Nurse Anesthetists

The roles of APRN, clinical nurse specialist (CNS), clinical nurse leader (CNL), CNM, and CRNA have been expanding in many hospitals just as APRNs in primary care are also increasing. Nurse practitioners who work in acute care are acute care nurse practitioners (ACNPs) and have completed educational programs that focused on hospitalized patients. Hospitals also use CNSs in a variety of areas to assist staff and work to improve care. Some hospitals are using

ACNPs and CNSs in the same way they use house staff or as hospitalists. The new role of the CNL is also expanding. Many of the decisions to expand the usage of these nurses are driven by costs and the pressure on hospitals to reduce costs. The ACA will increase the need for more APRNs, with the increasing number of insured over the next four years, physician shortage, increased need for primary care, and the recommendation from the IOM to increase primary care services provided by nurse practitioners (Institute of Medicine, 2011c).

Alternative/Complementary Therapies

Alternative/complementary therapies are now found in many types of healthcare settings. Acute care hospitals are no exception to this growth. Insurers are beginning to cover some of these services. Acute care hospitals might offer massage therapy, acupuncture, and other methods within the hospital setting, in their ambulatory care services, and in their wellness centers. It is not yet clear the direction this will all take in the future. Nurses may find that they are more involved in these services.

Continuum of Care and Acute Care

Understanding and participating in the changing healthcare environment requires an appreciation of the importance of the continuum of care and its relationship to acute care. **Continuum of care** focuses on assessment of patient needs, ensuring that the patient gets the care at the level needed and from the appropriate healthcare provider to meet positive patient outcomes. Quality and cost are critical factors in the continuum of care. The Institute of Medicine emphasizes the need for greater care coordination across the continuum by identifying care coordination as a major priority area to decrease fragmented care (2001). The continuum includes health promotion, disease and illness prevention, ambulatory care, acute care, tertiary care, home health care, long-term care, and hospice care as it takes place within HCOs and across organizations. Since more patients move into and out of the acute care setting quickly due to shorter lengths of stay, nurses must become facilitators, actively using coordination skills to ensure that patients receive the care they need despite the shortened length of stay.

Case management has become common in many hospitals, and it is considered to be an important insurer strategy to reduce costs and ensure quality as the patient moves through the continuum of care (Finkelman, 2011). Hospitals have also found that case management is useful in assisting with care coordination and rapid discharge, which are both critical to cost reduction. The case manager is also used to ensure that quality care is provided along the patient's treatment trajectory. Nurses are frequently chosen to be case managers in hospitals and may also be insurer case managers, collaborating with hospitals to ensure care coordination.

CASE STUDY

Health Care Delivery Systems: Changing

You have been chosen to be on a committee that will plan the implementation of critical new changes within a hospital. Administration and medical staff have decided to open up some new positions: two intensivists and four clinical nurse specialists. You are serving on the newly formed interprofessional planning committee. The plan is due in three months and should include critical implementation issues. This is the first time the hospital has had an interprofessional team work on descriptions of new staff roles within the hospital. You are not sure why you are on the committee. Although you have worked on a number of units over the past seven years, you still lack confidence in this type of setting (a committee, especially one that is interprofessional). The first meeting is used to discuss purpose and plan the work of the committee.

Questions:

1. Why would the new roles of intensivist and clinical nurse specialist be helpful to the hospital and its staff?
2. What might be some reactions from medical and nursing staff about these new roles?
3. What needs to be done to prepare staff for the change?
4. Describe the critical elements that need to be clarified before staff is hired into these positions.

Primary Care Providers

Primary care has grown in the past decade. A particular level of provider offers this care, for example, family medicine, general internal medicine, general pediatrics, obstetrical/gynecological, and advanced practice nurses. Insurers have pushed the use of primary care providers to reduce costs. The primary care provider should serve as the gatekeeper to the healthcare system, providing care at the primary care level and referring the patient to others for specialty care. The primary care provider should be aware of the patient's entire treatment plan and monitor the patient's progress. Does this happen? Not always but the goal is to improve in this area. However, most recently there have been fewer physicians going into primary care, mostly due to low reimbursement rates. Healthcare reform legislation should alter this picture, driving a return to increasing use of primary care providers, though the decreasing number of primary care providers continues to be a problem that will need to be resolved.

Nurses and Acute Care Hospital Changes

Nurses in hospitals are members of the system, and they need to learn to be more assertive to ensure that nursing care is recognized as critical to successful acute care. Nurses have much to offer in acute care settings, although they do not always get recognized. They also need to use their leadership skills to improve their position and role in hospital decision making. Unwillingness to change and inability to explore new ideas that might be more cost effective and yet provide quality care have a negative impact on improvement. Nurses with this attitude will eventually find that they are not part of the chapter, feel left out of the healthcare system, and may be out of jobs. This victim mentality acts as a barrier to the roles that nurses could assume within healthcare organizations, acute care, and others. Staffing continues to be a problem in some hospitals, as discussed in Chapter 8.

Patient outcomes are also monitored more now. If patients do not reach expected outcomes and experience complications, this increases the cost of health care. Hospitals and insurers do not want their patients/enrollees to experience complications that then require longer hospital stays, additional treatment, and extended care after hospitalization. Complications usually mean more medications are prescribed, and this is of particular concern since the cost of drugs is increasing. Nurses need data to demonstrate that decreasing nursing staff in hospitals will increase patient complications and affect outcomes negatively. Nurses need to gather more data about the positive effects that nursing care has on patient outcomes in the acute care setting.

Nurses who work in acute care settings have found that their work has changed. Skills that are more important now are advocacy, negotiation with a variety of internal and external staff, collaboration, coordination, delegation, and an understanding of the need to provide culturally appropriate care that considers language, religion, nutrition, culture, and family relationships. All of these are leadership competencies and are discussed in this text.

MOVING FORWARD TO LEADERSHIP IN ACUTE CARE: GUIDANCE FROM THE NURSE MANAGER ENGAGEMENT PROJECT

A major national study (Nurse Manager Engagement Project [NMEP]) focused on nurse manager engagement, funded by the Robert Wood Johnson Foundation, and included a sample of 30 nurse managers from six major U.S. medical centers. These nurse managers demonstrated experience and excellence. They were interviewed extensively about why they stay in the job—focusing more on why they are engaged rather than using the term "retention" (Mackoff, 2011). This chapter discusses acute care and nursing in hospital environments, which is where undergraduate nursing students have much of their clinical experience for their nursing programs and where many new graduates first practice. This text is about leadership and management for all nurses and for those who assume manager roles. The NMEP is particularly relevant as it assists in understanding the nurse manager role and challenges for those in the role, considering the role, and for staff who work daily with nurse managers.

The conclusions from this study help to better understand acute care and nursing in hospitals. The emphasis is on the following:

- Staff nurses' satisfaction is linked to their relationship with their manager.
- Future nursing leadership comes from development of middle managers.
- Nurse managers' satisfaction and longevity are currently at an all-time low (Mackoff, 2011, p. 2).

The Mackoff study describes the importance of the line of sight (LOS) that was originally discussed by Boswell and Bourdreau (2004). Line of sight is "the way the individual understands how his or her day-to-day work contributes to the larger vision, values, and objectives to the organization" (Mackoff, 2011, p. 102). Even without consideration of this study, looking back at earlier content in this text, for example Chapters 1, 3, and 4, this description of the line of sight ties in with current views of leadership and management such as importance of transformational leadership, organization vision and objectives, staff engagement in decisions, and need to embrace change as opportunity. Later chapters focus on the National Academy of Medicine (NAM) core competencies of healthcare professions, which are also related directly to the line of sight and the nurse manager. The Mackoff study supports the view that leaders and managers can be developed, as noted in earlier chapters, but it takes time and planned effort. Chapter 20 provides content about staff education for nurse leaders and managers, including ongoing education for the management level. The following strategies are suggested to develop and maintain the line of sight, with additional comments connecting the strategies to this text:

- Introduce the idea of the line of sight into the organization's culture to create a shared vocabulary about aligning individual goals and the organizational mission. *[This emphasizes the need to view the organization culture as something more than a description but rather integral to how staff at all levels function, including managers. All goals and missions, whether they be the organization, unit/division/department, or even individual staff and manager goals, should sync.]*
- Involve nurse managers in rounding to enable contact with patients. *[Nurse managers often feel disconnected from practice, and in some cases this may drive a nurse manager away from engagement in management. Providing methods for nurse managers to be visible and participate in practice is critical for the manager and for staff.]*
- Include explicit statements about the importance and challenge of maintaining the line of sight in the transition from staff nurse to nurse manager in nursing education, job descriptions, interviews, and mentoring. *[Nurse managers need to be reminded in concrete ways how what they do connects to the overall HCO goals and missions. Goals and missions are often viewed as words on paper and not connected to work done.]*
- Use behavioral interviewing to select and assess candidates' capacity for mission clarity, generativity, and identification in talent assessment. *[When interviewing for new positions, both the interviewer and the interviewee need to discuss these issues and provide examples.]*
- Create a teaching module for new nurse managers' orientation to describe and strategize about refocusing the LOS in their new role. *[As noted in Chapter 20, orientation is required for all staff, even for staff who change positions. The latter is often neglected or inadequately provided. This strategy reinforces the need for this but also emphasizes that there is need to recognize changing from staff to manager is a major shift in orientation and response.]*
- Seek opportunities to streamline the work of unit managers to keep them on the unit and focused on the mission (e.g., elimination of unnecessary meetings, designation of meeting-free days, or putting the office on the unit). *[Nurse managers and the entire HCO leadership team should frequently consider methods to make management work more effectively, such as the examples provided here. Managers need time to think and analyze—to be creative and innovative.]*
- Encourage nurse managers to get out of their offices and manage by walking around—talk to staff nurses and patients. *[This strategy connects with moving management into the care delivery area and also supports patient-centered care and staff-centered management. Nurse managers need to be seen by the staff in the work area and engaged in the processes.*

Observing care delivery provides information about how care is delivered; it is much more effective then viewing records or data. The latter are important, but if done without more hands-on management, information will be missed.]

- Assess the span of control for all nurses and set a ratio that facilitates more staff and patient contact. *[Span of control is an important part of organizational structure. The more staff a nurse manager supervises, the more difficult management and leadership become.]*
- Remove obstacles that block nurse managers' line of sight to the results of patient care by evaluating their workload and adding additional personnel as needed (e.g., a clinical instructor, business assistant). *[Providing the nurse manager with staff who can assist the manager will provide more time for the manager to engage in the work process of the staff—to understand it better and provide more effective support.]*
- Design annual line of sight surveys that evaluate how nurse managers' time is being spent and that underline how nurse managers' work contributes to meeting goals of patient care and supporting the organization's goals and values. *[Emphasizing personal appraisal that focuses on the positive is important, and expecting this to happen is even more effective.]*
- Assign each manager to write his or her own mission statement in light of larger organization mission. *[This strategy focuses on making the mission something the individual nurse manager can connect with. Does the nurse manager's version of the mission connect with the organization and unit/division/department missions? If not, why not? Reflecting on this can help the nurse manager better understand the line of sight and maybe why there is frustration. Then changes may be needed.]*
- Create visual reminders of success and reinforce performance that matters (e.g., patient letters, unit scorecards or staff achievement newsletters). *[Asking nurse managers to provide methods to share achievements—staff, unit, and others—supports the line of sight for all.]*
- Make stories of achievements and good news in patient care part of the daily routine in staff and management meetings and the subject of recognition notes from senior leadership. *[This strategy draws the focus to the patient—supporting patient-centered care.]*
- Include evaluation of positive identification, mission clarity, and generativity as part of performance reviews. *[Evaluation of nurse managers should include more than statistics and technical issues. How the nurse manager views self and the connection to the organization should be reviewed periodically. Nurse managers also have a major role in generativity or development of others and recognizing its importance as a contribution.]*
- Solicit nurse managers' high point experiences and contributions in evaluation and coaching sessions to create reminders of meaningful work. *[It is very easy to lose sight of what one has done—especially positive accomplishments—as we tend to focus on problems and how to solve them. Having a structured way to remind oneself and discuss this with a mentor or a supervisor helps to have a more balanced perspective.]*
- Cultivate identification with the organization through communication about accomplishments, grants, research, patient satisfaction scores, and completion of benchmarks. *[Recognition of manager and staff accomplishments should be routine.]* (Mackoff, 2011, p. 86)

The study results discuss the importance of reflection, or the ability to learn from our experiences. Reflection is "a systematic way of thinking about our actions and responses to change future actions and responses" (Sherwood & Horton-Deutsch, 2012, p. xxvii). In reviewing these strategies, all of them require some reflection on the part of the nurse manager. It is very easy to get into just doing the job, day-to-day routines, confronting problems and maybe resolving them, losing the line of sight. In addition to organizational strategies to recognize the importance of the line of sight for the organization, its patients, staff, and management, each nurse manager needs to develop methods to maintain the line of sight. The strategies described above came from an extensive analysis of the nurse manager interviews, identifying issues, concerns, and the need for improvement and support of nurse managers. Effective healthcare organizations need to keep development and engagement of managers as a major goal at all times. Doing so impacts quality of care and staff satisfaction, engagement, and productivity.

One could take this information to the next step and apply it to staff nurses. Go back and substitute "staff nurse" for "nurse manager" in the above comments. What is the result? *The Future of Nursing* report discusses the scope of practice and other matters, though it primarily focuses on advanced practice. The report comments:

> This report begins with the assumption that nursing can fill such new and expanded roles in a redesigned health care system. To take advantage of these opportunities, however, nurses must be allowed to practice in accordance with their professional training, and the education they receive must better prepare them to deliver patient-centered, equitable, safe, high-quality health care services; engage with physicians and other health care professionals to deliver efficient and effective care; and assume leadership roles in the redesign of the health care system. (Institute of Medicine, 2011c, p. xi)

The staff nurse, along with physicians, is the major provider of care in acute care, but staff nurses are there 24/7. The work is difficult and stressful, and few stop to consider and reflect— to connect as described for the nurse manager above. What would happen if staff nurses also engaged in the same manner with a nurse manager who was engaged? This would have a major impact on care—all aspects of health care where the nurses practiced or were managers. *The Future of Nursing* report comments that all nurses do not begin their careers thinking about being managers, but many end up managers. Even if they are not managers, being a staff nurse requires leadership, and staff nurses must work with nurse managers. Nurses can lead and should lead more.

> Nurses' unique perspectives are derived from their experiences in providing direct, hands-on patient care; communicating with patients and their families about health status, medications, and care plans; and ensuring the linkage between a prescribed course of treatment and the desired outcome. In care environments, being a full partner involves taking responsibility for identifying problems and areas of waste, devising and implementing a plan for improvement, tracking improvement over time, and making necessary adjustments to realize established goals. (Institute of Medicine, 2011c, p. 1–11)

The American Organization of Nurse Executives (AONE) supports development of nurse leaders and managers in its many initiatives discussed in this text. The American Association of Colleges of Nursing (AACN) identifies Hallmarks of the Professional Nursing Environment:

1. Manifest a philosophy of clinical care emphasizing quality, safety, interdisciplinary collaboration, continuity of care, and professional accountability.
2. Recognize contributions of nurses' knowledge and expertise to clinical care quality and patient outcomes.
3. Promote executive level nursing leadership.
4. Empower nurses' participation in clinical decision-making and organization of clinical care systems.
5. Maintain clinical advancement programs based on education, certification, and advanced preparation.
6. Demonstrate professional development support for nurses.
7. Create collaborative relationships among members of the health care provider team.
8. Utilize technological advances in clinical care and information systems (American Association of Colleges of Nursing, 2014).

All of this ties in with the Nurse Manager Engagement Project. To develop nurse managers for acute care and for any healthcare setting requires support and guidance from the major nurse executive organization (AONE) and from nursing education.

A CONCLUSION AND THE FUTURE

In 2009 the IOM in collaboration with the Robert Wood Johnson Foundation (RWJF) held three forums in three different areas of the country as part of the IOM Initiative on the Future of Nursing, which resulted in the publication of *The Future of Nursing: Leading Change, Advancing Health* (2011c). The focus of these forums was acute care nursing with the goal of gathering more information. The summary recognizes the complex issues of acute care practice and identifies concepts for imagining the future of nursing:

- Core Concept 1: Leverage the power of the electronic health record.
- Core Concept 2: Achieve a balance among technologies, disruptive business models, and human needs.
- Core Concepts 3 and 4: Implement rapid translational teams and interdisciplinary teams of designers.
- Core Concept 5: Create an infrastructure for rapid network exchange of successful system design innovations.

The IOM report *The Future of Nursing: Leading Change, Advancing Health* emphasizes that nurses must become partners and leaders in improving health care and specifies some critical recommendations to accomplish this. The report is based on the IOM Quality Series reports and supports the need for a greater role for nursing (Institute of Medicine, 2011c). Key recommendations are as follows:

1. Remove scope-of-practice barriers.
2. Expand opportunities for nurses to lead and diffuse collaborative improvement efforts.
3. Implement nurse residency programs.
4. Increase the proportion of nurses with a baccalaureate degree to 80 percent by 2020.
5. Double the number of nurses with a doctorate by 2010.
6. Ensure that nurses engage in lifelong learning.
7. Prepare and enable nurses to lead change to advance health.
8. Build an infrastructure for the collection and analysis of interprofessional healthcare workforce data.

Nurse managers need to examine these recommendations and integrate them into their organization. Nursing staff need to be aware of them and consider how they apply to the practice environment. Nurse leaders are responsible for guiding this process.

APPLYING LEADERSHIP AND MANAGEMENT

My Hospital Unit: An Evolving Case Experience

Now it is time to return to the unit you created when you started this textbook to apply some of this chapter's content to your own unit. The hospital is getting its application ready for the Magnet Recognition Program® (American Nurses Credentialing Center, 2015a). The Magnet website identifies the Forces of Magnetism used in this program and the Magnet model. Review the requirements on the American Nurses Credentialing Center website (American Nurses Credentialing Center, 2015b). What is this program, and what are its requirements? Describe the approach you would take on your unit to prepare for this process. What would be in your preparation plan? How would you communicate the importance of the recognition program to the staff? How would you include the staff? What would you share with the medical staff on your unit?

BSN and *Master's Essentials:* Application to Content

BSN Essentials (American Association of Colleges of Nursing, 2008) as Applied to this Chapter:

- II. Basic Organizational and Systems Leadership for Quality Care and Patient Safety
- III. Scholarship for Evidence-Based Practice
- VI. Interprofessional Communication and Collaboration for Improving Patient Health Outcomes
- VIII. Professionalism and Professional Values

Master's Essentials (American Association of Colleges of Nursing, 2011) as Applied to this Chapter:

- II. Organizational and Systems Leadership
- III. Quality Improvement and Safety
- IV. Translating and Integrating Scholarship Into Practice
- VII. Interprofessional Collaboration for Improving Patient and Population Health Outcomes

Applying AONE Competencies

Identify which of the AONE competencies found in Appendix A apply to the content of this chapter.

Engaging in the Content: Critical Thinking and Clinical Reasoning and Judgment

Discussion Questions

1. What are the common criteria used to classify hospitals?
2. Describe the process that may be used to create and maintain a hospital's policies and procedures.
3. What are some of the issues today related to emergency services? (Online Application Option)
4. Why is continuum of care important? (Online Application Option)
5. How would you apply the Nurse Manager Engagement Project to yourself as a staff nurse? (Online Application Option)

Application Exercises

1. What do you know about the acute care hospitals in your community? Select a hospital and learn more about its organization and services. You may find some of the information on the hospital's website, in hospital documents, and through interviews with managers and discussions with staff. Share your information with your classmates. You may want to do this activity in small teams. Then compare the different hospitals that different teams examined. There is no right answer. This response requires you to search for information and apply chapter content. Describe the levels of management. Have any mergers occurred in the past 5–10 years? Is so, describe them. Is the hospital accredited? If so, by whom? What is the accreditation status? When is the next scheduled accreditation? Is this a teaching or nonteaching hospital? What difference does this make? Does the hospital have Medicare certification? What is this and why is it important? How is the hospital organized (review an organizational chart)? Is it a Magnet hospital or on the Pathway to Excellence? Search the literature for a current study on Magnet hospitals. Summarize the study.

2. Many healthcare professionals and different departments in an acute care hospital are required to provide care. Explore more about the hospital you examined in #1. Select one non-nursing department described in this chapter. What can you find out about the service or department? Consider its purpose, type of staff, and how this department relates to other departments. What are two problems that the department staff feel need to be improved? How does the department staff relate to nursing?

3. Committees can be found in most organizations—student organizations, employer-related, professional, and other organizations. What has been your experience with committees? Describe an experience you have had on a committee. Consider whether you understood the purpose of the committee, leadership of the committee, your role or reason for participating, and whether or not this was a valuable experience for you.

4. What can you learn about specific healthcare policies and procedures? Ask to see a policy or procedure manual in one of your clinical sites. Some hospitals now have them computerized. You do not have to choose a hospital. You could do this in any clinical site where you do practicum. Get an idea about the types of policies and procedures that are available. What have you learned about policy and procedure development? Consider the following: focus, primary responsibility, content, evidence base, reaction of staff to the policy or procedure, problems that have been encountered with the policy or procedure, and usefulness of the policy or procedure.

5. Debate the benefits of the Magnet Recognition Program®. Be specific about the benefits, and apply them to a hospital in which you have had clinical experiences. (Online Application Option)

References

American Association of Colleges of Nursing. (2008). *The essentials of baccalaureate education for professional nursing practice*. Washington, DC: Author.

American Association of Colleges of Nursing. (2011). *The essentials of master's education in nursing.* Washington, DC: Author.

American Association of Colleges of Nursing. (2014). *Hallmarks of the professional nursing practice environment.* Retrieved from http://www.aacn.nche.edu/publications/white-papers/hallmarks-practice-environment

American Nurses Association. (2010). *Nursing: Scope and standards of practice.* Silver Spring, MD: Author.

American Nurses Credentialing Center. (2015a). Announcing a new model for ANCC's Magnet Recognition Program®. Retrieved from http://nursecredentialing.org/Magnet-Model

American Nurses Credentialing Center. (2015b). Magnet Recognition Program® overview. Retrieved from http://nursecredentialing.org/Magnet/ProgramOverview

Boswell, W., & Bourdreau, J. (2004). How "line of sight" helps with "big picture": How do you view your firm? *Human Resources Management International Digest, 129*(3), 15–17.

Dunn, L., & Becker, S. (2013). 50 things to know about the hospital industry. *Becker's Hospital Review*. Retrieved from http://www.beckershospitalreview.com/hospital-management-administration/50-things-to-know-about-the-hospital-industry.html

Finkelman, A. (2011). *Case management for nurses*. Upper Saddle River, NJ: Pearson Education.

Institute of Medicine. (2001). *Crossing the quality chasm*. Washington, DC: National Academies Press.

Institute of Medicine. (2003). *Health-care professions education*. Washington, DC: National Academies Press.

Institute of Medicine. (2006). *Emergency medical services at the crossroads*. Washington, DC: National Academies Press.

Institute of Medicine. (2007a). *Emergency care for children: Growing pains*. Washington, DC: National Academies Press.

Institute of Medicine. (2007b). *Hospital-based emergency care: At the breaking point*. Washington, DC: National Academies Press.

Institute of Medicine. (2008). *Knowing what works in healthcare*. Washington, DC: National Academies Press.

Institute of Medicine. (2010). Excerpt from *A Summary of the October 2009 Forum on the Future of Nursing: Acute Care*. National Academies of Science, Engineering, and Medicine. Washington, DC: National Academies Press.

Institute of Medicine. (2011a). *Clinical practice guidelines we can trust*. Washington, DC: National Academies Press.

Institute of Medicine. (2011b). *Finding what works in healthcare: Standards for systematic reviews*. Washington, DC: National Academies Press.

Institute of Medicine. (2011c). *The future of nursing: Leading change, advancing health*. Washington, DC: The National Academies Press.

Institute of Medicine. (2011d). *Learning what works: Infrastructure required for comparative effectiveness research*. Washington, DC: National Academies Press.

Mackoff, B. (2011). *Nurse manager engagement*. Boston, MA: Jones & Bartlett Publishers.

Sherwood, G., & Horton-Deutsch, S. (2012). *Reflective practice: Transforming education and improving outcomes*. Indianapolis, IN: Sigma Theta Tau International.

Study, E. (2011, November 17). Collaboration brings home health to forefront of hospital discharge process. *Home Healthcare News*. Retrieved from http://homehealthcarenews.com/2014/11/collaboration-brings-home-health-to-forefront-of-hospital-discharge-process/?utm_source=Home+Health+Care+News&utm_medium=email&utm_campaign=68b37638b4-RSS_EMAIL_CAMPAIGN&utm_term=0_8874f00bf0-68b37638b4-75697

COMMUNITY

CHAPTER 7

Public/Community Health: Expansion and Need for Leadership

KEY TERMS

- health promotion and prevention
- medical model
- nurse-managed health centers (NMHCs)
- population health
- primary care
- primary prevention
- public health
- secondary prevention
- tertiary prevention

● LEARNING OUTCOMES

Before you begin, take a moment to familiarize yourself with the learning outcomes for this chapter.

> Discuss the influence of the Institute of Medicine reports on public health.
> Examine various government initiatives that support public/community care at the federal, state, and local levels.
> Examine *Healthy People 2020* and its relevance to the nation's health.
> Compare and contrast population health and the medical model.
> Examine examples of health promotion and prevention strategies and their relationship to public/community health.
> Examine the multiple public/community health services.
> Explain the importance of disaster preparedness and related nursing roles.
> Discuss critical global health concerns and their relationship to U.S. health care.
> Apply leadership requirements to nursing leadership in the community.

WHAT'S AHEAD

Content in this text focuses on leadership and management that applies to nursing roles found in a variety of healthcare settings. Nurses typically think of management positions in acute care; however, with the expansion of care in the community, there are more and more leadership positions for nurses in public/community health settings. The same leadership and management competencies apply with some additional competencies described in this chapter. Nurses who provide direct care in the community and those who hold leadership positions need to have knowledge about the organization of these services and models used in public/community health, related health policies, role of government, health promotion and prevention, and the various public and private initiatives that focus on public/community health. This discussion also includes content related to disaster preparedness and global health, two topics that have become more and more important in the U.S. healthcare system and both of which provide leadership opportunities for nurses. Terminology in this area of nursing can be confusing, with advocates for one side or the other; however, this text will leave the determination of whether or not nursing should use the term "community health nursing" or "public health nursing" in courses and textbooks that focus on this topic. This chapter does not replace extensive content that is provided in public/community health courses but rather recognizes that when nursing leadership and management are considered, there should be inclusion of leadership and management content related to public/community practice.

INSTITUTE OF MEDICINE: *THE FUTURE OF THE PUBLIC'S HEALTH IN THE 21ST CENTURY*

Initially the Institute of Medicine's (IOM) examination of the quality of health care in the United States focused on acute care; however, it was always recognized that the healthcare delivery system was more than just acute care. In addition, during the early years of the IOM reviews, care in the community became a more critical concern. *The Future of the Public's Health in the 21st Century* (2002a) was the IOM's first report to focus on public/community health. As noted in this report, "health is a primary good because many aspects of human potential such as employment, social relationships, and political participation are contingent on it" (2002a, p. 2). This IOM report discusses the importance of public health, which impacts all areas of society, and how it has often been ignored or there has been limited attention focused on it. As the IOM moved into adding public health in its review of health care in the United States, it published several other reports related to public/community health: *Guidance for the National Healthcare Disparities Report* (2002c); *Who Will Keep the Public Healthy?* (2003c); *Unequal Treatment: Confronting Racial and Ethnic Disparities in Healthcare* (2003b); and *Health Literacy: A Prescription to End Confusion* (2004). All of these reports are relevant to nurses who hold leadership positions in public/community health. The reports are accessible through the National Academy of Medicine (NAM) website.

The Future of the Public's Health in the 21st Century (2002a) is directly tied to the *Healthy People* national initiative, which focuses on healthy people in healthy communities. The report emphasizes the public health system partners: the community, the healthcare delivery system, employers and business, the media, and academia. The key IOM recommendations focus on:

- Adopting a focus on population health that includes multiple determinants of health.
- Strengthening the public health infrastructure.
- Building partnerships.
- Developing systems of accountability.
- Emphasizing evidence.
- Improving communication (2002b, p. 2).

Nurses need to be involved at the community level and work toward meeting these recommendations, all of which relate to the leadership and management requirements for nurses. The report notes that the

> recommendations are directed to many parties, because in a society as diverse and decentralized as the United States, achieving population health requires contributions from all levels of government, the private business sector, and the variety of institutions and organizations that shape opportunities, attitudes, behaviors, and resources affecting health. Government public health agencies have the responsibility to facilitate and nurture the conditions conducive to good health. But without the active collaboration of other important institutions, they cannot produce the health outcomes envisioned in *Healthy People 2010*. (Institute of Medicine, 2002c, p. 7)

[Note since this IOM report came out, there is now a new version: *Healthy People 2020;* it is discussed in this chapter.]. **Public health** affects many aspects of a nation: health and lifespan, morbidity and mortality, families, economics, employment, education, social relationships, lifestyles, productivity, politics, and the ability of a community to respond to a disaster whether it is at the local, state, or national level.

The IOM expansion into a review of public health led to a discussion about the type of public health professional who will be required in the future, *Who Will Keep the Public Healthy?* (2003c). This IOM report addressed the needs for public health in a world that is affected by globalization, rapid travel, scientific and technological advances, and demographic changes. To address public health problems, public health professionals need to be prepared to deal with the potential problems. "A public health professional is a person educated in public health or a related discipline who is employed to improve health through a population focus" (Institute of Medicine, 2003c, p. 4). The eight content areas that are important for current and future public health professionals are informatics, genomics, communication, cultural competence, community-based participatory research, global health, policy and law, and public health ethics. These content areas are in addition to the long-held core components of public health: epidemiology, biostatistics, environmental health, health services administration, and social and behavioral science. This report provides an in-depth exploration of the educational needs for improved public health. Public health/community health services are an integral part of the full healthcare delivery system, but to be effective, this requires a prepared healthcare workforce. The examination of the knowledge base for public health professionals is partnered with a similar discussion in the significant IOM report *Health Professions Education* (2003a). The core competencies from this report form the framework for this text and also apply to health professionals who provide public/community services. The IOM recognized that to improve care in all settings and communities, the United States requires health professionals who are ready to take on the tasks and provide quality care.

Nursing education has also focused more on population health, as noted at the end of the chapter identifying the *Essentials of Baccalaureate Education for Professional Nursing Practice* (American Association of Colleges of Nursing, 2008) and the *Essentials of Master's Education in Nursing* (2011). The American Association of Colleges of Nursing (AACN) has a partnership with the Centers for Disease Control and Prevention (CDC) to meet the following goals:

- Improved integration of public health concepts into nursing education programs.
- Increased hands-on experience for students working with communities and public health partners.
- An expanded fellowship model that opens the door for field placements in health agencies and communities.
- Fostering inter-professional collaboration and learning in health professional education.
- Providing options for workforce improvement projects proposed by CDC program offices (American Association of Colleges of Nursing, 2014).

APPLYING EVIDENCE-BASED PRACTICE

Evidence for Effective Leadership and Practice

CITATION: American Association of Colleges of Nursing. (2013). *Public health: Recommended baccalaureate competencies and curricular guidelines for public health nursing.* Retrieved from http://www.aacn.nche.edu/education-resources/BSN-Curriculum-Guide.pdf

OVERVIEW: With the challenges of the 21st century of expanding public health needs and changes in the U.S. healthcare system due to the Affordable Care Act of 2010 (ACA), nursing education needs to increase its emphasis on public/community nursing in its curricula and in its learning strategies. The goal needs to be to better prepare nurses to practice in the public/community settings to ensure that these services are effective and efficient and meet the quality aims (Institute of Medicine, 2001, pp. 5–6).

1. *Safe:* Avoiding injuries to patients from the care that is intended to help them
2. *Effective:* Providing services based on scientific knowledge (evidence-based practice) to all who could benefit and refraining from providing services to those not likely to benefit (avoiding underuse and overuse)
3. *Patient centered:* Providing care that is respectful of and responsive to individual patient preferences, needs, and values and ensuring that patient values guide all clinical decisions

4. *Timely:* Reducing waits and harmful delays for both those who receive and those who give care
5. *Efficient:* Avoiding waste, including waste of equipment, supplies, ideas, and energy
6. *Equitable:* Providing care that does not vary in quality because of personal characteristics such as gender, ethnicity, geographic location, and socioeconomic status (disparity concern)

With this comes more emphasis on wellness, promotion of health, and prevention of disease, all areas that nurses can actively participate in.

APPLICATION: This AACN supplement to the AACN *Essentials of Baccalaureate Education for Professional Nursing Practice* (2008) provides recommendations to nursing undergraduate faculty with resources and curriculum suggestions to assist in introducing population health into baccalaureate curricula.

Questions:

1. What are the additions per *Essential*?
2. Why are these additions important to public/community health nursing leadership and management?
3. Develop an assessment tool to determine if you think your nursing program has met these recommendations. If not, how could the curriculum and learning experiences be improved?

In 2013 AACN published additional information focusing on public health nursing. These competencies are added to the baccalaureate competencies noted in the documents mentioned previously for baccalaureate and master's nursing education. Competencies related to public/community health were also influenced by the work done by the IOM and the projected changes in health care due to the Affordable Care Act (ACA) (American Association of Colleges of Nursing, 2013).

Several years later in 2009, the IOM published a report on the U.S. Department of Health and Human Services (HHS), *HHS in the 21st Century: Charting a New Course for a Healthier America*. Chapter 2 includes information about HHS, and Box 2-2 on page 34 describes its organization. The government requested a review of HHS, asking the IOM to complete this review. The IOM follow-up report describes the results of the review. The report did not recommend a major reorganization of the department, so it stays basically as it has been; however, there were other recommendations focused on the following goals:

- Define a 21st century vision.
- Foster adaptability and alignment.
- Increase effectiveness and efficiency of the U.S. healthcare system.
- Strengthen the HHS and U.S. public health and healthcare workforces.
- Improve accountability and decision making (Institute of Medicine, 2009).

HHS is the most important department at the federal level for health care, both acute and public/community, and the department needs to coordinate its services to be effective. HHS is also a very large department with many agencies. The HHS website provides current information about its strategic plans, programs and services, and role in improving public health.

GOVERNMENT INITIATIVES SUPPORTING COMMUNITY-BASED CARE: FEDERAL, STATE, AND LOCAL

Healthy People 2020

Healthy People 2020 is a national initiative begun in 1979, which was based on the surgeon general's report that identified the need to improve the health of citizens, emphasizing prevention and health promotion and developing a plan to do so (Healthy People, 2014c, 2014a). The initiative was set up to project 10 years forward, and there have been several revised plans: 1979, 1999, 2010, and 2020. The IOM quality series of reports are influenced by *Healthy People* initiatives. *Healthy People* is reviewed every 10 years, and changes are made. For example, the 2020 version added new measures/indicators related to adolescent health, blood disorders and blood safety, dementias, early and middle childhood, genomics, global health, lesbian/gay/bisexual/transgender health, older adults, disaster preparedness, sleep health, and social determinants of health. The vision proposed by *Healthy People 2020* is a society in which all people live long, healthy lives, and its mission is to:

- Identify nationwide health improvement priorities.
- Increase public awareness and understanding of the determinants of health, disease, and disability and the opportunities for progress.
- Provide measurable objectives and goals that are applicable at the national, state, and local levels.
- Engage multiple sectors to take actions to strengthen policies and improve practices that are driven by the best available evidence and knowledge.
- Identify critical research, evaluation, and data collection need (Healthy People, 2014c, 2014a).

It includes three overarching goals that support the vision and mission:

1. Attain high-quality, longer lives free of preventable disease, disability, injury, and premature death.
2. Achieve health equity, eliminate disparities, and improve health of all groups.
3. Create social and physical environments that promote health for all (Healthy People, 2014c, 2014a).

Healthy People 2020

A society in which all people live long, healthy lives

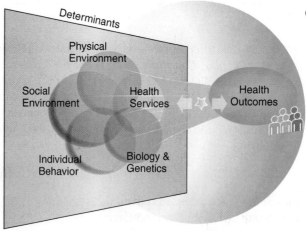

Overarching Goals:

• Attain high quality, longer lives free of preventable disease, disability, injury, and premature death.

• Achieve health equity, eliminate disparities, and improve the health of all groups.

• Create social and physical environments that promote good health for all.

• Promote quality of life, healthy development and healthy behaviors across all life stages.

Figure 7-1 Healthy People 2020

Source: U.S. Department of Health and Human Services. (2010). Healthy People 2020 (2nd ed.). Washington, DC: U.S. Government Printing Office. http://www.healthpeople.gov, U.S. Government.

Figure 7-1 describes the *Healthy People* model. Several critical determinants are integrated in the model: policy making, social and physical, individual behavior, biology and genetics, and health services. For example, the determinants and the model help to guide planning and management of public/community services through established policies. Other examples related to these determinants are the location of care, ease of access (social and physical); housing concerns; community members involvement in planning and assessing services in their communities such as serving on a community clinic advisory board; high level of smoking in the community that impacts individual behavior, biology, and genetics; and development of strategies to improve communication and collaboration among the various healthcare provider organizations such as city health department, clinics, acute care hospitals, home care agencies, emergency services, and so on. Nurses who work in public/community health are involved in many of these activities and need to develop even stronger positions, leading healthcare initiatives in many of these settings. The information found in Box 7-1 provides direction for public/community health leaders as they make plans for services and address critical needs.

Healthy People includes four health measures to assess *Healthy People* outcomes. These measures focus on:

• general health status.
• health-related quality of life and well-being.
• determinants of health.
• disparities.

In March 2014 a progress report commented on the current outcomes of the *Healthy Examples of People 2020* leading health measures/indicators. The data published in 2014 include:

• Four indicators (15.4%) have met or exceeded their HP2020 targets.
• Ten indicators (38.5%) are improving.
• Eight indicators (30.8%) show little or no detectable change.
• Three indicators (11.5%) are getting worse.
• One indicator (3.8%) has only baseline data (Healthy People, 2014b).

BOX 7-1	PUBLIC HEALTH CORE FUNCTIONS AND 10 ESSENTIAL SERVICES

Assessment

1. Monitor environmental and health status to identify and solve community environmental health problems.
2. Diagnose and investigate environmental health problems and health hazards in the community.

Policy Development

3. Inform, educate, and empower people about environmental health issues.
4. Mobilize community partnerships and actions to identify and solve environmental health problems.
5. Develop policies and plans that support individual and community environmental health efforts.

Assurance

6. Enforce laws and regulations that protect environmental health and ensure safety.
7. Link people to needed environmental health services and assure the provision of environmental health services when otherwise unavailable.
8. Assure a competent environmental health workforce.
9. Evaluate effectiveness, accessibility, and quality of personal and population-based environmental health services.
10. Research for new insights and innovative solutions to environmental health problems.

Source: Centers for Disease Control and Prevention. (2011). Core functions of public health and how they relate to the ten essential services. Retrieved from http://www.cdc.gov/nceh/ehs/ephli/core_ess.htm

This result is both positive and negative; thus, more work is needed to improve the health of citizens. The progress report also indicates that noteworthy outcomes have been reached for many of the measures/indicators:

- Fewer adults smoke cigarettes.
- Fewer children are exposed to secondhand smoke.
- More adults meet physical activity targets.
- Fewer adolescents use alcohol or illicit drugs (Healthy People, 2014b).

How might a nurse in a management position at a city health department use this information? Applying it is critical to ensuring better health in communities. First, nurses need to know about the information, where to find it, assess current community status, and develop strategies for improvement. For example, two health topics and measures/indicators are getting worse: (1) suicide and (2) adolescents with major depressive episodes. The nursing director of the city health department wants to address these concerns but first asks for community data about these problems. The director finds that the rates seem to be increasing in the community and contacts the director of school nurses for the public schools to discuss the problem. Leadership requires collaboration. Key mental health providers are contacted to join them in further assessment of the status of these two measures/indicators in their own community. They recognize that *Healthy People* describes national trends, which may or may not apply to their own community. This is an example of nursing leadership and emphasizes the need for knowledge, collaboration, coordination, and communication and use of evidence. If there is a local problem, the team needs to plan strategies to address the problem and develop and implement an assessment plan to improve health in the community, particularly for a vulnerable population—children. This initiative may also require political activities and advocacy. One example of this would include working with state-level government officials and elected officials to get funding for a new program in the schools to educate students about depression. Such a program may become a statewide initiative, thus expanding the number of stakeholders who would need to be involved. This process may also lead to concerns about disparities related to ethnic background or other cultural factors. Nurses can be very active in this type of approach to healthcare delivery by lobbying members of their state legislature, developing strong collaborative communication with state agency staff, serving as expert consultants to state officials, serving as elected officials, or holding state agency staff positions.

Healthy Communities

Healthy People provides resources for communities and health professionals to develop strategies to address needs that develop and support healthy communities. The recommended framework for communities to use is called MAP-IT (Healthy People, 2014d). The steps are:

- **M**obilize partners.
- **A**ssess the needs of your community.
- **P**lan: Create a plan to reach *Healthy People 2020* objectives.
- **I**mplement: Apply the plan.
- **T**rack your community's progress.

These steps were taken in the example about adolescent suicide described above. Additional current information and data can be found at the *Healthy People* website.

The Centers for Disease Control and Prevention (CDC) is also involved in ensuring healthy communities.

> CDC works with communities through local, state and territory, and national partnerships to improve community leaders and stakeholders' skills and commitments for establishing, advancing, and maintaining effective population-based strategies that reduce the burden of chronic disease and achieve health equity. Communities create momentum that assist people in making healthy choices where they live, learn, work, and play through sustainable changes that address the major risk factors—tobacco, physical inactivity, and unhealthy eating. Currently, 331 communities and 52 state and territorial health departments have been funded. (Centers for Disease Control and Prevention, 2014a)

The program is called the Community Health Assessment and Group Evaluation (CHANGE) (Centers for Disease Control and Prevention, 2010). This approach is based on teams and collaboration to develop an effective action plan that is then implemented by the community. Part of the evaluation process is to engage and understand stakeholders (government officials, business leaders, education leaders, healthcare leaders, healthcare professionals, religious leaders, nonprofit organization leaders, community members, needs, and others) and to use an evidence-based decision-making process. All of this requires commitment to the process and its implementation. The objectives are:

- Identify community strengths and areas for improvement.
- Identify and understand the status of community health needs.
- Define improvement areas to guide the community toward implementing and sustaining policy, systems, and environmental changes around healthy living strategies (e.g., increased physical activity, improved nutrition, reduced tobacco use and exposure, and chronic disease management).
- Assist with prioritizing community needs and consider appropriate allocation of available resources (Centers for Disease Control and Prevention, 2010, p. 6).

The American Public Health Association (APHA) also promotes healthy communities (2014). Other aspects of healthy communities to consider are environmental health, policies that relate to health issues, health equity, access for persons with disabilities so they can meet their personal needs, school health, transportation to get personal and health needs met, health reform, injury, safe neighborhoods and roads, safe work environments, and substance abuse and violence prevention.

POPULATION HEALTH VERSUS MEDICAL MODEL

Public health focuses on three major core functions and 10 essential services as described in Box 7-1 on page 189 and Figure 7-2. There are many aspects of population health that are not actively considered in the **medical model** of care, a model that primarily focuses on diagnosis and treatment. **Population health** pays more attention to many factors that can impact the health of individuals, families, and communities, whether they be local, state, or the national community. These factors include the work environment, physical environment, education, access to

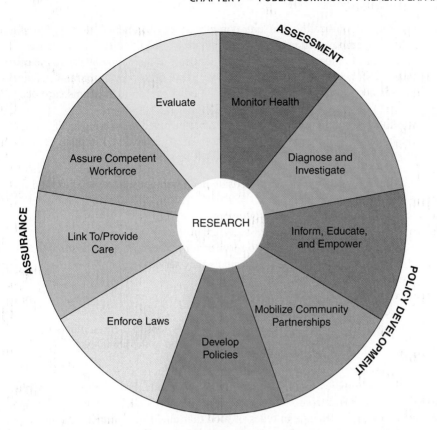

Figure 7-2   Core public health functions and essential services

Source: Centers for Disease Control and Prevention. (2014). Retrieved from http://www.cdc.gov/nceh/ehs/ephli/core_ess.htm

basic needs such as food, fresh water, housing, safety, transportation, education, and risky behaviors (substance abuse, violence, and so on). The World Health Organization (WHO) identifies the social determinants of health as geographic region and condition of birth and life, environment, age, and health care that is available and accessible (World Health Organization, 2014c). The National Healthcare Disparities Report (NHDR) is an important quality report card focusing on an annual review of disparities in the U.S. healthcare system, and it also relates to the healthy communities initiative (Agency for Healthcare Research Quality, 2013). This report is discussed along with the National Healthcare Quality Report in Chapters 10, 17, and 18.

HEALTH PROMOTION AND PREVENTION

Health promotion and prevention are critical aspects of community/public health at the local, state, and national levels. They are an integral part of *Healthy People 2020* and have been throughout the existence of the *Healthy People* initiative. The Affordable Care Act of 2010 (ACA), though mainly focused on reimbursement and getting more people insurance, does include some provisions related to health promotion and prevention. Some of these provisions include increasing access to screening, greater emphasis on primary care, which is typically based in the community, employer wellness programs, and funding to expand community-based transition programs, medical homes, and community health centers.

The surgeon general developed a National Prevention Strategy (NPS) with the following vision: "Working together to improve the health and quality of life for individuals, families, and communities by moving the nation from a focus on sickness and disease to one based on prevention and wellness" (U.S. Department of Health and Human Services, 2014). This vision highlights certain themes found in many common organizations involved in public/community health: collaboration, teamwork, inclusion of major stakeholders, assessment, planning, and so on. The NPS focuses on healthy and safe community environments, clinical and community preventive services, empowered people, and elimination of health disparities. There is also need to improve tracking of outcome data as an important part of managing health in the community. With the increase in people living with chronic illness, both prevention and management of chronic illnesses need to be part of the care provided because much of this care occurs in the community.

Nurses who work within the community are more involved in assuring health promotion and prevention than nurses who practice in acute care. They get involved in many aspects of daily living such as the following:

- Housing (fire safety, cleanliness, access, safe neighborhoods, access to heat and cooling during excessive temperatures)
- Communication access (telephone for emergencies)
- Environment (air quality, sanitation, safety, clean water)
- Transportation to ensure people get to services for health-related or personal reasons when needed (shopping, education, access to emergency services)
- Violence
- Substance abuse
- Health literacy
- Social support that might be provided by religious groups to their members in need or to the broader community (assisting with providing food to the homeless)

Nurses in public/community health practice are also more aware of diversity concerns and the impact of demographics on the community and its needs. For example, an increase in the number of immigrants in a community impacts health needs such as health status, number of children and older adults, change in types of food that might be common and their availability, language differences, religious concerns, and so on. Understanding risk is an important concern because this will help nurses plan community assessment and implement interventions required to promote health and prevent illness. Nurses are involved in community assessment and develop response plans with follow-up evaluation. Nurses do this work in collaboration with other health-care providers and within the community. Leadership and management are required for effective health promotion and prevention programs, whether they are at the local, state, or national level.

Health promotion and disease and illness prevention are strategies that focus on encouraging people to become partners in maintaining their own health. The National Academy of Medicine (NAM) includes health promotion, prevention, and wellness in its perspective of patient-centered care. These are also critical strategies used by insurers, primary care, and public/community health. Medicare is also providing more reimbursement for these strategies. Education is a key method for accomplishing this partnership. Each time an insurer develops health promotion and disease and illness prevention services, it reassesses the costs and benefits of these services. The health maintenance organization (HMO) is the managed care model most likely to cover preventive services though now many third-party payers are covering some of these services, and the ACA now requires insurers to cover some preventive services.

The goals of health promotion are to help people modify their lifestyles and make choices to improve their health and quality of life. Health education is very important in helping community members to accomplish this goal. There are three types of disease and illness prevention strategies: primary, secondary, and tertiary.

1. **Primary prevention** focuses on wellness behaviors and prevention of illness or prevention of the natural course of an illness. Examples of interventions include prenatal clinics, stress management courses, AIDS prevention education, nutrition education, safety for children, smoking clinics, alcohol usage, and seat belt safety.
2. **Secondary prevention** focuses on early diagnosis of symptoms and treatment after the onset of disease or illness and recognizes that early treatment may decrease complications. Mammograms, parent education, and screening for diabetes or glaucoma are examples of intervention at this level.
3. **Tertiary prevention** focuses on rehabilitative strategies to decrease disability from a disease or illness. Examples of interventions include chemotherapy education for a cancer patient and bladder training for a stroke patient.

The U.S. Preventive Services Task Force publishes a guide that can be accessed through its website (2010). Preventive services are frequently inadequately provided. Some of the reasons for this have been inadequate reimbursement, fragmentation of healthcare delivery, and insufficient time with patients. Even when these factors have been removed, the services are often not provided. This is partially due to lack of knowledge about what to provide and questions about their effectiveness. Patients may also be unaware of their own needs for preventive services and, thus, do not request them. Some preventive services are best provided on a community basis rather than with an individual focus in a clinical setting. This approach may become more common in the future. In addition, insurers may develop their own clinical guidelines for preventive services, which would increase the variability of these services.

After a community agency or HCO identifies the health promotion and disease and illness preventive services to offer, it must develop the services, ensure that providers provide the services, and communicate availability of preventive services. Newsletters, personal letters, information provided at the worksite, and the Internet may be used to share this information or involving local media as an important stakeholder.

PUBLIC/COMMUNITY HEALTH SERVICES

Description of Public/Community Health Care

The second part of the healthcare delivery system is the public/community or population system, which provides care for a specific population or community. The personal system focuses on acute care for individuals, and the public system provides a variety of services, including health promotion, prevention and early detection of disease, diagnosis and treatment of disease with a focus on cure, rehabilitative/restorative care, and custodial care.

Healthcare settings can be described by a variety of important characteristics, including the type of services offered, size, location (urban or rural), type of people served, healthcare providers within the setting, and reimbursement methods. The following are examples of healthcare settings that are important in public/community health.

Types of Services

PUBLIC HEALTH OR GOVERNMENT DEPARTMENTS AND AGENCIES (FEDERAL, STATE, OR LOCAL)

The government is involved in public/community care. It provides services through organizations funded primarily by taxes and administered by elected or appointed officials. Local health departments, for example city or country, and state departments of health develop and carry out programs to meet the health needs of groups within the community and those of the community as a whole. The government also provides important funds for public/community care.

CLINICS

Clinics represent a major setting in public/community health. The organization of clinics can vary. Some clinics may be directed by the city or by the county. Other clinics may be part of a healthcare system and not formally part of a city or county health department. Clinics should be located in areas of need to limit access concerns. Funding is often limited and can vary depending on changes in local and state government budgets. Nurses provide direct care and also serve as managers of clinics. In addition, there is increasing use of advanced practice registered nurses (APRNs) in clinic settings. Many clinics include patients on their advisory boards and also develop systems to obtain evaluation feedback from their consumers or patients to improve services.

PRIMARY CARE

The IOM was asked to examine how best to integrate primary care and public health and how the Health Resources and Services Administration (HRSA) and the CDC could promote this integration. The IOM uses the following as its definition of **primary care**: "the provision of integrated, accessible healthcare services by clinicians who are accountable for addressing a large majority of personal healthcare needs, developing a sustained partnership with patients, and practicing in the context of family and community" (Institute of Medicine, 1996, p. 1). Later, the IOM identified the following principles as important in supporting this integration:

- A shared goal of population health improvement
- Community engagement in defining and addressing population health needs

- Aligned leadership that bridges disciplines, programs, and jurisdictions to reduce fragmentation and foster continuity; clarifies roles and ensures accountability; develops and supports appropriate incentives; and has the capacity to manage change
- Sustainability, key to which is the establishment of a shared infrastructure and building for enduring value and impact
- The sharing and collaborative use of data and analysis (Institute of Medicine, 2012, p. S-5).

The HRSA and the CDC provide resources, data collection, and analysis that are important in providing effective public health services, including integration of primary care into the public health system; however, there needs to be greater coordination between the two agencies (Institute of Medicine, 2012). Both agencies are designated as key sources to improve population health and need to develop new programs to accomplish this goal, as noted in the ACA provisions. Examples of these programs are community assessment, prevention, and expansion of community health centers, accountable care organizations (ACOs), and medical homes. **Nurse-managed health centers (NMHCs)** are also increasing with the ACA authorization of additional funds for expansion. NMHCs must be associated with a school of nursing or with a community-based nonprofit organization. These centers provide care for patients covered by Medicare, Medicaid, and the Children's Health Insurance Program (CHIP), addressing the complex needs of underserved populations including typical services such as comprehensive primary care, family planning, prenatal services, mental/behavioral health care, health promotion, and disease prevention (Institute of Medicine, 2011). NMHCs are located in the communities they serve, and leadership/administration is provided by nurses, although other health professionals such as physicians, social workers, and others are also hired. APRNs are now more active in primary care, and the IOM report on the future of nursing (2011) strongly supports the need for greater use of APRNs in primary care including NMHCs, clinics, and other primary care settings.

HOME HEALTH   Home care has had its ups and downs and is now increasing due to shorter lengths of stay and the increased emphasis on keeping patients in the community for care. Telehealth, as discussed in Chapter 19, may also be used in some home health situations. Home health agencies may be managed and owned by city or county health departments, hospitals, or may be part of home health chains such as a national home health agency that has sites in multiple states. Home health is focused on getting patients what they need in the community and, more important, at the level of their own home. Nurses who work in home health have to be knowledgeable about the community, resources, specific healthcare interventions, best methods for providing care in the home, and reimbursement. They must also work with an interprofessional team such as physicians, pharmacists, physical therapists, social workers, and others. The patient's family or significant others also need to be involved in the team. Typically the nurse leads the home care team.

HOSPICE AND PALLIATIVE CARE   Hospice and palliative care are often structured in similar ways to home health agencies. They may be freestanding organizations located in the community or part of a chain of hospice services. Some hospitals provide these services, though they are often located on acute care floors or may be in separate buildings from the hospital in the community. Nurses provide many of the services but also must work with an interprofessional team and the patient's family or significant others. Hospice and palliative care may also be provided in the patient's home.

REHABILITATION   These services are found in various organizations in a community. They are often provided in ambulatory care settings, although some HCOs include them as part of long-term care settings and, in some cases, part of acute care. The role of the nurse is to ensure that patients can access rehabilitative services in the community; however, other healthcare providers provide most of these services.

EXTENDED CARE AND LONG-TERM CARE   The number and type of settings for extended care and long-term care are dependent on the characteristics of the community. Age range is one such example. These services are typically located in areas of the community where the need is greatest. Size and specific services vary among communities. Nurses provide direct care and serve in leadership positions in these HCOs. Some of the organizations offer a community-based residential setting that can progress to additional care services where people live and access multiple services such as assistance in their individual homes (apartments, suites, and so on), food service, social services and psychological support, primary health care, rehabilitation, exercise, social activities, and religious activities.

OCCUPATIONAL HEALTH   This is a service that is directly connected with businesses and industry, but not all businesses and industries provide occupational health services to employees. If they do, it is primarily provided on-site by occupational health nurses who not only provide direct care such as assessment, screenings, emergency care, and so on but are also involved in providing employee health education, work safety education, and work with management to improve workplace safety. Some of these nurses have master's degree in occupational health, and all need to be knowledgeable about the National Institute for Occupational Safety and Health (NIOSH) and the Occupational Safety and Health Administration (OSHA) requirements and resources. Websites for both of these federal government agencies provide extensive information about occupational health.

SCHOOL HEALTH   The CDC comments about school health: "Establishing healthy behaviors during childhood is easier and more effective than trying to change unhealthy behaviors during adulthood. Schools play a critical role in promoting the health and safety of young people and helping them establish lifelong healthy behavior patterns" (Centers for Disease Control and Prevention, 2014b). School nurses may work in public or private schools and often cover more than one school. They are a critical part of the heathcare system, particularly the public/community health system. Services are varied and in some schools, full clinic services are provided by APRNs. Other healthcare providers, such as psychologists, speech therapists, and social workers, may also be included as needed. School nurses are also involved in health education focused on students and families and are involved with teachers to ensure more effective health education initiatives for all students. As noted later in this chapter, school nurses also need to be involved in disaster preparedness planning as they can be very helpful in identifying family issues, getting information out to families, assisting during the response phase with the communities associated with their schools, and assisting with the recovery phase. School nurses need to know their communities to provide effective school health. Some nurses provide direct care or school nursing services while others serve in management positions in the community's school nursing service, often as part of the city or county health department.

DISASTER PREPAREDNESS

The United States recognizes that there are situations in which the country, either as a whole or its parts (cities, states) encounters emergency needs that would be considered a disaster, which are typically broadly classified as chemical, biological (including pandemic influenza), radiological/nuclear, and explosives. However, there are other disasters that occur such as natural disasters (e.g., floods, hurricanes, fires) and structural problems such as major blackout that can be very difficult during times of extreme heat or cold. Disease outbreaks that may be global and impact the United States or may be within the United States are also of major concern, as was seen with the Ebola virus in 2014. The three major phases of disaster preparedness are prevention, response, and recovery. Different organizations such as WHO, Red Cross, HHS, CDC, Homeland Security, and Federal Emergency Management Agency (FEMA) are involved in disaster preparedness depending on the type and location of the disaster. They may provide prevention and preparedness training, direct services during time of emergency, support services, resources such as water and food, equipment repair, funding, and so on. The American Nurses Association (ANA) also provides information for nurses on disaster preparedness. The websites for these organizations provide details about their disaster preparedness services and resources.

National Health Security Strategy (NHSS)

Recognizing that there is a potential problem is the first step in disaster preparedness. The next step is to prepare for it. The National Health Security Strategy (NHSS) was developed in 2009 to serve as the guide for the U.S. disaster preparedness process (see Figure 7-3) (U.S. Department of Health and Human Services, 2014). HHS is required to report a new plan to Congress every

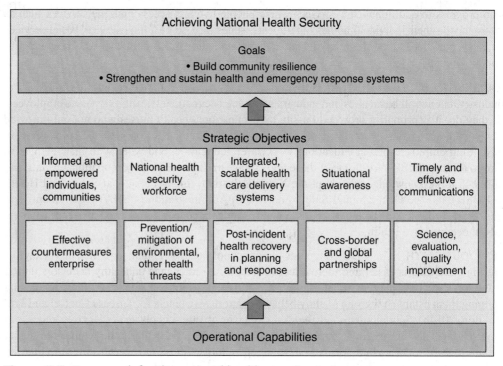

Figure 7-3 Framework for the national health security strategy

Source: U.S. Department of Health and Human Services. (2009). *National Health Security Strategy of the United States of America*. Washington, DC: Author.

four years, with the next one due by the end of 2018. The NHSS goals are to build community resilience and strengthen and sustain health and disaster response systems. The objectives related to these goals are to:

- foster informed, empowered individuals and communities.
- develop and maintain the workforce needed for national health security.
- ensure situational awareness.
- foster integrated, scalable healthcare delivery systems.
- ensure timely and effective communications.
- promote an effective countermeasure enterprise.
- ensure prevention or mitigation of environmental and other emerging threats to health.
- incorporate postincident health recovery into planning and response.
- work with cross-border and global partners to enhance national, continental, and global health security.
- ensure that all systems that support national health security are based on the best available science, evaluation, and quality improvement.

The report and requirement that HHS assume a major role in disaster preparedness indicates that the federal government is assuming the major leadership role in planning, providing resources (information, expertise, funds, and so on), guiding others such as state preparedness initiatives, and evaluating outcomes for improvement.

Planning

An effective plan needs to address prevention, response, and recovery and include multiple stakeholders: government (local, state, national), nongovernmental agencies/relevant nonprofit organizations, usual responders (police, fire, emergency transport services, emergency departments, and so on), healthcare organizations/providers, the community, and individuals in the community. Prevention is the first phase. Although many disasters cannot necessarily be prevented, the community can prevent major problems and protect its community from further harm by having a plan for response. The federal government can do a lot to provide funding, resources, and expertise, however when a disaster occurs in a community, it is the community that must provide the immediate and long-term response with help from others such as federal resources. Many factors determine a community's level of preparedness and its ability to recover after an emergency (U.S. Department of Health and Human Services, 2014). These factors include the following:

- The general health of a population
- Individual behaviors, lifestyles, and social interconnectedness
- Individual community members planning and preparing for an emergency
- Economic and social conditions
- Extensively prepared health services
- Access to health services

These factors need to be considered in the community's assessment and applied to the plan. For example, if a flood damages a low- to moderate-low-income sector of the community, this sub-population will have a harder time coping with disaster effects compared to members of the community who are at a higher socioeconomic level with more available resources (insurance, employment).

The plan needs to consider the potential types of disasters and how this might impact service limitations and needs. For example, a flood will limit transportation, impacting how people get to safe areas; determine if and how emergency responders can get into flood areas to assist people who may need to be removed or who are injured; and impact disbursement of food and drinking water. Healthcare providers may have a difficult time getting to centers of care; communication methods such as telephones may be damaged; loss of electricity can endanger people, especially in extreme heat or cold; and so on. These problems may last for a long time (e.g., Hurricane Katrina). Whereas a terrorist attack, such as the bombing at the Boston Marathon, may be localized with time-limited need for emergent critical services. Long-term follow-up care for victims and their families may be required. There may also be an impact on many people who may not even be directly involved and yet may require a high level of support services over a long period of time. This is not to say that one disaster is less important than another to a community, but prevention, response, and recovery are different for these disasters. However, there are some common issues that need to be assessed. Some of these issues may be eliminated depending on the type of disaster. Examples of these general concerns include:

- access to food and drinking water.
- safety from physical harm.
- access to healthcare services (e.g., emergencies, chronic conditions, access to medications, and so on).
- transportation.
- communication.
- crisis intervention, assessment, and long-term psychological support.
- funding for repairs.
- housing (short term/long term), including access to utilities (e.g., electricity, water).
- assessment of needs for individuals, families, and the community.
- structure/organization to ensure that needs are met in a timely manner.
- interprofessional team to implement the plan.

Each community needs to have a method for identifying responders and maintain a current list. Typically healthcare providers, nursing students, and other community members volunteer for these situations. The community needs to identify how responders will be notified and what procedures to employ. Media and virtual methods are also used to contact individuals and groups that may be needed. Training may be required for procedures and roles in advance of an emergency. This group then works with other responders such as EMTs, police, firefighters, and healthcare providers from acute care and health departments. A specific team should lead and coordinate the disaster response and recovery. This requires careful planning and organizing as well as keeping information current as community emergencies are not common occurrences.

A critical component of any community disaster preparedness plan is community education. Individuals, families, and businesses need to have a plan for their own response. They need to know the type of emergency supplies they should routinely keep such as first-aid supplies and bottled water, equipment such as flashlights and battery-operated radios, how to maintain mobile phone batteries for as long as possible, and the need to develop a response and communication plan. Emergency preparedness is typically more prevalent in communities at higher risk for emergencies such as hurricanes or major snowstorms. The threat of a terrorist attack or spread of an infectious disease can also drive individuals to be more prepared in times of high stress and fear. The news media can be a positive or negative factor in getting people motivated to be prepared. Sometimes the media can increase stress rather than present a realistic picture. On the other hand, media can communicate quickly with the community; therefore, the disaster preparedness planning team needs to include key community media leaders. Today, with the increased use of electronics, there are many ways to alert people about potential or actual emergencies. Alerts on smartphones can get through to a large number of people very quickly. This, however, still requires a plan for who will initiate communication and how the message will be communicated.

Leadership During Disasters

What is the responsibility of nurses during times of disaster (American Nurses Association, 2010)? Most nurses do feel compelled to help, although many do not feel qualified or prepared if their practice specialty is unrelated to the disaster needs. Others are concerned about the care of their own families and their needs, which is true for any responders. Safety of responders must always be considered, and the types of safety concerns vary depending on the disaster. For example, is the nurse legally required to respond? There needs to be more consideration of national standards related to legal and ethical concerns in disaster situations to better ensure that responders are protected legally and know what is expected. All health professionals then need to understand these standards so they can be effectively enacted. There are also recommendations to establish a national registry of volunteers, though individual communities should not wait for this and should include this in their own disaster preparedness plan.

Emergency preparedness requires an interprofessional team. Nurses need to be involved in two major ways. Community or public health nurses, nurses who work in emergency services, home health nurses, school nurses, and other direct sites may have to provide direct services in a disaster, depending on the type of disaster. Working directly with acute care providers is critical as they must continue to maintain services that are not related to the disaster and respond as needed to care for patients who are injured by the disaster, either physically or psychologically. Nurses also need to be part of the team that develops the community response plan, including preventive efforts. This activity requires competency in teamwork and effective communication, coordination, and collaboration skills. Nurses need to be knowledgeable about resources, needs of the community before and during disasters, health education, crisis intervention, and coping with change. This type of nursing requires that nurses "think on their feet," handle stress, use ongoing evaluation to adjust the plan as needed, and remember that not only are community members affected by the emergency but so are the healthcare providers who must respond and care for their own families and friends who may be struggling with the impact of the emergency. Nurses must take an active role in evaluation of the response and recovery to improve procedures for the next possible disaster. Evaluation measures must consider that the type of disaster makes a difference in the planning and implementation process.

GLOBAL HEALTH CARE: CRITICAL CONCERNS TODAY

Global health care is an important topic, more so than in the past. Why is this so? Today there is more interaction globally through sharing of information and resources among countries, need for collaboration due to disasters and wars, and greater travel that increases communication but also increases the risk of spread of infectious diseases and even terrorism. Nurses are involved in a variety of ways related to global health care. Many nurses either take international positions or may do short-term work particularly providing health expertise in countries that need assistance as either direct care providers or for consultation and training—providing nursing leadership to assist local nurses. Other nurses assume leadership roles in global health policy due to their expertise.

Nurses also hold staff positions in a variety of organizations that focus on global health or are involved in these organizations as members, consultants, and in other roles. They also serve as advocates for healthcare improvement and the need to improve population health. Some of these organizations are WHO, the International Committee of the Red Cross (ICRC), Sigma Theta Tau International (STTI), and the International Council of Nurses (ICN). (Detailed information about these organizations can be found on their websites.)

- *World Health Organization:* WHO is part of the United Nations (UN) and is responsible for United Nations (UN) global health matters: "Providing leadership on global health matters, shaping the health research agenda, setting norms and standards, articulating evidence-based policy options, providing technical support to countries and monitoring and assessing health trends" (World Health Organization, 2014a, 2014b). WHO assumes an active role in global public health by providing leadership, developing research agendas and stimulating global public health research, establishing standards and assessing outcomes, developing and supporting ethical and evidence-based policies, providing technical support for effective change, and monitoring health situations and health trends. Nurses are involved in WHO at the organizational level, working in specific projects such as providing care or acting as consultants or trainers to improve health provider education in designated locations.

- *International Committee of the Red Cross:* The ICRC is related to the American Red Cross and other country-specific Red Cross organizations (International Committee of the Red Cross, 2014). Its funding source is primarily through donations from countries, individuals, and other organizations. Nurses work with the ICRC, which provides health planning, health care, ensuring needs of communities such as safe water, sanitation, emergency housing, food, and response to disasters and wars. Refugees are a key vulnerable population of concern for many of the global health organizations.

- *Sigma Theta Tau International:* STTI is the nursing honor society whose goal is to support efforts that nurses make to improve global health. The organization has chapters in 86 countries (Sigma Theta Tau International, 2014). STTI provides training and resources to develop nursing leadership that has an impact on global health. Some of the issues that are of concern for STTI and its members are global health, international nurse migration that has an impact on shortages in countries when nurses emigrate, diversity, evidence-based nursing and research, staffing, and other topics. Its conferences bring nurses together from all over the world to address nursing and global health concerns, to share and provide support, and to develop nursing leadership in many countries.

- *International Council of Nurses:* The ICN is the international organization that was developed by nurses and is led by nurses to provide support to nurses internationally and to act as a voice for international nursing (International Council of Nurses, 2014a, 2014d). ICN provides resources to nurses such as position papers that cover topics related to nursing roles in healthcare services, the nursing profession, socioeconomic welfare for nurses, healthcare systems, and social issues (International Council of Nurses, 2014c). The organization particularly focuses on strategic leadership to empower nurses globally. In 2004 the ICN launched the Global Nursing Review initiative, which includes the Global Nursing Leadership Institute (GNLI) (International Council of Nurses, 2014b). This institute provides extensive training options for nurses and/or midwives in senior level and executive positions in developed and developing countries, focusing on leadership and management and negotiation skills development. An international faculty of nurses and other experts developed the training program and work with nurses to develop leadership competencies and collaboration. This program is now known as the ICN Leadership for Change™.

NURSING LEADERSHIP IN THE COMMUNITY

Is leadership in the community different from leadership in other healthcare settings? As the level of healthcare delivered in the community increases, nurse leadership will need to become more effective in this setting, and today more nurses are needed to assist in developing leadership within the community. By 2020, the United States is expected to need 250,000 additional public health professionals (*Orlando Business Journal*, 2008). Nurses who function in the community should not take over the leadership and direct the community, but rather should facilitate the building of community leadership by providing their expertise and guidance to empower the community.

The Future of Nursing: Leading Change, Advancing Health (Institute of Medicine, 2011) is a significant report from the IOM focusing on current needs, the future, and nursing leadership. This report does not just address the acute care segment of the healthcare delivery system, but also comments on the need for nurses to increase their roles and leadership in public health. One example includes APRNs to provide community assessment, screenings, and disease surveillance. APRNs may also practice in school health and occupational health. The report notes that to provide effective care in the community, there needs to be changes in public/community infrastructure and resources. These are changes that should involve nurses. "One of the major challenges facing the U.S. healthcare system is its high degree of fragmentation. Nowhere is this fragmentation more evident than in the transitions patients must undergo among multiple providers or different services for a single health problem" (Institute of Medicine, 2011, p. 2-12). Effective use of coordination and collaboration is key to positive healthcare outcomes. With an increasing emphasis on community care rather than acute care, there is even more need for improvement in these areas. Public/community health is complex, and providers are not always located in the same building or even near each other, increasing the challenges. This requires innovative approaches and commitment to change. The public/community sector of the healthcare system is a place where nurses can redesign their roles, as there is much that needs to be done to improve health of individuals, families, and communities. The disconnect between public and private services needs to be resolved if the nation's health is to be improved (Institute of Medicine, 2011). Nurses with their healthcare knowledge and expertise, coupled with leadership and management competencies, can add to the expertise pool.

Nurse Leader Competencies in Public/Community Health

To be effective in public/community health roles, nurses in the community require the same leadership and management competencies as acute care settings such as planning, teamwork, communication, coordination, collaboration, and quality improvement, but there are variations of competencies.

BUDGET   Though budgeting is a basic management competency in the public/community sector, the budget also often relies heavily on funds from government budgets (local, state, federal), grants, and nonprofit organizations. Government budgets change and nurses need to be involved

CASE STUDY

Disaster Preparedness

A year ago you took the position as director of school nursing for a city health department. The school nurses provide services to 20 schools ranging from elementary through high school. You live in a community located in a state that has frequent tornados. It is now December, and you have been asked to attend a city council meeting along with other stakeholders to discuss emergency preparedness. A nearby city experienced a major tornado last summer. A representative from that community shares their experiences at the city council meeting with an assessment of what took place. The council concludes with a charge that all key areas of the community must get prepared. You leave the meeting overwhelmed. You were sitting next to the director of nursing from the only local hospital who felt the same way you did. You both agree to work together and mentor each other as you develop your plans.

Describe how you will approach this planning. Identify the stakeholders and resources you might use to help you with the planning process.

Questions:

1. What might be included in the plan when it is completed, and how will the plan be implemented?
2. When you meet with your colleague from acute care, how might your plan differ from his or her plan?

in advocating for health services to ensure that funding is available, which requires political competencies. Funding is often limited, which means nurse leaders and managers must plan carefully, track budget outcomes, and may need to use innovative strategies to get needs met and stay within the budget.

POLITICAL AND ADVOCACY STRATEGIES   Public/community healthcare services require interaction with many stakeholders who may not be as common to nurses in acute care unless they are in high-level executive positions. This includes stakeholders from businesses, religious institutions, nonprofit organizations, government (staff and elected officials), media, and responders such as police and fire departments. Citizens are major stakeholders and need to be involved. Working with all of these groups is not easy and requires knowledge of what each can offer, their needs, and how to engage them. This requires some political skills. The nurse is advocating for best care for multiple population groups and for many different situations. This may require more assertiveness when dealing with complex issues in the community and multiple stakeholders who may not be directly related to or knowledgeable about health care and in situations where nurses work more autonomously. Nurses need to be more social change agents. "Community and public health nurses learn to expect the unexpected" (Institute of Medicine, 2011, p. 5-11). Political engagement and pursuit of leadership roles in policy development may also be part of many public/community healthcare positions.

HEALTH EDUCATION   Nurses in acute care typically think of patient education as focused on one patient, and if a patient agrees, staff may include the patient's family or significant others. Nurses in public/community health must envision health education for large groups. For example, health education may be focused on a specific neighborhood or for members of the community with a specific chronic illness, such as prevention of cardiac disease. This effort might include distribution of print materials, availability of information on the Internet, collaboration with park services to increase exercise equipment, partnership with a food bank and nutritionist to offer healthier food options, work with city clinics to identify patients at risk, engagement of the local chapter of the American Heart Association to provide community education on prevention of cardiac disease, education of home health nurses to work with families and improve care for patients with cardiac disease, involvement of school nurses to include more health teaching about exercise and healthy eating and so on. These are not strategies one typically thinks of in acute care nursing. All of this requires high-level communication and planning.

PLANNING   All nurse leaders and managers are involved in planning. Some of the examples above provide support for the complexity of planning needed in the community to improve the health of the community and provide care needed in the community. Nurses have to move away from the typical "healthcare delivery" box and be open to including anyone who might make a plan more effective and efficient.

IMPROVING HEALTH LITERACY   Health literacy is discussed in more detail in Chapter 10; however, it is important to recognize that nursing leadership in public/community health requires knowledge of health literacy and its significance. Nurses need to know how to assess health literacy including the usual demographics of the community and identify changes to be proactive. Strategies must then be developed to improve health literacy. This information should be part of all public/community plans. As compared with acute care concerns and health literacy, nurses in the community must still consider individual needs but also must think in the aggregate—vulnerable populations and others who need to improve health literacy; an important aspect of prevention and wellness. The IOM report on health literacy is an important resource on this topic (2004).

STAFFING   Staffing is always a challenge for nurse managers. In public/community health settings, nurse managers need to think about the competencies that are needed to practice effectively. Certainly nursing expertise is required, but nurse managers must also need to consider the nurses' ability to communicate and work with others—varied stakeholders. Staff safety also requires different measures. For example, nurses may travel into neighborhoods that may not be safe, work in clinics that may be in high-risk areas for substance abuse, question safety in the patient's home, travel during bad weather, and so on. This impacts recruitment and requires staff education. Salaries are often not as high as in some acute care organizations; often nurses are working for the city, county, or state and thus are government employees.

CONTINUOUS QUALITY IMPROVEMENT (CQI)   CQI is discussed in detail in Chapters 17 and 18; however, it is also important in public/community health. Nurses are often working in more isolated situations such as in home care, clinics with few staff, or a school nurse in one school. These nurses have less opportunity to turn to a colleague for advice, which can impact quality care and errors. All public/community health services need to have a defined CQI plan with clear outcomes, methods for data collection, data analysis, and interventions for improvement. This information needs to be shared and discussed. Getting staff engaged is critical. This is no different than acute care, but it may be more challenging. In acute care you may have a unit with staff who frequently see each other and it is easier to focus on a discrete physical location, small number of patients, and a clearer view of the stakeholders. In the community this is often not the case—the discrete unit may be a neighborhood offering multiple services such as a clinic, school, large factory with occupational health services, administering the flu vaccine for a city or county, planning for disaster (particularly more common weather-related disasters such as storms), and the continued need to access acute care with emergency services and regular hospital services. This is much more complicated with many variables that may impact CQI. For example, a neighborhood has a section where the rate of violence and substance abuse is high and the homeless population is increasing. Are staff knowledgeable about CQI and their role? What is the priority? What data collection methods are used, and how is the data recorded? There may not be access to computers in all the areas of service, and when there is access to computers, do the computer systems communicate with one another? Who organizes this into a plan? Are the segments connected and thus influence outcomes of one another? How is data analysis conducted and by whom? All of this takes time, planning, and expertise. Later in the text, consider the content in Chapters 17 and 18 and how it may or may not apply to a CQI plan for public/community health.

WORKFORCE EFFECTIVENESS   Developing an effective workforce that can provide public/community health services is important. Nursing education has included public/community health nursing in the nursing undergraduate curriculum, typically as one course. However, as noted earlier in this chapter, the AACN recently recognized that more needs to be done in nursing education to prepare nurses in public/community health nursing. Nurse residencies are discussed in other chapters; however, most of these residencies are in acute care. *The Future of Nursing* report comments that there needs to be nurse residency programs in nonacute care (Institute of Medicine, 2011). This type of program provides more intensive experiences with mentoring in public/community health services. Transition to practice needs to be more fully developed as most nurses who apply for their first positions in public/community health have had clinical experience only in their undergraduate programs. Some who apply may have master's degrees in public/community health nursing, so they have more experience. This means the majority of the responsibility for preparing staff who are new to this area of nursing falls on the employer, and mostly on the nurse manager or director. Public/community services often have limited budgets and lack on-site staff with expertise in staff education. This makes it difficult to provide effective staff education. Chapter 20 discusses staff education in more detail as a critical concern for any nurse manager. All of this impacts the quality of public/community health care as was noted by the *Quality Chasm* series and its identification of the need to improve health professions education and need for core competencies, which are also applicable to public/community health care.

Public/community health nursing has become more important in nursing. Leadership should not be ignored in this setting; however, nurses may need to consider new and different competencies for this environment. There is also no doubt that, despite the many exciting new opportunities, the U.S. healthcare delivery system has major problems, and this text discusses many of them. The IOM (2001) suggests that a major reason for the chaotic healthcare delivery system is that the system has lost its focus on what is truly important to the people it serves, the patients. The emphasis on the five core competencies of health professions indicates the need to have a common base from which all health professions practice (Institute of Medicine, 2003a). In addition, the healthcare system requires greater healthcare consumer participation, which is also emphasized in the core competency to provide patient-centered care, which in the case of the community would be community-based care. Nursing leadership can have a major impact in public/community health, but it must make a concerted effort to achieve this.

APPLYING LEADERSHIP AND MANAGEMENT

My Hospital Unit: An Evolving Case Experience

One problem that has been discussed in the hospital is the need for better collaboration between the community and the hospital. Each nurse manager has been asked to prepare a short presentation of eight slides with notes describing a strategy that might be used to improve relations with the community. You decide you need to collaborate directly with a community stakeholder. Whom might you choose and why? Related to this management task, what is the role of the staff in your unit? What will you include in your presentation?

BSN and *Master's Essentials:* Application to Content

BSN Essentials (American Association of Colleges of Nursing, 2008) as Applied to this Chapter:

 II. Basic Organizational and Systems Leadership for Quality Care and Patient Safety
 V. Healthcare Policy, Finance, and Regulatory Environments
 VI. Interprofessional communication and collaboration for improving patient health outcomes.
VII. Clinical prevention and population health. The baccalaureate program prepares the graduate to:

Master's Essentials (American Association of Colleges of Nursing, 2011) as Applied to this Chapter:

 II. Organizational and Systems Leadership
 III. Quality Improvement and Safety
 VI. Health Policy and Advocacy
VIII. Clinical Prevention and Population Health for Improving Health

Applying AONE Competencies

Identify which of the AONE competencies found in Appendix A apply to the content of this chapter.

Engaging in the Content: Critical Thinking and Clinical Reasoning and Judgment

Discussion Questions

1. What are the impact and recommendations from the IOM public health reports?
2. How is *Healthy People 2020* relevant to public/community health? (Online Application Option)
3. How is population-based care different from the medical model?
4. Why is disaster preparedness important? Describe nursing roles. Using the experience with the Ebola virus in the United States, discuss how this was handled within communities. How could it have been improved?
5. What are examples of public/community care that you know about in your community? How do the roles relate to content in this chapter? (Online Application Option)

Application Exercises

1. Divide into teams. Each team should select a public/community health issue of interest and research its current status within the state. Share this information and include recommendations for nursing involvement. (Online Application Option)
2. Find out about your community's disaster preparedness. Include nurses from acute care so you can compare the disaster preparedness approaches taken by acute care and public/community health nursing. Does your school participate in the community's disaster preparedness? If not, could this be changed and how?
3. Divide into teams and identify a global health issue to investigate. Have each team present their findings and then discuss roles for nurses.
4. Examine current data from *Healthy People 2020* found on the *Healthy People* website. What has improved? Identify problems and consider strategies to resolve two of the problems you identify.
5. In teams, use large paper to create a graphic that describes the public/community health system in your community. Each team should present their graphic to the class, and the teams should compare and contrast the visual representations.

References

Agency for Healthcare Research and Quality. (2013). National healthcare quality and disparities reports. Retrieved from http://www.ahrq.gov/research/findings/nhqrdr/index.html

American Association of Colleges of Nursing. (2008). *Essentials of baccalaureate education for professional nursing practice.* Washington, DC: Author.

American Association of Colleges of Nursing. (2011). *Essentials of master's education in nursing.* Washington, DC: Author.

American Association of Colleges of Nursing. (2013). *Public health: Recommended baccalaureate competencies and curricular guidelines for public health nursing.* Retrieved from http://www.aacn.nche.edu/education-resources/BSN-Curriculum-Guide.pdf

American Association of Colleges of Nursing. (2014). Public/population health nursing. Retrieved from http://www.aacn.nche.edu/public-health-nursing

American Nurses Association. (2010). Who will be there? Ethics, the law, and a nurse's duty to respond to disaster. Retrieved from http://www.nursingworld.org/MainMenuCategories/WorkplaceSafety/Healthy-Work-Environment/DPR/Disaster-Preparedness.pdf

American Public Health Association. (2014). What is public health? Retrieved from http://www.apha.org/what-is-public-health

Centers for Disease Control and Prevention. (2010). *Building a foundation of knowledge to prioritize community needs. An action guide.* Retrieved from http://www.cdc.gov/nccdphp/dch/programs/healthycommunitiesprogram/tools/change/pdf/changeactionguide.pdf

Centers for Disease Control and Prevention. (2014a). Healthy communities program. Retrieved from http://www.cdc.gov/nccdphp/dch/programs/healthycommunitiesprogram/

Centers for Disease Control and Prevention. (2014b). School health.

Retrieved from http://www.cdc.gov/healthyyouth/schoolhealth/

Healthy People. (2014a). About Healthy People. Retrieved from http://www.healthypeople.gov/2020/about/default.aspx

Healthy People. (2014b). *Healthy People 2020 Leading Health Indicators: Progress update.* Retrieved from http://www.healthypeople.gov/2020/leading-health-indicators/Healthy-People-2020-Leading-Health-Indicators%3A-Progress-Update

Healthy People. (2014c). History & development of Healthy People. Retrieved from http://healthypeople.gov/2020/about/history.aspx

Healthy People. (2014d). MAP-IT. Retrieved from http://healthypeople.gov/2020/implement/MapIt.aspx

Institute of Medicine. (1996). *Primary care: America's health in a new era.* Washington, DC: National Academies Press.

Institute of Medicine. (2001). *Crossing the quality chasm.* Washington, DC: National Academies Press.

Institute of Medicine. (2002a). *The future of the public's health in the 21st century.* Washington, DC: National Academies Press.

Institute of Medicine. (2002b). *The future of the public's health in the 21st century: Report brief.* Washington, DC: National Academies Press.

Institute of Medicine. (2002c). *Guidance for the national healthcare disparities report.* Washington, DC: National Academies Press.

Institute of Medicine. (2003a). *Health professions education.* Washington, DC: National Academies Press.

Institute of Medicine. (2003b). *Unequal treatment: Confronting racial and ethnic disparities in healthcare.* Washington, DC: National Academies Press.

Institute of Medicine. (2003c). *Who will keep the public healthy?* Washington, DC: National Academies Press.

Institute of Medicine. (2004). *Health literacy: A prescription to end confusion.* Washington, DC: National Academies Press.

Institute of Medicine. (2009). Excerpt from *HHS in the 21st Century: Charting a New Course for a Healthier America.* Washington, DC: National Academies Press.

Institute of Medicine. (2011). *The future of nursing: Leading change, advancing health.* Washington, DC: National Academies Press.

Institute of Medicine. (2012). Excerpt from *Primary Care and Public Health: Promoting Integration to Improve Population Health.* Washington, DC: National Academies Press.

International Committee of the Red Cross. (2014). Health. Retrieved from https://www.icrc.org/en

International Council of Nurses. (2014a). Who we are. Retrieved from http://www.icn.ch/who-we-are/who-we-are/

International Council of Nurses. (2014b). The global nursing review initiative. Retrieved from http://www.icn.ch/publications/the-global-nursing-review-initiative/

International Council of Nurses. (2014c). Position statements. Retrieved from http://www.icn.ch/publications/position-statements/

International Council of Nurses. (2014d). Strategic plan 2014–2018. Retrieved from http://www.icn.ch/images/stories/documents/about/ICN_Strategic_Plan.pdf

Orlando Business Journal. (2008, February 29). 250,000 more health care workers needed by 2020. Retrieved from http://www.bizjournals.com/orlando/stories/2008/02/25/daily37.html

Sigma Theta Tau International. (2014). About us. Retrieved from http://www.nursingsociety.org/aboutus/Pages/AboutUs.aspx

U.S. Department of Health and Human Services. (2014). National health security strategy. Retrieved from http://www.phe.gov/

Preparedness/planning/
authority/nhss/Pages/default.
aspx

U.S. Department of Health and Human
Services. (2014). National Prevention Strategy. Retrieved from
http://www.surgeongeneral.gov/
initiatives/prevention/strategy/
index.html

U.S. Preventive Services Task Force.
(2015). Recommendations.
Retrieved from http://www.
uspreventiveservicestaskforce.org/
BrowseRec/Index

World Health Organization. (2014a).
About WHO. Retrieved
from http://www.who.int/
about/en/

World Health Organization. (2014b).
The role of WHO in public health.
Retrieved from http://www.who.
int/about/role/en/

World Health Organization. (2014c).
What are social determinants of
health? Retrieved from http://
www.who.int/social_determinants/
sdh_definition/en/

8 Recruitment and Retention: Meeting Staffing Requirements

KEY TERMS

- background check
- competency
- full-time equivalent (FTE)
- human resources (HR) department
- job analysis
- job screening
- job stress
- performance appraisal
- position description
- reality shock
- recruitment
- résumé
- retention
- self-scheduling
- staffing
- staffing mix
- termination
- 360-degree evaluation
- turnover

◉ LEARNING OUTCOMES

Before you begin, take a moment to familiarize yourself with the learning outcomes for this chapter.

> Explain how the human resources department assists the healthcare organization and its employees in recruitment and retention of staff.
> Discuss why staff recruitment is important and effective methods to improve the process.
> Explain how a position description is developed.
> Apply the employment process to nursing staff recruitment.
> Apply critical guidelines that a nurse should consider when applying for a position.
> Analyze the issue of retention and its impact on staff and quality care.
> Apply the performance appraisal process.
> Examine strategies that can be used to prevent or decrease stress and incivility in the work setting.
> Discuss staffing issues that impact care and staff retention and recruitment.

WHAT'S AHEAD

The link between recruitment and retention is clear—recruiting the right staff for the right job is the first step in long-term **retention** of staff. Staff turnover is a major problem today in health care along with the variable nursing shortage. The National Academy of Medicine (NAM) core competencies for healthcare professions relate to recruitment and retention of staff. The goal is to hire qualified staff in appropriate numbers, maintain staff satisfaction, and display a willingness to apply evidence-based practice. This impacts effective patient-centered care, interprofessional teamwork, quality improvement, and proficient use of informatics. Dissatisfied, overworked, and stressed staff are less interested in improving care.

The work environment and many other factors also affect retention, as well as the ability to recruit. Recruitment and retention may be seen as functions of human resources (HR); however, it is a wise nurse leader who recognizes that nursing staff need to be involved in this process. Effective staff recruitment and retention requires active leadership. Staff need to help identify factors that drive recruitment and retention. Nurse managers, and in many cases staff, need to be involved in the staff interview and selection process. Word of mouth can be a critical factor in the community; nurses let other nurses know the best places to work. Nurses in the community know which healthcare organizations (HCOs) have problems hiring and retaining staff. Organizational culture also has a strong effect on recruitment and retention. In many situations nurses in the community can identify the factors that drive recruitment and retention problems, but HCOs do not always ask for this feedback. This chapter speaks to two perspectives: (1) HCO's recruitment and retention efforts from the employer's and the candidate's/employee's perspectives and (2) the need for active management involvement. There are many factors that impact staffing levels and shortages.

HUMAN RESOURCES

The **human resources (HR) department** in an HCO is responsible for ensuring that staff are recruited, hired, promoted, transferred, retained, and terminated according to the organization's policies, procedures, and relevant laws. The goal is to hire and retain the best staff possible to meet the mission and goals of the organization and its components. HR should collaborate with nursing management to ensure the goal is met.

Functions and Activities

The Joint Commission, the primary organization for accreditation of HCOs, includes management of human resources in its standards. The key focus areas are human resources planning; orienting, training, and educating staff; assessing competence, and managing staff requests.

It is not only important to find staff to fill openings, but it is also important to find competent staff. This is difficult to do with new graduates, as confirmed by the Institute of Medicine (IOM) and also the recent report on nursing education (Benner, Sutphen, Leonard, & Day, 2010; Institute of Medicine, 2004). The IOM emphasized in its report on nursing that

> Pre-licensure and pre-employment education cannot provide sufficient frequency and diversity of experiences (and sometimes offer no experience) in the performance of every clinical nursing intervention needed for every clinical condition found in patients, especially as the breadth of knowledge and technology expands. Nurses, therefore, like physicians, come to their initial place of employment as novices, without certain skills and knowledge—their limited skill and expertise reflecting the limitations of time and experience in their academic education. (2004, p. 202)

Benner and colleagues recommend that new graduates should have a one-year, high-quality postgraduate residency (2010, p. 31). This landmark nursing education report recognizes that there is also much more that needs to be done to improve pre-licensure nursing education, as does the IOM (Benner et al., 2010). In addition, *The Future of Nursing* report also includes a recommendation that nurse residency programs should be expanded (Institute of Medicine, 2011). Chapter 20 provides more information on nurse residency programs.

Meeting the goal of hiring competent staff requires planning by leaders to identify guidelines related to qualifications, competencies, and staffing requirements. Competent staff must be provided to ensure that patient care outcomes are met. Staff competencies need to be assessed, maintained, and improved, which should be an ongoing process. A culture needs to be established in which self-development and learning are supported, as discussed in Chapter 20. When the Joint Commission standards are reviewed, it is clear that HR does not work in isolation, but rather the HCO's leaders or management set the tone and guide HR. It takes a coordinated and collaborative effort to ensure that recruitment and retention processes are functioning and effective, and this requires clear communication about the functions and activities to be carried out by human resources and management. Effective HR departments have strong positive relationships with management, and staff feel that HR is a support service for them, not a department that acts against them.

Human Resources Policies and Procedures

The HR department, in collaboration with management, develops policies and procedures related to employment and staffing. Issues that are typically considered include hiring, promotion, transfers, termination, staffing and scheduling, performance appraisal, benefits, and other related issues. Procedures to ensure effective communication related to these policies and procedures are a critical concern as ineffective communication is a typical problem area. For example, staff may not be informed about a change in policy about work schedules, or a manager may not be informed about the hiring process. Required employment documentation needs to be clearly identified and implemented because this can have serious consequences on staff performance. Monitoring the implementation of policies and procedures is used to determine if standards are met. HCOs with labor unions must factor this into the management of their human resources. Labor contracts affect policies and procedures, documentation, monitoring, human resources decision making, staff involvement, and decisions made about staff. Nurse managers need to understand the contract requirements and work closely with HR on these issues. In HCOs with union supervisors, staff who have the right to hire, fire, evaluate, assign, or direct other staff are excluded from union contracts. Managers then need to be clear on how this impacts their responses to staff and decisions made (Westrick, 2014).

Legal Issues

Laws, both federal and state, protect employers and employees. It is important for both the HR staff and management to understand these laws and their implications to the hiring, promotion, and termination processes. It is equally important for employees to understand the implications of these laws, many of which are not explained during orientation. The following descriptions highlight the major laws and how they affect employers and employees.

AMERICANS WITH DISABILITIES ACT (ADA)   The Americans With Disabilities Act of 1990 prohibits discrimination in hiring and job assignments based on disability (Westrick, 2014). Reasonable accommodation must be made (e.g., equipment for the hearing challenged, ramps for wheelchairs, allowing employees to work in an area of the building that is easier to get to, allowing reasonable time for medical appointments, and so on). Substance abuse is classified as a disability, as is mental illness. A history of problems in these areas cannot be used to disqualify a qualified person for employment. If, however, the employee is unable to do the job due to absences or errors or if the employee has a history of this work behavior in a previous position, the employee can be terminated for poor work habits. However, the employee may not be terminated for a disability. The employer can refuse to hire the candidate based on poor work habits, but not a history of substance abuse or mental illness.

EQUAL EMPLOYMENT OPPORTUNITY COMMISSION (EEOC)   The Equal Employment Opportunity Commission (EEOC) is the federal agency that administers the Civil Rights Act/EEO, the Age Discrimination in Employment Act, and the Americans With Disabilities Act (Westrick, 2014). The EEOC is the agency that receives complaints when these laws may be violated. It conducts the investigation, makes the decisions as to who is at fault, and designates the penalties. The EEOC can make an employer keep an employee or hire a candidate, require an employer to pay back pay, and even require that employee's/candidate's legal fees be covered by the employer. The EEOC does not have to inform an employer that it is coming to investigate a complaint; however, records should not be turned over without presentation of a subpoena or a search warrant nor should staff be interviewed without legal counsel. Methods for avoiding EEOC problems include use of routine and appropriate management education about the laws and implications, implementation of policies and procedures that comply with the laws, recruitment that does not discriminate, use of a standardized interviewing process, use of application forms that meet legal requirements, and documentation of accurate notes regarding application and hiring, promotions, and terminations. Additional information is provided on the EEOC website.

CIVIL RIGHTS ACT OF 1964   The Civil Rights Act of 1964 and its amendments have had a major effect on the workplace (Westrick, 2014). This law prohibits discrimination in employment based on race, color, sex, religion, or national origin. Questions on applications and during interviews cannot address these factors. Employment tests must be designed so as not to discriminate in these areas. The law also addresses discrimination based on religion, as businesses must now make reasonable accommodation for religious practice (for example, wearing of religious clothing and days off for religious holidays). Allowing for the latter does not mean that the business cannot make the employee use personal leave days for these days off nor are they required to pay for these days. If meeting this requirement is an undue hardship for the business, pay does not have to be provided. Businesses, however, can prohibit proselytizing in the workplace. This law also protects against discrimination on the basis of gender. Businesses can identify gender-specific positions; however, they must be clearly defined. Pregnancy cannot be used to discredit a woman for a position.

AFFIRMATIVE ACTION   Despite the fact that the Civil Rights Act of 1964 clearly states an employer cannot discriminate based on race, religion, national origin, or sex, giving preference to special groups continues to be a concern and is a highly controversial issue. Several presidential executive orders, beginning with those issued by President Johnson, require affirmative action for protected classes (African Americans, Hispanics, Asians or Pacific Islanders, Native Americans or Alaskan Natives, and women), which applies to all federal contractors and subcontractors that have contracts of more than $50,000 and have 50 or more employees (Westrick, 2014). Executive orders are not laws and only apply to government agencies and organizations that do business with the government. Most HCOs do business with the federal government, so many must meet these requirements. This business occurs when HCOs accept Medicare and Medicaid payments for healthcare services they provide. What does this mean to the employer? Employers must actively seek candidates from these minority groups. Over the years this effort has also led to accusations of reverse discrimination. In these cases the complaint is that in giving members of the protected classes preference, this denies or discriminates against someone who does not belong to one of the classes but is qualified for the position.

FAMILY AND MEDICAL LEAVE ACT (FMLA)   The Family and Medical Leave Act of 1996 (FMLA) applies to employers of 50 or more employees who work within a 75-mile radius (Westrick, 2014). For employees who are eligible (and not all are eligible), FMLA covers 12 weeks of unpaid leave during a 12-month period for medical reasons, which may include the birth or adoption of a child as well as care of a spouse, child, or parent who has a serious medical problem. The medical problem may be mental or emotional illness. This law is complex, and when applied, it requires careful review. The employer may require that the employee submit medical certification of the claimed medical condition. If the employer has concerns about the validity of the certification, the employer can ask for a second medical opinion and even a third; however, the employer is responsible for these costs. The employer may select the provider who will give additional medical opinions; however, this healthcare provider cannot be an employee of the employer (e.g., a physician who works in the employer's hospital or clinic). Until all of the opinions are complete, the employee should receive FMLA benefits. For long-term or chronic conditions, the employer can request recertification but not second and third opinions.

SEXUAL HARASSMENT   What is sexual harassment? First, it is a form of sex discrimination and a violation of the Civil Rights Act of 1964. When an employee initiates a complaint, the employee must prove that there is a causal connection between the harassment and the job benefit in question or a quid pro quo. The EEOC further defines sexual harassment:

- It is unlawful to harass a person (an applicant or employee) because of that person's sex. Harassment can include "sexual harassment" or unwelcome sexual advances, requests for sexual favors, and other verbal or physical harassment of a sexual nature.
- Harassment does not have to be of a sexual nature, however, and can include offensive remarks about a person's sex. For example, it is illegal to harass a woman by making offensive comments about women in general.
- Both victim and harasser can be either a woman or a man, and victim and harasser can be the same sex.
- Although the law doesn't prohibit simple teasing, offhand comments, or isolated incidents that are not very serious, harassment is illegal when it is so frequent or severe that it creates a hostile or offensive work environment or when it results in an adverse employment decision (such as the victim's being fired or demoted).
- The harasser can be the victim's supervisor, a supervisor in another area, a coworker, or someone who is not an employee of the employer, such as a client or customer (U.S. Equal Opportunity Commission, 2014b).

Sexual harassment is one type of harassment. A second type is a hostile work environment that interferes with the employee's ability to perform the job. The EEOC decides whether or not the situation qualifies as a hostile environment. The EEOC describes this harassment as:

> Harassment is unwelcome conduct that is based on race, color, religion, sex (including pregnancy), national origin, age (40 or older), disability or genetic information. Harassment becomes unlawful where 1) enduring the offensive conduct becomes a condition of continued employment, or 2) the conduct is severe or pervasive enough to create a work environment that a reasonable person would consider intimidating, hostile, or abusive. Anti-discrimination laws also prohibit harassment against individuals in retaliation for filing a discrimination charge, testifying, or participating in any way in an investigation, proceeding, or lawsuit under these laws; or opposing employment practices that they reasonably believe discriminate against individuals, in violation of these laws. Petty slights, annoyances, and isolated incidents (unless extremely serious) will not rise to the level of illegality. To be considered unlawful, the conduct must create a work environment that would be intimidating, hostile, or offensive to reasonable people. Offensive conduct may include, but is not limited to, offensive jokes, slurs, epithets or name calling, physical assaults or threats, intimidation, ridicule or mockery, insults or put-downs, offensive objects or pictures, and interference with work performance. Harassment can occur in a variety of circumstances, including, but not limited to, the following:
>
> - The harasser can be the victim's supervisor, a supervisor in another area, an agent of the employer, a coworker, or a nonemployee.
> - The victim does not have to be the person harassed, but can be anyone affected by the offensive conduct.
> - Unlawful harassment may occur without economic injury to, or discharge of, the victim. (U.S. Equal Opportunity Commission, 2014a)

Other types of harassment are verbal, harassment of men, and harassment of homosexuals. Organizations should have harassment policy that describes how complaints are made. The EEOC has specific guidelines that need to be followed when complaints are filed with the EEOC (for example, there are time limits for filing complaints related to the alleged discriminatory act). Sexual harassment is a very emotional issue. Power over others plays a major role in this type of discrimination. There is abuse of authority, which is frightening. Harassers can be found at all levels and types of staff, in all types of organizations, and can be of any gender. Sexual harassment is extremely serious.

AGE DISCRIMINATION IN EMPLOYMENT ACT (ADEA) The Age Discrimination in Employment Act of 1967 (ADEA) and its amendments focus on age by prohibiting discrimination against anyone 40 years or older (Westrick, 2014). In addition to this federal law, some states have their own laws protecting persons 18 years and older. This law covers businesses with 20 or more employees. As long as the person meets the requirements of the position, persons who fall in this age range cannot be denied the job. Many applications no longer include birth date or age, and most people do not include birth date on their résumés. How do some businesses try to get around this law? They say that the candidate is overqualified; the candidate made more money in his or her last position than this position offers, or this is a trainee position. Businesses cannot say they will not provide healthcare coverage to older employees. The law, which was established by the Older Workers Benefits Protection Act of 1990, requires that the benefit plan, if it is offered, cover all employees.

FEDERAL DRUG-FREE WORKPLACE ACT The Federal Drug-Free Workplace Act of 1988, which covers certain federal contractors and grantees and federal agencies, does not make screening for alcohol and drug use a requirement for employment; however, it does not make these tests illegal. This screening may be done as part of the preemployment physical exam or at other times within an employment setting. Urine tests are usually used first, and if a potential problem is identified, blood tests may follow (U.S. Department of Labor, 2015).

WORKERS' COMPENSATION Workers' compensation is a very expensive type of insurance for employers (Westrick, 2014). This insurance is an important part of the national healthcare delivery system. Workers' compensation provides medical benefits and replacement of lost wages that result from injuries or illnesses that arise from the workplace. When an employee receives these benefits, the employee cannot then sue the employer for the injury. Typically employees are provided workers' compensation coverage, as mandated by state law, employee medical benefits, and often disability benefits. Workers' compensation is not equivalent to employee medical benefits, although workers' compensation was the first form of social insurance used in the United States. It is a social contract, a form of mutual protection for the employee and the employer, and is required by a federal law and delegated to states. The employer must follow state requirements related to benefits and limits. The financial status of the employer is not a factor in determining the type of plan it offers. The state's workers' compensation commission is the authority that supervises these healthcare services. States, however, do vary in the benefits they require.

Disability costs are an important part of workers' compensation costs. Workers' compensation is not, strictly speaking, health coverage. Most employers offer short-term disability coverage that is a portion of the worker's pay for up to three to six months after an incapacitating accident or illness. These policies may cover pregnancy and maternity leaves for a specified time period. Paying for this care without any insurance can be a major financial crisis for most employees. Disability management is critical for most employers because it is used to control costs. Many workers who experience a disability feel a sense of entitlement; they feel that this benefit is a "right." This can lead to workers' demanding excessive medical care, and this in turn delays their return to work. As a result, employer costs also increase. Employee secondary gain comes from the wages the employee receives during the disability period without working.

Keeping workers' compensation separate from the traditional healthcare delivery system has not always proven to be the most cost-effective method of providing medical care for work-related injuries and illnesses. Workers' compensation is regulated under state laws. States vary in benefit levels, medical reimbursement schedules, and the amount of control the employer has over employee medical choices. Occupational health nurses may be involved in prevention of work-related injuries and illnesses as well as providing on-site treatment and follow-up.

THE WAGNER ACT OF 1935 AND THE TAFT-HARTLEY ACT OF 1948 The Wagner Act of 1935 (also known as the National Labor Relations Act) and the Taft-Hartley Act of 1948, which amended the original law of 1935, cover issues related to employer-union relations (National Labor Relations Board, 2014; Nolo, 2014). These laws prohibit discrimination based on union membership. Employers may not ask candidates if they are members of a union. Employers are no longer required to hire union members, but union contracts may specify that nonunion employees must join the union within a specific time period after they are hired. This is called "union shop." This issue has been taken over by some state laws, known as "right to work" laws, which prohibit "union shop" or fair-employment laws. This is an area that requires careful review of specific state law in addition to federal law.

EQUAL PAY ACT OF 1963 The Equal Pay Act of 1963 prohibits the determination of pay based on gender (Westrick, 2014), referred to as "equal pay for equal work." The person must be legally able to work in the United States. Comparable worth is more than equal pay for equal work, and it is more than just addressing appropriate values to the employer. The process to determine comparable work includes job analysis with points assigned to jobs so even jobs that seem completely different may be of comparable worth based on such factors as education, training, responsibility, and so on.

IMMIGRATION REFORM AND CONTROL ACT OF 1986 The Immigration Reform and Control Act of 1986 prohibits the denial of employment due to nationality (U.S. Citizenship and Immigration Services, 2014). However, there are key responsibilities that must be met when hiring immigrants, such as examining required documentation to prove identity and citizenship, or documents authorizing employment of noncitizens. This area is undergoing change because immigration issues have increased and are highly political.

HR must be informed of changes in labor laws and share relevant information with management. If an HCO is unionized, then this information must be factored in and managers must be knowledgeable about the union contract requirements and any changes in the contract.

Figure 8-1 The recruitment process

RECRUITMENT

Recruitment focuses on timely recruitment of the right staff for the right job. Issues that are included in this discussion are HR's responsibilities, policies and procedures, employment legal issues, job analysis, and the employment process. Nurses are involved in all of these issues as managers, team leaders, staff nurses, new employees, or potential employees. **Recruitment** is a planned and coordinated effort to ensure that competent and appropriate staff are available to meet the goals and provide the organization's services. The recruitment process includes five steps, which are described in Figure 8-1.

After this process is completed and a candidate accepts employment, the final steps of employment and orientation take place. There is no doubt that recruitment is critical for any organization; without competent and adequate number of staff, organizations will not be effective and will not survive. The goal is to hire the right person for the right job at the right time.

How do HR and management get the right person in the right job at the right time? The first step is to have a clear understanding of the job or position then develop a **position description**. The goal is to hire staff who meet the position description criteria and have a chance of succeeding in the position to decrease turnover and ensure work is done effectively. This is not easy to accomplish, particularly if the position criteria do not effectively address critical characteristics. Employers want to hire employees who will be committed to the position and the organization—to find the right match.

During interviews, interviewers can ask candidates about examples of when they made an extra effort to get something done or were enthusiastic about something at work. What examples can be described to indicate a drive toward success, leadership, and a pattern of growth? Other issues to consider in hiring criteria are (a) education and work experience, (b) problem-solving skills, (c) personal values, (d) specific clinical skills, and (e) cultural fit. Cultural fit with the organization is important as staff tend to stay in organizations where they feel there is a match between their values and the organization's values. Since change is ever present today, asking candidates to describe their experiences with change can be helpful in identifying the right employee for the job by assessing their coping styles when change occurs.

Job analysis includes a clear description of responsibilities and skills for a specific job. How does HR arrive at this description? Various methods such as observation of performance, interviews of staff who hold the position, interviews of supervisors/managers, discussions with team members, and descriptions from other organizations of similar positions are used to gather data about jobs/positions. The result should be the written position description, which lays out the job expectations to be used for hiring and performance evaluation, including such content as education, work experience and history, competencies, and references.

The Employment Process

The employment process is long and complex and begins with recruitment of candidates. Typical methods used to attract job candidates include print advertising (newspapers, professional journals), the Internet, job fairs, and the use of nurse recruiters. Word of mouth is also an important method, though electronic methods have increased and become even more important. Sometimes employers offer incentives to encourage their staff to refer job candidates. To attract new graduates, many employers are now meeting with nursing students in schools of nursing. Some schools of nursing have required or optional co-op programs where students spend some time employed in a guided situation. For example, Northeastern University School of Nursing has a required co-op program. Another strategy used by some hospitals is nurse internship programs offered to nursing students between their junior and senior years. These internship programs offer opportunities for HCOs to see how students function. These students may then be offered positions after graduation. Students' familiarity with working in the HCO influences the type and amount of orientation needed when these students are hired as staff.

After receiving résumés, candidates then need to be screened. During **job screening**, applications are reviewed in more detail, and selections are made for interviews. Preparation for interviews takes time. After the interviews, decisions need to be made to determine if additional interviews are required or additional candidates are needed or to make final decision to offer a position to a candidate. The offer is then made, and negotiation may take place. It is important to frequently evaluate the process, which is highly dependent on communication that can easily fail.

It is very important to remember that the initial contact in the employment process is a potential employee's first impression of the employer. Many potential employees are lost when they are unimpressed with the process and the staff they encounter and thus decide the HCO is not the best place for them. When telephone calls go unanswered, staff members do not respond when they say they will, applications are lost, or staff is rude on the telephone, potential employees may look elsewhere for employment.

SCREENING   The goal of screening is to identify those candidates who should be evaluated further. Screening actually can take place more than once. The first time may be when potential candidates call or email for further information. A second opportunity for screening is after candidates submit résumés and, in some cases, applications to determine which candidates will be interviewed. The third screening is directly involved in the final decision when choices are made about additional interviews or a candidate is selected for the position. Sources of data that are used in screening may include telephone and email communication, application, references, résumé, licensure, certification status, and in-person interview contact.

PROS AND CONS OF APPLICATION FORMATS   Applications are important. A candidate may send a résumé and indicate on the application: "See résumé." Candidates, however, should be required to complete the organization's application. First, this protects the organization legally; the organization is meeting the requirements of employment laws. Applications also provide a standard record of information about candidates that can be used when recruitment is evaluated and to provide consistent types of application data for comparison of candidates. When candidates are compared, the application is the best source for comparison data.

Despite the fact that applications provide a consistent format for information about candidates, it is important to approach application review with some flexibility. First, this requires a clear understanding of the position and need. If the position description says the candidate must have five years of experience but the candidate only has three years, this should be considered with an open mind. In some cases a candidate may not have the required experience but has some characteristics that indicate the candidate could quickly adapt and learn to meet the position requirements. Reviewing the application form with a rigid eye may lead to missing out on an important candidate. Another problem that can occur is reviewing candidates too quickly because positions need to be filled. If there is a shortage in nursing, it is easy to think any nurse is better than none. In this case little or no consideration may be given to the position requirements and matching them with the best candidate. This can lead to serious future performance problems and possibly future staffing problems if staff are not retained.

RÉSUMÉ   In reviewing **résumés**, the format or style does make a difference. The chronological style, the most commonly seen résumé, is an easy style to review and provides an overall picture of the candidate with a listing of jobs by dates of employment. The functional style is organized around functions that the candidate performed in previous jobs (for example, direct care, management, and patient education functions). This style may not provide as much detailed information and also may not describe duration of employment, but it does describe experience over time in a logical manner. Red flags that require further investigation are gaps in dates, more information supplied on earlier positions than more current ones, overemphasis on education and nonjob factors, and poor grammar and spelling.

REFERENCES   References are typically requested at some time during the hiring process. HR contacts references via telephone or requests written information. Candidates supply names, telephone numbers, and addresses for their references.

LICENSURE   Licensure is very important to many positions in the healthcare setting such as registered nurses. During the application process, employers ask for the nurse's professional license number, renewal date, and the state that issued the license. Typically after the position is accepted, the candidate must show the license and/or submit a copy of it; however, in many states employers can check licensure status online. This is required by state licensure boards to ensure that appropriate staff, for example registered nurses, are licensed. Checking licensure of a nurse candidate with the state board of nursing may lead to information about professional misconduct. However, the reporting of misconduct and disciplinary action process is not perfect. It is the employer who needs to make the decision about offering employment, but only licensed professionals can hold positions that require licensure.

CERTIFICATION STATUS   Certification is also important for some positions. The most common certification that many who work in health care have is cardiopulmonary resuscitation certification. Candidates may be asked if certified and, when hired, to show documentation. Other certifications that may be relevant are nursing certifications for specific clinical practice specialties such as community health, gerontology, maternal-child, and other specialties; advanced practice registered nurse specialties such as family, adult, and pediatric; and other clinical specialists.

THE INTERVIEW PROCESS   The interview is a critical step in the hiring process; in fact, it is the most important method used in selecting staff. It is costly and time consuming and therefore must be done with careful consideration, including the selection of candidates to interview, preparation for the interviews, the interview itself, and analysis of the interview results so the best possible decisions can be made.

INTERVIEWER: PLANNING FOR THE INTERVIEW   The interview step begins as soon as candidates are selected for interviews, which will affect the number and types of interviews as well as when they will take place. Interview appointments must be made, frequently requiring coordination of schedules among many people. The candidate needs to be told who will be conducting the interviews and their positions, interview location, time frames, and any other pertinent information such as parking and information to bring to the interview. All staff involved in the interviews need to review the candidate's résumé and application. Interview questions should be developed prior to the interview. There may be standard questions asked and questions focused on the individual candidate's experience and the needs of the position. Although both the interviewer and interviewee are interviewing one another, the interviewer should be in charge of the process. There may be more than one interview; therefore, after the first interview, the interviewer must decide whether or not to ask the candidate to return for a second interview. All of this requires planning with multiple people and consideration of their feedback. The interviewee/candidate should be told the steps that follow the interview (for example, when decisions will be made and how the candidate will be informed).

INTERVIEW GUIDELINES   An interview is a formal discussion, although some interviewers approach it using an informal style of interviewing. An effective result requires some thought and homework. It is, however, not helpful to have an overly structured interview in which the interviewer does not allow for some flexibility. Follow-up questions and/or asking for more information can be critical during the interview. Effective interviewers are cognizant of the relevant laws and how these laws can impact interview questions and the employment process.

Another concern is actually saying too much about the position to the candidate before the candidate is given the opportunity to share information. This allows the candidate more opportunity to formulate responses that match the position requirements, which may or may not be an accurate reflection of the candidate or the candidate's experiences.

It is easy for many interviewers to quickly jump to a conclusion about a candidate soon after the interview begins or even in initial telephone conversations. Biases—what is seen or heard—can lead to positive or negative responses to the candidate. This can also work in the reverse, in that the candidate can have biases about the employer and also jump to conclusions before all the facts are known.

There are structured and unstructured interviews; however, there needs to be some structure in every interview for it to be effective. This is where planning becomes important—considering what needs to be asked and why. There may be a list of standard questions that are routinely asked then supplemented with more job-specific and individual candidate questions. Having a list of questions better ensures that all questions are asked. Some organizations use group interviews with a group of key staff sitting in on the same interview. In this case the group should work out procedures about asking questions and follow-up. Again, this is done to ensure that everything is covered. If the interview appears disorganized, the job candidate may then conclude that the staff are disorganized. Candidates should be told if a group interview is part of the process.

The interview should begin with establishing rapport. Privacy, of course, is important during the entire process. Introductions of all staff members present should be done with some brief statement about their roles. After a few introductory comments to put the candidate at ease, the interview should begin. Most of the questions should be open ended. Box 8-1 provides some sample questions and content to consider.

The interviewer should allow the interviewee/candidate time to respond and not feed the interviewee answers or cut the interviewee off. The interviewer should stay on task and not allow the interview to get off focus. As the interview progresses, information found in the candidate's résumé and application should be explored. This might include "Tell me more about …" Nodding of the head, asking for more information, and using other methods to indicate interest will lead the candidate to say more. HCOs are using more situational questions by asking nurse candidates to respond to hypothetical situations. When candidates discuss their own experiences, this can provide information about how they might handle similar problems. This allows the interviewer to gauge the interviewee's critical thinking/clinical reasoning and judgment abilities and capability to handle multiple problems. Of course, the interviewer must be knowledgeable about the situation proposed to assess the response and ask follow-up questions. Another technique is to end with summarizing questions by asking the candidate to summarize some aspect of the discussion. The candidate might also be asked about examples of when the candidate was resourceful, received criticism, worked under supervision, and worked with others. The candidate may be asked to describe him- or herself. At the end of the interview, the candidate needs to be given the opportunity to ask additional questions, and information about the next steps in the process should be shared. During the interview, the interviewer should take notes to ensure that information is not forgotten.

Interviewers can make serious mistakes during the interview that may lead to obtaining inadequate information and to poor decision making. If the interview is a group interview, a leader should be identified ahead of time to guide the interview. Talking too much can be a "deal breaker" as it limits time for the candidate to respond. Cutting the candidate off by jumping in too soon with another question or comment is also not helpful. The interviewer does need to be in control of the interview. To accomplish this, the interviewer needs to be clear about the position, know the interview questions that need to be asked, and be aware of the content of the candidate's résumé and application. Interviewers need to listen and follow up on questions, or important information may be ignored. Throughout the interview, the interviewer's body language and communication techniques are important. The candidate will watch for cues and interest. For example, if the interviewer communicates through body language that there is limited interest in the candidate even though this may not be the case (the interviewer may just be tired or distracted), the candidate may decide that this is not the best match for employment. If there are concerns about the candidate's experience, this might open up the discussion, allowing the candidate to further expand on experiences and skills, and help in the selection process.

BOX 8-1	SUGGESTED QUESTIONS FOR INTERVIEW FOR A PROFESSIONAL NURSING PRACTICE POSITION

1. **Manifest a philosophy of clinical care emphasizing quality, safety, interdisciplinary collaboration, continuity of care, and professional accountability.**
   - Does the organization have a written philosophy and mission statement that reflect an emphasis on quality, safety, interdisciplinary collaboration, continuity of care, and professional nursing accountability?
   - Does the organization have committees with nursing representation that provide input into policy development and operational management of issues related to quality of care, safety, continuity of care, patient-to-staff ratios, and clinical outcomes?
   - Does the organization have a formal mechanism for quality assurance that includes criteria to assess whether nursing practice is based on the most current research evidence?
   - What is the nurse-to-patient ratio?
   - What support staff are available on the unit to assist nurses?

2. **Recognize the contributions of nurses' knowledge and expertise to clinical care quality and patient outcomes.**
   - *Request a copy of the job description(s) of the registered nurse.*
   - How does the organization hold professional nurses accountable for high-quality practice?
   - Does the annual performance evaluation have explicit criteria related to level of practice expertise?
   - Are there differentiated practice levels or roles for nursing congruent with differences in educational preparation, certification, and other advanced preparation in nursing (i.e., continuing education)?
   - Does the organization have differentiated pay scales that recognize role distinctions and educational preparation among staff nurses?
   - Does the organization recognize professional role distinctions among all disciplines by title on nametags, etc.?
   - Does the organization use clinical nurse specialists, nurse practitioners, nurse scientists, and/or educators to support and enhance the work of staff nurses in clinical care?

3. **Promote executive-level nursing leadership.**
   - What are the key responsibilities/accountabilities of the top nurse executive? (Request a copy of the job description.)
   - *Request a copy of the organizational chart of the governing body and hospital structure to determine:*
     - Where is the top nursing voice in the organizational chart?
     - Where are nurses represented in key committees and activities of governance?
   - *Request a copy of the organizational chart of the patient care/nursing services:*
     - What is the chain of command?

   - What resources and functions fall under the domain of the nurse executive?
   - What professional development, educational, and research functions are included in nursing services?

4. **Empower nurses' participation in clinical decision making and organization of clinical care systems.**
   - Do nurses control decisions directly related to nursing practice and delivery of nursing care, such as staffing, nursing quality improvement, and peer review?
   - Do nurses have input into the systems, equipment, and environment of care?
   - How is nurse staffing addressed in the hospital plan of care? *(Request a copy of the hospital plan of care.)*
   - *Request a copy of the unit/department plan of care to determine:*
     - What is the specific patient population and nature of nursing care on this unit?
     - What issues are evident in the performance improvement plans for this department?
     - What role is defined for nursing staff in the unit plan?
   - *Request a copy of the policy/procedure regarding the patient classification system to determine:*
     - How are nurses involved in establishing and monitoring the workload measurement system?
     - How does this system influence daily staffing?
   - *Request a copy of the hospital performance improvement plan to determine:*
     - Is the role of nursing evident?
     - What are the key issues reflected in this overall hospital plan?

5. **Maintain clinical advancement programs based on education, certification, and advanced preparation.**
   - Are bachelor's graduates distinguished from other nursing personnel in terms of:
     - employment responsibilities?
     - opportunities for advancement and promotion?
     - initial pay schedule or salary?
   - If yes, what are the differences?
   - What rewards based on educational preparation are available?
   - How are clinical competencies and professional contributions evaluated?
   - How does this evaluation relate to the promotion process?
   - Does the evaluation of clinical advancement, competencies, and professional contributions include consideration of:
     - patient satisfaction?
     - self-initiated education?
     - dissemination of clinical information (e.g., nursing rounds, case presentations, articles)?
     - improvement of clinical outcomes and efficiency?
     - evidence-based practice?

BOX 8-1   (CONTINUED)

- ability to delegate to and guide nonbachelor's prepared nursing staff?
  - Serving as mentor, consultant, or preceptor to students and recent graduates?
  - demonstrated ability to work in an interdisciplinary context?
  - leadership role in institutional self-governance and practice committees?
- How are nurses recognized for meeting the professional practice criteria listed above (e.g., public acknowledgment, salary increases, time release, additional education, support to attend conferences, etc.)?
- How do peers, patients, and supervisors provide input into the review process?
- *Request a copy of procedures or information regarding the performance evaluation process and any clinical advancement system:*
  - Is peer review included in this process?
  - What are salary increases based on?

6. **Demonstrate professional development support for nurses.**
   - What resources are committed to the ongoing professional development of nurses (i.e., tuition, continuing education, and certification)?
   - How much is budgeted annually per staff nurse for attendance at professional development activities?
   - Do you provide tuition reimbursement for nursing course work completed toward obtaining the next higher degree?
   - Is there an internship or its equivalent in your institution for bachelor's degree nursing students?
   - Is there an internship or mentorship program to prepare nurses for clinical leadership positions?
   - Do the graduates who have completed an internship program in your institution as students start at a higher pay scale/salary than those who have not?
   - What are the opportunities for promotion within the clinical practice model?
   - What types of incentive programs exist for licensed practical nurses and other nonnurse healthcare personnel who wish to pursue registered nurse education?
   - Do you use case managers or their equivalent in your institution, and what is the minimum nursing education required for that role?
   - What are the opportunities for my own professional growth? What can I learn here, and how would employment here facilitate my career goals?

7. **Create collaborative relationships among members of the healthcare provider team.**
   - How is the quality of patient care and safety reviewed?
   - Who is involved in this process? Is it a peer review process?
   - Do nursing units or departments of the practice setting have interdisciplinary or shared leadership models?

- Does the practice setting have interdisciplinary standing committees for peer review, patient safety, quality care, or disease state management?
- Does an interdisciplinary team participate in the process for quality improvement and review of patient care errors?
- Does the practice setting offer clinical practice privileges to advanced practice nurses and other healthcare providers as part of the medical staff bylaws and credentialing system?
- Are nursing units or departments of the practice setting organized from a discipline-centered perspective or from a patient-centered perspective?
- Do nurses from the practice setting refer to other members of the patient care team when discussing their roles or work?
- Do nursing units or departments of the practice setting hold routine interdisciplinary care planning sessions?
- What collaborative, interdisciplinary articles, books, or research reports have been published by clinicians from the practice setting?

8. **Use technological advances in clinical care and information systems.**
   - Does this institution use an electronic patient care documentation system? If yes, who has access to this system and who inputs information?
   - If a patient goes to a unit/department outside of this building, do the staff in that unit/department have access to the system?
   - Do nurses have electronic access to clinical nursing and healthcare knowledge and research results, including Web access? Is this access available on nursing units or departments of the practice setting?
   - Does the practice setting allocate budgeted resources for new equipment and patient care technology?
   - Do clinical care providers have routine opportunities to provide input to the budget planning process?
   - What clinical information system, including patient care documentation, does the practice setting use? Is the system integrated throughout all or most clinical departments?
   - Do nurses feel that their practice is supported by up-to-date clinical care technology?
   - What continuing nursing education programs are in place to help nurses and other providers assimilate new technologies and information systems?

Other key statistics and information that should be requested:
- RN vacancy rate and RN turnover rate
- Patient satisfaction scores (preferably percentile ranking)
- Employee satisfaction scores
- Average tenure of nursing staff
- Education mix of nursing staff
- Percentage of registry/travelers used

At some point in the application process, it is important to offer the candidate the opportunity to visit units or other worksites. Usually, this opportunity is offered only to serious candidates. This allows the candidate to see the work environment and staff. As this is a time-consuming and costly process, the visit should be planned with staff accompanying the candidate and should not disturb work or interfere with patient care. With the increasing concern and legal requirements about patient privacy and confidentiality, consideration needs to be given as to patient privacy during the tour. Staff members who escort the candidate need to be briefed as to their roles and should be willing to perform them, or it will not provide the most positive view of the organization. However, this should not be a staged experience with the staff member told what to say or not to say to the candidate. The candidate will notice this, and it will not be a positive experience for the candidate. After the tour, the staff member can share information with HR or a manager about questions the candidate asked, concerns expressed by the candidate, and the candidate's communication skills.

EVALUATION CRITERIA   Evaluation and selection of candidates involves reviewing all the available candidate information. All staff members who were involved in the process need to share their feedback in a timely fashion, whether this is written or verbal. The hiring criteria are used to make a final determination. The identification of person or persons who will make the final decision should be clear to all involved in the process.

THE JOB CANDIDATE AND THE INTERVIEW   The job candidate should arrive at least 10 minutes early to allow time to unwind and collect thoughts before the interview. Parking information and directions should be clarified before going to the interview to avoid getting lost and being late. When entering the room for the interview, it is best to first see if the interviewer offers direction to a specific seat. If this does not occur, the best seat is one that is directly opposite the interviewer. During the interview, sharing of personal information should be limited. It is important to be aware of and avoid behaviors that indicate nervousness such as swinging legs, clenching hands, pencil tapping, knuckle cracking, and chewing gum. Dress should be business attire.

Before the interview, the interviewee should consider personal career goals and experiences. If the candidate is a new graduate, the candidate should consider clinical experiences from courses taken. These may serve as examples during the interview. Coming to the interview with prepared questions that address critical issues demonstrates an understanding of the position. Finding out about the HCO, its nursing services, and its nursing staff prior to the interview is helpful and communicates interest.

The type of position may also affect the interview questions that might be asked (for example, questions about responsibilities and types of patients and patient problems). Other issues that might be considered are the HCO's culture, mission and vision, communication within the nursing department, interprofessional and organization-wide policies, scheduling, staff development and career advancement, differential for education and certification, use of career ladders, and ability to change positions and receive promotions. It is important for the candidate to listen to the interviewer and to clarify questions that might be confusing before answering them. As the candidate goes through the process, the candidate should consider if the HCO is a good match with his or her career goals, experience, and desired work environment.

Interviewing provides experience in how to evaluate organizations and positions. Even an interview for a position that might be of limited interest can provide nurses with more experience about the process. Some nurses even work for temporary agencies so they can get into an HCO and learn more about it before pursuing a long-term position in the organization.

SELECTION PROCESS   References should be checked carefully, although responses are frequently vague. When this occurs, the person who calls for references should push for more information. This does not, however, mean that attempts to obtain this information from references should not be made.

Due to federal regulations, there are **background check** requirements for some healthcare providers who apply for clinical privileges, such as physicians and dentists. This information is checked in the National Practitioner Data Bank every two years. Initial registered nurse licensure now requires fingerprinting to be used for a background check. Background checks regarding patient abuse and neglect, rape, and child abuse are of particular interest to the employer.

Alcohol and drug screening may be included, but it must meet the requirements of the Federal Drug-Free Workplace Act of 1988. The candidate cannot be discriminated against based on disability.

Selection of candidates for positions must be done thoughtfully. This decision needs to include all staff who had a formal role in the process and all relevant information (the résumé, application, information from interviews, and reference information). Many HCOs have forms that are used to evaluate candidates based on specific criteria. The staff member who is responsible for making the job offer should be clearly identified, and typically this is someone in HR. This staff member needs to know what is negotiable and what is not before contacting the candidate. The staff person needs to know who in the HCO needs to be consulted about the negotiation with the candidate and kept informed of the progress.

The candidate is involved in the negotiation of salary. What should the candidate consider? The first step is a self-assessment of worth. This is also important when a nurse wants an increase in salary. The self-assessment should consider factors such as education, experience, past salary, certification, cost of coverage by a temporary agency nurse or outsourcing compared with the employee, and contributions that the nurse has made in previous positions (or in the present position if seeking a promotion rather than a new position). Arguments for the salary need to be clearly made and discussed, and at the end of the meeting, there should be a summarization of the critical reasons used to support the salary change. After the position is accepted, the candidate is informed about the next steps to take and what the employer will do. If the candidate rejects the position, it is helpful to know the reason(s) so this information may assist in understanding possible recruitment problems.

WHEN IS THE JOB THE RIGHT JOB?   There are many factors to consider when deciding to accept or reject a job offer. The benefits package is the description of services or additional pay that the employer offers employees. Benefits are important factors when accepting a position; typical benefits are health insurance plans, personal leave days, holidays, retirement, and investment. Employers may cover these benefits, or the employee and employer may share the costs for them, often at a reduced rate for the employee. The benefits that are offered vary from employer to employer. Benefits are not required, but they go a long way to attract potential competent employees to accept positions. The Affordable Care Act (ACA) has had an impact on insurer benefits, type, and amounts. Labor unions affect the types of benefits offered as this is part of the negotiated labor contracts; however, not all HCOs are unionized. Potential employees should evaluate benefits carefully. It is important to understand individual needs and then evaluate the benefits package based on this information. If information is not clear or there are questions, candidates for positions, new employees, and even current employees should address these with the organization's HR staff. During new employee orientation, benefits are typically discussed. If a nurse changes positions, there could be an effect on benefits, so this needs to be addressed.

Most nurses will work in a variety of settings and hold several different types of positions during their careers. Some of this will be due to changes in educational levels or moves, but it is also due to changes in interest and personal requirements such as scheduling and level of responsibility. An advantage of nursing as a profession is there are many different ways and settings in which a nurse can practice. With the variety of positions available, there are a number of job-related factors that the nurse needs to consider when evaluating a new position:

- The nurse applicant needs to decide whether or not the level of work required meets the nurse's personal needs and career goals. This might include working part time or full time or shifts (day, evening, night, 12-hour shift, or short shifts, which are used to cover busy times and when there are short staff periods).
- The type of HCO may make a difference whether or not the nurse is able to meet individual needs, goals, and skill levels.
- A critical issue is whether or not the position focuses on direct or indirect care. Making this decision will eliminate or clarify which positions to pursue.
- As positions are evaluated, the nursing delivery model that is used may be important to candidates.

- Selection methods for team leaders may be important. If the candidate has no interest in being a team leader at the time and team leadership is rotated among team members, then this may not be the position for the nurse.
- Many candidates are interested in educational support to pursue advanced degrees.
- Candidates need to know about promotions and career advancement.
- Another area of concern that each nurse should assess is the nurse's strengths and weaknesses. Weaknesses can be changed with education and/or additional experience, but to do this, those weaknesses need to first be acknowledged. The areas that need consideration when identifying strengths and weaknesses are technical skills and competencies, interpersonal relationship skills, communication, leadership, and management skills and competencies. It is not expected that a nurse demonstrate a high level of functioning in all these areas, but an honest appraisal is helpful. Certain positions require more of some skills than others. For example, psychiatric/mental health nurses need to communicate on all levels and be proficient in establishing interpersonal relationships. They do, however, still need some basic technical nursing skills. A nurse who works in the community also needs to be able to establish interpersonal relationships, communicate with individuals and groups, apply epidemiologic concepts, and demonstrate leadership and management. If the nurse is working in the community as a home health nurse, technical skills will be a critical part of the position competencies.
- The last consideration is specialty area, something that also may change over time. Specialty positions are also affected by education and certification. Some specialty decisions may be driven by prerequisite experience level before employment in that specialty area. Some organizations offer internships to further prepare nurses for work in the specialty, such as in intensive care or the operating room.

RETENTION: WHY IS IT IMPORTANT?

HCOs that ignore staff retention soon experience problems with quality of care and costs. Staff retention keeps the organization going and meeting its mission and goals. Staff are needed to meet these goals. When staff do not mesh with the organizational culture, problems occur such as staff frustration, unsatisfactory job performance, and decreased quality of care. These all affect staff negatively and can lead to loss of staff members. Problems with retention are extremely costly for HCOs. Every organization has to make a concerted effort to create an environment that helps to retain staff, particularly nursing staff. Registered nurses' rights should be considered as HCOs and the managers assess retention of staff. Box 8-2 describes the American Nurses' Association Bill of Rights for Registered Nurses.

BOX 8-2	BILL OF RIGHTS FOR REGISTERED NURSES

1. Nurses have the right to practice in a manner that fulfills their obligations to society and to those who receive nursing care.
2. Nurses have the right to practice in environments that allow them to act in accordance with professional standards and legally authorized scopes of practice.
3. Nurses have the right to a work environment that supports and facilitates ethical practice, in accordance with the *Code for Nurses* and its interpretive statements.
4. Nurses have the right to freely and openly advocate for themselves and their patients, without fear of retribution.

5. Nurses have the right to fair compensation for their work, consistent with their knowledge, experience, and professional responsibilities.
6. Nurses have the right to a work environment that is safe for themselves and their patients.
7. Nurses have the right to negotiate the conditions of their employment, either as individuals or collectively, in all practice settings.

Turnover: Costs, Reasons, and Prevention

Turnover problems are related to retention. As commented on earlier in this chapter, there are turnover problems particularly with new graduates. The *RN Work Project* is a 10-year study of newly licensed registered nurses (NLRNs) that began in 2006 and represents a major multistate, longitudinal study of new nurses' turnover rates, intentions, and attitudes. The study also examined intent, satisfaction, organizational commitment, and preferences about work. The sample included nurses from 34 states, covering 51 metropolitan areas and 9 rural areas, including 3 cohorts of newly licensed RNs. The conclusions from the study estimated that 17.5% of newly licensed RNs left their first nursing position within the first year and 33.5% left within two years. In comparing clinical sites, turnover was lower in hospitals compared to other HCOs (Kovner, Brewer, Fatehi, & Jun, 2014). The researchers also commented on the association of increased pressure ulcers, physical restraints, patient falls, and nursing care. All of these are included in the Medicare and Medicaid events that are no longer covered for reimbursement if they are identified as having occurred during a hospitalization.

The costs of turnover are great: most notably the costs incurred during the recruiting and hiring process, orientation, and additional staff member support, such as human resources records, staff development, and so on. The study discussed above noted that cost can be as much as $6.4 million for a large acute care hospital. The variation in cost depends on the type of nursing. For example, the turnover costs for an intensive care nurse are higher due to the need for more specialized orientation and training. In addition, turnover causes great strain on work teams. The first thought when considering turnover costs is that it is simply money, but it is not. Staff morale is impacted by costs related to reduced productivity, increased need for orientation and training, team problems, increased cost to cover empty positions, recruitment costs, orientation preceptor time, increased overtime, and staff stress due to dealing with staff changes.

When new staff are oriented and become part of the team, this affects the overall productivity of a unit or a team, which is costly. If the turnover becomes a more extensive problem, the HCO as a whole suffers, leading to stress and frustration as more and more staff try to cope with empty positions, orient new staff, and adjust to new team members or temporary staff. Work teams eventually develop communication and methods of working together, but all of this takes time. Turnover rates need to be monitored and analyzed. It is important to identify the reasons for the turnover as they impact productivity.

There are, of course, reasons for turnover that are related to natural life events, such as births, ill family members, spousal job changes and subsequent relocation, a need to stay home with younger children, and return to school. If a move is required and the HCO is a state or national organization, encouraging staff to stay in the system can be helpful for the healthcare system (e.g., if a nurse works for the VA system and is able to transfer to another VA hospital). Employers need to monitor the reasons staff members are leaving their jobs. Some reasons can be addressed through prevention methods (e.g., providing child care on site, encouraging nurses to work part time while in school, altering the staff schedule, and supporting staff with educational benefits). Staff members view reasons for turnover differently as their personal perspectives come into play. One of the simplest interventions that can be used to help prevent retention problems is to let staff know they are appreciated; recognition and "thank you" is one place to start when addressing retention problems. It is also important for organizations to ask: What is good about the organization? What does it offer its staff? What is unique about it? What needs to improve? Answers to these questions help an HCO develop an action plan to retain staff. Organizations want to retain their best people, but this takes effort. When management assumes that staff must be satisfied when they are good at their jobs, this may lead to a false sense of security. It is important to understand staff satisfaction and dissatisfaction to improve the work environment. If this process is turned over to HR, it will not be effective because it needs to come from management. Listening to staff is the place to begin. What excites a staff member? Using performance review time to discuss what makes the staff member excited about work can be very helpful and involves the staff member in assessment and improvement process. However, there are many times when there is no one else who can do the parts of the job the staff member does not like to do. Managers must be careful about promising too much as this can lead to even greater staff frustration and retention problems.

APPLYING EVIDENCE-BASED PRACTICE

Evidence for Effective Leadership and Management

CITATION: Bae, S., Mark, B., & Friend, B. (2009). Impact of nursing unit turnover on patient outcomes in hospitals. *Journal of Nursing Scholarship, 42*(1), 40–49.

OVERVIEW: This secondary analysis study examined how nursing unit turnover impacts workgroup processes. The review also considered how these processes mediate the impact of nurse turnover on patient outcomes. RN and patient data from 268 nursing units at 141 hospitals were used. Researchers examined the turnover rates for six consecutive months; used a questionnaire to gather data about workgroup processes; and analyzed data on patient outcomes (unit-level average lengths of stay, patient falls, medication errors, and patient satisfaction). Results indicate that moderate levels of turnover rates have lower workgroup learning levels (how groups learn from their experiences), lower turnover levels have fewer patient falls, and workgroup cohesion and relational coordination have a positive impact on patient satisfaction.

APPLICATION: Nursing unit turnover is a critical concern throughout the country in all types of healthcare settings. This study offers an interesting perspective on the interrelationship of nurse unit turnover, workgroup issues, and patient outcomes.

Questions:

1. Why do you think nurse unit turnover impacts patient outcomes and workgroup effectiveness?
2. What other factors might impact workgroup cohesion?
3. As a chief nurse executive, how might you use the results of this study in your management decisions?

Staff Role in Retention

Staff have a major role in retention of other staff. How staff work together can make an important difference in whether or not staff feel comfortable in the work environment. Motivation has a major impact. What motivates staff to work? Motivation is complex and very individual. It helps to explain why one staff member works differently or better than another, and this has a direct effect on performance. Motivation may be influenced by the need to have a job, for another pay level, or for a different work schedule. Nurse managers and their actions have an impact on staff motivation: providing positive feedback, recognizing work effort, providing some degree of flexibility, asking staff to take part in decision making, providing resources staff need to complete their work, and trying to find the best staff to fill empty positions and retain staff to improve the level of productivity—all demonstrate that management is concerned about staff.

Another important factor in staff retention is HCO efforts made to support career advancement. Identifying staff with skills and expertise for promotion is an important management responsibility. The Peter Principle, or promoting past one's ability, is not what should be done, but rather staff members who can succeed should be the ones promoted (Peter & Hull, 1969). Organizations must also provide support, training, and opportunities for further education to staff. (See Chapter 20.) This can be very effective in retaining staff; staff who feel recognized may be more motivated to stay.

Losing Staff

Losing staff, whether through resignation or termination, should be an organizational concern. Terminating staff is never easy. It needs to be done thoughtfully with a clear understanding about the reasons for the **termination**. Staff are often given the opportunity to resign rather than be terminated. A manager may use the time to counsel the staff member, particularly if the manager feels that the position or type of nursing specialty or position is not the best fit for the staff member. Most staff members, however, are usually quite upset and have difficulty hearing this advice. The way in which terminations are handled and why staff are terminated has a tremendous effect on staff morale. Although termination is initiated by the HCO, this does not mean that the organization should ignore the reasons for the terminations (e.g., staff who have been terminated due to an inability to fulfill job requirements). Causes for this type of turnover should also be analyzed. Staff may not be clear about expectations, not know how to do the job, lack continuing education required for the job responsibilities, have been hired with the wrong competencies needed for the position, and so on.

A staff member may be unsure how to resign in a way that does not have a negative impact on career goals. For example, when an employee publicly criticizes the manager or HCO during resignation, this may lead to a problem when seeking references for other employment opportunities. The first resource a nurse should consult is the employee policies and procedures, which should describe what is expected of employees at the time of resignation. It is also important that the immediate supervisor is informed before gossip reaches the supervisor about the resignation, which can come from an internal or external source. After verbal notice is given, a written resignation letter should be submitted and addressed to the immediate supervisor. Copies should be sent to the department director and human resources. This letter needs to be clear about the decision with a date provided. It is not appropriate to use the letter as an avenue for negative feedback. The letter will be kept in personnel files and referred to if references are sought. The way in which a nurse terminates from a position can make a difference in obtaining future positions. Following the appropriate process is important because one never knows when references or a recommendation will be needed from an employer or supervisor. The exit interview is an important tool for gathering information about the work environment and retention issues: reasons for resigning; the staff member's view of the HCO, the unit where the staff member works, management, and coworkers; the positive and negative aspects of the organization; and what the staff member thinks would help to retain staff in the future.

The interviewer should not be defensive when hearing negative comments about the organization or the job. The goal is to collect information and to try to end the exit interview on a positive note. It is important to remember that ex-employees will talk about past employers in the community, which is a public relations concern. Former employees who feel efforts have been made to listen to them, even though it may be late in the process, may feel more positive about the organization.

Orientation: Its Role in Retention and Improving Quality Improvement

Orientation is discussed in detail in Chapter 20; however, it is important to mention in this chapter. The orientation program is an important factor for a job candidate to consider. When staff get the orientation they need, they are usually more satisfied in their jobs, thus boosting retention and positively impacting continuous quality improvement efforts. The goal of orientation should be to assist new graduates in becoming knowledgeable about the HCO and the new position, competent, efficient, and confident nurses with strong communication skills.

PERFORMANCE APPRAISAL

Performance appraisal is an important part of retention. During the process, management decides if staff members are fulfilling position requirements and determines how to improve staff performance. By doing so, management provides guidance that will help to retain staff. All employers have some type of performance appraisal, but a performance appraisal may be called by many other terms such as performance review, performance evaluation, performance assessment, and performance rating. Accreditation organizations require that HCOs implement a performance evaluation process, although there can be great variation in the type and effectiveness of the process. The traditional view of performance appraisal focuses on job competence and areas that need improvement; however, there are other important reasons for conducting a performance appraisal. This formal discussion provides uninterrupted time to discuss staff member views of personal performance, management, functioning of the unit and organization, need for improvement (employee and manager), and plans for the future. The basic theme should be improvement.

Evaluation is also an opportunity to reinforce the HCO's vision, mission, and goals and to draw the employee into the organization's culture. The formal performance appraisal should not be the only time that the supervisor has a discussion with an employee or shares positive feedback. If this is the case, there are 364 days of lost opportunities to ensure staff improvement and growth. Staff will feel disconnected from the organization, and this affects performance, quality care, staff dissatisfaction, and workplace stress and burnout. The ultimate result may be loss of staff and major problems with retention and recruitment if the word gets out that the organization or a unit/service is not concerned about its staff.

The idea of preparing for and participating in performance appraisal, despite its positive attributes, is rarely seen as a positive experience, and many dread it. The process is therefore conducted quickly and with less consideration. Employees sense this dissatisfaction as something that just needs to get done. Feeling incompetent while conducting a performance appraisal is a major problem. Another potential problem is inadequate position descriptions that do not set clear performance standards for employees or for the person conducting the appraisal. If there are insufficient rewards, staff may not see the process as being positive. Recruitment is another factor. If staff are just hired to fill positions with limited concern about being a suitable match, there will be problems in the future with performance appraisal when staff cannot meet the standards of the position. This does not, however necessarily mean that the staff member will lose the position. There will be more of a struggle for the appraiser to find reasons to keep the staff member, especially when there are staff shortages. Ultimately this dilutes the performance appraisal process and its results and has a direct impact on productivity, quality of care, and costs. A major tool typically used for appraisal is the appraisal interview; however, before the interview can take place, there are other concerns. The goal is to implement an effective performance appraisal process that provides honest, constructive feedback to the employee and includes the employee in the process to better ensure quality of care as well as improve staff performance and the HCO's goals. What issues or factors need to be considered?

Performance Standards and Position Descriptions

HCOs establish performance standards in their position descriptions. HR is responsible for oversight of personnel issues, including performance appraisal. This department ensures that the process is maintained, keeps records, assists with development and review of standards and position descriptions, and consults with supervisory staff about performance issues and disciplinary concerns. There should be a positive relationship and effective communication between HR and management. When this is lacking, there are major problems for all concerned.

The position description identifies the standards or competencies that need to be met. This information needs to be given to all employees as they begin a new position. If changes are made in the description, then employees should be informed in writing. Organizations typically use a standard format for their position descriptions. Position descriptions are very important documents, and each staff member should have a copy of the description of his or her staff position. Typically the position includes job title, department (if applicable), status of the job (for example, full time, part time, or temporary), reporting relationship or to whom the employee reports (not a specific person but position, such as nurse manager), job summary, essential functions of the job or duties, qualifications, any physical requirements, and the date the description was approved. Position descriptions are also important for staff who are supervising other staff. They need to know about position expectations for their staff. For example, a team leader needs to have an understanding of the job that an unlicensed assistive personnel (UAP) is expected to perform. (See Chapter 15 on delegation.)

Competency-Based Performance Appraisal

Competency is a frequently used term today. The American Nurses Association (ANA) defines competency as "an expected and measurable level of nursing performance that integrates knowledge, skills, abilities, and judgment, based on established scientific knowledge and expectations for nursing practice" (2010, p. 64). The goal of staff education within HCOs is to maintain nursing competency throughout employment. Maintaining competency requires evaluation, but this is not easy to accomplish. The best approach is a proactive one that helps staff improve and prepare for changes and thus better ensure competency. Nursing organizations also emphasize the need to develop and maintain competencies, as does the Joint Commission and the IOM report on nursing (2011).

How competency is demonstrated continues to be a problematic issue. The Institute of Medicine report (2001) on quality care indicated that retooling practicing clinicians is critical today, and assessing this is part of performance appraisal. This is also highlighted in the IOM report *Health Professions Education* with the identification of five core competencies of healthcare professions (2003). Should nurses be required to take only one exam in a lifetime career to demonstrate competency? How does attendance at continuing education programs demonstrate competency? Certification has been used as one method to demonstrate competency; however, it, too, has limitations. After the exam is taken for certification, if there are no other exams and only continuing education requirements, is competency demonstrated over time? Should this be left in the hands of professional organizations? These are complex questions that cause stress among nurses in practice and for which the profession has no clear answers.

Components of a performance management program have been changing, and there are now several new approaches that can be used. Some of these approaches are a greater emphasis on self-appraisal, continuous feedback, peer appraisal, and 360-degree appraisal.

Self-appraisal/evaluation should be part of every performance management program. Staff members need to assess themselves and to include this information in their performance appraisal. How do they view their own performance? What are their strengths and limitations? What would staff recommend for improvement strategies? It is not easy to do self-evaluation, but it is an important skill to learn. Every nurse should be evaluating performance daily and striving for improvement.

Continuous feedback lets staff members know routinely about their strengths or need for performance improvement. Staff members need to receive clear recognition when their performance goes beyond expectations, improves, or worsens. Documenting this performance in the personnel file is important. This form of evaluation also helps to clarify expectations on a regular basis and offers more direct contact with staff. The timing for giving feedback is very important. During a stressful incident, it is best to give feedback when the situation is calmer. Feedback should be given in private, although it is important to provide public recognition when a staff member accomplishes something special or when a team performs effectively. When appointments are made with staff, it is best to state the purpose of the meeting, or staff may become concerned and spend time wondering about its purpose, perhaps blowing it out of proportion.

Peer appraisal is used in some organizations, with people giving feedback to peers about job performance. This can be a very sensitive process that requires trust in peers to provide objective, constructive feedback. All staff need to understand the process and how to provide constructive feedback. This feedback should not be the only method used in the performance appraisal process, but it can be helpful to know how peers respond to a staff member's performance.

Another method of evaluation is **360-degree evaluation**, which includes a variety of people in the feedback loop, thus forming a complete circle. This evaluation includes constructive feedback from supervisors, peers, other subordinates, and self and may include patients, family members, and others. All staff need to understand this method, why it is being used, and how it will be done. In some HCOs staff members may choose who will do the evaluation, specifying a number of potential reviewers. This feedback should be anonymous and subsequently needs to be summarized. It is critical that those involved understand the criteria and that the focus is on performance, not on personality issues. This type of evaluation should be used for development, not to make critical decisions such as salary increases.

Legal and Regulatory Issues

Some of the laws that were discussed earlier in this chapter are relevant to the performance appraisal process. Performance appraisal must focus on performance and not individual characteristics such as gender, age, race, or sexual orientation. If any of these factors are used to determine a performance appraisal decision or a decision about salary, promotion, or any other job-related decision, then there is great risk of discrimination and noncompliance with required legal regulations. During the evaluation, there needs to be a conscious effort to avoid generalizations, labels, personality issues, gender-based comments, and subjective language. The focus should be on job performance, and clear examples should be provided to the staff member to support feedback comments.

Performance Appraisal/Evaluation Process

THE APPRAISER'S ROLE   The appraiser is expected to provide an honest, thorough evaluation of an employee. This should not be viewed as competition among staff but an evaluation of each staff member's performance. Objectivity is critical throughout the process. If the supervisor does not understand or feel competent to evaluate a staff member, then that supervisor is obligated to get direction and assistance with the process. Staff need to view the process as important and feel respected during the entire process.

Certain types of information need to be collected to prepare for performance appraisal. Methods that might be used are observation, maintenance of a log of observations, or anecdotal notes. The information should be collected throughout the year. These observations take place as the staff member is providing care, during meetings and interactions with other staff, and with patients and families or whenever the job requires. Checklists, particularly for tasks, can be used to structure observation and to keep a record. Rating scales may also be used. Patient care documentation may be reviewed to better ensure accuracy and quality. Quality improvement data may also provide helpful data. If information is collected and reviewed throughout the year, the task of the annual performance appraisal should not be viewed as such a heavy burden. After data are collected and reviewed, then the required performance appraisal forms must be completed and should provide clear information about the employee's performance.

Implementation of the following year's performance appraisal process actually begins as the current year's performance appraisal process ends. Goals are established for the next year. Throughout the coming year, feedback should be provided before the formal, annual review takes place. Employees need notice when the annual performance review is due so they can prepare for it, and they need to know what is expected from them during the appraisal process.

THE PERFORMANCE APPRAISAL INTERVIEW The purpose of the interview can be categorized in the following ways.

1. *Probationary.* To determine if the employee has met the job's requirements; typically used for orientation to determine if the new employee meets the competency requirements for the position.
2. *Annual.* To determine the current competency of the employee, provide feedback, and plan for professional goals for the coming year as past year goals are reviewed.
3. *Ongoing/continuous.* Performance appraisal should not occur just once a year but should be ongoing. Feedback needs to be given when the employee demonstrates competence or when the employee needs guidance to improve.
4. *Transfer.* If an employee is transferring to another area within the organization or receiving a promotion, a performance appraisal should take place before changing position and after orientation to a new position.
5. *Exit.* If an employee is leaving an organization, a terminal performance appraisal should be completed. As is true with all evaluations, the results should be documented in the employee's personnel file for either voluntary resignations or terminations.

The supervisor (e.g., nurse manager) contacts the employee to arrange a time and place for the performance interview. There should be sufficient time for the meeting with no interruptions. Privacy, of course, should be maintained. Both parties should come to the interview prepared to discuss performance. The general format of the interview includes initial greetings and comments, review of expectations, review of previous year's goals, performance data and discussion with input from the employee, and establishment of goals for the coming year. It is easy to conduct the interview by telling the employee what is wrong or right about the employee's performance with limited mutual communication and self-evaluation by the employee; however, this is an ineffective approach. It is important for the employee to be able to use self-evaluation as this is a skill that the employee needs throughout the year. Staff may also be more defensive if the approach is to tell staff what is wrong without allowing staff the opportunity to comment or to only focus on the negative. Bias based on personal feelings should be avoided during the evaluation process and the interview. This may be difficult sometimes as there are personalities that just do not do well together; however, this needs to be recognized so the parties can work toward a more positive viewpoint. Beginning the interview with positive comments and a clear focus on job performance can get the interview off to a productive start. The interviewer needs to avoid patronizing, doing all the talking, focusing too much on negative feedback, not listening to the employee, not answering questions, and allowing interruptions to occur. Beginning with an open-ended question will draw the staff member into the process quickly, setting the standard of a dialogue instead of a lecture.

HCOs typically use a standard form during the process, and it is reviewed with the employee during the appraisal interview. Appraisal forms indicate that the organization has thought about what should be included in the evaluation process, provide some consistency, and should reflect the organization's vision and goals. Regulatory requirements need to be demonstrated in the form's content. The form guides the interview; however, the supervisor needs to be flexible, encouraging the employee to participate in all aspects of the interview. If the approach is one of problem solving, identifying problems or issues, and working together to figure out the best strategy for improvement, this will stimulate more staff development. It is important that both the supervisor and the employee provide specific examples to support comments. The focus should be on behavior and facts and, while doing this, encouraging the employee to contribute comments. Both the supervisor and employee should sign the appraisal form, which only indicates that the employee has read the form but may not necessarily mean that the employee agrees with its content. Forms should have space for employees to make their own comments about the evaluation.

All appraisal interviews must be documented with records kept in the employee's personnel file. The employee should be given a copy of the completed performance appraisal form. The supervisor may keep notes along with data about the employee. A copy of future goals should also be kept.

THE EMPLOYEE'S ROLE   The employee should have an active role in performance appraisal. Preparing for performance appraisal is key for the employee, just as it is for the supervisor. It begins with self-evaluation. The employee should review position requirements, past year's goals, past year's evaluations, and ask colleagues for feedback. A portfolio may be developed or updated for the evaluation. This all requires time and should be a thoughtful process, not a hurried one. The goal is to have a positive experience that focuses on improvement and recognizes accomplishments, not to emphasize failures. The performance evaluation may be a time to discuss or negotiate a salary increase, change in position, promotion, and other job-related matters. Since mutually established goals should be agreed on in the interview, the employee should develop goals for the coming year in preparation for the performance appraisal interview. These goals need to be clear, specific, and relate to the position and professional growth. Examples of content for goals are to improve documentation by describing clinical problems more clearly, to attend one conference in a specialty area, to organize work better so the employee can leave work at the scheduled time, to develop more specific patient education plans, and so on. Some topics are not appropriate for the performance interview, such as critique related to personal issues that are not related to job performance.

CASE STUDY

A First Experience With Complicated Performance Appraisal

Six months ago you were promoted to a nurse manager position on a surgical unit. The first six months have been rocky with short staff, high census, high acuity, and several critical incidents such as a medical error that led to a patient being transferred to ICU. You have been trying to learn more about your new role. Staff seem to be accepting of you, but a couple of nurses do not think you have enough experience. You have heard this through the grapevine. Two of these nurses are now up for their annual performance appraisals. The hospital uses competency-based performance appraisal. The following briefly describes the two nurses:

a. Jane has been working on the unit for eight years longer than you. She has experienced three nurse managers in this time period. She has a BSN. When there are staff issues, she is the first to lead the charge and can get very emotional. She has had three arguments with physicians in the past six months. This nurse has also been involved in four medication errors over the past eight months. This year her documentation meets required criteria.

b. Sue has worked on the unit for three years. She had an AD but just completed her BSN five months ago. Her behavior has changed in the past five months. She has not worked well with the certified nurse assistants (CNAs) and had an argument with a new nurse. She told this nurse, "You don't know what you are doing." The new nurse is ready to leave the job. Sue has never been an effective delegator, but no one has ever addressed this. She has no known errors, but her documentation does not consistently meet required criteria. You wonder if her attaining her BSN has made a difference—and not necessarily a positive difference.

You now have to prepare for both nurses' performance appraisals.

Questions:

1. What information would you need to prepare for the meetings? Use information described here in this chapter and any additional information.
2. What are the critical issues for each nurse that you think you should address during the performance appraisal meetings, and how will you address them?
3. During the meeting with Jane, she says, "I have to tell you that I think you are not an effective nurse manager." How would you respond to her?
4. Sue tells you in the interview that since she got her BSN, she is better than the other nurses, particularly the three AD nurses on the unit. How would you respond to her?
5. Describe the plan you would recommend to each nurse to improve in the next year. Include a time line for review.

Problems With Employees

As with any relationships, there can be problems in the employer-employee relationship. How these problems are handled can affect retention and staffing. Problems may occur during the performance appraisal or throughout the year.

Employees and supervisors may encounter problems with one another. As managers and team leaders supervise staff, they may wonder why staff members are not doing what is expected of them. Some of the reasons for the inability to meet expectations may be because staff members and managers do not understand their own roles and how these roles interact. Sometimes it is due to a disagreement as to how a job should be done or may be because staff do not want to do what is expected. Communication is often a critical factor in any staff problem.

Personal problems on either the manager's or the staff's side can be a barrier, and there are situations in which a manager and a staff member just do not like or respect one another. After the job or work begins, staff members may think that they are doing what they are supposed to do. They may not recognize any positive consequences for doing their job. Obstacles beyond their control may get in the way of doing the work. It may be that staff members think there are more important tasks they should be doing. Sometimes staff members do not do what they are asked to do because they are punished for doing it or they may be rewarded for not doing it. If staff members do not see any negative consequences for poor performance, they may not feel the need to do the job well or to improve. The goal is to prevent these barriers from occurring so the work gets done effectively. It is important to try to understand the causes of these problems. The manager should use the following prevention strategies:

- Keeping lines of communication open
- Offering positive feedback
- Providing negative feedback (if warranted) privately and in a constructive manner
- Observing and listening
- Being fair
- Respecting staff
- Asking for staff input
- Dealing with problems early before they get bigger and harder to resolve

These strategies are not just preventative but also may be used to solve problems when they occur.

There has also been a growing problem with lateral violence in HCOs in nurse-to-nurse relationships. This mostly occurs in the form of verbal comments, lack of support for one another, negativity, and lack of teamwork. Stress plays a big role in this problem. In addition, experienced nurses may not be as supportive and helpful to new staff. This has an impact on job satisfaction of new staff and retention. When staff do not feel welcomed and supported, this can lead to staff quitting.

Not all evaluation meetings go smoothly. The appraiser/manager might know before the meeting that problems exist. This is particularly true if the employee's performance has been less than anticipated. In this case the appraiser needs to be very careful about preparing for the meeting and spend time thinking through the evaluation and how to discuss it. The appraiser should not become defensive but stay on the subject of performance and expectations. Honest feedback that includes some positive comments should be provided. The employee may express emotion during the meeting. Job satisfaction is easy to handle, but frustration and anger about performance will be stressful for both managers and staff. Giving the staff member some time to get in control is important. It allows the manager to also gain some composure and not respond with emotion. If the staff member cannot control emotions at the time, the meeting may need to be rescheduled, although this is not preferable. If there is any threat of aggression, then the manager should stop the meeting and reschedule if possible. Safety is a priority. Workplace violence should never be tolerated. The supervisor may recommend that the employee seek assistance from the Employee Assistance Program (EAP) if one is available. This program provides counseling for emotional problems and substance abuse problems, and many organizations offer this service to their staff. If there is concern prior to a meeting with staff that the employee might respond with aggression, the meeting should not be conducted alone. Employees who are not meeting expectations need to be treated with respect in a safe environment for both the manager and staff. The meeting should allow time to discuss performance objectively and to work on an improvement plan that includes deadlines and a clear description of what is required to improve performance. The employee needs to understand the plan and feel that it represents a joint effort.

STRESS ON THE JOB

Job stress can be defined as

> the harmful physical and emotional responses that occur when the requirements of the job do not match the capabilities, resources, or needs of the worker. Job stress can lead to poor health and even injury. The concept of job stress is often confused with challenge, but these concepts are not the same. Challenge energizes us psychologically and physically, and it motivates us to learn new skills and master our jobs. When a challenge is met, we feel relaxed and satisfied. Thus, challenge is an important ingredient for healthy and productive work. (Centers for Disease Control and Prevention, National Institute for Occupational Safety and Health, 2014)

Individuals and Stress

Individuals respond differently to stress, making it difficult to predict who will experience job stress. However, there are work environment factors that can impact the risk of stress. Figure 8-2 describes the NIOSH model of job stress.

The following are examples of factors that impact job stress (Centers for Disease Control and Prevention, National Institute for Occupational Safety and Health, 2014):

The Design of Tasks. Heavy workload, infrequent rest breaks, long work hours and shift-work, hectic and routine tasks that have little inherent meaning and do not use workers' skills and provide little sense of control.

Management Style. Lack of participation by workers in decision making, poor communication in the organization, lack of family-friendly policies.

Interpersonal Relationships. Poor social environment and lack of support or help from coworkers and supervisors.

Work Roles. Conflicting or uncertain job expectations, too much responsibility, too many "hats to wear."

Career Concerns. Job insecurity and lack of opportunity for growth, advancement, or promotion; rapid changes for which workers are unprepared.

Environmental Conditions. Unpleasant or dangerous physical conditions such as crowding, noise, air pollution, or ergonomic problems.

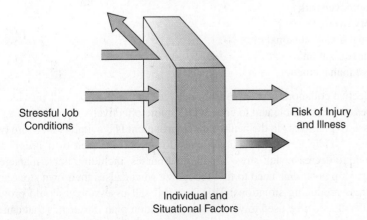

NIOSH Model of Job Stress

Stressful Job Conditions

Risk of Injury and Illness

Individual and Situational Factors

Figure 8-2 NIOSH model of job stress

Source: Centers for Disease Control and Prevention. National Institute of Occupational Safety and Health. (2014). Retrieved from http://www.cdc.gov/niosh/docs/99-101/default.html

How to Change the Organization to Prevent Job Stress

- Ensure that the workload is in line with workers' capabilities and resources.
- Design jobs to provide meaning, stimulation, and opportunities for workers to use their skills.
- Clearly define workers' roles and responsibilities.
- Give workers opportunities to participate in decisions and actions affecting their jobs.
- Improve communications—reduce uncertainty about career development and future employment prospects.
- Provide opportunities for social interaction among workers.
- Establish work schedules that are compatible with demands and responsibilities outside the job.

—*American Psychologist*

Figure 8-3 Preventing stress at work: A comprehensive approach

Source: From *How to Change the Organization to Prevent Job Stress*. Published by American Psychological Association (APA) © 2014.

Job stress not only impacts job performance and productivity, but it can also lead to employee health problems, such as cardiovascular disease; musculoskeletal disorders; psychological disorders; and in some cases suicide, impaired immune functioning, and ulcers. Workplace injuries also increase putting staff and patients at risk. Typical psychological responses are headaches, upset stomach, sleep problems, concentration problems, irritability, and fatigue. Responding to stress first requires understanding that job stress exists and some stress cannot be eliminated; however, HCOs can take steps to prevent some stress and respond when it increases. NIOSH describes a comprehensive approach to preventing job stress in Figure 8-3.

The healthcare work environment is no different from other work environments. Staff are experiencing stress and frustration with staff shortages and changes in healthcare and in HCOs. Nurses often identify the following as reasons for their stress:

- Staff shortage
- Increasing responsibility with less time
- Excessive and/or redundant paperwork
- Interdisciplinary/interprofessional issues
- Job dissatisfaction
- Working different shifts
- Fatigue and overwork
- Mandatory overtime
- Decreasing quality personal time
- Poor communication
- Ineffective management

An active, effective collaborative relationship between managers and staff provides a solid base to prevent stress when possible and to cope with it more effectively when it occurs.

Since it seems that stress in the healthcare environment is inevitable, there are two key questions to consider: (1) What can individual nurses do to decrease their own stress? and (2) What can the HCO do to decrease staff stress? Individual nurses, including nurse managers and other nurses in leadership positions, need to first recognize what causes their own stress and how they respond to stress-producing situations. This personal self-assessment should provide valuable information that can then be used to work out a prevention plan. Strategies that can help a nurse prevent or decrease stress are as follows:

- Set reasonable priorities.
- Ask for help and do not see this as a weakness.

- Do one task at a time.
- Take a few minutes to slow down several times during the day.
- Get sufficient sleep, eat a healthy diet, and exercise.
- Focus on what *is* happening rather than worrying about what *could* happen.
- Use appropriate self-assertion.
- Remove yourself from stressful discussions, such as complaint sessions with other staff.
- View problems as challenges and opportunities.
- Laugh and take time for self.

Understanding how one responds to stress is an important first step for each staff member, including leaders and managers, as all experience job stress. For example, when a person feels overwhelmed by stress, time should be taken to write down what another person said or did that might have influenced the person's reaction. Faulty beliefs are often behind these responses. Some HCOs are now offering opportunities for stress reduction such as yoga classes, exercise opportunities, nutrition classes, and so on.

New graduates are particularly vulnerable to stress as they learn their new professional roles. **Reality shock**, which was identified and defined in the 1980s and still applies today as "the shock-like reaction that occurs when an individual who has been reared and educated in that subculture of nursing that is promulgated by schools of nursing suddenly discovers that nursing as practiced in the world of work is not the same—it does not operate on the same principles" (Kramer, 1985, p. 291). New graduates need an organized orientation and staff preceptors who take an interest in and assist them with transition from the classroom to practice. Staff members on the unit can make a difference in how well a new graduate adjusts. It is important for nurses to feel an obligation to assist new nurses in the profession. Reaching out is critical, as many new nurses do not feel comfortable reaching out themselves for help. Patient assignments need to be done with care as new nurses further develop their skills and learn their way around. They need time to analyze what was done and their reactions; preceptors for new staff can help with this process, but it takes time. In doing so, the new nurse can talk through an experience and use critical thinking in a safe environment—one that focuses not on punishment but rather growth. Self-confidence builds slowly; however, if there is a staff shortage, experienced nurses often expect new nurses to gain experience quickly and carry a regular workload, although this is an unrealistic expectation. The pressure and stress that experienced nurses feel increases their impatience with colleagues. Taking time to help new nurses with the transition and supporting them will go a long way to decrease problems of rapid turnover of this vulnerable staff group, who may change jobs, thinking it will get better, or eventually leave the nursing profession.

Disruptive Behavior and Incivility: Goal of Civility and a Healthy Work Environment

Some hospitals are now using "Code Pink" (Trossman, 2014). What does this mean? It is used to call for assistance when other nurses are experiencing unacceptable behavior on behalf of other staff. The fact that such a code is needed illustrates the frequency of incivility in HCOs. Nurses respond by going and standing with the nurse who is being bullied and support the nurse. Other areas in the workforce also experience incivility. Incivility can be viewed on continuum from negative facial expressions, to more direct verbal abuse, to threats. A key principle is everyone needs to be accountable for their own behavior. HCOs should have zero tolerance for incivility from anyone, including from managers to staff and between managers (American Nurses Association, 2014a).

Others have expressed concern about incivility. For example, in 2008 the Joint Commission issued a *Sentinel Event Alert* "Behaviors Undermine a Culture of Safety" (Joint Commission, 2008). The ANA has resources on its website to help nurses address this problem. Students also experience incivility in the school setting and when in clinical (2014a). The ANA content discusses workplace violence, lateral violence, bullying, and advocacy. Lateral violence includes actions that colleagues take against one another. Bullying often involves actions taken by a staff person who is in a higher position against a staff person in a lower position. All of this behavior may lead to staff stress and reduced productivity and may impact the quality of care.

Incivility can be difficult to cope with in the work environment, and it is something that all staff will undoubtedly experience with colleagues. When coping with a staff member who exhibits this type of behavior, it is important to clarify expectations, particularly those related to assignments. The overall expectation should be that the work will be done. Apologies and excuses will not be enough. When complaints are made, it is important to consider the facts and avoid defensiveness.

STAFFING AND VARIABLE SHORTAGE: CRITICAL ISSUES

Staffing is a critical concern in all HCOs. Competent staff are required to ensure that quality patient care is provided and outcomes met, including cost outcomes. With the increasing costs of health care, staffing is an expense that must be considered daily. Staffing can be viewed from several different perspectives. There is the general perspective of a possible nursing shortage in the near future—limited resources to fill healthcare demand experienced by many HCOs. This can be focused in a local area, in a state, or nationally. Another perspective is that an individual HCO cannot hire enough nurses to fill budgeted positions. The reasons for this may vary, such as poor recruitment, poor reputation as an employer, inadequate pay and/or benefits, lack of local new graduates, undesirable work setting (e.g., long-term care), and degree requirements (requiring a BSN when most applicants have associate degrees). The third perspective is simply staffing is inadequate for a given shift, day, week, or longer.

The IOM includes staffing issues in its report on nursing (2004). The ACA addresses the shortage in its provisions. The law establishes a healthcare Workforce Advisory Committee to develop workforce strategy, and it identifies needs for funding to increase nursing education capacity, support training programs, provide loan repayment and retention grants, and create a career ladder to nursing. The American healthcare workforce includes more than 14 million people and accounts for about 10% of the national workforce. This total includes those employed within the health sector in hospitals, clinics, practitioners' offices, and nursing homes as well as those employed in other sites such as insurance companies, worksites, schools, and government at all levels. The workforce job classifications encompass a rich mix of occupation types and professional qualifications. The largest estimated numbers by category are found in registered nurses (2.8 million); nursing, psychiatric, and home health aides (2.3 million); personal care aides (1 million); physicians (861,000); medical assistants and other healthcare support personnel (845,000); and licensed practical and licensed vocational nurses (690,000) (Health Resources and Services Administration, 2013).

Tied in with the ACA, the presidential proposed 2015 budget includes modernizing graduate medical education to create more residencies focused on community-based ambulatory care; expansion of the National Health Service Corps (NHSC) to provide more providers in areas of need; and extension of enhanced Medicaid primary care payments. Expansion of access to healthcare reimbursement increases the need for more healthcare providers in the workforce (U.S. Department of Health and Human Services, 2014). The presidential report on the 21st-century healthcare workforce specifies five key principles that are emphasized:

1. Moving toward a value-based system.
2. Using workforce levers to improve access to primary care.
3. Making full use of every member of the healthcare team.
4. Aligning the workforce to population needs.
5. Transforming healthcare delivery through workforce innovation (U.S. Department of Health and Human Services, 2014, p. 2).

These principles are integrated into the examples from the 2015 budget mentioned above. The report notes that many factors impact the need for more providers other than increased reimbursement, which increases need for health services access. Other factors include an aging population, new medical technologies, anticipated retirement of baby boomer providers (nurses, physicians, and others), and growing need for care of chronic diseases.

Staffing Basics

This discussion provides some general information about staffing basics. Each nurse needs to become familiar with the staffing policies and procedures that are used in his or her HCO and specific unit/service. During the recruitment process, it is important that the nurse candidate ask about staffing levels, skill mix, and scheduling. All of these issues directly affect staff, including new staff members.

Staffing is the method used to ensure that the appropriate staff members—qualifications and quantity—are available to provide the care that is needed for patients to meet their needs and thus provide quality, safe care. This is not easy to accomplish with patients changing and the unstable nursing workforce. Factors that must be considered in staffing are as follows:

- Types of patients and care required.
- Number of patients.
- Workload patterns such as when patients are admitted and discharged.
- Times of procedures and other treatment.
- Average daily census.
- Hours of work (e.g., an inpatient unit is operational 24 hours a day, 7 days a week; a clinic might be operational 5 days a week but may have variable and evening hours); split shifts when staff work hours in more than one shift.
- Types of nursing staff used (e.g., RNs, LPNs/LVNs, and UAP).
- The use of support staff such as a unit secretary and staff to transfer patients to exams and procedures can make a big difference, as does the communication system (e.g., use of pagers, mobile phones, and handheld computers). The documentation system also is a critical factor, with the electronic medical/health record systems typically providing effective documentation and effective use of time.

Other terms and issues that arise in staffing are the following:

- **Full-time equivalent (FTE)** is the term used to designate a position equal to 40 hours of work per week for 52 weeks, or 2,080 hours per year. As scheduling is considered, one person or two or three persons can fill one FTE, with hours divided.
- Nursing care hours or the number of hours of patient care provided per unit of time.
- **Staffing mix** is also important, describing the type of staff needed to provide the care. To determine the staff mix, it is important to identify the type of care that is required and who is qualified to provide that care. Staff mix also includes an assessment of staff competency to fulfill care needs. This becomes important, for example, when staff members are transferred from their usual work environment into a new one, even if temporarily; they must, nonetheless, be competent to carry on the assigned tasks.
- Daily patient census is calculated every 24 hours, providing data on the number of patients at the time of the count and factoring in admissions, transfers, and discharges.
- Staff distribution is another important factor that focuses on times when staff are needed. (For example, if a surgical unit gets most of its admissions on Sunday evening for Monday surgeries, if a unit has medical procedures that are done in the morning, if admissions occur from 11 a.m. to 6 p.m. and discharges occur by 11 a.m., these factors need to be considered in the schedule.)

Nurse practice acts and other state regulations must always be met when staffing decisions are made. For example, if the patient requires more activities of daily living care such as would be found in a long-term care facility, then UAP should be included in the staff mix with RNs providing supervision, assessment, and other procedures that require RN competency.

Scheduling can be a challenge for the scheduler and for staff members who want their individual schedule needs met. Getting a schedule, preferably a cyclical schedule, established that is acceptable to management and staff is the goal. However, there will always be times when adjustments need to be made because of staff illness, vacation, and other factors. Shift hours have changed over the years with 8-, 10-, and 12-hour shifts used. Twelve-hour shifts have become more common; however, the Institute of Medicine report indicates that when shift durations exceed 12 hours, errors increase (Institute of Medicine, 2004). This means multiple reports and handoffs. In this situation there are risks for communication problems and errors related to frequent handoffs, and patients and families feel they have no anchor when the staff changes multiple times in one day. This can also cause staff stress as staff try to keep up with the rotating staff and do their jobs well.

Some HCOs have moved to **self-scheduling**, with staff directly involved in developing the work schedule. Supplemental staff issues are a concern when an HCO experiences a shortage.

Extra staff hours are also needed to cover vacations, illness, and other such situations; vacancies; and times when patient acuity demands more staff. How do HCOs handle these situations? Some have their own internal pools of staff who float as needed. Others use agency nurses who are hired per diem. Others use travel nurses. These are nurses who are hired by travel nurse agencies and contracted to work for specific hospitals and positions for specific time periods through a contract between an agency and an HCO. These nurses move from one community to another, assigned for extended times, then move on to another position. Use of agency nurses and travelers is expensive for HCOs. Overall, scheduling has implications for staff, their workload, and for patient care outcomes and quality.

The Nursing Shortage: A Changing Variable

In 2009 the United States began to see a reduction in the nursing shortage that had increased since the 1990s. This improvement was not experienced in all areas of the country, and there were some HCOs that had more problems finding staff than others. In some instances the poor economy caused nurses to postpone retirement due to financial needs. In addition, nurses who had been out of practice or had been working part time wanted and needed more full-time work had an impact on filling positions. Though this reduced the shortage, this had a negative impact on new graduates getting jobs, particularly if they were unwilling to move from their own communities. Even with the gradual decrease in the shortage, this does not eliminate the projected nursing shortage that has been discussed for years. There are still many nurses who will retire in the next decade, and there are still major problems with having enough clinical sites and faculty to meet the demands of expanding enrollment in nursing programs.

> The Bureau of Labor Statistics' Employment Projections 2012–2022 released in December 2013 provides important data about the future that should not be ignored. Registered Nurse (RN) is listed among the top occupations in terms of job growth through 2022, with numbers expected to grow from 2.71 million in 2012 to 3.24 million in 2022, an increase of 526,800 or 19 percent. The projection indicates there will need to be 525,000 replacement nurses in the workforce bringing the total number of job openings for nurses due to growth and replacements to 1.05 million by 2022. (Bureau of Labor Statistics, 2013)

Fifty-five percent of the RN workforce is 50 years of age or older, so retirement numbers will significantly increase. The American Association of Colleges of Nursing (AACN) reports that in 2012 U.S. nursing schools could not enroll 79,659 qualified applicants to baccalaureate and graduate nursing programs due to insufficient faculty, clinical sites, classroom space, clinical preceptors, and budget constraints. Almost two-thirds of the nursing schools responding to the survey pointed to faculty shortages as a reason for not accepting all qualified applicants into their programs (2014). This makes the potential future shortage even more difficult; there will have to be an increase in graduates to fill future empty positions. Staffing needs have always been difficult to project, and projections are estimates.

Another important perspective of staffing needs relates to quality care. There have been a number of studies focused on staffing and quality care. For example, Needleman's study analyzed the records of nearly 198,000 admitted patients and 177,000 eight-hour nursing shifts across 43 patient-care units within large academic health centers. The data show that the mortality risk for patients was about 6% higher on units that were understaffed as compared with fully staffed units. The study also indicated that increasing a nurse's workload due to high patient turnover also increases mortality risk (Needleman et al., 2011). *The Future of Nursing: Leading Change, Advancing Health* discussed the need for more accurate and current healthcare workforce data so we can prepare for workforce fluctuations (Institute of Medicine, 2011). The report also included the recommendation to increase the proportion of nurses with baccalaureate degrees (BSNs) to 80% by 2020. The push to increase nurses with BSNs has led to more HCOs supporting RNs who need to get the degree, increasing expansion of RN-BSN degree programs. It has also been problematic for new graduates from associate degree programs who live in areas where the local HCOs hire only RNs with BSNs. Many areas of the country have sufficient numbers of RNs, and in some instances they have an abundance. Rural areas, on the other hand, fall short in number required or need to cover staffing for certain specialty areas. Potential shortage, number of graduates, quality care, and level of education are integrated concerns when staffing is examined.

The Institute of Medicine commented on the shortage, retention, and staffing in several of its healthcare quality reports. In the report on nursing (2004), the need to maximize the capability of the workforce is discussed along with the nursing shortage. Maximizing the workforce requires attention to promote safe staffing levels, support knowledge and skills acquisition and clinical decision making, and foster interprofessional collaboration—all in keeping with the NAM's five core competencies of healthcare professions. The report states there is a connection between patient outcomes and elements that are needed to maximize the workforce. A study published in 2012 also concluded that staff satisfaction, use of teams, staff engagement in decision making, offering staff education, and retention of nurse managers and administrators impact quality of nursing care (Flynn, Liang, Dickson, Xie, & Suh, 2012). Given these examples of studies and professional organization perspectives, effective recruitment and retention of competent staff are critical issues to resolve to meet the current requirements and future ones, even for HCOs that have sufficient staff. With the variable shortage of nursing staff, recruitment, retention, and related staffing activities have become critical functions within HCOs.

Examples of Strategies to Resolve Shortage Problems

In the fall of 2002, Congress passed and funded the Nurse Reinvestment Act. This legislation addressed the issue of the nursing shortage, both of nursing staff and nursing faculty. In the interim, other laws have been passed for support of professional training. Prior to the Nurse Reinvestment Act, a federal law, California adopted a major policy related to nurse-to-patient ratios in general acute care hospitals, acute psychiatric hospitals, and specialty hospitals by passing a law in 1999 about this issue. This model of nurse staffing policy is called fixed minimum ratios. California's health services department was mandated to develop regulations that require nursing staff to be based on the following:

- Severity of illness
- Need for specialized equipment and technology
- Complexity of the clinical judgment needed to develop, implement, and evaluate patient care
- Ability of patients to provide self-care
- Licensure of the professional

The law also prohibits assigning RN functions to UAP, and it requires that certain functions be assigned to UAP only with supervision. In California this law was strongly supported by RNs and included major nursing input. Since then, other states have moved in the same direction. It should be noted that the law itself does not specifically state what the nurse-to-patient ratio must be but rather directs the state health services department to develop these regulations based on the criteria identified in the new state law. Over time there have been changes made to the law. This type of model had little research to support its use and does not address the problem of funding for staff. However, a significant study (Aiken et al., 2010) sampled 22,336 hospital staff nurses in California, Pennsylvania, and New Jersey and the state hospital discharge databases in these three states. The purpose of the study was to determine whether nurse staffing in California hospitals, which had state-mandated minimum nurse-to-patient ratios, were different from two states that did not have this mandate and if the differences were associated with nurse and patient outcomes. The conclusion from the study is "hospital nurse staffing ratios mandated in California are associated with lower mortality and nurse outcomes predictive of better nurse retention in California and in other states where they occur" (Aiken et al., 2010, p. 904). This model has had an impact on other states. As of December 2013, 13 states have staffing laws (American Nurses Association, 2013). The ANA supports a legislative model in which nurses are empowered to create staffing plans specific to each unit (American Nurses Association, 2013). This approach is preferred to staffing specifics mandated by law.

Using patient classification systems (PCSs) is another nurse staffing approach, and it is not a new one. These systems provide a structured method to assess patient acuity and needs then assign the number and type of staff who are expected to meet the needs effectively. If this method is used, it is important to select a PCS that has been tested and review results to determine if the system is a good match for the HCO or the unit.

The ANA emphasizes that staffing should recognize individual characteristics of the clinical setting and have awareness of differences throughout the day. It is important to assess patient acuity; use of unlicensed personnel; and the skills, education, and training needed for specific settings (American Nurses Association, 2012, 2014b). Staffing levels that are planned and meet identified needs may reduce errors, decrease patient complications, decrease mortality, improve patient satisfaction, reduce nurse fatigue, decrease nurse burnout, and improve nurse retention and job satisfaction. Staffing makes a major difference in care outcomes.

Pay-for-performance is now frequently used by insurers. In this model there is greater reimbursement for care that meets expected outcomes—performance. This is not easy, and currently there are more questions than answers about it (Robert Wood Johnson Foundation, 2013). This has also been influenced by the IOM report on quality (2001). The ACA also supports this approach. Pay-for-performance is focused particularly on incentives for physicians and hospitals to influence decisions and, it is hoped, improve care and reduce costs. In some cases advanced practice registered nurses are now also included in pay-for-performance assessments and reimbursement. It would be easy for direct care staff nurses and nurse managers to say this is of no concern to them but it is. Pay-for-performance influences treatment decisions, length of stay, and patient acuity. All of these factors impact nursing care and staffing—type of care needed; status of patients admitted and discharged; length of stay; and shortened length of time to provide care, provide patient education, and prepare for discharge.

Though many states are trying to develop and pass staffing laws, there are experts who believe that mandatory staffing is not the best approach. It takes years to determine if this type of policy change is effective. Mandatory staffing requires financial support. States that mandate staffing levels do not address the funding required to meet the staffing levels. HCOs then must find the funding to meet these requirements. Welton (2007) recommends that HCOs unbundle nursing care from room and board charges. Currently hospitals do not specifically identify nursing costs from other costs but rather include these costs in a flat rate for room and board. Using nursing intensity ratings to determine a level of nursing care needed and then provided allows for more specific billing. This would be an incentive to hospitals to improve nurse staffing levels. The HCOs would have a better chance of covering the actual costs of providing nursing care and would then staff for these needs and be paid for the staff hours.

Many of the provisions of the ACA of 2010 relate to staffing. There is now greater need for nurses because more people who were uninsured in the past have obtained access to health insurance; more patients equals an increased need for nurses. The legislation addresses this by including provisions to establish the Workforce Advisory Committee to develop a national workforce strategy and also to increase workforce supply and support training of health professionals through scholarships and loans. Nurse practitioners will also be in greater demand to assist in areas that have medical shortages.

What are some other strategies that have been tried or could be tried to address the staffing problems? It is clear that there needs to be a multistrategy approach. The following represent some strategies that are used or might be used. Most of these strategies depend on the environment in which they are used and the support that is given to the strategy.

- Communities are joining together to form task forces to look at the problems with representatives from healthcare providers and nursing education. Regional workforce task forces identify common issues and possible strategies to resolve them. This collaboration includes nursing education, practice, and consumers, which can lead to effective partnerships.
- Many hospitals and other large HCOs are using nurse retention specialists to help with recruitment and retention. The difference between a recruiter and a retention specialist is the latter focuses on not only hiring good staff but also keeping them—recruitment *and* retention.
- Education and training is a critical strategy that is used in many types of situations. Cross-training has benefits for some HCOs as it may increase availability of staff who have the skills that are needed in short-term specialty care; provide opportunity for professional development; and allow some of the staff who may wish to eventually transfer to ICU staff, which then decreases the cost of recruitment and training. Rapid response teams (RRTs) are also used in many hospitals, and this has an impact on staff satisfaction and quality care. The Rapid Response Team—known by some as the Medical Emergency Team—is a team of clinicians who bring critical care expertise to the bedside (Institute of Health Improvement, 2010).

- The use of UAP has been discussed in this text. Using this strategy for coping with RN shortages has caused much conflict. HCOs have supported it as a strategy to reduce costs. The nursing profession needs to assume active leadership in this type of decision to determine its impact on patient care and the profession. It is easy to assume that unlicensed means unskilled or uneducated, but this is not a fair assumption. UAPs can be skilled with the right education, training, and supervision; however, short training periods and lack of follow-up will lead to problems with quality and safety and require even more RN supervisory time—time that is rarely available. HCOs need to recognize the time needed for RNs to supervise UAP.

- Teaching staff how to cope with inadequate staffing is a strategy that can be incorporated in any HCO. Staffing shortages can be short term or long term; just having a shift when staff call in sick and the staffing level is then not at the expected level has an impact on care and workload.

- Use of "float" staff is a strategy that is used to respond to staff shortages. One of the major concerns with this strategy is whether or not the nurse is qualified and competent to practice in the clinical area where the nurse is asked to work. Nurses have the right to refuse to go but then should request training and orientation. Nurses need to know their state's practice laws and regulations about performing care a nurse is not qualified to do.

- The image of nursing is a critical factor that needs to be addressed. Nurses need to be the drivers of the effort to improve this image. This topic is important in much of this text's content. The ANA and other nursing professional organizations have been working on the image of nurses. Nursing used ads on television and radio as well as in print media. It is important that collaborative efforts are made with other groups to communicate a realistic image of nursing and health care. Consumers need to know what a nurse is and what a nurse can do. Image also affects recruitment and interest of young people in the profession. Some communities have nurses and nursing students go to high schools to talk about nursing. Recruitment fairs are also common, though less so today due to use of electronic recruitment methods.

- Use of mandatory overtime has become a common strategy for handling a staffing shortage and one that has serious consequences, affecting ability to work, health of staff, retention, quality, and safety. It is a stopgap or crisis approach that will not solve the problem long term. Many states are passing legislation to limit the use of mandatory overtime. The RN Work Study Project, a 10-year longitudinal study of newly licensed RNs that began in 2006, examined the issue of overtime (Bae, Brewer, & Kovner, 2012). The study notes that by 2010, 16 states were regulating hospital nurse overtime—setting maximum mandatory overtime or setting maximum total work hours. The researchers comment that the regulatory approach does control overtime and total worked hours, but it also removes the RNs from regulating themselves, noting that RNs can work multiple jobs and thus not fall under these regulations.

- The Magnet Recognition Program® is another strategy that has been used to improve recruitment, retention, and staffing during staff shortages. These HCOs meet certain standards that support effective staff recruitment and retention.

- Increased compensation will not be enough to solve the problem, although it does help some and should not be ignored.

- Job sharing, which has been used in a variety of work settings, is now also used in some HCOs. It is an innovative approach, but it will not work for all positions. Some key issues are selecting the job that can be done by two people and finding the right staff matches. It requires partnership and sharing. This strategy can attract nurses who want to work part time and still make a contribution.

- Providing clinical practice opportunities and responsibility that match the nurse's knowledge and skills can help to retain nurses. This approach is supported by *The Future of Nursing* report (Institute of Medicine, 2011).

- The *Code for Nurses* (American Nurses Association, 2010) requires that nurses participate in the development of workplaces so they are environments in which quality care can be provided. Nurses must advocate for their patients. This type of workplace should help to retain nurses and also to attract nurses, decreasing job dissatisfaction.

- Nurses need more assistance with developing delegation skills because delegation is required more and more with the increased use of non-RN caregivers. (See Chapter 15.)
- The decreasing number of nursing faculty is a serious problem. Attracting more nurses into teaching is critical. There is now more funding available for graduate education, which is supported by *The Future Report* (Institute of Medicine, 2011). Schools of nursing need to develop programs to educate future faculty to develop alternative effective strategies for coping with the faculty shortage (American Association of Colleges of Nursing, 2010).
- Nursing curricula need to be current. Graduates must be prepared to practice. If they are not, there is a risk of losing the new nurse early in the career track, as noted in the 2010 nursing education report (Benner et al., 2010).
- Greater attention needs to be given to orientation, preceptorships, internships and residencies, and other creative methods to assist in helping new graduates adjust to the workplace and retain them (Benner et al., 2010; Institute of Medicine, 2011). (See Chapter 20.)
- As hospitals begin to realize that they must figure out how to deliver quality care more effectively even if there are days or longer periods when staff are short, they will develop their own staffing strategies. This requires planning (operational and strategic) for current staffing problems and the future projected shortage.
- One particular area of concern in HCOs is documentation, which is often affected by regulations and accreditation requirements. Documentation is complex and time consuming for staff. It can be very repetitive, and staff may not see its value. Documentation needs to be streamlined, standardized, and must take advantage of computers. The electronic medical record and other electronic methods may assist in making work more efficient and safer and thus impact staffing. (See Chapter 19.)
- HCOs need to explore how staff spend work time and if there are better ways of doing things to decrease activities that could be better done by someone else. Nurses spend more time than they need on nonnursing tasks. Over the years, these tasks have only increased. Effective management requires that work be allocated according to who is the best person to do the work. Managers need to help staff to develop better skills in prioritizing, planning, and delegating and provide effective technology to improve communication and make it easier such as use of smartphones, tablets, special pagers, and so on. All of this should be directed at effective staff use and allocation of limited resources (Institute of Medicine, 2004).
- Some HCOs are using their own staff to increase the pool of RNs. Identifying nonprofessional staff who might be interested and have the ability to pursue nursing education is one approach. This is an excellent example of an HCO supporting career advancement. In addition, many HCOs are supporting RN efforts to obtain BSN and graduate degrees. Support can be in the form of tuition reimbursement, scheduling flexibility, and other types of services to make it easier to go back to school. Some organizations have partnered with nursing schools to conduct courses on-site or to develop online programs. These efforts indicate that the organizations really do want to help staff develop themselves.

APPLYING LEADERSHIP AND MANAGEMENT

My Hospital Unit: An Evolving Case Experience

Your hospital and your unit are experiencing major staffing problems. You do not feel you have a good relationship with the human resources department. In reviewing your staffing data for the past two years, you notice that new graduates are not staying long, with an average of six to seven months. This impacts your budget, staff morale with complaints of constantly orienting new staff, and patient outcomes. The latter is of concern as there are documentation and medication errors and patients complain that staff are not tuned in to their needs. This is a major challenge for you. What do you need to do? Develop a plan to address this problem given the facts you have here and based on previous decisions you have made about your unit.

BSN and *Master's Essentials:* Application to Content

BSN Essentials (American Association of Colleges of Nursing, 2008) as Applied to this Chapter:

  I. Liberal Education for Baccalaureate Generalist Nursing Practice

 II. Basic Organizational and Systems Leadership for Quality Care and Patient Safety

 V. Healthcare Policy, Finance, and Regulatory Environments

VII. Interprofessional Communication and Collaboration for Improving Patient Health Outcomes

Master's Essentials (American Association of Colleges of Nursing, 2011) as Applied to this Chapter:

   I. Background for Practice from Sciences to Humanities

  II. Organizational and Systems Leadership

VII. Interprofessional Collaboration for Improving Patient and Population Health Outcomes

Applying AONE Competencies

Identify which of the AONE competencies found in Appendix A apply to the content of this chapter.

Engaging in the Content: Critical Thinking and Clinical Reasoning and Judgment

Discussion Questions

1. How do laws related to human resources apply to healthcare human resources? Why should a nurse manager be concerned about these laws? (Online Application Option)
2. What are some of the current issues related to nursing staff turnover? (Online Application Option)
3. How should a nurse manager provide effective performance appraisal?
4. What are some common reasons for job stress?
5. Complete a literature search on patient acuity classification systems. What can you learn about them? Does a hospital in your area use a system, and if so, what can you find out about it? How does this method impact staffing?

Application Exercises

1. What does it feel like to be an interviewer or an interviewee for a position? This exercise should be done in small teams of four. Go online and find sites that advertise nursing positions. Review the information and select several ads for RN positions to use in the exercise. Two members of the team should role-play a job interview, one as interviewer and the other as interviewee. Use the information found in this chapter to guide the role-play. The other two members should observe and critique the interview. Then those observing can role-play for a different job, switching roles. As you role-play, you should consider the questions suggested in this chapter content and add others that you think are important. Effectiveness of communication is also important to observe. How comfortable did the interviewer and interviewee feel doing the role-play? Which role was easier to do, and why do you think so? What can you learn from this exercise to help you improve your interviewing skills?

2. There are some important questions that should be asked by the interviewee. The following are questions that could be asked in an interview for a position in an HCO. Review the questions; then select an HCO and see how much of the information you can find out about the organization. This exercise might be done in small teams. It is best to select a number of different types of HCOs (e.g., hospital, long-term care, home health agency, and so on) as well as some that are the same (for example, several acute care hospitals) so you can compare and contrast the data.

   - What are the goals of the organization for the next five years?
   - What are the goals of patient services or nursing services?
   - What has been the nurse turnover rate for the past two years?
   - What is the nurse-to-patient ratio? (It is best to clarify the department or services as ratios can vary.) What is the staff mix? What is the scheduling method used?
   - Do they use competency-based performance appraisal?
   - What is the leadership style of nursing management? Ask for examples.
   - How does management view staff suggestions? Ask for a recent example and what happened with the suggestion.
   - What is the staff satisfaction rate?
   - Does nursing services use a specific care model, and if so, what model? How effective has it been?
   - Is there shared governance? Ask for a description.
   - Is there a clinical ladder or something similar? Ask for a description.
   - What is done for employees in relationship to safety on the job?
   - Is mandatory overtime used?
   - What is the organizational structure, and to whom does the particular position sought report?

3. Your answers to questions in Number 2 will depend on the individual organizations that you select. After the information is collected, compare and contrast it, and judge what would be important for you to consider in your own job search. Discuss these with your classmates to understand different viewpoints. Not everyone looks for the same factors in a job or an employer.
4. What is the status of nursing staffing in your local area? What strategies are HCOs using to recruit staff? Are they effective? What do you think should be done to improve the staffing?

Does your state or local area have a nurse or healthcare workforce group, and if so, what can you find out about it? (Online Application Option)
5. In teams discuss incivility in the workplace. Provide examples you have observed in clinical. Do not provide names or any other identifiers. What could be done to reduce passive-aggressive behavior? (Online Application Option)
6. Why is retention important? Search for current studies on this topic and discuss.

References

Aiken, L., Sloane, D., Cimiotti, J., Clarke, S., Flynn, L., Seago, J., … Smith, H. (2010). Implications of the California nurse staffing mandate for other states. *Health Services Research, 45*(4), 904–921.

American Association of Colleges of Nursing. (2008). *The essentials of baccalaureate education for professional nursing practice.* Washington, DC: Author.

American Association of Colleges of Nursing. (2010). New AACN data show growth in doctoral nursing programs. Retrieved from http://www.aacn.nche.edu/news/articles/2010/enrollchanges

American Association of Colleges of Nursing. (2011). *The essentials of master's education in nursing.* Washington, DC: Author.

American Association of Colleges of Nursing. (2014). Nursing shortage. Retrieved from http://www.aacn.nche.edu/media-relations/fact-sheets/nursing-shortage

American Nurses Association. (2010). *Scope and standards of practice in nursing.* Silver Spring, MD: Author.

American Nurses Association. (2012). *Principles for nurse staffing.* (2nd ed.). Silver Spring, MD: Author.

American Nurses Association. (2013). Nurse staffing plans and ratios. Retrieved from www.nursingworld.org/MainMenuCategories/Policy-Advocacy/State/Legislative-Agenda-Reports/State-StaffingPlansRatios

American Nurses Association. (2014a). Bullying and workplace violence. Retrieved from http://www.nursingworld.org/Bullying-Workplace-Violence

American Nurses Association. (2014b). Nurse staffing. Retrieved from http://www.nursingworld.org/nursestaffing

Bae, S., Brewer, C., & Kovner, C. (2012). State mandatory overtime regulations and newly licensed nurses' mandatory and voluntary overtime and total work hours. *Nursing Outlook, 60*(2), 50–71.

Benner, P., Sutphen, M., Leonard, V., & Day, L. (2010). *Educating nurses.* San Francisco, CA: Jossey-Bass Publishers.

Bureau of Labor Statistics. (2013, December 19). Economic news release. Retrieved from http://www.bls.gov/news.release/ecopro.t08.htm

Centers for Disease Control and Prevention, National Institute for Occupational Safety and Health. (2014). Stress … at work. Retrieved from http://www.cdc.gov/niosh/docs/99-101/

Flynn, L., Liang, Y., Dickson, G., Xie, M., & Suh, D. (2012). Nurses' practice environments, error interception practices, and inpatient medication errors. *Journal of Nursing Scholarship 44*(2), 180–186.

Health Resources and Services Administration. (2013, November). The U.S. Health Workforce Chartbook—In brief HRSA/National Center for Health workforce analysis. Retrieved from http://bhpr.hrsa.gov/healthworkforce/supplydemand/usworkforce/chartbook/index.html

Institute for Health Improvement. (2010). *Rapid response teams.* Retrieved from http://www.ihi.org/Topics/RapidResponseTeams/Pages/default.aspx

Institute of Medicine. (2001). *Crossing the quality chasm.* Washington, DC: National Academies Press.

Institute of Medicine. (2003). *Health professions education.* Washington, DC: National Academies Press.

Institute of Medicine. (2004). *Keeping patients safe.* Washington, DC: National Academies Press.

Institute of Medicine. (2011). *The future of nursing: Leading change, advancing health.* Washington, DC: National Academies Press.

Joint Commission. (2008). Behaviors undermine a culture of safety. *Sentinel Event Alert, 40.* Retrieved from http://www.jointcommission.org/sentinel_event_alert_issue_40_behaviors_that_undermine_a_culture_of_safety/

Kovner, C., Brewer, C., Fatehi, F., & Jun, J. (2014). What does nurse turnover rate mean and what is the rate? *Policy, Politics, & Nursing Practice,* Online First, as doi:10.1177/1527154414547953

Kramer, M. (1985). Why does reality shock continue? In J. McCloskey & H. Grace (Eds.), *Current issues in nursing* (pp. 891–903). Boston, MA: Blackwell Scientific Publication.

National Labor Relations Board. (2014). 1947 Taft-Hartley substantive provisions. Retrieved from http://www.nlrb.gov/who-we-are/our-history/1947-taft-hartley-substantive-provisions

Needleman, J., Buerhaus, P., Pankratz, S., Leibson, C., Stevens, S., & Harris, M. (2011). Nurse staffing and inpatient hospital mortality. *New England Journal of Medicine, 364,* 1037–1045.

Nolo. (2014). National labor relations act. Retrieved from http://www.nolo.com/legal-encyclopedia/content/nlra-act.html

Peter, L., & Hull, R. (1969). *The Peter Principle: Why things go wrong.* New York, NY: William Morrow.

Robert Wood Johnson Foundation. (2013). New study challenges conventional wisdom of pay-for-performance incentive programs. Retrieved from http://www.rwjf.org/en/library/articles-and-news/2013/09/new-study-challenges-conventional-wisdom-on-pay-for-performance-.html

Trossman, S. (2014, November 21). Toward civility. *The American Nurse.* Retrieved from http://www.theamericannurse.org/index.php/2014/02/27/toward-civility/

U.S. Citizenship and Immigration Services. (2014). Immigration Reform and Control Act of 1986 (IRCA). Retrieved from http://www.uscis.gov/tools/glossary/immigration-reform-and-control-act-1986-irca

U.S. Department of Health and Human Services. (2014, February). A 21st century healthcare workforce for the nation. Washington, DC: Author.

U.S. Department of Labor. (2015). Drug-free workplace advisor. Retrieved from http://www.dol.gov/elaws/asp/drugfree/menu.htm

U.S. Equal Opportunity Commission. (2014a). Harassment. Retrieved from http://www.eeoc.gov/laws/types/harassment.cfm

U.S. Equal Opportunity Commission. (2014b). Sexual harassment. Retrieved from http://www.eeoc.gov/laws/types/sexual_harassment.cfm

Welton, J. (2007). Mandatory hospital nurse to patient staffing ratios: Time to take a different approach. *The Online Journal of Nursing, 12*(3).

Westrick, S. (2014). *Essentials of nursing law and ethics.* (2nd ed.). Burlington, MA: Jones & Bartlett Learning.

HEALTHCARE PROFESSIONS CORE COMPETENCIES

This section focuses on the National Academy of Medicine's core competencies for healthcare professions. The competencies are as follows:

- Provide patient-centered care
- Work in interprofessional teams
- Employ evidence-based practice
- Apply quality improvement
- Utilize informatics

The twelve chapters in this section emphasize these core competencies and include content related to managing patient-centered care, consumers, diversity and disparities, building interprofessional teams, improving teamwork through collaboration, coordination, conflict resolution, effective communication, evidence-based practice and management, and healthcare informatics. Two chapters focus on healthcare quality and policy issues with the second chapter examining implementation of quality improvement. The last chapter addresses staff education, a critical need in all healthcare organizations to assist in maintaining staff competencies and improvement of care. These core competencies relate to practice in all settings, but they also are important aspects of effective leadership and management.

Managing Patient-Centered Care

KEY TERMS

- chronic care model
- clinical judgment
- clinical pathway
- clinical practice guideline
- clinical reasoning
- disease management
- patient-centered care
- self-management
- variances

▣ LEARNING OUTCOMES

Before you begin, take a moment to familiarize yourself with the learning outcomes for this chapter.

> Explain how patient-centered care impacts the healthcare delivery system and nursing care.
> Analyze the implications of care planning, clinical reasoning and judgment, and patient/family education on patient-centered care.
> Examine the relationship between self-management and patient-centered care.
> Apply the chronic illness model to a specific chronic illness, and relate it to patient-centered care.
> Compare and contrast tools used to manage care such as a clinical pathway or practice guideline so care is more patient-centered.

WHAT'S AHEAD

Collaboration is important within clinical settings and between HCOs and is an important part of each patient's care, serving as a critical part of patient-centered care and its related National Academy of Medicine (NAM) core competency focused on interprofessional teams. Patient care cannot be delivered alone; it requires different healthcare providers to work together and provide their specific expertise. Chapter 13 discusses collaboration in more detail, but here in this chapter it is necessary to recognize that to achieve patient-centered care, it requires collaboration (Finkelman & Kenner, 2016). This chapter examines the NAM patient-centered care core competency. The content includes a discussion about patient-centered care and factors that impact it such as care planning, clinical reasoning and judgment, patient/family education, self-management, and health promotion. The NAM emphasizes the need for patient-centered care for all patients and highlights the increasing number of patients with chronic illnesses. Chronic illness and disease management are examined. Two examples of tools used by different healthcare settings and providers to assist in managing care for individuals, families, and communities are described: clinical pathways and practice guidelines.

THE CORE COMPETENCY: PATIENT-CENTERED CARE

The Institute of Medicine (2003a) identifies five core competencies for healthcare professions, all of which are emphasized in this text. Provide patient-centered care is the key competency around which the other four competencies (work in interprofessional teams, employ evidence-based practice, apply quality improvement, utilize informatics) function. The core competency of **patient-centered care** is described by the Institute of Medicine (IOM) (2003a): "identify, respect, and care about patients' differences, values, preferences, and expressed needs; relieve pain and suffering; coordinate continuous care; listen to, clearly inform, communicate with, and educate patients; share decision making and management; and continuously advocate disease prevention, wellness, and promotion of healthy lifestyles, including a focus on population health" (p. 4). With the IOM describing the healthcare system as "in need of fundamental change" (Institute of Medicine, 2001, p. 1), providing patient-centered care is a critical need that continues to be important. Healthcare delivery systems need to be "carefully and consciously designed to provide care that is safe, effective, patient-centered, timely, efficient, and equitable. Such systems must be designed to serve the needs of patients, and to ensure that they are fully informed, retain control and participate in care delivery whenever possible, and receive care that is respectful of their values and preferences" (Institute of Medicine, 2001, p. 7). The main issue is to move away from a focus on disease or medical problems to focus on the individual. Patients who are involved in their own care have better outcomes (Institute of Medicine, 2003a). Over the past 15 years researchers and experts have examined the skills required by healthcare professionals to provide effective patient-centered care. The following are identified as important:

- Share power and responsibility with patients and caregivers.
- Communicate with patients in a shared and fully open manner.
- Take into account patients' individuality, emotional needs, values, and life issues.
- Implement strategies to reach those who do not present for care on their own, including care strategies that support the broader community.
- Enhance prevention and health promotion (Institute of Medicine, 2003a, pp. 52–53).

Effective patient-centered care requires that staff collaborate and coordinate care. The patient—and when appropriate and acceptable to the patient, the patient's family—needs to be engaged in the care delivery process. Diversity issues need to be considered to better ensure that the patient's values and preferences are integrated into the care process, discussed in Chapter 10. As discussed in a later chapter (Chapter 11), consumerism is more important today in health care. Patient-centered care is directly related to consumerism and the need for patient advocacy—advocacy in which the patient is supported and makes decisions, not the healthcare provider making the decisions for the patient. Informatics is also an area that supports patient-centered care. Patients can get more current information and access experts when they need it, and staff can get information easily to plan care with the patient. Chapter 19 discusses the core competency of utilizing informatics.

HCOs may take different approaches to implementing patient-centered care, and how this is done may be influenced by the vision of the HCO and the needs. However, there are some negative results that may occur if an HCO focuses mostly on customer service and amenities, thinking this is the meaning of patient-centered care. A study looked at this issue and concluded that this can lead to an environment where customer service tasks may supersede nursing tasks. Outcomes may be that the nurse-patient relationship is limited, professional roles are questioned, and care that is needed is no longer the priority (Mikesell & Bromley, 2012).

The Role of Management in Patient-Centered Care

A nurse manager or a team leader must recognize the need for patient-centered care and keep this need in the forefront when making decisions. How does management actually relate to providing patient-centered care? The following are some examples:

- The structure of a unit is designed to meet individual patient needs through an interprofessional team.
- Care planning is interprofessional and includes the patient.

- Patient care rounds include the patient and, when possible and agreeable with the patient, the patient's family.
- Shift report focuses on the individual patient, recognizing the patient's values, preferences, diversity, rights, and needs.
- Patient-staff relationships and communication focus on the patient (e.g., listen to the patient, take time to focus on the patient, avoid acting hurried, use open communication, and so on).
- Nurse managers should routinely visit patients to assess status, talk with the patient and family, and determine issues that need addressing.
- The unit processes put the patient first, for example, how meals are served, communication system with the patient, and so on.
- The organizational culture considers the patient to be the center of the culture influencing systems, communication, and the environment so the patient feels comfortable in a healing environment.
- Errors are disclosed to patients in an effective manner, and patients are considered a part of quality improvement—engaged in identifying possible risks.
- Quality improvement evolves with patient outcomes.
- Delegation is guided by patient needs.
- Assignment is guided by patient needs.
- Staffing includes patient needs and acuity, consideration of required staff, and competencies of staff to ensure effective patient outcomes.
- Staff education is designed so the patient and his or her needs are the center of content and learning experiences—to ensure that care is effectively and efficiently provided.
- Self-management is incorporated into care so patients are better able to care for themselves long term; family is included as appropriate and agreeable with the patient.
- The admission process focuses on the patient with a complete assessment and identification of needs and problems, engaging the patient and, when appropriate and agreeable with the patient, the family in the process. The patient is oriented to the unit and care processes.
- The discharge process prepares the patient for discharge and care needs after discharge, engaging the patient and, when appropriate, the family in the process.
- Performance appraisal focuses on the ability of the employee to provide patient-centered care and achieve effective patient outcomes.
- Support services recognize that the patient is the center of concern.
- Patient privacy and confidentiality (Health Insurance Portability and Accountability Act of 1996 [HIPAA]) is maintained (e.g., sharing of patient name and other information is controlled, asking the patient's permission to share information with family members and include them in planning, etc.). If the patient says no, then the family cannot be included.

Just as transformational leadership engages staff and focuses on inclusion in the decision-making process, transformational leadership should keep the patient at the center of the process. Davis, Schoenbaum, and Audet (2005) identify seven attributes of patient-centered care:

1. *Superb access to care.* Patients can easily make appointments and select the day and time. Waiting times are short. Email and telephone consultations are offered. Off-hours service is available.
2. *Patient engagement in care.* Patients have the option of being informed and engaged partners in their care. Practices provide information on treatment plans, preventive and follow-up care reminders, access to medical records, assistance with self-care, and counseling.
3. *Clinical information systems that support high-quality care, practice-based learning, and quality improvement.* Practices maintain patient registries; monitor adherence to treatment; have easy access to lab and test results; and receive reminders, decision support, and information on recommended treatments.
4. *Care coordination.* Specialist care is coordinated, and systems are in place to prevent errors that occur when multiple physicians are involved. Posthospital follow-up and support are provided.
5. *Integrated and comprehensive team care.* There is a free flow of communication among physicians, nurses, and other health professionals. Duplication of tests and procedures is avoided.

6. *Routine patient feedback to doctors.* Practices take advantage of low-cost, Internet-based patient surveys to learn from patients and inform treatment plans.
7. *Publicly available information.* Patients have accurate, standardized information on physicians to help them choose a practice that will meet their needs.

Implications of Care Planning, Clinical Reasoning, and Clinical Judgment to Patient-Centered Care

Patients need to be as active in the care planning process as possible given their medical status. Planning that is done separate from the patient and delivered as a final decision acts as a barrier to patient-centered care. Patients tolerate this type of care approach less today than they did in the past. Most patients expect to be the decision maker. Communication with the patient needs to be clear and open. Health literacy has been a concern in health care, as discussed in Chapter 11. Health literacy is "the ability to read, understand, and act on healthcare information" (Institute of Medicine, 2004, p. 52). Health literacy can be a major barrier to patient-centered care. Care plans that are developed by an interprofessional team with an emphasis on collaboration, coordination, and continuity of care are more patient-centered focused. The plan guides the care for individual patients but also informs teams and unit management about patient needs and interventions that need to be considered in the management of services such as staff number, mix, and competencies.

Throughout the care process, nurses need to actively use clinical reasoning and clinical judgment. **Clinical reasoning** is the "practitioner's ability to assess patient problems or needs and analyze data to accurately identify and frame problems within the context of the individual patient's environment" (Murphy, 2004, p. 227). This is the ability to reason as a clinical situation unfolds (Benner, Sutphen, Leonard, & Day, 2010). **Clinical judgment** requires that a nurse apply, analyze, and synthesize knowledge considering the patient context. It is the "ways in which nurses come to understand the problems, issues, or concerns of clients/patients, to attend to salient information, and to respond in concerned and involved ways" (Benner, Tanner, & Chesla, 1996, p. 2). This is deliberate, conscious decision making. If done effectively, it should allow the nurse to reflect on the patient, communicate effectively, respond to uncertainty, and avoid snap judgments. The 2010 national report on nursing education expresses strong concern that nursing education is not preparing students to use clinical reasoning and clinical judgment and that this has an impact on care (Benner et al., 2010).

Implications of Patient/Family Education to Patient-Centered Care

Patient and family education has long been a nursing responsibility. It has become more difficult to provide effective education, particularly in the acute care setting due to the acuity of patients and shorter lengths of stay. Different methods are used to deliver patient education such as videos, downloads onto computers or smartphones, and the typical brochures and handouts. Health literacy needs to be carefully monitored as the nurse determines if the patient understands the information and can apply it. Follow-up with home health care may be required. If the patient agrees, the family should be involved whenever possible as they are often the primary caregivers when patients return to their homes. All patient education needs to focus on the individual patient and not just provide broad information. Understanding the patient's medical history, assessment data, needs, and home situation is important in developing patient-centered education. This also requires patient engagement—for example, asking what the patient identifies as needs, problems, and so on. To include family participation, patient permission is required.

Self-Management

Self-management support is the "systematic provision of education and supportive interventions to increase patients' skills and confidence in managing their health problems, including regular assessment of progress and problems, goal setting, and problem-solving support" (Institute of Medicine, 2003b, p. 52). Health promotion and disease and illness prevention, as discussed in Chapter 7, are part of self-management. The Institute of Health Improvement comments that there needs to be more support of self-management rather than focusing on the patient following orders (Institute of Health Improvement, 2014). The strong movement toward

CASE STUDY

Is the Patient First?

A rehabilitation hospital wants to implement a patient-centered approach. The chief executive officer has requested this change after reviewing the Institute of Medicine reports on quality and health care professions. The senior management team has just concluded a meeting discussing this topic. The hospital has many patients with chronic illnesses and disabilities. These patients are often referred to the rehab hospital after acute care and stay long periods of time for physical therapy, occupational therapy, and nursing care. The hospital looks like a typical hospital with little personal features. Visiting hours tend to be regulated with staff members saying that they want patients to focus on their treatment. Considering the content in this chapter and earlier chapters on change and organizations, what would you recommend as chief nursing executive to respond to this directive?

Questions:

1. What does patient-centered care mean?
2. Identify strategies that this organization could take to implement a patient-centered approach.
3. How might patient-centered care impact nursing care in this hospital? How might patient-centered care impact other services?
4. How might the hospital use its consumers (patients and families) in this change process?
5. You recommend that the hospital use clinical pathways. Why would this recommendation be connected with patient-centered care?

patient-centered care indicates that there is recognition to improve this situation. A patient-centered focus requires that patients have a greater role in their care and, in some instances, providers have less of a role, supporting more self-management. The IOM identifies four areas that need improvement and lead to effective programs:

1. Providers communicate and reinforce patients' active and central role in managing their illness.
2. Practice teams make regular use of standardized patient assessments.
3. Evidence-based programs are used to provide ongoing support.
4. Collaborative care planning and patient-centered problem solving result in an individualized care plan for each patient and support from the team when problems are encountered (Institute of Medicine, 2003b, p. 52).

An example of a patient-centered model of care is provided in Figure 9-1.

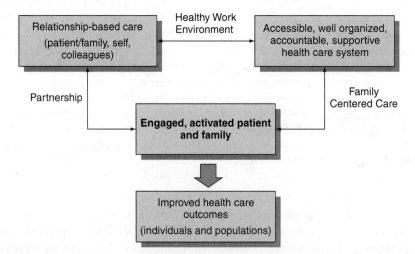

Figure 9-1 Patient Engagement and Activation Model of Care

Source: From "Action Brief: Patient Engagement and Activation: A Health Reform Imperative and Improvement for Nursing" by Luc R. Pelletier and Jaynelle F. Stichler from *Nursing Outlook, 61*, 51–54. Copyright © 2013 by Elsevier Inc. Used by permission of Elsevier Inc.

CHRONIC ILLNESS: A KEY HEALTHCARE CONCERN

More people are living longer and often with multiple chronic illnesses, mostly because of advances in medical science and technology. It is not uncommon for these patients to have comorbid conditions, increasing the complexity of their problems and requiring more collaboration and coordination. Many people are in relatively good health, though chronic illness is a problem. The United States spends 85% of its healthcare dollars on chronic disease (Centers for Disease Control and Prevention, 2014c). The following bulleted list provides some data about the status of chronic illness and costs (Centers for Disease Control and Prevention, 2014b). As is true for most government reported data, current data are typically one to two years or more behind the current year. Chronic diseases and conditions—such as heart disease, stroke, cancer, diabetes, obesity, and arthritis—are among the most common, costly, and preventable of all health problems.

- As of 2012, about half of all adults—117 million people—have one or more chronic health conditions. One of four adults has two or more chronic health conditions.
- Seven of the top 10 causes of death in 2010 were chronic diseases. Two of these chronic diseases—heart disease and cancer—together accounted for nearly 48% of all deaths.
- Obesity is a serious health concern. During 2009–2010, more than one-third of adults, or about 78 million people, were obese (defined as body mass index [BMI] ≥ 30 kg/m^2). Nearly one of five youths aged 2–19 years was obese (BMI $\geq$ 95th percentile).
- Arthritis is the most common cause of disability. Of the 53 million adults with a doctor's diagnosis of arthritis, more than 22 million say arthritis caused them to have trouble with their usual activities.
- Diabetes is the leading cause of kidney failure, lower limb amputations other than those caused by injury, and new cases of blindness among adults.

The majority of U.S. healthcare and economic costs associated with medical conditions are from the costs of chronic diseases and conditions and associated health risk behaviors (Centers for Disease Control and Prevention, 2014b).

- Eighty-four percent of all healthcare spending in 2006 was for the 50% of the population who have one or more chronic medical conditions.
- The total costs of heart disease and stroke in 2010 were estimated to be $315.4 billion. Of this amount, $193.4 billion was for direct medical costs, not including costs of nursing home care.
- Cancer care cost $157 billion in 2010.
- The total estimated cost of diagnosed diabetes in 2012 was $245 billion, including $176 billion in direct medical costs and $69 billion in decreased productivity. Decreased productivity includes costs associated with people being absent from work, being less productive while at work, or not being able to work at all because of diabetes.
- Medical costs linked to obesity were estimated to be $147 billion in 2008. Annual medical costs for people who are obese were $1,429 higher than those for people of normal weight in 2006.
- For the years 2009–2012, economic cost due to smoking was estimated to be more than $289 billion a year. This cost included at least $133 billion in direct medical care for adults and more than $156 billion for lost productivity from premature death estimated from 2005 through 2009.
- The economic costs of drinking too much alcohol were estimated to be $223.5 billion, or $1.90 a drink, in 2006. Most of these costs were due to binge drinking and resulted from losses in workplace productivity, healthcare expenses, and crimes related to excessive drinking.

Given the status and need for chronic care, the Affordable Care Act of 2010 (ACA) has numerous provisions about chronic illness from reimbursement to delivery provisions. Examples are establishment of medical homes and nurse-managed health centers; establishment of a Prevention and Public Health Fund and Council; providing new options for home and community-based services through Medicaid, and so on. (See Appendix B.) Typical disease management goals for chronic illnesses are to improve quality of life, decrease disease progression, and reduce hospitalizations. Chronic illnesses that are typically monitored are diabetes, heart disease/hypertension, asthma, cancer, depression, renal disease, low back pain, and obesity.

Chronic Illness Care Model

Wagner, Austin, and Von Korff (1996) developed a **chronic care model**, which is described in Figure 9-2. This model is also described on the website Improving Chronic Illness Care sponsored by the Robert Wood Johnson Foundation. The model focuses on an informed, activated patient who is supported by a prepared, proactive practice team. The model elements are:

1. Health system
2. Delivery system design
3. Decision support
4. Clinical information systems
5. Self-management support
6. The community (Improving Chronic Illness Care, 2014)

In 2003 the following were added to the identified elements:

- Patient safety (in Health System)
- Cultural competency (in Delivery System Design)
- Care coordination (in Health System and Clinical Information Systems)
- Community policies (in the Community)
- Case management (in Delivery System Design)

It is easy to see the influence of the IOM reports and recommendations on this model and the impact of patient-centered care. Nursing needs to consider the impact of increasing chronic illness on its practice and nursing delivery processes.

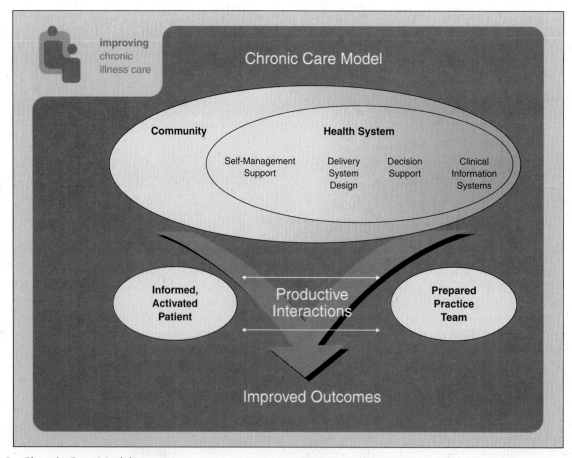

Figure 9-2 Chronic Care Model

Source: Republished with permission of American College of Physicians, from Chronic Care Model 2008; permission conveyed through Copyright Clearance Center, Inc.

The six fundamental elements of the Chronic Care Model describe a system that encourages high-quality chronic disease management. To improve chronic care, HCOs need to focus on these six elements as well as develop productive interactions between patients who take an active part in their care and providers backed up by resources and expertise.

EXAMPLES OF TOOLS TO MANAGE PATIENT-CENTERED CARE

Examples of tools or methods that providers use to manage care that are particularly relevant to chronic illness are disease management programs, clinical pathways, and clinical practice guidelines. Even though these tools are developed from a general patient standpoint, any time they are used, the nurse, physician, or other provider must ensure that the disease management program, pathway, or guideline is individualized to meet the patient's needs and to ensure that all care is patient centered.

Disease Management Programs

Disease management programs can be effective in assisting patients with chronic illness and to better ensure patient-centered care.

DEFINITION AND PURPOSE **Disease management** is a service strategy or method used by third-party payers and also by some HCOs to control costs and improve care. Disease management focuses on the whole patient with a specific disease or illness, typically a chronic, long-term illness, identifying coordinated interventions to address typical problems encountered by the patient with the identified illness. The purpose of disease management programs is to provide patients with education and preventive care that improves the quality of their lives and prevents complications that may increase healthcare costs. Examples of illnesses that are often targeted for disease management are asthma, arthritis, cancer, diabetes, hypertension, osteoporosis, high-risk pregnancy, congestive heart failure, depression, high cholesterol, and human immunodeficiency virus/acquired immune deficiency syndrome (HIV/AIDS). Why would an insurer develop a disease management program that takes time to develop and is expensive to develop and offer?

Disease management programs are similar to continuous quality improvement (CQI) programs that have been used by HCOs to improve their functioning. CQI programs focus on identification, intervention, and measurement, just as do disease management programs. Disease management programs can vary from one insurer to another, but they usually include all or some of these elements:

- Prevention
- Early detection/diagnosis
- Treatment
- Management

Some programs just monitor medication treatment. Other programs offer only patient education or behavior modification. The more complex disease management programs use case management for their patients to provide coordinated care over a long period of time and to ensure that there is collaboration within interprofessional teams. The major goal is to prepare the patient to understand the disease and increase the patient's self-management of the disease, but also to reduce costs, improve outcomes, and support the patient when needed to better ensure that treatment plan is followed.

How does a disease management program really work? For example, an insurer groups its enrollees into disease-specific populations and, based on the numbers within a specific disease category, it then focuses its disease management program on this population. Patients chosen for disease management services typically have high cost; experience long-term problems; and are at risk for complications, increased hospitalizations, and longer lengths of stay. Patients need to agree to participate. Patients with chronic illnesses are the most common type of patient for whom disease management can be effective. Usually the physician's role is to continue to provide appropriate interventions for the patient; however, other healthcare professionals—often nurses—provide education that focuses on prevention and health maintenance based on the disease and individual needs of the patient. Case managers may be involved to help coordinate care. Case managers may be

BOX 9-1	DISEASE MANAGEMENT: EXAMPLES OF COMMON DISEASES

- Arthritis
- Diabetes
- Asthma
- Cardiac diseases

- Chronic obstructive pulmonary disease
- Mental illness
- Stroke

nurses and in some cases are social workers. The major goal is to prepare the patient to understand the disease and increase the patient's self-management of the disease. Disease management programs typically focus on chronic illnesses such as the examples found in Box 9-1.

DEVELOPMENT OF DISEASE MANAGEMENT PROGRAMS   Developing disease management programs takes time and is costly. Many insurers are turning to other groups or organizations that have developed these programs or contract with experts to design a customized program. HCOs, insurers, and healthcare businesses, such as healthcare consulting businesses, develop disease management programs that are then sold as a package or contracted to providers and insurers. Disease management also provides an opportunity for partnerships between insurers and other organizations to create innovative programs. Some of these programs offer nurse call lines and nurse-led education programs and support; consider readiness to learn and behavior modification; encourage partnerships that are formed between the patient and the primary care provider; and track critical data such as hospital admissions, length of stay, and use of emergency services and prescriptions. These programs offer great opportunities for nurses.

PROVIDER RESPONSE TO DISEASE MANAGEMENT PROGRAMS   Provider concerns about disease management programs are similar to those with practice guidelines and clinical pathways. Is this "cookbook" health care with little regard for the individual? Program supporters and developers insist that these programs offer individual assessment of needs and an opportunity to incorporate individual treatment needs. Some providers do not understand the concept and thus have problems accepting disease management programs. Others are concerned that this is an effort to take over their treatment decisions. Supporters of disease management emphasize that the programs augment the provider's treatment and help patients better accept treatment and encourage compliance. Comorbidities continue to be a problem, particularly with older patients. To increase physician support, physicians need education about the program and its purposes. They need to be recognized as coordinators of patient care and understand that disease management programs offer support to their treatment but does not replace their treatment.

In addition to physicians benefiting from disease management programs, advanced practice registered nurses (APRNs) can benefit by using these programs, but they must also understand disease management and its application to their practice. Including the nurses and physicians, as well as other healthcare providers, in the development or adaptation of these programs is critical for their success. Insurers collect data on the outcomes then use these data to demonstrate results to physicians and other providers.

Pharmacists have also taken an active role in disease management programs. Pharmacy costs are a major concern for providers and insurers. Disease management programs may focus on the use of medications and medication education for specific diagnoses to decrease costs. Pharmaceutical companies are also developing disease management programs that they sell or contract to insurers. The danger with these programs is the potential of pushing specific drugs on the insurer and its providers. This could result in ethical dilemmas. The companies are, however, providing a variety of services that could be very helpful such as development of patient information resources.

Clinical Pathways

DEFINITION AND PURPOSE OF CLINICAL PATHWAYS   HCOs are dependent on providing effective, efficient care, which requires a clear framework of practice for the interprofessional team. Collaborative care and interprofessional care are intertwined, as the development of clinical pathways and their implementation requires interprofessional collaboration.

There is no universally accepted definition of **clinical pathways** (Kinsman, Rotter, James, Snow, & Willis, 2010). The following are some of the common characteristics of clinical pathways:

- A structured multidisciplinary plan of care
- Translation of guidelines or evidence into practice
- A description of steps in the treatment process or care in a plan, pathway, algorithm, guideline, protocol, or other listing of actions
- A description of time frames or criteria-based progression in treatment
- Standardized care for a specific clinical problem, procedure, or episode for a specific population

One can conclude from these characteristics that there are some common elements, including the following:

- Provide guidelines for practice.
- Define outcomes.
- Focus on timelines.
- Use resources efficiently.
- Emphasize the need for coordination, communication, and collaboration.
- Include the patient and family.
- Provide interdisciplinary effort.
- Collaborate.

Pathways provide direction in the coordination of care, focus on efficient and effective use of resources, and ensure that outcomes are met within a designated time frame. Pathways have an interprofessional focus, and thus include all aspects of the patient's care that are critical to meeting outcomes. They can be used to demonstrate compliance with standards of care, accreditation, and regulatory requirements. These tools assist staff during orientation and in teaching nursing and medical students and others. Some institutions have developed patient versions of pathways that are given to the patient/family on admission or when treatment begins.

What are the advantages and disadvantages of using clinical pathways? Because they have been used for some time, there is considerable information about their use and difficulties in using them.

Critics of pathways question pathways as rigid requirements and with limited individuation. This could be a major disadvantage; however, HCOs have considered this potential problem. They require that there is assessment of pathway content each time it is used with a patient to ensure that individual patient needs are met. Pathways should not be used without thought and consideration of the individual circumstances because this can lead to errors and care that is not appropriate for the patient. Patient-centered care requires that patient values and preferences along with needs be integrated into the decision making and must include the patient. The physician, nurses, and other providers need to document changes or adaptations per individual patient. Another disadvantage is the cost and time required to develop and implement pathways. The most expensive part of the project is the development of the first pathway. It takes time to develop the process, policies and procedures, and forms. Then more time is spent to conduct the review of the literature required to ensure the pathway is evidence based and to get started. In addition, it takes time to educate the project committee, interprofessional teams, and all of the staff.

Selection of the illnesses or conditions that require pathways should be done carefully. If there are few patients in a category (illness or condition), it may not be cost effective to spend time on developing pathways that may make little difference in care, outcomes, and expenses. For example, if a hospital does not do transplants of any kind, developing a pathway for transplant care is not useful. A negative staff attitude toward pathways can also be a major disadvantage. If staff view the development of pathways as just another project with excessive paperwork, requiring redundant documentation, and view it as a new gimmick to endure, then the process of implementing pathways will be an arduous one. Staff will be waiting for it to pass and will not feel committed to the project. This is particularly problematic in HCOs that have instituted many "new projects" only to have them fall by the wayside due to a lack of commitment, a lack of knowledge about their use and implications to practice, or a lack of funding to complete the project. If care and systems do not change as a result of pathway outcomes, staff will wonder about all the effort that is expended on the project. If staff are fearful that pathways may be used to identify individual staff performance problems rather than used as assessment of process and system to improve care, then staff will be reluctant to participate. HCOs that spend time considering these disadvantages and staff concerns, resolving them, and increasing staff commitment and participation will be much more successful.

EVOLUTION OF PATHWAYS   Why have HCOs developed clinical pathways? Oil and chemical refineries were the first industries to use pathways as a method for defining their work processes, and pathways were adopted by the engineering, construction, and computer industries as they discovered that it was a good tool for managing projects. Karen Zander, a nurse, then borrowed the idea in the mid-1980s and adapted it to the acute care setting (1992). These early clinical pathways focused on nursing interventions and use of technology to provide care. Zander was interested in decreasing the cost of care without decreasing quality. The process to develop clinical pathways was very similar to the nursing process and the nursing care plan. As is true of all new ideas, they grow and change and, it is hoped, improve.

The initial efforts to use pathways were restrained by limitations. Because of the generic nature of these plans, they did little to control the use of resources, types of medications, routes of administration, or other factors related to cost and quality. Pathways, however, have changed and improved as they no longer focus on only nursing interventions. Instead, they focus much more on interprofessional treatment and the effect of interventions on cost and quality.

One issue with the evolution of pathways was their name. Initially they were called "critical pathways." Now pathways may be called "care paths," "care maps," "case management plans," "anticipatory recovery plans," "care guides," "collaborative plans," "coordinated plans," "integrated plans," "plans of action," and (probably the most common name) "clinical pathways." This does cause confusion, as some healthcare professionals think that each of these represents a unique tool, yet they are all basically the same. There are other tools that add to this confusion (for example, algorithms, practice guidelines, practice parameters, and disease management programs).

Clinical practice guidelines focus on general treatment for a specific illness or condition, whereas pathways are more specific and unique to the healthcare agency in which they are used. Pathways are also individualized for patients and meet the practice concerns of the providers. These characteristics make it more difficult to use pathways developed by other institutions and organizations. All pathways need to be adapted to meet the individual needs of the institution, its providers, and its patient population.

A common misperception is that clinical pathways and case management are the same. How did this come about? The case management plan used by case managers confuses the issue, as it focuses on case manager responsibilities, while the clinical pathway focuses on shared accountability of the interprofessional team. More case managers are using pathways as they coordinate care with the interprofessional team.

PATHWAY DEVELOPMENT AND THE IMPLEMENTATION PROCESS   The pathway development process must be considered carefully as this is not a simple project. Typically a project committee develops the framework that will be used for all pathways and oversees the project. This committee should have a broad-based representation. Some of the departments or services that might be in an HCO include nurses, physicians, and representatives from social service, case management, admissions, finance, administration, medical records, utilization review, quality improvement, risk management, and materials management. Laboratory, radiology, claims processing, and other specialized areas, such as respiratory therapy and physical therapy, may also be on the interprofessional teams that develop the content for specific pathways.

Before any specific plans are made for this project, the organization's environment for change needs to be assessed. As is true of all change efforts, the commitment of key staff is the critical element for the success of pathway development. Change has become an all too common experience in health care today, and it is unlikely to go away. There are steps that can be taken, however, to make it easier on the staff and to maintain an environment that is supportive of change. If pathways are to be used, the organization's leaders must support the effort, communicate this support to all staff, and ensure that the project is completed. Too frequently, projects are begun but never seem to be completed. A lack of commitment to complete projects affects future projects in the organization. Staff is then not enthusiastic or supportive, knowing the organization's history of failure with new projects. Open and consistent communication assists staff members as they adjust to new requirements.

Because instituting the use of pathways or any of the other tools or strategies highlighted in this chapter is a major undertaking, beginning other major projects at the same time needs to be considered carefully. Too much stress at one time may affect the success of all new projects. There must also be a clear definition of the goals and identification of those staff members who will have leadership responsibilities in instituting clinical pathways. Because this is not a quick fix, a reasonable timeline is required, with identified key points for reassessment of progress. With these decisions made, the project committee can begin work on specific pathways. The first phase of the project is the development of the pathways, and the second is implementation. Evaluation is incorporated throughout the project. (See Chapter 3 for information on change and planning.)

Pathway development requires an interprofessional team/committee that is willing to openly discuss issues and research information (evidence-based practice), be receptive to change, and be committed to the project. It is, however, helpful to have some staff members who are skeptical as they provide the "other viewpoint" that is critical in the development of realistic pathways. It is hoped these team members will not be so negative that they are destructive to the process, but rather they will identify issues and concerns that staff will undoubtedly experience. The committee finds out more about the topic, uses this information to develop the pathway using a designated standard format, gets feedback from other staff, tests the pathway to get more feedback, implements the pathway, and evaluates the outcomes.

The project committee and interprofessional teams need education about project development, change, and clinical pathways. It is helpful to provide this education prior to beginning the project or in the initial stages. Content should include the following:

- Project development and organizational change
- Definition and purposes of a pathway
- Advantages and disadvantages of pathways
- Implementation of pathways
- Research resources
- Variances and variance analysis
- Project evaluation
- Listing of references used to support the pathway content

The final draft should be dated and include a list of staff who participated in developing the pathway and identification of approval and by whom.

Providing committee members and teams with resources such as current articles and books on pathways, library access, and even sample pathways from similar organizations is a good way to begin. The project committee and the teams that develop the content for specific pathways need access to data such as length of stay (LOS), common admission diagnoses, readmission rates, laboratory tests, and quality improvement data. Some staff may not know what data are available within the HCO, so including information management system (IMS) staff who can assist the committee and the teams is very helpful.

It is best if there is a standard pathway format that will be used throughout the HCO. Reviewing formats used by other HCOs is a good way to understand what can be done, and many examples are found in the literature. The committee may also want to contact similar organizations and ask about their pathway formats as well as their experiences with using clinical pathways. The format that is chosen needs to be easy to use and clear and should not seem so overwhelming that staff will immediately complain that it will only add more work. Staff appreciate brevity, relevance, and conciseness.

What is included in the clinical pathway format? The scope of clinical pathways can vary; for example, a pathway might focus on inpatient care, a complete episode of care, specialized applications, or health management. Specific pathway content may also vary among organizations; the most common categories of information that are included in pathways are identified in Box 9-2; however, a pathway does not have to include all of these categories. The committee selects the categories of information that are important to include for the specific patient population and its providers.

BOX 9-2	PATHWAY DEVELOPMENT PROCESS

PROJECT COMMITTEE SELECTED

- Assess environment for change.
- Identify target populations.
- Design pathway format.
- Select medical record and documentation issues.
- Develop variance tracking and analysis requirements.
- Develop policies and procedures.
- Select interdisciplinary teams for specific pathways.
- Provide education about pathways to the teams.
- Develop and implement general staff education.

INTERPROFESSIONAL TEAMS

- Research to prepare content for specific pathway.
- Retrospective chart review.
- Current practice patterns.
- Benchmarking.
- Standards of practice.
- Literature review.

- Review pathway samples from other institutions and literature.
- Review financial data.
- Review use data.
- Review outcome studies.
- Request expert opinions.
- Identify outcomes, length of stay, and timeline.
- Define required content.
- Pilot test.
- Make changes based on pilot test data.
- Repeat pilot as necessary.
- Final approval of pathway by project committee and administration.
- Implementation of pathway.
- Variance tracking and analysis.
- Continue overall project evaluation.

Source: Author created; summarized from Finkelman, A. (2001). *Managed care* (p. 154). Upper Saddle River, NJ: Prentice Hall.

Key indicators are a very important part of the pathway. These indicators are the interventions that must be implemented to attain specified outcomes. During the development phase of pathways, it is important to understand the key indicators; however, overemphasis on indicators can be a problem. This usually happens when staff are concerned about missing something important. Nurses and other healthcare providers need to continuously remind themselves to focus on the most important care needs. This is not easy to do in today's stressful healthcare environment with its complex patients.

The development team needs to document its work so there is a record of the planning and development process. The HCO must make a decision about whether or not the pathways will be a permanent part of the medical record. If it is optional, confusion and inconsistency often occur. Accrediting agencies may question records that are not consistent. Pathways that are not part of the medical record may be viewed as less important by the staff. In the past nurses experienced this with nursing care plans when some hospitals included them in their medical records and others did not. If staff members are concerned that using the pathways does not really cover documentation needs, they may overdocument. As the interprofessional teams develop specific pathway content, it is essential to review the current documentation system and how it relates to the specific content and use of pathways. How will documentation need to change in the medical record and on the clinical pathway? HCOs or providers who use computerized information management systems need to incorporate their pathways into these systems. These are critical questions that need to be repeated for each new pathway that is developed.

Including medical records staff on the project committee is critical. Their participation and input will prevent many future documentation problems. Decisions about access to the pathway are important. Digital access is the best method today as this is easier for staff, but the electronic methods used need to be easy to use and accessible. If the pathway is to be included in an individual patient's record and it is describing care the patient is receiving, then this has to be part of the planning.

Identification of the target population is a critical decision for the project committee as time should not be wasted on the wrong population. It is costly and will only aggravate staff. A typical way to approach classifying diagnoses for pathway development is to use the International Classification of Diseases, Version 10 Conversion Manual (ICD-10-CM) (Centers for Disease Control and Prevention, 2014a). This is the primary resource for medical diagnoses and third-party payer reimbursement coding. The pathway committee considers the following as it reviews the typical illnesses or conditions in its patient population (e.g., patients in the hospital or home care agency, insurer enrollee, etc.):

- High volume
- High risk

- Complex care requirements
- High cost
- Variations in length of stay compared with the "norm" or benchmarks
- Readmission data
- Variations in practice patterns
- Quality improvement data
- Payer request or interest in the illness or condition
- Opportunity for improved care

With increasing emphasis on interprofessional issues, interprofessional staff teams that are selected to develop specific pathway content need to be qualified in the particular clinical area or some aspects of the delivery of care. For example, a pathway for a surgical condition should include surgeons, registered nurses from surgical units, operating room, and recovery room and might include representatives from anesthesia, transportation, pharmacy, laboratory, medical records, admission, finance, utilization review (UR), quality improvement (QI), risk management (RM), and information management system (IMS). The team begins by brainstorming but must focus on the routine, not the exceptions. Developing a flowchart often provides a helpful picture of the steps required from the routine care for the identified illness or condition. The team considers all aspects of care, a timeline that corresponds to the LOS goal, outcomes, and the key indicators for reaching the outcomes. As the team prepares to develop content, they review medical records of cases with the same diagnosis or condition, research literature, utilization and outcome data, current practice, and local practice patterns (both internal and external), and seek expert opinions. Identification of outcomes is a critical aspect of the process. Outcomes need to be specific, objective, and quantitative, and they should be reviewed periodically to ensure that they are current with new research, technology, medications, and clinical practice. Pathways need to be evidence based. (See Chapter 16.)

With the increasing emphasis on care in the community, acute care hospitals need to consider what is the best setting in which to deliver the care and how to better collaborate with community providers and resources. The development of pathways is a good time to discuss these questions to collaborate with public/community providers.

Another approach to the development of pathways is to use pathways that have been developed by other HCOs or professional healthcare organizations or that are found in the literature. It is critical that all selected pathways are then adapted to the specific provider organization. It is important to critically review the examples and determine if the needs of the HCO and its patients can be met using the examples, and if the examples are based on sound evidence.

The reviewers must also consider how current the references are that were used to develop pathway content. Outdated references can be a problem in reflecting the currency of the pathway content. With the increasing emphasis on evidence-based practice, it is important that practice guides such as pathways are based on best practice and updated.

Many drafts of the pathways are required as the team works through the content, discusses it with other staff, and reviews the literature. The project committee identifies the final review process that should be followed for all pathways that are developed. This process includes key persons in the HCO and the project committee. Consensus is critical for successful implementation, but it is not always easy to reach. Negotiation and collaboration often are needed to reach consensus.

New clinical pathways need to be pilot tested prior to their final approval. The project committee determines the pilot testing process, including its length, number of times the pathway should be implemented with patients, and data collection procedures and analysis. Undoubtedly changes will need to be made, and some of these may be major. If so, another pilot may be required. Obtaining staff members' feedback as they use the pathway in the pilot is critical for obtaining helpful information. If this feedback is ignored, staff feel left out and less inclined to support the pathways when they are implemented. Once pathways are approved, implementation begins; however, there are two issues that are important throughout the development and implementation phases: collaboration with other HCOs or other organizations such as insurers that might require the use of clinical pathways or HCOs that might receive patient referrals for additional services.

Implementation of clinical pathways requires time and patience. Staff members will be uncomfortable and have concerns about how their use will affect their practice. Pathways should not be seen as a method for improving all of an organization's problems. For example, using clinical pathways will not improve overall communication in an organization that has a long-standing problem of poor communication. During the implementation of pathways, problems are often encountered that need to be resolved to prevent project failure. The following are examples of potential problems that may interfere with pathway implementation:

- There is concern that pathways represent cookbook medicine in that they standardize care without regard to individual patient needs or individual provider practice. Pathways ignore practice pattern differences that occur when physicians and nurses care for the patients with the same diagnosis. Staff education is required to ensure that clinical staff understand the purpose of pathways and emphasize the need for individualizing pathways to meet individual patient needs.

- Pathways can become just one more record to keep or follow, particularly if the documentation system is not evaluated at the time of pathway development. Duplication is a frequent complaint and serves only to frustrate staff and increase documentation errors. Consolidating the progress notes often helps. In addition, there is a tendency to include too many indicators or too much detail in the pathways. This makes them cumbersome to use. If a pathway is long, staff may assume that using it is a complex process that will only increase the workload. Using electronic versions helps, but if the pathway is complex and lengthy, then there may still be a problem to reach effective application.

- If pathway outcomes are based on only data from within the institution and do not consider relevant external information and outcomes, the pathways may represent only the internal current standards rather than the optimal. In this case, patient care may not improve.

- Turf battles may become serious, particularly if they were present prior to implementing pathways. Who is in charge of the pathways? Physicians? Utilization review? Nursing staff? Case managers? Job boundaries need to be reviewed prior to implementation. When project leadership is defined, staff needs to be included in discussions. Gaining consensus is an important part of the implementation process for all levels of staff. As was discussed in Chapter 3, effective change requires understanding and buy-in from staff. Clearly defining purpose and responsibility will help to prevent many future problems.

- A common problem in pathway development is to overestimate or underestimate the expected LOS. This can lead to increased staff stress. Using pathways is the best way to assess the LOS, and their use helps to determine the best expected LOS.

- Comorbidities are also problematic. Pathways usually are developed for one illness or condition; however, patients often have more than one. How should staff use the pathways for these patients? This needs to be clarified before implementation. One way to resolve this problem is to develop copaths. This prevents confusion and problems with increased documentation. The copath is usually used across departments as typically these are problems that are experienced with different types of patients.

- Physicians usually are concerned about pathways, as they need to be reassured that pathways do not replace physician orders. They are also concerned about losing their autonomy. To decrease this fear, physician input is absolutely necessary during pathway development, implementation, and evaluation. The HCO may require a physician's order for the use of a pathway; however, there is usually a method for physicians to alter or choose not to use a pathway. This is important to ensure patient-centered care.

  Of course, these approaches could defeat the purpose of the pathways, and the healthcare organization would need to monitor the use of these alternatives to ensure that pathway implementation is not sidetracked. Data obtained from the pathways about patient outcomes may also be affected by these physician options.

Staff resistance in using pathways must be dealt with directly. Often, recognizing that it might be a problem and taking steps to alleviate staff concerns can prevent it. The first step is to recognize it as a problem and to understand the reasons for the resistance. This understanding should then lead to developing strategies to address the concerns that are supporting staff resistance to use pathways. In addition, it is important to identify if there are specific groups that are resisting. Understanding resistance helps to develop strategies to reduce resistance.

If a pathway is blindly followed, this can have a negative impact on its use and decisions based on the pathway. If a pathway contains errors or represents substandard care, the provider is still responsible for the care provided. Nothing relieves the professional, such as a nurse, of the responsibility for using professional judgment. If pathways are used, every healthcare professional who uses them must be responsible for learning how to use them correctly in the best interest of individual patients or take the risk of making an error. Disclaimers may be used with pathways. General disclaimers should state that the pathway provides guidance for the plan of care, but staff recognizes that each patient requires individualized care. The disclaimer should convey that the practitioner makes treatment decisions after an assessment of the patient's condition. In all these situations, the HCO should consult its legal counsel.

PATHWAY EVALUATION Pathway evaluation should not be made into a complicated process. The areas of most concern are whether costs are changing per patient diagnosis and for itemized costs, such as laboratory tests, pharmacy, physical therapy, and radiology, and whether the quality of care is compromised. Are outcomes met? Evaluation also focuses on the LOS or the length of treatment. Particularly important in the evaluation process is variance analysis.

Variances are deviations from the expected or that which is defined in the clinical pathway. Variances are tracked and used to assess achievement of outcomes. Comments about general variance data should never be documented in individual medical records. They may be positive or negative. Negative variances indicate that the patient has not achieved expected outcomes or that activities have not been completed. A positive variance indicates that the patient achieved an outcome or activity prior to the expected deadline. If the trend is toward more positive variances, it may mean that the deadlines need to be reviewed and could be shortened. Negative variances might relate to HCO, provider, or patient issues. With today's complex HCOs and concern about quality, it is important to analyze the causes for negative variances. (See Chapters 17 and 18.) System or operational variances focus on hindrances in the system or the organization that prevent the achievement of patient outcomes. Examples are delays in laboratory results, lack of bed space, hours of service, delayed transfers to a long-term care facility, lack of supplies, and so on. Provider variances focus on the variances that may be caused by the provider. Examples include the following:

- The physician does not respond to a telephone call from a nurse about a patient's condition.
- A mislabeled medication is given to a patient.
- A staff member is unable to do a procedure due to lack of experience or knowledge.
- Orders are misread and a patient is sent for the wrong procedure.
- Inadequate nursing staff decreases the time a nurse has to review a patient's history.
- A patient variance identifies factors related to the patient that prevent the achievement of patient outcomes; for example, a patient refuses medication, a patient experiences complications (e.g., elevated temperature that interferes with proceeding with treatment), a patient experiences inadequate pain relief, or a patient arrives late for his admission for ambulatory care surgery.

It is important to avoid blame when assessing variances but rather to look at reasons and resolution; this is a key recommendation from many of the IOM reports about quality and patient safety. Staff need to consider all aspects of an issue (for example, a patient's medication problem). Why is the patient refusing medication? Is the patient afraid of the medication and its side effects? Does the patient lack understanding of the purpose of taking the medication? Does the patient have the money to pay for the medication? Does the patient lack transportation to pick up the medication or feel that the medication will not help? Jumping to conclusions is not helpful and limits true understanding as to the reason for the variance. Variance data are most critical in understanding outcome achievement or lack of achievement and also provide direction for change. Data should be shared with the pathway development team and relevant staff. Involving them in resolution development is also important.

Variance analysis assists in identifying patterns of concern or problems that are seen in a number of patients. These problems may require more intensive action for every patient who experiences these problems. It might, however, be due to a repetitive problem in the system. Algorithms are created to resolve these variances and prevent future variances. Generally algorithms are not developed until variance data indicate a need. Algorithms are developed in the same way as pathways. Typically they are formatted as decision-making trees. For example, if a patient experiences an elevated temperature, then specific treatment is begun.

Documenting these variances can be problematic due to liability risk. Staff need to avoid blaming a staff member in the medical record; for example, to state in the medical record that because a physician did not respond to a call from the nurse about the patient's condition, the patient developed a complication. Documenting variances must be done with care. Reasons for the variance, if known, need to be identified but should be based on factual data. When treatment that is not in the pathway is added or deleted, this must be documented. Nurses document most of the variances because they have the most contact with patients, particularly in acute care, home care, and long-term care. Variance documentation requires accurate and complete documentation. The HCO develops documentation policies and procedures and prepares staff in their use.

Patient and staff satisfaction are also critical evaluation issues. Patient satisfaction is a very important factor in the evaluation of the use of pathways and should consider three key questions:

1. Does the patient/family feel involved in the care?
2. Were the patient's goals met?
3. Did staff discuss the patient's progress with the patient?

Patients need to first understand what a clinical pathway is and how it is used to engage the patient in the process and improve patient-centered care. Individual nurses best provide this explanation because they interact more with patients and families. Other issues that have been discussed as factors that might be affected by the use of pathways are patient education, continuity of information, continuity or care, quality of care, length of stay, and reduction of costs.

Staff satisfaction should also not be overlooked in pathway evaluation. Important questions to consider include the following:

- Do you understand the reasons for using pathways?
- Did you feel prepared to use the pathways?
- If you participated in the development of the pathways, do you feel that your input was respected?
- How has the use of pathways affected your daily practice/work?
- How has the use of pathways affected your relationship with your patients/families?
- Do you think that pathways support interprofessional collaboration? If so, how?
- How has the use of pathways affected your documentation?
- What would you like to see changed with the pathways and their implementation?
- Is staff using the pathways and using them correctly?

These questions are particularly important for HCOs that use temporary nurses, part-time staff, and travel nurses, which may make it difficult to ensure that all staff are knowledgeable about pathways and committed to using them. Full-time staff may carry the burden of ensuring that pathways are used correctly. This can lead to increased staff stress and affect patient care delivery.

There are many questions that can be asked in the evaluation process. HCOs need to develop questions relevant to their environment, patients, and staff. Gathering data can be overdone, so question selection and related data should be carefully considered. When evaluation is complete, a summary of the results and any pathway revisions should be shared with the staff. In many organizations, staff find out about changes when changes affect them, but this is too late. Staff members should not pick up a copy of a pathway when they need to use it and find out it has been changed. This does not allow time for staff to understand the changes and how they affect patient care delivery.

Clinical Practice Guidelines

Insurers and HCOs use clinical practice guidelines. Healthcare professional organizations also recognize the value in using guidelines. This interest in tools to manage care stems from the need to decrease costs and yet provide quality care, and the IOM reports as well as the ACA strongly recommend their use. Guidelines are used in conjunction with clinical pathways. The goal is to narrow the gap between an organization's current care and optimal care. Practice guidelines are used to assist with treatment decision making and to evaluate care.

DEFINITION AND PURPOSE   **Clinical practice guidelines** (CPGs) are "systematically developed statements that assist practitioners in making decisions about appropriate healthcare for specific clinical conditions" (Agency for Healthcare Research and Quality, 2014). As with clinical pathways, practice guidelines are called by many names. Some of the more common names are appropriateness indicators, practice parameters, medical review criteria, and standards. Their purpose is to pull together research information from the literature, evaluate these results, and access expert opinions about the clinical condition. CPGs should be evidence based, as noted by the Institute of Medicine in its report *Clinical Practice Guidelines We Can Trust* (2011). This information is then prepared in a usable form. Practice guidelines are different from standards of care in that guidelines do not define treatment but rather provide information and options. National Guideline Clearinghouse, sponsored by the Agency for Healthcare Research and Quality (AHRQ), is a major source for evidence-based clinical practice guidelines and provides access to the CPGs on its website (Agency for Healthcare Research and Quality, 2014).

INSURER INTEREST IN PRACTICE GUIDELINES   Insurers often support the use of practice guidelines. The common reasons for this support are to do the following:

- Reduce healthcare costs.
- Improve the quality of care.
- Ensure consistency of care.
- Provide performance data for comparison with other insurers, as well as comparison of individual provider performance levels.
- Comply with accreditation and regulatory requirements.

DEVELOPMENT AND IMPLEMENTATION OF PRACTICE GUIDELINES   Most insurers, HCOs, and healthcare providers typically use CPGs that have been developed by professional organizations, the AHRQ, or other resources. Guidelines are then selected and adapted to meet the needs of the HCO or provider. Public and private sector organizations, including professional organizations, healthcare organizations, and researchers, develop practice guidelines. Condition-specific organizations (e.g., American Heart Association, Arthritis Foundation) have also developed guidelines. As members of these various organizations, nurses have been active in the development of guidelines. Governmental agencies that have been involved in the development are the AHRQ through the National Guideline Clearinghouse, the National Institutes of Health, the Centers for Disease Control and Prevention, the U.S. Preventive Services Task Force, Centers of Medicare and Medicaid Services, and the U.S. Department of Health and Human Services. Active participation from many types of organizations and the government indicates the level of interest in practice guidelines. The AHRQ guidelines are well-known sets of statements that may be used to assist practitioners and/or patients in making healthcare decisions for specific clinical problems. Interprofessional panels of experts develop these guidelines. CPGs accepted by the National Guideline Clearinghouse must meet requirements, which are described on its website.

What are the problems or factors that are keeping providers, such as physicians and nurse practitioners, from using practice guidelines? One major problem is the accessibility of the information while the provider (such as a physician, nurse, or nurse practitioner) is with the patient. If the provider has access to a computer in the examining room, then this information could be discussed with the patient in the examining room. This would save time and be more relevant to the patient. This is, however, an expense. With so many guidelines in existence, making decisions about which ones to use is problematic. Information overload is a major complication today, and it can actually increase stress rather than decrease it or control it. A common approach made by providers is to amalgamate the guidelines by considering providers' personal experiences and approaches with the specific condition.

Nonadherence to guidelines can often be traced to limited provider input in guideline development, disagreement about a specific guideline, or dislike of guideline use in general. Change that is instituted from outside is rarely successful. In addition, change that brings limited rewards often fails. Some insurers encourage guideline use by paying incentives to providers who use them and by tracking their use when they evaluate provider performance. A final concern with practice guidelines is coverage of comorbidities, which is also true with clinical pathways. For example, what does the provider do when a patient has a cardiac condition and diabetes? There are guidelines for the cardiac condition and also guidelines for diabetes. The guidelines may not consider the impact of one illness on the other and may actually offer conflicting treatment options. Often the provider chooses not to use any practice guideline rather than deal with conflicting and confusing recommendations.

Nurse practitioners also encounter the same problems with practice guidelines as they use them in their practice. With more nurse practitioners entering private practice and clinics, they will need to review these guidelines and determine their relevance to advance practice nursing. Nurses who work in the community can make use of the guidelines to help plan community health education and services that focus on specific problems.

Informatics can be used to support implementation of guidelines as well as assist with evaluation of their use and outcomes. The National Guideline Clearinghouse is based on the Internet. As noted in Chapter 19, informatics has become more important in all areas of health care. Informatics can provide quick access to the guidelines. Within the information system, staff should be able to get to the guidelines when they are needed, review them, and apply them to planning and patient education, development of policies and procedures, and application to individual patient care planning. The information system can also be set up to remind staff to use guidelines and integrate these guidelines into the documentation system. Information systems also allow for easy updates of guidelines, but for this to be successful, it must be built into the system to ensure that it gets done.

Evaluation of the implementation of clinical practice guidelines is important, and there is need to have more research that assesses the value of CPGs, as well as use of clinical pathways and disease management. What are the outcomes both from quality and costs perspectives? We need to ensure that these tools are evidence based and current and they are easily accessible for review and use when appropriate.

The IOM report *Clinical Practice Guidelines We Can Trust* (2011) examines the use of CPGs and their importance. Chapter 16 describes this report in more detail. The report can be accessed from the National Academy of Medicine website.

CURRENT APPROACHES TO PATIENT-CENTERED CARE

HCOs are approaching patient-centered care in a variety of ways. The following concludes this discussion about patient-centered care by highlighting some of them. Other chapters in this text pertain to patient-centered care such as chapters about diversity and disparities, consumers, teams, delegation, evidence-based practice, communication, and others. Typically patient-centered care is viewed as a new concept; however, it is not.

> Organizing the delivery of health care around the needs of the patient may seem like a simple and obvious approach. In a system as complex as health care, however, little is simple. In fact, thirty years ago when the idea of patient-centered care first emerged as a return to the holistic roots of healthcare, it was swiftly dismissed by all but the most philosophically progressive providers as trivial, superficial, or unrealistic. Its defining characteristics of partnering with patients and families, of welcoming—even encouraging—their involvement, and of personalizing care to preserve patients' normal routines as much as possible, were widely seen as a threat to the conventions of healthcare where providers are the experts, family are visitors, and patients are body parts to be fixed. Indeed, for decades, the provision of consumer-focused healthcare information, opportunities for loved ones' involvement in patient care, a healing physical environment, food, spirituality, and so forth have largely been considered expendable when compared to the critical and far more pressing demands of quality and patient safety—not to mention maintaining a healthy operating margin. (Frampton et al., 2008, p. 3)

The movement to patient-centered care was long and variable. Today with the push through the IOM quality series of reports, including recognition that all healthcare professions should meet the core competency of providing patient-centered care, the need for this approach has now been recognized as critical. Key now is how to get it done effectively. Care should be organized around the patient, but this is not simple to accomplish—and may not even be desirable to some healthcare providers and HCOs. To accomplish this requires commitment from leadership, management, and staff but also must be done in a way that makes sense. HCOs need to use self-assessment to better understand the status of the organization culture and what will need to be done to make it more patient centered. Frampton et al. provide a sample self-assessment tool (2008). Looking at this self-assessment provides a perspective of the critical issues related to patient-centered organizations.

- The foundation of the organization (such as values, expectations, engagement, "walking the talk")
- Communicating effectively with patients and families
- Personalization of care (respecting patient preferences, preserving patient dignity, promoting patient and family empowerment, encouraging caring interactions, using patient-centered approaches to food and nutrition, creating signature moments, and responding to diverse cultural expectations)
- Continuity of care
- Access to information
- Family involvement
- Environment of care (comfort, healing)
- Spirituality
- Integrative medicine
- Caring for the community
- Care for the caregiver (reward and recognition, promoting work-life balance, promoting employee wellness)
- Patient satisfaction

As often happens with "new ideas," myths develop about them. These myths can act as barriers to developing a patient-centered environment. The following are common myths:

- Providing patient-centered care is too costly.
- Patient-centered care is "nice" but not important.
- Providing patient-centered care is the job of the nurses.
- To provide patient-centered care, we will need to increase staffing ratios.
- Patient-centered care can be effective in only a small hospital.
- There is no evidence to prove patient-centered care is an effective model.
- Many patient-centered practices compromise infection control efforts.
- The first step in becoming a patient-centered hospital is construction.
- Patient-centered care is a magic bullet.
- A shared medical record policy violates HIPAA.
- We have already received a number of quality awards, so we must be patient centered.
- Being patient centered is too time consuming (Frampton et al., 2008).

None of these myths are correct; however, it is important for leaders and managers to know about them because they keep staff and even leaders and managers from engaging in the process.

The Planetree Designation is a "voluntary review and identification of hospitals that excel in the providing patient-centered care. It provides a process and structure that inspires and enables caregivers to transform the healthcare experience" (Planetree, 2014). This is discussed further in Chapter 10. The Joint Commission recognizes the Planetree Designation on its Quality Check website. The Centers for Medicare & Medicaid Services (CMS) also compares the Planetree Designation with CMS core measures, and typically these hospitals do better than others (Frampton & Guastello, 2010).

There is some research on the impact of patient-centered care on outcomes, though more is needed. For example, one study retrospectively examined data from two comparable medical-surgical units over five years—one that had implemented the Planetree model and one that had not (Stone, 2008, p. 60). In each of the five one-year cohorts studied, the Planetree unit consistently demonstrated:

- shorter average lengths of stay.
- statistically significant lower costs per case (this resulted largely from the shorter lengths of stay but also from "slightly reduced" RN hours per patient day and an increased use of "lower-cost personnel," such as aides).
- higher average overall patient satisfaction scores.
- higher scores in nearly all the dimensions of patient satisfaction measured.

APPLYING EVIDENCE-BASED PRACTICE

Evidence for Effective Leadership and Practice

CITATION: Fowler, F., Levin, C., & Sepucha, K. (2011). Informing and involving patients to improve the quality of medical decisions. *Health Affairs, 30*(4), 699–706.

OVERVIEW: Quality care requires both use of appropriate and effective procedures, treatments, and diagnostic tests, but also should involve a well-informed patient to support patient-centered care. The patient is not always given the option to participate in decision making and may not be informed enough to do so. There need to be more incentives for providers to ensure that the patient is informed and participates if the patient chooses to do so. This article looks at methods and tools used to meet this important goal.

APPLICATION: Shared decision making must be part of effective care. To accomplish this, healthcare providers need more information about patient understanding and how to integrate the patient into decision making. With the growing use of healthcare technology, there are many more methods for accomplishing this goal.

Questions:

1. What is known about obtaining information about the patient's knowledge and desire to participate in decision making?
2. How is the Affordable Care Act related to this topic?
3. What are some common patient surveys that are used in health care to get patient feedback?

The Joint Commission also provides guidance to hospitals regarding development and implementation of patient-centered care by offering resources to hospitals such as *Advancing Effective Communication, Cultural Competence, and Patient- and Family-Centered Care: A Roadmap for Hospitals* (2010). The guide not only offers general background information about patient-centered care but also offers suggestions for how hospitals can make admission, assessment, treatment, end-of-life care, and discharge and transfer more patient centered. Nurse managers and staff need to consider how care is provided at points along the patient trajectory and what is done or could be done to make the experience more patient centered. The Joint Commission provides some first steps to doing this and associates the recommendations with its standards and requirements. The guide focuses on communication and cultural competence and their relationship to patient- and family-centered care.

All staff, clinical, management, and nonclinical, in an HCO can contribute to the implementation of patient-centered care, though nurses have a major role in ensuring this type of care setting. To accomplish meaningful changes, hospitals must consider staff training and also review policies and procedures to determine if they are in sync with a patient- and family-centered approach. Leadership must be knowledgeable about this approach and committed to it—and not just verbally, but in actions. Many HCOs are now stating they are patient and family centered or attempting to change so they can be more patient and family centered. Health care has gone through many "bandwagon" experiences where HCOs made changes to be more like a certain model of care or philosophy of care. In this case, as noted earlier, patient-centered care is really not new as some in health care have discussed it for many years, but it never became a serious issue nor was it broadly implemented until recently. There are many approaches to implementing patient-centered care; however,

the first step in understanding patient-centered care is an understanding that patients must be asked to rate or judge their healthcare; providers often believe that we know everything about our patients and their care, but we are simply unable to accurately assess our patients' perceptions of their care—what is important to them, how well we are delivering care, what factors in our patient care improve outcomes. We need to attempt to move from "what's the matter" with our patients to "what matters" to our patients. (Rickert, 2012)

Patient-centered care is about relationships (provider-patient), communication, and empathy. We have to be careful that we do not just use words to say patient-centered care exists, but rather we need change and actions that demonstrate it exists. HCOs and individual providers, including nurses, can say they agree with patient-centered care, but the real test is if it is practiced.

APPLYING LEADERSHIP AND MANAGEMENT

My Hospital Unit: An Evolving Case Experience

You have to decide on your priority strategic goal for your unit for the coming year. You and your staff decide that it will be to improve patient-centered care. A meeting is scheduled with the staff to discuss how this might be achieved. You do not want the plan to be broad and want clear direction of strategies. What might you and your staff develop to describe the strategies you will use to meet this goal? How will you measure and then apply goal achievement to your specific unit? The strategies need to be clear, specific, and measurable.

BSN and *Master's Essentials:* Application to Content

BSN Essentials (American Association of Colleges of Nursing, 2008) as Applied to this Chapter:

III. Scholarship for Evidence-Based Practice
VI. Interprofessional Communication and Collaboration for Improving Patient Health Outcomes
VII. Clinical Prevention and Population Health
IX. Baccalaureate Generalist Nursing Practice

Master's Essentials (American Association of Colleges of Nursing, 2011) as Applied to this Chapter:

IV. Translating and Integrating Scholarship into Practice
VII. Interprofessional Collaboration for Improving Patient and Population Health Outcomes
IX. Master's-Level Nursing Practice

Applying AONE Competencies

Identify which of the AONE competencies found in Appendix A apply to the content of this chapter.

Engaging in the Content: Critical Thinking and Clinical Reasoning and Judgment

Discussion Questions

1. Discuss examples from a clinical setting to illustrate that the healthcare organization is patient centered. Identify examples that are not patient centered, and assess why they are not and how you would improve them.
2. Compare and contrast disease management, clinical pathways, and clinical guidelines.
3. What is self-management, and how does it relate to patient-centered care? Why is it important to nursing management?
4. What is your opinion of patient-centered care? (Online Application Option)

Application Exercises

1. Find an example of a *clinical pathway* from a clinical site, nursing literature, or the Internet. Review the example. Apply what you have learned in this chapter. Describe the critical elements of the pathway and, if possible, how it was developed. You should consider the following: purpose of the pathway, the process used to develop it (including who developed it, how it was reviewed, and what type of data was used to develop it), the target population and why it would be selected, type and quality of content, identification of any possible legal and ethical issues, use of the clinical pathway (Is it easy to use? What does staff think about using it? Could you follow it for a patient?), and what is the evaluation process for the pathway (frequency of review, by whom, and who can provide feedback about its use)?

2. Find an example of a *clinical guideline* from a clinical site, nursing literature, or the Internet. Review the example. Apply what you have learned in this chapter. Describe the critical elements of the pathway and, if possible, how it was developed. You should consider the following: purpose of the pathway, the process used to develop it (including who developed it, how it was reviewed, and what type of data was used to develop it), the target population and why it would be selected, type and quality of content, identification of any possible legal and ethical issues, use of the clinical guideline (Is it easy to use? What does staff think about using it? Could you follow it for a patient?). What is the evaluation process for the guideline (frequency of review, by whom, and who can provide feedback about its use)?

3. Visit the Institute of Health Improvement website and find information on patient-centered care. Explore the toolkit of strategies for hospital leaders to improve patient-centered care. How might these apply to nursing management?

4. Find an example of the application of health promotion or illness prevention in one of your clinical sites. What is the example? How is it used? Is it effective, and what do you base this on? What is the role of the patient or consumer of health care? (Online Application Option)

5. Describe several examples of applying patient-centered care that you have observed in clinical. Share in teams. (Online Application Option)

References

Agency for Healthcare Research and Quality. (AHRQ). (2014). National guideline clearinghouse. Retrieved from http://www.guideline.gov

American Association of Colleges of Nursing. (2008). *The essentials of baccalaureate education for professional nursing practice*. Washington, DC: Author.

American Association of Colleges of Nursing. (2011). *The essentials of master's education in nursing*. Washington, DC: Author.

Benner, P., Sutphen, M., Leonard, V., & Day, L. (2010). *Educating nurses*. San Francisco, CA: Jossey-Bass Publishers.

Benner, P., Tanner, C., & Chesla, C. (1996). *Expertise in nursing practice: Caring, clinical judgment, and ethics*. New York, NY: Springer.

Centers for Disease Control and Prevention. (2014a). 2015 ICD-10-CM and GEMS. Retrieved from http://www.cms.gov/Medicare/Coding/ICD10/2015-ICD-10-CM-and-GEMs.html

Centers for Disease Control and Prevention. (2014b). Chronic disease overview. Retrieved from http://www.cdc.gov/chronicdisease/overview/

Centers for Disease Control and Prevention. (2014c). Chronic disease prevention and health promotion. Retrieved from http://www.cdc.gov/chronicdisease/

Davis, K., Schoenbaum, A., & Audet, A. (2005). Excerpt from "A 2020 Vision of Patient-Centered Primary Care" from *Journal of General Internal Medicine, 20*(10), 953–957. Society of General Internal Medicine.

Finkelman, A., & Kenner, C. (2016). *Professional nursing concepts*.

Competencies for quality leadership (3rd ed.). Boston, MA: Jones and Bartlett Publishers.

Frampton, S., & Guastello, S. (2010). Patient-centered care: More than the sum of its parts. Planetree's patient-centered hospital designation program. *AJN, 110*(9), 49–53.

Frampton, S., Guastello, S., Brady, C., Hale, M., Horowitz, S., Bennett Smith, S., & Stone, S. (2008). Excerpt from *Patient-Centered Care Improvement Guide*. Derby, CT: Planetree.

Improving Chronic Illness Care. (2014). The chronic care model. Retrieved from http://www.improvingchroniccare.org/index.php?p=Model_Elements&s=18

Institute of Health Improvement. (2014). Partnering in self-management support: A toolkit for clinicians. Retrieved from http://www.ihi.org/resources/Pages/Tools/SelfManagementToolkitforClinicians.aspx

Institute of Medicine. (2001). *Crossing the quality chasm*. Washington, DC: National Academies Press.

Institute of Medicine. (2003a). Excerpt from *Health Professions Education: A Bridge to Quality*. Washington, DC: National Academies Press.

Institute of Medicine. (2003b). *Priority areas for quality improvement*. Washington, DC: National Academies Press.

Institute of Medicine. (2004). *Health literacy*. Washington, DC: National Academies Press.

Institute of Medicine. (2011). *Clinical practice guidelines we can trust*. Washington, DC: National Academies Press.

Joint Commission. (2010). *Advancing effective communication, cultural competence, and patient- and*

family-centered care: A roadmap for hospitals. Oakbrook Terrace, IL: Author.

Kinsman, L., Rotter, T., James, E., Snow, P., & Willis, J. (2010). What is a clinical pathway? Development of a definition to inform the debate. *BMC Med.*, 8:31. Retrieved from http://www.ncbi.nlm.nih.gov/pmc/articles/PMC2893088/

Mikesell, L., & Bromley, E. (2012). Patient centered, nurse averse? Nurses' care experience in a 21st-century hospital. *Quality Health Research, 22*(12), 1659-1671.

Murphy, J. (2004). Using focused reflection and articulation to promote clinical reasoning. *Nursing Education Perspectives, 24*, 226–231.

Planetree. (2014). About us. Retrieved from http://planetree.org

Rickert, J. (2012, January 24). Patient-centered care: What it means and how to get there. Retrieved from http://healthaffairs.org/blog/2012/01/24/patient-centered-care-what-it-means-and-how-to-get-there/

Stone, S. (2008). A retrospective evaluation of the impact of the Planetree patient-centered model of care on inpatient quality outcomes. *HERD: Health Environments Research and Design, 1*(4), 55–69.

Wagner, E., Austin, B., & Von Korff, M. (1996). Organizing care for patients with chronic illness. *Milbank Quarterly 74*, pp. 511–544.

Zander, K. (1992). Quantifying, managing, and improving quality. Part II: The collaborative management of quality care. *The New Definition, 7*(3), 1–2.

10 Diversity and Disparities in Health Care

◉ LEARNING OUTCOMES

Before you begin, take a moment to familiarize yourself with the learning outcomes for this chapter.

〉 Discuss the problem of health disparities.
〉 Analyze the status of patient diversity in health care.
〉 Apply strategies to improve health literacy and the role of the nurse manager.
〉 Examine the implications of a diverse patient population for the staff and organization.
〉 Explain how organizational culture impacts the healthcare organization, patient care, and professional competency.
〉 Examine workplace diversity in healthcare organizations.
〉 Apply strategies that may be used to improve an organization's culture.

KEY TERMS

- baby boomers
- consonant culture
- cultural competence
- culture
- dissonant culture
- Generation X
- Generation Y
- health disparity
- health literacy
- Nexters
- organizational culture
- workforce diversity

WHAT'S AHEAD

The U.S. healthcare system has seen an increase in diverse patients representing many cultural backgrounds. The Institute of Medicine (IOM) examined the healthcare system, and as a result, there is now recognition of a serious problem with health disparities in the United States and understanding that culture and diversity is a key part of the strategies to improve the disparity problem. Organizational culture influences how consumers view healthcare organizations (HCOs) and staff who work in HCOs. **Culture** is "the accumulated store of shared values, ideas (attitudes, beliefs, values, and norms), understandings, symbols, material products, and practices of a group of people" (Institute of Medicine, 2002, p. 522). The following discussion focuses on patient culture and diversity, health disparities, health literacy, HCO culture, and workforce diversity.

HEALTHCARE DIVERSITY AND DISPARITIES

The National Academy of Medicine's (NAM) core competencies for healthcare professions ensure patient-centered care includes cultural issues: identify, respect, and care about patients' differences, values, preferences, and expressed needs (2003). The IOM states that

> a culturally diverse population poses challenges that go beyond simple language competency and include the need to understand the effects of lifestyle and cultural differences on health status and health-related behaviors; the need to adapt treatment plans and modes of delivery to different lifestyles and familial patterns; the implications of a diverse genetic endowment among the population; the prominence of nontraditional providers, as well as family caregivers. (2003, p. 40)

Nurses hold many different positions in HCOs, often positions covering 24/7 care such as staff nurse. They can have a major impact on improving care for all patients and ensuring equitable care.

Critical definitions related to cultural competence and diversity include (Centers for Disease Control and Prevention, 2014):

- Cultural competence: Culture is the blended patterns of human behavior that include "language, thoughts, communications, actions, customs, beliefs, values, and institutions of racial, ethnic, religious, or social groups." **Cultural competence** is "a set of congruent behaviors, attitudes, and policies that come together in a system, agency, or among professionals that enables effective work in cross-cultural situations." "Competence" in the term *cultural competence* implies that an individual or organization has the capacity to function effectively "within the context of the cultural beliefs, behaviors, and needs presented by consumers and their communities" (U.S. Department of Health and Human Services, Office of Minority Health, 2014).
- Health disparity: "A type of difference in health that is closely linked with social or economic disadvantage. Health disparities negatively affect groups of people who have systematically experienced greater social or economic obstacles to health. These obstacles stem from characteristics historically linked to discrimination or exclusion such as race or ethnicity, religion, socioeconomic status, gender, mental health, sexual orientation, or geographic location. Other characteristics include cognitive, sensory, or physical disability" (U.S. Department of Health and Human Services, National Partnership for Action, 2011). The IOM defines **health disparity** as "racial or ethnic differences in the quality of healthcare that are not due to access-related factors or clinical needs, preferences, and appropriateness of intervention" (Institute of Medicine, 2002, pp. 3–4).
- Health equity: "Providing care that does not vary in quality because of personal characteristics such as gender, ethnicity, geographic location and socioeconomic status" (Institute of Medicine, 2001, p. 6).
- Health inequity: A difference or disparity in health outcomes that is systematic, avoidable, and unjust.
- Health literacy: "Whether a person can obtain, process, and understand basic health information and services that are needed to make suitable health decisions" (Institute of Medicine, 2004, p. 2). **Health literacy** includes the ability to understand instructions on prescription drug bottles, appointment cards, medical education brochures, doctor's directions, and consent forms. It also includes the ability to navigate complex healthcare systems. Health literacy is not simply the ability to read. It requires a complex group of reading, listening, analytic, and decision-making skills and the ability to apply these skills to health situations. The American Association of Colleges of Nursing (AACN) emphasizes the five NAM core competencies in its 2008 publication *Essentials of Baccalaureate Education for Professional Nursing Practice*, which includes cultural competency. AACN has also developed an online toolkit, found on its website, to assist in developing cultural competency. Nursing education has made improvements to include content and learning experiences to improve cultural competency, though current reports on disparities indicate that more improvement is required.

The U.S. Department of Health and Human Services (HHS) Action Plan to Reduce Racial and Ethnic Health Disparities outlines goals and actions. The HHS will take appropriate steps to reduce health disparities among racial and ethnic minorities. The Office of Minority Health is leading the work to implement the HHS Disparities Action Plan at all levels of the HHS and in communities. With the HHS Disparities Action Plan, the HHS commits to continuously assessing the impact of all policies and programs on racial and ethnic health disparities. The HHS will promote integrated approaches, evidence-based programs, and best practices to reduce these disparities. The HHS Action Plan builds on the strong foundation of the Affordable Care Act (ACA) and is aligned with programs and initiatives such as *Healthy People 2020*, First Lady Obama's Let's Move initiative, and President Obama's National HIV/AIDS Strategy (U.S. Department of Health and Human Services, Office of Minority Health, 2012).

The ACA influenced content in the HHS Disparities Action Plan. The legislation not only includes provisions related broadly to health insurance coverage, health insurance reform, and access to care but also provisions related to disparities reduction, data collection and reporting, quality improvement, and prevention. The ACA includes these provisions to reduce health disparities by investing in prevention and wellness and giving individuals and families more control over their own care. Box 10-1 provides additional details on the

BOX 10-1	PROVISIONS IN THE AFFORDABLE CARE ACT THAT ADDRESS HEALTH DISPARITIES

Expanding Coverage and Access to Care: Over time, the mechanisms such as Medicaid expansion (2014) and Health Insurance Exchanges (2014) will give millions of people and small businesses access to affordable coverage. The Medicaid program provided services to an average of 50 million people in 2009; with the expected expansion (2014), the number could potentially increase by 16 million by 2019. Health Insurance Exchanges and new private competitive health insurance markets will help individuals and small employers select and enroll in high-quality, affordable private health plans. These will make purchasing health insurance easier and more understandable. Special efforts should be made to reach target populations and put greater choice in the hands of individuals and small businesses. In addition, the Affordable Care Act requires health plans and encourages state Medicaid programs to place a strong emphasis on prevention, specifically by encouraging coverage for any clinical preventive service recommended with a grade A or B by the U.S. Preventive Services Task Force (USPTF) and for immunizations recommended by the Advisory Committee on Immunization Practices (ACIP). Through the Medicare program, beneficiaries can now receive personalized prevention plans, an initial preventive physical examination, and any Medicare-covered preventive service recommended (grade A or B) by the USPTF.

Nondiscrimination: Section 1557 of the Affordable Care Act extends the application of existing federal civil rights laws prohibiting discrimination on the basis of race, color or national origin, gender, disability, or age to any health program or activity receiving federal financial assistance; any program or activity administered by an executive agency; or any entity established under Title I of the act or its amendments. Entities subject to §1557 must provide information in a culturally and linguistically appropriate manner to comply with the relevant antidiscrimination provisions of Title VI of the Civil Rights Act of 1964. (Section 1557 explicitly references the legal protections of Title VI of the Civil Rights Act of 1964, Title IX of the Education Amendments of 1972, the Age Discrimination Act of 1975, and section 504 of the Rehabilitation Act of 1973.)

Data: Section 4302 of the Affordable Care Act contains provisions to strengthen federal data collection efforts by requiring that all federally funded programs to collect data on race, ethnicity, primary language, disability status, and gender.

HRSA Community Health Center Program: The Affordable Care Act expands access to primary health care by investing $11 billion into the HRSA Community Health Center program over the next five years. Together with funds from the American Recovery and Reinvestment Act of 2009, the Affordable Care Act will enable the Community Health Center programs to nearly double the number of patients served over the next five years. A key component of the health center program will be the implementation of the New Access Points (NAPs) grant program. For fiscal year 2011, HRSA has committed to support 350 NAPs to increase preventive and primary healthcare services for eligible public and nonprofit entities including tribal, faith-based, and community-based organizations. Overall there should be funding of up to $335 million for expanded services in existing health centers and $10 million for 125 planning grants to help communities without a health center to develop one. The Community Health Center program provides care to vulnerable populations by assuring access to comprehensive, culturally competent, quality primary healthcare services. Of the nearly 19 million patients currently served through these HRSA-funded health centers, 63 percent are racial and ethnic minorities, and 92 percent are below the federal poverty level.

Health Professional Opportunity Grants (HPOGs): HPOGs are human service program grants that primarily assist organizations that serve populations with high concentrations of Native American, Hispanic, and African American people. The Temporary Assistance for Needy Families (TANF) program provides grants to states to administer a time-limited welfare program to assist needy families in achieving self-sufficiency. Recognizing the need for a larger, well-trained healthcare workforce, HPOG will provide comprehensive healthcare-related training to low-income workers and TANF participants to improve their ability to enter various health professions. To increase their opportunity for success, HPOG will work with community partners to enhance supportive services such as transportation, dependent care, and temporary housing for low-income workers and TANF participants.

Maternal, Infant, and Early Childhood Home Visitation Program: The Affordable Care Act provides support for the Maternal, Infant, and Early Childhood Visitation Program. Home visiting is an effective and relatively low-cost strategy used by public health and human services programs to foster child development and improve prenatal and postnatal health outcomes. The families that benefit from these visits are in communities with concentrations of premature births, low-birth-weight infants, infant mortality, poverty, crime and domestic violence, high rates of high school dropouts, substance abuse, and unemployment.

National Health Service Corps (NHSC): The Affordable Care Act provides $1.5 billion over five years to expand the NHSC. Of note, since the 1970s, the NHSC funds and places health professionals in Health Professional Shortage Areas to provide healthcare services to underserved populations. Currently 7,000 NHSC clinicians are providing healthcare services in underserved areas in exchange for loan repayment or scholarships, with approximately half of them in health centers. Approximately one-third of these clinicians are minorities.

Prevention and Public Health Funds, Community Transformation Grants: The Affordable Care Act authorizes Community Transformation Grants to state and local governmental agencies, tribes and territories, and national and community-based organizations for the implementation, evaluation, and dissemination of evidence-based community preventive health activities to reduce chronic disease rates, prevent development of secondary conditions, and address health disparities. This program is intended to build on the CDC's Communities Putting Prevention to Work program.

Promotoras, also known as peer leaders, community ambassadors, patient navigators, or health advocates: The Affordable Care Act authorizes promotion of these community health workers uniquely skilled in providing culturally and linguistically appropriate services, particularly in diverse, underserved areas. Community health workers can play a critical role in providing enrollment assistance to racial and ethnic minorities.

Source: U.S. Department of Health and Human Services. (2011). HHS action plan to reduce racial and ethnic health disparities. A nation free of disparities in health and health care. Retrieved from http://minorityhealth.hhs.gov/assets/pdf/hhs/HHS_Plan_complete.pdf

provisions that will affect health disparities. Two important initiatives mandated by the ACA are the National Quality Strategy, focused on priorities to improve the delivery of health care, and the National Prevention and Health Promotion Strategy, focused on prevention and wellness as a national policy issue (U.S. Department of Health and Human Services, National Partnership for Action, 2011, p. 10). The five goals of the HHS Disparities Action Plan are to:

1. Transform health care.
2. Strengthen the nation's health and human services infrastructure and workforce.
3. Advance the health, safety, and well-being of the American people.
4. Advance scientific knowledge and innovation.
5. Increase the efficiency, transparency, and accountability of HHS programs (U.S. Department of Health and Human Services, 2012).

A DIVERSE PATIENT POPULATION

There is no doubt that nurses are caring for patients who come from a variety of cultural backgrounds. It is also important for nurses to consider how their own cultural backgrounds affect the care they provide and their leadership. What is done with this information? How does it impact the healthcare delivery system? Why should a nurse leader/manager be concerned? Nurse managers need to understand the implications of staff members' personal cultural backgrounds and how this relates to patients' cultural backgrounds, the cultures in the local community, and the culture of the HCO. The American Organization of Nursing Executives' (AONE) competencies listed in Appendix A include diversity under the first category (communication and relationship building) and also discusses the relationship of nursing leadership and diversity principles.

Demographics

The total minority population in the United States increased by 1.9% from 2011 to 2012 and accounted for 116 million people, or 37% of the total U.S. population, in July 2012 (U.S. Census Bureau, 2012). Racial and minority populations are defined as Asian American, Black or African American, Hispanic or Latino, Native Hawaiian or Other Pacific Islander, and American Indian and Alaska Native. The U.S. Census Bureau publishes current data on its website and identifies the following projected diversity in the U.S. population:

- The non-Hispanic white population is projected to peak in 2024, at 199.6 million, up from 197.8 million in 2012. Unlike other race or ethnic groups, however, its population is projected to slowly decrease, falling by nearly 20.6 million from 2024 to 2060.
- The Hispanic population is projected to more than double, from 53.3 million in 2012 to 128.8 million in 2060. Consequently, by the end of the period, nearly one in three U.S. residents would be Hispanic, up from about one in six today.
- The African American population is expected to increase from 41.2 million to 61.8 million over the same period. Its share of the total population would then rise slightly, from 13.1% in 2012 to 14.7% in 2060.
- The Asian population is projected to more than double, from 15.9 million in 2012 to 34.4 million in 2060, with its share of the nation's total population climbing from 5.1% to 8.2% in the same period.
- Among the remaining race groups, American Indians and Alaska Natives are projected to increase by more than half from now to 2060, from 3.9 million to 6.3 million, with their share of the total population edging up from 1.2% to 1.5%. The Native Hawaiian and Other Pacific Islander population is expected to nearly double, from 706,000 to 1.4 million. The number of people who identify themselves as being of two or more races is projected to more than triple, from 7.5 million to 26.7 million over the same period (U.S. Census Bureau, 2012).

The United States is projected to become a majority-minority nation for the first time in 2043. While the non-Hispanic white population will remain the largest single group, no group will make up a majority. Minorities, now 37% of the U.S. population, are projected to comprise 57% of the population in 2060. The total minority population would more than double, from 116.2 million to 241.3 million over the period. These data are published on the Internet, but they are typically one to two years behind the current year.

How do these demographic facts and projections affect the healthcare delivery system? There are new demands to provide more culturally appropriate health care. This means more than language competency, which is highly problematic in many areas and for individual HCOs that must provide interpreters when needed. Where to find this resource and the cost factors are major problems. Also important are understanding of multiple cultures and religions and using this understanding to provide patient-centered care.

The last issue of differences in healthcare quality for minority Americans was addressed in a report, *Diverse Communities, Common Concerns: Assessing Healthcare Quality for Minority Americans* (Collins et al., 2002). This report identified "three factors in ensuring that minority populations receive optimal medical care: effective patient–physician communication, overcoming cultural and linguistic barriers, and access to affordable health insurance" (p. 6). These factors continue to be important. In many communities, minority groups are the primary groups that have been affected by lack of health insurance, underinsurance, and limited access to providers. Migrant health care is also a critical issue in many areas—and a complex one. There are some common barriers that limit care for this diverse population. For example, in some states some families, such as illegal aliens, are concerned about sharing information required for registration for health care. In addition, the process is complex. Language and culture also affect willingness to share information. Fear of government intervention(s) is a concern with some groups. Many states have been successful in addressing some of these critical barriers, and others have been less successful. Programs that assist multicultural populations need to consider these concerns as they can act as barriers to success.

Another aspect of a diverse healthcare system is staff education about other cultures. How should this be done to ensure that staff have the needed information and apply it? This content has been increased in nursing education. This, however, does not get to staff who have practiced for a time and yet still need updates. HCOs are providing staff education focused on diversity, and there are many educational resources offered online through government agencies such as the Health Resources and Services Administration (HRSA). The IOM describes three conceptual approaches to cross-cultural education: (1) focus on attitudes (cultural sensitivity/awareness approach), (2) knowledge (multicultural/categorical approach), and (3) skills (cross-cultural approach) (Institute of Medicine, 2002, p. 19).

Healthcare Disparities: Impact on Quality and Cost

The IOM report *Unequal Treatment* (2002) opened up an area of major concern for healthcare delivery by identifying problems with bias, prejudice, and stereotyping issues in the healthcare system. The report recommended that the United States needed to monitor the problem routinely. Healthcare disparities occur consistently, which is a difficult fact for healthcare professionals to accept.

Consideration of who is considered to be within a health-disparity population has policy and resource implications. The IOM defines healthcare disparity as a difference in treatment provided to members of different racial (or ethnic) groups that is not justified by the underlying health conditions or treatment preferences of patients (Institute of Medicine, 2002). These differences are often attributed to conscious or unconscious bias, provider bias, and institutional discriminatory policies toward patients of diverse socioeconomic status, race, ethnicity, and/or gender orientation (Finkelman & Kenner, 2012). The reasons for disparities are varied and can be a "function of the overall performance of the health system where one lives or of the quality of providers that care for many minorities" (Mead, Cartwright-Smith, Jones, Ramos, & Woods, 2008, p. 1).

As discussed in Chapters 17 and 18, the IOM in its healthcare quality series of reports recommended that it was time for the United States to annually monitor the quality of care and disparity. The HHS directed the Agency for Healthcare Research and Quality (AHRQ) to implement this recommendation. The annual National Healthcare Disparities Report (NHDR) provides extensive data on the status of healthcare disparities (Agency for Healthcare Research and Quality, 2013). It is typically two years behind the current date as it takes time to collect and

APPLYING EVIDENCE-BASED PRACTICE

Evidence for Effective Leadership and Management

CITATION: Chin, M., Walters, A., Cook, S., & Huang, E. (2007). Review of interventions to reduce racial and ethnic disparities in health care. *Medical Care Research and Review, 64*, October, 29S–100S.

OVERVIEW: This systematic review of more than 200 published articles addresses the question: What actually works for reducing racial and ethnic disparities in health care? The review focused on care for patients with cardiovascular disease, diabetes, depression, breast cancer, and disparities. The conclusions indicate that the following strategies are often part of successful interventions: multifaceted programs that include providers, patients, and the community; a focus on cultural relevancy or culturally tailored interventions to ensure that the patient's culture is included; and nurse-led programs.

APPLICATION: As has been discussed in this chapter and by the Institute of Medicine reports on diversity, there is a major problem with health disparities. Much more needs to be known about the impact of culture on care and what interventions can be more effective. What needs to be considered to redesign interventions so they include cultural issues? Cultural leverage is identified by

this study as very relevant to care delivery. This is "a focused strategy for improving the health of racial and ethnic communities by using their cultural practices, products, philosophies, or environments as vehicles that facilitate behavior change of patients and practitioners. Building upon prior strategies, cultural leverage proactively identifies the areas in which a cultural intervention can improve behaviors and then actively implements the solution" (Fisher, Burnet, Huang, Chin, & Cagney, 2007, p. 245S).

Source: Fisher, T., Burnet, D., Huang, E., Chin, M., & Cagney, K. (2007). Cultural leverage: Interventions using culture to narrow racial disparities in health care. *Medical Care Research and Review, 64* (5 Suppl.), 243S–282S.

Questions:

1. What is your opinion of "cultural leverage"?
2. What has been your experience with the impact of culture on patient care?
3. Why do you think nurse-led programs are considered successful strategies?

analyze the data. The NHDR is available online through the AHRQ. The IOM recommended the following goals for this report:

- Analyze racial and ethnic disparities, considering socioeconomic status.
- Conduct research to determine how to best measure socioeconomic status as it relates to healthcare access, service utilization, and quality.
- Recognize that access is a critical element of healthcare quality.
- Measure high and low utilization of certain healthcare services; include data state by state.
- Work with public and private organizations that provide data to increase standardization.
- Provide AHRQ with resources to compile an annual survey of disparity in health care (Institute of Medicine, 2002, p. 7).

This annual national report includes data about racial, ethnic, socioeconomic, and geographic disparities in health care. Quality of health care includes effectiveness of care for common clinical conditions and for care across the lifespan, patient safety, timeliness, patient centeredness, care coordination, efficiency, health system infrastructure, access to care, and priority population. Box 10-2 provides some highlights from the 2013 report. (The current report can be found on the AHRQ website.) HCOs can use the NHDR data to identify current national disparities problems and compare these with their own disparity issues. The NHDR is correlated with the National Healthcare Quality Report (NHQR) as recommended by the IOM. (See Chapters 17 and 18.)

HEALTHCARE LITERACY

Health literacy impacts patient-provider communication, both verbal and written communication. HCOs need to carefully review forms and information given to patients to ensure that the content is understandable and to check with patients and families to confirm that they understand the information. Vulnerable populations are more at risk for healthcare literacy problems; however,

---

BOX 10-2   **2013 NATIONAL HEALTHCARE DISPARITIES REPORT: HIGHLIGHTS**

Disparities in quality of care are common:

- African Americans and Hispanics received worse care than Whites for about 40% of quality measures.
- American Indians and Alaskan Natives received worse care than Whites for 33% of quality measures.
- Asians received worse care than Whites for about 25% of quality measures but better care than Whites for about 30% of quality measures.
- Poor people received worse care than high-income people for about 60% of quality measures.
- People with basic or complex activity limitations received worse care than people with neither type of activity limitation for about 33% of quality measures and better care for about 25% of quality measures.

Access to Care:

- African Americans had worse access to care than Whites for 33% of measures, and American Indians and Alaskan Natives had worse access to care than Whites for about 40% of access measures.
- Asians had worse access to care than Whites for 25% of access measures but better access to care than Whites for a similar proportion of access measures.
- Hispanics had worse access to care than Whites for about 60% of measures.
- Poor people had worse access to care than high-income people for all measures but one.
- People with basic or complex activity limitations had worse access to care than people with neither basic nor complex activity limitations for about 60% of measures.

Improvement:

- Most disparities in quality of care related to race, ethnicity, or income showed no significant change, getting neither smaller nor larger.
- The number of disparities that were getting smaller exceeded the number of disparities that were getting larger for African Americans, Hispanics, Asians, and poor people.
- Of the few disparities related to activity limitations that could be assessed, most were not changing.

Source: Agency for Healthcare Research and Quality. (2013). National Healthcare Disparities Report. Retrieved from http://www.ahrq.gov/research/findings/nhqrdr/nhdr13/2013nhdr.pdf

---

staff need to be alert to this potential problem with all patients. The major barriers to quality health care associated with health literacy are inability to access care, manage illness, and process information (DeWalt & Pignone, 2008).

1. *Accessing care:* Critical issues are obtaining health insurance, finding healthcare providers, and knowing when to seek health care. (For example, making an appointment, finding the number, and keeping a record of the appointment may all be difficult for someone who cannot read.)
2. *Illness management:* Managing illness today, both acute and chronic illness, can be complex with complicated prescription recommendations, testing schedules, and appointments with different providers. Patients need to know the right questions to ask as information is often not freely shared. Healthcare transitions are very common; patients move from provider to provider even within the same HCO, increasing the risk of errors but also requiring the patient adapt to changes and new providers.
3. *General information processing:* Patients are presented with informed consents and other documents, often written in a manner they cannot understand, especially under stressful situations. Family members often can be very helpful with this type of information. Medical bills can easily overwhelm even someone who reads English well, and for those who do not, this inability to read bills can lead to major problems and stress.

What impact does health literacy have on care? Recognizing the importance of culture to each patient and family is the first step. It has an impact on the patient understanding information about the illness and treatment and the discharge plan. It may have an impact on communication. Health literacy problems can make a difference on reaching expected outcomes. It is important to incorporate cultural competency into healthcare education and practice to decrease health disparities and improve care for all. Connected to all of this is the HCO. The organization has its own culture that then interacts with the diversity in its patients and also its workforce diversity.

CULTURE AND CLIMATE: BUILDING ORGANIZATIONAL CULTURAL COMPETENCY

What is it that makes an organization feel like a comfortable place to work or receive services? How is an HCO described? How do individual staff members affect an HCO's culture? Understanding this part of an organization is not easy. It is even harder to change an HCO's culture. For an organization to build its cultural competency, it must first understand what **organizational culture** is then assess its present culture. Is it a **consonant** (functional or effective) culture or a **dissonant** (dysfunctional or ineffective) culture? The goal is to be an effective culture. As this process occurs, there are legal issues that also need to be considered related to the organization's culture. Staff have a key role in the HCO's culture. This section of the chapter discusses these critical issues. It is not simple to address diversity issues in an HCO when the organization as a whole and all its component parts need to be considered: staff, patients, and families. The community in which the organization exists is also an important factor that impacts organizational culture.

Definition of Organizational Culture and Climate

A HISTORICAL REVIEW   In the late 1920s and early 1930s, a study conducted at an electric company focused on employee performance, productivity, and motivation (Shuttleworth, 2009). Why would this study be important to the topic of organizational culture today? The results of this study identified a phenomenon, which became known as the Hawthorne Effect. During the study, environmental factors such as light and noise were altered, and productivity was monitored. Changes in the environment affected productivity. The study also noted that when employees participated in decisions, their job satisfaction increased. In the long term, these particular experiments have been questioned; however, they did begin the process of increased interest in productivity, work environment, and job satisfaction factors, which are related to an organization's culture.

Healthcare organizational culture is more complex than cultures found in other businesses as it also includes a particular professional culture: healthcare professionals. The Institute of Medicine also describes the healthcare delivery system as dysfunctional (Institute of Medicine, 2001).

MAJOR THEORETICAL VIEW OF ORGANIZATIONAL CULTURE: SCHEIN   Schein defined the culture of a group as "a pattern of shared basic assumptions that was learned by a group as it solved its problems of external adaptation and internal integration, that has worked well enough to be considered valid and, therefore, to be taught to new members as the correct way to perceive, think, and feel in relation to those problems" (2010, p. 17). The organization's culture is passed on to new members through the process of socialization. This theory identifies three levels of organizational culture (Schein, 2010). The *artifacts* are the visible structures and processes. The *espoused beliefs and values* are found in the vision, mission, goals, and strategic plans. The *underlying assumptions* are the taken-for-granted beliefs and perceptions. Shein also emphasizes the critical need to align the subcultures in an organization so as to be effective. These subcultures are the following: *operators* (based on human interaction, high levels of communication, trust, and teamwork), *engineers* (elegant solution, abstract solutions to problems, automation, and systems), and *executives* (financial focus, lone hero, sense of rightness and omniscience). Operators would primarily be staff who provide care; engineers would be management level; and the executives are the high-level leaders in an HCO. This description neglects an important subculture (patients and families) and an external subculture (the community). The theory was not specifically developed for HCOs but applies on most levels to understanding organizational culture. Organizations need to ensure a shared understanding and consensus on vision, mission, values, goals and strategies, and measurement and correction (improvement or repair strategies). In addition, organizations need to:

- create a common language.
- define group boundaries and criteria for inclusion and exclusion.

- distribute power authority and status.
- develop norms of trust, intimacy, friendship, and love.
- define awards and punishments.
- explain the unexplainable.

Consonant and Dissonant Organizational Cultures

If an organization ignores its culture, this can lead to major problems for the organization. To prevent this, leaders within the organization must recognize the importance of culture and shared values to the organization and work toward developing a consonant or an effective organizational culture. New people come into the organization and learn about the culture by making a connection between behaviors and their consequences. An adaptive organizational culture is able to meet the challenge of change to become more effective and meet their outcomes. Rigid organizational cultures are not able to do this and become a dissonant or ineffective organizational culture.

Shared values have a major effect on organizations and provide direction for organizations, which can be demonstrated in staff loyalty and commitment to the organization. Organization values influence when decisions and judgments are made. Do values always mesh? No, they do not, and when they do not, problems often arise. As noted by Schein, integration is critical. There is no doubt that there are major problems with burnout and turnover in healthcare delivery systems today. As these HCOs struggle to understand these issues and resolve them, gaining a better understanding of the status of the organizational culture—whether it is dissonant or consonant—may help. It is initially important to identify what is a dysfunctional or dissonant culture. Dysfunctional organizations do not meet the requirements described by Schein.

An Effective, Creative, and Productive Workplace

The HCO's culture identifies the acceptable attitudes and values within the organization. The formal framework includes the organization's structure, chain of command, rules and regulations, and so on. The informal framework includes use of open-door policies, accessibility of management, dress codes, special events and rituals, standard manners of speech and behavior, and so on. Both frameworks are important and interrelated.

Some HCOs are more driven by financial issues, and in other organizations, staff interpret that this is the case when it may not actually be true. Both perspectives affect the organization's culture. Why is this the case? Many healthcare professionals feel a real conflict in their work environment. They want to advocate for the patient, yet they feel extreme stress at work, which makes it difficult to provide the required care. While blaming administration for real and unreal problems, perceptions can become part of an organization's culture, making it an ineffective culture. Organizational caring has been studied within the hospital organizational culture. Content regarding organizational theories and models found in Chapter 1 indicates that structure impacts how leaders lead in an organization, staff roles, and the organization's function—in short, how the organization works. Developing an environment of caring must come from leadership so it is part of the entire organizational environment. As noted earlier, transformational leadership supports an environment that is more personal and caring and engages staff in the organization and its functioning. There is greater management/staff trust, and trust is important for effective work, decision making, and responses to change.

HCOs need to develop strategies to stay ahead of the need to change their orientation and culture—to project and plan ahead. In today's healthcare environment, most HCOs recognize the need to be more flexible and to respond more to both external and internal factors, not just one. These organizations then need to change their staff orientation to accomplish this effectively. Typically organizations focus on financial projections and monitoring, but there are other factors of importance such as changing patient population, changes in treatments and drugs, staffing issues, staff education, healthcare professional issues related to regulation, health policies, and other factors. Many HCOs have incorporated a shared governance model to improve organizational culture, as discussed in Chapter 4. An organization's culture can be changed, but it takes leadership and a planned effort to accomplish this change. The first step should be to assess the culture.

Assessment of Organizational Culture

HCOs need to assess their culture, and Schein's descriptors can be used to formulate an assessment. Earlier information about leadership and management styles (Chapter 1) is also relevant to understanding and assessing organizational culture. The subject of organizational culture assessment is now an important activity for many organizations. Formal assessment surveys are available on the Internet and through publications.

A place to begin the assessment is to consider the many factors within the HCO that have an impact on the organizational culture. These factors include the following:

- Vision, values, and goals
- Structure and process
- Communication, both formal and informal (e.g., use of memos, email and other digital communication methods, effect of gossip, accessibility of information, secrecy, how soon staff know about changes, how effective it is, information overload, grapevine, and so on)
- Acceptance of new members/staff
- Willingness to allow new members to offer suggestions or new ideas
- Management's willingness to include staff in decision making and change process
- Management and staff morale
- Staff turnover rate
- Staff vacancy rate
- Feedback (staff, patients, families) and how it is used
- Reputation in the community
- Financial status and changes including competition and reimbursement—impact on culture

The organization's vision, mission, values, goals, and strategic plans reveal important information about the organization and how the organization views itself and its staff; however, these documents may be just more paper to put into binders. The key is to decide if what is written in these documents is actually demonstrated in behavior and communication. Organizations with a consonant culture emphasize the sum of their parts rather than their many separate parts. An organization that is tied up in focusing on its parts and has problems with viewing itself as a whole may have a dissonant culture. It will feel out of sync. From a systems perspective, the organization will not be as effective as it could be. Some aspects of an organization are helpful in describing and understanding the organizational culture such as artifacts (e.g., written policies and procedures, position descriptions) mentioned in the Schein theory. Patterns of behavior can be used to identify traditions, written and verbal comments, and staff behaviors. The values and beliefs are a critical part of the culture, often described in stories staff share about the organization. Managers, team leaders, and preceptors need to be directly involved in clarifying expectations about organization values to the staff and to the students, but to do this effectively, they need to understand the culture.

CASE STUDY

What Is It With This Place?

Tom has been working in the local acute care hospital for about 10 years. The hospital has grown from a 150-bed facility to a 200-bed facility in that time, but recently there have been comments made about cutting some beds due to a lower census. He works on a cardiac unit as one of the team leaders. Sue graduated from nursing school two years ago and has recently joined the staff. This is her second position since graduation. After working on the unit for three months, Sue comes to Tom and says, "What is it with this place?" He is confused and asks what she means. Her response is spoken with much emotion, "People here don't seem to care about one another. I don't trust anyone I work with. Do you?" He responded, "Sure I do. Seems like a comfortable place to me. Just go with the flow, and you will be fine." Sue ponders this but still struggles. Another new nurse begins to work on the unit. This nurse has five years of experience and recently moved from out of state. A few weeks after her arrival, she and Sue have lunch together. The new nurse tells Sue that she is discouraged. She has always liked working and now dreads coming in. "I just don't feel that staff is connected here. No one really talks to one another. I don't even think that staff members have any pride in their work." Sue connects with these comments and discusses how she has felt. It is great to have someone who understands, but she wishes that staff who have been working on the unit longer would be more helpful and connect to these concerns.

Questions:

1. Why do you think Tom responded in the way he did?
2. How would you describe the culture of this organization?
3. Do you think the culture described applies to the specific unit or the entire organization? What would you base your answer on?
4. Is this a consonant or dissonant culture, and what is your rationale?
5. What possible effects can an organization's culture have on patient care delivery?
6. If you were either of the new nurses, what would you do?

WORKFORCE DIVERSITY

The people within an organization—its staff, patients, and families who receive the healthcare services—affect an organization's culture and how the staff responds to the diverse patient population that exists today. The Sullivan Commission report (Sullivan, 2004) examined the problem of disparity in the healthcare workforce as a major contributor to the healthcare delivery disparity problem. The report recommends an increase in minority representation in healthcare professions, expanding **workforce diversity** (e.g., minority, gender, age, degrees). The critical federal regulations and state labor laws that affect workforce diversity are Title VII of the Civil Rights Act of 1964 and Executive Order 11246, which prohibits employer discrimination on the basis of race, color, religion, sex, or national origin, and the Americans With Disabilities Act of 1990. (Other relevant laws are discussed in Chapters 2 and 8.) Since most HCOs receive reimbursement from Medicare, which is a federal payment system, and Medicaid, which is a joint federal and state reimbursement system, most HCOs must meet the requirements of these federal laws and regulations. This means that staff must be prepared with education and training for work in a culturally diverse environment. There is an ongoing problem with diversity within the profession of nursing. Efforts have been made to improve this, and although there has been improvement, the problem is not yet resolved. In 2013 the National Council of State Boards of Nursing (NCSBN) and the Forum of State Nursing Workforce Centers reported that only 19% of all U.S. registered nurses were members of an ethnic or racial minority (American Association of Colleges of Nursing, 2014). Enrollment and graduation data provide a picture of the future workforce, indicating there are still limitations in minority representation: BSN and higher degree programs with minorities representing 28.3% of BSN students, 29.3% of students in master's-level programs, and 27.7% of students in PhD programs (American Association of Colleges of Nursing, 2014). To accomplish more diversity in the nursing profession, we not only need more student representation from the minority populations but also more faculty and HCO nurse leaders and managers. Carthon's study shows "pipeline" programs to increase student diversity are improving the situation for some minorities; however, this is not only an issue of applications and enrollment but also of graduation (Robert Wood Johnson Foundation, 2014). For example, in schools with special programs to increase enrollment, African American student graduation rates dropped at schools with special emphasis/programs on increasing minority representation as compared to those schools without such emphasis/program.

The nursing profession is less diverse than the general population, and this is noted as a concern in *The Future of Nursing: Leading Change, Advancing Health* report. This report emphasizes that because nurses are the largest proportion of the healthcare workforce in every type of healthcare setting, changing the demographic composition of nurses will have a major impact on the level of diversity in the healthcare workforce (Institute of Medicine, 2011).

Cultural barriers for staff and patients within HCOs must be assessed and resolved. Language barriers are particularly important as noted by the IOM and its comments about health literacy (2004). This, of course, includes availability of interpreters when they are needed to assist staff. Family members are not the best choice for interpreters; they are too personally involved, and their culture may affect how and what they translate. Patients from different cultures need time to understand what is said and what it means, and they will also process the communication through their own cultural filters. Cultural filters are the way that individuals perceive the world and their experiences. These filters are created and adopted by members of a culture. For example, how a person communicates, verbally, nonverbally, and behaviorally, goes through this filter. If staff members are not sensitive and aware of culture and do not have knowledge of other cultures, they may misinterpret words and behaviors. This filter also affects how people define health and illness, whether or not they seek care, from whom they seek care, and their attitudes about the quality of their lives.

Organizational culture also includes how staff respond to persons with disabilities as employees. Laws dictate some of this response. The Americans With Disabilities Act of 1990 (ADA), which became effective in 1992, has had a major impact on healthcare workforce issues (Westrick, 2014). This law makes it illegal for employers to discriminate against persons with disabilities in employment and provides for enforcement of equal access to jobs and accommodations. Employers of 15 or more are affected by this law, which certainly includes most HCOs as they typically have more employees. Chapters 2 and 8 include additional information on this law, but it is relevant to this chapter on diversity.

The Staff and Its Culture

Healthcare staff affect an organization's culture and vice versa. The staff brings its own personal culture into the organization; in addition, the staff represent several generations, which has a major impact on the organizational culture. Staff members and their personal cultures represent a critical component of building cultural competency in an organization. Many HCOs now have required staff education about culture. Despite these efforts, there continue to be healthcare disparities.

Management and a Culturally Diverse Staff

Managers need to understand the impact of cultures on the HCO, the daily work, the staff, and know how to use cross-cultural management. This requires an open mind and understanding. Acceptance of others who may be different is critical, as is encouragement of staff members to share their feelings and reactions appropriately. Staff members need to be appreciated for their individual strengths and differences. The focus is on differences, not on right and wrong.

Some HCOs have hired more nurses from other countries who have come to work in the United States during times of nursing shortages, and there is also a more diverse physician pool today. The common reasons for this migration are differences in income, job satisfaction, organizational environment, governance, protection and risk, and social security and benefits (International Centre for Nurse Migration, 2014). The International Centre for Nurse Migration, collaborating with the CGFNS International (formally the Commission on Graduates of Foreign Nursing Schools) and the International Council of Nurses, provides resources about nurse migration on its website. Its role is to establish dynamic, effective global and national migration policies and practices that facilitate safe patient care and positive practice environments for nurse migrants (International Centre for Nurse Migration, 2014).

Diversity, however, is not just found in staff who migrate from other countries for short periods of employment. There are many staff members from other cultural backgrounds who have lived in the United States for some time or were born in the United States though they are members of minority cultures. The multicultural work environment means that nurse managers must consider its impact on productivity, recruitment, and retention. This requires an awareness of cross-cultural issues. Staff members may respond to other staff and patients from cultures different from their own in ways that may be ineffective. This must be addressed to build cultural competency.

A Historical and Current View of Generational Issues and Their Effects on Organizational Culture

Some authors have discussed the importance of understanding the generation that staff members represent and how this influences their different responses to the work environment (Gerke, 2001; Wieck, Prydun, & Walsh, 2002; Zemke, Raines, & Filipczak, 2000). "Managing diversity here is defined as creating and maintaining an environment in which each person is respected because of his or her differences" (Davis, 2001, p. 161). Nursing now has the unique experience of including four generations working in the same place (Gerke, 2001). This situation can lead to a rich diversity of viewpoints and practice; however, it can also lead to conflict and problems within the organizational culture. Key questions to consider include: What are the four generations? What are their characteristics? What can be done to gain the most for this matrix of generations? The focus of this discussion will be on the last two generations; however, to appreciate these two generations, it is necessary to briefly describe the first two generations. Box 10-3 highlights the four key generations in nursing.

BOX 10-3	THE FOUR KEY GENERATIONS IN NURSING

1. Traditional Generation	Born 1930–1940
2. Baby Boomers	Born 1941–1964
3. Generation X	Born 1965–1980
4. Generation Y	Born 1981–2000

The traditional, silent, or mature generation, born from 1930 to 1940. This generation is less apparent due to its age, but it had a major impact on nursing. Many from this generation were nurses in World War II. They can be characterized as hard working, loyal, duty bound, and family focused. They accepted hierarchy as an important characteristic of the organizations in which they worked.

Baby boomers, born from 1941 to 1964. This generation fills most of the nursing positions, both in practice and nursing education. Typically this group had a choice of only two careers, nursing or teaching (Bertholf & Loveless, 2001). This group is beginning to retire, leading to a greater nursing shortage in both practice and education. This generation works independently, accepts authority, causes few problems, feels that loyalty is an important work value, is less able to cope with new technology, and has been described as workaholic. Gerke (2001) describes this group as preferring consensus leadership, competitive, and more focused on material gain. It is important to recognize that there is variation within the generational group (for example, many in this generation have been the leaders and pushed for greater use of technology in health care). This can be supported by the increased use of computer technology in nursing education and in practice documentation. This would have never happened if some members of the generation had not pushed for it.

Generation X (born from 1965 to 1980) and Generation Y (born from 1981 to 2000). Why is it important to understand the differences in the last two generations of staff? At this time, they are the major age groups that are increasing in nursing and will assume the leadership of the profession as the baby boomers retire. It is believed that characteristics of the age groups affect how they work, why they work, and leadership that is required within HCOs (American Hospital Association, 2002). Generation X is different from the baby boomer generation (Santos & Cox, 2002) and are described as the "original 'latch key kids' who have grown up mastering information technology and creative thinking" (Bertholf & Loveless, 2001, p. 169). They have grown up during a time of extreme change. Generation X nurses want to be led, not managed. They need to develop self-confidence and empowerment. They want effective, intelligent leaders who mentor staff, and they want to be trusted and respected by their leaders. Nurturing is a key leadership characteristic that is important to Generation X, and it forms the base for their other important characteristics: motivated, receptive, positive, good communicator, team player, good people skills, approachable, and supportive (Wieck et al., 2002). This generation is not made up of joiners, and this is a problem for professional organizations. They do not value job longevity, which has an impact on loyalty to employers. They also feel strongly about maintaining a balance between work and personal life.

The core values of Generation X staff are diversity, thinking globally, balance, technoliteracy, fun, informality, self-reliance, and pragmatism. The job assets of this generation are adaptable, technoliterate, independent, intimidated by authority, and creative. How might their values affect their assets? Generation X staff is motivated by organizational messages such as:

- "Do it your way."
- "We've got the newest hardware and software."
- "There aren't a lot of rules here."
- "We're not very corporate."

Generation Xers are pessimistic and rightfully so given the world they grew up in. They are loyal to themselves and the people with whom they have familial-like relationships. They like to feel that they are part of something bigger. They expect and respond well to things that contribute to their own professional knowledge and competency. Xers are flexible and very comfortable with change. . . . They are technoliterate. . . ." Because Generation X often views a job as a stepping stone to the next job, benefits and rewards geared to the present rather than the future are the most valuable in recruitment and retention." (Ulrich, 2001, p. 152)

This description of Generation X explains some of the conflict or tension that can be seen between these nurses and baby boomer nurses, who are just ahead of them. Baby boomer nurses are more willing, although not happy about it, to work overtime and are often shocked when younger nurses say they are leaving. This is driven by the fact that more baby boomer nurses have a long-term commitment to employers (Santos & Cox, 2002). These are not characteristics found in the generation that is replacing the baby boomers.

Generation Y (**Nexters**; Millennials, Generation Next, MyPod generation, GenY, and other titles) (Ruby, 2007), the newest generation entering nursing, demonstrates the core values of optimism, civic duty, confidence, achievement, social ability, morality, street smarts, and diversity. Their important on-the-job assets are collective action, optimism, tenacity, heroic spirit, multitasking capabilities, and technology savvy. They are interested in technology and feel competent around it. Compared to Generation X, they have more trust in centralized authority (Gerke, 2001). Change is part of their lives, and thus they tolerate it better. Related to this, they are seen as being greater risk-takers and want to be challenged and excited about their work.

The first step is to recognize the importance of distinguishing between generations, and the second is to develop strategies that improve collaboration and culture. It is clear that these generational groups need to communicate with one another to increase understanding of where each group is coming from and recognize the values that are important to each group. Some strategies that have been recommended to accomplish this include the following:

- Develop coaching behaviors in preceptors/educators to enable learning by doing and supporting the newer employee in asking "why" questions.
- Design care delivery models to support collaborative practice.
- Use participatory management strategies to develop relationships.
- Recognize and accept that all employment is temporary.
- Lighten up.
- Be specific.
- Realize that you have more commonalities than differences.
- Assess the organization for its ability for inclusion.
- Discuss openly how you see your team working with new members (Bertholf & Loveless, 2001, pp. 170–171).

STRATEGIES FACILITATING CULTURAL DIVERSITY IN HEALTHCARE ORGANIZATIONS

As organizations assess their cultures and realize that changes are needed, they will find that increasing participation from all levels of the HCO will go a long way in improving the organization and increasing trust among staff and between staff and the organization. Lack of trust can be a major barrier to improving the HCO's culture, as was noted earlier in this chapter. How do organizations get a better match between employee values and those of the organization? The HCO's values should be communicated regularly to staff and patients, but more important, the values should be demonstrated in actions. When new staff are hired, HCO values should be discussed in the hiring process and included in staff orientation. Position descriptions, policies, and procedures should reflect the values, as should all organizational planning and the HCO's quality improvement plan and its implementation.

If an HCO concludes after an extensive assessment of its culture that improvement is needed, what should the organization do? Leaders who want to change an organization's culture need to develop and implement strategies to improve the organization's culture. Engagement of all staff is critical.

A key aspect of the HCO's culture is how staff and managers view diversity and their level of cultural competency. The basic components of cultural competency in nursing care are a set of behaviors, attitudes, and skills that enables nurses to work effectively in cross-cultural situations (U.S. Department of Health and Human Services, Office of Minority Health, 2014). In 2008 the AACN published a toolkit for nurse educations to assist in the development of cultural competency. The material identifies five competencies:

1. Apply knowledge of social and cultural factors that affect nursing and healthcare across multiple contexts.
2. Use relevant data sources and best evidence in providing culturally competent care.

3. Promote achievement of safe and quality outcomes of care for diverse populations.
4. Advocate for social justice, including commitment to the health of vulnerable populations and the elimination of health disparities.
5. Participate in continuous cultural competence development (2008b, p. 2).

Cultural competence is demonstrated in the following examples:

- Awareness of personal culture, values, beliefs, and behaviors
- Knowledge of and respect for different cultures
- Skills in interacting and responding to individuals from other cultures
- Acknowledgment about importance of culture and incorporation at all levels
- Assessment of cross-cultural relations
- Vigilance toward the dynamics that result from cultural differences
- Expansion of cultural knowledge
- Adaptation of services to meet culturally unique needs (American Association of Colleges of Nursing, 2008b, p. 13)

These are helpful guidelines for developing staff/manager competencies. Do they have these competencies? If not, training and education need to be addressed to increase the level of cultural competency. Culture is a sensitive subject, so it is important that education programs consider the best learning methods and relevancy of content to the staff and the HCO. It is important to avoid a paternalistic approach, stereotyping, and biases when this content is presented.

The Institute of Medicine report *Crossing the Quality Chasm* (2001) addresses some key issues related to organizational culture in healthcare delivery systems. The process of developing this report included the participation from experts in medicine, nursing, safety, pharmacy, and health administration, which resulted in a broad base of viewpoints and the following recommendations:

- **Care based on *continuous healing relationships*:** Patients need a healthcare system that is responsive to their needs when they require care. The type of services or entry into services should consider all possible methods, including innovative ones when necessary, such as Internet, telephone, and so on.
- ***Customization* based on patient needs and values:** Healthcare delivery must consider the needs that are frequently found in the population; however, it must be flexible enough to address those unexpected needs and consider individual patient choices and preferences.
- **The *patient as the source of control*:** To be in control, patients need information, and healthcare providers need to be able to accommodate differences.
- ***Shared knowledge* and the free flow of information:** Patients need access to their health information in an easily accessible manner. The focus should be on sharing information.
- ***Evidence-based* decision making:** The best possible scientific information needs to be used in providing care.
- ***Safety* as a system property:** All healthcare provider settings and providers need to offer a safe environment in which to receive safe and appropriate care.
- **The need for *transparency*:** Information needs to be shared with patients, which includes information about the provider's performance on safety, evidence-based practice, and patient satisfaction.
- ***Anticipation* of needs:** Healthcare providers need to be proactive with regard to patient needs.
- ***Continuous* decrease in waste:** Resources should not be wasted, and this includes patients' time.
- ***Cooperation* among clinicians:** Individual providers and provider organizations need to collaborate to ensure appropriate, timely care and exchange of information (Institute of Medicine, 2001).

Each one of these descriptors is directly related to nursing care.

The most effective organizational cultures will be those that have a credible culture. These cultures build and maintain trust and feature leaders who are role models and set the culture's tone. Communication is recognized as important and is viewed as being effective. Staff and management are clear about expectations.

Cultural Perceptions of Health and Illness: Need for a Caring, Healing Environment

As HCOs and their cultures are considered, it is important to recognize that healthcare delivery organizations are more than just organizations in which people work. This is one part of the culture but not the only part. Whether or not the organizational culture supports an environment in which patients can be cared for by providing a healing environment is another critical issue. This section discusses factors related to a caring, healing environment.

WHAT IS A HEALING ENVIRONMENT?   Defining healing environments is not easy. There are a variety of components that are associated with healing environments such as privacy, air quality, noise levels, views, and visual characteristics. As needs among people vary, there is no doubt that the perfect environment for healing cannot be developed, but there has been recognition that efforts should be taken to develop healing environments. "Throughout history healthcare providers, architects, and psychologists have noted a strong link between the environment and human behavior" (McCullough & Wille, 2001, p. 111). Florence Nightingale commented on the need for healing environments that she associated with fresh air, warmth, cleanliness, quiet, diet, and light (McCullough & Wille, 2001). Historically physicians and nurses were the center of health care, but today there is emphasis on patient- and family-centered care as has been discussed in this chapter and in Chapter 9. This approach has been recognized by the IOM and has become part of the healthcare delivery system, and as noted earlier, even part of the ACA. Changing to this approach is not easy, and it is not yet a reality for the healthcare delivery system. Some have been more successful than others. An important component to patient-centered care is the need for healing environments.

If one reflects on personal experiences in acute care facilities as well as other types of healthcare settings, the environment often is not all that conducive to healing—noise interferes with rest and relaxation, lack of cleanliness, difficulty finding one's way around, the lack of warmth as far as color and furnishings, confusion over staff identities, and unresponsive staff. Some organizations, of course, have made successful efforts to improve their environments. One model that focuses on healing environments is the Planetree Model. This is a patient-centered, holistic approach to health care, promoting mental, emotional, spiritual, social, and physical healing. Patient and family empowerment is important and related to the exchange of information and encourages healing partnerships with caregivers. Positive healthcare outcomes are important and should be supported by appropriate treatment (Planetree, 2014). In this type of environment, the focus of care is on the whole patient—body, mind, and spirit—with active consumer involvement—the patient is at the center. The following beliefs are part of the Planetree Model:

- We are human beings, caring for other human beings.
- We are all caregivers.
- Care giving is best achieved through kindness and compassion.
- Safe, accessible, high quality care is fundamental to patient-centered care.
- Use a holistic approach to meet people's needs of body, mind, and spirit.
- Families, friends, and loved ones are vital to the healing process.
- Access to understandable health information can empower individuals to participate in their healthcare.
- The opportunity for individuals to make personal choices related to their care is essential.
- Physical environments can enhance healing, health, and well-being.
- Illness can be a transformational experience for patients, families, and caregivers (Planetree, 2014).

The Planetree Model and organization were developed prior to the IOM reports. The concept emphasizes the need for a patient-centered approach to care. This initiative recognized a need and responded to it. Due to the IOM reports, there now is greater movement to embrace and operationalize patient-centered care. Some hospitals have applied the Planetree Model to make necessary changes to improve their healing environments. The key strategies that support the Planetree Model are integral to quality nursing care. They are also highly supportive of a positive culture that not only moves the patient into an important role but also provides a more positive work culture.

THE PHYSICAL ENVIRONMENT AS PART OF A HEALING ENVIRONMENT   The Planetree Model considers not only behavior and attitudes but also the physical environment: Is it conducive to healing? Making HCOs more appealing spaces is also important to developing healing environments. In the past 15 to 20 years, more efforts have been made by hospitals to make their environments more comfortable and soothing (Leighty, 2003). The Center for Health Design identified consumer environmental rights in healthcare facilities. Environments should do the following:

- Be easy to navigate.
- Offer restricted access to nature through views, gardens, landscaped patios, terraces, courtyards, atria, and natural elements.
- Have an easy-to-control personal environment including lighting, noise and sound reduction, odor elimination, thermal comfort, and privacy.
- Offer the capability to select positive distractions including television, games, videotapes, computers, art, telephone, music, social opportunities, access to nature, and reading material.
- Have activities in spaces conducive to their purpose.
- Make it easy for staff to bring food, medicine, and other supplies related to the care.
- Have access to furniture and equipment that is comfortable and user-friendly.
- Allow maximum opportunities for regular lifestyle activities.
- Have access to a continuous sequence of environments that support one's dignity and the dignity of others.
- Be clean, neat, and orderly.
- Be free from hazards.
- Provide for personal safety and security for personal possessions. Inspire trust and confidence.
- Symbolize values appropriate to patients and others.
- Provide for local cultural backgrounds and diversity in the community.
- Be appropriate for the various ages, genders, and physical and cognitive abilities of the people who use it.
- Support interaction with others including care-partners.
- Decrease unnecessary stress for all patients or residents, visitors, and staff.
- Be aesthetically appealing (Center for Health Design, 2014).

This effort can also be seen in other types of healthcare settings too (for example, clinics, physician offices, and long-term care facilities).

Some evidence exists that these strategies actually have an important impact on patient outcomes and staff. The study described in this chapter's *Applying Evidence-Based Practice* feature emphasizes unit design factors and their impact on patient outcomes. A nurse-friendly environment is one in which the work environment is conducive to safe practice. Examples of these strategies are reducing travel time between work areas, better lighting, and providing space for staff to take breaks. These efforts decrease staff stress, fatigue, and physical burden, thus improving efficiency and nurses' attitudes, which may affect retention and recruitment. When nurses are asked to participate in renovation planning or in new expansions, the environment typically is a more nurse-friendly environment; nurses who are patient centered understand what is meant by a healing environment. The staff members are the ones who really know what they need to get their work done. Leighty (2003) noted that increased use of private patient rooms (a) decreases requests for transfers, which decreases costs and increases patient satisfaction; (b) increases patient sleep and rest, which affects outcomes and patient satisfaction; (c) along with location of sinks and airflow, decreases nosocomial infections, which affects costs due to complications and outcomes; and (d) can even affect market share because patients want to come to hospitals where they get private rooms. More research needs to be done about environmental factors and how they affect organizational culture. Most would agree that it is much easier to work in a pleasant, attractive environment and that these factors make it easier for patients and families during times of stress. However, more information is needed on the effect of these strategies and how they can be improved.

APPLYING LEADERSHIP AND MANAGEMENT

My Hospital Unit: An Evolving Case Experience

The goal is to have an effective, creative, and productive workplace. What does this goal mean to you? Make a list of the critical factors that you think your unit and the hospital would have to demonstrate to meet this goal. You might share your unit list in small teams in your class and find out if your views are similar or different from your classmates' in their own units. Discuss why there may be differences. What have you listed as factors that describe a hospital's culture? Some of the factors that might be found on your list (although there are many more and your list does not have to agree) include the following:

- Clear vision, mission, goals, and objectives.
- Vision/mission/goals/objectives that can be demonstrated in your unit's and in the hospital's actions.

- Staff trust management and vice versa.
- Clear communication with staff input into decisions.
- Staff care for one another.
- Management cares about staff as individuals.
- Safe work environment is supported.
- Staff loyalty.
- Staff empowerment.
- Positive reputation in the community.
- Visible, accessible management.
- Demonstration of organization partnership and collaboration.

Describe three strategies you might use in your unit to improve the culture. Remember to consider past decisions you have made about your unit and plans you completed in earlier chapters for your unit.

BSN and *Master's Essentials:* Application to Content

BSN Essentials (American Association of Colleges of Nursing, 2008a) as Applied to this Chapter:

  I. Liberal Education for Baccalaureate Generalist Nursing Practice
VIII. Professionalism and Professional Values

Master's Essentials (American Association of Colleges of Nursing, 2011) as Applied to this Chapter:

  I. Background for Practice from Sciences and Humanities
 VI. Health Policy and Advocacy

Applying AONE Competencies

Identify which of the AONE competencies found in Appendix A apply to the content of this chapter.

Engaging in the Content: Critical Thinking and Clinical Reasoning and Judgment

Discussion Questions

1. How did the Institute of Medicine influence disparities in health care?
2. What are some of the critical issues related to healthcare diversity and disparities?
3. What are the generations that are in practice today, and how do their characteristics impact the work environment and patient care? (Online Application Option)
4. What does "organizational culture" mean?
5. What is the management role in improving the organizational culture? (Online Application Option)
6. How is the healthcare workforce influenced by diversity? (Online Application Option)

Application Exercises

1. Consonant and dissonant cultures can be found in many organizations. It is important to understand the differences between a consonant and a dissonant organization culture to improve an organization's culture. Select an organization (a hospital unit, home care agency, school, or other clinical site that you have worked in as a student or staff or you might choose your school, other schools attended, an organization you belong to, and so on). Determine if the culture of that

organization is consonant or dissonant, and provide your rationale. When you are doing your assessment, use the characteristics of a dysfunctional or dissonant organization culture. You will also want to consider how members of the organization share values, group behavior norms, and communication methods with new members. Is the organization adaptive, and in what ways? Is it rigid and what effect does this have on its members (staff)? What is your feeling about the organization? We all get these feelings when we have been in an organization. How comfortable does it feel to be in the organization? What influences your reaction? (Online Application Option)

2. Interview or ask a member of the human resources department in a local hospital to discuss how diversity in the workforce affects what the human resources department does and its processes. Share your work in teams. (Online Application Option)

3. Why is diversity considered part of the patient-centered competency? Describe examples of this connection. (Online Application Option)

4. Review the current National Healthcare Disparities Report on the Agency for Healthcare Research and Quality website. What are the current concerns and status of healthcare disparities? This can be done in teams, with teams reporting on different sections of the current report. Discuss implications for nursing care and nurses.

5. Review the AONE diversity principles. How do you think these could be applied in a healthcare organization? Review the AONE website.

References

Agency for Healthcare Research and Quality. (2013). 2013 national healthcare disparities report. Retrieved from http://nhqrnet.ahrq.gov/inhqrdr/reports/nhdr

American Association of Colleges of Nursing. (2008a). *The essentials of baccalaureate nursing education for professional nursing practice.* Washington, DC: Author.

American Association of Colleges of Nursing. (2008b). Excerpt from *Tool Kit Of Resources For Cultural Competent Education For Baccalaureate Nurses* by American Association of Colleges of Nursing. Published by American Association of Colleges of Nursing. Washington, DC: Author.

American Association of Colleges of Nursing. (2011). *The essentials of master's education in nursing.* Washington, DC: Author.

American Association of Colleges of Nursing. (2014). Enhancing diversity in the workplace. Retrieved from http://www.aacn.nche.edu/media-relations/fact-sheets/enhancing-diversity

American Hospital Association. (2002). *In our hands. How hospital leaders can build a thriving workplace.* Chicago, IL: Author.

Bertholf, L., & Loveless, S. (2001). Baby boomers and Generation X: Strategies to bridge the gap. *Seminars for Nurse Managers, 9*(3), 169–172.

Center for Health Design. (2014). Healthcare design. Retrieved from https://www.healthdesign.org/

Centers for Disease Control and Prevention. (2014). Definitions. Retrieved from http://www.cdc.gov/socialdeterminants/definitions.html

Collins, K., Hughes, D., Doty, M., Ives, B., Edwards, J., & Tenney, K. (2002). *Diverse communities, common concerns: Assessing healthcare quality for minority Americans.* (Findings from the Commonwealth Fund 2001 Healthcare Quality Survey). New York, NY: The Commonwealth Fund.

Davis, S. (2001). Diversity and Generation X. *Seminars for Nurse Managers, 9*(3), 161–163.

DeWalt, D., & Pignone, M. (2008). Advocacy and patient literacy: What healthcare professionals can do to help patients overcome patient literacy barriers. In J. Earp, E. French, & M. Gilkey (Eds.), *Patient advocacy for healthcare quality* (pp. 215–239). Sudbury, MA: Jones and Bartlett Publishers.

Finkelman, A., & Kenner, C. (2012). *Teaching IOM: Implications of the Institute of Medicine reports* (3rd ed.). Silver Spring, MD: American Nurses Association.

Gerke, M. (2001). Understanding and leading the quad matrix: Four generations in the workplace: The traditional generation, boomers, gen-X, nexters. *Seminars for Nurse Managers, 9*(3), 173–181.

Institute of Medicine. (2001). *Crossing the quality chasm.* Washington, DC: National Academies Press.

Institute of Medicine. (2002). *Unequal Treatment. What healthcare providers need to know about racial and ethnic disparities in healthcare.* Washington, DC: National Academies Press.

Institute of Medicine. (2003). *Health professions education.* Washington, DC: National Academies Press.

Institute of Medicine. (2004). *Health literacy.* Washington, DC: National Academies Press.

Institute of Medicine. (2011). *The future of nursing: Leading change, advancing health.* Washington, DC: National Academies Press.

International Centre for Nurse Migration. (2014). About us. Retrieved from http://www.intlnursemigration.org/about/

Ruby, B. (2007). The new workforce—dealing with nexters (Generation Y). Retrieved from http://cmsreport.com/articles/the-new-workforce-dealing-with-nexters-generation-y--3442

Leighty, J. (2003). Healing by design. *NurseWeek Midwest/Great Lakes, 2*(5), 14–16.

McCullough, C., & Wille, R. (2001). Healing environments. In C. McCullough (Ed.), *Creating responsive solutions to healthcare change* (pp. 109–134). Indianapolis, IN: Center Nursing Press.

Mead, H., Cartwright-Smith, L., Jones, K., Ramos, C., & Woods, K. (2008, March 13). *Racial and ethnic disparities in U.S. health care: A chartbook.* Retrieved December 3, 2009, from http://www.commonwealthfund.org/publications/chartbooks/2008/mar/racial-and-ethnic-disparities-in-u-s--health-care--a-chartbook

Planetree. (2014). Approach. Retrieved from http://planetree.org/approach/

Robert Wood Johnson Foundation. (2014). Study: Nursing school diversity initiatives mostly successful. Retrieved from http://www.rwjf.org/en/about-rwjf/newsroom/newsroom-content/2014/05/nursing-school-diversity-initiatives-mostly-successful--study-fi.html

Santos, S., & Cox, K. (2002). Generational tension among nurses. *American Journal of Nursing, 102*(1), 11.

Schein, E. (2010). *Organization culture and leadership* (4th ed.). San Francisco, CA: Jossey-Bass.

Shuttleworth, M. (2009, October 10). Hawthorne Effect. Retrieved from https://explorable.com/hawthorne-effect

Sullivan, L. (2004). *Missing persons: Minorities in the health professions, a report of the Sullivan Commission on diversity in the healthcare workforce.* Retrieved January 2, 2010, from http://www.aacn.nche.edu/Media/pdf/Sullivan-Report.pdf

Ulrich, B. (2001). Successfully managing multigenerational workforces. *Seminars for Nurse Managers, 9*(3), 147–153.

U.S. Census Bureau. (2012). U.S. Census Bureau projections show a slower growing, older, more diverse nation a half century from now. Retrieved from https://www.census.gov/newsroom/releases/archives/population/cb12-243.html

U.S. Department of Health and Human Services. (2012). HHS action plan to reduce racial and ethnic health disparities. A nation free of disparities in health and health care. Retrieved from http://minorityhealth.hhs.gov/assets/pdf/hhs/HHS_Plan_complete.pdf

U.S. Department of Health and Human Services, National Partnership for Action. (2011). Health equity and disparities. Retrieved from http://www.minorityhealth.hhs.gov/npa/templates/browse.aspx?lvl=1&lvlid=34

U.S. Department of Health and Human Services, Office of Minority Health. (2012). HHS disparities action plan. Retrieved from http://minorityhealth.hhs.gov/omh/browse.aspx?lvl=2&lvlid=10

U.S. Department of Health and Human Services, Office of Minority Health. (2014). Culturally competent nursing care: A cornerstone of caring. Retrieved from https://ccnm.thinkculturalhealth.hhs.gov/

Westrick, S. (2014). *Essentials of nursing law and ethics* (2nd ed.). Burlington, MA: Jones & Bartlett Learning.

Wieck, K., Prydun, M., & Walsh, T. (2002). What the emerging workforce wants in its leaders. *Journal of Nursing Scholarship, 34*(3), 283–288.

Zemke, R., Raines, C., & Filipczak, B. (2000). *Generations at work.* New York, NY: American Management Association.

11 Consumers and Nurses

🔴 LEARNING OUTCOMES

Before you begin, take a moment to familiarize yourself with the learning outcomes for this chapter.

> Examine the history of healthcare consumerism and its impact on health care.
> Assess the relationship between public policy and the healthcare consumer.
> Compare and contrast the consumer implications of *Healthy People* and the Institute of Medicine reports (*Quality Chasm* series).
> Assess the importance of the role of technology in consumer healthcare information.
> Examine the relationship between patient education and healthcare consumerism.
> Critique how consumers are involved in evaluating the quality of care.
> Apply patient advocacy to the role of the nurse manager.

KEY TERMS

- advocacy
- consumer health informatics
- consumerism
- macroconsumer
- microconsumer

WHAT'S AHEAD

The consumer's role has changed as health care has undergone major changes. This chapter addresses the role of the consumer or the patient in the healthcare delivery system. By its very nature, the nursing process places both the patient and the patient's family in a major role. The recent work by the Institute of Medicine (IOM) also emphasizes patient-centered care, which is a consumer-oriented approach. (See Chapter 9.) Viewing patients as consumers of healthcare services has been gaining strength as consumers speak out about their health care. They are concerned about the quality of care and its cost. Nurses have had a role in this as well, as patient advocacy is an important component of nursing care and of healthcare management. Healthcare organizations (HCOs) now focus more on consumers in their planning, services, and evaluation processes.

There is no doubt that the patient is paying more for care as employers pay less. Premiums are higher, as are copayments and deductibles. Recognition of consumer priorities and understanding the criteria that consumers use as they evaluate their healthcare services are critical to maintaining a positive relationship with the healthcare consumer. HCOs, providers, and insurers need to know more about consumer issues: What does the patient want and need? Is the outcome what the patient wanted? With the greater focus on interprofessional teams, the patient is viewed as part of the team (Institute of Medicine, 2003). For a long period of time, consumer rights and protection were not addressed, but now there is legislation to provide some protections (Health Insurance Portability and Accountability Act of 1996 [HIPAA]). (U.S. Department of Health and Human Resources, 2014). It is difficult to develop and pass effective legislation that balances the needs of all consumers including patients/enrollees/employees, employers, the government, providers, and insurers. This process involves many constituents, often with conflicting agendas.

Patients are turning more to nurses and asking questions about their health care and health-care delivery; therefore, nurses need to be prepared to answer their questions or know how to help patients seek answers about health care. Consumer- or patient-centered health care means the nurse must be more aware of patient/customer needs. This chapter discusses consumerism, the role of the consumer or patient in healthcare policy, healthcare information, patient evaluation of health care, and the nurse as patient advocate. Similar content in this text includes leadership, patient-centered care, HCO structure and function, quality improvement, and informatics.

THE CONSUMER AND HEALTH CARE

Who Is the Consumer?

Consumers can be described in a variety of ways. A **macroconsumer** is a large purchaser of healthcare services (e.g., employers, government). The macroconsumer may also be called the customer. Clearly this type of consumer has a major voice in healthcare decisions due to its size and acts as a liaison between the insurers and employees. A **microconsumer** is the employee, the employee's family, and people who buy insurance as individuals rather than through an employer. They are the users of the healthcare services, or patients. All consumers, whether macro or micro, make decisions about the purchase of healthcare coverage, but the microconsumers are involved in more decisions about healthcare services that directly affect them. Choice is an important aspect of health care, and some consumers feel their choices have diminished (e.g., choice of health plan has decreased as employers offer fewer plans and more tightly control the types of plans; the choice of provider, when the provider can be consulted, and so on; and in some cases the choice of using specialty care has diminished). As healthcare reimbursement has changed, choice has become an important healthcare consumer issue and one that is integral in many consumer complaints about health care.

History of Healthcare Consumerism

Consumerism has been evolving over many years. With the development of managed care, consumerism became even more important, and we see even more involvement today with the development of the healthcare reform of 2010 (Affordable Care Act [ACA]). What is the history of healthcare consumerism? How did it evolve? In the 1970s consumers were informed and assertive about their active participation in health care (Armer, 1998). During that time, the focus was on patient satisfaction and use of healthcare services. For example, in the 1970s, as consumerism was gaining some strength, a 1971 study found that 75% of the families surveyed believed that there was a crisis in health care, but only 10% said they were dissatisfied with the quality of their care (Andersen, Kravits, & Anderson, 1971). This is a confusing result; despite the fact that a high percentage felt that the healthcare system was in a crisis, few were critical of that care's quality. At the time this study was conducted in the 1970s, managed care was growing strong and influencing not only reimbursement but also delivery of care. Patient satisfaction is a very complex issue, and it is not always easy to know what a patient is responding to during a satisfaction survey. Quality is also difficult to define, and the perspective of the person defining quality has a major impact on the definition. Cost has also become more and more important to consumers as their personal costs (e.g., insurance premiums and copayments) have increased.

In addition, accessing health care is important and a growing concern for vulnerable populations (e.g., people who live in rural areas, are poor, are elderly, are mentally ill, and are minorities). Diversity and disparities in health care are discussed in Chapter 10. Quality care and access to services have been important issues throughout the healthcare consumer movement, and these issues are even more important today.

As managed care became the dominant player in the healthcare system in the 1990s, a change developed regarding healthcare consumerism. Consumers were not as active in the early 1990s as they were by the end of the decade. Managed care developed on the West Coast then jumped to the East Coast. Then managed care slowly moved toward the interior of the country, with some areas not feeling its effect until the mid-1990s. As this occurred, managed care did not affect enough consumers to cause them to organize and protest against it. The media were not as cognizant of the changes, so it was not a forefront news item. However, as more consumers were affected by managed care, consumers became stronger and made a major impact on healthcare delivery when the problems affected their personal care. Consumers reached a point of dissatisfaction to say, "Enough!" This cry came from the soon-to-be-seniors generation. The baby boomers, in contrast, are not new to protesting and being assertive. They had an impact on managed care, which has now lost much of its influence in health care; however, managed care strategies were adopted by many insurers/third-party payers and integrated into all types of health insurance plans. Consumers are now addressing their concerns about healthcare delivery.

One such example is the role of consumers in the healthcare reform process of 2009–2010 and passage of the ACA in 2010. Proponents for different approaches reached out to consumers via ads in print, television, radio, and the Internet. Consumers had an active voice through their representatives in Congress. Sometimes these issues became very emotional. Members of Congress used patient or consumer experiences to make their points. There is no doubt that as consumers experience problems with health care, they often criticize the system and have been successful as they demanded changes in managed care and other aspects of reimbursement. There are, however, positive aspects of managed care that should not be ignored, such as its gradual increased emphasis on preventive care, health promotion, and continuity, which are now supported by ACA. Nonetheless, it is easy to lose sight of the positive aspects of managed care. Emotions sometimes undermine rational policy changes and criticism. If the goal is to control costs, provide quality care, and increase care delivery to those who cannot afford care, it is critical to find a balance and identify the strengths and limitations of managed care and reimbursement, while building on its strengths.

Healthcare providers and third-party payers recognize the need to listen more to consumer criticisms and are more willing to make some changes that address these criticisms. Today "patient centered" is a frequently heard term, although it does not always significantly affect health care in practical changes. More effort has been made to provide patient-centered care, and this includes providing the consumer with information. In 2010 preexisting conditions was a critical issue that was addressed during healthcare reform legislation. Preexisting conditions can no longer be used to exclude persons from insurance coverage. Prior to passage of the ACA, this was a key consumer issue. Insurers did not want this to be part of the legislation as this does impact the insurer enrollee pool and can increase cost for insurers; however, insurers were not able to influence the final bill that was signed into law in 2010.

Nurses have long supported a more consumer-based approach, but why would HCOs and insurers be interested? HCOs are increasingly aware of the need to develop satisfied consumers who participate in their care, and in turn, this does affect HCO budgets. Certainly the need to obtain contracts from employers is one driving force. Insurers also want consumers to have more understanding about their healthcare needs so they can be informed purchasers of care and informed users of healthcare services. They believe that an informed healthcare consumer will reduce healthcare costs. At the same time, consumers are turning more to government and legislation to influence healthcare policy making and get their needs met.

PUBLIC POLICY AND THE HEALTHCARE CONSUMER

HCOs and healthcare providers need to understand how consumers view their organizations and services as well as their expectations of care. This understanding is needed at local, state, and national levels. Effective health policy, as noted in Chapter 2, depends on this understanding so it can be integrated into policy. The IOM strongly supports this with its emphasis on patient-centered care. The IOM reports and the need for patient-centered, quality care influence the ACA provisions. Nursing organizations have a responsibility to advocate in the legislative arena for the consumer, so they partner with consumer groups, and they frequently do this because collaboration can result in a win-win outcome. However, more could be done. The examples of healthcare fraud and abuse found in Chapter 2 indicate that nurses do get involved in situations when the consumer needs assertive nurses who will take risks for them. This can be very difficult for nurses, but situations such as these can demonstrate nurses' leadership skills.

The consumer must also become involved in the development of healthcare public policy. This is usually done through organizations such as the American Diabetes Association, National Alliance for the Mentally Ill, the American Association of Retired Persons, the Arthritis Foundation, the Susan G. Komen Breast Cancer Foundation, and other organizations that advocate for specific policies while representing their membership. Frequently these organizations also have healthcare professional members such as nurses who participate in their policy advocacy and other organizational activities. Individual consumers also go directly to their legislators, on both the state and federal levels, to have a voice in policy decision making. Television, the Internet, and newspapers keep the public informed of healthcare policy issues. Nurses can be supportive of consumer involvement by ensuring that consumers get accurate information, through serving as experts while writing letters to editors, and by keeping up with media content. Typically the media turns to physicians for comments about health care, but nurses are also good resources for this information. Nurses have to let the media know that they are competent and available to do this. Nursing organizations usually let the media know that they have representatives who are willing to be interviewed. Chapter 2 discusses other lobbying and legislative activities.

An example of the consumer voice occurred in late 2009 when the U.S. Preventive Services Task Force reversed its recommendation about the use of mammography screening for women age 40 and older in addition to changes in its recommendation for cervical cancer screening. The task force supported this decision with evidence-based practice after a review of current research. Consumers, primarily women, were angry about the decision and concerned that this would mean insurers would no longer cover this screening at the age of 40 but rather only cover based on the age recommended, 50 years old. This decision was a very important topic on news channels, newspapers, and so on with consumers expressing their concerns (Aronowitz, 2009; Grady, 2009; Kolata, 2009; U.S. Preventive Services Task Force, 2009). This complex decision struck a negative cord with consumers, particularly women. There is greater emphasis on basing medical decisions on evidence, which is also an IOM recommendation (2008) and also one of the healthcare professions' core competencies (Institute of Medicine, 2003). In this case, however, when the evidence was reviewed and indicated a need for change, consumers did not agree with the change. It was a complex issue for consumers and providers. This will not be the only medical decision issue that arises as more evidence-based practice is implemented. Consumers know how to voice their opinions, and in this case, they did—through the media, their government officials, and their healthcare providers—whether or not they supported evidence-based decisions.

Consumer Rights

Consumer rights have slowly become a major issue in healthcare policy, particularly due to dissatisfaction with managed care. States are active in establishing requirements related to information that the insurer must supply to the consumer and to identify grievance and appeal requirements. The Patient Self-Determination Act of 1990 (PSDA) is a law that applies to all HCOs (hospitals, long-term care facilities, home health agencies, clinics, primary care sites) that participate in Medicare or Medicaid by receiving reimbursement from these government sources (Westrick, 2014). What does this law require? All HCOs that receive Medicare and Medicaid funding must provide their patients with information about patients' rights, which are typically referred to as a Patient's Bill of Rights. In reality, this means very few HCOs do not receive this federal funding through reimbursement. Some of the rights that are important are confidentiality, consent, right to make medical decisions, right to be informed about diagnosis and treatment, right to refuse treatment, and use of advance directives. As noted earlier, six years after the passage of PSDA, HIPAA legislation was passed, a law that is important in supporting patient rights.

The consumer rights issue is highly controversial. If too many consumer rights are recognized, how will this affect the ability of insurers to meet their goals to reduce healthcare costs? Reducing costs is a concern for all, not just the insurers. What effect will patient rights have on healthcare providers? For example, changes in patient privacy protection are costly to implement, yet they represent an important consumer issue. Consumers also want costs lowered; however, the critical factor is what must be given up to reach this goal. HCOs such as hospitals, clinics, long-term care facilities, and home care agencies must consider how particular patient's rights might impact care and costs.

Consumer Assessment of Healthcare Providers and Systems

The Consumer Assessment of Healthcare Providers and Systems (CAHPS) is a program funded and administered through the Agency for Healthcare Research and Quality (AHRQ) that develops patient surveys to assess patient perspectives of their ambulatory and facility level care (Consumer Assessment of Healthcare Providers and Systems, 2014). The goals of this program are to assess patient-centeredness, compare contract performance, and improve quality of care. The data provide benchmarking opportunities for comparison of health plans (commercial plans, Medicare, and Medicaid), clinician groups, and hospitals. The CAHPS website is a valuable resource about consumer views of their health care. The site provides an interactive benchmarking database. A quality improvement process described on the site includes content related to plan strategy, development and testing of strategy, monitoring strategy, and reassessment and response. The level of content and resources this site provides indicates that consumer viewpoints about their health care are much more important today.

The end of the 1990s brought major efforts to pass additional federal legislation to establish a greater patient or consumer protection bill of rights. There have been many proposals in Congress, and in the fall of 1999, the Senate and the House passed two very different bills, requiring compromises on their part; however, no patient's rights legislation was passed.

All of this activity indicates how the late 1980s and the 1990s were an active time for patient consumerism. Although probably initiated by dissatisfaction with managed care, many of the changes had little to do directly with managed care and really focused more on health care in general. Today emphasis on patients' rights is an integral part of the healthcare delivery system; however, ensuring that they are implemented effectively to meet consumer needs and encourage participation requires ongoing work.

SPECIAL REPORTS AND INITIATIVES: IMPLICATIONS FOR HEALTHCARE CONSUMERS

Healthy People and the Institute of Medicine reports on quality in the healthcare delivery system are very important for the consumer. These reports and initiatives, one led by the government and the second by a nongovernmental agency, The National Academy of Medicine, that serves in an advisory capacity for the government, have had a major influence on healthcare professions, the delivery system, healthcare professionals' education, and consumers.

Healthy People 2020

Healthy People is a national prevention initiative that identifies opportunities to improve the health of all Americans by identifying goals and objectives that are used by the U.S. Department of Health and Human Services (HHS), as well as many HCOs and institutions, to promote health and prevent disease and illness (U.S. Department of Health and Human Services, 2015). Chapter 7 includes more information about Healthy People.

A major goal of the Healthy People national initiative is to eliminate health disparities. This is a difficult goal to meet; it requires improved access to care for all persons as well as new knowledge about the determinants of disease and effective interventions. With the large number of uninsured in the United States, this has been a challenge. Socioeconomic disparities, demographic changes, education-related differences, race, and ethnicity are significant barriers to the success of this goal. The IOM report on disparities further clarified major problems in healthcare disparities (2002). The Healthy People website provides current information about the status of its goals and objectives. Why does the Healthy People initiative have relevance to this chapter's content? Healthy People is an example of an initiative that provides methods to improve the health status of individual consumers and communities. One of its major overall goals is to improve the quality of health-related decisions through effective communication with patients. Interwoven into its other goals and their objectives is the need for consumer education, advocacy, and self-management of illness via health promotion and disease and illness prevention, all of which are supported by the IOM quality reports.

The Institute of Medicine Reports on Quality Care

The IOM reports on quality are discussed in most chapters in this text. The IOM strongly recommends the need for patient-centered care, collaboration, care coordination, and advocacy. Patients as consumers need to assume an active role in their care decisions and in their treatment and should be considered members of the interprofessional team. Self-management is an important part of the IOM recommended changes (2003), as noted in Chapter 9. The IOM discusses the consumer perspectives of healthcare needs—including staying healthy, getting better, living with illness or disability, and coping with the end of life (2001, p. 61). What does each of these elements mean?

- *Staying healthy:* The individual needs to get health care to stay well and avoid illness.
- *Getting better:* The individual requires care to reach recovery.
- *Living with illness or disability:* The individual needs assistance in learning how to manage and cope long term.
- *Coping with end of life:* The individual needs support and care during terminal stages of illness.

If the patient agrees, families and caregivers need to be involved in each of these elements of the consumer dimension. HIPAA requires that the patient provide permission for sharing of information, and this includes with the family.

INFORMATION RESOURCES AND THE CONSUMER

Consumer Health Informatics is the field devoted to informatics from multiple consumer or patient views. These include patient-focused informatics, health literacy, and consumer education. The focus is on information structures and processes that empower consumers to manage their own health (e.g., health information literacy, consumer-friendly language, personal health records, and Internet-based strategies and resources). The shift in this view of informatics analyzes consumers' needs for information; studies and implements methods for making information accessible to consumers; and models and integrates consumers' preferences into health information systems. (American Medical Informatics Association, 2014)

Interactive technology has certainly changed the availability of information, particularly email, websites, intranets, interactive voice response systems, mobile phones, and smartphones. These new technologies offer additional ways to communicate with patients and to collect, manage, and use healthcare information. Who uses this technology and for what reasons? Patients use the information to learn more about their own health. An example is the growth in the use of apps, and some of them have a consumer health focus (e.g., display general health information, personal health information, provide alerts, instruct, and record information). This use of informatics will increase as more and more consumers find value in the options.

National organizations and the government often provide the most accurate patient information. Information and education are important in promoting health; preventing, managing, and coping with disease; and supporting appropriate decisions across the spectrum of health care. For individuals, effective health communication can help raise awareness of health risks, provide motivation and skills to reduce them, bring helpful connections to others in similar situations, and offer information about difficult choices, such as health plans and providers, treatments, and long-term care. As discussed in Chapter 19, nurses also should be active in ensuring better informatics for patients/families/consumers.

APPLYING EVIDENCE-BASED PRACTICE

Evidence for Effective Leadership and Management

CITATION: Agency for Healthcare Research and Quality. (2008, November). *Barriers and Drivers of Health Information Technology Use for the Elderly, Chronically Ill, and Underserved.* Rockville, MD. Retrieved from http://www.ahrq.gov/clinic/tp/hitbartp.htm

OVERVIEW: This is a systematic review of 563 full-text articles including 129 articles for abstraction. Few of the studies were specifically designed to compare the elderly, chronically ill, or underserved with the general population. Of the studies that reported the impact of the interactive consumer health information technology (IT) on health outcomes, a consistent finding was that these systems tended to have a positive effect when they provided a complete feedback loop that included the following:

- Monitoring of current patient status
- Interpretation of data in light of established, often individualized, treatment goals
- Adjustment of the management plan as needed
- Communication back to the patient with tailored recommendations or advice
- Repetition of this cycle at appropriate intervals

The most common factor influencing the effective use of interactive technology for these specific populations is that the consumers perceived a benefit from using the system. Convenience is an important factor. Effective data entry is not cumbersome, and the intervention needs to fit into the user's daily routine. Clinicians who respond in a timely and frequent manner increase use and user satisfaction. The researchers identify questions that need further examination.

APPLICATION: The consumer's perception of benefit, convenience, and integration into daily activities facilitates effective use of the interactive technologies for the elderly, chronically ill, and underserved. Nurses who are involved in the development and/or implementation of consumer health technology should be aware of research results to improve consumer health technology.

Questions:

1. What is meant by a complete feedback loop in this systematic review?
2. How would you see the feedback loop impacting nursing care, and in what types of settings might this be particularly helpful?
3. What is your opinion of the three questions that are mentioned in the conclusion? How might these questions relate to nursing and nurses?

PATIENT SATISFACTION AND QUALITY

In today's highly competitive healthcare delivery environment, patient satisfaction and quality have become more important (Institute of Medicine, 2001). This text discusses many aspects of leadership and management, yet sometimes it is difficult to see how this all relates to patient care. Do the healthcare environment and culture, services, satisfaction, staff retention, and type of organizational structure matter to patients? Do they just go through the system untouched by it? Patients report greater satisfaction with their care in shared governance organizations, which tend to have greater staff retention and work satisfaction. Clearly the contexts in which staff work and patients receive their care are interrelated and affect patients' views of their care.

Patients and their families can assist in identifying near misses, catching errors before they occur by asking questions and being informed about their care, and participating in evaluating care at a minimum on the four elements of the consumer dimension mentioned earlier.

Besides addressing difficulties in determining satisfaction, other issues need to be considered. One issue that comes up is whether the patient, as a healthcare consumer, is able to judge what quality care is. This question tends to generate strong feelings on both sides—from the patient and the provider. How does the patient's illness affect the patient's impression of the treatment, and how does the patient express the evaluation? This is an important consideration during assessment—finding out about the patient's past experiences. This may reveal potential problems and concerns that need to be addressed to prevent patient satisfaction problems. Today asking for feedback is common in almost all experiences from the restaurant to the shopping center and, of course, health care. Access to a variety of Internet sites for many different purposes often elicits a request for feedback. Who completes these surveys? First, surveys take time even if short and people are busy. Language may be an issue, so knowledge of English is usually required, though many HCOs have other language options. To effectively use surveys with different groups, reading level needs to be considered. Sometimes patients do not want to share their thoughts or feel if they do, it will result in a negative response from caregivers. Some patients wonder what is done with the information and if care really changes. In many situations when negative feedback is provided, there is no follow-up with the patient. Providing feedback in person is even more problematic (e.g., when the patient recognizes a near miss or possible error or the nurse does not wash her hands). Will the patient say something at the time? In the past this happened less often, but today more patients will speak up; however, more need to do this. As is true for many problems that may be identified in the evaluation process, management/staff may tend to trivialize complaints by saying the patient or family member was annoying or a constant complainer. This is a way of avoiding complaints and not working on improvement.

Patient satisfaction data are also an important component of HCO report cards. Report cards are discussed in Chapter 18. As more is learned about the type of data that are really helpful, the report cards should become more useful and reliable for the patient, employer, all types of providers, and insurers. It is important to recognize that the variables of satisfaction need to be identified by the patient, not the healthcare professional. For example, a patient may associate quality care with "nice" responses from nurses, doctors who spoke to the patient, food quality, and reasonable wait times for an appointment, whereas the healthcare provider or the HCO focuses on outcomes met, errors, what the provider views as patient-centered care, and so on. This presents a problem as the perspectives may be very different, yet both may conclude there is satisfaction or dissatisfaction. Patient satisfaction is a core element of quality of care. It is now easy for patients to go on the Internet and review a lot of data about HCO quality and rankings within the local, state, and national levels. This does not necessarily mean that the rankings are always accurate or ensure quality. The variables used to determine the rankings and who did the ranking are critical factors that most consumers are not aware of or even consider. A study published in 2015 illustrates how difficult it is to rank healthcare services (Austin et al., 2015). In this study four different rating systems applied to 844 hospitals were compared. None of the HCOs were rated high performers by all four systems. The rating systems used different variables/measures, making it very difficult to compare them. If a consumer seeks HCO rating information, looking at one rating may not be effective, but when considering multiple systems, the consumer may get variable results.

CASE STUDY

Consumer Satisfaction Is Not My Problem!

A community health center received its annual patient satisfaction data, a summary provided to staff from patient satisfaction surveys that are mailed to all current patients by an external organization. The return rate this year was 40% of surveys mailed, which was up from 20% the previous year. The center has a new director who has asked staff to respond to the data. Staff members are rather surprised as in the past they were lucky if they even saw the data. Many staff members do not feel it is their job to make the center better or solve consumer problems; this is management's job. Over the past year, more patients and their families have been verbal about their complaints to staff. Some of the complaints, which also were included in the summarized data, were increased wait times for getting an appointment, longer wait times when arriving for appointments, staff attitude (rude, abrupt, uncaring), little patient education, inadequate parking, and confusion over payment.

Questions:

1. Why is it important for staff to be involved in improving consumer satisfaction?
2. Who are the consumers in this case?
3. What type of structure would be most effective to make a plan for improvement? Consider who should participate, size, purpose, and so on.
4. After considering the major complaints highlighted, how might the center respond to improve consumer satisfaction? (Be specific in the interventions that might be taken.)

THE NURSE AS PATIENT ADVOCATE

Advocacy has always been a major aspect of the nursing role with the consumer. Nursing standards developed by the American Nurses Association (ANA), nursing specialty organizations, and HCOs, as well as those developed by accrediting organizations and other healthcare professional organizations, support many of the critical aspects of advocacy and consumerism. The ANA includes advocacy in its code of ethics and standards (2010a, 2010c). The documents focus on patient-centered care, recognizing that advocacy is a fundamental aspect of nursing with the obligation to influence health policy and care delivery and wellness for the consumer (patient). This view is also supported by the ANA *Nursing's Social Policy* statement (2010b). The ANA standards for nursing administration expand on advocacy by describing the nurse administrator role in advocating for staff and for a healthy work environment, indicating that advocacy is relevant to more than just patient advocacy (2009).

Patient education, patient satisfaction and complaint process, quality improvement, patient participation in healthcare decision making, and all components of advocacy and consumerism are found in both of the ANA standards.

There are two important components of **advocacy**: (1) providing information that is useful to the patient and (2) supporting the patient's decision, which may not be the decision the nurse thinks is best but nonetheless must be supported. To be successful, collaboration must be part of this process. The nurse provides services through a collaborative relationship with the patient and the patient's family and advocates for the patient. To be an advocate, the nurse needs to be persuasive with the patient and with others with whom the nurse may interact on behalf of the patient. Advocacy does not mean that the nurse takes over for the patient, but rather that the nurse helps the patient to be more independent, recognizing that the patient is a stakeholder in the care process. Changes in reimbursement such as the expansion of managed care and its strategies have certainly also affected physician-patient relationships. An advocate must also recognize his or her own limits and refer patients to appropriate resources.

Advocacy needs to be part of practice. One perspective of advocacy described by Gilkey, Earp, and French (2008) focuses on advocacy as a continuum:

- The individual level focuses on informing patients, and considers "interventions that target the personal beliefs, attitudes, and knowledge needed to achieve health" (p. 17). This would include self-management and patient education. Chronic illness, discussed earlier in this book, is a critical concern. E-health has become more and more important as consumers turn to the Internet for information.
- The next level is the interpersonal level focusing on supporting and empowering patients. Interventions such as "advice giving, emotional support, and provision of resources and other help" (p. 18) are an integral part of this level, and all require interpersonal interactions. Families and significant others need to be brought into this process, when the patient agrees.
- The third level is the organizational and community levels focusing on transforming culture. What are organizations and communities doing to support patient advocacy?
- The fourth level is the policy level focusing on translating consumer voice into policy and laws. "In patient advocacy, important policies are those that (1) control access to patient care; (2) regulate healthcare organizations, especially with regard to patient safety surveillance; and (3) protect healthcare consumers" (p. 21).

Advocacy is also associated with health informatics as noted in the ANA *Nursing Informatics: Scope and Standards of Practice* (2014). Examples that are given are the need for nurses to be involved in the development and implementation of health informatics, particularly those with expertise. In doing this, nurses advocate for the information that consumers need and in a format that provides easy consumer access. Nurses may also be involved in advocating for health information access in areas where it may be difficult for patients to get information, such as advocating for Internet access in rural areas. Nurses also need to advocate for careful consideration of confidentiality and security of data.

What can the nurse do to assist and advocate for the patient? Ensuring that the nursing process is complete and includes active patient and family/significant other participation is the critical first step. Built into the process are individualized care, patient rights, respect for the patient, and patient education. The nurse also needs to empower the patient with information and support the patient and the family as healthcare choices are made. Accessing care, which includes services, supplies, and medical equipment, is not always easy. Doing this in a healthcare environment in which patients have shortened lengths of stay or who do not come in for care early enough is very difficult. Patient education takes time. More and more of this load has shifted to the community. It takes commitment on the part of the nurses to ensure that it happens and that the patient education is appropriate to meet the needs of the patient. Nurses will have to be more creative in meeting the needs, probably by turning more to technology. Care, however, does need to be taken to ensure that individual needs and human contact are still present. The nurse can help the patient understand the complex healthcare system and reimbursement issues related to the system to receive care when it is needed. Prevention is important in today's healthcare environment, and helping the patient understand the need for prevention and how it can benefit the individual patient is part of the nurse-patient relationship.

APPLYING LEADERSHIP AND MANAGEMENT

My Hospital Unit: An Evolving Case Experience

Your hospital has an initiative to increase consumer involvement in hospital activities and services. Today you are meeting with your staff to discuss how consumerism impacts the unit and what can be done to improve consumer- or patient-centered care.

Remember that families and significant others should also be involved when the patient agrees. How would you (1) determine the current status of patient involvement, (2) identify what needs to change, (3) plan for change, and (4) evaluate the outcomes? Who should be involved?

BSN and *Master's Essentials*: Application to Content

BSN Essentials (American Association of Colleges of Nursing, 2008) as Applied to this Chapter:

IV. Information Management and Application of Patient Care Technology
V. Healthcare Policy, Finance, and Regulatory Environments

Master's Essentials (American Association of Colleges of Nursing, 2011) as Applied to this Chapter:

V. Informatics and Healthcare Technologies
VI. Health Policy and Advocacy

Applying AONE Competencies

Identify which of the AONE competencies found in Appendix A apply to the content of this chapter.

Engaging in the Content: Critical Thinking and Clinical Reasoning and Judgment

Discussion Questions

1. What is the difference between a microconsumer and macroconsumer?
2. Describe the history of healthcare consumerism.
3. How is public policy related to the healthcare consumer?
4. Why are consumer rights important in health care? (Online Application Option)
5. What is your vision of the role of the nurse as patient advocate? Provide examples. (Online Application Option)

Application Exercises

1. This is a good time to assess healthcare consumerism in your community. What are the healthcare consumer groups? What do they do? Are they effective? Are nurses involved in any of these groups? In what ways? Is your school of nursing or its students involved in any of these groups? What could be done to increase this involvement? It might be helpful to first develop a list of consumer organizations in your class then divide the organizations for further research by smaller teams or individual students. Then information can be shared.

2. Working in small teams, determine how you might get information about the nurse as a patient advocate in your community. Consider the data you would want to collect and where you might obtain the data. What methods are you going to use?

3. Select an example of health communication such as from a television ad, pamphlet, Internet health site, and so on. Using the attributes related to health communication discussed in this chapter, assess the example. This could be done in class so students can share their examples and assessments.

4. Find out more information about how a local healthcare organization evaluates patient satisfaction. Consider the content, frequency, analysis of the data, and who gets the information. Has the assessment of patient satisfaction made a difference and how?

5. Review the Consumer Assessment of Healthcare Providers and Systems (CAHPS) (through the Agency for Healthcare Research and Quality) website. What can you learn about this program? How does it relate to nursing leadership and management?

References

American Association of Colleges of Nursing. (2008). *The essentials of baccalaureate education for professional nursing practice.* Washington, DC: Author.

American Association of Colleges of Nursing. (2011). *The essentials of master's education in nursing.* Washington, DC: Author.

American Medical Informatics Association. (2014). Consumer health informatics. Retrieved from http://www.amia.org/applications-informatics/consumer-health-informatics

American Nurses Association. (2009). *Nursing administration: Scope and standards of practice.* Silver Spring, MD: American Nurses Publishing.

American Nurses Association. (2010a). *Guide to the code of ethics for nurses.* Silver Spring, MD: American Nurses Publishing.

American Nurses Association. (2010b). *Nursing's social policy statement.* Silver Spring, MD: American Nurses Publishing.

American Nurses Association. (2010c). *Scope and standards of practice.* Silver Spring, MD: American Nurses Publishing.

American Nurses Association. (2014). *Nursing informatics: Scope and standards of practice.* Silver Spring, MD: American Nurses Publishing.

Andersen, R., Kravits, J., & Anderson, O. (1971). The public's view of the crisis in medical care: An impetus for changing delivery systems? *Economic and Business Bulletin, 24,* 44–52.

Armer, J. (1998). Consumers as allies or partners in care. In T. Sullivan (Ed.), *Collaboration: A healthcare imperative* (pp. 515–533). New York, NY: McGraw-Hill.

Aronowitz, R. (2009, November 20). Addicted to mammograms. *New York Times.* Retrieved from http://www.nytimes.com/2009/11/20/opinion/20aronowitz.html?pagewanted=all&_r=0

Austin, J., Jha, A., Romano, P., Singer, S., Vogus, T., Wachter, R., & Pronovost, P. (2015). National hospital ratings systems share few common scores and may generate confusion instead of clarity. *Health Affairs, 34*(3), 423–430.

Consumer Assessment of Healthcare Providers and Systems. (2014). CAHPS. Retrieved from https://cahps.ahrq.gov/

Gilkey, M., Earp, J., & French, E. (2008). What is patient advocacy? In J. Earp, E. French, & M. Gilkey, *Patient advocacy for healthcare quality,* pp. 3–28. Sudbury, MA: Jones and Bartlett.

Grady, D. (2009, November 20). Guidelines push back age for cervical cancer tests. *New York Times.* Retrieved from http://www.nytimes.com/2009/11/20/health/20pap.html

Institute of Medicine. (2001). *Crossing the quality chasm.* Washington, DC: National Academies Press.

Institute of Medicine. (2002). *Unequal treatment: Confronting racial and ethnic disparities in health care.* Washington, DC: National Academies Press.

Institute of Medicine. (2003). *Health professions education.* Washington, DC: National Academies Press.

Institute of Medicine. (2008). *Knowing what works in healthcare.* Washington, DC: National Academies Press.

Kolata, G. (2009, November 17). Panel urges mammograms at 50, not 40. *New York Times,* p. 74.

U.S. Department of Health and Human Services. (2014). Health information privacy. Retrieved from http://www.hhs.gov/ocr/privacy/index.html

U.S. Department of Health and Human Services. (2015). *Healthy People 2020.* Washington, DC: U.S. Government Printing Office.

U.S. Preventive Services Task Force. (2009). Screening for breast cancer: U.S. Preventive Services Task Force recommendation statement. *Annals of Internal Medicine, 151*(10), 716–726.

Westrick, S. (2014). *Essentials of nursing law and ethics.* Burlington, MA: Jones & Bartlett Learning.

◼ LEARNING OUTCOMES

Before you begin, take a moment to familiarize yourself with the learning outcomes for this chapter.

- ❭ Discuss the importance of teams in the healthcare delivery system.
- ❭ Compare and contrast the different types of teams.
- ❭ Assess team leader characteristics and how these relate to the team leader's tasks and responsibilities.
- ❭ Explain the important considerations related to team development, structure, and functions.
- ❭ Examine issues related to effective teams.
- ❭ Discuss the roles of charge nurse or shift manager and teams.
- ❭ Examine how TeamSTEPPS® may be used to improve teams.

WHAT'S AHEAD

With an increasing outcome-oriented healthcare delivery system, synergy from teams can work to the health system's benefit. **Synergy** requires good communication, particularly through listening and clarifying; supporting and encouraging one another; use of differing and confronting skills; a commitment to quality; acceptance of the value of teams and their collective contributions; and use of constructive feedback for the betterment of the team and outcomes. In addition to increased use of teams in practice settings, nursing education has experienced an increased use of collaborative learning experiences for students. One reason for this is it can improve learning, but another reason is it facilitates student learning about teams—how teams function, roles and responsibilities, setting an agenda, working with team members, and evaluation. It helps students appreciate that multiple views and knowledge is better than just one (Michaelsen, Parmelee, McMahon, & Levine, 2008). The content in this text is related to teams, how they function, and how they impact health care, thereby supporting the Institute of Medicine's (IOM's) recommendation for more effective teams. This chapter specifically provides information about critical team elements and the team's functioning or the structure and process of teams that are important for nurses. Content in Chapter 13 continues the discussion on teams.

TEAMS IN TODAY'S HEALTHCARE ENVIRONMENT

No one person can do it all. This fact is even more relevant in today's healthcare environment with its dynamic and frequent changes. The information explosion has made it impossible for any one person to know it all. Expertise is developed over time, and some staff have different types of expertise. The IOM emphasizes that teams improve skills, communication, participation, and effectiveness (2003) and identifies the use of interprofessional teams as one of the five key core competencies of healthcare professions. The 2004 IOM report on nursing identifies six major concerns about direct care and nursing, with the sixth concern described as integration and coordination of care (2004). Teams play a critical role in ensuring integration and coordination of care. All healthcare organizations (HCOs) desire to perform effectively, although clearly many do not. The IOM has commented in its reports that the healthcare system is not working effectively; it is dysfunctional. There continues to be a lack of continuity and coordination and poor communication (2001, 2003). "An interdisciplinary [interprofessional] team is composed of members from different professions and occupations with varied and specialized knowledge, skills, and methods. The team members integrate their observations, bodies of expertise, and spheres of decision making to coordinate, collaborate, and communicate with one another in order to optimize care for a patient or a group of patients" (Institute of Medicine, 2003, p. 54). Interprofessional teams can improve care and reduce costs (Institute of Medicine, 2003). Salmon stated,

> I must say I have grown tired of us saying that we are making major strides in collaboration and partnership with others beyond nursing. I worry that we in nursing have fought so hard for our professional identity and autonomy that we see being separate from others as a condition for future success. I see our separateness as antithetical to our most basic professional values. How can we reconcile our commitment to providing the best possible care when we still grapple with the place that nursing assistants, technicians, and others have in relation to our work? (2007, p. 117)

Achieving the competence of using interprofessional teams effectively is not easy to accomplish, and developing and maintaining teamwork has been a long-term issue in health care.

Teams, Teamwork, and Groups

What is the difference between teams and teamwork? A **team** represents the structure and **teamwork** the function, or how the team works together. Shared governance, discussed in Chapter 4, might be confused with use of teams; however, they are not the same, though teams are an important part of shared governance. An HCO may not use the model of shared governance yet still use teams in the clinical area to support management functions and to develop and implement projects.

Another area of confusion comes from comparing teams and groups. Most assume that teams and groups are synonymous, but they are not. In HCOs the more common term is "teams." It is rare for staff to refer to its "work group" as a "group." A group is more commonly viewed as less organized than a team. For example, a group of people may get together for social activities, but a team is structured. It should have clear goals and purpose, membership requirements, leader and follower responsibilities, and evaluate its work. There is less emphasis on a shared vision and mission with a group as compared to a team. Teams typically feel committed to one another. Teams have operating guidelines, decision-making processes, and a defined relationship with other parts of the organization. For example, a patient unit may have several nursing staff teams that cover the care of the patients, or there may be interprofessional teams of nurses, physicians, social workers, and other healthcare providers. Sharing, acceptance, collaboration, and communication are critical elements of effective team functioning.

The Future of Nursing report recognizes the importance of teams and the need for nurses to know more about teamwork by including teamwork in its priorities for future research:

- Identification of the main barriers to collaboration between nurses and other healthcare staff in a range of settings.
- Identification and testing of new or existing models of care teams that have the potential to add value to the healthcare system if widely implemented.

- Identification and testing of educational innovations that have the potential to increase healthcare professionals' ability to serve as productive, collaborative care team members (Institute of Medicine, 2011, p. 7-5).

Types of Teams

Teams have been classified in many different ways, although two broad common categories for classifying teams within organizations are formal and informal. **Formal teams** are created by the organization with a specific purpose in mind, and the team may be permanent or temporary. Examples of formal teams are clinical teams, policy committees, nurses' councils, and quality improvement committees. **Informal teams** or groups are quite different in that the members form these teams, and typically members share something in common. There is less structure, and the team would not really be recognized as a team by the HCO. An informal team may simply be a social or support group, but may also serve as a resource to resolve problems or provide a service. Formal teams may be formed for different reasons. The most common is the patient care team that is assigned specific patients and ensures that the care is provided. HCOs may form teams to work on special projects such as a project to change to an electronic medical record. Other teams may work on long-term projects such as policy and procedures and in this case may be called a "committee." With the greater emphasis on patient-centered care, there is more focus on patient-centered teams—the patient is the center with the team focusing on ensuring patient needs are met (Spitzer, 2008).

Some HCOs use the team nursing model. These teams are composed of nonprofessional nursing staff who provide most of the direct care with an RN directing the team and may include other staff nurses. The team leader plans and supervises the care delivered to a group of patients, which means the team leader probably spends less time providing direct care.

The team and its members must learn how to set goals for the team and evaluate its performance. Teams need training and education so they can be effective and obtain the skills that are needed to work together. Role transition may be very difficult and takes time. Over time, however, most teams develop into cohesive work units.

Examples: The Nursing Team and the Interprofessional Team

Nursing teams have been organized in a variety of ways over the years. The typical method has been to organize according to function. Understanding some of the history of the development of nursing teams is beneficial to appreciate the current status of teams. This type of work team might include a medication nurse, treatment nurse, and unlicensed assistive personnel (UAP). Team members see patients based on need and related tasks. If no one staff member reviews the patient's total care needs, this approach may lead to segmented care that is not patient centered and may result in inadequate coordination. It is important to note that just decentralizing an organization will not automatically make different healthcare professionals more inclined to collaborate and work effectively on teams. It takes much more than this organizational change.

Today there is a greater need to move to interprofessional teams (Institute of Medicine, 2003). The literature refers to **interdisciplinary, interprofessional**, transdisciplinary, and **multidisciplinary** teams, which can be confusing. The multidisciplinary team process implies that team members practice relatively independently with respect to goal setting and treatments. Team members may meet regularly or communicate in other ways, but their lack of common goals and their autonomous practice can result in lack of coordination and conflict over priorities and decision making. Teams that adopt an interdisciplinary (transdisciplinary, interprofessional) approach focus more on integration of activities to meet shared goals with team members contributing assessment data and meeting to synthesize information, identify issues, and plan to meet goals that are shared by the team. Both interdisciplinary/interprofessional and transdisciplinary teamwork require considerable educational preparation of team members. They must agree on leadership, team process, priority setting, and methods to resolve conflicts. Transdisciplinary teams are highly collaborative, and role boundaries are often blurred and skills transferred across professional boundaries. Today the more common term for this type of team is "interprofessional." The terms "cross disciplinary" and "multiskilled" have been applied to teams where members extend their skills well beyond the boundaries of their parent discipline (Encyclopedia.com, 2014).

The interprofessional approach considers a more collective action and is process oriented, which is the approach that the IOM recommends. Here are some advantages of using interprofessional teams:

- Decreased fragmentation in a complex care system
- Effective use of multiple expertise (e.g., medicine, nursing, pharmacy, allied health, social work, and so on)
- Decreased utilization of repetitive or duplicate services
- Increased creative and innovative solutions to complex problems
- Increased learning for team members about different roles and responsibilities, communication and coordination, and how to better plan care
- Motivation and increased self-esteem in team and individual performances
- Greater sharing of responsibility
- Empowerment to speak up (Finkelman & Kenner, 2016, p. 337)

Another approach to a clinical team is to view it as a microsystem (Nelson et al., 2008). A healthcare delivery microsystem (such as a clinical unit) focuses on a small staff team working together on a regular basis to provide care to patients. Some of the critical components of the microsystem are its communication system, need for shared information, work processes, and performance outcomes. Microsystems are part of a larger system. For example, multiple patient care units form a hospital. Clinical microsystems are the front-line units that provide most health care to most people. The patient should be the center of this microsystem, and the microsystem is the place where:

- care is made.
- quality, safety, reliability, efficiency, and innovation are made.
- staff morale and patient satisfaction are made.

Microsystems are the building blocks that form hospitals (Dartmouth College, 2010). Microsystems as well as mesosystems and macrosystems were discussed in Chapter 4, with a strong focus on patient-centered care.

THE TEAM LEADER

The **team leader** is very important to a team's effectiveness. RNs are the team leaders on many healthcare teams. Their leadership and management skills assist the team as it works toward its goals. This is a leadership role that new graduates typically assume early in their careers: Who is the team leader? How does the leader function? What are some issues that affect the team leader?

Team Leader Characteristics

In most organizations the team leader has less formal authority than individuals in management positions; however, a team leader should have the necessary authority to meet the position requirements. Self-confidence and the ability to act as a role model for team members are important characteristics. Team leaders often must act as the "cheerleader" to move the team along with enthusiasm, but this should be done appropriately. No one wants to work with someone who is always "cheery." Team leaders need to demonstrate facilitative leadership, although how this is implemented may vary. This means that the leader leads with a vision and is willing to become a learner. Coaching is an important part of team leadership by supporting and encouraging team members. If the leader is effective, the leader gradually relinquishes control as the team gains strength, though may not transfer all control or decisions to the team.

The leader's role changes over time as the team develops, and the leader slowly gives some direct control to team members and becomes a facilitator. Not all teams fully develop. This means the team leader needs to assess team performance over time and provide guidance as needed. Less experienced RNs who are developing their leadership and management skills usually have more difficulty recognizing when a team is ready to be more independent due to a lack of self-confidence, lack of trust, and fear that something will go wrong if they do not make all decisions for the team. They also have greater difficulty communicating, delegating, and assessing team members. With time, experience, and mentoring, less experienced RNs can further develop these important competencies.

The team leader focuses on the team's process as well as on its outcomes. Process is how the team works together. The facilitative leadership approach offers coaching and development to members. Team leaders, as is true with other types of leaders, need to have an understanding of communication, psychology, change, problem solving and decision making, motivation, and systems. It is important to encourage team members to give honest feedback and to provide an environment in which members can feel comfortable and safe in doing so. By establishing open communication when the team meets, the team leader sets the stage for a comfortable work environment. In addition, the team leader moves the team from the use of first-person singular to words that focus on the team as a group with joint responsibilities (for example, "we" and "us" to emphasize the team and interdependence rather than "I" and "me"). Team leaders provide praise to the team and, during stressful times, support. This does not mean, however, that individual members should never be praised as there are clearly times when an individual team member shines through in the team. "There's no 'I' in 'team.' Healthcare is a team sport, but too often practitioners act as individual players" (Weinstock, 2010).

Tasks and Responsibilities

Team leaders who approach the position with an attitude that they are different from team members or better than team members will not be successful. Effective leaders must jump in and work too, although they must continue to see the whole—what needs to be done and how best to accomplish it. Guiding from above will not be effective, but guiding from within the team will. The organization needs to be clear about the decision-making boundaries for its teams. Competitiveness between teams is not uncommon, but under most circumstances, this is not helpful in developing a positive organization culture of collaboration. The key tasks and responsibilities of the team leader are the following:

- Guide the team by helping to establish goals and objectives.
- Provide an environment where team members are active in all stages of team planning and feel comfortable in this role.
- Reinforce the focus on the patient, if this is the focus of the team's task or project.
- Ensure that the team's tasks are clear, planned, and accomplished in a timely manner.
- Ensure that standards and rules are established, and encourage team members to monitor their use.
- Link the team to key resources and with others in the HCO, and when necessary with the community.
- Assist the team to stay on task.
- Challenge the team to improve and develop.
- Remove barriers to collaboration.
- Follow up on problems in a timely fashion.
- Recognize and value team member contributions.
- Minimize micromanaging and encourage team members to assist in management issues.
- Use conflict management to benefit the team and help it reach its outcomes.
- Ensure that team self-evaluation occurs with an emphasis on outcomes.
- Accept feedback from team members.
- Provide appropriate and timely evaluation of team members' performance and team effectiveness.

Gender Issues and Team Leadership

There can be no doubt that literature about leadership and theories of leadership have been more interested in masculine leadership than feminine leadership. Some of this can be understood because historically women did not hold many leadership positions. Today, however, this is not true. Women are found in leadership positions in all major types of organizations, although clearly more are needed as the majority of women are found in the lower ranks and in lower management positions. Health care is no exception.

How are masculine and feminine leaders described? In a study of women leaders in 19 different businesses, including health care, women were found to have different characteristics than men (Caliper, 2005). Female leaders usually prefer a more participatory approach to leadership and encourage others to be involved. They are more empathetic, flexible, and willing to take risks

CASE STUDY

So You Are the Team Leader Now

The unit you are working on had an opening for a team leader position. You applied and, to your surprise, you get the position. You begin leading the team next week. After the excitement dies down, you begin to get nervous about the new position. Can you really do this job? You know that the team includes two RNs, one LPN, and two CNAs. You have worked with all of the members, but you don't know any of them well. Your nurse manager tells you that one of the RNs has a reputation of being quiet and passive and the other is "pushy." He has made most team leaders wish he would go away. The LPN has worked on the unit longer than any of the other team members and is a hard worker. The two CNAs also have a lot of experience. Now what do you do?

Questions:

1. What information about teams do you need to consider?
2. Describe the type of team leader you want to be and how this might impact decisions you need to make now.
3. What additional information about the team members might you ask the nurse manager?
4. What would be the expected phases of team development?
5. How will you build team cohesiveness? Consider the barriers and strategies to address.

than men. Men also scored high in these areas but not as high as women. Sharing power is seen as a positive characteristic, as is sharing information to reach the goals. Improving staff perceptions of themselves can improve the work environment and performance. Often female leaders focus more on process than on "the bottom line." They are concerned with broader issues. It is important to recognize that this description of female leaders can become a stereotypical viewpoint. The approach should also not be viewed as a negative or ineffective approach just because it is more commonly found in women. Notably these characteristics are emphasized more in current leadership theory and styles such as transformational leadership. There are certainly men in leadership positions who have these characteristics, and there are female leaders who do not. Focusing too much on gender issues ignores the importance of individual differences in leaders regardless of gender.

Followership: A Critical Concept

Followership can be defined as "the willingness to cooperate in working towards the accomplishment of the group [team] mission, to demonstrate a high degree of teamwork and to build cohesion among the group [team]" (Holden Leadership Center, 2009). Team leaders must recognize that teams do not exist without **followers**, the team members. Followers are critical to the success of any organization. Followers have become more important as leadership theory has turned more and more to a participatory approach. Leadership means that followers are developed; just telling staff to follow does not mean they will follow a leader. Common reasons that staff follow are listed here:

- Fear of retribution: The follower is fearful of some action and therefore follows the leader.
- Blind hope: The follower believes in the leader and the leader's ability to find a solution.
- Faith in the leader: The follower believes in the leader rather than focusing on the potential solution the leader offers.
- Intellectual agreement: The follower understands the solution offered by the leader.
- Buying the vision: The follower commits to the vision proposed by the leader (ChangingMinds, 2014).

Despite the importance of understanding this concept, it is still not a critical topic in many nursing management and leadership publications or in nursing curricula when leadership is discussed. In many publications there are direct and indirect messages that followership is negative; however when this is seriously considered, how could this be true? Without followers, no work would be done and there would be no need for leaders.

What does it take to be an effective follower? Every new graduate should consider this question, as it is a role that all will assume. Even leaders experience situations when they are followers.

It takes energy to be a follower, although some may think that following is just an automatic response. To be effective, it is not automatic nor is it a passive role that does not involve thinking. It requires development and use of expertise, sharing, understanding of problems, effective communication, and collaboration. It is important, however, to understand that followers do not exist just to become leaders; they have responsibilities as followers and most will not become leaders.

Followers who are contributing to the team or the work environment are eager to add their ideas to the process, to participate actively in decision making, and to feel committed to the process and the vision. These followers trust the leader and recognize the importance of sharing feelings and concerns. They also feel comfortable discussing their own limitations. One should not view followers as insignificant or invisible because if they are, they are not effective followers. It is important for leaders to develop trust in their relationships with team members/followers. An important strategy that increases mutual trust between leaders and others is leaders who keep promises and, when promises cannot be kept, offer explanations, give and encourage honest feedback, and reward followers. All of these strategies build mutual trust.

TEAM STRUCTURE AND PROCESS

Teams do not just appear as fully functioning effective teams; rather they develop through team leadership and team members who are committed to team goals. The team's structure and processes are gradually developed. Team leaders need to assess the individual team members and the team as a whole, considering styles of followers, communication team purpose, roles, and so on, to determine what needs to be improved to make the team even more effective.

Team Tasks and Functions

Typical team roles besides the leader role are participant and service roles such as recorder, observer, resource person, and timekeeper. Participants are the real team workers when they focus on doing the job, whatever it might be. The leader is the team guide who facilitates the work of all members of the team. To ensure that there is documentation of team activities, the recorder or secretary records minutes from team meetings. Some teams also have an observer who observes the process and shares this information with the team, a timekeeper to watch the time for specific discussions and meetings, and a resource person who provides specific content or expertise. The latter three roles are typically used for specific tasks or periods of time. An example might be when a team must produce a particular report or a team is having a thorough discussion that is conflictual. Clinical teams usually do not have all of these service roles, and the leader may have a more formal role defined in a specific organizational position description.

Teams that develop an identity are more successful. "Effective teams have a culture that fosters openness, collaboration, teamwork, and learning from mistakes" (Institute of Medicine, 2001, p. 132). The team leader and members may actively move toward developing this identity. Some methods for developing identification are matching coffee mugs and T-shirts and use of a team name. These may appear to be unimportant, but they do support the idea that "we are in this together." Teams begin to develop inside jokes and stories that mean something to them, and if they interact in informal situations, this also builds team cohesiveness. All of this also develops team spirit, which affects outcomes and how team members pitch in to help one another. They will be more tolerant of one another and more able to recognize when team members need help. Team members will also feel more comfortable asking for help. Sharing knowledge and skills then becomes the norm in the team because the team feels connected and has a team identity.

Teams exist to get a job done, and they need to be active. This involves both talking and doing. The major **team function** is to complete the assigned task(s). This task can vary from planning and development to actually implementing a proposed action such as delivering patient care or providing an educational program for the staff. The team needs to clearly understand its purpose(s), timeline, and relationship to other parts of the organization. Effective team function also means that members need to be committed to improvement—both in how they work together and in their outcomes. Delegation is also a critical skill for team leaders and team members who will be delegating. (See Chapter 15.) It can make a key difference in the effectiveness of the team.

The type of team affects its tasks and functions. A clinical team provides care, and thus, tasks and functions are centered on patient care. A team that is formed to complete a specific project such as change in documentation would include tasks and functions related to literature research and contacting other HCOs to learn about their documentation review, development of forms, methods for ensuring that standards are met, planning staff orientation, and planning and implementing a pilot.

Team Size and Composition

Team size is a common concern when teams are developed. In some situations, such as a clinical team, the size may be predetermined based on the number and types of staff required to provide care for a specific number of patients. A general principle related to size is that the team should include the smallest number necessary to do the assigned task. Size is directly related to team effectiveness. Seven or more members are difficult to manage in a team. Another issue that is related to team composition is whether or not participation in the team is voluntary or involuntary. Again, in a clinical situation if the team model is the delivery model, then all clinical staff, such as RNs, licensed practical/vocational nurses (LPN/LVN), unlicensed assistive personnel (UAP), and so on, would be assigned to teams. Volunteer team membership can be found in some organizational committees, while in other situations staff may be assigned to project teams or to committees. Volunteer membership is better as staff will usually then feel more committed, although this is not always clear. For example, a nurse may be told that participation on a committee will improve chances for a promotion. The nurse may have a choice in which committee to join or may be assigned or elected. Professional organizations are, for the most part, run by volunteers through committees. Again, this fact may not be so clear. A nurse may volunteer for a committee because this will "look good" on the nurse's résumé, but commitment to the committee's work may be variable and not known.

EFFECTIVE TEAMS

What is an effective team? Various characteristics have been used to describe effective teams, including the following tips for effective team functioning:

- Learn about other team members' expertise, background, knowledge, and values.
- Learn individual roles and processes required to work collaboratively.
- Demonstrate basic group skills, including communication, negotiation, delegation, time management, and assessment of group dynamics.
- Ensure that accurate and timely information reaches those who need it at the appropriate time.
- Customize care and manage smooth transitions across settings and over time, even when the team members are in entirely different physical locations.
- Coordinate and integrate care processes to ensure excellence, continuity, and reliability of the care provided.
- Resolve conflicts with other members of the team.
- Communicate with other members of the team in a shared language, even when the members are in entirely different physical locations (Institute of Medicine, 2003, p. 56).

Stages of Team Development

In 1965 Tuckman, a psychologist, developed a method for describing team development, which is easy to apply to teams (MindTools®, 2014b; Tuckman, 1965). These stages are highlighted in Box 12-1.

1. ***Forming, or the initial orientation.*** During the first stage, **forming**, the team members are learning about one another, and trust is not likely to be high at this time. If the task(s) is complex or unclear, anxiety may be experienced. As the team meets, it focuses on developing trust and team member working relationships, although this may not actually be stated. Team members begin assessing their roles in the context of the team. A leader is identified or may be identified prior to the first meeting. For a clinical team, there is typically an identified person or position that is always the formal leader, such as the nurse team leader. Informal leaders, however, may develop within the team as time goes by.
2. ***Storming, or the stage of conflict and confusion.*** At the time of the second stage, **storming**, team members see themselves as individuals and want to respond to the task in the manner

BOX 12-1	STAGES OF TEAM DEVELOPMENT

1. Forming	3. Norming
2. Storming	4. Performing

they would respond to tasks as individuals. Some members may be reluctant to really work as a team, and others may be restless with the need to get through the **team building** activities to the task. It may be noticed at this time that some members attempt to control the team and its communication. Other team members should step in to avert this move so the members function as a team. Conflict can arise from this process. As this stage begins to change into norming, the next stage, the team will formulate team rules that will guide team members in their performance, interaction, decision making, and how they accomplish their goals (MindTools®, 2014b). Ideally these rules are developed during the norming stage; however, during the storming stage, the team begins to consider these rules. When rules are considered, one needs to factor in the HCO's requirements that may affect team rules such as meeting requirements, minutes, and attendance. What might be included in these team rules?

- Definition of purpose
- Meeting schedule, days, time, and place
- Documentation requirements for meetings
- Attendance at meetings, requirements, and what happens if one does not attend
- Confidentiality
- Roles and responsibilities
- Assignment of tasks
- Sharing of information
- Collaboration and assisting one another
- Consensus process and decision making
- Evaluation of work

3. *Norming, or the stage of consolidation around tasks.* The **norming** stage starts as team members begin to work together, establish their roles, and help one another see value in this; thus, team cohesion develops. At this point, members must appreciate one another's strengths and limitations.

4. *Performing, or the stage of teamwork and performance.* When work is getting done and the team feels positive about this, the **performing** stage has arrived. If interpersonal issues arise, they can be worked through within the team. An important part of this stage is consensus building that occurs as decisions are made. Time is an important issue, which is dependent on the nature of the decisions that need to be made. Clinical decisions typically have the highest pressure for decision making. Many clinical decisions do not require consensus, or the consensus may be decided outside the team (for example, by using a clinical pathway). The team then decides when to use the clinical pathway. Individual team members may need to make some decisions (for example, a physician may need to order a medical procedure or medication). Other issues that the patient may encounter, such as discharge problems, may be something the treatment team discusses before reaching a consensus to determine the best approach.

As the team members suggest ideas and approaches for the team to take, there are some factors that need to be considered. When suggestions are made, the reasons behind the suggestions and opinions should also be provided. It is important to ask others for information and their opinions. This would, of course, be other team members, but it may also mean seeking out others outside the team who have specific expertise. As one presents a suggestion or opinion, the team should be open to ideas and contributions made by others to make the team's work even better.

Conflict can arise when consensus is developed. However, this is not necessarily a negative situation as long as the conflict addresses the issues and does not focus on personalities of team members. The latter situation will be destructive to the team's work. Team members have the responsibility for suggesting alternatives when they disagree with other team members (MindTools®, 2014b). Consensus is also not a unanimous agreement but rather a general agreement. All team members must agree to support the decision although all may not totally agree with it. All feelings or reactions to the decision should then be expressed appropriately, and if needed, are dealt with to allow the team to function effectively.

Motivation and Team Success

It is difficult to discuss any work issue without considering motivation. Motivation relates to individual staff members, teams, management, components of the organization (units, divisions, departments), and the organization as a whole. Theories of leadership and management often address motivation. Motivation is important to the team leader and the team members because it affects whether or not the team works effectively; therefore, it is important to understand motivation. What is motivation and how does it affect work?

MOTIVATION THEORIES   The willingness to work and the ability to work go hand-in-hand. **Motivation** is the desire to do something. Knowledge about what drives a person to work is key for all who hold any leadership position and for those who work on teams. Motivation is related to behavior, performance, satisfaction, and rewards. Mobilizing the team to meet the outcomes is an important role for the team leader. Motivation theories vary, and there is no one correct or universally accepted motivation theory. The following is a brief historical review of some of the major motivation theories and their impact on management.

- **Maslow:** Maslow's theory of motivation focuses on a need hierarchy (Maslow, 1943). These needs are physiological (the lowest level); safety and security; belongingness, social, and love; esteem; and self-actualization. People attempt to satisfy the lower needs first. His theory emphasizes that once a need is met then it no longer motivates the person. If a need is not satisfied, the person may feel stress, frustration, and conflict, which can affect performance.
- **Herzberg:** Herzberg's two-factor theory of motivation, extrinsic (dissatisfiers) and intrinsic (satisfiers) was originally based on research of engineers and accountants (Herzberg, Mausner, & Snyderman, 1959). It was thought to oversimplify the nature of job satisfaction, as it did not look at unconscious factors that might affect motivation.
- **McClelland:** McClelland's learned needs theory focuses on three needs: (1) the need for achievement, (2) the need for affiliation, and (3) the need for power (McClelland, 1962). The achievement need encourages a person to set goals, challenging one to achieve those goals. The affiliation need pushes a person toward social interaction, which affects motivation as few things can be achieved without others. The need for power focuses on the person's efforts to obtain and exercise power and authority. The theory supports the idea that people learn about these needs as they learn to cope with their environment. If they are learned, then behavior that is rewarded will probably increase. This theory is different from Maslow's and McClelland's in that it focuses on socially acquired needs.
- **Skinner:** Skinner's theory identifies reinforcement as its key factor. By accepting the importance of reinforcement, one understands that rewarding behavior encourages continuation of the behavior, and punishing for specific behavior may decrease or stop the behavior (Skinner, 1953).
- **Equity theory:** Equity theory emphasizes that staff make comparisons of their own efforts and rewards with those of others who work in similar jobs or situations. The critical question for the employees is "Are they equivalent?" (Adams, 1963). If inequity is felt, then staff tension rises, which affects motivation. This tension, however, may work one of two ways. The staff member may feel that less work is required because some staff may be getting the same reward with less effort. The staff members may also feel that more work or effort are required if they recognize that others are working at a higher level and receiving additional rewards. This is a theory that most staff can probably relate to easily.
- **Theory X and Theory Y:** Theory X and Theory Y are related and based on earlier theories of staff motivation described by McGregor in 1960 (McGregor, 1960). Theory X focuses on authoritarian management and Theory Y on participative management, with Theory Y focusing on staff motivation gained from working rather than forcing or controlling staff (MindTools®, 2015).

ASSESSMENT OF THE MOTIVATIONAL CLIMATE   Understanding a person's motivation is helpful in developing strategies to increase a person's motivation and to better understand the team's motivation. The critical questions are: "What makes a person work?" and "What makes a person want to improve work performance?" Methods that might be used to increase motivation include observation, asking staff, and comparing and contrasting outcomes with rewards that staff receive. When people are identified as having poor motivation, how are they usually described? Typical descriptors a person demonstrates are lack of energy, lack of initiative, poor communication, lack of follow through, low socialization at work, and no "get up and go." It is helpful to watch for changes in self and others. Motivation at work is also affected by personal problems and thus may interfere with staff motivation.

STRATEGIES TO IMPROVE MOTIVATION   Rewarding team members for achieved outcomes and effective performance is critical in developing the team and improving and supporting motivation. Recognizing effort should never be taken for granted. There will be times when team members or the team as a whole will excel, and it is particularly important to recognize these times. There will also be times when things do not go well, and these times cannot be ignored. The focus should be on improvement and moving forward, not on dwelling on errors (although they do need to be analyzed if improvement is to take place). Typical methods used to motivate staff are salary/pay, benefits, position titles, recognition awards that may also be monetary, positive feedback, and asking a staff member to assume a leadership function, which may be short term or long term. If the latter is just done to add on more work, then this will not be viewed as a motivator. The decision to use the reward method depends on the individual, situation, policies and procedures, roles and responsibilities, and timing.

Building Team Power and Spirit

The development of effective teams does not just happen nor is there an end point as teams are always evolving and developing. One cannot just put a group of staff members together, call them a team, and assume they will function as a team with very little change and be motivated to meet team goals. As described in the stages of team development, it takes time and effort to really build a team. Empowerment is also relevant to team functioning. When people work together, such as on a team, power issues do arise. There are different agendas, personal and team, that may conflict. Teams and individual team members can feel powerless when they think their ideas are not considered or no one is listening. **Power** means a person can influence others and decisions. To empower is to enable to act. **Empowerment**, however, means that some may lose power and prestige. In organizations that truly practice shared participation in decision making, middle management tends to lose the most, turning over power and authority to teams. A key question that those who are empowered often ask and should ask is, "What am I empowered to do?" If this is not clear, then more questions need to be asked. Muddled empowerment is worse than no empowerment because this often increases errors, frustration and conflict, and decreases motivation.

Empowered teams are involved in a process of self-control and feel a responsibility for the team's performance. Empowerment does not mean telling someone or a team exactly what he or she must do but rather giving some direction when required and giving the team authority to do the task(s) without having to wait for approval and other management control methods. More content about continuous quality improvement is found in Chapters 17 and 18, but quality is also related to teamwork and empowerment. What happens to a team that feels empowered? An empowered team feels confident to make decisions and to assess its own work. The team recognizes its role and responsibilities and knows it will get the support needed to get the job done. The development of team relationships is critical. Developing team spirit and a concern for one another will go a long way in setting up an environment in which the team can function effectively. Providing informal time for team members to get to know one another may develop positive team function. Developing communication on multiple levels also builds team spirit as well as commitment to a common vision and goals that recognize the value of individuals and the team. Team conflict typically interferes with productivity, though there are times when conflict may lead to recognition of problems that need to be resolved to improve teamwork. See Chapter 13 for information about conflict and conflict resolution.

Barriers to Team Success

As teams improve their functioning, which needs to be continuous improvement, teams do encounter barriers. Teams must address these barriers to become more effective, and this, too, should be a continuous process. Barriers come and go and are affected by many factors. Ineffective

APPLYING EVIDENCE-BASED PRACTICE

Evidence for Effective Leadership and Practice

CITATION: Hassmiller, S. (2009). Envisioning a future of nurse leaders in the boardroom. *NSNA Imprint*, November–December, pp. 28–30. Retrieved from http://campaignforaction.org/sites/default/files/Hassmiller-Envision-Future-Nurse-Leaders.pdf

OVERVIEW: Healthcare organization boards are the top-level decision-making body for healthcare organizations. Nurses have slowly developed as leaders in healthcare organizations, starting with positions as director of nurses and moving to positions of leadership that are responsible for more than just nursing services. Are nurse leaders ready for the next step?

APPLICATION: What do nurse leaders need to do to serve on healthcare organization boards and to be active participants on this critical type of HCO team? The Board of Directors is a team, a high level administrative team.

Questions:

1. What data are presented describing the engagement of nurse leaders on healthcare organization boards?
2. Why is it important that nurse leaders serve on healthcare organization boards? Why is a board a team?
3. What does the author mean by the "bigger issues"? Why are they important?

teams may be focused on just an individual team or system-wide problems in implementing effective work teams. When the nursing staff is not prepared or does not understand teams and teamwork, this has a major impact. Inadequate intrapersonal skills and communication competency are barriers. If the nursing staff is unwilling to assume leadership roles and ownership of work, this leads to problems within teams. Shared governance relies heavily on teams, but if the organization supports shared governance in name only and not in action, then teams are not empowered. Ineffective communication throughout an HCO interferes with team communication and the effectiveness of communication as it moves outside the team. If the staff are not given time to complete work required for the team functions, then many staff members will be passive about the team's work and assignments. It takes time for a team to form and become productive, and sometimes administration and even team members do not recognize this. This leads to frustration and giving up before the team can really function.

A team typically recognizes when it is not meeting its goals. Every team needs to take time to assess its outcomes and use this information and process to improve. This is no different than evaluating patient care for an individual patient. A nurse knows there are problems with the patient's care when patient outcomes are not met. Another indicator of unproductive teams is the use of cautious or guarded communication, which indicates a low level of trust among team members or inadequate team communication with others in the organization. The level of disagreement can also be used to evaluate a team as it is not healthy. People should not agree all the time, but disagreement should not be frequent or interfere with work—team members should be able to move forward after disagreement and resolve concerns.

Groupthink can be another barrier to effective team functioning. This occurs when the team members reach a unanimous agreement that is based on pressure to conform. This limits the team from considering options that might actually be better solutions (Mindtools®, 2014a). Why does this happen? The common reasons are as follows:

- There is team pressure on each member to agree with everyone else.
- The team feels separated from the consequences of its actions.
- General closed-mindedness prevails.
- The team ignores suggestions and demonstrates irrational thinking.
- Members censor thoughts that go against team ideas.

This type of approach to decision making leads the team to poor judgment because the team is unable to effectively consider alternative courses of action. To prevent groupthink, it is important to recognize the value of some level of disagreement and the need for all team members to stretch themselves and consider alternatives.

Dysfunctional meetings can indicate a lack of enthusiasm, inability to reach decisions, control by some team members or unclear communication. How might a staff nurse evaluate a team meeting? A meeting should have a clear purpose that is stated so everyone who attends the meeting knows it. Minutes of previous meetings should be available. The team leader should set an agenda and ensure that it is followed. If the discussion wanders off the agenda, the team needs to be pulled back on track. Maybe the topic needs to be added to another agenda. All members should be respected and allow one another to express opinions. Some teams develop rules for their meetings. Everyone should agree to follow the rules. The team leader or whoever is leading the meeting should not dominate the discussion or cut off team members. There may be times, however, when the leader indicates it is time to conclude a discussion to maintain the agenda. At the end of the meeting, there should be a short summary of what was accomplished, identifying next steps, responsibilities, and timelines. Having a lively discussion does not mean the meeting is dysfunctional as long as the discussion stays on the planned agenda. Team members need to be engaged as this is a sign of commitment, plus there will be more sharing of more ideas. If a team member dreads going to a meeting and feels nothing is accomplished in meetings, then there are problems in the team meeting. The best approach is to discuss this with the team and determine strategies to use to improve teamwork.

Getting the Job Done

Using teams to better ensure effective care can lead to good outcomes (Fabre, 2005). Workload can be distributed so staff are not overburdened. This can decrease the risk of errors and staff fatigue, stress, and frustration. Teams build on synergy so more is accomplished. "Synergy occurs when a group (team) achieves more together than the sum of what the group/team members could have accomplished individually" (Fabre, 2005, p. 117). Working together using the best each member has to offer leads to better use of everyone's intellectual capacity and experience. This should lead to improved patient care and other team outcomes. Teams promote accountability and staff retention. If a team thinks as one, this can be a disadvantage. Yes, consensus is needed for decisions, but there are times when first it is best to explore multiple solutions and select the best. Team members need to value diversity, think critically and use clinical reasoning and judgment, and use synergy. Each member needs to build self-esteem. Clear communication is critical to getting the job done effectively. (See Chapter 14.)

THE CHARGE NURSE OR SHIFT MANAGER AND THE TEAM

Methods used for selecting charge nurses or shift managers vary from one HCO to another. Common methods are permanent charge nurses per shift (who may be assistant nurse managers) or rotating charge nurses per shift. The charge nurse is typically not the nurse manager. The major responsibility of the charge nurse is to ensure that the unit is managed effectively and patient care is delivered in a quality, safe manner for a specific shift. A charge nurse needs to understand the organization, job responsibilities, and those who are supervised and must also demonstrate clinical and managerial competencies. The charge nurse considers the broad unit perspective, and the team leaders focus on their individual groups of patients. All nurses who hold the position of charge nurse or team leader either permanently or temporarily need to practice self-evaluation. Nurses who are charge nurses or team leaders should be able to assess themselves by considering the following: whether they listen to staff, trust staff, are consistent, communicate clearly, and guide rather than dictate to staff.

Both the charge nurse and the team leader must spend a lot of time making decisions and ensuring that work gets done. Typically a charge nurse is responsible for several teams that are providing care, and each team has a team leader. If teams are not used, the charge nurse supervises a large number of staff who have individual assignments. As has been pointed out in this text, the work will be easier and more effective if the charge nurse cultivates staff participation in decision making and encourages collaboration. Working with several teams requires the nurse manager and charge nurse to understand team strengths and limitations; share appropriate, timely information with the teams; and assist teams by providing needed resources whenever possible. The latter requires an awareness of team needs and also asking teams what resources they need. Interpersonal skills are constantly tested as work is assigned and evaluated and staff coordinates care; therefore, it is important for nurses who hold either of these positions to be competent in these areas just as it is for a team leader. Both the charge nurse and team leaders hold similar positions with related required competencies; however, the charge nurse carries a larger responsibility for the unit or service during a specific shift, while the team leader focuses on part of that unit or service. Figure 12-1 provides an example of teams and competencies for success.

Creates a Positive Environment **Leaders have the responsibility to establish and maintain positive expectations and attitudes that produce the setting for healthy relationships and effective work behaviors. Leaders are charged with improving the organization while accomplishing missions. They should leave the organization better that it was when they arrived.**	
Fosters teamwork, cohesion, cooperation, and loyalty	• Encourages people to work together effectively. • Promotes teamwork and team achievement to build trust. • Draws attention to the consequences of poor coordination. • Acknowledges and rewards successful team coordination. • Integrates new members into the unit quickly.
Encourages subordinates to exercise initiative, accept responsibility, and take ownership	• Involves others in decisions and keeps them informed of consequences that affect them. • Allocates responsibility for performance. • Guides subordinate leaders in thinking through problems for themselves. • Allocates decision making to the lowest appropriate level. • Acts to expand and enhance subordinate's competence and self-confidence. • Rewards initiative.
Creates a learning environment	• Uses effective assessment and training methods. • Encourages leaders and their subordinates to reach their full potential. • Motivates others to develop themselves. • Expresses the value of interacting with others and seeking counsel. • Stimulates innovative and critical thinking in others. • Seeks new approaches to problems.
Encourages open and candid communications	• Shows others how to accomplish tasks while remaining respectful, resolute, and focused. • Communicates a positive attitude to encourage others and improve morale. • Reinforces the expression of contrary and minority viewpoints. • Displays appropriate reactions to new or conflicting information or opinions. • Guards against groupthink.
Encourages fairness and inclusiveness	• Provides accurate evaluations and assessments. • Supports equal opportunity. • Prevents all forms of harassment. • Encourages learning about and leveraging diversity.
Expresses and demonstrates care for people and their well-being	• Encourages subordinates and peers to express candid opinions. • Ensures that subordinates and their families are provided for, including their health, welfare, and development. • Stands up for subordinates. • Routinely monitors morale and encourages honest feedback.
Anticipates people's on-the-job needs	• Recognizes and monitors subordinate's needs and reactions. • Shows concern for the impact of tasks and missions on subordinate morale.
Sets and maintains high expectations for individuals and teams	• Clearly articulates expectations. • Creates a climate that expects good performance, recognizes superior performance, and does not accept poor performance. • Challenges others to match the leader's example.
Accepts reasonable setbacks and failures	• Communicates the difference between maintaining professional standards and a zero-defects mentality. • Expresses the importance of being competent and motivated but recognizes the occurrence of failure. • Emphasizes learning from one's mistakes.

Figure 12-1 Competency: Creates a positive environment and associated components and actions

Source: U.S. Army. (2006). *Army leadership: Competent, confident, and agile.* Retrieved from http://fas.org/irp/doddir/army/fm6-22.pdf.

TeamSTEPPS®: AN ORGANIZED APPROACH TO TEAMS

Teams are also used to address quality care issues in healthcare organizations. One of the processes used today is TeamSTEPPS®, which was developed by the government. This process is described in Box 12-2. It is a structured team analysis approach that assists in the development of solutions for healthcare quality problems. There are numerous resources available on the TeamSTEPPS® website (Agency for Healthcare Research and Quality, 2015).

BOX 12-2	TeamSTEPPS®

ABOUT TeamSTEPPS®

TeamSTEPPS® is a teamwork system designed for health care professionals that is:

- A powerful solution to improving patient safety within your organization.
- An evidence-based teamwork system to improve communication and teamwork skills among health care professionals.
- A source for ready-to-use materials and a training curriculum to successfully integrate teamwork principles into all areas of your health care system.
- Scientifically rooted in more than 20 years of research and lessons from the application of teamwork principles.
- Developed by Department of Defense's Patient Safety Program in collaboration with the Agency for Healthcare Research and Quality.

TeamSTEPPS® provides higher quality, safer patient care by:

- Producing highly effective medical teams that optimize the use of information, people, and resources to achieve the best clinical outcomes for patients.
- Increasing team awareness and clarifying team roles and responsibilities.
- Resolving conflicts and improving information sharing.
- Eliminating barriers to quality and safety.

TeamSTEPPS® has a three-phased process aimed at creating and sustaining a culture of safety with:

- A pretraining assessment for site readiness.
- Training for onsite trainers and healthcare staff.
- Implementation and sustainment.

The TeamSTEPPS® curriculum is an easy-to-use comprehensive multimedia kit that contains:

- Fundamentals modules in text and presentation format.
- A pocket guide that corresponds with the essentials version of the course.
- Video vignettes to illustrate key concepts.
- Workshop materials, including a supporting CD and DVD, on change management, coaching, and implementation.

THREE PHASES OF THE TeamSTEPPS® DELIVERY SYSTEM

The three phases of TeamSTEPPS® are based on lessons learned, existing master trainer or change agent experience, the literature of quality and patient safety, and culture change. A successful TeamSTEPPS® initiative requires a thorough assessment of the organization and its processes and a carefully developed implementation and sustainment plan.

PHASE 1—ASSESS THE NEED

The goal of Phase 1 is to determine an organization's readiness for undertaking a TeamSTEPPS®-based initiative. Such practice is typically referred to as a training needs analysis, which is a necessary first step to implementing a teamwork initiative. For more information about conducting a needs assessment see website.

PHASE 2—PLANNING, TRAINING, AND IMPLEMENTATION

Phase 2 is the planning and execution segment of the TeamSTEPPS® initiative. Because TeamSTEPPS® was designed to be tailored to the organization, options in this phase include implementation of all tools and strategies in the entire organization, a phased-in approach that targets specific units or departments, or selection of individual tools introduced at specific intervals (called a "dosing strategy" in TeamSTEPPS® parlance). As long as the primary learning objectives are maintained, the TeamSTEPPS® materials are extremely adaptable. For more information about planning, training, and implementing see the TeamSTEPPS® website.

PHASE 3—SUSTAINMENT

The goal of Phase 3 is to sustain and spread improvements in teamwork performance, clinical processes, and outcomes resulting from the TeamSTEPPS® initiative. The key objective is to ensure opportunities exist to implement the tools and strategies taught, practice and receive feedback on skills, and provide continual reinforcement of the TeamSTEPPS® principles on the unit or within the department. For more information on sustaining TeamSTEPPS® initiatives, go to the website.

DETAILS OF A SITE ASSESSMENT

A site assessment entails identifying opportunities for improvement; determining the readiness of the institution, such as leadership support; identifying potential barriers to implementing change; and deciding whether resources are in place to successfully support the initiative. Each part of the Phase 1 assessment is described below.

1. Establish an organizational-level change team.
   - The organizational-level change team should consist of a multidisciplinary group that represents the breadth of health care professionals within the organization. Successful change teams are comprised of organizational leaders who are committed to changing the current culture.

BOX 12-2   (CONTINUED)

2. Conduct a site assessment.
   - A site assessment, also called team training needs analysis, is a process for systematically identifying teamwork deficiencies so training programs can be developed to address those deficiencies. This information is then used to identify critical training and develop training objectives.
3. Define the problem, challenge, or opportunity for improvement.
   - The team must identify the recurring problem that threatens patient safety and then determine how this problem results from existing processes and procedures. The team should devise a flowchart or map of the process during which the problem occurs. With information and processes properly mapped, it becomes clear what interventions are needed, what the objective of these interventions should be, and how ready the organization is to engage in these interventions.
4. Define the goal of your intervention.
   - List the goals that will reduce or eliminate the risk to safe patient care. For each goal, state in one sentence what will be achieved, who will be involved (whose behavior will change), and when and where the change will occur. Ideally, a team process goal, a team outcome goal, and a clinical outcome goal will be defined.

DETAILS FOR PLANNING, TRAINING, AND IMPLEMENTATION OF TeamSTEPPS®

The tools and strategies needed to address opportunities for improvement in an organization will be determined by the Phase 1 assessment. The next step is to develop a customized Implementation and Action Plan, followed by training and implementation. Below is a brief description of steps for planning, training, and implementation.

1. Define the TeamSTEPPS® intervention.
   - Decide whether "whole training" (all the tools in one sitting) or "dosing" (specific tools targeted to specific interventions) is the best intervention tactic. Whole training optimizes teamwork but does not maximize learning. It can also lead to overload or uncertainty about which tools best fit improvement opportunities. Dosing is the recommended approach because it allows for direct linking of tools and strategies with specific opportunities for improvement to minimize training fatigue and overload.
2. Develop a plan for determining the intervention's effectiveness.
   - There are a variety of ways to evaluate the impact of training. The plan should assess whether trainees have acquired new knowledge, skills, or attitudes at the end of training; if individuals are taking their learning back to the workplace and using it on the job; and organizational outcomes.
3. Develop an implementation plan.
   - Assess what groups will be trained, the order in which they will be trained (if not together and all at once), and what level of training they will receive. Include in the plan who will conduct training and where and when training will take place.

4. Gain leadership commitment to the plan.
   - Inform leaders of all facets of the plan, including how much time will be used for training and the desired resources to support it. Leadership commitment often yields plan refinement. The key is to know what elements of the plan cannot be altered.
5. Develop a communication plan.
   - Develop a plan for communicating what will be done and how the goal will be achieved. Leaders (both designated and situational) should provide information to all those in their departments or units about the initiative. It is crucial to tie together all activities that will take place with the overall goal for the initiative (i.e., improved patient safety).
6. Prepare the institution.
   - For any initiative to be fully successful, transfer of training must be achieved. Transfer is achieved by ensuring new knowledge or skills are learned and applied in the work environment. The change team must ensure the work environment is prepared to foster transfer of training so new tools and strategies are applied on the job.
7. Implement training.
   - The most effective strategy for delivering the training initiative is one that involves teams of trainers that include physicians, nursing staff, and support staff. A combination of the curricula is recommended when training different sets of staff independently. The TeamSTEPPS® system includes three different medical team training curricula and a complete suite of multimedia course materials:
     1. **Train-the-Trainer.** This 2.5-day training course is designed to create a cadre of teamwork instructors with the skills to train and coach other staff members.
     2. **TeamSTEPPS® Fundamentals.** This curriculum includes 4 to 6 hours of interactive workshops for direct patient care providers.
     3. **TeamSTEPPS® Essentials.** This curriculum is a 1- to 2-hour condensed version of the Fundamentals Course and is specifically designed for nonclinical support staff.

DETAILS FOR SUSTAINING A TeamSTEPPS® INTERVENTION

The designated change team manages sustaining interventions through coaching and observing team performance. An effective sustainment plan should account for ongoing assessment of the effectiveness of the intervention, sustainment of positive changes, and identification of opportunities for further improvements. Below is a brief description of the steps to include in a TeamSTEPPS® sustainment plan.

1. Provide opportunities to practice.
   - Any TeamSTEPPS® based initiative will be much more successful if the change team accounts for opportunities to practice these behaviors. It is important to embed opportunities for practice in day-to-day functions.
2. Ensure leaders emphasize new skills.
   - Leaders play a critical role in sustainment because they are responsible for emphasizing daily the skills learned in

(continued)

BOX 12-2	TeamSTEPPS® (CONTINUED)

TeamSTEPPS® training. The goal is for leaders to engage in activities that will ensure continuous involvement in teamwork.

3. Provide regular feedback and coaching.
   - Regular feedback and coaching are key to ensuring interventions are sustained. Change team members, champions from the unit, and leaders should develop and use a coaching and feedback plan that allows for sufficient observation and feedback opportunities.

4. Celebrate wins.
   - Celebrating wins bolsters further sustainment and engagement in teamwork. When using a TeamSTEPPS®-based initiative, it is critical to celebrate successes for two reasons. First, it recognizes the efforts of those who were engaged from the beginning, and second, it provides detractors or laggards a tangible example of how teamwork has improved the current operations.

5. Measure success.
   - The change team should measure success by demonstrating satisfaction with training, learning, the effective use of tools and strategies on the job, and changes in processes and outcomes. It is useful to ensure that measurement of pretraining factors is parallel with post-training factors so changes can be assessed.

6. Update the plan.
   - The final stage in any TeamSTEPPS®-based intervention is to revise the plan as the organization's needs change. The change team should determine when organizational needs have changed and ensure the sustainment plan continues to focus on the needs of the organization or unit where the intervention has been implemented.

Source: Agency for Healthcare Research and Quality. About TeamSTEPPS®. Retrieved May 20, 2010, from http://teamstepps.ahrq.gov/about-2cl_3.htm

APPLYING LEADERSHIP AND MANAGEMENT

My Hospital Unit: An Evolving Case Experience

You are developing your annual plan for your unit. From data you have received from staff, other care providers, patients and families, and quality improvement, you recognize that the unit does not use teams effectively. The entire hospital is moving to interprofessional teams. Develop your plan to move your unit to interprofessional teams, including how you would work with other healthcare providers on the unit. The plan should be clear and identify steps you will take and whom you will involve in the process. How will you evaluate whether or not you have met your goals? This is your unit, so past decisions you have made may impact current decisions.

BSN and *Master's Essentials*: Application to Content

BSN Essentials (American Association of Colleges of Nursing, 2008) as Applied to this Chapter:

II. Basic Organizational and Systems Leadership for Quality Care and Patient Safety

VI. Interprofessional Communication and Collaboration for Improving Patient Health Outcomes

Master's Essentials (American Association of Colleges of Nursing, 2011) as Applied to this Chapter:

II. Organizational and Systems Leadership

VI. Interprofessional Collaboration for Improving Patient and Population Health Outcomes

Applying AONE Competencies

Identify which of the AONE competencies found in Appendix A apply to the content of this chapter.

Engaging in the Content: Critical Thinking and Clinical Reasoning and Judgment

Discussion Questions

1. How do you function in a team? Team members need to practice self-evaluation of their own participation as a team member or performance as a team member or follower. What might be included in this self-evaluation? A member might begin by keeping a log for a specified period of time that includes contributions to the team as well as those ideas that were not given but were considered by the individual staff member. At the end of the time period, what was the members' overall impact on the team? What was contributed, and what was its value? What was the knowledge level, interest in the topic, willingness to listen to others, and comfort level in participating? Attitudes and behaviors demonstrated in the team should also be considered. Besides the log and evaluation of its content, a team member might ask a coworker or the team leader to critique team participation. Reasons behind effectiveness or ineffectiveness should be analyzed. The final step is to develop a plan of action that addresses improvement areas. This process is the same as that used for any self-assessment process. (Online Application Option)

2. Based on your own experience, do you think the team approach is effective? Provide rationale and examples for your response. (Online Application Option)

3. How is an interprofessional team different from other types of teams?

4. How is a nursing team different from an interprofessional team? What are the advantages to these two types of teams?

5. How does motivation impact teamwork?

6. What is the difference between a group and a team?

Application Exercises

1. Attend a team meeting in a clinical site. Do not participate but simply observe the interactions. Describe the team according to size and composition. Consider the following when you write up your analysis: What were the key team tasks for that meeting? Was the leader clearly identified? What role did the leader take? How did team members interact with each other and with the leader? Did you notice differences in team members based on their positions or disciplines? If so, what did you observe? How would you evaluate the effectiveness of the team based on the meeting you attended?

2. If you have an opportunity to lead a team meeting, do so. You may belong to groups or organizations where you are in a leadership position or there are opportunities to do this. Then evaluate your experience. What would you include in your self-evaluation?

3. Review the material on TeamSTEPPS® provided in the chapter, and go to the TeamSTEPPS® website. Analyze with a team of students how the information on TeamSTEPPS® relates to content in this chapter. Discuss this in your team in class. (Online Application Option)

4. What is your opinion of interprofessional teams? Discuss this in class with your team. Provide examples to support your viewpoint. Each team should then provide a brief summary report to the entire class. (Online Application Option)

5. Review the current literature (past five years) to identify nursing studies that focus on teams. How many studies do you find? What type of studies (quantitative or qualitative)? (Online Application Option)

6. Review the following report: U.S. Department of Health and Human Services report on diabetes prevention (U.S. Department of Health and Human Services, National Diabetes Education Program, 2013). Discuss in teams how this report emphasizes teams and how it relates to content in this chapter. Continue the discussion after reading Chapters 13 and 14.

References

Adams, J. (1963, November). Toward an understanding of inequity. *Journal of Abnormal and Social Psychology, 11*, 422–436.

Agency for Healthcare Research and Quality. (2015). TeamSTEPPS®. Retrieved from http://teamstepps.ahrq.gov/

American Association of Colleges of Nursing. (2008). *The essentials of baccalaureate education for professional nursing practice*. Washington, DC: Author.

American Association of Colleges of Nursing. (2011). *The essentials of master's education in nursing*. Washington, DC: Author.

Caliper. (2005). *The qualities that distinguish women leaders*. Princeton, NJ: Author.

ChangingMinds. (2014). Five reasons to follow. Retrieved from http://changingminds.org/disciplines/leadership/followership/follower_five_reasons.htm

Dartmouth College. (2010). Transforming microsystems in health care. Retrieved May 5, 2010, from https://clinicalmicrosystem.org/

Encyclopedia.com. (2014). Multidisciplinary team. Retrieved from http://www.encyclopedia.com/topic/Multidisciplinary_Team.aspx

Fabre, J. (2005). *Smart nursing*. New York, NY: Springer Publishing Company.

Finkelman, A., & Kenner, C. (2016). *Professional nursing concepts. Competencies for quality leadership* (3rd ed.). Boston, MA: Jones and Bartlett Publishers.

Herzberg, F., Mausner, B., & Snyderman, B. (1959). *The motivation to work*. New York, NY: John Wiley and Sons.

Holden Leadership Center. (2009). Followership. Retrieved from http://leadership.uoregon.edu/resources/exercises_tips/skills/followership/

Institute of Medicine. (2001). *Crossing the quality chasm*. Washington, DC: National Academies Press.

Institute of Medicine. (2003). Excerpt from *Health Professions Education: A Bridge To Quality* by Committee on the Health Professions Education Summit. Washington, DC: National Academies Press.

Institute of Medicine. (2004). *Keeping patients safe: Transforming the work environment for nurses*. Washington, DC: National Academies Press.

Institute of Medicine. (2011). *The future of nursing: Leading change, advancing health*. Washington, DC: National Academies Press.

Maslow, A. (1943, July). A theory of human motivation. *Psychological Review, 4*, 370–396.

McClelland, D. (1962, July–August). Business drive and national achievement. *Harvard Business Review, 4*, 99–112.

McGregor, D. (1960). *The human side of enterprise*. New York, NY: McGraw-Hill.

Michaelsen, L., Parmelee, D., McMahon, K., Levine, R. (Eds.). (2008). *Team-based learning for health professions education: A guide to using small groups for improving learning*. Sterling, VA: Stylus Publishers, Inc.

MindTools®. (2014b). Forming, storming, norming, and performing. Retrieved from http://www.mindtools.com/pages/article/newLDR_86.htm

MindTools®. (2014a). Avoiding groupthink. Retrieved from http://www.mindtools.com/pages/article/newLDR_82.htm

MindTools®. (2015). Theory X and Theory Y. Retrieved from http://www.mindtools.com/pages/article/newLDR_74.htm

Nelson, E., Godfrey, M., Batalden, P., Berry, S., Bothe, A., McKinley, K. . . . Nolan, T. (2008). Clinical microsystems, part 1: The building blocks of health systems. *The Joint Commission Journal on Quality and Patient Safety, 34*(7), 367–378.

Salmon, M. (2007). Guest editorial: Care quality and safety: Same old? *Nursing Outlook, 55*(3), 117–119.

Skinner, B. (1953). *Science and human behavior*. New York, NY: Simon and Schuster.

Spitzer, R. (2008). Teamwork, teams, and reality. *Nurse Leader, 6*(6), 6, 49.

Tuckman, B. (1965). Development sequence in small groups. *Psychological Bulletin, 63*(6), 334–399.

U.S. Department of Health and Human Services, National Diabetes Education Program. (2013). Redesigning the healthcare team: Diabetes prevention and lifelong management. Retrieved from http://ndep.nih.gov/publications/PublicationDetail.aspx?PubId=113#main

Weinstock, M. (March 3, 2010). Team-based care: There's no "I" in team. *H&HN*. Retrieved from http://www.thefreelibrary.com/Team-based+care%3a+there%27s+no+%27I%27+in+team.-a0222555625

13 Improving Teamwork: Collaboration, Coordination, and Conflict Resolution

● LEARNING OUTCOMES

Before you begin, take a moment to familiarize yourself with the learning outcomes for this chapter.

> Analyze key aspects, barriers, and strategies related to collaboration and their impact on staff and healthcare delivery.
> Analyze key aspects, barriers, and strategies related to coordination and their impact on staff and healthcare delivery.
> Examine conflict management, strategies, and their impact on staff.

WHAT'S AHEAD

This chapter continues the discussion about teams, focusing on collaboration, coordination, and conflict resolution as critical competencies needed by every nurse regardless of position, specialty, or type of setting. These skills are directly related to effective leadership and management and teamwork. Healthcare organizations (HCOs) in which staff members collaborate with one another, work together to coordinate care delivery, and strive to resolve conflicts that inevitably will occur will be successful in meeting their goal—to provide quality, safe care. This chapter discusses these three critical competencies and their importance to nursing.

COLLABORATION

The American Nurses Association (ANA) defines **collaboration** as "recognition of the expertise of others within and outside the profession, and referral to those other providers when appropriate. Collaboration involves some shared functions and a common focus on the same overall mission" (2010b, p. 40). This is a critical competency required to practice in any healthcare setting today or to participate in any aspect of healthcare delivery—critical for effective patient-centered, quality care. The increased emphasis on using interprofessional teams to meet the patient's needs across the continuum of care requires collaboration. Team members and different healthcare providers must be able to work together; recognize strengths and limitations; respect individual responsibilities and expertise; and maintain open, effective communication.

Nurses who have long worked on teams should be familiar with teamwork. Despite this, there continues to be a separation between physicians and nurses, who often work in silos. Nurses

KEY TERMS

- **coercive power**
- **collaboration**
- **collaborative planning**
- **conflict**
- **consensus**
- **coordination**
- **empowerment**
- **expert power**
- **felt conflict**
- **informational power**
- **latent conflict**
- **legitimate power**
- **manifest conflict**
- **mediation**
- **negotiation**
- **perceived conflict**
- **persuasive power**
- **power**
- **powerless**
- **referent power**
- **reward power**

and physicians need to work together to ensure that the patient receives the care that is required when it is required. Collaboration involves cooperative effort among all healthcare providers offering care for a patient. This will result in more effective decision making with healthcare professionals working together to accomplish identified outcomes. This is not easy to do. There are professional issues, territory issues, conflicting goals, inadequate communication, and multiple differences; however, despite all of this, effective and efficient care requires collaboration. The system is just too complex to function well without collaboration. The nurse is often the person who must lead the effort to ensure collaboration occurs.

Key Definitions Related to Collaboration

Collaboration is a cooperative effort that focuses on a win-win strategy. To collaborate effectively, each individual needs to recognize the perspective of others who are involved and eventually reach a **consensus** of a common goal(s). The ANA notes that collaboration involves recognition of expertise and some shared functions (2010a, 2010b). The ANA's *Nursing: Scope and Standards of Practice* (2010b) and the *Nursing Administration Scope and Standards of Practice* (2009) also identify the need for collaboration, emphasizing that all nurses are expected to collaborate. The American Organization of Nurse Executives (AONE) also includes the need for collaboration in its descriptions of leadership competencies, as described in Appendix A.

Key concepts related to collaboration are partnership, interdependence, and collective ownership and responsibility. Considering these concepts helps in understanding the impact of collaboration. Collaboration is also a process. It is not stagnant but rather changes, which requires staff to make adjustments to collaborate with others as situations change. The American Association of Critical-Care Nurses' nurse competencies in its Synergy Model™ states: "working with others (e.g., patients, families, healthcare providers) in a way that promotes/encourages each person's contributions toward achieving optimal/realistic patient/family goals; involves intra- and interdisciplinary work with colleagues and the community" (American Association of Critical-Care Nurses, 2014). Most people can remember experiences when working with others where the work just seemed to flow with less stress and good communication. This probably means that the people working together were collaborating.

Collaboration should be a positive experience, but this is not always the case. If it is not positive, it will not be effective. If a group of nurses were surveyed, it would be surprising to get a consensus that collaboration was always a positive experience. Often attempts at collaboration mean struggle, conflict, and sometimes ineffective results. Some research has been conducted to assess the effectiveness of collaboration. The Institute of Medicine (IOM) recognizes the importance of collaboration in its rules to guide healthcare provider behavior in the 21st-century healthcare system (2001). The 10th rule, cooperation among clinicians, emphasizes, "cooperation in patient care is more important than professional prerogatives and roles" (p. 93). To meet this rule, staff need to collaborate and use effective teamwork, which is weak in the healthcare delivery system.

The Future of Nursing: Leading Change, Advancing Health (Institute of Medicine, 2011) includes collaboration in its content. For example, by noting that nursing leadership competencies need to be applied in "a collaborative environment" (p. 8) and "future, primary care and prevention are central drivers of the healthcare system where interprofessional collaboration and coordination are the norm" (p. 2). In its recommendations for priorities in research that focus on teamwork, the report lists "identification of the main barriers to collaboration between nurses and other healthcare staff in a range of settings" (p. 275).

Barriers to Effective Collaboration

As noted by the IOM, working in isolation with concern for only your own profession is not effective; however, nursing also has much work to do to improve the image of nursing and nursing leadership. Salmon (2007) comments that "improvements in care quality and safety will simply not happen with nurses working by themselves. To take it a step beyond what may seem obvious, it can't happen just by adding physicians to the equation. It's going to take the partnered engagement of other clinicians, health administrators, and, ultimately, the public" (p. 117). Given these issues, how does the nursing profession arrive at the right balance, one that focuses on nursing and its professional role and needs, while simultaneously developing nurses who can work collaboratively with others to meet positive patient outcomes? Collaboration requires an interactive process. If staff are not willing to interact or have any other barrier to interaction, collaboration cannot take place. Lack of understanding about the roles and responsibilities of others and lack of respect for what others have to contribute interferes with effective collaboration. How much do nurses know about what physicians or social workers or physical therapists or others do and vice versa? If there is distrust, collaboration is hindered because distrust affects willingness to share information, which is an integral component in the collaborative relationship. Collaboration has an impact on whether or not a team is effective or ineffective as team members need to work with each other to develop effective teams and also need to work with others external to the team. Conflict may arise as teams and individual staff work together. Conflict and conflict resolution are discussed in more detail later in this chapter. Although each nurse must develop individual expertise, this expertise must come together with others' expertise. Few nurses really can work effectively in isolation. Nursing is a profession that requires contact with others—patients, other nursing staff, other healthcare professionals, families, community members, and so on.

Competencies and Strategies to Achieve Effective Collaboration

The increased emphasis on interprofessional teams to meet the patient's needs across the continuum of care requires effective use of collaboration. The very nature of a team implies that there is more than one idea or approach and not all can usually be accomplished. Decisions need to be made, and this is where collaboration comes into play. It is important to remember that collaboration is also a critical factor in the nurse-patient relationship. Nurses need to actively pursue patient collaboration to ensure that patients are involved in their own care—patient-centered care. The nursing profession has long emphasized patient participation in planning care and in patient education. Collaboration is also important in the development of effective management. To be effective in collaboration, staff require a number of skills:

- Communication skills are critical. Verbal skills are the focus; however, in some instances written communication is also important when information and process are described in written format.
- Staff members also need to be aware of their own feelings, as was discussed in some of the leadership theories such as emotional intelligence.
- Staff need to be able to make decisions to solve problems effectively.
- As is discussed in this chapter, coordination is also important when collaborating with others.
- Conflicts will arise, which may interfere with collaboration. Staff need to develop negotiation skills to be used in resolving difficult conflicts.
- Assessment skills are needed to collect and analyze information as collaborative relationships develop. Box 13-1 highlights these skills.

Collaborative care is central to the success of efficient, outcome-driven care. With the complex healthcare system, specialization of many healthcare professionals, variety of healthcare settings, complex reimbursement systems, technology, and new drugs, collaboration is the only way that patients will receive quality, cost-effective care. Today the healthcare system is an interdependent system with multiple settings and a variety of healthcare professionals, who are dependent on one another. Delivery of care in this complex system requires sharing of information, analysis, critical thinking, clinical judgment, reasoning, clear communication, and ability to use team problem solving. These activities are integral to successful care as the nurse works with many different healthcare providers, within many different healthcare settings, and with the patient and family to ensure quality, cost-effective care for the patient.

Collaborative planning recognizes that collaboration has a positive effect on achieving patient outcomes (Institute of Medicine, 2001). Collaborative planning requires that all parties agree on the mission and goals of the partnership so they have common expectations. All members

BOX 13-1	COLLABORATION: SKILLS NEEDED

- Effective communication
- Awareness of personal feelings
- Problem solving

- Negotiation
- Assessment
- Recognition of expertise: Self and others

of the collaborative effort need to commit to open and honest communication, which is essential to sharing. This can be difficult in some HCOs, components of an organization such as specific units or departments, and for some individuals. Those who fear competition and are concerned about power will struggle with the need to share.

Regular evaluation needs to be built into collaborative planning. This evaluation should not only focus on the content of the planning but also on the process—how the collaborative relationship is working. This is something that is often neglected. Power, which is discussed later in this chapter, is related to collaboration. Usually some of the partners in a relationship have more power than others. When partners work through the collaborative planning process, some issues, such as weak communication, level of commitment, expertise, and an understanding that working together is better than working against one another, may interfere with the process. Recognizing these potential issues should be a priority to prevent barriers to success. What can be done to prevent them? Clear communication about purpose, particularly identifying issues from the past that may affect the collaborative planning, can help to clear up misconceptions. Team members need to accept the importance of effort and commit to it. All efforts should be made to keep team members committed. Evaluation data about the collaborative effort can help to improve team functioning.

Application of Collaboration

What is gained from collaboration? The complex healthcare delivery system requires many competencies, and no one healthcare profession has all of the necessary competencies to provide all the care that is required. Effective interprofessional teams and collaboration are critical. The IOM report on nursing (2004) identifies practices that have an impact on the delivery system, and these practices require collaboration to be effective. The practices are to create and maintain trust throughout the organization, deploy staff in adequate numbers, create a culture of openness so errors are reported, involve staff in decision making pertaining to work design and work flow, and actively manage the change process.

How do healthcare professionals develop the skills necessary for effective collaboration? There is a great need to incorporate more interprofessional educational experiences in all healthcare professional education, including nursing (Interprofessional Education Collaborative, 2011; World Health Organization, 2010). Students from the various healthcare professions need to have some experiences learning together in the same classroom and participating in clinical experiences together. Learning separately makes it very difficult to expect that at the time of graduation new healthcare professionals will easily collaborate when they have had limited collaborative experience with other healthcare professional students or healthcare professionals. They do not understand or respect the knowledge and learning experiences of other students or their roles and typical communication methods and processes. They may not even value or respect what other healthcare professionals offer to the team and to the patient. This causes serious problems as new healthcare professionals begin to work and are then confronted with working with one another. In addition, nurses need to have a positive understanding of their own roles and responsibilities—what they have to offer is valuable—so they can approach collaboration while understanding that they have important knowledge and competencies to add to the collaboration. This, however, must be accomplished *not* from the perspective of "I am better than you" but rather "How can we bring our respective skills and knowledge together to provide comprehensive, consistent care?" (Chapter 20 discusses staff education in more detail.)

Interprofessional relationships and activities can result in positive, collaborative outcomes; however, it is not easy to establish these relationships and maintain them over time. It takes time to develop an effective interprofessional environment. Other recommendations are to set realistic goals with commitment from all involved professionals, negotiate the means to meet the goals, avoid battles that serve only as barriers such as turf battles, and measure success based on established goals.

COORDINATION

The IOM identifies care coordination as one of the critical priority areas of care that need be monitored and improved. The purpose of care coordination is "to establish and support a continuous healing relationship, enabled by an integrated clinical environment and characterized by a proactive delivery of evidence-based care and follow-up" (Institute of Medicine, 2003b, p. 49). Patient-centered care is discussed in Chapter 9; however, patient-centered care is an important theme throughout this text. There needs to be greater attention on how care is coordinated across people, functions, activities, and sites to provide effective and efficient care that leads to the patient's specific desired outcomes. Coordination requires that the nurse understands patient needs and the resources that are available to meet these needs. An awareness of the association of costs and services is part of coordinating patient care. The healthcare delivery system has become more complex, which has made communication and coordination more complex, all of which leads to increased risk of errors. There is greater need for interprofessional teams. Team members may not always view the patient, problems, or priorities in the same way, yet it is critical that the team find a way to work collaboratively to provide coordinated patient care. Team members need to have a better understanding of individual responsibilities and stress to appreciate each other and develop more realistic working relationships. As noted by the IOM healthcare core competency, all healthcare professionals need to know how to work in interprofessional teams (Institute of Medicine, 2003a). Recognizing this will make coordination less frustrating.

Key Definitions Related to Coordination

Coordination is the process of working to see that "the pieces and activities fit together and flow as they should" (Finkelman & Kenner, 2016, p. 328). Effective coordination requires working across services that are complementary—across clinicians or settings—to ensure quality care across patient conditions, services, and settings over time (Institute of Medicine, 2001). Examples might be physicians, nurses, social workers, pharmacists, informatics specialists, and administrators working together to improve documentation through an electronic medical record or staff from a hospital and an ambulatory care center working together to coordinate better care for patients. Coordination is related to collaboration, and in fact, it is very difficult to do one without the other. When considering patient care, however, there is a critical difference between the two. Collaboration with a patient requires a direct interaction with the patient. Coordination of care usually takes place before or after patient care is provided, or it is interwoven in the care process. In the latter situation, a nurse may ensure that all the plans for the patient's discharge are complete or that the various treatment and exam procedures are scheduled appropriately for the patient's needs. Coordination does not mean that the patient is not involved because patient input is critical to achieve patient-centered care, but the nurse may do the coordination such as calling for supplies or making sure a treatment is scheduled when not in the presence of the patient or while providing direct care. Both coordination and collaboration are also found daily in staff-to-staff interactions. Collaboration focuses on solving a problem with two or more people working toward this goal. Coordination is done to ensure that something happens such as the provision of services. The ANA *Nursing Administration Scope and Standards of Practice* (2009) includes a standard on coordination recognizing the need for nurses in administration/management to be competent in coordination, which is needed for planning and implementation of plans, implementation of the management functions, teamwork with other nurses and interprofessional teams, and is part of effective communication with staff and patients/families/significant others. The ANA supports the need for care coordination as an important component of improving the quality of care and providing for efficient and effective use of resources. Care coordination needs to be a critical competency that all registered nurses demonstrate (American Nurses Association, 2012).

Barriers to Effective Coordination

As HCOs and services become more complex and use more interprofessional teams, team members may not always have the same view of the patient, problems, or priorities. It is, however, critical that the team find a way to work collaboratively to provide coordinated patient care and prevent errors, disorganized care, and care that does not reach effective outcomes. Team members need to have a better understanding of individual responsibilities and their own stress to appreciate each other and develop more realistic working relationships. Coordination is also more effective when involved staff have a better understanding of their respective roles and work stresses. Recognizing this will make coordination less frustrating. If resources are not available

APPLYING EVIDENCE-BASED PRACTICE

Evidence for Effective Leadership and Practice

CITATION: American Academy of Nursing. (2012, March 5). The imperative for patient, family, and population centered interprofessional approaches to care coordination and transitional care. Policy Brief 3.5.1.2. Retrieved from http://www.aannet.org/assets/docs/PolicyResources/aan_care%20coordination_3.7.12_email.pdf

OVERVIEW: The American Academy of Nursing (AAN) praises the Centers for Medicare & Medicaid Services (CMS) for its support of evidence-based care coordination and transitional care, which has been applied to Medicare and Medicaid services. The AAN recommends that the CMS consider the framework it will use to implement care coordination and the evidence to support that framework.

APPLICATION: This paper from AAN suggests various models and measurement methods to assist CMS in the implementation of greater use of care coordination, which requires an interprofessional team approach.

Questions:

1. What are the guiding principles recommended by the AAN?
2. Why is this change important?
3. What models are described? How is measurement included?
4. Analyze the recommendations made by the AAN.

---

when and in the manner required, this will act as a barrier to coordination. Staff who are not willing to listen and include others will find that coordination may not be as successful as planned. Other barriers are a lack of interprofessional understanding, lack of resources, and inadequate communication. Ineffective problem solving is also a critical barrier. Coordination needs to include the patient and, when appropriate and agreeable with the patient, the family. If patient engagement is not present, it is a major obstacle to care.

Competencies and Strategies to Achieve Effective Coordination

For staff to provide effective coordination, they need to make decisions to solve problems, plan, use the abilities of other staff, identify resources required, communicate, and be willing to collaborate. Delegation often is required, so delegation skills are important. (See Chapter 15 for more discussion on delegation.) The nurse also needs to develop evaluation skills to determine if outcomes are met as well as when to change course or make adjustments. The skills required for coordination are the same ones required for collaboration, with the primary goal of working together to reach agreed-upon goals. Box 13-2 highlights the skills needed for effective coordination.

Application of Coordination

Coordination is integral to daily operations, short- and long-range planning, and the daily care process. All of these activities require coordination of clinical and administrative resources. The following strategies are helpful in improving coordination (Finkelman & Kenner, 2016):

- All staff need to understand the importance of coordination.
- All staff should have a clear understanding of purpose and goals.
- All staff should have knowledge of policies and procedures with an understanding of what has to be done, by whom, and how it will help to facilitate coordination.
- Improved organizational performance will depend on coordination at all levels in the organization.
- Communication needs to be clear and timely. (See Chapter 14.)
- Orientation and staff development programs should emphasize the importance of coordination and how to use it.

BOX 13-2	COORDINATION: SKILLS NEEDED
• Problem solve • Plan • Use abilities of others • Identify needed resources	• Communicate • Collaborate • Delegate • Evaluate

- Coordination requires effective communication and collaboration.
- Staff/team members need to appreciate the expertise of other team members.
- Delegation should be used as needed. (See Chapter 15.)

Health care uses many tools that focus on coordination of care to ensure patient-centered care. Some of these are case management, clinical pathways, practice guidelines, and disease management. To be successful and meet expected outcomes, these tools or methods also require collaboration with the patient, patient's family and significant other, and other healthcare staff, and they are very useful when coordination is required. With insurers emphasizing more effective and efficient care, coordination plays a major role in reaching this goal. Coordination requires that the nurse understand patient needs and the resources that are available to meet these needs. An awareness of the association of costs and services is part of coordinating patient care. In addition, coordination is a very important part of management within the healthcare delivery system. This system has become more complex, which has made communication and coordination more complex. Coordination is required to get resources, schedule staff, plan work activities, implement quality improvement, and perform all types of management functions. With the growth of informatics in documentation and decision-making tools, additional methods are now available and new ones will be developed. (See Chapter 19.) Figure 13-1 describes one view of competencies needed to get results.

NEGOTIATION AND CONFLICT RESOLUTION

There may be conflict between professions, but there is also conflict within the nursing profession and with coworkers. In these situations, staff members may attack one another by asserting their position or by criticizing ideas. In some cases, they attack one another personally. Collaboration is used frequently to reach an agreement during a conflict. This is often true with nurse-physician collaboration, though ideally collaboration should be part of all of their interactions. Nurse-physician relationships are complex. There is overlapping focus in that both are concerned about the patient, though each may come from different points of view, which is not always understood or appreciated. There is also some confusion about roles, which can lead to problems. In some cases there is a certain amount of competition, which really is a sad statement; the goal should be focused on what is best for the patient and not what is best for individual staff or individual professions.

Conflict can never be eliminated in organizations; however, conflict can be managed. Typically conflict arises when people feel strongly about something. Conflicts may take place between individual staff, within a unit, or within a department. They may be interunit and interdepartmental, affect the entire HCO, or even occur between multiple organizations, between or within teams or units, or between an HCO and the community. When people disagree, this may lead to **conflict**—having views that are different and do not seem to be easy to resolve (MindTools®, 2014a).

Key Definitions Related to Conflict

There are three types of conflict: individual, interpersonal, and intergroup/organizational (Mind-Tools®, 2014a).

- *Individual conflict.* The most common type of individual conflict in the workplace is role conflict, which occurs when there is incompatibility between one or more role expectations. When staff do not understand the roles of other staff, this can be very stressful for the individual and affects work. Staff may be critical of each other for not doing some work activity when in reality it is not part of the role and responsibilities of that staff member, or staff members may feel that another staff member is doing some activity that really is not his or her responsibility.
- *Interpersonal conflict.* This conflict occurs between people. Sometimes this is due to differences and/or personalities; competition; or concern about territory, control, or loss.
- *Intergroup/organizational conflict.* Conflict also occurs between teams (e.g., units, services, teams, healthcare professional groups, agencies, community and a healthcare provider organization, and so on). Sometimes this is due to competition, lack of understanding of purpose for another team, and lack of leadership within a team or across teams within an HCO.

Gets Results

A leader's ultimate purpose is to accomplish organizational results. A leader gets results by providing guidance and managing resources, as well as performing the other leader competencies. This competency is focused on consistent and ethical task accomplishment through supervising, managing, monitoring, and controlling of the work.

Prioritizes, organizes, and coordinates taskings for teams or other organizational structures/ groups	• Uses planning to ensure each course of action achieves the desired outcome. • Organizes groups and teams to accomplish work. • Plans to ensure that all tasks can be executed in the time available and that tasks depending on other tasks are executed in the correct sequence. • Limits overspecification and micromanagement.
Identifies and accounts for individual and group capabilities and commitment to task	• Considers duty positions, capabilities, and developmental needs when assigning tasks. • Conducts initial assessments when beginning a new task or assuming a new position.
Designates, clarifies, and deconflicts roles	• Establishes and employs procedures for monitoring, coordinating, and regulating subordinates' actions and activities. • Mediates peer conflicts and disagreements.
Identifies, contends for, allocates, and manages resources	• Allocates adequate time for task completion. • Keeps track of people and equipment. • Allocates time to prepare and conduct rehearsals. • Continually seeks improvement in operating efficiency, resource conservation, and fiscal responsibility. • Attracts, recognizes, and retains talent.
Removes work barriers	• Protects organization from unnecessary taskings and distractions. • Recognizes and resolves scheduling conflicts. • Overcomes other obstacles preventing full attention to accomplishing the mission.
Recognizes and rewards good performance	• Recognizes individual and team accomplishments; rewards them appropriately. • Credits subordinates for good performance. • Builds on successes. • Explores new reward systems and understands individual reward motivations.
Seeks, recognizes, and takes advantage of opportunities to improve performance	• Asks incisive questions. • Anticipates needs for action. • Analyzes activities to determine how desired end states are achieved or affected. • Acts to improve the organization's collective performance. • Envisions ways to improve. • Recommends best methods for accomplishing tasks. • Leverages information and communication technology to improve individual and group effectiveness. • Encourages staff to use creativity to solve problems.
Makes feedback part of work processes	• Gives and seeks accurate and timely feedback. • Uses feedback to modify duties, tasks, procedures, requirements, and goals when appropriate. • Uses assessment techniques and evaluation tools (such as AARs) to identify lessons learned and facilitate consistent improvement. • Determines the appropriate setting and timing for feedback.
Executes plans to accomplish the mission	• Schedules activities to meet all commitments in critical performance areas. • Notifies peers and subordinates in advance when their support is required. • Keeps track of task assignments and suspenses. • Adjusts assignments, if necessary. • Attends to details.
Identifies and adjusts to external influences on the mission or taskings and organization	• Gathers and analyzes relevant information about changing situations. • Determines causes, effects, and contributing factors of problems. • Considers contingencies and their consequences. • Makes necessary, on-the-spot adjustments.

Figure 13-1 Competency: Gets results and associated components and actions

Source: U.S. Army. (2006). *Army leadership: Competent, confident, and agile.* Retrieved from http://fas.org/irp/doddir/army/fm6-22.pdf

When conflict occurs, something is out of sync, usually due to a lack of clear understanding of one another's roles and responsibilities. Sometimes conflict is open and obvious, and sometimes it is not as obvious; this latter type may be more destructive as staff may be responding negatively without a clear reason. Everyone has experienced covert conflict. It never feels good and increases stress quickly. Distrust and confusion about the best response are also experienced. Acknowledging covert conflict is not easy, and staff will have different perceptions of the conflict since it is not clear and below the surface. Overt conflict is obvious, at least to most people, and thus coping with it is usually easier. It is easier to arrive at an agreement when overt conflict is present and easier to arrive at a description of the conflict.

The common assumption about conflict is that it is destructive, and it certainly can be. There is, however, another view of conflict. It can be used to improve if changes are made to address problems related to the conflict. The following quote speaks to the need to recognize that conflict can be viewed as an opportunity.

> When I speak of celebrating conflict, others often look at me as if I have just stepped over the credibility line. As nurses, we have been socialized to avoid conflict. Our *modus operandi* has been to smooth over at all costs, particularly if the dynamic involves individuals representing roles that have significant power differences in the organization. Be advised that well-functioning transdisciplinary teams will encounter conflict-laden situations. It is inevitable. The role of the leader is to use conflicting perspectives to highlight and hone the rich diversity that is present within the team. Conflict also provides opportunities for individuals to present divergent yet equally valid views that allow all team members to gain an understanding of their contributions to the process. Respect for each team member's standpoint comes only after the team has explored fully and learned to appreciate the diversity of its membership. (Weaver, 2001, p. 83)

This is a positive view of conflict, which on the surface may appear negative. If one asked nurses if they wanted to experience conflict, they would say no. Probably behind their response is the fact that they do not know how to handle conflict and feel uncomfortable with it. However, if you asked staff, "Would you like to work in an environment where staff at all levels could be direct without concern of repercussions and could actively dialogue about issues and problems without others taking comments personally?" many staff would most likely see this as positive and not conflict. Avoidance of conflict, however, usually means that it will catch up with the person again, and then it may be more difficult to resolve. There may then be more emotions attached to it, making it more difficult to resolve.

Causes of Conflict

Effective resolution of conflict requires an understanding of the cause of the conflict; however, some conflicts may have more than one cause. It is easy to jump to conclusions without doing a thorough assessment. Some of the typical causes of conflict between individuals and between teams/groups are "whether resources are shared equitably; insufficient explanation of expectations, leading to performance being questioned; unexplained changes that disturb routines and processes and that team members are not prepared for; and stress resulting from changes that team members do not understand and may see as threatening" (Finkelman & Kenner, 2016, p. 336).

Two predictors of conflict are the existence of competition for resources and inadequate communication. It is rare that a major change on a unit or in an HCO does not result in competition for resources (staff, financial, space, supplies), so conflicts arise between units or between those who may or may not receive the resources or may lose resources. Causes of conflict can be varied. An understanding of a conflict requires as thorough an assessment as possible. Along with the assessment, it is important to understand the stages of conflict.

Stages of Conflict

There are four stages of conflict that help describe the process of conflict development (MBA, 2014):

1. ***Latent conflict.*** This stage involves the anticipation of conflict. Competition for resources or inadequate communication can be predictors of conflict. Anticipating conflict can increase tension. This is when staff may verbalize, "We know this is going to be a problem," or may feel this internally. The anticipation of conflict can occur between units that

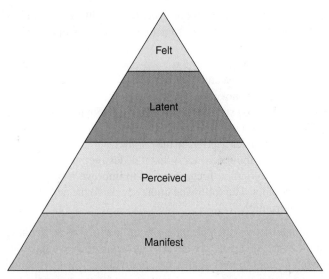

Figure 13-2 Stages of conflict

accept one another's patients when one unit does not think that the staff members on the other unit are very competent yet must accept orders and patient plans from them.

2. *Perceived conflict.* This stage requires recognition or awareness that conflict exists at a particular time. It may not be discussed but only felt. Perception is very important as it can affect whether or not there really is a conflict, what is known about the conflict, and how it might be resolved.

3. *Felt conflict.* This occurs when individuals begin to have feelings about the conflict such as anxiety or anger. Staff feel stress at this time. If avoidance is used at this time, it may prevent the conflict from moving to the next stage. Avoidance may be appropriate in some circumstances, but sometimes it just covers over the conflict and does not resolve it. In this case the conflict may come up again and be more complicated. Trust plays a role here. How much do staff trust that the situation will be resolved effectively? How comfortable do staff members feel in being open with their feelings and opinions?

4. *Manifest conflict.* This is overt conflict. At this time the conflict can be constructive or destructive. Examples of destructive behavior related to the conflict are ignoring a policy, denying a problem, avoiding a staff member, and discussing staff in public with negative comments. Examples of constructive responses to the conflict include encouraging the team to identify and solve the problem, expressing appropriate feelings, and offering to help out a staff member. (Figure 13-2 highlights the stages of conflict.)

Prevention of Conflict

Some conflict can be prevented, so it is important to take preventive steps whenever possible to correct a problem before it develops into a conflict. A staff team or HCO that says it has no conflicts is either not aware of conflict or prefers not to acknowledge it. Prevention of conflict should focus on the typical causes of conflict that have been identified in this chapter. Clear communication, known expectations, appropriate allocation of resources, and delineation of roles and responsibilities will go a long way toward preventing conflict. If the goal is to eliminate all conflict, this will not be successful because it cannot be done.

Since not all conflict can be prevented, managers and staff need to know how to manage conflict and resolve it when it exists. It is important to identify potential barriers that can make it more likely that a situation will turn into a conflict or will act as barriers to conflict resolution. First and foremost, if all staff make an effort to decrease their tension or stress level, this will go a long way in preventing or resolving conflict. In addition to this strategy, it is important to improve communication, recognize team members as members with expertise, listen and compromise to get to the most effective decision given the available data, understand the roles and responsibilities of team/staff members, and be willing to evaluate practice and team functioning.

Conflict Management: Issues and Strategies

Conflict management is critical in any HCO. When conflicts arise, then managers and staff need to understand conflict management issues and strategies. The major goals of conflict management are as follows:

1. To eliminate or decrease the conflict
2. To meet the needs of the patient, family/significant others, and the organization
3. To ensure that all parties feel positive about the resolution so future work together can be productive

POWERLESSNESS AND EMPOWERMENT   When staff experience conflict, powerlessness and empowerment, as well as aggressiveness and passive-aggressiveness, become important. When staff members feel that they are not recognized, appreciated, or paid attention to, then they feel **powerless**. What happens in a work environment when staff feel powerless? First, staff members do not feel they can make an impact; they are unable to change situations they think need to be changed. Staff members will not be as creative in approaching problems. They may feel they are responsible for tasks yet have no control or power to effect change with these tasks. The team community will be affected negatively, and eventually the team may feel it cannot make change happen. Staff may make any of the following comments: "Don't bother trying to make a difference," "I can't make a difference here," and "Who listens to us?" Morale deteriorates as staff feel more and more powerless. New staff will soon pick up on the feeling of powerlessness. In some respects, the powerlessness really does diminish any effort for change. As was discussed in Chapter 3, responding to change effectively is very important today. In addition, when staff feel powerless, this greatly impacts the organizational culture.

Power is about influencing decisions, controlling resources, and affecting behavior. It is the ability to get things done—access resources and information, and use them to make decisions. Power can be used constructively or destructively. The power a person has originates from the person's personal qualities and characteristics, as well as the person's position. Some people have qualities that make others turn to them—people trust them, consider their advice helpful, and so on. A person's position, such as a team leader or nurse manager, has associated power.

Power is not stagnant. It changes as it is affected by the situation. There are a number of sources of power. Each one can be useful depending on the circumstances and the goal. An individual may have several sources of power. The common sources of power include the following:

- *Legitimate power.* This power is what one typically thinks of in relation to power. It is power that comes from having a formal position in an organization such as a nurse manager, team leader, or vice president of patient services. These positions give the person who holds the position the right to influence staff and expect staff to follow requests. Staff members recognize that they have tasks to accomplish and job requirements. It is important to note that a leader must have legitimate power. This is a critical concept to understand about leadership and power. However, it takes more than power to be an effective leader and manager. The leader must also demonstrate competency.
- *Reward power.* A person's power comes from the ability to reward others when they comply. Examples of reward power include money (such as an increase in salary level), desired schedule or assignment, providing a space to work, and recognition of accomplishment.
- *Coercive power.* This type of power is based on punishment initiated when a person does not do what is expected or directed. Examples of punishment may include denial of a pay raise, termination, and poor schedule or assignment. This type of power leads to an unpleasant work situation. Staff will not respond positively to coercive power, and this type of power has a strong negative effect on staff morale.
- *Referent power.* This informal power comes from others recognizing that an individual has special qualities and is admired. This person then has influence over others because they want to follow the person due to the person's charisma. Staff feel valued and accepted.
- *Expert power.* When a person has expertise in a particular topic or activity, the person can have power over others who respect the expertise. When this type of power is present, the expert is able to provide sound advice and direction.

BOX 13-3	TYPES OF POWER
• Legitimate • Reward • Coercive • Referent	• Expert • Informational • Persuasive

- *Informational power.* This type of power arises from the ability to access and share information, which is critical in the Information Age.
- *Persuasive power.* This type of power influences others by providing an effective point of view or argument (Finkelman & Kenner, 2016). (Box 13-3 highlights the types of power.)

All HCOs experience their own politics, and this usually involves some staff trying to gain power, hold on to power, or expand power. As has been said, power can be used negatively, and this can also lead to the unethical use of power or not doing the right thing with the power. Chapter 2 discusses examples of ethical issues. There is no doubt that there are managers who use their power to control staff, as well as staff who use power to control other staff, but this is not a healthy use of power. Rather, it is a misuse of power and does not demonstrate nursing leadership.

A self-appraisal of a person's personal view of power allows the individual to better understand how the person uses power and how it then affects the person's decisions and relationships. This can lead to more effective responses to change during planning and decision making, coping with conflict, and the ability to collaborate and coordinate.

Empowerment is often viewed as the sharing of power; however, it is more than this. "To empower is to enable to act" (Finkelman & Kenner, 2016). Power must be more than words; it must be demonstrated. Participative decision making empowers staff but only if staff really do have the opportunity to participate and influence decisions. Recognizing that one's participation is accepted makes a difference. True empowerment gives the staff the right to choose how to address issues with the manager.

Should all staff be empowered? A critical issue to consider when answering this question is whether or not staff can effectively handle decision making. This implies that staff members need leadership qualities and skills to make sound decisions and participate together collaboratively. They need to be able to use communication effectively. When staff members are selected, all these factors become important. Empowerment is not gained just by being a member of the staff, but rather staff members become empowered because they are able to handle it. Management who want to empower staff must transfer power over to the staff, but management must first feel confident that staff can handle empowerment.

When staff are empowered, some limits or boundaries need to be set, or conflict may develop. Some of these boundaries are established by the HCO's policies, procedures, and position descriptions; education and experience; standards; and laws and regulations (for example, state nurse practice acts). The manager must be aware of these boundaries and establish any others that may be required (for example, direct involvement of staff in the selection process for new equipment). If staff members are involved in the decision making, then they should first be given a list of several possible equipment choices that meet the budgetary requirements and criteria to use in the evaluation process. It is critical that the manager make clear the boundaries, or staff members will feel like their efforts are useless if their suggestions are rejected because they were not given the boundaries. Setting staff up by not giving them full information leads to poor choices and is not effective. What does this mean? Roles and responsibilities need to be clearly described, and if they change, they need to be discussed. At the same time, the nurse manager or the team leader must not control, domineer, or overpower staff. This type of response is usually seen in new nurse managers or team leaders who feel insecure. Ineffective use of empowerment can be just as problematic as a lack of empowerment.

Although empowering oneself may seem like an unusual concept, it is an important one. The amount of power a person has in a relationship is determined by the degree to which someone else needs what the other person has. Anger is related to expectations that are not met, and when these expectations are not met, the person may act out to gain power. It is the responsibility of the nursing profession to communicate what nurses have to offer to patient care and to the healthcare delivery system, but individual nurses also need to understand what they have to offer as nurses. To have an impact, this communication and development must be ongoing. Empowerment can be positive if the strategies that are used to gain empowerment are constructive (for example, gaining new competencies, speaking out constructively, networking, using political advocacy, increasing involvement in planning and decision making, getting more nurses on key organization committees, improving image through a positive image campaign, and developing and implementing assertiveness). There are many other strategies that can result in empowerment that improves the workplace and the nurse's self-perception.

AGGRESSIVE AND PASSIVE-AGGRESSIVE BEHAVIOR   Aggressive and passive-aggressive behavior can interfere with successful conflict resolution and might even be the cause of conflict. When staff members are hostile to one another, the team leader, or the nurse manager, anxiety rises. Hostile behavior can be a response to conflict. It is important to recognize personal feelings. The first response should be to get emotions under control and communicate control to the hostile staff member. The nurse manager or team leader may be the one who is hostile, which makes it even more complex and requires assistance from higher-level management. It is hoped someone will recognize the need to bring the situation under control and try to move to a private place. Demonstrations of open conflict with hostility should not take place in patient or public areas. If the suggestion to move to a private area does not work and the situation continues to escalate, simply walking away may help set some boundaries. Cool down time is definitely needed.

There are many times when more information is really required before a response can be given. If this is the case, everyone concerned needs to be told that when information is gathered, the issue or problem will then be discussed. No one should be pressured to respond with inadequate information as this will lead to ineffective decision making and may lead to further hostility. It is critical that after further assessment is completed there be additional discussion and a conclusion.

When there are conflicts with patients and families, what is the best way to cope? Many of the same strategies mentioned earlier can be used. Safety is the first issue, as it must be maintained. It is never appropriate to allow patients or families to demonstrate anger inappropriately. When this occurs, someone needs to set reasonable limits that are based on an assessment of the situation. There may be many reasons for anger and inappropriate behavior, such as pain, medications, fear and anxiety, psychosis, dysfunctional communication, and so on. Staff need to avoid taking things personally as this will interfere with thoughtful problem solving. When one gets defensive or emotional, interventions taken to resolve a conflict may not be effective. Active listening is critical to cope with emotions. If a different culture is involved, then this factor needs to be considered. (For example, some cultures consider it appropriate to be very emotional, and others do not.) In the long term, clear communication is critical during the entire process.

HOW DO INDIVIDUAL STAFF MEMBERS COPE WITH CONFLICT?   Not everyone responds to conflict in the same way, and individuals may vary in how they respond dependent on the circumstances. Four typical responses to conflict are avoidance, accommodation, competition, and collaboration (MindTools®, 2014a).

- Avoidance occurs when a person is very uncomfortable and cannot cope with the anxiety effectively. This person will withdraw from the situation to avoid it. There are times when this may be the most effective response, particularly when the situation may lead to negative results, but in many situations this will not be effective in the long term. This response might occur when a staff member is in conflict with a manager and disagrees with the manager. The staff member must consider whether it is worthwhile to disagree publicly. Typically avoidance occurs when one side is perceived as more powerful than the other. It is a helpful approach when more information is needed or when the issue is not worth what might be lost.
- A second response is accommodation. How does this occur? The person tries to make the situation better by cooperating. The critical issue may not be resolved or not resolved to the fullest satisfaction. The goal is just to eliminate the conflict as quickly as possible.

Accommodation works best when one person or team is less interested in the issue than the other. It can be advantageous as it does develop harmony, and it can provide power in future conflict since one party was more willing to let the conflict deflate. Later interaction may require that the other party cooperate.

- A third response is competition. How does this work? Power is used to stop the conflict. A manager might say, "This is the way it will be." This closes further efforts from others who may be in conflict with the manager.
- Collaboration is the fourth response, which has been discussed in this chapter. This is a positive approach, with all parties attempting to reach an acceptable solution, and in the end, both sides feel they won something. Collaboration often involves some compromise, which is a method used to respond to conflict.

Using the best conflict resolution style can make a difference in success. There are many ways that a conflict can be resolved. When conflict occurs, each person involved has a personal perspective of the issue and conflict. Today there is more conflict in the healthcare delivery environment with increased workplace stress that may lead to misunderstandings, ineffective communication, and reduced productivity and dysfunctional organizations, as noted in the Institute of Medicine reports (2001, 2004).

GENDER ISSUES   Are there differences in the ways in which women and men negotiate? There are differences in how women and men approach leadership issues such as conflict (Greenberg, 2005). Men tend to negotiate to win, while women focus more on what is fair. It is believed that this is related to the way children play through sports and activities. Women will make an effort to reach win-win solutions. Men will test the limits that have been set more overtly than women, so it is important for women to ensure that limits are set and maintained. It is important, despite the differences described, to avoid stereotyping.

NURSE-PHYSICIAN RELATIONSHIPS   Though the nurse-physician relationship should be the strongest relationship that nurses have to meet the needs of the patient, it frequently is not. Both sides have a role in the inadequacies of this relationship. Conflict does occur and this conflict can act as a barrier to effective patient care. Collegial relationships are those where there is equality of power and knowledge. In contrast, collaborative relationships between nurses and physicians focus on mutual power, but typically the physician's power is greater. The nurse's power is based on the nurse's extended time with patients, experience, and knowledge. In addition to power, this relationship requires respect and trust between the nurse and physician. Due to these factors, it is a complex relationship.

Nurses have long worked on teams, mostly with other nursing staff. However, the nurse-physician relationships have become more important in the changing healthcare environment with the greater emphasis on interprofessional teams. Nurse-physician interactions and communication have been discussed for a long time in healthcare literature.

Physicians, however, are not the only healthcare providers nurses must work with while they provide care. (For example, nurses work with other nursing staff, social workers, support staff, laboratory technicians, physical therapists, pharmacists, and many others.) There are also other members joining the healthcare team such as alternative therapists (massage therapists, herbal therapists, acupuncturists, etc.), case managers, more actively involved insurers, and so forth. The future will probably bring other new members into the healthcare delivery system. Nurses need to develop the skills necessary to participate effectively on the team, which requires collaboration, communication, coordination, delegation, and negotiation. Communication and delegation are discussed in other chapters. It is difficult to practice today in any healthcare setting without experiencing interprofessional interactions such as nurse to physician. Effective teams:

- work together (collaborate).
- recognize strengths and limitations.
- respect individual responsibilities.
- maintain open communication.

Positive professional communication is critical. Both sides should initiate positive dialogue rather than adversarial positions. Cooperation and collaboration are also integral to the success of this relationship. A frequent question discussed in the literature is "Why is there conflict between nurses and physicians?" The structure of work is different for physicians and for nurses, and this has an impact on understanding, communicating, collaborating, and coordinating. This perspective identifies the key elements as sense of time, sense of resources, unit of analysis, sense of mastery, and type of rewards as described by the following:

- The nurse is focused on shorter periods of time, and time is usually short, with frequent interruptions. The physician's sense of time focuses on the course of illness.
- If a physician gives a stat order, the physician has problems understanding what might interfere with the nurse's making this a priority. There is a lack of understanding of the nurse's work structure.
- Physicians often are not concerned with resources, though this is certainly changing as physicians recognize that there may be a shortage of staff as well as issues about costs and reimbursement for care. They, however, may not be willing to accept these factors as relevant when their patients need something. There are, of course, other resources such as equipment availability, supplies, and funds that can cause problems and conflicts. Nurses are typically more aware of the effect that these factors have on daily care and the work that needs to be done.
- Unit of analysis is another factor; for example, nurses are caring for groups of patients even though care is supposed to be individualized. Physicians may not have an understanding of this if they have only a few patients in the hospital.
- Physicians also do not have an understanding of nursing delivery models, and often nurses themselves are not clear about them. This affects nurses' ability to explain how they work.
- The sense of reward is different. Nurses work in a task-oriented environment and typically get paid an hourly rate. Most physicians are not salaried and are independent practitioners, though some are employees of the organization (hospital, clinic, and so on).

Conflict and verbal abuse are related. Verbal abuse occurs in healthcare settings between patients and staff, nurses and other nurses, physicians and nurses, and all other staff relationships. This abuse can consist of statements made directly to a staff member or about a staff member to others. A common complaint from nurses regards verbal abuse from physicians. In addition to impacting quality care, verbal abuse affects turnover rates and contributes to the nursing shortage, so it is has serious consequences.

How can this problem be improved? A critical step is to gain better understanding of each profession's viewpoint and demonstrate less automatic acceptance of inappropriate behavior. This requires that management become proactive in eliminating negative communication and behavior. Some hospitals have tried a number of strategies to deal with verbal abuse. The IOM recommends increased interprofessional approaches to care delivery and the need for increased

CASE STUDY

A Verbal Explosion Leads to Confrontation of a Problem

As a nurse manager in a busy operating room (OR), you have to ensure that all staff are collaborating and communicating well. In the past six months, you have noticed more problems with poor communication between nurses and physicians, which had an impact on the quality of care. Nurses are also frequently complaining that they are "second-class citizens" in the department. The number of last-minute call-ins has increased by 25% over the past six months, causing staffing problems. Today was the last straw when a nurse and a surgical resident had a shouting match in the hallway. The nurse left the encounter crying, and the resident said he would not work with the nurse anymore. The nurse manager went into the OR medical director's office. They have had a positive collaborative relationship over several years. She went in and said, "We have a problem!" As she described the problems, he said, "I was unaware there was so much tension and lack of collaboration. Why didn't you tell me this earlier?"

Questions:

1. How would you respond to the medical director's question?
2. What do you and the medical director need to do?
3. How can you avoid this being a we/they situation?
4. How will you involve all staff?
5. What can you do about the powerlessness the nurses feel?

interprofessional education among health professions so all health professions are prepared to work together on teams (2003a). What can nurses do about this? One suggestion is to improve their knowledge base and thus develop more self-confidence. Another problem is that nurses think they must resolve all problems and "make things" work correctly when this may not be realistic. The nurses then become scapegoats. Verbal abuse, no matter who—physician or nurse—is doing it, should not be tolerated. Those involved need to be approached in private to identify the need for a change in behavior. Staff needs to be respected. The AONE *Guiding Principles for Excellence in Nurse-Physician Relationships* is found in Box 13-4.

Application of Negotiation to Conflict Resolution

Negotiation is the critical element in making conflict a nightmare or an opportunity. Negotiation can be used to resolve a conflict, and some types of negotiation, such as mediation, can be very structured. When two or more people or organizations disagree or have opposing views about a problem or solution, a conflict exists. To resolve the conflict, the involved people need to discuss resolution in a manner that is acceptable to all involved. Although it does not have to take long, in some cases it may be very long, such as what might occur in a union-employer negotiation for a contract. Conflict resolution includes the use of a variety of skills and strategies. As the process begins, it is important to clarify all of the issues and parties who are involved in the conflict. Performance or potential outcomes should be established early in the process. Questioning is important throughout resolution. For example, it is important to ask about behaviors that started the conflict and how to avoid them in the future. Management needs to be clear about expectations and provide these in writing, which helps to decrease conflict over critical issues. Since conflict is inevitable, all staff nurses will encounter it. Knowing how to manage conflict will be of great benefit to the individual nurse as well as improve the working environment and ability to better reach patient outcomes.

Patients should not become part of staff or organizational conflicts, and there is risk that this may occur. Consider these examples:

- The interprofessional team cannot agree on a treatment approach and must do this by the end of the team meeting.
- A patient's insurer refuses to allow the patient to stay two more days in the hospital. As the hospital's nurse case manager, you must work with the insurer representative to reach a compromise.
- Staffing in a hospital has been reduced, and the nurses are convinced that the new staffing level will be unsafe for patients. Something must be done to resolve this issue.
- A home healthcare agency learned that the Medicare contract has changed and specific patients will receive fewer visits.

How can these examples be resolved satisfactorily so the quality of care does not suffer and staff still work together collaboratively? Finding a mentor to discuss the process as well as vent feelings may be helpful. Developing negotiation skills makes conflicts easier to handle and less stressful. Nurses who become involved in unions will find that negotiation skills are also very important. If negotiation is not used effectively, all of these conflict examples can lead to major problems for the patient and/or staff.

When approaching conflict resolution, it is important to recognize that both sides contributed to the conflict. One side cannot have a conflict by itself; it takes at least two. Consider how each side has contributed to the conflict. Another critical issue is to carefully consider if this is the time and place to address the conflict. When the environment is too emotional, conflict resolution will be difficult. Stepping back or taking a break may be the best position to take. The following are strategies that can be used to negotiate effectively (MindTools®, 2014b):

- Negotiate for agreements—not winning or losing. Clearly state that your desire is to find a solution and to work together.
- Separate people from positions.
- Establish mutual trust and respect.
- Avoid one-sided or personal gains.
- Allow time for expressing the interests of each side/party.
- Listen actively during the process, and acknowledge what is being said; avoid defending or explaining yourself.

BOX 13-4	AONE GUIDING PRINCIPLES FOR EXCELLENCE IN NURSE-PHYSICIAN RELATIONSHIPS

INTRODUCTION TO THE GUIDING PRINCIPLES

Excellent working relationships between nurses and physicians are key to creating a productive, safe, and satisfying practice environment. The patient and the patient's family benefit from care delivered by a team practicing within this environment.

Senior leadership in healthcare organizations must support the development of excellent relationships and, more importantly, create an environment that sustains and nurtures these critical relationships.

GUIDING PRINCIPLES FOR EXCELLENCE IN NURSE-PHYSICIAN RELATIONSHIPS

Institutions that are committed to establishing and maintaining environments that promote excellence in the nurse/physician relationship adhere to the following principles.

1. Interdisciplinary collaborative relationships are promoted, nurtured and sustained.
2. This requires that practitioners be proficient in communication skills, leadership skills, problem solving, conflict management, utilizing their emotional intelligence, and functioning within a team culture.
3. Excellence in relationship building begins with hiring, continues with learning and developing together and is reinforced over time.
4. The organization has specific systems for reward, recognition, and celebration.
5. The organization supports the "Platinum Rule" with a specific Professional Code of Conduct that includes a system to support it. A "No Tolerance" standard exists for those unable to adhere to the Code.
6. The organization creates and supports a "Just & Fair" environment.
7. The work of all professional caregivers is seen as interdependent and collegial.
8. Cross-discipline job discovery is supported and encouraged.
9. Patient-focused care and better patient outcomes are the organizing force behind creating a collaborative environment.

IMPLEMENTATION GUIDELINES

Interdisciplinary collaborative relationships are promoted, nurtured and sustained.

1. Nurses and physicians are given formal training in communication skills, leadership development, problem solving, conflict management, development of emotional intelligence, and team functions. Education and training is provided to nurse/physician teams and is not discipline specific.
2. Specific education is provided in team building.
3. Organization governing bodies and committees have representative members from all disciplines.
4. Nurse/physicians leadership teams are identified to lead the work at the unit level. (Microsystem Management)
5. All organizational task forces include representatives from those stakeholders closest to the issue.
6. Interdisciplinary collaborative relationships are assessed, unit-by-unit. Each unit has a development and improvement plan for continued growth of the relationship.

7. Teams develop common values for their interdisciplinary collaboration.
8. Teams develop common language for their interdisciplinary collaboration.
9. Nurse/physician collaborative champions are identified at the hospital and unit level.

Excellence in relationship building begins with hiring, continues with learning and developing together and is reinforced over time together and is reinforced over time.

1. Nurses and physicians work collaboratively to identify the behaviors that they want in team members.
2. Employees, both nurse and physician, are hired using behavioral interviewing to ascertain a good fit with the organization, teams, values, culture, and behavioral expectations.
3. Nurses and physicians do 360 degree performance reviews.
4. Credentialing criteria includes behavioral attributes and expectations, as well as clinical skills.
5. The Graduate Medical Education competencies are used as hiring criteria and for performance review.
6. Education and team training is done in work teams, as described in the Institute of Medicine reports.
7. Personal accountability for demonstrating team behaviors is rewarded.

The organization has specific systems for reward, recognition, and celebration.

1. There is alignment of purpose among the disciplines regarding reward/recognition & celebration.
2. Mechanisms for reward and recognition are easy to access.
3. Performance appraisal is linked to patient satisfaction measurements.
4. Awards, recognition and celebration are public and visible and across disciplines and teams—Example: Physicians identify the Nurse of the Year; Nurses identify the Physician of the Year.
5. Rewards and Recognition programs promote team accomplishments.

The organization supports the "Platinum Rule" with a specific Professional Code of Conduct that includes a system to support it. A "No Tolerance" standard exists for those unable to adhere to the Code.

1. The Golden Rule states: "Do unto others as you would have them do unto you." The Platinum Rule states: "Do unto others as they would have you do for /unto them." Thus, this principle speaks to treating others as they want to be treated, not necessarily how you would want to be treated.
2. Code of Conduct Guidelines/Policies exists for all professionals that outline behavioral expectations.
3. Work improvement plans and measures hold the team accountable, not just individual.
4. Individual professional codes of ethics/conduct are known and honored.
5. Contacts and processes/procedures for the impaired professional are easily accessible to all staff.

(continued)

| BOX 13-4 | AONE GUIDING PRINCIPLES . . . (CONTINUED) |

6. There are identified coaches and mentors for the professionals on site in the hospital to help with performance issues.
7. All professionals receive team training that focuses on communication skills and processes.
8. Processes exist to identify and address conflict situations before they become a crisis and/or deteriorate.

The organization creates and supports a "Just & Fair" environment.

1. There is a systems approach to management and decision-making.
2. Internal trends and reporting processes are multidisciplinary.
3. Language for reporting and safety is analyzed to assure that it is "Just & Fair".
4. Processes exist for multidisciplinary critical incident debriefing.
5. Decision-making tools are used that support the "Just & Fair" processes, such as the "Just Model".
6. The processes outlined in the patient-safety literature that creates cultures of safety are used as blue prints for culture changes.
7. Remedial training is offered when needed.

The work of all professional caregivers is seen as interdependent and collegial.

1. The culture of team includes all disciplines providing care on a unit.
2. Behavioral expectations are defined for all disciplines.

Cross-discipline job discovery is supported and encouraged.

1. All disciplines are educated in the role/responsibility of their colleagues.
2. Opportunities for shadowing different professions are encouraged.

Patient-focused care and better patient outcomes are the organizing force behind creating a collaborative environment.

1. Work is directed toward identifying and measuring those outcomes that are sensitive to the function of collaboration.
2. Patients and families are appointed to internal committees.
3. Patient-centeredness is a key focus for processes.

Source: From *AONE Guiding Principles For Excellence In Nurse–Physician Relationships.* Copyright © 2005 by American Organization of Nurse Executives. Used by permission of American Organization of Nurse Executives.

- Use data/evidence to strengthen your position.
- Focus on patient care interests.
- Always remember that the process is a problem-solving one, and the benefit is for the patient and family.
- Clearly identify the priority and arrive at common goal(s).
- Avoid using pressure.
- Identify and understand the real reasons underlying the problem.
- Be knowledgeable about organizational policies, procedures, systems, standards, and the law, applying this knowledge as needed.
- Try to understand the other side, and ask questions and seek clarification when unsure or uncertain; understanding the other side first before explaining yours increases effectiveness.
- Avoid emotional outbursts and overreacting if the other party exhibits such behavior; depersonalize the conflict.
- Avoid premature judgments, blame, and inflammatory comments.
- Be concrete and flexible when presenting your position.
- Be reasonable and fair.

There are some conflicts that require a third-party negotiator to reach a more effective resolution. This is needed when there is no opportunity for cooperative problem solving and objectivity is required. "Mediation is an informal and confidential way for people to resolve disputes with the help of a neutral mediator who is trained to help people discuss their differences. The mediator does not decide who is right or wrong or issue a decision. Instead, the mediator helps the parties work out their own solutions to problems" (U.S. Equal Employment Opportunity Commission, 2014). Mediators are facilitators, not decision makers (as in the case of arbitrators). In **mediation**, the people with the dispute have an opportunity to tell their story and to be understood, as well as to listen to and understand the story of the other party. A key factor in mediation is the need for all parties to willingly participate in the process. The mediator guides the process and discussion. Certain guidelines are established for the discussion that all parties must follow throughout the process (for example, allowing each party time to speak and complete a statement without interruption, calling for a break when needed, enforcing time-limited meetings, substantiating comments with facts, and so on). With these guidelines and the presence of a mediator, this type of negotiation can result in positive outcomes. It provides protection for both sides.

APPLYING LEADERSHIP AND MANAGEMENT

My Hospital Unit: An Evolving Case Experience

When you arrive at work today, you are confronted with several staff members upset that work is not being done effectively, particularly with other departments. Successful coordination requires identification of barriers and strategies to resolve barriers to coordination. Coordination also requires collaboration. Identify the barriers to effective coordination and collaboration. Clearly describe them. Then consider what strategies could be used to prevent the barriers or to decrease the barriers on your unit. Your strategies need to be applicable to your unit as you have designed it.

BSN and *Master's Essentials:* Application to Content

BSN Essentials (American Association of Colleges of Nursing, 2008) as Applied to this Chapter:

I. Liberal Education for Baccalaureate Generalist Nursing Practice

II. Basic Organizational and Systems Leadership for Quality Care and Patient Safety

VI. Interprofessional Communication and Collaboration for Improving Patient Health Outcomes

Master's Essentials (American Association of Colleges of Nursing, 2011) as Applied to this Chapter:

I. Background for Practice from Sciences to Humanities

II. Organizational and Systems Leadership

VII. Interprofessional Collaboration for Improving Patient and Population Health Outcomes

Applying AONE Competencies

Identify which of the AONE competencies found in Appendix A apply to the content of this chapter.

Engaging in the Content: Critical Thinking and Clinical Reasoning and Judgment

Discussion Questions

1. What does collaboration mean to you? (Online Application Option)
2. What does coordination mean to you? (Online Application Option)
3. How do you personally respond to conflict? Is it effective? If not, how might you improve your response?
4. What are the stages of conflict?
5. What may be the impact of conflict in the healthcare setting? (Online Application Option)

Application Exercises

1. Select one of the following issues to discuss with RNs. (Students should not all choose the same questions so when data are discussed, there will be different issues described.) Questions to include: (1) Is collaboration with other healthcare professionals part of your practice? If so, describe some examples. If not, why do you think collaboration does not exist? (2) How is coordination used in your practice? (3) How might you and others improve coordination in your workplace? (4) Describe your worst experience with conflict at work and how it was resolved or not resolved. What were the long-term consequences of the conflict? (5) Do you feel empowered at work? Why or why not? How do you think the situation could be improved?

2. The examples of strategies to improve nurse-physician relationships are broad. What do you think about them? Divide into teams and have each team take one of the strategies. Switch off strategies among the teams in the class, and discuss the advantages and disadvantages of the strategy identified by another team. How would you respond to the strategy? Have you experienced or observed any abusive behavior yourself or among staff? Do you think one of these strategies might prevent this type of behavior? Each team should explore the strategy. How would it work? Would it be offensive to staff (nurses or physicians)? It is important to consider the nurses' and physicians' viewpoints. (Online Application Option)

3. Conflict is complex yet there are guidelines for understanding it. Select an example of a conflict, which can be one you experienced or observed. Describe the conflict, identify the type of conflict, and explain your rationale for selecting the type. Apply the four stages of conflict described in the chapter to your example. What resulted from the conflict?

4. Provide an example of collaboration that you observed or participated in during clinical. Apply content from this chapter to your example. Share with your team. (Online Application Option)

References

American Association of Colleges of Nursing. (2008). *The essentials of baccalaureate education for professional nursing practice*. Washington, DC: Author.

American Association of Colleges of Nursing. (2011). *The essentials of master's education in nursing*. Washington, DC: Author.

American Association of Critical-Care Nurses. (2014). The AACN synergy model for patient care. Retrieved from http://www.aacn.org/wd/certifications/content/syn-model.pcms?menu=

American Nurses Association. (ANA). (2009). *Nursing administration scope and standards of practice*. Silver Spring, MD: Author.

American Nurses Association. (ANA). (2010a). *Nursing: Scope and standards of practice*. Silver Spring, MD: Author.

American Nurses Association. (ANA). (2010b). *Nursing's social policy statement* (2nd ed.). Silver Spring, MD: Author.

American Nurses Association. (2012). *The value of nursing care coordination*. Silver Spring, MD: Author.

Finkelman, A., & Kenner, C. (2016). *Professional nursing concepts. Competencies for quality leadership* (3rd ed.). Boston, MA: Jones and Bartlett Publishers.

Greenberg, H. (2005). *The qualities that distinguish women leaders*. Retrieved from http://www.setsale.com/uploadedFiles/Women%20Leader%20White%20Paper%20setsale.pdf

Institute of Medicine. (2001). *Crossing the quality chasm*. Washington, DC: National Academies Press.

Institute of Medicine. (2003b). *Priority areas for national action*. Washington, DC: National Academies Press.

Institute of Medicine. (2003a). *Health professions education*. Washington, DC: National Academies Press.

Institute of Medicine. (2004). *Keeping patients safe: Transforming the work environment of nurses*. Washington, DC: National Academies Press.

Institute of Medicine. (2011). *The future of nursing: Leading change, advancing health*. Washington, DC: National Academies Press.

Interprofessional Education Collaborative. (2011). *Core competencies for interprofessional collaborative practice: Report of an expert panel*. Washington, DC: Author. Retrieved from http://www.aacn.nche.edu/education/pdf/IPECReport.pdf

MBA. (2014). What are the different stages in a conflict? Retrieved from http://www.mbaofficial.com/mba-courses/human-resource-management/management-of-conflict/what-are-the-different-stages-in-a-conflict/

MindTools®. (2014a). Resolving team conflict. Retrieved from http://www.mindtools.com/pages/article/newTMM_79.htm

MindTools®. (2014b). Win-win negotiation. Retrieved from http://www.mindtools.com/CommSkll/NegotiationSkills.htm

Salmon, M. (2007). Guest editorial: Care quality and safety: Same old. *Nursing Outlook, 55*(3), 117–119.

U.S. Equal Employment Opportunity Commission. (2014). Mediation. Retrieved from http://www.eeoc.gov/employees/mediation.cfm

Weaver, D. (2001). Transdisciplinary teams: Very important leadership stuff. *Seminars for Nurse Managers, 9*(2), 79–84.

World Health Organization. (2010). *Framework for action on interprofessional education and collaborative practice*. Retrieved from http://whqlibdoc.who.int/hq/2010/WHO_HRH_HPN_10.3_eng.pdf

14 Effective Staff Communication and Working Relationships

🔵 LEARNING OUTCOMES

Before you begin, take a moment to familiarize yourself with the learning outcomes for this chapter.

> Distinguish between the critical elements of communication: lines of communication, communication process, and verbal and nonverbal communication.
> Assess a team's communication.
> Compare the four communication methods, including the most effective use of the method.
> Apply two strategies for resolving communication problems.
> Assess your own communication style.

WHAT'S AHEAD

Communication is part of everything that is done within the healthcare system. It can appear as staff-to-staff communication and patient-to-staff communication and can be in verbal, nonverbal, written, or electronic form. The major goal of staff communication is the effective exchange of information that assists staff in meeting outcomes. The survival of each organization is dependent on the transfer of information and actions taken based on information or communication; therefore, this process serves to integrate the organization's activities. Respect for another's values, feelings, opinions, and trust are critical to effective communication. Typically when a team or teams work together, one of the first signs that productivity is low will be an increase in communication problems. Decreasing communication has a direct negative effect on decision making, collaboration, coordination, and prevention of conflict. Communication is costly because it consumes staff time and affects the organization and patient outcomes. When outcomes are not met, this affects costs. New information technology, such as computer hardware, software, information specialists, maintenance, repair and upgrade of hardware and software, and staff training in use of information technology (IT), is very costly. This chapter discusses many of these issues concerning communication and how communication affects the work environment and outcomes. Informatics is discussed more fully in Chapter 19.

KEY TERMS

- active listening
- communication
- communication process
- context
- decoding
- diagonal communication
- downward communication
- encoding
- feedback
- lateral (horizontal) communication
- medium
- message
- selective listening
- sender
- storytelling
- upward communication
- videoconferencing

COMMUNICATION: WHAT IS IT?

Communication, a key to successful teamwork, is a complex process that should never be ignored. Nurses need to be competent communicators in their work as they work with patients, families, coworkers, physicians and other healthcare providers, administrators and managers, support staff, case managers, quality improvement staff, management staff, community agencies, and so on. The American Nurses Association (ANA) nursing standards include communication as an important part of nursing practice (2010), and the ANA nursing administration standards integrate the need for effective communication (2009). Communication cannot be avoided, and inadequate or ineffective communication often occurs. The Joint Commission has noted that the most common and important reason for causes of sentinel events is ineffective communication (2007).

Definition of Communication

Communication is a two-way process that is used to convey a **message** or an idea between two or more people. This process is used to share thoughts, attitudes, information, and feelings. Effective care, which should be the goal, requires a focused exchange of ideas, feelings, and attitudes. Communication is best described as a complementary process with sender and receiver(s) roles and is a process that happens between people and within people. Healthcare organizations (HCOs) must exert considerable effort in ensuring that effective communication occurs within the organization, with external organizations, and with people who are important to the HCO. Key issues are who says what, to whom, in what way, when, and with what effect. Even after focusing on these key issues, it is still important to remember that the interpretation phase of the communication is important and can impact how the original message is understood (Finkelman & Kenner, 2016).

Nurses need to understand the communication process and use it to benefit patient care and the work that needs to be done to reach identified outcomes. With greater interest on patient-centered care, much of communication needs to be focused on the patient. The Institute of Medicine (IOM) includes information about communication in its discussion about the core competency to provide patient-centered care:

> Communicate with patients in a shared and fully open manner. Allow patients to have unfettered access to the information contained in their medical records. Communicate accurately in a language that patients can understand. Offer patients' preferred communication channels (e.g., face-to-face, e-mail, other Web-based communication technologies). Explore a patient's main reason for a visit, associated concerns, and need for information. (Institute of Medicine, 2003a, pp. 52–53)

As staff members communicate, they become involved in discussions and in dialogue mostly about patients but also about the work effort related to patient care. There is also personal conversation that takes place among coworkers. This personal conversation is very important in building teamwork; members feel more connected to one another. Effective communication broadens an individual's and a team's view of issues and how best to work with one another. The result should be better outcomes for patients and the HCO.

Communication Systems and Lines of Communication

Typically communication is thought of as taking place in a straight line, from the sender to the receiver; however, in most situations communication is much more complex. Its direction can be downward, upward, lateral, or diagonal.

DOWNWARD COMMUNICATION Communication is downward when a team leader tells a team member that a specific task must be done. Lines of communication typically relate to the organizational structure. The organizational chart provides the best illustration of these lines of communication. Management communicates to staff in lower levels and so on. **Downward communication** is the most typical type of communication flow and is found in the traditional bureaucratic organization, although it is used in many types of organizational structures. In line with this type of organizational structure, this communication is directive and used primarily to coordinate activities to ensure that outcomes are reached. Downward communication might be used when there are issues related to the HCO's policies and procedures, position descriptions, employee rules and regulations, written communication from administration, and other forms of organizational communication that come from above. Performance evaluations traditionally have been primarily downward; however, this type of performance evaluation is less effective, as was discussed in Chapter 8. Most organizations now require that staff participate in their own performance evaluations, thereby changing this communication line.

Changing organizational structures and leadership approaches have required changes in communication. Consider what was discussed about transformational leadership in Chapter 1. Dictating from above, or downward communication, is not a communication approach that supports this type of leadership. As a consequence of leadership change, downward communication is less common as more staff are encouraged to participate in organizational decisions and to be innovative and initiate changes. This encourages more upward communication and other communication forms in which staff interact in a participatory environment such as shared governance.

Downward communication is also not as effective as other communication lines. Why is this so? Communication really is the act of the message's receiver. If there is no active receiver, does communication really occur? Downward communication can only send commands or directions. Communication needs to begin with the intended receiver rather than the sender. Downward communication occurs after upward communication has been successful.

UPWARD COMMUNICATION   Communication is upward for example when a staff nurse tells a nurse manager that the schedule for the month does not meet the staff nurse's needs or when staff are involved in decision making at the unit level. Examples of **upward communication**, which are increasing in most HCOs, include staff meetings, team meetings, staff-to-staff or staff-to-manager communication, and communication that occurs on a daily basis in the work setting. Other examples are a manager's use of an "open door" policy so staff can feel free to come to the manager with issues or concerns, shift reports, team or project communication and written reports, grievance procedures, staff development evaluation feedback, exit interviews, use of a suggestion box, staff satisfaction surveys, union communication, and the grapevine. Shared governance, a form of organizational process and structure discussed in Chapter 4, requires that staff participate actively in organizational decision making, which is upward communication. Downward and upward communication are similar in that communication goes from one level to another. Those who receive the message last may not receive the exact original message that was sent. This can be a disadvantage as it is critical that the message is received as sent. This can be an advantage if the message's content has been improved with the creative process of the ideas of more than one staff member, but this still means that not all staff received the same message. The issues of perception and expectations will always be factors in limiting consistent communication.

LATERAL COMMUNICATION   **Lateral (horizontal) communication** is typically used to coordinate activities. This type of communication takes place between staff who are in the same or similar hierarchical level or departmental level in that one does not have formal power over the other (for example, between a staff nurse and another staff nurse or between two nurse managers, one from the cardiac care unit and the other from a medical unit). Typically this communication is informal and might involve sharing information about patients, committee communication, communication among team members, interprofessional communication, and communication among work team project members. As HCOs begin to incorporate more teamwork and emphasize the value of working in teams, this type of communication develops and becomes critical for success.

DIAGONAL COMMUNICATION   **Diagonal communication** is informal communication. This communication typically occurs when staff members who are from different hierarchical levels are working on a project together, but when they work on the project, they are equal. This form of communication is increasing because more staff from different departments or units are working together, increasing collaboration. It also applies to the relationship between a nurse and a physician or a nurse and a patient. For example, if an HCO is developing a new admission procedure, the project's team ideally should include a physician, several nurse managers, several staff nurses, a patient transportation supervisor, the director of medical records, the director of information system management, an ombudsman or patient advocate, an admission department representative, an administrator, and the chief financial officer. In some HCOs a patient representative may be included. This team has representatives from different departments, units within departments, management, administration, and an insurer representative; different hierarchical levels; consumers; and external representatives. The goal of diagonal communication is to improve communication so all can collaborate to meet the team's goal.

There is increasing evidence suggesting that clinical errors are often related to ineffective communication patterns and miscommunication between members of the healthcare team. The Institute of Medicine report *To Err Is Human* discusses the problem of increasing errors in health care (Institute of Medicine, 1999). (See Chapter 17.) The report defines an error as "the failure of a planned action to be completed as intended or the use of a wrong plan to achieve an aim" (Institute of Medicine, 1999, p. 3). Considering this definition, it is difficult to exclude communication as a major factor in errors. Ineffective communication, problems with communication flow, poor feedback, and difficulty in getting relevant patient information are all mentioned in the report. As noted earlier, the Joint Commission has also commented on communication and errors, noting that communication problems often are the cause of common errors in health care. When we do not use patient-centered care and fail to engage the patient to obtain accurate and complete information, there is risk of errors, and care may not meet positive outcomes (O'Daniel & Rosenstein, 2008).

THE COMMUNICATION PROCESS

The transmission of information and understanding of that information in the message takes place on many different levels: individual to individual, in small teams, in large organizations, and between organizations.

The Steps in the Communication Process

Each level of the **communication process** or cycle is highlighted in Figure 14-1 and includes the following (MindTools®, 2014a):

1. Aim: The sender clarifies the goal of the message.
2. **Encoding**: The communicator's ideas are translated into language (compose the message).
3. Transmit: The sender delivers the message in some format (e.g., face-to-face, memo, medical record, team meeting, computer, policy statement); it can also be an unintended message that is sent by silence or inaction.

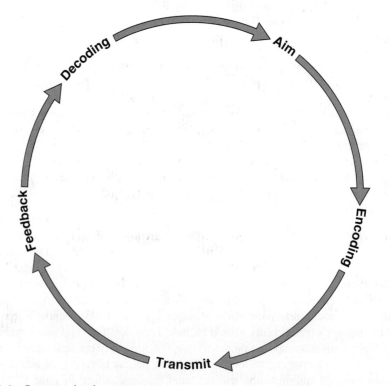

Figure 14-1 Communication process

4. **Feedback**: The receiver communicates back to the sender, an important component of two-way communication.
5. **Decoding**: The receiver analyzes and interprets the message.

The communication process is made up of five elements. It is important to recognize the use of the term "process," which indicates that communication is a dynamic interaction. The following are the five elements:

1. The **sender** is the individual who initiates the message, which may be verbal and/or non-verbal. Communication may also be written. Verbal communication always includes non-verbal communication. There are many factors that affect the sender and the message (e.g., the sender's attitude toward self and toward the receiver, the situation in which the message is sent, timing, and purpose of the message). The sender uses encoding when decisions are made about what to include in the message and how to transmit the message. Then the message is sent.
2. The message includes both verbal and nonverbal information as well as the sender's attitude toward self, receiver, and the message.
3. The receiver is the person(s) to whom the message is sent. The receiver decodes the message so it can be fully understood. This includes the actions necessary to understand the message (for example, listening, reading a memo or an email message, or reviewing a chart of data).
4. The feedback is the message or response that the receiver may send back to the sender. Feedback may be verbal, nonverbal, or both. Clearly the receiver's feelings, attitudes, experiences, relationship with the sender, the communication climate, cultural factors, and so on affect the decision to respond—the message and method chosen for the response. As discussed earlier, the receiver's perception and expectations are important. This is often referred to as "noise," or that which might interfere with communication. If response occurs, the process may then turn around with the receiver becoming the sender and the original sender becoming the receiver. The receiver may also then communicate with other receivers. Two-way communication has then occurred.
5. The **context** is the situation or environment in which the communication takes place (for example, the nurse's station, a patient's room, a patient's home, the hallway, the clinic, the school nurse's office, a staff meeting, or during shift report). This aspect of the process is very important and takes into consideration factors such as noise, number of people present, stress level, emergency or routine, presence of management or supervisors, privacy in the patient care area, organizational culture, morale, ethics and legal requirements, technology and information systems, and so on (Finkelman, 1996).

Why should one be concerned about this process? First, the process can be used to analyze communication. Where was communication effective or ineffective? Was there a problem when the communicator developed the message? For example, if a nurse is too tired to be clear when giving directions to an unlicensed assistive personnel (UAP), this then affects the message (e.g., instead of telling the UAP to take blood pressures on four patients, one patient is forgotten). Sometimes a less effective **medium** is chosen; for example, a memo may be sent when it would have been better to call the person to get more immediate feedback. Analyzing communication by using these levels and elements of the communication process as a framework can help to identify where the communication process needs to be improved.

The communication process is affected by many factors that are external to the environment in which the communication may take place. For example, reimbursement issues and dealing with insurers can be problems, such as just trying to get approval for a patient procedure can strain a staff member's patience and impact communication. There may need to be telephone calls; written documentation of needs; and in some cases, actual face-to-face contact, and the result may still be unsatisfying. Some external factors cannot be controlled. An example is state health departments require the reporting of all cases of child abuse. If there is a breakdown in this legally mandated communication, the child may suffer physically, and the HCO may experience severe consequences such as fines and discipline of specific healthcare providers. In this situation, the HCO has no choice but to develop a communication process to ensure that this information is communicated via policy and procedure to guide staff about reporting possible child abuse.

Communication Process Components: Verbal and Nonverbal

VERBAL COMMUNICATION   Verbal communication is considered to be the most common type of communication. It is complex and can be described as written or oral, and by its tone, language, volume, frequency, choice of words, rate, and accent. Verbal communication, like all other types of communication, is affected by a person's gender, age, culture, stereotypes and biases, education, and impairments such as hearing or sight loss. Individuals are highly dependent on verbal communication and often are less aware of nonverbal communication.

NONVERBAL COMMUNICATION   Nonverbal communication is frequently used in clinical situations when staff assess patients and their responses. Staff members, however, are often not as aware of their own use of nonverbal communication with other staff, patients, and families. The major functions of nonverbal communication are expression of emotion; expression of interpersonal attitudes; maintenance of rituals; support of verbal communication; establishment, development, and maintenance of relationships; and self-presentation. Nonverbal communication is not something that is always in the awareness or control of the individual. To improve communication, a person needs to increase awareness of the impact of nonverbal communication and increase assessment of nonverbal communication during the communication process. Nonverbal communication can consist of facial expressions, body movements or posture, gestures, volume of speech, tone of voice, gait, and physical appearance. Body language typically includes facial expression, eye movements, body movements, posture, gestures, and proxemics (distance between individuals). This assessment must not only include nonverbal communication that the other party uses but also self-assessment of nonverbal communication. It is more difficult to be aware of how one is using nonverbal communication while one is using verbal communication. For example, when a nurse is discussing a procedure with a patient, is the nurse aware of personal facial expressions, body language, and tone of voice, or is the nurse just focused on the procedure? Some strategies that might be used to improve nonverbal communication are as follows:

- Maintain eye contact and a relaxed manner as this communicates sincerity.
- Smile if it is appropriate to the content, but do not smile constantly because this tends to make the receiver distrust the sender and the message.
- A neutral environment might be useful in circumstances in which meeting in one's office or on one's own territory might make the other person feel uncomfortable.
- If a person stands over or leans over another, it can make that person uncomfortable and feel a loss of power.
- Pulling away or appearing too casual may communicate superiority or disinterest.

Cultural issues are also important because there is great variation in nonverbal communication among different cultures and interpretation of nonverbals. Examples of questions to consider with different cultures are the following: Do men look directly at women who are not their wives? How do people greet one another? Does the husband speak for the wife? Answers to these questions and many others are important to know if a nurse is trying to teach a woman with her husband present. The IOM supports the need for the importance of cultural communication factors in all communication with patients, families, and staff (workforce diversity): "Sociocultural differences between patient and provider influence communication and clinical decision-making" (Institute of Medicine, 2003b, p. 214).

Nonverbal communication frequently causes problems because it is often difficult to assess and interpret. This communication includes anything other than the spoken word. It can be deliberate or unintentional, and when it is unintentional, it is out of the control of the sender or the receiver. When there is doubt about the interpretation, the best approach is to ask for clarification about the meaning; however, this is not always easy to do. The receiver may be hesitant, feel incompetent, be concerned that asking for information may be threatening, or not know how or what to ask. Comparing the nonverbal with the verbal may assist in greater understanding, but this is not always the case as a person's nonverbal communication may be different from the verbal. Nurses tend to use comparison of verbal and nonverbal communication more during their communication with patients than with coworkers. Nonverbal communication, however, is very important in work-related communication and should not be ignored. Delegation is a time when asking for clarification is critical, from the perspective of both delegator and delegatee. (See Chapter 15.)

ASSESSMENT OF COMMUNICATION EFFECTIVENESS

Communicators want to have productive communication when the sender sends a message. The goal is that the message will be received and understood as sent. Productive communication can lead to many positive benefits for individual staff, teams, structural units within the HCO, the HCO, the community, and for the patient and family. Some of these benefits are as follows:

- A team spirit with a common understanding and staff working toward common goals
- Participative management providing the staff with the opportunity to express different points of view and develop the best approach to problems
- Quick resolution of misunderstandings
- A comfortable environment that supports a motivational climate
- More creative thinking by nursing management and nursing staff
- Less staff turnover
- Less evidence of a rumor mill
- Clarification of responsibilities (Finkelman, 1996, pp. 1–1:13–14)

Communication Assessment Questions and Methods

Nurse managers, team leaders, and charge nurses need to periodically evaluate the effectiveness of the communication—their own communication, individual staff members, and team communication, which could be a team, unit, department, or the entire HCO. The following are questions that can be used to help evaluate communication effectiveness:

- What might be some indicators of staff communication problems?
- Do staff members feel comfortable expressing their feelings and opinions?
- Are some staff members trying to get on the good side of the nurse manager or leader and not communicating effectively?
- During meetings or in shift report, do staff ask questions?
- Do staff members contribute their ideas to the discussion when there are problems? Silence may be positive as it can allow time for thinking before responding; however, if the staff are silent for long periods without contributing to the discussion, this can be an indicator of a communication problem.
- What happens when messages do not seem to be understood or are misinterpreted?

Staff-to-staff communication provides the critical framework in which care occurs. Imagine how a nurse might provide care without using communication. The care would have to occur on an isolated island, and even in that situation, the nurse would still have to communicate with the patient. Problems, however, do occur even in the best communication situations. The following are some examples:

- Discussing patients and their care is part of staff responsibilities. This takes time and needs to be considered a critical aspect of each staff member's role. This is not to say that in some cases too much time can be spent talking about care rather than providing care. Undoubtedly every nurse encounters staff members who seem to talk too much, neglect work, interrupt others' work, and cause tension. This may mean that the nurse manager or team leader needs to talk to the staff member and determine the reason for this type of communication problem, discuss how it interferes with work and care of patients, and arrive at strategies to improve the staff member's communication and reduce the interruptions. Other staff may even discuss it with the staff member; however, this should be offered in private as positive criticism.
- Competition among staff can interfere with productive communication. It can lead to withholding of information, distortion of information, and poor morale. Why would staff be competitive? They might be seeking recognition for their work, better assignments, improved work schedules, or they might feel that some staff members are treated differently. Clearly this indicates that there are major problems in the work environment that need to be addressed so communication can improve.
- Confidentiality is an ever-present need in all clinical setting interactions, which is reinforced by the HIPAA law. (See Chapter 2.) Discussing staff and patient issues where others

who should not hear about them might hear the conversation is very easy to do. Staff get involved and forget; however, the problems that can result from this can be very serious. Staff members are busy, so when they can "reach out" to other staff for these discussions, they may do so in areas that are not private, for example in the hallway, elevator, or cafeteria. Even the nursing station must be considered an open area unless it is enclosed. Telephone conversations can also be easily overheard. Many HCOs now give staff mobile telephones to use in the clinical setting. These telephones are frequently used where conversations may be overheard. Nurses who work in the community must be particularly aware of this as they frequently use mobile telephones where the public can overhear confidential information or misinterpret what might be said by a healthcare professional (for example, taking calls while on a lunch break in a public restaurant or telephoning a patient while in another patient's home during a home visit).

- There needs to be greater consideration of staff feelings in the workplace. With heavy workloads, it is easy to forget about the feelings of coworkers. Dashing around, communicating in short sentences, and moving on creates an environment in which staff forget to connect and to listen. A critical element of positive communication is the comfort level. Do staff feel comfortable saying, "I need help," "I am overwhelmed"? Or do staff feel that this will be seen in a negative light? Staff communication may be sharp and caustic, leading to hurt feelings or anger, setting up barriers to future effective communication.

- Medical records and documentation are very important parts of communication in the healthcare delivery system. This form of communication must be clear and provide critical information that is required. Requirements come from the nursing profession; state boards of nursing; standards; state and federal laws and regulations; insurers; legal cases; and the HCO's policies, procedures, and quality improvement program. Assessment of this type of communication must include consideration of these regulations. It is particularly important today to follow insurer requirements, especially when describing patient problems, plan of care, and outcomes. This information affects decisions that are made and changes that are instituted, directs care evaluation, communicates responsibilities, identifies outcomes that should be met and (if they are met) determines reimbursement, and guides staff. The common response to medical malpractice issues, "If it is not documented, it did not happen," says much about the importance of this documentation. If a list were made of healthcare communication concerns, documentation would be a top priority.

- When a staff member does not understand something or what needs to be done, it is important to ask to have the information or instruction repeated or explained. If it is something that makes the staff member feel uncomfortable, these feelings should be discussed. This is very important in delegation, as is discussed in Chapter 15.

- Mutual trust is something that is not easy to accomplish or assess today. Poor or inconsistent communication, inadequate staff input during the change process, and fears such as job loss or change can damage trust. This trust is a critical component of communication. Developing strategies to build mutual trust is important. Effective timing is something that should be considered for important communication and assessment of the communication process.

- At times there seem to be several different "stories" or versions of information from various staff. This causes major communication and morale problems. Getting facts from the source and discussing them openly helps to resolve this problem.

- Many people use intuition, often unconsciously, and when it is used, it may predict what will happen within communication or within a situation. This may or may not be helpful as it may cause the sender or receiver to make the wrong assumption.

- Sometimes it is difficult to know when to use face-to-face communication and when to use the telephone or email. Telephone, text messages, and email communication usually take less time, but if it is important to have a face-to-face conversation, then time needs to be taken for this. When there is major conflict and miscommunication, blasting with a lot of emails is not effective. This is the time for a face-to-face meeting. Telephone, text messages, and email offer more control. When these methods are used, the sender selects the time when it is done, the time it takes is usually shorter, and it is easier to take notes while in the middle of the communication. Plus, email provides more time to think about what will be said. Although physical nonverbal communication cannot be observed with these methods, tone and use of words in email can communicate some aspects of nonverbal communication.

- Staff should not be left hanging. Feedback and follow-up are necessary for the development and maintenance of trust and to encourage two-way communication. It takes time to provide feedback, but it is time well spent.
- Interdepartmental/unit communication helps the nurse manager and staff see problems from the other department/unit's point of view. Without this communication, it is easy to be isolated and see only one viewpoint.
- There are times when communication in the nursing station, desk area, or the work area (such as in a clinic) is impossible or undesirable. If it is very busy, the message may be lost amid the confusion. If a sensitive topic needs to be discussed, this location is too public. Never assume that this area is private.
- Selecting the appropriate time to discuss a sensitive issue or even to communicate daily work-related information can make a critical difference. If a staff member is busy with patient care, administering medications, or documentation, this is not the best time. There are times such as immediately after a critical clinical incident that the staff are not able to discuss fully what has occurred due to emotions or fatigue. Often the first response is to discuss the situation; however, the best approach is to identify another time within a reasonable time frame to discuss the incident. Putting off a discussion is not always negative if it is done thoughtfully and follow-up action is actually taken (Finkelman, 1996, p. 1–1:14–15).

Barriers to Communication

The exchange of information and transmission of meaning (communication) among several individuals or teams throughout the HCO is not always successful. There are many barriers to communication that an organization, its management, and staff need to be aware of that affect short-term and long-term activities. The following list is far from complete, but it provides many critical examples of these barriers.

- **Failing to listen to others and not recognizing them:** This leads to negative feelings and responses. Active listening can improve this problem.
- **Using selective listening so one hears only what one wants to hear:** This is often due to the inability to recognize the needs and problems of others. Active listening and gaining more understanding of others' expectations can also improve this problem.
- **Failing to probe or inquire further when encountering vague information, obtaining inadequate answers, reaching a confusing interpretation, or following procedures and standards so closely that the message is missed:** Using open questions will make a difference with this problem.
- **Making overly judgmental statements:** This often occurs when the receiver decides the overall value of the message (e.g., a staff member who always complains may not be heard when there is legitimate need for complaint). Active listening, trying to understand other viewpoints, and stopping before responding may decrease this barrier.
- **Expressing opinions while intentionally or unintentionally intimidating others:** Asking for feedback can be helpful so steps can be taken to improve. Being direct rather than aggressive avoids setting up barriers.
- **Overusing reassuring statements and rejecting statements:** These types of statements cut off communication. More open communication that respects the other person can limit this barrier.
- **Using a defensive stance stops open communication:** The communicator needs to be more open and recognize that there is more than one point of view.
- **Making a false inference:** This often occurs when someone jumps to a conclusion without enough information. Getting more information before responding or communicating can limit this barrier.
- **Using personal criticism, profanity, and crudity:** These responses act only as barriers to effective communication and are very destructive to the work climate. Respecting others is critical in communication and can help to limit this barrier.
- **Responding to spatial issues:** Space can be a barrier. If too close, people may feel uncomfortable, particularly if a person crosses too far into the person's safe zone. If

there is a lot of space, people may feel distant from one another. Spatial factors to consider are:

- How close are the receiver and sender?
- Has one of them crossed into personal space that makes the other person uncomfortable?
- What are the cultural issues related to space?
- What is the space between the staff and the patient?
- In a team meeting, what is the arrangement of the seating area: at a table, in a circle, in another layout?
- What is the distance between them?
- Is it easy to have eye contact?

- **Keeping secrets:** Secrecy is very destructive to communication and to HCOs. It decreases staff trust and interferes with team building. This leads to ineffective communication. Communicating fully and openly will increase effective communication and keeps the channels of communication open. It is not easy to develop and maintain a culture in which open communication is valued. Chapter 1 emphasizes the importance of this type of communication in leadership theories such as emotional intelligence.

In an open communication environment, staff know that ideas are respected and should be shared. Effective managers openly discuss the communication process and actively pursue greater communication with staff. Communication is considered when organizational goals are evaluated; assessment of the HCO's communication is integrated into the process. Leaders and managers advocate that each staff member has a responsibility to contribute ideas and opinions, and they ask staff to contribute and give them time to respond. Communication should be part of performance evaluation for each staff member throughout the organization.

Information Overload

Today in most HCOs, it is very easy for staff to experience information overload. Information is coming from multiple sources at one time. It is difficult to decide what is important, and it seems that everyone feels that his or her needs are more important and require an immediate response. With the growth of information technology, there is now an increased burden of too much communication and often done too quickly with less real people contact. Emails, text messages, and the Internet add a layer to the ability to communicate memos, letters, and reports. Medical record documentation also increases the amount of information that nurses have to cope with today. With the increase in quantity, there is also increased speed; staff get information faster and feel compelled to respond faster. This increasing speed of communication receipt has also spoiled staff to expect information quickly, and when it does not come quickly, staff experience stress and maybe criticism.

What are the critical issues with information overload? Staff need to consider the following questions: What information is important, and what is extraneous? How quickly is a response expected, and what is a realistic response time? What is the purpose of the information? Does the information need to be saved? How should it be saved? Is this the end point of the information, or should it be sent on to another? If so, to whom and why? What is the quality of the information? Who sent the information? What is the source of the information? It is very helpful when the sender indicates a time frame for response. This simple intervention can do much to decrease the stress of feeling compelled to respond quickly.

Importance of Feedback: Giving and Receiving Feedback

Feedback is a part of all communication. To become an effective communicator, nurses need to learn how to give and receive feedback. First and foremost, feedback should not be described as something that is negative. Most staff immediately assume that feedback means "bad news." Positive feedback, what has been done well and so on, is critical. Now feedback can be given in many forms such as face-to-face orally or written—even through email, though this is not ideal, and in other written forms. Face-to-face provides opportunity for immediate response and dialogue. This is usually better as clarification can be provided and questions can be asked and answered.

Feedback should flow in four directions in HCOs: (1) from manager to staff, (2) from staff to managers, (3) from staff to staff, and (4) from staff to patients and families/significant others. The first two types, between managers and staff, can be difficult, especially if staff feel uncomfortable and threatened in the work setting. How can HCOs encourage staff to give feedback to managers so it is not just manager to staff? Typical methods that are used to increase staff feedback are:

- managers asking directly for feedback.
- allowing time in staff meetings for feedback.
- suggestion boxes.
- surveys.
- informal meetings such as at lunch or during break times.
- problem solving or project teams.
- an open-door policy when the manager has open office hours.
- walk-around management in which the manager is present on the clinical units and staff can approach the manager with comments and issues.

When feedback can be given freely and received without undue stress, the work environment is a much more positive environment. Feedback should focus on performance and outcomes with clear description of the issues. Staff need time to respond to the feedback and to ask questions.

How should staff respond to supervisory feedback? The most common response is to jump to a defensive response, but the better approach is to carefully consider what is shared. Listening is just as important in this type of communication as in other types. The tendency is to immediately try to explain actions or become defensive rather than to first listen. Sometimes a supervisor is only offering an alternative solution that needs to be thought about. If managers or supervisors do not offer feedback, the staff need to ask for it. The staff sometimes think that supervisory feedback means that all of the coworkers think the same thing as the nurse manager. Supervisory feedback should represent the manager's opinion. Though every HCO should have a formal performance review for all staff, this does not mean that feedback should not be shared at other times or that staff should not ask for feedback.

Improving feedback communication can be done by using several techniques and considering some factors related to feedback:

- Think before you speak.
- Jargon and unfamiliar terms can confuse a conversation, requiring additional feedback for clarification. Keep language clear and simple. Consider your tone and pace, and make eye contact.
- Actively listen and use what you hear and observe (nonverbal communication) to better understand the communication.
- Be aware that making assumptions may lead to problems in understanding the communication and in your response.
- Questions can help clarify and stimulate feedback; repeat information if needed for clarification.
- Feedback to the staff needs to be constructive and positive, avoiding downgrading comments and making remarks that are hurtful and not effective feedback.
- Follow-up is also an important technique to improve communication. In the busy clinical setting, it is easy to forget to follow up.
- Empathy is important. It means that the sender needs to be receiver oriented or have a greater understanding of the receiver to better understand the receiver's perspective. This is closely related to the need for mutual trust between the sender and receiver. Those who use empathy recognize that it is important to understand another person. Questioning and active listening improve empathy. This process requires that the person focus on what is happening and avoid thinking of other things or allowing one's mind to wander.

Feedback should include examples and allow time to discuss them. The focus should be on performance and expectations, engaging the staff member in providing feedback about the work as well as the manager.

Grapevine: Is It Good or Bad?

The grapevine is present in every HCO, within its service areas, units, and departments. The grapevine can be positive or negative. Clearly information can be distorted in the grapevine, individual feelings can be hurt, and information can be very difficult to control. The grapevine can

Exchanging Information Across Shifts

The ICU has been having problems with communication between shifts, particularly on the weekends. This problem is brought up in the monthly staff meeting. A nurse says, "I think the night shift has not shared important patient information. It has led to serious errors, and I don't want to be held responsible for these errors." Silence follows this statement. As the nurse manager, you know you need to respond, so you say, "What is going on?"

Questions:

1. What do you think of the nurse manager's response?
2. What information do you need?
3. What is the best way to frame the problem?
4. How might you go about assessing communication in the unit?
5. What are strategies you might use to resolve the communication problems?

affect staff morale when information that should not be communicated is shared, when communication is distorted and its meaning causes damage, or when staff feel left out. Efforts to eliminate the grapevine will undoubtedly fail as grapevines seem to be ingrained in all organizations and have a life of their own. Managers need to learn how to use the grapevine to their advantage. However, using the grapevine can be risky as once a message is put into the grapevine, one loses control of the message and how it is presented. If the manager wants to get a message out quickly, the grapevine can be used if the leader knows how to access it. In addition, corrected information can be put into the grapevine. Given this information about the grapevine, what is the best way to decrease the damage the grapevine can cause? The best approach is keeping staff informed. This is particularly important when there are critical issues (for example, budget, staffing, and plans for change). Staff need to also be careful with the grapevine, recognizing that factual information may not always be found in communication that is received via the grapevine.

COMMUNICATION METHODS

There are four common communication methods that are used by staff and management: written, face-to-face, storytelling, and information technology. With each of these methods, timing needs to be considered. What is the best time to use a particular communication method? Sometimes it is better to talk to someone face-to-face, while at other times, an email will be just as effective. The time it takes to complete the communication is another concern. How quickly does the communication need to occur? Today, with the technology that is available, communication can be delivered quickly. This may or may not be a positive outcome. What is the best time to initiate communication? The situation, sender, receiver, stress, energy level, and support that might be needed are some of the factors to consider as well as timing. Each of the following communication methods is important for nurses in their daily practice.

Written Communication

With so many communication options available today, it is often difficult to know when to use each method. Written communication provides a paper trail—documentation of the communication, which for some communication is important. It is particularly important to use this method when a record needs to be kept (e.g., document an important one-to-one meeting; minutes of a team, staff, or project meeting; disciplinary meeting; performance evaluation; reimbursements; and so on). Written communication may be not only in emails now, but also as attachments to emails. It is important to remember that longer messages do not necessarily include more useful information. Time is important so messages need to get to the point and include required information.

Effective written communication requires thought from the sender. There are two types of messages: direct and indirect. The latter is typically used when the sender expects the receiver to have a negative response to the message. This is the message that begins with general comments, and the bad news is buried near the end. An example might be the letter that comes after a job interview with an introduction describing the wonderful candidates who applied and how difficult the decision was to make, which is followed by the section that says someone else got the job. A direct message gets right to the point, and this type is often used when the receiver is expected to respond positively to the information. This does not mean, however, that bad news should not be communicated with a more direct style. Often the sender's comfort level determines the method. Breaking bad news gently seems to make it less bad or less difficult for the sender, not necessarily for the receiver. Written communication needs to be reviewed and edited before sending. A timely response is always appreciated. This communication method, as is true of all communication, needs to be adapted for the audience. Graphics and other visuals may be appropriate and added to written communication, but they should augment the message, not detract from it.

Written communication can be sent in several ways: hard copy via interdepartmental mail, email, fax, U.S. Postal Service, other delivery companies, or hand delivered by the sender. The form that this type of communication takes can also vary: an informal note, memorandum (memo), formal letter, minutes, policy or procedure, surveys, data collecting tools, or performance evaluation. Most organizations have specific forms or formats that need to be used for memos, emails, minutes, policies, procedures, and performance evaluations. Memos need to follow the HCO's format with a clear identification of the subject or topic. Careful consideration needs to be given as to who should receive the memo. Content should be concise and relevant. A memo is not a lengthy report, but rather short and to the point. Clearly all patient care documentation is a critical component of written communication.

Face-to-Face Communication

Face-to-face communication is one of the most frequently used communication methods; however, electronic communication has had a major impact causing a move away from face-to-face communication. There are times, however, when face-to-face communication is the preferred method, particularly when personal sensitive information needs to be discussed. When a dialogue is needed with greater give-and-take, in-person communication is better. If in-person communication cannot be done and is needed, then the next choice is to use the telephone or, when possible, synchronous online conversation. Some HCOs, especially large healthcare networks, have equipment for videoconferencing, which is discussed later in this chapter. This is another alternative to in-person communication. Box 14-1 provides other examples of communication techniques to improve trust and effective communication.

Active listening, a technique that is critical for effective communication, means listening for the message's full meaning and ensuring that judgment of interpretations does not interfere with the understanding of the message. This takes concentration and involvement on the part of the listener. Listening also means that the person is willing to listen even when it means that what is heard may be negative or unpleasant. Seeking out information sometimes means taking risks. It is not uncommon for staff to tell nurse managers what they think the nurse manager wants to hear rather than providing a full disclosure. This does not demonstrate that the staff feel empowered, and it is not productive communication. Staff members want to feel that managers and other staff

BOX 14-1	**EXAMPLES OF TECHNIQUES DESIGNED TO PROMOTE TRUST AND EFFECTIVE COMMUNICATION**

- Demonstrate respect.
- Recognize differences and individuality.
- Show warmth and caring.
- Use active listening and silence when needed.
- Give sufficient time to answer questions.
- Maintain confidentiality.
- Demonstrate congruence between verbal and nonverbal behaviors.
- Use appropriate tone of voice.

- Use appropriate eye contact.
- Use nonverbal communication appropriately.
- Be honest and open.
- Give complete, consistent information.
- Plan best time to discuss difficult issues.
- Control distractions.
- Set limits when conversation is emotional.
- Use questioning, restating, paraphrasing, clarification, and summarizing.
- Confirm message received as intended.

are communicating *with* them, not *to* them, and the presence of listening increases the chance that communication will be a joint endeavor. Barriers to effective listening include making assumptions before one hears the communication, noninterest in the topic or issue, history of problems with the sender, and feeling as if the sender is dictating to the receiver. Another barrier today can be electronic communication when staff members are looking at their mobile phones to read and send emails or text messages or are using their laptops or tablets in meetings for more than note taking. These tools have improved communication, but they can also interfere with active listening as staff members multitask their way through meetings and as they work.

Questioning can help to resolve some communication problems to get more information and open up the communication. An open-ended question is a question that requires a more extensive answer that a simple "yes," "no," or "I agree." Why is this type of question more effective in most cases than the closed question? Mainly because it expands and facilitates the dialogue between the sender and the receiver, allowing for greater exchange of information.

Storytelling

Storytelling is a useful communication technique that can be used to clarify a confusing message, inspire others, and make communication more interesting. As Denning (2011) describes, storytelling is a way to get to important information and share it in a meaningful way with others—in this case staff or other managers. Storytelling is really used naturally by all managers but may not be used in a thoughtful manner to get the most out of it. Storytelling can be used in many situations, but it is particularly effective during times of change when innovation is needed. It supplements analytic thinking in organizations. Springboard stories are used to enable staff to move to the next level of understanding. As Denning notes, not all stories result in this type of effect. Typically stories that have the perspective of a single protagonist who is in a predicament that is prototypical of the organization are the most successful. It needs to be familiar to the staff for it to be effective, yet it must get their attention. When stories are told, they need to be brief and get to the point. Storytelling can be difficult, particularly if the audience is skeptical, but even under normal circumstances, the storyteller, just like any sender of a message, must consider the situation, the receiver, and the nature of the message. The storyteller needs to identify and understand the purpose of communication; choose the right method and time while considering contextual factors; and above all, adapt when cues are picked up indicating that the communication is not effective.

Information Technology and Communication

Information technology has become important in healthcare communication. It is used for organization, staff-to-staff, and staff-to-patient communication. This is done through the HCO website, email, and other methods such as smartphones. Hand-held devices are used in many hospitals to assist with communication. With the increased development of communication technology, there has also been an increase in problems that are encountered with this type of communication (for example, hackers, viruses, multitasking, and information overload). The information highway grows, and those who want to meddle with communication and productivity increase. Hackers who interfere with computer transmission and can break into secure information are of major concern for healthcare providers due to the need of maintaining records and patient information confidentiality. In addition, viruses can also destroy software and crucial databases of patient and organization information. Healthcare providers, like all who use or interact with computers, have experienced times when the "system was down" or inaccessible. This is a major problem in HCOs when clinical staff need this information and access to interactive communication to provide care. Backup plans are clearly critical for every HCO. Staff need to be informed about these plans and when they should be used. Information technology has radically changed communication—personal and work related. (See Chapter 19 for more information on technology and communication.)

TELEPHONE The telephone is certainly the most basic of the technology options available today and continues to be a very important communication method. Use of mobile telephones is now the norm with growth in use of smartphones that have Internet connection and text messaging. Some hospitals are giving their staff mobile phones to use while at work so they can be reached, working around paging systems. Here are some simple reminders to improve the telephone communication method:

- Answer the phone with your name and title.
- When taking a message, repeat the information for the caller.
- With the increasing use of voice message systems, be prepared to leave a message.
- Keep emotions under control. Some callers may not be doing this and may say things that increase emotions. Stick to the point and get the information you need. If you do not have the answer, tell the caller you will return the call by a certain date/time or ask someone else to call.
- When you conclude a conversation that requires action, summarize the key issues and actions to be taken.
- Healthcare staff frequently receive calls that must be transferred. Check the number you are transferring to and tell the caller the number.

Voice mail has become so much a part of the workplace that it is easy to get frustrated when someone does not have voice mail or it is not working. This method can be used to send routine information and information that does not require a response. It can be used at any time and, in fact, is a method that is often used when the sender does not really want to talk to the receiver but rather just wants to get the message sent. When a message is left, clearly identify who is calling; from what location or organization, if relevant; date and time; purpose of call; and, if a response is required, provide suggested times and method for a return communication. Callers need to speak slowly, repeating numbers and email addresses. Some thought needs to be given to the content of the message so the caller does not appear confused and the message remains clear. Long messages should be avoided. If possible, identify good times to return the call. Confidentiality is important, so it is important to consider the message that is left and the nature of the message, which may be heard by others, for example, if leaving a message for a patient who does not want any healthcare information shared with others.

EMAIL Many HCOs have email policies and procedures, and these policies need to be communicated to staff members when they receive their email addresses. One can never assume that work-related email systems are private as the employer has the right to review emails in its email system. Email etiquette has been developing over the years. It is easy to forget in the world of rapid-fire messaging that there are important legal and confidentiality issues that need to be considered. Patient names and other significant personal information or identifiers should not be used. Care needs to be taken when sending copyrighted material. As this requires permission, policies and procedures should be followed. Security within the organization's email system is an important concern and HCOs need to review security with staff. Common topics are using passwords, not sharing passwords, and noting that when messages are deleted they may stay on the server and thus are accessible long term to the HCO. HCOs have policies about who may access sensitive information, and these policies must be followed. Some organizations have policies about using the organization's email system for personal messages. Thought needs to be taken when writing messages, remembering that once they are sent, they cannot be retrieved. Email is a good method for sending routine messages and reminders about meetings, sharing reports, and so on. The following are some email etiquette guidelines (MindTools®, 2014b):

- Remember that email may not be read quickly, so when the message is urgent, a telephone call may be a better method. At a minimum, indicate the message is "urgent" or "priority" and request receipt reply.
- Email should be used thoughtfully. Sending too many messages that are unimportant may mean that important messages are ignored.
- Specify the subject in the subject line.
- It has become more acceptable to attach formal letters or résumés to an email, but the sender should first inquire if this is acceptable such as with contracts.
- Acronyms and emoticons (symbols) should not be used in business emails.
- Break up content by using paragraphing. This makes it easier to read. Use bulleting or numbering to highlight information. Put the most important information at the beginning of the message to ensure it is read.
- Color can also be used for emphasis, but it should be used carefully. Some colors do not show up well on the screen. When printed, the message probably will be printed in black

and white. Complex graphics, such as graphic letterheads, should be avoided as they take longer to download.

- When forwarding messages, include only relevant information from the original message to reduce the amount of reading required and length of time for receiving the message. The forwarded message should be clearly distinguished from the original message. When a message is forwarded, consideration should be given as to who are the appropriate people to receive the message. The sender may not have intended for the message to be sent to others.

- When using reply, check to make sure that the reply message should go to all recipients automatically or just one recipient. A common error is to click "reply all" when really one wants the message to go to only one sender.

- There are times when a recipient may need more time to respond to a message, for example, to obtain more information. When this occurs, the recipient should acknowledge receipt of the message and indicate when a more detailed message will be sent.

- Not all messages sent via email are received, and messages stating that there was a problem sending the message are not always sent. It is a good idea to ask the recipient to acknowledge receipt of important messages so the sender can be sure the message was received.

- Use of virus protection is critical. Downloading messages, attachments, and information from the Internet is a good way for an entire system to get a virus, so it is important to make it a practice to check for viruses first.

- When an attachment is sent, double-check to see if the correct attachment is attached before hitting the send button. Another common problem is to say a document is attached then forget to attach it. Extremely large attachments should be avoided unless the receiver has been consulted about the size.

- There is a tendency to ignore grammar, spelling, and so on in emails, but this should be considered in business-related emails.

- Do not use all caps, as this indicates shouting.

- Care needs to be taken with using the "reply all" option as there may be people included on the email who should not get the information.

- Posting an out-of-office message is helpful, sharing when a response can be expected and whom to contact if there is need for an immediate response or information.

VIDEOCONFERENCING, WEBINAR, AND OTHER WEB-BASED CONFERENCING The advantage to **videoconferencing** is it is a live interaction with visual images while the communication takes place. It also can reduce costs and time, as staff do not have to travel to another physical location. However, the initial cost of the equipment must be considered. Staff require some training in the use of the equipment, but it is not difficult. Videoconferencing is also used in telehealth. One example of its use is in providing medical consultations between rural healthcare providers and academic medical centers. More common uses are to conduct meetings and educational programs. Webinars and other types of Internet-based group communication systems are important today. They can save travel time and costs yet keep staff and others in contact and able to work collaboratively.

WEBSITES Websites are very common today; most HCOs have them. They are used by organizations to communicate to a broad audience such as staff, patients, families, healthcare providers, consumers, the public, and so on. They need to be designed carefully with consideration given to ease of use, accuracy, timeliness and current information, level of information that might require secure entry, ethics of advertising on the page, and graphics and audio. Nursing staff should be involved in the development of web pages and consider what should be included that would be helpful to the nursing staff and the care they provide. Websites can be useful in sharing patient and family health prevention education material, contact information for questions and further information, guidance for admission preparation, links to reliable websites that can provide additional information, and support information (for example, related to cancer, diabetes, arthritis, new mothers, breastfeeding, and many other health issues). It is critical that the website is monitored and updated. Responsibility for the monitoring needs to be clearly defined. If information is not current, this acts as a barrier to effective communication.

SOCIAL NETWORKING There is rapid growth of social networking methods through the Internet. Facebook and other methods are used to post information and connect with others who have similar interests. How this will be used in work settings is still unknown but no doubt will be used more. Twitter is another type of short Internet communication method that has grown rapidly.

APPLYING EVIDENCE-BASED PRACTICE

Evidence for Effective Leadership and Practice

CITATION: Mayor, E., Bangerter, A., & Aribot, M. (2011). Task uncertainty and communication during nursing shift handovers. *Journal of Advanced Nursing, 68*(9), 1956–1966.

OVERVIEW: This study examines handovers and communication related to task uncertainty as the team works. Nurse managers from 80 units in 18 hospitals were interviewed, and content-analysis was used to examine the interview data. Communication and other factors had an impact on handovers.

APPLICATION: Handovers are connected to teams and communication. As patients are "passed" from team members to other teams, errors occur, many associated with communication.

Questions:

1. What is the aim of this study?
2. Describe the researchers' review of the problem of handovers and methods used to implement handovers.
3. What were the results of the study? If you were a nurse manager, how would you apply this information to the work you do—to your unit, teams on your unit, handovers, and communication?

Staff need to be careful about sharing work-related content in social networking methods as this is not acceptable and can lead to employee-employer problems and even to legal problems.

RESOLVING COMMUNICATION PROBLEMS AND IMPROVING COMMUNICATION

The nurse manager plays a critical role in setting the tone for communication and maintaining open communication channels so staff can do their work and positive patient care outcomes can be reached. The manager must continuously assess the communication climate to ensure that it supports effective communication.

Asking others for feedback about their communication needs is helpful, and this information should be considered carefully. Include an assessment of nonverbal communication as it can make the difference between effective and noneffective communication. Specific methods that can be used to improve communication when it occurs are increased use of paraphrasing, reflection, and summarization. When paraphrasing is used, a person restates what another person has said and asks for confirmation of what was said. The focus is on facts, and the statement should be short. Reflection focuses on the speaker's feelings, and the receiver of the message restates what the receiver thinks are the feelings expressed. Again, this is done for confirmation. Summarization combines content and feelings by restating both of these elements for confirmation. Additional strategies that can be used to improve staff communication include the following:

- Communicate the "why" behind the "what."
- Realize that effective communication takes time.
- Accept negative news as information, and do not take it personally.
- Respond nondefensively when people express differing or contradictory ideas and views.
- Report situations as accurately as possible, and avoid downplaying negative factors.
- Send important organizational messages by at least two methods (for example, email and a written memo or verbally and written).
- Do not rely so much on written communication as people often do not read it.
- Use active listening in all conversations.
- Select the location for discussing sensitive issues carefully.
- Say what you mean; avoid assumptions and ensure that the receiver has less need to turn to assumptions.
- Validate to ensure that what has been said has been heard and understood.
- Stress can interfere with communication, while managing stress can improve communication.
- Use appropriate eye contact.
- State information clearly, backed up with research, to get to the facts.
- Think before speaking.

- When you cannot answer a question, state that you do not have the information you need and that you will look for the information and follow up.
- Summarize at the end of a lengthy conversation and ask for confirmation from the other party.
- Use "I" statements, which are more effective than "you" statements and are less likely to put the other person on the offensive.
- Thank others for their feedback and suggestions as this recognizes they have been heard and supports further communication.
- Provide credible information; trust can make or break how a message is received and interpreted.
- Select the time to communicate carefully when difficult questions must be asked or there is a difficult discussion; a time when the other person (receiver) might be more receptive.

Different people have different ways or styles of communication. Recognizing one's style will help to improve communication and to use the most effective approach to communication. Figure 14-2 provides an example of a perspective of competencies related to effective communication.

Communication is complex and requires that staff use a thoughtful process to communicate effectively. It is something that is used daily in practice and management and often is not viewed as important until there is a problem with it. Throughout this text, communication is a driving element for effective managers who are leaders.

Communicates	
Leaders communicate effectively by clearly expressing ideas and actively listening to others. By understanding the nature and importance of communication and practicing effective communication techniques, leaders will relate better to others and be able to translate goals into actions. Communication is essential to all other leadership competencies.	
Listens actively	• Listens and watches attentively. • Makes appropriate notes. • Tunes into content, emotion, and urgency. • Uses verbal and nonverbal means to reinforce with the speaker that you are paying attention. • Reflects on new information before expressing views.
Determines information-sharing strategies	• Shares necessary information with others and subordinates. • Protects confidential information. • Coordinates plans with higher, lower, and adjacent individuals and affected organizations. • Keeps higher and lower headquarters, superiors, and subordinates informed.
Employs engaging communication techniques	• States goals to energize others to adopt and act on them. • Speaks enthusiastically and maintains listeners' interest and involvement. • Makes appropriate eye contact when speaking. • Uses gestures that are appropriate but not distracting. • Uses visual aids as needed. • Acts to determine, recognize, and resolve misunderstandings.
Conveys thoughts and ideas to ensure shared understanding	• Expresses thoughts and ideas clearly to individuals and groups. • Uses correct grammar and doctrinally correct phrases. • Recognizes potential miscommunication. • Uses appropriate means for communicating a message. • Communicates clearly and concisely up, down, across, and outside the organization. • Clarifies when there is some question about goals, tasks, plans, performance expectations, and role responsibilities.
Presents recommendations so others understand advantages	• Uses logic and relevant facts in dialogue. • Keeps conversations on track. • Expresses well-thoughtout and well-organized ideas.
Is sensitive to cultural factors in communication	• Maintains awareness of communication customs, expressions, actions, or behaviors. • Demonstrates respect for others.

Figure 14-2 Competency: Communicates and associated components and actions

Source: U.S. Army. (2006). *Army leadership: Competent, confident, and agile.* Retrieved from http://fas.org/irp/doddir/army/fm6-22.pdf

APPLYING LEADERSHIP AND MANAGEMENT

My Hospital Unit: An Evolving Case Experience

You are concerned about several staff complaining to you that there is poor communication on your unit. They do not feel that staff are sharing, and there is poor communication among nurses and the interprofessional teams. You had not noticed this and are concerned that you missed the signals of a problem. What might you do to better ensure that you are on top of and ahead of problems like this in the future? What can you do to improve this situation? Describe the steps you would take. Consider how you would involve staff.

BSN and *Master's Essentials:* Application to Content

BSN Essentials **(American Association of Colleges of Nursing, 2008) as Applied to this Chapter:**

- I. Liberal Education for Baccalaureate Generalist Nursing Practice
- II. Basic Organizational and Systems Leadership for Quality Care and Patient Safety
- VI. Interprofessional Communication and Collaboration for Improving Patient Health Outcomes

Master's Essentials **(American Association of Colleges of Nursing, 2011) as Applied to this Chapter:**

- I. Background for Practice from Sciences to Humanities
- II. Organizational and Systems Leadership
- VII. Interprofessional Collaboration for Improving Patient and Population Health Outcomes

Applying AONE Competencies

Identify which of the AONE competencies found in Appendix A apply to the content of this chapter.

Engaging in the Content: Critical Thinking and Clinical Reasoning and Judgment

Discussion Questions

1. What are the critical elements of effective communication?
2. Describe the four directions of communication and how they are different.
3. What are three common barriers to effective communication?
4. Assess your own communication, identifying strengths and weaknesses.
5. Make a list of communication technology methods and the pros and cons for using each one.

Application Exercises

1. When communication problems are analyzed, it is important to consider all of the process's components: the sender, the message, the receiver, feedback, and the context. Assessment of communication should include these factors with the understanding that communication is rarely perfect. This chapter has discussed many of the elements associated with the communication process. If you were a team leader, what might you routinely include in your assessment of the team's communication? Develop a checklist of critical elements to assess.
2. With your team, review the communication barriers and discuss methods to prevent them. (Online Application Option)
3. Errors in healthcare delivery are a serious concern, as has been noted in the Institute of Medicine report *To Err Is*

Human (1999). Interview a nurse manager or a team leader, and ask for examples of errors that have occurred. What are they? Are the examples related to ineffective communication? If so, in what way? How could future similar errors be prevented? What is the healthcare organization doing to improve communication? Share your results. (Online Application Option)
4. With your assigned team, determine how you might assess the team's communication using information in this chapter. Then use your assessment plan to assess the team's communication. (Online Application Option)
5. Discuss with your team examples of storytelling you have experienced. What was the impact of this communication method? (Online Application Option)

References

American Association of Colleges of Nursing. (2008). *The essentials of baccalaureate education for professional nursing practice*. Washington, DC: Author.

American Association of Colleges of Nursing. (2011). *The essentials of master's education in nursing*. Washington, DC: Author.

American Nurses Association. (2009). *Nursing administration: Scope and standards of practice*. Silver Spring, MD: Author.

American Nurses Association. (2010). *Nursing: Scope and standards of practice* (2nd ed.). Silver Spring, MD: Author.

Denning, S. (2011). *The leader's guide to storytelling: Mastering the art and discipline of business narrative* (2nd ed.). San Francisco, CA: Jossey-Bass.

Finkelman, A. (1996). *Psychiatric nursing administration manual*. Gaithersburg, MD: Aspen Publishers, Inc.

Finkelman, A., & Kenner, C. (2016). *Professional nursing concepts. Competencies for quality leadership* (3rd ed.). Boston, MA: Jones and Bartlett Publishers.

Institute of Medicine. (1999). *To err Is human*. Washington, DC: National Academies Press.

Institute of Medicine. (2003a). *Health professions education*. Washington, DC: National Academies Press.

Institute of Medicine. (2003b). *Unequal treatment*. Washington, DC: National Academies Press.

Joint Commission. (2007). "What did the doctor say?" Improving health literacy to protect patient safety. Retrieved from http://www.joint-commission.org/assets/1/18/improving_health_literacy.pdf

MindTools®. (2014a). The communication cycle. Retrieved from http://www.mindtools.com/pages/article/communication-cycle.htm

MindTools®. (2014b). Writing effective emails. Retrieved from http://www.mindtools.com/CommSkll/EmailCommunication.htm

O'Daniel, M., & Rosenstein, A. (2008). Professional communication and team collaboration. In R. Hughes (Ed.), *Patient safety and quality: An evidence-based handbook for nurses*. Rockville, MD: Agency for Healthcare Research and Quality. Retrieved from http://www.ncbi.nlm.nih.gov/books/NBK2637/

15 Delegation for Effective Outcomes

⬤ LEARNING OUTCOMES

Before you begin, take a moment to familiarize yourself with the learning outcomes for this chapter.

> › Examine the definition of "delegation" and related delegation roles.
> › Critique the benefits of using delegation.
> › Examine key legal issues related to delegation.
> › Compare and contrast responsibility, authority, and accountability as they apply to delegation.
> › Apply the delegation process in clinical situations when unlicensed assistive personnel are used.
> › Assess methods to monitor and improve delegation to reach effective patient outcomes.

WHAT'S AHEAD

With today's emphasis on teams, collaboration, and coordination in the healthcare system (Institute of Medicine, 2001, 2003) and a more diverse workforce, any type of leadership position eventually requires the use of delegation to ensure the job gets done and that effective patient and healthcare organization (HCO) outcomes are met. Delegation should be focused on the patient—what is best to ensure quality patient care. Not only do nurse managers need to use delegation, but nurses in staff positions must also use delegation daily. **Delegation** makes the best use of the talents and expertise of all staff as it facilitates the HCO's work. To perform delegation effectively, nurses need to develop competencies in delegation and supervision. As has been discussed in several chapters in this text, no one person can do it all. Delegation is essential to productive organizations.

KEY TERMS

- accountability
- assignment
- authority
- competent
- delegatee
- delegation
- delegator
- perform
- responsibility
- standards of practice
- supervision
- unlicensed assistive personnel (UAP)
- vicarious liability/ respondeat superior

DELEGATION: WHAT IS IT?

It seems there should be a simple definition for "delegation," but it is not a simple process. First, delegation can relate to assigning a specific task, a range of tasks, or a major job such as a project or leadership of a team. Registered nurses (RNs) must consider delegation carefully in their roles to protect patients and advocate for them. The RN transfers the responsibility yet retains outcome accountability (American Nurses Association, 2005). For example, the RN, in delegating a task such as giving a patient a bath to an assistive individual, transfers the responsibility for the performance of the bath but retains professional accountability for the outcome.

Typically what drives a leader or a staff nurse to use delegation is simply that he or she cannot do it all. The nursing process is the domain of the RN; the following describes how this impacts delegation related to what part of the process can be delegated and is also included in Figure 15-1 (American Nurses Association & National Council of State Boards of Nursing, 2006):

- Assessment: Cannot be delegated because input is solicited
- Diagnosis: Cannot be delegated because this requires professional nursing knowledge and experience
- Planning: Cannot be delegated because input is solicited
- Intervention: Can be delegated with supervision; not all interventions can be delegated
- Evaluation: Cannot be delegated because input is solicited

Some key terms are important to consider as one discusses delegation (American Nurses Association, 2005). The **delegator** is the person who does the delegation, and the **delegatee** is the person who receives it. Supervision has a major role in delegation. This involves guidance or direction, including evaluation and follow-up provided by the delegator to the delegatee. Much of this discussion will focus on delegation to **unlicensed assistive personnel (UAP)** who are nonprofessional staff, often trained by the HCO or in a state training program, which may offer a certification status. They assist RNs and licensed practical/vocational nurses (LPNs/LVNs) and have limited interventions they may perform. The titles for UAP vary considerably, but some examples are nurses' aides, orderlies, attendants, and technicians.

Benefits of Delegation

Delegation offers many benefits to the HCO and to the staff. It is a process that, if done following recommended principles, increases the opportunity to provide quality care that meets outcomes. This is the overall benefit, but it also offers a method for allocation of resources that should be more efficient and effective (American Nurses Association & National Council of State Boards of Nursing, 2006). Dividing up the work in a logical manner allows the RN to focus on higher-level tasks while still being accountable for the patient's overall care. This also then impacts cost of care, for example, when salaries are considered and the HCO can then have a mix of staff at various salary levels, which supports cost effectiveness. In this sense, the RN is a broker of patient care resources (Weydt, 2010). There is also a time-saving aspect to delegation as activities are allocated among others, thereby multiplying the ability to get work done more efficiently. Professional growth can occur when staff members are challenged to develop new skills as they take on new opportunities. The delegator, who might be a manager, team leader, or staff nurse, has more time available to do other activities. When delegation is done in a thoughtful manner, the environment is typically one in which staff feel valued and trusted.

Delegation has always been present in nursing and, at different points in its history, has been more important than other tools. With the increasing use of UAP, delegation is now a skill that every nurse must have and use effectively. This includes newly licensed nurses, as it is difficult for even new nurses to avoid delegation in any healthcare setting. Delegation is dependent on transferring a task to a competent staff member, which implies a process as well as indicates that it is something the nurse would do but is giving the responsibility to someone else. **Competent** means the person who will do the task has the required skills and experience. The nurse must be able to determine that the staff member can do the task. **Authority**, or the power to act, is given to the staff person. **Perform** means that an action must take place, and this action is described as a selected nursing task in a selected situation. The nurse must tell the staff member what needs to be done. It is important that the RN delegate with thought—considering what needs to be delegated and who is qualified to complete the task or activity. The RN will most likely not be present when the work is done.

LEGAL ISSUES RELATED TO DELEGATION

Decisions the nurse makes must be consistent with law, for example the nurse cannot delegate a task to another if that staff member is not allowed by law to perform that task (American Nurses Association, 2005).

(*text continues on page 361*)

Decision Tree – Delegation to Nursing Assistive Personnel

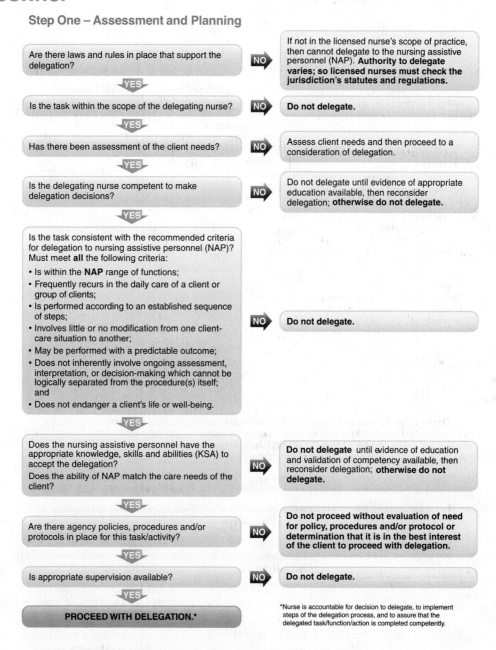

The Delegation Decision Tree above represents the first step in the delegation process. The other three steps are summarized below.

Figure 15-1 National Council of State Boards of Nursing Decision Tree for Delegation to Nursing Assistive Personnel

Source: From *Joint Statement on Delegation*, American Nurses Association (ANA) and the National Council of State Boards of Nursing (NCSBN). Copyright © 2006 by American Nurses Association. Reprinted with permission. All rights reserved.

(continued)

Decision Tree – Delegation to Nursing Assistive Personnel continued

Step Two – Communication

Communication must be a two-way process

The nurse:	The nursing assistive personnel:	Documentation:

• Assesses the assistant's understanding of:
  • How the task is to be accomplished
  • When and what information is to be reported, including:
    – Expected observations to report and record
    – Specific client concerns that would require prompt reporting
• Individualizes for the nursing assistive personnel and client situation
• Addresses any unique client requirements and characteristics, and expectations
• Assesses the assistant's understanding of expectations, providing clarification if needed
• Communicates his or her willingness and availability to guide and support assistant
• Assures appropriate accountability by verifying that the receiving person accepts the delegation and accompanying responsibility
	• Asks questions regarding the delegation and seek clarification of expectations if needed
	• Informs the nurse if the assistant has not done a task/function/activity before, or has only done infrequently
	• Asks for additional training or supervision
	• Affirms understanding of expectations
	• Determines the communication method between the nurse and the assistive personnel
	• Determines the communication and plan of action in emergency situations
		Timely, complete and accurate documentation:
		• Facilitates communication with other members of the health care team
		• Records the nursing care provided

Step Three – Surveillance and Supervision

The purpose of surveillance and monitoring is related to nurse's responsibility for client care within the context of a client population. The nurse supervises the delegation by monitoring the performance of the task or function and assures compliance with standards of practice, policies and procedures. Frequency, level and nature of monitoring vary with needs of client and experience of assistant.

The nurse considers the:	The nurse determines:	The nurse is responsible for:

• Client's health care status and stability of condition
• Predictability of responses and risks
• Setting where care occurs
• Availability of resources and support infrastructure
• Complexity of the task being performed
	• The frequency of onsite supervision and assessment based on:
	  • Needs of the client
	  • Complexity of the delegated function/task/activity
	  • Proximity of nurse's location
		• Timely intervening and follow-up on problems and concerns. Examples of the need for intervening include:
		  • Alertness to subtle signs and symptoms (which allows nurse and assistant to be proactive, before a client's condition deteriorates significantly)
		  • Awareness of assistant's difficulties in completing delegated activities
		  • Providing adequate follow-up to problems and/or changing situations is a critical aspect of delegation

Figure 15-1 National Council of State Boards of Nursing Decision Tree for Delegation to Nursing Assistive Personnel (CONTINUED)

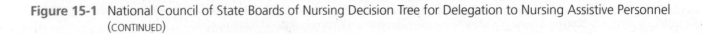

Decision Tree – Delegation to Nursing Assistive Personnel continued

Step Four – Evaluation and Feedback

Evaluation is often the forgotten step in delegation.

> In considering the effectiveness of delegation, the nurse addresses the following questions:
>
> - Was the delegation successful?
>   - Was the task/function/activity performed correctly?
>   - Was the client's desired and/or expected outcome achieved?
>   - Was the outcome optimal, satisfactory or unsatisfactory?
>   - Was communication timely and effective?
>   - What went well; what was challenging?
>   - Were there any problems or concerns; if so, how were they addressed?
> - Is there a better way to meet the client need?
> - Is there a need to adjust the overall plan of care, or should this approach be continued?
> - Were there any "learning moments" for the assistant and/or the nurse?
> - Was appropriate feedback provided to the assistant regarding the performance of the delegation?
> - Was the assistant acknowledged for accomplishing the task/activity/function?

Figure 15-1 (CONTINUED)

State Law and Delegation

Critical legal and regulatory issues and factors that impact delegation are related to the state boards of nursing, scope of practice and nurse practice acts, labor unions, and standards of care. Each one of these issues and factors affects the "who," "what," "when," and "how" of delegation. Every nurse is responsible for knowing how these factors might affect delegation. The legal authority for delegation comes from state laws and regulations. State statute or law establishes the state board of nursing, and professional groups establish professional standards.

The nursing board in each state is the governing body that ensures the safe practice of nursing is provided to its citizens. Note that the focus is on the patient, not the nurse. The board in each state is also involved in approving the schools of nursing and granting and revoking licenses, as discussed in Chapter 2, regulating nursing practice, although states vary in how this is implemented. The National Council of State Boards of Nursing (NCSBN) serves as the umbrella organization for all state boards. It is also involved in delegation and standards. It provides guidance to the state boards on practice issues such as delegation. The nurse practice act of each state and its associated rules and regulations represent the law that every nurse needs to know. The law's associated rules and regulations and description of the scope of practice are also important (Westrick, 2014). The law itself may appear to be very general, and it usually is. This is why it is important to also be aware of the related rules and regulations, which direct how the law is to be implemented. Every registered nurse needs to know what is in the scope of practice and the legal limits, which relate to delegation. In addition, every registered nurse needs to know what certified and unlicensed personnel can do. Position descriptions within HCOs are critical, but they cannot conflict with guidelines developed by the board of nursing. Nurses are responsible for knowing when a position description might conflict with board regulations. One cannot say, "I followed the position description," when it does not meet state requirements related to what tasks can be delegated, to whom, and when. The board of nursing is also responsible for clearly describing the principles related to delegation or what is expected of nurses in the state when they delegate, for example, limitations in what may be delegated and other critical information. Guidelines as provided in Figure 15-1 are also useful as well as the American Nurses Association (ANA) *Principles of Delegation* (2005). Nurses can obtain a copy of the state's nurse practice act from their state board of nursing; each state website provides this information.

Standards of Practice

Standards of practice are also important documents, although not legal documents. Why would standards be discussed under legal issues related to delegation? When delegation occurs, the tasks performed must meet the standards of practice, as well as the organization's policies and procedures. Nurses are expected to know what these are and how they apply. The RN takes responsibility and accountability for individual nursing practice and determines the appropriate delegation of tasks consistent with the nurse's obligation to provide optimum patient care (American Nurses Association, 2010). Registered nurses may delegate certain nursing tasks to LPNs/LVNs and UAP. Some states allow LPNs/LVNs to delegate certain tasks within their scope of practice to UAP. What happens if the nurse's employer wants tasks delegated when the nurse does not think that this delegation is appropriate (for example, the delegatee is unable to do the task safely)? Using professional judgment through the application of the nursing process and the delegation process, the nurse must act as the patient's advocate by only delegating action that is appropriate for the patient. This also means that the HCO cannot just have a list of tasks that can be delegated because nursing judgment and the nursing process must also be applied to the delegation process. If the nurse does not use professional judgment and delegates when it is inappropriate, even if told to do this by supervisors, the nurse is still accountable for errors in delegation. This might result in disciplinary action from the board of nursing and increase liability concerns (American Nurses Association, 2005). Liability means the person/RN is legally responsible for one's own professional practice and for those actions that are delegated. Nurse managers must also be very aware of the delegation process and expect that delegation is followed in a manner that does not put the patient at risk.

Malpractice and Delegation

If there is an issue of malpractice, the nurse practice act and standards may be used to support a case or dispute it. One might ask if the HCO itself has any liability when there are problems with delegation that is done by its staff. The legal principle of corporate liability is important to understand. HCOs are responsible or have a legal duty to provide the resources needed to provide care to the public, such as equipment, facility, staff, and safe care (Westrick, 2014). In addition to this principle, the organization is also responsible based on the principle of **vicarious liability/** *respondeat superior*. This means the organization is responsible for the acts of its employees when they are performing their jobs (Westrick, 2014). The delegator needs to know about the competency level of the staff member to whom a task is delegated (delegatee). However, when staff delegate to UAP or LPNs/LVNs, the staff nurse as well as the nurse manager need to supervise the work. Delegation does not mean a task is delegated then forgotten.

Critical Delegation Issues: Authority, Responsibility, and Accountability

As was discussed in Chapter 4, organization structure illustrates how work is assigned and describes relationships among staff by identifying authority, responsibility, and accountability. The assignment of work and delegation are closely tied to the HCO's structure. The scalar chain that describes the organizational chart with vertical lines and how employees are responsible to one another is an important resource to learn more about authority. It is easy to view delegation at the micro level, viewing one RN delegating to UAP, but this approach is ineffective. Not only do nurse managers and supervisors need to be aware of delegation and monitor it but also the chief nurse executive should provide overall guidance and monitoring to ensure that the process is effective as it is an important part of the healthcare delivery system. This aspect of leadership is embedded in the American Organization of Nurse Executives competencies. (See Appendix A.)

ACCOUNTABILITY **Accountability** identifies who is answerable for what has been done. How is this different from responsibility? A nurse delegates a task to the nursing assistant. The nursing assistant is responsible for his or her performance, and the nurse is accountable for the decision to delegate and to whom to delegate (American Nurses Association, 2005; American Nurses Association & National Council of State Boards of Nursing, 2006). The delegator must take accountability seriously, and this involves identifying the best person for the task or job. Although this is not always easy to determine, it must be done thoughtfully. For example, can a UAP delegate to an RN or LVN? No, this cannot be done. A key question is whether or not the task or job is within the position description of the delegatee and whether the delegator is allowed to delegate the task or job. Overlapping accountability by having more than one person responsible often leads to problems unless this is very clear and both parties are aware of this potential overlap. There are, however, times when shared accountability is appropriate. When this is used, the same principles that are used for individual accountability need to be defined. The American Nurses Association (2005) defines it as

> the state of being responsible or answerable. Nurses, as members of a knowledge-based health profession and as licensed healthcare professionals, must answer to patients, nursing employers, the board of nursing and the civil and criminal court system when the quality of patient care provided is compromised or when allegations of unprofessional, unethical, illegal, unacceptable or inappropriate nursing conduct, actions or responses arise. (p. 4)

RESPONSIBILITY   **Responsibility** is important as it implies an obligation to do something.

AUTHORITY   **Authority** is the power or right to give orders such as to delegate. Position descriptions should clarify the nurse's authority, which should not conflict with the state nurse practice act. Delegation requires thought, and it also requires that the delegator use assessment; critical thinking; and consideration of accountability, authority, and responsibility. Responsibility can be applied when delegation is assigned. The delegator is responsible for selecting the best person to do the job, explaining the task thoroughly and validating that the delegatee understands what needs to be done. When authority is given during delegation, knowledge about the job needs to be shared. Others within the HCO who need to be informed about which staff members are assigned the delegated task or job should also be told. Resources need to be assigned. Letting the delegatee control the job or task is part of giving the appropriate level of authority. In establishing accountability, the delegator identifies deadlines, feedback time periods, and evaluation criteria, with emphasis on success.

If the organization has labor unions, this will affect delegation. Why is this so? Union contracts typically cover issues that are important to delegation such as staffing, staff safety, position descriptions, work schedules, seniority, and a grievance procedure (Westrick, 2014).

APPLYING EVIDENCE-BASED PRACTICE

Evidence for Effective Leadership and Management

CITATION: Excerpt from "When Does Delegating Make You a Supervisor?" *OJIN: The Online Journal of Issues in Nursing*, Vol. 15, No. 2, Manuscript 3. Copyright © 2010 by Online Journal of Issues in Nursing.

OVERVIEW: Delegation is associated with supervision, and this can be complicated when a nurse is working in a healthcare organization that is unionized. This article examines the issue of delegation and supervision and their association with the National Labor Relations Act and the National Labor Relations Board.

APPLICATION: When working in an environment where there are unions, nurses need to understand the implications of their actions,

particularly in relation to supervision. This discussion provides information about this topic with response examples. It also illustrates how this issue can impact legal decisions.

Questions:
1. Why are supervision and delegation a concern?
2. What does the author say about charge nurses and their management decisions and labor unions?
3. How are nursing organizations involved in increasing the understanding of delegation and how this process impacts other aspects of care?

THE DELEGATION PROCESS AND THE NCSBN GUIDELINES

The ANA and the NCSBN in their joint statement identify the key delegation principles applicable to all registered nurses. (See Figure 15-1.) These two organizations address issues such as roles, responsibility and accountability, the delegation process, communication, and supervision.

When delegation is considered, it is important to note that not all tasks or activities should be delegated. How does one determine what might be delegated? Management is involved is setting the HCO standards and processes, which should reflect the state board of nursing nurse practice act and professional nursing standards. This information should be included in orientation and in staff education on a routine basis to ensure that the staff are current in their understanding of delegation. In addition, the following key questions should be asked as the delegation process begins:

1. What is the task or job to be delegated? Consider the complexity and skills that are required for the task or job. Is it clear what needs to be accomplished?
2. To whom should the task or job be delegated? Consider if the delegatee has the skills and time to perform the task or job effectively.
3. How should the task or job be assigned? Consider how much information and explanation needs to be given to the delegatee.
4. How often and in what depth should the delegator follow up to see that the task or job has been performed effectively?

What activities and tasks can be delegated? Activities and tasks that frequently occur are considered technical by nature, considered standard and unchanging, demonstrate predictable results, and with minimal potential for risks are the typical types of tasks that are delegated (American Nurses Association, 2005). Box 15-1 identifies the five rights of delegation. Box 15-2 provides some criteria that can be used to determine when to delegate.

Hansten and Jackson (2009) describe delegation as a cyclical process, similar to the nursing process, as summarized in the following steps and supported in Figure 15-1:

1. The assessment phase focuses on delegators' understanding of the environment in which they practice and their own strengths and limitations and knowledge about the delegatee's competencies.
2. Delegators need to know what needs to be done so the delegated task can be clearly defined for the delegatee.
3. Intervention means that delegators need to be able to prioritize and match the job to the delegatee. Effective communication, which includes the initial directions and follow-up, is critical. If the delegator does not understand what needs to be done, when, where, to whom, and how, then the task will not be completed as expected. Conflicts and errors may increase during the process, which require collaboration and negotiation.
4. Evaluation is ongoing throughout the delegation process. Delegators need to know how to give constructive feedback to motivate the delegatee. Evaluation does require problem solving, particularly if the results or outcomes were not what you expected. Supervision is part of evaluation.

BOX 15-1	FIVE RIGHTS OF DELEGATION

I. Right Task: One that is delegable for a specific patient or situation.

II. Right Circumstances: Appropriate setting, available resources, and other relevant factors considered.

III. Right Person: Right person is delegating the right task to the right person to be performed by the right person.

IV. Right Direction/Communication: Clear, concise description of the task, including its objective, limits, and expectations.

V. Right Supervision: Appropriate monitoring, evaluation, intervention (as needed), and feedback.

BOX 15-2	TO DELEGATE OR NOT

The following are some criteria that are used to determine if one should delegate an activity or a task:

- Patient's condition, including complications and stability
- Complexity of the assessment
- Intricacy of the task
- Repetitiveness of the task
- Capabilities of the UAP
- Amount of technology required
- Infection control and safety precautions
- Potential for harm
- Level of supervision that the RN will need to provide

- Predictability of outcome
- Extent of patient interaction
- Environment

Sources: Summarized by author from: Yoder-Wise, P. (2007). *Leading and managing in nursing* (4th ed.). St. Louis, MO: Mosby. American Nurses Association. (2005). *Principles of delegation*. Silver Spring, MD: Author. American Nurses Association & National Council of State Boards of Nursing. (2006). *Joint statement on delegation.* Retrieved from https://www.ncsbn.org/Joint_statement.pdf. Hansten, R., & Jackson, M. (2009). *Clinical delegation skills* (4th ed.). Boston, MA: Jones and Bartlett Publishers.

Selecting a staff member to do a task who will be honest when he or she needs help or if there are questions or concerns is paramount to effective delegation. Staff members who often take initiative can be good choices for some tasks. Staff members who are analytic, organized, and able to look at problems carefully will also be more successful. It is easy to fall into the trap of making decisions about delegation too quickly. Sometimes a situation calls for a quick decision; however, whenever possible, it is best to take time and be as objective as possible. Some tasks, activities, or projects may require that the delegatees obtain additional training to do the delegated work. If this is the case, it should be provided. This is an investment, and it will help the HCO reach its goals. This training needs to be planned and directed at the needs.

EFFECTIVE DELEGATION

Assessment of the Delegation Process

The delegation process, like other processes, is fluid and thus must be frequently assessed as to its quality. Are the steps followed? What are the outcomes—for the patient, staff members, team, unit, and organization? Nurse managers should plan to assess staff delegation processes on a routine basis.

Characteristics of Effective Delegation

Effective delegation requires that the delegator have delegation skills as delegation is not simple. Elements essential for effective delegation include:

1. Emphasis on professional nursing practice
2. Definition of delegation, based on the nurse practice act and regulations
3. Review of specific sections of the law and regulations regarding delegation; identification of disciplinary actions related to inappropriate delegation
4. Emphasis on tasks/functions that cannot be delegated nor routinely delegated
5. Focus on RN judgment for task analysis and decision to delegate
6. Determination of the degree of supervision required for delegation
7. Identification of guidelines for lowering risk related to delegation
8. Development of feedback mechanisms to ensure that task is completed and to receive updated data to evaluate the outcome (American Nurses Association, 2005, p. 12).

Effective delegation does not just happen. Every nurse has to learn how to delegate. It takes practice. Even if a nurse has the best intention, delegation may still be difficult. There are also barriers that can interfere with delegation. Effective delegation helps to get work done efficiently and effectively, can reduce budget, meet outcomes, use expertise effectively, and facilitate teamwork.

Reimbursement is connected more and more to performance outcomes, and these outcomes are related to delegation as well to increasing use of quality report cards reflecting outcomes.

There is no doubt that in the hectic healthcare delivery system, communication is difficult. As discussed in earlier content on communication, interpretation of a message makes a difference, and for delegation this interpretation may lead to ineffective outcomes and even to errors and poor quality care. The handoff of a task to another is also the handoff of information (Anthony & Vidal, 2010). We use policies and procedures to standardize required work, but patients vary and situations vary, so there needs to be thoughtful use of policies and procedures in delegation. Adaptation may be needed, and this should be clearly communicated. This all requires thought and openness to change; delegating on automatic pilot is not effective.

Barriers to Effective Delegation

Barriers to effective delegation require attention before, during, and after the process. Delegating may mean something different to different staff. Some staff members even think that if they delegate to others, this means they are not competent. This indicates that the staff member does not understand delegation. Some staff members may not even be aware of their inner feelings about delegation. The following are some of the typical barriers to effective delegation:

- The attitude of "I would rather do it myself" leads to the question of whether or not this is a good use of time and skills.
- Some staff or managers may think that delegation overburdens the staff who are already overworked. In this case the delegator is not going through all the delegation process, which requires an assessment of the delegatee's ability to do the job. This involves more than just knowing if the delegatee has the skills, but also if he or she has the time.
- Staff members sometimes have a lack of knowledge and experience about delegation. Realizing they do not know how to delegate is sometimes difficult for staff to recognize. There are often few resources for teaching and guiding staff who need further knowledge and delegation experience.
- Inexperienced delegators will often hesitate to delegate, not knowing what to do. To prevent more problems, they avoid delegating. They try to do everything themselves, which will eventually lead to serious problems.
- Staff members may not even think that delegation is a possibility, or they may use denial (for example, a potential delegator may think that a certain task cannot be delegated when it can be).
- Staff fear loss of control, which is related to lack of trust in others to do the job right, insecurity, and suspiciousness. This interferes with delegation.
- The organization's policies and procedures can be helpful but also can act as barriers if not updated or applied correctly.
- Position descriptions that do not clearly state responsibilities and accountability are a problem. This applies to both the delegator's and the delegatee's positions descriptions.
- Concern about education and training of the delegatee is important. If the delegatee is expected to do a task and the delegatee is not prepared, the delegatee must receive appropriate training and education.
- Sometimes there does not seem to be enough time to consider delegation. Sometimes the situation is so complicated and must move so quickly, it seems to the delegator that it would be easier and faster to do the task rather than delegate it.
- Some delegators want staff to like them, so delegation is not used in order to lighten workloads.
- The Supernurse syndrome, or feeling that others cannot do what you can do so you try to do it all, acts as a barrier.
- Lack of organization is always a barrier to effective work. The delegator needs to think through what needs to be done, by whom, when, and so on. This all requires planning and organization.
- Staff turnover does not allow time for developing trust and confidence in staff. Working with the same staff over time allows the delegator to get to know staff and feel more comfortable with delegation.
- Lack of role models to learn how to delegate effectively can be found in most HCOs. Student nurses and new graduates need experienced RNs to act as their role models.
- An RN supervising the delegatee may have limited contact with the patient. This means the RN must trust the delegatee. It is better for the RN to have some patient contact.

- Poor communication interferes with all steps in the delegation process. Much sharing of information goes on in this process, which requires effective communication.
- If staff have difficulty taking a risk, delegation is difficult. Delegation involves some level of risk. If delegation follows the process, the risk level is less, but it can never be totally eliminated. Much more needs to be done to develop environments where risk taking is valued and not punished.
- Some staff experience the Supermartyr syndrome by refusing to ask others to help. This is particularly important when the delegatee does not ask for help when needed.
- Lack of self-confidence interferes with the delegator's ability to delegate, and when experienced by the delegatee, this can interfere with effective completion of work that has been delegated.
- Fear of criticism is a barrier, both for the delegator and delegatee. More needs to be done to help staff understand evaluation and feedback.
- Poor relationships with staff block effective delegation. Staff may not be motivated to respond appropriately or may not trust the delegator. Lack of respect for staff will be a major barrier as staff who are respected and appreciated are more motivated and productive (American Nurses Association, 2005; American Nurses Association & National Council of State Boards of Nursing, 2006; Weydt, 2010).

Additional barriers to effective delegation that need to be considered relate to delegator involvement. Delegators who get too involved in work details (called micromanaging) are not effective. This gets back to earlier comments about the delegator's ability to turn over control and to trust. This does not mean, however, that the delegator does not need feedback at regular intervals to monitor progress because this is an important step in the delegation process. Another barrier is when delegators delegate only the unpleasant or boring activities, keeping tight control over the more interesting activities, or delegate the better tasks to certain staff. Empowering staff, which may be done through delegation, requires that staff be given some responsibility for the more interesting activities, not just the boring or less important ones. It is also important to understand the reasons that individual staff are selected for tasks.

How can barriers be overcome? The most important strategy to remove barriers is for the RN to fully understand why delegation would be used and the delegation process. Following this, the RN needs to accept that delegation is part of the job and that the RN cannot do everything. The RN uses experience and judgment to arrive at delegation decisions. New graduates need help with delegation from their nurse managers and team leaders. Assuming new graduates are able to effectively delegate is risky.

Assignment, Delegation, and Supervision

It is difficult to discuss delegation without considering supervision and assignment. All three can be confusing, particularly to new graduates. **Supervision** is defined by the American Nurses Association (2005) as

> the active process of directing, guiding and influencing the outcome of an individual's performance of a task. Supervision is generally categorized as on-site (the RN being physically present or immediately available while the task is being performed) or off-site (the RN has the ability to provide direction through various means of written and verbal communications). Individuals engaging in supervision of patient care should not be construed to be managerial supervisors on behalf of the employer. (p. 4)

An example of supervision is when a nurse visits all of the team's patients to ensure that the UAP/delegatee has completed an assigned task. **Assignment** is determining which staff will do which task or series of tasks. Assignment may also include work schedule, though this is not covered in this chapter but discussed in Chapter 8. What does assignment mean in practice? A staff member is assigned to do an activity (responsibility and accountability) based on need, competency, number of available staff, and scope of practice and state practice act. When a nurse is told to care for a group of patients by the nurse manager, this is an assignment. In this example, the nurse manager is accountable only for making the assignment and selecting who will be responsible for the care of the patients. The staff nurse is accountable and responsible for actually providing the care or ensuring that it is provided. In turn, the staff nurse can only delegate work to others, such as UAP, but cannot typically assign work. Delegation is different in that it is a temporary transfer of a task to another with accountability and responsibility remaining with the delegator.

Monitoring progress of a delegable task, activity, or project can be difficult. Too much or too little monitoring may get in the way of success. Figure 15-1 describes supervision, as do the ANA *Principles of Delegation* (2005). General principles of supervision apply to delegation as noted in these documents. It is important to allow the delegatee some space to do the work and not to oversupervise, unless there is serious concern about outcome, in which case the delegation should not have occurred. Ask the delegatee questions and to share if he or she has questions or needs help. Communicating verbally and nonverbally and trust in the delegatee to do the job effectively are important. This is often easier when the staff know one another and work together on a team; it is easier to communicate and understand one another. New RNs are often hesitant to delegate, and this is communicated to the delegatee and may be viewed as lack of trust. In reality the underlying process is the new RN may fear the delegatee knows more. The nurse manager expects the RN to complete the work assigned. Even if the RN delegates to other staff, the RN must still ensure effective completion of the work. The RN as the delegator must analyze and evaluate the outcome of the delegated task or activity.

A key question that now becomes important is what activities can be delegated to the UAP (American Nurses Association, 2007; American Nurses Association & National Council of State Boards of Nursing, 2006). Nursing practice delineates between UAP direct patient care activities and indirect ones by describing them in the following manner:

- **Direct patient care activities:** These activities assist the patient in meeting basic human needs within the HCO, at home, or in other healthcare settings. This includes activities such as assisting the patient with feeding, drinking, ambulating, grooming, toileting, dressing, and socializing. It may also involve the collecting, reporting, and documentation of data related to the previous activities. Data are reported to the RN, who uses the information to make a clinical decision or judgment about patient care.
- **Indirect patient care activities:** These activities support the patient and the patient's environment and only incidentally involve direct patient contact. These activities assist in providing a clean, efficient, and safe patient care milieu and typically encompass chore services, companion care, housekeeping, transporting, clerical, stocking, and maintenance tasks.

It is important to note that there are specific types of activities that cannot be delegated to UAP. These include health counseling; teaching; and those activities that require independent, specialized nursing knowledge, skill, or judgment.

It may seem clear what activities can be delegated and what activities cannot; however, this is a topic that does lead to discussion and debate. Efforts have been made by various groups to change what certain healthcare providers can or cannot do. This is a great example of when it is important for nurses to become politically active, and many have done this to ensure that RNs have a voice in setting these parameters. There is, however, no consensus on this issue other than what is defined by state boards of nursing.

Methods that might be used to monitor and supervise delegation include observation, verbal feedback, written feedback, review of records such as medical records and other standard records, and email. During monitoring, it is important to praise and reward delegatees. Finding something positive to comment on is important even when progress may not be all that was hoped for. Recognizing effort sometimes falls by the wayside because it is taken for granted. There are times when difficulties are identified during monitoring. How should the delegator handle these difficulties? The first step is to analyze the difficulties before jumping to conclusions. Then talk to the delegatee in a nonthreatening manner. Getting the delegatee engaged in solving the problem can be used to help the delegatee improve and also feel a commitment to assisting in problem solution. There are some circumstances where performance is an issue, and in these cases, the organization's procedure for performance evaluation and documentation should be followed. The nurse manager or whoever is the delegator's and delegatee's supervisor would need to lead this process.

CASE STUDY

Getting the Work Done to Reach the Best Outcomes

A new team leader is struggling with learning a new role and getting the work done. It is like learning on the run. This day is particularly difficult on the surgical unit. There were four new admissions last night; one is from a serious automobile accident, and a second, a gunshot wound. Five patients are scheduled for morning surgery. A nursing student is assigned to a patient who is one of the team's patients. This student can provide only basic care as this is the student's first clinical course. The team is composed of the team leader; another RN, who graduated six months ago; two LPNs; and one UAP, who has worked on the unit for 10 years and must be shared with another team depending on need. The night shift reported that two patients have elevated temperatures and both are one-day postop. Today there are eight patients assigned to the team; six patients have

IVs, with two to be discontinued. Two patients will be discharged, and three admissions for elective surgery are expected toward the end of the shift. The report has been given, and the team leader is meeting with the team to plan the day.

Questions:

1. Identify the key team member characteristics that the team leader needs to consider as potential strengths or limitations.
2. What should the team leader remember about delegating to LPNs and to UAP?
3. What should the team leader consider about assignments for the nursing student and working with the student? What are the priorities?
4. Considering the patients assigned to the team and possible tasks and responsibilities, describe how the team leader might delegate to the team.
5. How should the team leader supervise the team members' work?

APPLYING LEADERSHIP AND MANAGEMENT

My Hospital Unit: An Evolving Case Experience

You have just reviewed your unit's quality improvement data and the most current staff performance appraisal information. You are concerned about a trend that you identify: delegation is not as effective as it should be. Using the information in this chapter, particularly the ANA and the NCSBN information and information from these organizations' websites, develop a staff education module on delegation.

Develop the content and describe the teaching methods you will use, how staff will access the content, and evaluation methods. Remember evaluation of the educational experience should not just focus on the learning experience but also on its impact on care outcomes. Consider how you need to individualize the content for your unit as you have described your staff and unit over time in this course. Use the information found in Figure 15-1.

BSN and *Master's Essentials:* Application to Content

BSN Essentials (American Association of Colleges of Nursing, 2008) as Applied to this Chapter:

  II. Basic Organizational and Systems Leadership for Quality Care and Patient Safety
  V. Healthcare Policy, Finance, and Regulatory Environments
 VI. Interprofessional Communication and Collaboration for Improving Patient Health Outcomes
VIII. Professionalism and Professional Values
 IX. Baccalaureate Generalist Nursing Practice

Master's Essentials (American Association of Colleges of Nursing, 2011) as Applied to this Chapter:

  II. Organizational and Systems Leadership
 VII. Interprofessional Collaboration for Improving Patient and Population Health Outcomes
 IX. Master's-Level Nursing Practice

Applying AONE Competencies

Identify which of the AONE competencies found in Appendix A apply to the content of this chapter.

Engaging in the Content: Critical Thinking and Clinical Reasoning and Judgment

Discussion Questions

1. How do accountability, authority, and responsibility relate to delegation?
2. Consider one of your current clinical sites. Identify barriers to effective delegation that you observe or experience. For each barrier, describe a strategy that might be used to prevent or overcome the barrier. (Online Application Option)
3. What are the benefits of using delegation?
4. Identify three barriers to effective delegation.
5. Why is the state nurse practice act important in delegation?

6. Find your state's nurse practice act on the Web or in your library. Why is it important for you to be aware of this law? Compare your state's nurse practice act with a UAP position description from a local HCO. Does the law say anything about delegation, and if so, how does it relate to the position description? Is there other information on your state's board of nursing website on delegation, and how might this information be useful? Sharing information may allow the team to look at position descriptions from different HCOs. (Online Application Option)

Application Exercises

1. What are some of the critical aspects of delegation that have been identified by the nursing profession? Visit the National Council of State Boards of Nursing website to learn more about the critical issues related to delegation. Explore the following content areas: the delegation decision-making tree, five rights of delegation, and delegation terminology. This is important information to know as you begin to delegate to others.
2. You should identify a task or activity and describe how you would delegate it to a UAP. Respond to each of the questions in the tree found on the website. How might you remember this decision-making tree so you can apply it in your practice?
3. Standards for UAP have been a major concern, as noted in this chapter's content. Obtain a copy of a UAP position description from a local healthcare organization. Working in small teams, review the descriptions collected. Summarize your review. What resources might you use to determine the quality of the position description? Your review should consider UAP qualifications, what the UAP may do (tasks and activities), who must supervise the UAP, any restrictions

noted, and any information about staff education. Are there any conflicts with the information that you find in your search for information about UAP? Resources that you might use are the HCO's standards of care, state board of nursing practice act and other related information, nursing literature, observation, and interviews (nurse managers, team leaders). With sicker patients, shorter lengths of stay, increased use of UAP, and heightened demand for cost-effective care, it is imperative that RNs delegate some aspects of patient care to others.

4. For one week in clinical, consider the following:
   - What tasks or patient care activities that your patients require could be delegated and to whom?
   - Apply the delegation decision-making tree and five rights of delegation.
   - Discuss delegation with a team leader and staff nurses. Document your data.
   - When tasks are delegated to UAP, how do they respond?
   - If you have an opportunity to observe an RN delegating to a UAP, evaluate the communication, attitude, and response. (Online Application Option)

References

American Association of Colleges of Nursing. (2008). *The essentials of baccalaureate education for professional nursing practice*. Washington, DC: Author.

American Association of Colleges of Nursing. (2011). *The essentials of master's education in nursing*. Washington, DC: Author.

American Nurses Association. (2005). *Principles of delegation*. Silver Spring, MD: Author.

American Nurses Association. (2007). Position statement: Registered nurses utilization of nursing assistive personnel in all setting. Silver Spring, MD: Author.

American Nurses Association. (2010). *Guide to the code of ethics for nurses. Interpretation and application*. Silver Spring, MD: Author.

American Nurses Association & National Council of State Boards of Nursing. (2006). *Joint statement on delegation*. Retrieved from https://www.ncsbn.org/

Delegation_joint_statement_
NCSBN-ANA.pdf

Anthony, M., & Vidal, K. (2010). Mindful communication: A novel approach to improving delegation and increasing patient safety. *OJIN: The Online Journal of Issues in Nursing, 15*(2). Retrieved from http://www.nursingworld.org/MainMenuCategories/ANAMarketplace/ANAPeriodicals/OJIN/TableofContents/Vol152010/

No2May2010/Mindful-Communication-and-Delegation.html

Hansten, R., & Jackson, M. (2009). *Clinical delegation skills* (4th ed.). Boston, MA: Jones and Bartlett Publishers.

Institute of Medicine. (2001). *Crossing the quality chasm*. Washington, DC: National Academies Press.

Institute of Medicine. (2003). *Healthcare professions education*. Washington, DC: National Academies Press.

Westrick, S. (2014). *Essentials of nursing law and ethics*. Burlington, MA: Jones & Bartlett Learning.

Weydt, A. (2010). Developing delegation skills. *OJIN: The Online Journal of Issues in Nursing, 15*(2). Retrieved from http://www.nursingworld.org/MainMenuCategories/ANAMarketplace/ANAPeriodicals/OJIN/TableofContents/Vol152010/No2May2010/Delegation-Skills.html

KEY TERMS

- applied research
- basic research
- evidence-based management
- evidence-based practice
- institutional review board
- meta-analysis
- outcome
- outcomes research
- PICO or EBP question
- research
- systematic review

LEARNING OUTCOMES

Before you begin, take a moment to familiarize yourself with the learning outcomes for this chapter.

> Critique the research process, including differences in basic and applied research.
> Discuss the importance of ethics, informed consent, and institutional review boards.
> Discuss the barriers and strategies related to research and implications for nurses.
> Discuss the implications of research for nursing leaders and managers.
> Critique the evidence-based practice process and the governmental initiatives addressing EBP.
> Critique the implications of evidence-based practice for nursing leaders and managers.
> Critique the implications of using evidence-based management.
> Compare and contrast research, evidence-based practice, evidence-based management, and quality improvement.

WHAT'S AHEAD

The Institute of Medicine (IOM) recommends that healthcare providers "integrate best research with clinical expertise and patient values for optimum care, and participate in learning and research activities to the extent feasible" (2003, p. 4). This is one of the five core competencies for healthcare professions described by the National Academy of Medicine (NAM). This chapter discusses the relationship of research to evidence-based practice (EBP) and the importance of EBP to nursing management. EBP is a topic that is typically covered in nursing research courses and clinical courses; however, nurse managers have a key role in ensuring that EBP is implemented in practice. Evidence-based management (EBM) is a newer term, and it is critical that nurse leaders and managers use EBM to better ensure more effective management decisions.

RESEARCH

Research is a critical component of providing quality care and is integral to better understanding effective leadership and management. Research results provide evidence that can be used to answer practice and management questions. The following content provides an overview about research.

Description of Research

To understand EBP and EBM, it is important to review certain basic information about research. Nursing has an active research initiative that is present in most clinical and university settings.

Nurses are researchers guiding their own research, participating in interprofessional studies with other researchers, managing clinical trials, and guiding patients who are considering participating in clinical trials. The National Institute of Nursing Research (NINR) is the major U.S. nursing research organization. It is part of the National Institutes of Health (NIH) located in the Washington, DC, area. According to the NINR strategic plan, nursing research develops knowledge to:

- Enhance health promotion and disease prevention
- Improve the quality of life by managing symptoms of acute and chronic illness
- Improve palliative and end-of-life care
- Enhance innovation in science and practice
- Develop the next generation of nurse scientists (2011)

Research is "the systematic collection and analysis of information (data). It is planned, organized, and carefully thought out before being done" (Tappen, 2011, p. xiv). The two major types of research approaches are basic and applied. The goal of **basic research** is to broaden the base of knowledge rather than solve an immediate problem. Results from basic research may then be used to develop applied research. The goal of **applied research** is to find a solution to a practical problem. Nurses typically are involved more in applied research, though some do basic research, and these results may then be identified as evidence for best practice.

Outcomes research is another type of research, though not as common as the two major types. We need to know much more about outcomes and relationship to nursing care delivery, particularly for nursing leadership and management. An **outcome** is the result of some action and provides a method to measure results. Examples of outcomes are absence of skin ulcers or fluid restriction compliance. The goal of **outcomes research** is to determine the effectiveness of healthcare services and patient outcomes, which is critical today if care is to be effective and improved. Nurses are involved in identifying patient outcomes and intervening to better ensure outcomes are met, and with this expertise, nurses should be and are involved in outcomes research. Nurse managers and leaders need to be active in directing this type of research within their healthcare organizations (HCOs). Comparative effectiveness research is related to this issue and discussed later in this chapter.

The NINR supports clinical or applied research, basic research, and research training that focus on health and illness across the lifespan (National Institute of Nursing Research, 2013). The NINR's research focus encompasses health promotion and disease prevention, quality of life, health disparities, and end of life. The NINR sponsors research by outside investigators at colleges, universities, and other research sites (extramural research) and conducts its own research at the NIH (intramural research).

- The extramural program, managed through the Division of Extramural Activities, accepts unsolicited, investigator-initiated applications, as well as those submitted in response to a published request for applications (RFA) or program announcement (PA).
- The intramural program, managed through the Division of Intramural Research, is composed of the Symptom Management Laboratory, the Pain Research Unit, and the Research Training Section.

The mission of the NINR is "to promote and improve the health of individuals, families, communities, and populations. The Institute supports and conducts clinical and basic research and research training on health and illness across the lifespan to build the scientific foundation for clinical practice, prevent disease and disability, manage and eliminate symptoms caused by illness, and improve palliative and end-of-life care" (National Institute of Nursing Research, 2013). This mission primarily focuses on care concerns and not leadership and management; however, this does not mean it is not important to expand knowledge of leadership and management through research. Ideally there should be more emphasis on leadership and management research.

Research design describes the details of a plan for a research project. Content that is typically included is the description of the problem, review of literature, type of study (research approach and design), sample description and sample selection method, setting for the study, data collection measurement and instrumentation, data collection process, timeline, data analysis plan, and a description of potential limitations. The research proposal is similar to a nursing care plan or a project plan in that it lays out the steps that will be taken prior to initiating the research project. Typically the proposal is used to request approval and funding to conduct the research. After approval and funding are received, the study is then conducted. The last part of the research process is data analysis and description of the results and conclusions. This is the important part of the study addressing two key questions: What did the analysis of data demonstrate, and what are the implications of the data?

Ethics, Informed Consent, and Institutional Review Board

History often guides decisions, and the area of research ethics is no exception. There are three examples of past negative experiences with research ethics that have led to major changes in how research is conducted. The Nazi medical experiments conducted during World War II violated basic human rights with little beneficial gain in scientific knowledge (U.S. Holocaust Memorial Museum, 2014). After World War II and the Nuremburg trials that focused on physicians who participated in these experiments on innocent people, an important result was the publication of *The Nuremberg Code* (U.S. Department of Health and Human Services, 2005). This code has provided a prototype for the development of many later codes of research ethics and identified the following rights that must be protected:

- Right to self-determination
- Right to privacy
- Right to anonymity and confidentiality
- Right to fair treatment
- Right to protection from discomfort and harm

Two other examples of serious ethical problems in research studies include the Tuskegee Syphilis Study (1932–1972) and the Willowbrook Study (mid-1950s–1970s), which occurred in the United States. The Tuskegee Study used African Americans to examine the natural course of syphilis, and the researchers did not give informed consent to participants (Centers for Disease Control and Prevention, 2013). Many of them did not even know they were in a study. This study resulted in participants' getting syphilis, acquiring complications of the illness, and in some cases dying. Following this study, which lasted for years, the federal government established a clearer ethical code for research in the Belmont Report by focusing on

> (i) the boundaries between biomedical and behavioral research and the accepted and routine practice of medicine, (ii) the role of assessment of risk-benefit criteria in the determination of the appropriateness of research involving human subjects, (iii) appropriate guidelines for the selection of human subjects for participation in such research and (iv) the nature and definition of informed consent in various research settings. (U.S. Department of Health and Human Services, 2014)

The Willowbrook Study examined hepatitis at an institution for developmentally disabled children. The study resulted in major health problems for many of the children in the study sample (National Institutes of Health, 2009). The parents gave consent but not informed consent as they were told the children were receiving vaccinations when in actuality they were infected with hepatitis.

As a result of these experiences and greater understanding of the need for rights and ethics in research, there are now greater protections for human subjects. The creation of **institutional review boards** (IRBs) has contributed to greater protections. The IRB is a committee that reviews research proposals before research is conducted to ensure the study is conducted ethically. An institution that receives federal funds and conducts research must have an IRB process, and most institutions now have some type of IRB process. All three examples of unethical research behavior mentioned earlier laid the groundwork for major reform in research ethics, particularly protecting vulnerable populations. The vulnerable populations that need *extra* protection in research as guided by ethics codes (although all research participants need protections) are as follows:

- Neonates (newborns)
- Children
- Pregnant women and fetuses
- Persons with mental illness
- Persons with cognitive impairment
- Persons who are terminally ill
- Persons confined to institutions (e.g., prisons, long-term care hospitals)

To better understand the IRB process, one might ask what the IRB is concerned about when research studies are conducted in an organization. Examples of questions that might be considered by the IRB are as follows:

1. Are the subjects being deceived, and if so, is this necessary for the integrity of the research?
2. Do the subjects understand the purpose of the project and completely understand his/her role in the project?
3. Are there obvious costs or any hidden costs to people if they participate?
4. Can subjects withdraw at any time?
5. What are the benefits, if any, to the subjects?
6. What are the risks, immediate and long-term, (if known) to the subjects?
7. How will the researcher(s) protect the subjects' right to confidentiality?
8. Whom should the subjects contact with questions?
9. What will be done with the results of the study (Finkelman & Kenner, 2014, p. 357)?

If research is conducted within the HCO's patient care areas, nurse leaders and managers have responsibilities related to that research. They need to be knowledgeable about the research process and about the specific research studies. What is the staff role? Are staff involved in collecting data, documentation of data, and so on? If studies include patients, the staff need to be informed. Nurse researchers may conduct studies and involve staff. Nonnurses such as physicians and other healthcare professionals may also conduct studies in clinical areas and include nursing staff. Nurses may also serve on the healthcare organization's IRB.

Regardless of the research structure used by the HCO, nurse managers need to develop methods for staff to learn about research, attend research conferences, present at conferences, publish their work, and so on. When staff members encounter a clinical question for which they need an answer and there is no available research, then it might mean that the question is appropriate for a research study. However, not all questions lend themselves to a research study, and not all staff members are qualified to conduct research as they may have little knowledge or experience in research. If resources are required for an effective research program, they might not be available at that time or in that setting. In addition, it takes time and funding to conduct studies.

Nurse leaders and managers who demonstrate a personal interest in research act as role models for staff. If patients are participating in clinical studies, then nurse managers must also ensure that patient rights are maintained at all times. Part of this responsibility is assisting staff to understand the research process and the importance of informed consent, participant rights, and the IRB process.

Research Barriers and Strategies

Research is not easy to accomplish. The following information describes some of the common barriers to research with examples of strategies that might be used to prevent or reduce these barriers:

1. *Lack of funding:* The need to get adequate funding, typically through grants.
2. *Lack of enough time:* Good research takes planning and time to accomplish. The researcher needs blocks of time to work on a study. Some do this full time.
3. *Lack of research competencies:* Research expertise needs to be developed over years. Finding a mentor(s) is important; working with researchers who have been successful can assist a novice researcher.
4. *Lack of participants for the sample:* If the study requires participants, it is not always easy to find them and in the number that is required. This takes time and creativity. The study needs to apply ethical principles in selecting the sample for the study and informing the participants about the study.
5. *Cannot find the right setting:* Finding and getting a setting to commit to participate in a study can be problematic; it takes contacts and communication.
6. *Lack of statistics expertise:* Using statistical expertise to consult on the study can be very helpful. Researchers work in teams (Finkelman & Kenner, 2014, p. 357).

Even if a study is funded by a grant, any study conducted in an HCO requires support such as time to work on the study, staff time, and other resources from the HCO and management. If this is not present, this will be a major barrier to success.

Clinical Research: Role of Leaders and Managers

Many HCOs are involved in conducting research studies. Some of these studies are nursing studies, and others may include nurses on the research team, for example, in managing a clinical trial or collecting data. Nurse leaders such as the chief nursing executive may advocate for the HCO to establish and maintain an active nursing research program with nursing staff involvement and support from leadership. Nurse researchers may be hired to lead the program. Nursing staff may initiate a study on a nursing problem of concern. Some of the staff may be qualified to conduct research, and others may need expert assistance. If nursing research is a goal of the HCO, staff need time and resources to ensure research is conducted effectively. When research is conducted, funding is required, which may come from internal or external sources. After a study is completed, the staff involved in the study should disseminate the results. This is done by presenting at conferences and publishing articles about the study. Nursing leadership needs to support this phase as much as they support the entire research process. It is the responsibility of the researcher to share results, and this is directly related to EBP. Results must be known before they can be considered in the EBP process. Nurse managers also need to be supportive and encourage staff who have an interest in research, either to continue their education or to initiate studies if they have the education background and expertise to do so.

One approach to increasing nursing research expertise in an HCO is to partner with a college of nursing. Nursing faculty might assist by providing mentoring and staff education about research. For example, nursing faculty and graduate students can be invited to consider conducting research in the HCO and also are encouraged to include staff. Some HCOs have a designated faculty member or other external nursing expert who acts as their research consultant. Requiring nursing faculty who conduct research in an HCO to present their findings or to ask faculty who may be doing research in another study to share information about the research process with staff are useful methods to emphasize research within an HCO and provide extended learning experiences for staff. Some HCOs have annual research days and EBP days where staff members present their work. Encouraging staff members to continue their education also helps to increase research expertise within the HCO. The American Organization of Nurse Executives (AONE) annually identifies research goals on its website and awards grants for nursing studies and program development and includes EBP in its nurse executive competencies, as seen in Appendix A. In its first priority in the AONE 2014–2016 strategic plan, the nursing leadership organization notes that the following should be a goal: Accelerate adoption of innovative best practices through educational resources, tools, and leadership development for nurse leaders at all stages of their careers (American Organization of Nurse Executives, 2014). Many hospitals now include EBP as a critical part of their nursing services and provide staff training about EBP to ensure its effective use, though there is less emphasis on evidence-based management limiting effective management decisions.

EVIDENCE-BASED PRACTICE

Description of Evidence-Based Practice

There is uncertainty in health care for nurses. How do you know the best intervention to apply? EBP is one method that is used to resolve this dilemma. Sometimes it can be very helpful; however, there is limited research in nursing, which makes finding the highest level of nursing research evidence—a randomized, controlled trial—difficult. The goal is to find evidence that will help the patient and improve care. This means the nurse needs to be able to apply EBP to patient care. Evidence-based practice has been integrated into more and more healthcare delivery systems. The recent IOM reports on quality care emphasize the need to apply EBP in practice. The IOM has also published three reports that specifically address EBP:

- *Knowing What Works in Health Care: A Roadmap for the Nation* (2008): This report discusses the need to use EBP so best evidence can identify diagnostic, treatment, and prevention services. The report identifies critical factors that need to be considered: healthcare costs, reducing geographic variation in the use of healthcare services, improving quality, empowering healthcare consumers, and making healthcare coverage decisions.
- *Clinical Practice Guidelines We Can Trust* (2011a): This report focuses on the importance of developing effective clinical guidelines based on best evidence and applying those

guidelines when appropriate. Guidelines should be based on systematic reviews, be developed by knowledgeable multidisciplinary experts, consider important patient subgroups and patient preferences, provide clear explanations of the logical relationships between alternative care options and health outcomes, and be revised as needed.

● ***Finding What Works in Health Care: Standards for Systematic Reviews* (2011b):** This report discusses research and EBP, emphasizing the importance of **systematic reviews**. Standards based on systematic reviews should be used to support quality and should include assessment of individual studies and synthesis of the evidence. This information should then be shared through publication, allowing for greater access to those who need the information.

Evidence-based practice was first defined using the term evidence-based medicine: "The conscientious, explicit, and judicious use of current evidence in making decisions about the care of individual patients … integrating individual clinical expertise with the best available external clinical evidence from systematic research" (Sackett, 1996, p. 71). Since that time the term more commonly used is evidence-based practice rather than evidence-based nursing or evidence-based medicine. Using a term that focuses only on one healthcare profession does support an interprofessional approach to care. The EBP process is a systematic process; however, it follows a somewhat different process from research. It is easy to overemphasize research as the only evidence source relevant for EBP, but there are other sources of evidence. These include clinical patient history and physical, expertise of the care provider, and the patient's values and preferences.

All four types of evidence are used in shared clinical decision making between the patient and the healthcare provider team to reach patient outcomes and ensure quality care. The following is an example of a five-step approach to EBP (Schmidt & Brown, 2015a, p. 419):

1. Ask or identify the research question. Determine if the question is well constructed to elicit a response or solution.
2. Acquire or search the literature for pre-appraised evidence or research. Secure the best evidence that is available.
3. Appraise or conduct a critical appraisal of the literature and studies. Evaluate for validity and determine the applicability in practice.
4. Apply or institute recommendations and findings and apply them to nursing practice.
5. Assess or evaluate the application of the findings, outcomes, and relevance to nursing practice.

Evidence-based practice helps to identify and assess high-quality, clinically relevant research that can be applied to clinical practice as well as the development of health policy. As one travels from one area of the country to the other, or even within one community, there can be great variation in practice and delivery. The IOM ties EBP together with other critical aspects and core competencies. "Individual clinical expertise should be integrated with the best information from scientifically based, systematic research and applied in light of the patient's values and circumstances. Centering decision-making on the patient is integral to improving the quality of healthcare and is also imperative if consumers are to take an active role in making informed healthcare decisions based on known risks and benefits. This report also recognizes that healthcare resources are finite. Thus, setting priorities for systematic assessment of scientific evidence is essential" (Institute of Medicine, 2008). There are critical reasons for doing this. Active use of EBP can have a positive impact on:

● constraining healthcare costs.
● reducing geographic variation in the use of healthcare services.
● improving quality.
● consumer-directed health care.
● making health coverage decisions (Institute of Medicine, 2008, p. 3).

Today patients are more knowledgeable about their illnesses and treatment, and technology allows access to much more information. Information increases control, and now more and more patients want the best care possible, supported by evidence. Management needs to keep this in mind. In order to meet patient goals, management and staff will need to know how to identify the EBP question, how to find and critique evidence, apply the evidence, and then evaluate the results or outcomes of using evidence to assist in patient care decision making.

A common method for nurses to use when searching for evidence to improve practice with the goal of asking a searchable and answerable question is to use a **PICO or EBP question**. This is an EBP focused question that clearly identifies the patient population, information needed regarding intervention, comparison of interest, and under what circumstances is the information to be applied (American Nurses Association, 2014).

Evidence-based practice requires that information is available for specific questions. The research literature is reviewed using explicit scientific methods and includes all relevant research. This valuable information is then available to practitioners and should be helpful in directing their care decisions. An obvious question is how does one get to this information and then how does one know what information is valid and reliable?

EBP is particularly concerned with synthesizing results found in professional research so that they can be used to improve care or the delivery of healthcare services. Systematic reviews provide a summary of best evidence based on published research studies, providing the highest level of evidence for decisions. Randomized controlled trials (experiments) provide the best evidence for systematic reviews. Clinicians (nurses, physicians, pharmacists, allied health), healthcare administrators and nursing administration, healthcare policy makers, and healthcare insurers use systematic reviews to find the most current best practice. These sources provide an overview and rating of quality and strength of evidence from primary research studies, **meta-analysis** or systematic reviews, published and unpublished, on a specific question. Experts complete these reviews in a systematic manner. Inconsistencies and weaknesses in the studies are identified. Most nurses do not develop systematic reviews themselves. EBP experts are best prepared to do these specialized reviews and analysis of research. Clinical nurses do not really have the time to do this type of review. The goal of the search for evidence is to find the evidence in a form that it can be applied to practice based on an EBP question.

The next level of research evidence is quasi-experiments without randomization. Case-control and cohort studies (descriptive studies) may provide evidence but not at the same high level as experiments (randomized controlled trial). Qualitative studies and expert opinions may also be reviewed.

The best sources of studies are research journals, and then clinical journals, and they should be peer-reviewed journals. There are several major EBP databases and other sources of EBP literature, and all have websites describing their initiatives and resources.

1. *Cochrane Center and Collaboration:* This center develops, maintains, and updates systematic reviews of healthcare interventions to allow practitioners to make informed decisions.
2. *Joanna Briggs Institute Evidence-Based Practice:* This institute represents an international collaboration among nursing and allied health centers.
3. *National Clinical Guidelines:* This source is government based although its guidelines derive from many different sources.
4. *Sigma Theta Tau International (STTI):* This nursing organization offers EBP resources through its online publication, *Online Journal of Knowledge Synthesis for Nursing.* This journal provides full-text systematic reviews to guide nursing practice.

There are many advantages for using systematic reviews within the healthcare delivery system (Academic Center for Evidence-Based Nursing, 2008). They are as follows:

- Reduces large quantities of information into a manageable form
- Establishes generalizability across participants, settings, treatment variations, and study designs
- Assesses consistency and explains inconsistencies of findings across studies
- Increases power in suggesting the cause and effect relationship
- Reduces bias from random and systematic error, improving true reflection of reality
- Integrates existing information for decisions about clinical care, economic decisions, future research design, and policy formation
- Increases efficiency in time between research and clinical implementation
- Provides a basis for continuous updates with new evidence

Nursing management should consider the implications of these advantages in developing a plan to prepare staff to effectively use EBP and EBM.

In order to apply EBP effectively, the IOM report on EBP recommends that professionals are able to do the following (Institute of Medicine, 2003, pp. 57–58):

- Know where and how to find the best possible sources of evidence.
- Formulate clear clinical questions.

- Search for the relevant answers to the questions from the best possible sources of evidence, including those that evaluate or appraise the evidence for its validity and usefulness with respect to a particular patient or population.
- Determine when and how to integrate these new findings into practice.

What happens after evidence is collected? This can be an overwhelming process: the result is often a large amount of information and some may conflict. The HCO needs to involve stakeholders who have knowledge of the problem or care concern to arrive at a decision about the problem or care concern. Interprofessional care is a major factor, and in most cases, the stakeholders should be an interprofessional team with team members who are involved in the patient's care.

Advantages and Barriers to Implementing Evidence-Based Practice

EBP emphasizes the importance of the knowledge worker, which relates to content in Chapter 1 about knowledge and leadership. There is need for nurses to see themselves as knowledge workers. The goal is for nurses to make clinically sound and autonomous decisions whenever possible. EBP increases clinical knowledge, impacts the nurse's autonomy (the nurse's freedom to act), and allows the nurse to make a sound decision with the patient. Implementing EBP is difficult to accomplish and takes time. What are the barriers to implementing EBP?

- Lack of knowledge about EBP
- Lack of acceptance of the value of EBP—impact on quality and costs
- HCO nursing shortage limits staff time and energy for change
- View that EBP represents cookbook approach to care
- Lack of knowledge and experience with technology and library searches
- Mistakenly view EBP as research and lack understanding of research
- Lack of understanding that EBP evidence is more than just research results
- Using one study as sufficient evidence for EBP decisions

This list of barriers can also be used by a nurse manager to plan for staff needs when implementing EBP.

Several of the major barriers in getting nurses prepared to use EBP include: Nurses need to know how to critique a research study, use systematic reviews, and apply best evidence to practice. With the average age of nurses being over 45 years, this is a challenge since most of these nurses did not have EBP content in their formal nursing degree programs. If nurses need to use an EBP approach, nurses will need to be more aware of the professional literature and have access to it during working hours. Nurse managers need to encourage staff to review the literature, provide training about literature searches and resources such as computer databases mentioned in this chapter and librarian assistance, all of which impacts budget. Staff education about EBP also needs to be planned, offered, and evaluated. (See Chapter 20.) Over the past 10 years, there have been more efforts by HCOs to prepare staff who have limited or no knowledge of EBP, and now this is a critical component in both undergraduate and graduate nursing programs, so graduates are more prepared than in the past when they enter practice.

Schmidt and Brown recommend strategies to overcome the common barriers to implementing EBP (2015b, pp. 10–11).

Barrier—Time:
- Devote 15 minutes to reading evidence related to a clinical problem.
- Sign up for emails that offer summaries of research studies in your area of interest.
- Use a team approach when considering policy changes to distribute the workload among members.
- To promote faster retrieval of information, bookmark websites with clinical guidelines.
- Evaluate available technologies to create time-saving systems that allow quick and convenient retrieval of information at the bedside.
- Negotiate release time from patient care to collect, read, and share information about relevant clinical guidelines.
- Search for already established clinical guidelines because they provide synthesis of existing research.

Barrier—Research in Practice Not Valued:
- Make a list of reasons healthcare providers should value research, and use this list as a springboard for discussions with colleagues.
- Invite nurse researchers to share why they are passionate about their work.
- When disagreements arise about a policy or protocol, find an article (preferably research) that addresses the question.
- When selecting a work environment, ask about the organizational commitment to EBP.
- Link measurement of quality indicators to EBP.
- Participate in EBP activities to demonstrate professionalism that can be rewarded through promotions or merit raises.
- Provide recognition during National Nurses Week for individuals involved in EBP projects.

Barrier—Lack of Knowledge About EBP and Research:
- Take a course or attend a continuing education offering on EBP.
- Invite a faculty member to a unit meeting to discuss EBP.
- Consult with advance practice nurses about EBP.
- Attend conferences where clinical research is presented, and talk with presenters about their studies.
- Volunteer to be on committees that set policies and protocols.
- Create a mentoring program to bring novice and experienced nurses together.

Barrier—Lack of Technological Skills to Find Evidence:
- Consult with a librarian about how to access databases and retrieve articles.
- Learn to bookmark important websites that are sources of clinical guidelines.
- Commit to acquiring computer skills.

Barrier—Lack of Resources to Access Evidence:
- Write a proposal for funds to support access to online databases and journals.
- Collaborate with a nursing program for access to resources.
- Investigate funding possibilities from others (i.e., grants, pharmaceutical companies, etc.).

Barrier—Communication Gap Between Researchers and Nursing Staff:
- Identify clinical problems and share them with nurse researchers. (It is easy for staff to confuse research and EBP.)
- Participate in ongoing unit-based studies.

Barrier—Resistance to Change:
- Listen to staff concerns about change.
- When considering an EBP project, select one that interests the staff, has a high priority, is likely to be successful, and has baseline data.
- Mobilize talented individuals to act as change agents.
- Create a means to reward individuals who provide leadership during change.

Barrier—Organization Does Not Embrace EBP:
- Link organizational priorities with EBP to reduce cost and increase efficiency.
- Recruit administrators/managers who value EBP.
- Form coalitions with other healthcare providers to increase the base of support for EBP.
- Use EBP to meet accreditation standards and gain recognition.

The Federal Government and Evidence-Based Practice

The federal government is very active in both developing resources for EBP and encouraging use of EBP. In some cases the federal government even makes use of EBP as a requirement when healthcare services are associated with federal health programs and services such as Medicare and Medicaid.

THE AGENCY FOR HEALTHCARE RESEARCH AND QUALITY (AHRQ)   Finding sources of data to support evidence-based practice in nursing may not always be easy. Clearly well-designed research is the best; however, there may be none available on a particular problem area. The AHRQ evaluates research and publishes guidelines based on their reviews. This can be a source of information to support evidence-based practice. In 1997 the Agency for Healthcare Policy and Research (AHCPR), now known as the AHRQ, began an initiative to promote EBP in daily care, and more recently it established the Evidence-based Practice Center (EPC) Program. The EPCs develop evidence reports and technology assessments on topics relevant to clinical and other HCO and delivery issues, focusing on common, expensive, and/or significant concerns for the Medicare and Medicaid populations. "With this program, AHRQ became a 'science partner' with private and public organizations in their efforts to improve the quality, effectiveness, and appropriateness of healthcare by synthesizing the evidence and facilitating the translation of evidence-based research findings" (Agency for Healthcare Research and Quality, 2014). Nonfederal partners that recommend topics include professional societies, such as the American Nurses Association; insurers; employers; and patient-focused organizations, such as the American Heart Association, American Cancer Society, and federal partners.

Another new program connected to the EPC is the Effective Healthcare (EHC) Program, which was created from the Medicare Prescription Drug, Improvement, and Modernization Act of 2003. EHC sponsors systematic reviews and the translation and dissemination of research findings to a variety of audiences, including clinicians, consumers, and policymakers (Agency for Healthcare Research and Quality, 2014). This initiative supports comparative effectiveness reviews, effectiveness reviews, and technical briefs focused on patient-centered outcomes.

> One of the unique aspects of the EHC Program is the involvement of a diverse range of stakeholders throughout the research process to ensure relevancy and transparency. Collaboration with a broad range of healthcare stakeholders is a cornerstone of AHRQ's work to develop effective EBP resources. AHRQ believes that "involving all stakeholders in the research enterprise from the beginning improves the end product and facilitates the diffusion and implementation of the research findings by ensuring that they reflect the various needs of all diverse users, are relevant to their unique challenges, and are applicable in real-world situations". (Agency for Healthcare Research and Quality, 2014)

The AHRQ Evidence-based Practice Center website describes details about past and current projects and reports.

ACCELERATING CHANGE AND TRANSFORMATION IN ORGANIZATIONS AND NETWORKS (ACTION) This is a "model of field-based research designed to promote innovation in healthcare delivery by accelerating the diffusion of research into practice. The ACTION network includes 15 large partnerships and collaborating organizations that provide healthcare to more than 100 million Americans" (Accelerating Change and Transformation in Organizations and Networks II, 2013). This initiative, begun in 2006, is designed to better ensure that research findings are applied in the healthcare delivery system and not lost. It includes a number of HCOs that have partnered with the AHRQ. Projects must have "direct relevance to practice, public policy, and/or the organization and management of healthcare delivery" (Accelerating Change and Transformation in Organizations and Networks II, 2013). Initiatives such as this one may help to move EBM into the mainstream of management, including nursing management.

THE NATIONAL GUIDELINE CLEARINGHOUSE This is an AHRQ initiative that provides access to many EBP-based clinical guidelines on its website. Its mission "is to provide physicians, nurses, and other health professionals, healthcare providers, health plans, integrated delivery systems, purchasers and others an accessible mechanism for obtaining objective, detailed information on clinical practice guidelines and to further their dissemination, implementation and use" (2014). Guidelines can be downloaded to computers, tablets, and smartphones for easy access when needed in practice.

COMPARATIVE EFFECTIVENESS RESEARCH Comparative effectiveness research (CER) is

> the conduct and synthesis of systematic research comparing different interventions and strategies to prevent, diagnose, treat, and monitor health conditions. The purpose of CER is to inform patients, providers, and decision makers, responding to their expressed needs, about which interventions are most effective for which patients under specific circumstances. To provide this information, comparative effectiveness research must assess a comprehensive array of health-related outcomes for diverse patient populations. (U.S. National Library of Medicine, 2014)

The Affordable Care Act of 2010 (ACA) requires greater emphasis on comparing available treatment options. It is not clear in the long run the impact that this type of initiative will have on quality and cost. There is need to compare interventions, but how to do this comparison and apply this information to practice is complicated. It is unclear if long term this might lead to some form of healthcare rationing.

PATIENT-CENTERED CARE OUTCOMES RESEARCH INSTITUTE   The ACA also includes provisions related to evidence-based practice. The nonprofit Patient-Centered Outcomes Research Institute (PCORI) was established to support comparative effectiveness research (Patient-Centered Outcomes Research Institute, 2014). The ACA also requires that a grant program be established to support delivery of evidence-based and community-based prevention and wellness services to improve prevention activities, reduce chronic disease, and address health disparities; develop a national strategy to improve the nation's health; and disseminate evidence-based recommendations.

How all of these new initiatives and programs mesh is not yet clear nor is their effectiveness. They are new, and it will take time to evaluate outcomes. Critical concerns are repetition; information overload; cost of the initiatives/programs; level of use by healthcare providers (individuals and organizations); and use of effective, objective evaluation.

Nursing Leadership to Implement and Maintain Evidence-Based Practice

How might the evidence-based approach be applied to nursing management or administration? Titler, Cullen, and Ardery (2002) addressed this question and emphasized the importance of interprofessional collaboration, which seems to be a key issue with so much of what is happening in health care today. This must be a continuous process, takes commitment, and includes:

1. Incorporating evidence-based practice terminology into the mission, vision, strategic plan, and performance appraisals of staff.
2. Integrating the work EBP into the governance structure of nursing departments and the healthcare system.
3. Demonstrating the value of evidence-based practice through administrative behaviors of the chief nurse executive.
4. Establishing explicit expectations about EBP for nursing leaders (e.g., nurse managers and advanced practice nurses) who create a culture that values clinical inquiry (Titler et al., 2002, p. 26).

From this description, it is clear that to be successful, EBP has to be incorporated into all aspects of the organization structure, culture, and systems. Examples that are given to implement these four factors are:

- Integrate EBP in all staff education.
- Monitor and act on results of key indicators for selected EBPs.
- Select a specific number of EBP examples each year that have been identified from operational or quality improvement data.
- Establish a documentation system that supports EBP and allows for tracking or monitoring of EBP application.
- Provide routine staff education on EBP.
- Incorporate EBP into orientation, and so on.

EBP does have much to offer management and the delivery of nursing care to improve care and the way in which nurses work; however, the HCO has to make a commitment to implement it. How might EBP evidence be used in practice, and how does one go about applying it? One method is through use of protocols that are evidence based and describe step-by-step approaches to care for specific problems or use of clinical guidelines. How can the evidence be applied in practice?

- Change care for one patient or a population.
- Revise or develop a policy or a procedure.
- Implement the use of an evidence-based clinical guideline.
- Use to revise or develop a clinical pathway or a protocol.
- Use in shared governance to improve care.

CASE STUDY

Developing Excellence for a Hospital Unit

One of two pediatric units in an acute care hospital has not demonstrated that it is applying evidence-based practice. The chief nurse executive of the hospital is meeting with the nurse manager of the unit, the director of the pediatric nursing division, and the pediatric medical director. They review the information about the unit and conclude there is a problem. The chief nurse executive requests that the unit improve in applying EBP and asks the nurse manager to lead the effort with assistance from the two directors. All agree with this direction. The nurse manager leaves the meeting stressed and sits down to think through what he needs to do.

Questions:

1. Why is it important for EBP to be effectively applied in all units?
2. If other units are applying EBP more effectively, how might this be helpful to you in your planning?
3. What steps will you take, and whom will you involve?

- Educate staff.
- Share information through written communication, on website, and other materials.
- Develop fact sheets and posters to educate staff.
- Discuss in staff meetings.
- Involve staff in improving care.
- Reduce errors; use in root cause analysis of errors.
- Educate nursing students.

It is always important to note that an HCO can have the best written documents such as evidence-based policies and procedures, protocols, and standards, but if these do not change practice and improve care or if they remain static and not reviewed and updated routinely, then they are ineffective. The nurse manager needs to ensure not only that documents describing care are evidence based but also that they are applied. This requires monitoring, and this is part of quality improvement. EBP should also have an impact on patient and family education in that patient/family education content and teaching methods need to be current and effective approaches. Development of infrastructure to better ensure effective EBP integration needs to be carefully planned, implemented, and evaluated. Nurse managers need to actively participate in this process and ensure that their staff participate.

The Future of Nursing report also supports the need for nursing research and use of best evidence in practice (Institute of Medicine, 2011c). Throughout the report, evidence is used to support the report's comments, conclusions, and recommendations. The report also identifies research priorities for transforming nursing practice, education, and leadership. Given the focus of this text is leadership and management, the following research priorities to transform leadership are relevant:

- Identification of the personal and professional characteristics most critical to leadership of healthcare organizations, such as accountable care organizations, healthcare homes, medical homes, and clinics.
- Identification of the skills and knowledge most critical to leaders of healthcare organizations, such as accountable care organizations, healthcare homes, medical homes, and clinics.
- Identification of the personal and professional characteristics most important to leaders of quality improvement initiatives in hospitals and other settings.
- Identification of the characteristics of mentors that have been (or could be) most successful in recruiting and training diverse nurses and nurse faculty.
- Identification of the influence of nursing on important healthcare decisions at all levels.
- Identification of the unique contributions of nurses to healthcare committees or boards (Institute of Medicine, 2011c, p. 277).

Nurse leaders and managers need to be involved in research focused on these goals and also other areas of nursing leadership and management concerns—requiring great investment in evidence-based management.

EVIDENCE-BASED MANAGEMENT

Reports of medical mistakes have splashed across newspapers and magazines in the United States. At the same time, instances of overuse, underuse, and misuse of management tactics and strategies receive far less attention. "The sense of urgency associated with improving the quality of medical care does not exist with respect to improving the quality of management decision making. A more evidence-based approach would improve the competence of the decision makers and their motivation to use more scientific methods when making a decision" (Kovner & Rundall, 2009, p. 53). Most nurse managers do not consider evidence such as research on a routine basis when they make management decisions, and many managers are not even familiar with the term "management evidence" though it has been highlighted in some nursing professional standards and literature. In the American Organization of Nurse Executives' (AONE) 2010–2012 strategic plan, the organization noted the importance of using "evidence-based management practice and sound research in the development of future patient care delivery systems and practice environments. Explore and support the interrelations of technology, facility design and patient care delivery models" (American Organization of Nurse Executives, 2010). In its 2014–2016 plan, EBM is not specifically identified, but one of its strategies is to communicate the value of nursing in health care across the care continuum to all stakeholders and to "support and disseminate best practices and research that demonstrate the link between nursing leadership, nursing sensitive indicators, quality, and value to validate the contribution of nursing to patient outcomes across all care settings" (p. 3).

What is **evidence-based management**? It would seem natural to think that if evidence is important in making clinical or practice decisions, it should be important in making management decisions. EBM is the "systematic application of the best available evidence to the evaluation of managerial strategies for improving the performance of health services organizations" (Kovner & Rundall, 2009, p. 56). This definition is not much different from the EBP definition. It is important for nursing leaders and managers to base their decisions on best management evidence whenever possible, preferably management research. The five principles of evidence-based management are as follows:

1. Face the hard facts, and build a culture in which people are encouraged to tell the truth, even if it is unpleasant.
2. Be committed to fact-based decision making, which means being committed to getting the best evidence and using it to guide actions.
3. Treat your organization as an unfinished prototype; encourage experimentation and learning by doing.
4. Look for the risks and drawbacks in what people recommend; even the best medicine has side effects.
5. Avoid basing decisions on untested but strongly held beliefs, what you have done in the past, or on uncritical "benchmarking" of what winners do (Evidence-Based Management, 2014).

Evidence-Based Management Process

Just as there is an EBP process, there is an EBM process. Both processes are similar. The steps include (Kovner & Rundall, 2009):

1. **Formulating the question:** Formulate the management question so research studies can be found. This may require a broader question than originally proposed, but if the question is too broad and vague, it will not yield research studies that are helpful. It is best to include clarification of the technique or tool, the setting, and outcome of interest. This is similar to the PICO question used in EBP.
2. **Acquiring research evidence:** Evidence can be obtained from experts, colleagues, personal experience, and published literature, similar to EBP sources that are more than just research evidence. This requires literature searches similarly done for EBP. The best source is research syntheses of a large number of studies on the question. It is not easy to find this type of evidence, particularly in nursing management. This is not an area that has a large research library to choose from. Many of the questions that a nurse leader or manager would propose may actually be addressed in healthcare delivery, business, and organization research, though it is difficult to find research on many of the questions that arise in management.

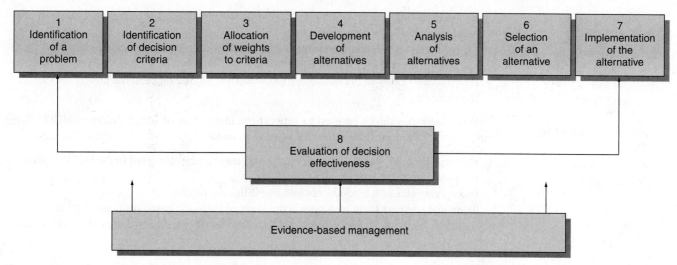

Figure 16-1 The eight-stage decision-making process

Source: Kovner, A. & Randall, T. (2009). Evidence-based management reconsidered. In A. Kovner, D. Fine, & R. D'Aquila (Eds.), *Evidence-based Management in Healthcare* (pp. 53–57). Adapted by Kovner & Randall from S. Robbins & D. Decenzo. (2004). Fundamentals of management: Essential concepts and applications (4th ed.). Upper Saddle River, NJ: Pearson Prentice Hall. Robbins, Stephen P.; Decenzo, David A. Fundamentals of management: Essential concepts and applications (3rd ed.). © 2001 Pearson Education, Inc., Upper Saddle River, New Jersey.

3. **Assessing the quality of the evidence:** Managers should assess the following aspects of the evidence: strength of the research design, study context and setting, sample size, control of confounding factors, reliability and validity of measurements, methods and procedures, justification of the conclusions, study sponsorship, and consistency of the findings with other studies. These criteria are very similar to the criteria used to assess EBP evidence.

4. **Presenting the evidence:** This is not a step that is actively considered in EBP, but it is in EBM. When a manager presents evidence to support a decision, the following should be considered in the presentation, whether it is oral or written. It should be timely, brief, and easily understood with limited use of jargon, and it should include a clear description of questions addressed, a description of context of the research, an assessment of the quality of the evidence, and the results and the implications for management. This is when the manager "makes the case" for a decision.

5. **Applying the evidence to the decision:** It is just as difficult to apply evidence in management as it is to apply evidence in clinical practice. Figure 16-1 provides another description of the decision-making process in relationship to EBM.

Identification of the problem is the description of "the discrepancy between an existing and desired state of affairs" (Kovner & Rundall, 2009, p. 57). Steps 5 and 6 in the figure are particularly important as they emphasize the need to analyze alternatives and select the best alternative based on the evidence on hand. Nurse managers need to take the time to do this. The tendency is to grab at a possible solution with limited consideration of alternatives and analyzing evidence supporting the alternatives.

Evidence-Based Management: Barriers and Strategies

There are many barriers to implementing EBM; some are similar to the barriers to implementing EBP. Examples of barriers are as follows:

- Lack of leadership support
- Lack of technology and library expertise
- Lack of knowledge about EBM and the confusion over the difference between EBM and EBP
- Limited or no recognition of the value of EBM with limited expectation that managers will use EBM
- Limited time

- Restrictions on decision making (e.g., centralized decision making, rigid policies and procedures, and other bureaucratic factors)
- Limited relevant research and limited EBM literature such as systematic reviews
- Lack of structure to implement EBM
- Resistance to EBM so the manager makes decisions based on personal preferences rather than evidence

What strategies might be used to support the integration of EBM within an HCO? Some examples of implementing systematic processes to make major decisions include the following:

- Periodically brief managers on recent management research related to the HCO's operational and strategic concerns.
- Incorporate research assessments into due diligence reports.
- Train management team members in the steps of evidence-based decision making.
- Establish ties with academic institutions and research centers (Rundall et al., 2009, p. 15).

APPLYING EVIDENCE-BASED PRACTICE

Evidence for Effective Leadership and Management

CITATIONS: Institute for Healthcare Improvement. (2009). *Using evidence-based environmental design to enhance safety and quality.* Retrieved from http://www.ihi.org/resources/Pages/IHIWhitePapers/UsingEvidenceBasedEnvironmentalDesignWhitePaper.aspx

Jha, A., Orav, J., Zheng, J., & Epstein, A. (2008). Patients' perception of hospital care in the United States. *New England Journal of Medicine, 359,* 1928.

Joint Commission. (2008). Guiding principles for the development of the hospital of the future. Retrieved from http://www.jointcommission.org/Guiding_Principles_for_The_Development_of_the_Hospital_of_The_Future_/

OVERVIEW: There is a connection between physical design and quality care (Institute for Healthcare Improvement, 2008). This connection needs to be understood by nurse managers. Nurse leaders in HCOs should be involved in environmental design decisions from new building, renovation, and day-to-day needs of the physical environment. The environment not only is important to patients, families, and visitors, but it also has an impact on staff safety and satisfaction. One such example is the Hospital Consumer Assessment of Healthcare Providers and Systems (HCAHPS) data mandated by the Centers for Medicare & Medicaid Services (CMS). In an article assessing patient perception of care in American hospitals, the authors examined several domains of the patient experience. The component that received the lowest composite score (52%) was a quiet room (Jha, Orav, Zhen, & Epstein, 2008). Changing the physical environment and building new facilities is costly, and many of the HCOs are old and need renovation.

APPLICATION: In 2008 the Joint Commission recognized the need for more consideration of decision making in HCO environmental design in its report *Guiding Principles for the Development of the Hospital of the Future.* To be cost effective and meet needs of the changes in healthcare delivery, it is important to use evidence, when possible, to make these critical decisions. It is noted that there is no perfect formula of interventions needed to develop the best physical environment, and there should be a comprehensive review of needs and a plan. Some examples of interventions identified by the Institute for Healthcare Improvement that emphasize multiple patient needs in the healthcare environment include the following:

- Install alcohol-based gel dispensers at each patient bedside and at all points of care.
- Install noise mitigation materials.
- Use music and art as positive distractions.
- Include clear directions throughout the facility.
- Improve task lighting in pharmacy, medicine rooms, and procedure areas.
- Build private rooms.
- Provide adequate space for families to stay overnight in patient rooms.
- Design space to support patient transfer from bed to stretcher, to wheelchair, and so on.
- Assess and build patient bathrooms to accommodate patient care needs.
- Provide access to natural light.
- Install ceiling-mounted lifts in many patient rooms.
- Design decentralized nursing stations.
- Provide choices for patients to control lighting, privacy, music, and visual images.
- Other general examples are furnishing that is calming in color, useful in design, and easy to clean. Floor surfaces should be safe, easy to clean, and coordinate with colors.

Questions:

1. How do the information from the Institute for Healthcare Improvement and the Joint Commission compare to one another?
2. Have you heard patients and families make comments about the environment in an HCO? What were the comments? If they had complaints, were they identifying problems that could be resolved easily or with more effort and how?
3. Take an experiential trip and enter an HCO only for the purpose of describing its environment. What do you see, hear, and smell?
4. Describe examples of how a nurse manager might improve the environment in the manager's unit.

These strategies should be incorporated into nursing management. The last strategy is an important one. Many nursing departments are associated with schools of nursing for EBP implementation. If the school has faculty experienced in leadership and management, then using this expertise can assist the HCO and also build stronger bridges with the school of nursing; collaboration will be more evident. D'Aquila (2009) also recommends incorporating EBM into performance evaluation of managers. Are they using EBM? This will need to be tracked or monitored. Strategic planning should also demonstrate use of EBM and should include a method for monitoring decision making.

RESEARCH, EVIDENCE-BASED PRACTICE, AND QUALITY IMPROVEMENT

It is easy to get nursing research (NR), evidence-based practice, and quality improvement (QI) confused. Chapters 17 and 18 discuss QI in more detail, but it is important here to clarify similarities and differences in them. A key difference in separating QI from research and EBP is that with QI the data are usually collected and reported internally, within the HCO, making generalizability difficult. The purpose is not to generate new knowledge as it is with research. Typically IRB approval is not required nor is participant consent required in the same manner as would be done for research; however, there have been recent situations where this has been questioned and has caused problems. The best approach is to ask the IRB committee if the QI project meets requirements for exemption from IRB requirements (Miller & Emanuel, 2008). The decision as to how to proceed, however, would be decisions made by leadership or management.

With QI, the gap is different from EBP as it is one of a knowing-doing gap. Staff know what to do, but they either do not do it or fail to do it correctly. Chapters 17 and 18 discuss the many causes for this gap. EBP is doing the right things, and QI is doing things right. The techniques of QI have focused on integrating what we know and moving it to how we should be doing it.

Common techniques to achieve this are reminder systems (paper or computer), simplification of processes (reducing unnecessary steps), structuring the system to do the right thing at the right time and place (putting hand-washing equipment and/or instructions in the right place) and testing new interventions to determine what works in this particular setting. This task is often a creative and iterative process of identifying barriers, and working out solutions to overcome these. (Glasziou, Ogrinc, & Goodman, 2011, p. i15)

Figure 16-2 describes the relationship.

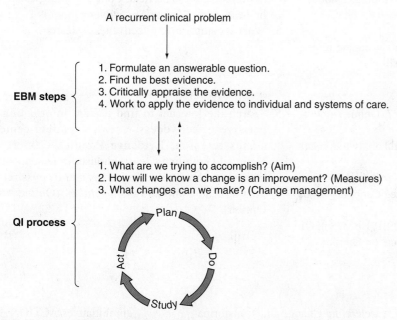

Figure 16-2 Proposed linkage between EBM and one model for QI

Source: From "Can Evidence-Based Medicine and Clinical Quality Improvement Learn from Each Other?" by Glasziou, P., Ogrinc, G., & Goodman, S. *BMJ Qual Saf, 20 (suppl 1)*, i13–i17; Published by BMJ Publishing Group © 2011.

APPLYING LEADERSHIP AND MANAGEMENT

My Hospital Unit: An Evolving Case Experience

You must make a lot of decisions as nurse manager on your unit. Select a problem that you might encounter on a daily basis on your unit, and apply the evidence-based management process as described in this chapter to your management question. Include references that you identify as relevant, and summarize the key points to answer your management question. What would you do to ensure that you use EBM in your daily work as nurse manager?

BSN and *Master's Essentials:* Application to Content

BSN Essentials (American Association of Colleges of Nursing, 2008) as Applied to this Chapter:

III. Scholarship for Evidence-Based Practice
IV. Interprofessional Communication and Collaboration for Improving Health Outcomes

Master's Essentials **(American Association of Colleges of Nursing, 2011) as Applied to this Chapter:**

III. Quality Improvement and Safety
IV. Translating and Integrating Scholarship into Practice
VII. Interprofessional Collaboration for Improving Patient and Population Health Outcomes

Applying AONE Competencies

Identify which of the AONE competencies found in Appendix A apply to the content of this chapter.

Engaging in the Content: Critical Thinking and Clinical Reasoning and Judgment

Discussion Questions

1. Discuss the barriers to research and strategies that might be used to overcome these barriers. Consider strategies not discussed in the chapter.
2. Discuss the four types of EBP evidence.
3. Develop an EBP question, and look for a systematic review or a clinical guideline to answer your question.

4. Discuss the barriers to EBP and strategies that might be used to overcome these barriers. Consider strategies not discussed in the chapter. (Online Application Option)
5. What is comparative effectiveness research?

Application Exercises

1. Why is it important for nurses to use EBP? (Online Application Option)
2. Describe the EBM process and how it might apply to nursing management. (Online Application Option)
3. Discuss the barriers to EBM and strategies that might be used to overcome these barriers. Consider strategies not discussed in the chapter.
4. In teams, compare and contrast research, EBP, EBM, and QI. Provide examples for each. (Online Application Option)

5. Search the Internet to find current information on comparative effectiveness research, patient-centered outcomes research, Evidence Practice Centers, and the National Guideline Clearinghouse. In teams, compare the current work of these initiatives and discuss relevance to nursing leadership and management. (Online Application Option)

References

Academic Center for Evidence-Based Nursing. (2008). ACE Star Model. Retrieved from http://www.acestar.uthscsa.edu/acestar-model.asp

Accelerating Change and Transformation in Organizations and Networks II. (2013). Retrieved from http://www.ahrq.gov/

cpi/initiatives/ACTION_II/index.html
Agency for Healthcare Research and Quality. (2014). Evidence-based

Practice Centers (EPC) Program overview. Retrieved from http://www.ahrq.gov/research/findings/evidence-based-reports/overview/index.html

American Association of Colleges of Nursing. (2008). *The essentials of baccalaureate education for professional nursing practice*. Washington, DC: Author.

American Association of Colleges of Nursing. (2011). *The essentials of master's education in nursing*. Washington, DC: Author.

American Nurses Association. (2014). Asking the question. Retrieved from http://www.nursingworld.org/Research-Toolkit/Asking-the-Question

American Organization of Nurse Executives. (2010). 2010–2012 strategic plan. Chicago, IL: Author.

American Organization of Nurse Executives. (2014). 2014–2016 strategic plan. Retrieved from www.aone.org/membership/about/docs/2014-2016%20AONE%20StratPlan.Final.pdf

Centers for Disease Control and Prevention. (2013). The U.S. Public Health Service syphilis study at Tuskegee. Retrieved from http://www.cdc.gov/tuskegee/timeline.htm

D'Aquila, R. (2009). Application of evidence-based management at an academic medical center: The Yale-New Haven Hospital experience. In A. Kovner, D. Fine, & R. D'Aquila (Eds.), *Evidence-based management in healthcare* (pp. 17–28). Chicago, IL: Health Administration Press.

Evidence-Based Management. (2014). Five principles of EBM. Retrieved from http://evidence-basedmanagement.com/

Finkelman, A., & Kenner, C. (2014). Excerpt from *Professional Nursing Concepts: Competencies For Quality Leadership*. Boston, MA: Jones & Bartlett.

Glasziou, P., Ogrinc, G., & Goodman, S. (2011). Can evidence-based medicine and clinical quality improvement complement each other. *BMJ Qual Saf, 20(Suppl 1)*, i13–i17.

Institute of Medicine. (2003). *Health professions education*. Washington, DC: National Academies Press.

Institute of Medicine. (2008). *Knowing what works in health care: A roadmap for the nation*. Washington, DC: National Academies Press.

Institute of Medicine. (2011a). *Clinical practice guidelines we can trust*. Washington, DC: National Academies Press.

Institute of Medicine. (2011b). *Finding what works in health care: Standards for systematic reviews*. Washington, DC: National Academies Press.

Institute of Medicine. (2011c). *The future of nursing: Leading change, advancing health*. Washington, DC: National Academies Press.

Kovner, A., & Rundall, T. (2009). Evidence-based management reconsidered. In A. Kovner, D. Fine, & R. D'Aquila (Eds.). (2009). *Evidence-based management in healthcare* (pp. 53–78). Chicago, IL: Health Administration Press.

Miller, F., & Emanuel, E. (2008). Quality improvement research and informed consent. *New England Journal of Medicine, 358*(8), 765–768.

National Guideline Clearinghouse. (2014). About NGC. Retrieved from http://www.guideline.gov/about/index.aspx

National Institute of Nursing Research. (2013). Mission & strategic plan. Retrieved http://www.ninr.nih.gov/aboutninr/ninr-mission-and-strategic-plan#.VJ51ODBI

National Institutes of Health. (2009). Willowbrook hepatitis experiments. Retrieved from http://science.education.nih.gov/supplements/nih9/bioethics/guide/pdf/Master_5-4.pdf

Patient-Centered Outcomes Research Institute. (2014). About us. Retrieved from http://www.pcori.org/about-us

Rundall, T., Martelli, P., McCurdy, R., Graetz, I., Arroyo, L., Neuwirth, E., … Hsu, J. (2009). Using research evidence when making decisions: Views of health services managers and policymakers. In A. Kovner, D. Fine, & R. D'Aquila (Eds.), *Evidence-based management in healthcare* (pp. 3–16). Chicago, IL: Health Administration Press.

Sackett, D. (1996). On some clinically useful measures of the effects of treatment. *British Medical Journal, 309*, 7055–7056.

Schmidt, N. A., & Brown, J. M. (2015a). *Evidence-based practice for nurses: Appraisal and applications of research*. Burlington, MA: Jones and Bartlett Learning. (Adapted from Straus, S. (2005). *Introduction to teaching evidence-based healthcare*. University of Toronto knowledge translation program—PowerPoint Presentation). Retrieved from http://www.cebm.net/?o=1021

Schmidt, N. A., & Brown, J. M. (2015b). *Evidence-based practice for nurses: Appraisal and applications of research*. Burlington, MA: Jones and Bartlett Learning.

Tappen, R. (2011). *Advanced nursing research*. Sudbury, MA: Jones & Bartlett Learning.

Titler, M., Cullen, L., & Ardery, G. (2002). Evidence-based practice: An administrative perspective. *Reflections in Nursing Leadership, 28*(2), 26–27.

U.S. Department of Health and Human Services. (2005). The Nuremberg code. Retrieved from http://www.hhs.gov/ohrp/archive/nurcode.html

U.S. Department of Health and Human Services. (2014). The Belmont report. Retrieved from http://www.hhs.gov/ohrp/humansubjects/guidance/belmont.html

U.S. Holocaust Memorial Museum. (2014). Medical experiments. Retrieved from http://www.ushmm.org/research/research-in-collections/search-the-collections/bibliography/medical-experiments

U.S. National Library of Medicine. (2014). Comparative effectiveness research (CER). Retrieved from http://www.nlm.nih.gov/hsrinfo/cer.html

17

Healthcare Quality: A Critical Health Policy Issue

KEY TERMS

- error
- high-reliability organization
- outcome
- process
- quality care
- safety
- structure
- system

● LEARNING OUTCOMES

Before you begin, take a moment to familiarize yourself with the learning outcomes for this chapter.

> Examine the content and implications of the Institute of Medicine and its healthcare quality and nursing reports.
> Examine the current status of healthcare quality.
> Discuss the relevance of legislation and governmental and nongovernmental initiatives and strategies to improve healthcare quality policy.
> Critique critical issues related to defining quality health care, including measurement, structure, process, and outcome elements.
> Explain the purpose of the National Quality Strategy and its relationship to other content in this chapter.

WHAT'S AHEAD

The National Academy of Medicine's (NAM) fourth core competency for healthcare professions is to apply quality improvement (QI). The NAM describes this core competency as "identify errors and hazards in care; understand and implement basic safety design principles, such as standardization and simplification; continually understand and measure quality of care in terms of structure, process, and outcomes in relation to patient and community needs; and design and test interventions to change processes and systems of care, with the objective of improving quality" (2003a, p. 4). As noted in this report and also in the IOM report *To Err Is Human* (1999), the U.S. healthcare system is dysfunctional and has problems with safety, quality, and inefficiency. Nurses encounter these issues as they try to ensure patients receive quality, timely care. The healthcare system is the focus of quality improvement (QI). A **system** is a perspective of the whole and its parts so there can be better understanding of the interactions of the parts and impact on the whole. The healthcare system is composed of a continuum of services (e.g., medicine, surgery, women's health, pediatrics, mental health, etc.), settings (e.g., hospitals, clinics, physician practices, long-term care facilities, home care agencies, hospice, pharmacies, laboratories, etc.), healthcare professionals (e.g., nurses, physicians, social workers, administrators, etc.), third-party payers/purchasers, and patients/consumers. Ideally the healthcare system should be an effective system for care to meet required outcomes. Each patient's care is part of this overall emphasis on healthcare improvement. Ultimately the goal is that each patient's outcomes will be met. Quality improvement now emphasizes continuous quality improvement (CQI) and describes problem identification as an opportunity to improve. The older term is "quality assessment" or "assurance." How can this approach be applied to the healthcare system that is rapidly changing? This chapter discusses the critical policy issues of quality care in the healthcare delivery system. Safety is a component of quality care. With this complex system that changes daily, the task of assessing quality of care and the best way to improve care are difficult to accomplish. Prior to the IOM examination of healthcare quality and its reports, the United States had no comprehensive system to monitor health care, judge improvement, or determine the best strategies to improve health care. The United States now has an annual report describing national healthcare quality data, and as discussed in this chapter, more robust national healthcare policies and initiatives to monitor and better ensure changes to improve care. This chapter focuses on healthcare quality from a health policy perspective and the history of its expansion. Chapter 18 continues the discussion by focusing on the implementation of healthcare quality improvement.

THE INFLUENCE OF THE INSTITUTE OF MEDICINE HEALTHCARE QUALITY REPORTS

In the past 17 years, there has been increasing interest in the quality of health care, particularly since the publication of the Institute of Medicine report *To Err Is Human* (1999). This report signaled that the healthcare system was experiencing frequent and important errors, and this report led to the IOM initiative to examine the healthcare system in more detail. How did this process begin, and where is it today?

President Clinton's Advisory Commission on Consumer Protection and Quality in the Healthcare Industry (1998) was a major reason the IOM decided to examine the issue of quality care. This commission addressed many of the concerns about quality care and the need to make changes to improve care. Three nurse leaders served on the 23-member commission. The purpose of the commission was to advise the president about the impact of healthcare delivery system changes on quality, consumer protection, and the availability of needed services. The commission consisted of four subcommittees:

1. The first subcommittee's purpose was to develop a Consumer Bill of Rights, Protections, and Responsibilities. Critical issues addressed were healthcare coverage/reimbursement, choice of practitioners, privacy and confidentiality, disclosure of practitioner qualifications, and external appeals processes. Despite the recommendations from this commission, the United States did not have a Consumer Bill of Rights until the Affordable Care Act of 2010 (ACA) included a provision on this issue, though the 1996 passage of the Health Insurance Portability and Accountability Act (HIPAA) does address patient privacy and confidentiality, which are aspects of patient rights.
2. The second subcommittee was created to identify performance measurement and quality oversight that would improve the validity and reliability of performance measurement data.
3. The third subcommittee, which was chaired by a nurse, considered the creation of a quality improvement environment and the internal and external barriers and facilitators of quality improvement.
4. The fourth subcommittee focused on the roles of public and private oversight entities, strategies to reach a balance between market-driven quality incentives and regulatory requirements, and the responsibilities of group purchasers to protect quality.

The final report from the commission, *Quality First: Better Health Care for all Americans*, was published in 1998. The commission was part of President Clinton's hopes for healthcare reform, but it was not successful. However, this commission and its report did stimulate the development of the Quality of Health Care in America project, which resulted in the development of the *Quality Chasm* series of reports initiated by the IOM in June 1998 and has been ongoing since then. The purpose of the project was to expand the work of Clinton's commission after it completed its charge and to develop strategies that would improve quality of care over the next 10 years. This has been expanded beyond 10 years. Box 17-1 highlights the key initial IOM reports that are a part of this project. As indicated by the number of reports and their content, much work has been done since Clinton's advisory commission in 1997–98, and many other reports continue to be completed by the National Academy of Medicine (NAM) today.

BOX 17-1	CURRENT REPORTS ON HEALTHCARE QUALITY

First report (Clinton administration) that stimulated IOM reports:

- Advisory Commission on Consumer Information and Quality in the Health Care Industry. (1998). *Quality first: Better health care for all Americans.*

The following reports can be accessed at the National Academy of Medicine (NAM) website:

- Institute of Medicine. (1999). *To err is human: Building a safer health system.* Washington, DC: National Academies Press.
- Institute of Medicine. (2001). *Crossing the quality chasm: A new health system for the 21st century.* Washington, DC: National Academies Press.
- Institute of Medicine. (2001). *Envisioning the national health care quality report.* Washington, DC: National Academies Press.
- Institute of Medicine. (2002). *Leadership by example: Coordinating government roles in improving health care quality.* Washington, DC: National Academies Press.
- Institute of Medicine. (2003). *Who will keep the public healthy? Educating public health professionals for the 21st century.* Washington, DC: National Academies Press.
- Institute of Medicine. (2003). *Health professions education: A bridge to quality.* Washington, DC: National Academies Press.
- Institute of Medicine. (2003). *Priority areas for national action: Transforming health care quality.* (2003). Washington, DC: National Academies Press.
- Institute of Medicine. *Keeping patients safe: Transforming the work environment of nurses.* Washington, DC: National Academies Press.
- Institute of Medicine. (2003). *Patient safety: Achieving a new standard for care.* Washington, DC: National Academies Press.

Examples of special focus IOM reports:

- Institute of Medicine. (2006). *Preventing medication errors.* Washington, DC: National Academies Press.
- Institute of Medicine. (2007). *Hospital-based emergency care: At the breaking point.* Washington, DC: National Academies Press.
- Institute of Medicine. (2007). *Emergency care for children: Growing pains.* Washington, DC: National Academies Press.
- Institute of Medicine. (2005). *Preventing childhood obesity: Health in the balance.* Washington, DC: National Academies Press.
- Institute of Medicine. (2005). *Quality through collaboration: The future of rural health.* Washington, DC: National Academies Press.
- Institute of Medicine. (2006). *Improving the quality of health care for mental and substance-use conditions.* Washington, DC: National Academies Press.
- Institute of Medicine. (2006). *From cancer patient to cancer survivor: Lost in transition.* Washington, DC: National Academies Press.
- Institute of Medicine. (2007). *Preterm birth: Causes, consequences, and prevention.* Washington, DC: National Academies Press.
- Institute of Medicine. (2007). *Cancer care for the whole patient: Meeting psychosocial health needs.* Washington, DC: National Academies Press.
- Institute of Medicine. (2008). *Retooling for an aging America: Building the health care workforce.* Washington, DC: National Academies Press.
- Institute of Medicine. (2010). *The future of nursing: Leading change, advancing health.* Washington, DC: National Academies Press.
- Institute of Medicine. (2011). *Relieving pain in America: A blueprint for transforming prevention, care, education, and research.* Washington, DC: National Academies Press.

The following discussion provides an overview of the content of these critical reports related to quality health care that have guided healthcare policy since 1999. All of the IOM reports are accessible through the NAM website.

TO ERR IS HUMAN The first report, *To Err Is Human: Building a Safer Health System* (Institute of Medicine, 1999), focused on safety within the healthcare delivery system. Data from the report indicated that there were serious safety problems. Examples included the following:

- When data from one study was extrapolated, the result was at least 44,000 Americans die each year as a result of a medication error. Another study indicated the number could be as high as 98,000 (American Hospital Association, 1999, as cited in Institute of Medicine, 1999).
- More people die in a given year as a result of medical errors than from motor-vehicle collisions (43,458), breast cancer (42,297), or AIDS (16,516) (Institute of Medicine, 1999).
- Healthcare costs represent over one-half of total national costs, which include lost income, lost household production, disability, and healthcare costs (Institute of Medicine, 1999).

There were clear problems, and the report focused on hospital errors. This, however, does not negate the presence of medical errors in home health care, long-term care, ambulatory care, primary care, and other healthcare settings. These settings require further exploration, and this is ongoing today. Currently the annual National Healthcare Quality Report includes measurement of some of the nonacute care variables, but the original annual reports recommended by the IOM focused on only acute care.

What are some of the outcomes from errors that cause further problems? Cost is certainly a concern, and errors can result in a variety of costs. Complications that result from errors may lead to increased healthcare costs. Opportunity costs occur when repeat diagnostic tests are required or interventions are needed to counteract adverse drug events. Another critical concern is patients' loss of trust in the healthcare system and its providers. If a patient experiences an error, this has a direct impact on the patient's trust in the healthcare system; however, the increase in media coverage of healthcare quality can also have just as serious an impact on patient trust in the system.

Historically, accrediting and licensing organizations had not focused much on the issue of errors, but this has changed. The decentralized and fragmented healthcare system certainly has been a factor in contributing to unsafe conditions, and it interferes with improvement (Institute of Medicine, 1999; 2001a). Multiple providers and ineffective communication also are other problems that affect patient safety. Third-party payers have become more involved in encouraging providers to improve performance as they recognize the impact errors can have on decreasing costs.

The IOM report on safety clearly indicated that there is not only one answer to solving this problem, and both safety and errors have to be considered. This report defines **safety** as "freedom from accidental injury" and defines **error** as "the failure of a planned action to be completed as intended or the use of a wrong plan to achieve an aim" (Institute of Medicine, 1999, p. 3). Errors are directly related to outcomes, which is a significant concern in quality improvement efforts. There are two general types of errors: errors of planning and errors of execution. Errors harm the patient, and some errors that do harm the patient may have been preventable adverse events. In 1999 the IOM identified three types of problems that are now used in the measurement of quality and have become more important as QI initiatives developed:

1. **Misuse:** avoidable complications that prevent patients from receiving full potential benefit of a service
2. **Overuse:** potential for harm from the provision of a service that exceeds the possible benefit
3. **Underuse:** failure to provide a service that would have produced a favorable outcome for the patient

The four key messages from the *To Err Is Human* report discussed important elements of the healthcare system and its safety needs. As noted earlier, the level of errors was high and continues to be (Subcommittee on Primary Health and Aging, U.S. Senate, 2014). Errors need to be viewed from a system perspective. There was no significant national monitoring or reporting system for healthcare quality. To accomplish improvement, the healthcare system will have to change (Institute of Medicine, 2001a). Nurses must be involved in developing plans to respond to safety problems on the local, state, and national levels, including the four key messages in the report. Chapter 18 extends this discussion on quality, focusing on QI implementation.

CROSSING THE QUALITY CHASM   The second major IOM report was *Crossing the Quality Chasm* (Institute of Medicine, 2001a), which focused on developing a new healthcare system for the 21st century, one that improves care. The first conclusion from the report was the system is in need of repair, one of fundamental change, which continued the emphasis on this concern from the *To Err Is Human* report. As this text emphasizes, the report called attention to the impact of the rapid change in the healthcare system: new medical science, new technology, rapid availability of information, and so on. Healthcare providers must work to maintain competence and knowledge of these changes and their impact on practice. Across the country there is variation in how both individual providers and healthcare organizations (HCOs) respond to change in healthcare and make the best use of resources (Institute of Medicine, 2001a). Content in Chapter 3 on change is relevant to the QI process, which is highly dependent on change for improvement.

Another conclusion from the report was that the increase of chronic conditions has had a major impact on the system. With people living longer, mostly due to advances in medical science and technology, more people are living with chronic conditions. The standard description of a chronic condition, which is supported by the IOM reports, includes illnesses that last longer than three months and are not self-limiting. These illnesses affect a large portion of the population (Institute of Medicine, 2001a). Many of these patients also have comorbid conditions. They have complicated problems and require collaborative treatment efforts. The complex, fragmented, and disorganized healthcare system is ineffective in dealing with these problems. In 2014 a major decision was made by the Centers for Medicare & Medicaid Services (CMS) to begin paying physicians a monthly fee for coordination of care for patients with chronic illness, effective January 2015 (Kaiser Health News, 2014). A comprehensive care plan will be developed for those patients who agree to participate. Though the outcomes of this proposal are not yet known, the fact that it has been implemented is supportive of the need for coordination and patient-centered care, both critical components of effective care for chronic illness.

The 2001 report identified quality as a system property and developed six aims or goals for improvement:

1. *Safe:* Avoiding injuries to patients from the care that is intended to help them
2. *Effective:* Providing services based on scientific knowledge (evidence-based practice) to all who could benefit and avoiding providing services to those not likely to benefit (avoiding underuse and overuse)
3. *Patient-centered:* Providing care that is respectful of and responsive to individual patient preferences, needs, and values and ensuring that patient values guide all clinical decisions
4. *Timely:* Reducing waits and harmful delays for both those who receive and those who give care
5. *Efficient:* Avoiding waste, including waste of equipment, supplies, ideas, and energy
6. *Equitable:* Providing care that does not vary in quality because of personal characteristics such as gender, ethnicity, geographic location, and socioeconomic status (disparity concern) (Institute of Medicine, 2001a, pp. 5–6)

These aims or goals, highlighted in Figure 17-1, are now part of continuous quality improvement. The aims are related to nursing practice and healthcare management and should be integrated into individual patient care planning and management of healthcare services.

As discussed in Chapter 3, the healthcare system has been undergoing change. The system was using ineffective work designs that also led to unsafe and poor quality care. These identified problems are complex and not easily resolved. Some of these problems have been addressed, such as with redesigning health care discussed in Chapter 3, but the results have not always

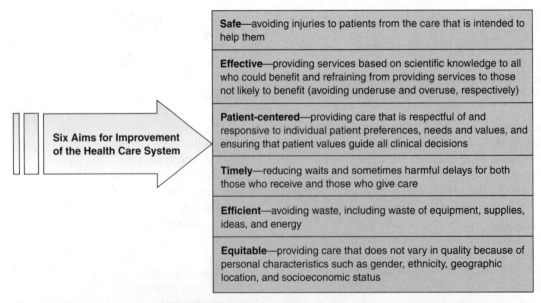

Figure 17-1 Six aims for improvement of the health care system

● Encourage data collection efforts needed to refine and develop quality measures and, ultimately, stimulate the development of a health information infrastructure to support quality measurement and reporting (Institute of Medicine, 2001b, p. 31).

The *Envisioning the National Health Care Quality* report described a framework that is now used to collect and organize annual data about healthcare quality, focusing on how the healthcare delivery system performs in providing personal health care. The framework for the annual report recommended by the IOM focused on two dimensions to describe quality. The first dimension focused on safety, effectiveness, patient centeredness, and timeliness. The second dimension of quality care focused on the consumer perspectives on healthcare needs and included staying healthy, getting better, living with illness or disability, and coping with the palliative or end-of-life needs.

These components continue to be key issues for individuals and are affected by the individual's age. Across the life span, individuals view these components differently. Particularly important and somewhat different is the second dimension in the matrix because this dimension expands on the patient or consumer of healthcare services and personal health issues and perspectives, reinforcing patient-centered care. Both dimensions emphasize quality and patient-centered care. Box 17-2 describes the key measurement areas for the current reports, which have been adapted as more experience was gained on collecting and analyzing national quality data.

BOX 17-2 — KEY MEASUREMENT AREAS FOR THE NATIONAL HEALTHCARE QUALITY REPORT (NHQR) AND THE NATIONAL HEALTHCARE DISPARITIES REPORT (NHDR)

Effectiveness of Care for Common Clinical Conditions: Organized around several clinical areas: cancer, cardiovascular disease, chronic kidney disease, diabetes, HIV and AIDS, mental health and substance abuse, musculoskeletal diseases, and respiratory diseases. New to the 2013 report are data from the Ryan White HIV/AIDS program that examine primary care and support services for people living with and affected by HIV disease.

Effectiveness of Care Across the Lifespan: Examines four types of health care services that typically cut across clinical conditions: maternal and child health, lifestyle modification, functional status preservation and rehabilitation, and supportive and palliative care. New to the 2013 reports are measures of adolescent receipt of counseling about birth control and of patient perceptions of home health care.

Patient Safety: Tracks safety within a variety of health care settings. In prior years, this chapter focused on hospitals, with an examination of healthcare-associated infections, postoperative and other hospital complications, and preventable hospital deaths. In the 2013 reports, this chapter has been expanded to include measures of patient safety in nursing homes, home health settings, and ambulatory care settings. Many new measures have been added from an assortment of new data sources.

Timeliness: Examines the delivery of time-sensitive clinical care and patient perceptions of how quickly they receive care. Among the measures reported in this chapter are the ability to get care when the patient needs it and emergency department wait times.

Patient Centeredness: Examines individual experiences with care in an office or clinic setting, as well as during a hospital stay. The 2013 reports include a new discussion of provider-patient communication for adults receiving home health care. Measures reported on perceptions of communication with providers and satisfaction with the provider-patient relationship.

Care Coordination: Presents data to assess the performance of the U.S. health care system in coordinating care across providers or services. Care coordination is measured, in part, using readmission measures as well as measures of success in transitioning across health care settings. The 2013 reports contain a new chapter on information gathering by home health care providers.

Efficiency: Discusses how well the health care system promotes quality, affordable care, and appropriate use of services. The emphasis in this chapter is on overuse of health services, as measures representing misuse or underuse overlap with other chapters of the report and are included in various chapters of the reports.

Health System Infrastructure: Explores the capacity of the U.S. health care system to support high-quality care. Infrastructure measures, which are primarily structural measures of quality, include adoption of computerized data systems and the supply of selected health care professionals. The 2013 reports contain a new discussion of nurse practitioners and physician assistants and a new discussion on e-prescribing.

Access: Presents measures that cut across several priority areas and includes measures that focus on barriers to care, such as lack of insurance, financial barriers to care experienced by the population with health insurance, and usual source of care.

Priority Populations: Continues to be unique to the NHDR. This chapter summarizes quality and disparities in care for populations at elevated risk for receiving poor health care, including racial and ethnic minorities, low-income populations, older adults, residents of rural areas, and individuals with disabilities or special health care needs. New to the 2013 report is a display of the prevalence of multiple chronic conditions among Medicare beneficiaries and additional data from California on lesbian, gay, bisexual, and transgender populations.

Source: Agency for Healthcare Quality and Research. (2014, May). *National healthcare quality report, 2013.* AHRQ publication No. 14-0005. Retrieved from http://www.ahrq.gov/research/findings/nhqrdr/nhqr13/2013nhqr.pdf

The Agency for Healthcare Research and Quality (AHRQ), an HHS agency, is mandated to collect the data for the national report on quality using the framework identified in the IOM reports. AHRQ then publishes the annual report describing the results, the National Healthcare Quality Report (NHQR), and also the National Healthcare Disparities Report (NHDR). These reports provide a consistent monitoring device so multiple stakeholders can have a view of the current status of healthcare quality that can then be used to provide direction for improvement. The reports serve as the U.S. annual national report card; however, this does not replace the need for individual HCOs to monitor their own organization's quality. HCOs, insurers, health policy makers, and health professions educators use the data and report analysis to evaluate and develop services and determine health professions education needs. This is also information that nurses in management positions and nurses who provide care can use to increase their awareness of current quality concerns and policies and apply the information to their specific healthcare organization's services. The current reports are available through the AHRQ website.

PRIORITY AREAS FOR NATIONAL ACTION   After identifying the problem in *To Err Is Human* and describing it further in *Crossing the Quality Chasm*, the IOM concluded that, along with the need for a healthcare monitoring system, there was need to conduct a systematic identification of the priority areas for quality improvement to make the necessary changes. In the *Priority Areas for National Action* the IOM identified 20 priority areas (Institute of Medicine, 2003b). The first two areas identified were promotion of care coordination and self-management/health literacy, both of which affect a broad range of groups and cross all the priority areas of care. The other areas are concerned with the continuum of care across the life span, preventive care, inpatient/surgical care, chronic conditions, end-of-life care, and behavioral care. The priority areas change over time, as can be seen in the current NHQR and NHDR. As areas improve, they may be dropped from the annual reports and other areas of concern added. Figure 17-2 provides a summary view of the development of the approach to monitor and assess U.S. healthcare quality.

LEADERSHIP BY EXAMPLE   This report, requested by Congress, examined the federal government's quality enhancement processes (Institute of Medicine, 2003b). It focused on six government

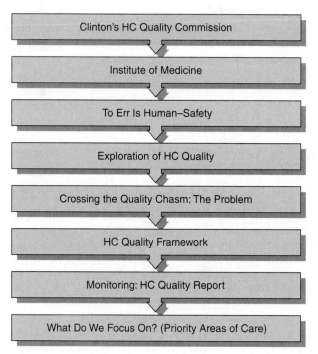

Figure 17-2 Development of the *Quality Chasm* series

Source: From *Teaching IOM: Implications of Institute of Medicine Reports For Nursing Education* by Anita Finkelman and Carole Kenner. Copyright © 2012 by American Nurses Association. Reprinted with permission. All rights reserved.

programs: Medicare and Medicaid (CMS), State Children's Health Insurance Program (SCHIP/CHIP), the Department of Defense TRICARE and TRICARE for Life programs, the Veteran's Administration program, and the Indian Health Services program. These programs cover more than 100 million people. In early 2009 President Obama signed legislation that renewed and expanded SCHIP. The IOM's leadership report's conclusion was that improvement in the government's QI process was particularly needed.

1. There is a lack of consistent performance measurement across and within programs.
2. The usefulness of quality information has been questioned.
3. There is a lack of a conceptual framework to guide the evaluation.
4. There is a lack of computerized clinical data.
5. There is a lack of commitment to guide decisions.
6. There is a lack of a systematic approach for assessing the quality enhancement activities.

Solving each of these problems requires substantial changes in the healthcare delivery system and relate directly to the results of the earlier IOM quality reports. The report supports the use of transformational leadership in government programs noted above (see Chapter 1).

In 2015 the problems continue: the problem with wait lists, fraud, and other leadership issues in the Veterans Affairs hospitals, requiring response and change in leadership in many of these hospitals, as discussed in Chapter 2 (Soergel, 2014). In addition, a report on the status of quality in military hospitals indicated that there are broad disparities in appointment wait times and quality of care. For example, some hospitals failed to meet expected standards for surgical complications; obstetrics measured poorly on some obstetrical care standards; collection of quality data was inconsistent (U.S. Department of Defense, 2014). Another example is from the fall of 2014 and the nation's response to Ebola. The errors made and poor public health planning led to public concern about the healthcare system's ability to respond to crises effectively and in a timely manner.

The IOM report notes that federal leadership is needed because the federal government is in a unique position to assume a lead role to develop a national healthcare quality improvement initiative due to its multiple roles as regulator; purchaser; healthcare provider; and supporter of programs for research, education, and training. As a regulator, the federal government can also affect many healthcare providers who are not in the federal system; for example, as was noted earlier in this text, HCOs that accept Medicare or Medicaid funds must comply with federal regulations, which often then impacts all patients, not just Medicare and Medicaid patients. It should be noted that regulation is not the best way to make improvement changes because it usually provides a broad strategy, not specific enough to drill down to the more focused need (Institute of Medicine, 2003b). Regulation should not be relied on as the only approach to the problem. The federal government provides direct care to many: military personnel and their families, Native Americans, and veterans. Through these programs, the federal government could establish models to improve care and address problems; however, these programs need to act as models and provide effective leadership. This has already been demonstrated through the CMS, which is not a provider approach but rather regulatory through reimbursement. Through sponsorship of research, education, and training, the federal government can also have a major impact. The report's conclusions recommended that the federal government should lead by example and coordinate government roles in improving healthcare quality. In doing this, the government will have an impact on all parts of the healthcare delivery system. However, as noted with recent problems in the Veterans Administration hospitals and military hospitals, these systems continue to need improvement. The federal government influence over health care in general occurs because most HCOs receive federal funding through CMS reimbursement, and if funding is received, then these HCOs must follow CMS standards. This is a very effective motivator and should be used to improve care, not make it more difficult to provide effective services.

HEALTH PROFESSIONS EDUCATION   The IOM recognized that a successful national effort to improve health care requires that all healthcare professions are competent in specific areas of concern (2003a). This applies to students in healthcare professional education programs and also maintaining competency through staff education and continuing education. The IOM did not specify certain competencies for specific professions, but rather identified five core competencies that apply to all healthcare professions. The competencies are discussed throughout this textbook, in this chapter and Chapter 18 as these pertain to QI, and in Chapter 20, which focuses on staff education.

KEEPING PATIENTS SAFE: TRANSFORMING THE WORK ENVIRONMENT OF NURSES The IOM report *Keeping Patients Safe: Transforming the Work Environment of Nurses* (Institute of Medicine, 2004) is an important report for nurses who work in all types of settings. This extensive report addressed critical quality issues with a particular focus on nursing care and nurses, examining these issues from the perspective of the work environment. The report strongly supported the important role of nurses in acute care who are with the patients most of the time and have a direct impact on patient care outcomes at a time when patients are most vulnerable. From the review of this critical work environment, the report described methods for designing the work environment so nurses may provide safer, quality patient care. The content identified concerns related to the nursing shortage, healthcare quality and errors, patient safety risk factors, the central role of the nurse in patient safety and quality improvement, and work environment threats to patient safety. Recommendations for resolving these concerns include the following:

- Developing patient safety defenses.
- Applying an evidence-based model for safety defenses.
- Addressing reengineering issues.
- Using transformational leadership and evidence-based management.
- Maximizing workforce capability through safe staffing levels, recognizing the need for knowledge and skills and clinical decision making.
- Applying interprofessional collaboration.
- Using workspace design.
- Building and creating a culture of safety.

This report should have had a major impact on the practice of nursing, healthcare delivery, and how nursing was taught. However, many in nursing did not know about the report at the time it was published. Its content and recommendations are still highly relevant and should not be ignored.

THE FUTURE OF NURSING: LEADING CHANGE, ADVANCING HEALTH As noted in Chapter 1, this report is highly significant for nursing (Institute of Medicine, 2011). If viewed with the earlier report of *Keeping Patients Safe* (2004), the two reports describe the important roles of nurses, all of which require leadership and knowledge of quality improvement. Both reports support the

CASE STUDY

Policy Development Is Not for Us

A local nursing organization is meeting to discuss what the organization's focus should be in the coming year. One member of the executive committee says, "I think we need to consider the IOM quality reports." The treasurer quickly responds, "Those reports have nothing to do with us or health care in our community or state!" The committee is quiet. The organization's president then joins the discussion as he agrees with the suggestion to focus on these reports, though he is not sure what to do with the idea.

Questions:

1. How might the president respond to this discussion in a positive manner?
2. What might the president say about the current status of national healthcare quality and quality health care in your state?
3. What strategies could the organization use to implement the reports' recommendations? Consider policy development, professional education including continuing education, and collaboration with other healthcare professions and with other professional organizations.
4. How is advocacy connected to this topic?

need for nurses to step up and assume more leadership in all aspects of quality improvement; however, the first report focused on acute care and the needs of nurses providing direct care, representing the majority of nurses. The second report is broader. Both reports are discussed in various chapters. *The Future* report includes the following as one of its recommendations, focused on quality improvement:

> **Recommendation 2: Expand opportunities for nurses to lead and diffuse collaborative improvement efforts.** *Private and public funders, health care organizations, nursing education programs, and nursing associations should expand opportunities for nurses to lead and manage collaborative efforts with physicians and other members of the health care team to conduct research and to redesign and improve practice environments and health systems. These entities should also provide opportunities for nurses to diffuse successful practices.* (Institute of Medicine, 2011, p. 7-10)

To this end:

- The Center for Medicare & Medicaid Innovation should support the development and evaluation of models of payment and care delivery that use nurses in an expanded and leadership capacity to improve health outcomes and reduce costs. Performance measures should be developed and implemented expeditiously where best practices are evident to reflect the contributions of nurses and ensure better-quality care.
- Private and public funders should collaborate, and when possible pool funds, to advance research on models of care and innovative solutions, including technology that will enable nurses to contribute to improved health and health care.
- Healthcare organizations should support and help nurses by taking the lead in developing and adopting innovative, patient-centered care models.
- Healthcare organizations should engage nurses and other front-line staff to work with developers and manufacturers in the design, development, purchase, implementation, and evaluation of medical and health devices and health information technology products.
- Nursing education programs and nursing associations should provide entrepreneurial professional development that will enable nurses to initiate programs and businesses that will contribute to improved health and health care.

THE CURRENT STATUS ON THE CHANGING VIEW OF QUALITY

Quality is a complex concept, with many factors affecting it. Assessing and improving care is not a static process, and changes continue, as do problems. As discussed later in this chapter, the road to improving health care is not a smooth one and includes successes, failures, and mediocrity. In 2012 the then current president of the Institute of Medicine, Dr. Harvey Fineberg, commented on the status of healthcare quality and reflected on the pursuit of quality. He emphasized the major aims as proposed by the IOM (effective, safe, timely, patient centered, equitable, and efficient) (Fineberg, 2012). Fineberg believed that there was need for a sustainable healthcare system that was an affordable, acceptable, and adaptable health system. The U.S. system was not meeting those requirements due to poor performance and high cost. The United States has a lower life expectancy than other similar countries, but it has one of the highest healthcare expenditure levels. Fineberg commented on the potential of the Affordable Care Act of 2010 to support more effective quality improvement. There is, however, no one answer to this problem, requiring that efforts should include different approaches then determine best outcomes. The HHS commented on patient safety in a December 2, 2014, press release (U.S. Department of Health and Human Services, 2014b). The implementation of the Hospital-Acquired Complications (HACs) Initiative for Medicare and Medicaid patients in 2010–2012 reduced the number of patient deaths to an estimated 50,000 or fewer and approximately $12 billion in healthcare costs were saved. This initiative is connected to the ACA and to the HHS Partnership for Patients, and demonstrates what can be done in a national initiative to improve care.

APPLYING EVIDENCE-BASED PRACTICE

Evidence for Effective Leadership and Management

CITATION: *More Than 1,000 Preventable Deaths a Day Is Too Many: The Need to Improve Patient Safety. Hearing before the Subcommittee on Primary Health and Aging,* 113th Cong (2014) (testimony of John James, PhD; Ashish Jha, MD, MPH; Tejal Gandhi, MD, MPH; Peter Pronovost, MD, PhD; Joanne Disch, PhD, RN; Lisa McGiffert). Retrieved from http://www.psnet.ahrq.gov/resource.aspx?resourceID=27773

OVERVIEW: "A group of patient safety experts, including Drs. Peter Pronovost, Ashish Jha, and Tejal Gandhi, testified to Congress that more must be done to track and prevent widespread patient harms. The title of the hearing was based on the seminal study estimating that as many as 200,000 to 400,000 patients experience harms that contribute to their death each year. The medical experts recounted the lack of significant progress since the landmark Institute of Medicine report in 1999, and they called on Congress to task the Centers for Disease Control and Prevention with tracking medical errors and patient harm. Dr. John James, a scientist who became engaged in patient safety efforts following the death of his son due to medical errors, recommended that lawmakers establish a National Patient Safety Board, similar to the current National Transportation Safety Board. A prior Agency for Healthcare Research and Quality (AHRQ) WebM&M perspective discussed the many challenges of measuring patient safety." *The congressional testimony can be found through the Agency for Healthcare Research and Quality, Patient Safety Network (PSNet).* The testimony reflected on current studies.

APPLICATION: This provides an example of how health policy is part of congressional work, and how key stakeholders may participate while emphasizing that evidence based on sound research can make a difference.

Questions:

1. Why is it important that this topic was presented to a congressional committee?
2. What might happen as a result of this examination of a healthcare policy problem?
3. What is your response to the status of errors mentioned in the overview?
4. Go to the AHRQ, PSNet website to review some of the congressional testimony representing eight perspectives. Select one, examine what was said, and identify some of the possible implications.
5. Did any nurses provide testimony? Why would it be important for nurses to participate?

EXAMPLES OF OTHER INDICATORS OF INCREASED INTEREST IN HEALTHCARE QUALITY

What are factors in the healthcare delivery environment that demonstrate there is increased interest in the quality of care?

Legislation

Increased legislation is one indication of public concern for quality care. In 2005 the Patient Safety and Quality Improvement Act was signed into law. Box 17-3 describes this legislation. Of course, the ACA is the current major healthcare legislation, though its primary focus is on reimbursement of healthcare costs, thus impacting access to care. It does include provisions related to QI, but the intent of the law was not focused on QI. The previous legislation that initiated HIPAA in 1996 was an early indication of need for healthcare policy changes, and this law was under consideration just as the IOM was beginning its work on healthcare quality.

The IOM reports from 1999 to 2003 and other related reports that have been published since this time certainly stimulated this legislative activity. The HHS has a major role in healthcare delivery in the United States and in assessing quality care. Box 17-4 highlights some of the HHS activities. The HHS is responsible for developing rules and regulations for most federal healthcare laws and serves as the administrator for Medicare and Medicaid through the CMS.

Affordable Care Act of 2010 and Changes in Quality Improvement Policy and Programs

The healthcare reform legislation of 2010 primarily focuses on reimbursement and increasing the number of citizens with healthcare insurance; however, the legislation does have other provisions. Some of these provisions are related to improving health and healthcare delivery, particularly noting

BOX 17-3	THE PATIENT SAFETY AND QUALITY IMPROVEMENT ACT OF 2005

The Patient Safety and Quality Improvement Act of 2005 (Public Law 109-41), signed into law on July 29, 2005, was enacted in response to growing concern about patient safety in the United States and the Institute of Medicine's 1999 report, *To Err is Human: Building a Safer Health System*. The goal of the Act is to improve patient safety by encouraging voluntary and confidential reporting of events that adversely affect patients.

The Patient Safety and Quality Improvement Act signifies the Federal Government's commitment to fostering a culture of patient safety. It creates Patient Safety Organizations (PSOs) to collect, aggregate, and analyze confidential information reported by health care providers. Currently, patient safety improvement efforts are hampered by the fear of discovery of peer deliberations, resulting in under-reporting of events and an inability to aggregate sufficient patient safety event data for analysis. By analyzing patient safety event information, PSOs will be able to identify patterns of failures and propose measures to eliminate patient safety risks and hazards.

Many providers fear that patient safety event reports could be used against them in medical malpractice cases or in disciplinary proceedings. The Act addresses these fears by providing Federal legal privilege and confidentiality protections to information that is assembled and reported by providers to a PSO or developed by a PSO ("patient safety work product") for the conduct of patient safety activities. The Act also significantly limits the use of this information in criminal, civil, and administrative proceedings. The Act includes provisions for monetary penalties for violations of confidentiality or privilege protections.

Additionally, the Act specifies the role of PSOs and defines "patient safety work product" and "patient safety evaluation systems," which focus on how patient safety event information is collected, developed, analyzed, and maintained. In addition, the Act has specific requirements for PSOs, such as:

- PSOs are required to work with more than one provider.
- Eligible organizations include public or private entities, profit or not-for-profit entities, provider entities, such as hospital chains, and other entities that establish special components.
- Ineligible organizations include insurance companies or their affiliates.

Finally, the Act calls for the establishment of a Network of Patient Safety Databases (NPSD) to provide an interactive, evidence-based management resource for providers, PSOs, and other entities. It will be used to analyze national and regional statistics, including trends and patterns of patient safety events. The NPSD will employ common formats (definitions, data elements, and so on) and will promote interoperability among reporting systems. The Department of Health and Human Services will provide technical assistance to PSOs.

Source: Agency for Healthcare Research and Quality. Retrieved from http://www.ahrq.gov/qual/psoact.htm

the need for a national healthcare strategy to improve the delivery of healthcare services, patient health outcomes, and population health. This initiative should include multiple stakeholders. Some examples of ACA provisions that address this need include the following, many of which go into effect over several years:

- Establish National Prevention, Health Promotion, and Public Health Council.
- Increase coverage of preventive services.
- Establish National Quality Improvement Strategy (NQIS) (later this changed to NQS).
- Establish Accountable Care Organizations (ACOs).
- Establish the Center for Medicare & Medicaid Innovation.
- Pay physicians based on value and not volume.
- Establish Center for Quality Improvement and Patient Safety (CQuIPS).
- Develop Hospital Readmission Reduction Program.
- Develop Care Transitions Program.
- Develop Hospital-Acquired Complications Program.
- Increase Primary Care Options.
- Establish Patient-Centered Outcomes Research Institute (PCORI).

Additional information on these changes can be found on the Internet and in Appendix B on page 493. All of these programs and centers are related to HHS and its agencies such as CMS and AHRQ.

Healthy People 2020

Healthy People 2020 is a national government initiative that sets goals and objectives for 10-year periods (U.S. Department of Health and Human Services, 2014a). It focuses on providing a science-based approach for improving the health of all Americans. Chapter 7 includes more extensive information on Healthy People, but it is important to understand that it is also a part of the national quality care strategies, and one of the earlier initiatives. Additional information can be found on the Healthy People website.

BOX 17-4	U.S. DEPARTMENT OF HEALTH AND HUMAN SERVICES

The Department of Health and Human Services (HHS) is the U.S. government's principal agency for protecting the health of all Americans and providing essential human services, especially for those who are least able to help themselves.

The department includes more than 300 programs, covering a wide spectrum of activities. Some highlights include:

- health and social science research.
- preventing disease, including immunization services.
- assuring food and drug safety.
- Medicare (health insurance for elderly and disabled Americans) and Medicaid (health insurance for low-income Americans).
- health information technology.
- financial assistance and services for low-income families.
- improving maternal and infant health.
- Head Start (preschool education and services).
- faith-based and community initiatives.
- preventing child abuse and domestic violence.
- substance abuse treatment and prevention.
- services for older Americans, including home-delivered meals.
- comprehensive health services for Native Americans.
- medical preparedness for emergencies, including potential terrorism.

HHS represents almost a quarter of all federal outlays, and it administers more grant dollars than all other federal agencies combined. HHS's Medicare program is the nation's largest health insurer, handling more than 1 billion claims per year. Medicare and Medicaid together provide healthcare insurance for one in four Americans.

HHS works closely with state and local governments, and many HHS-funded services are provided at the local level by state or county agencies or through private sector grantees. The department's programs are administered by 11 operating divisions, including eight agencies in the U.S. Public Health Service and three human services agencies. In addition to the services they deliver, the HHS programs provide for equitable treatment of beneficiaries nationwide, and they enable the collection of national health and other data.

The following are agencies in HHS:

U.S. Public Health Service Agencies

National Institutes of Health (NIH)—NIH is the world's premier medical research organization, supporting over 38,000 research projects nationwide in diseases including cancer, Alzheimer's, diabetes, arthritis, heart ailments, and AIDS. It includes 27 separate health institutes and centers. Established: 1887, as the Hygienic Laboratory, Staten Island, NY.

Food and Drug Administration (FDA)—The FDA assures the safety of foods and cosmetics and the safety and efficacy of pharmaceuticals, biological products, and medical devices—products that represent almost 25 cents out of every dollar in U.S. consumer spending. Established: 1906, when the Pure Food and Drugs Act gave regulatory authority to the Bureau of Chemistry.

Centers for Disease Control and Prevention (CDC)—Working with states and other partners, the CDC provides a system of health surveillance to monitor and prevent disease outbreaks (including bioterrorism), implement disease prevention strategies, and maintain national health statistics. It provides for immunization services, workplace safety, and environmental disease prevention and guards against international disease transmission, with personnel stationed in more than 25 foreign countries. The CDC director is also administrator of the Agency for Toxic Substances and Disease Registry, which helps prevent exposure to hazardous substances from waste sites on the U.S. Environmental Protection Agency's National Priorities List and develops toxicological profiles of chemicals at these sites. Established: 1946, as the Communicable Disease Center.

Indian Health Service (IHS)—Working with tribes, the IHS provides health services to 1.8 million American Indians and Alaska Natives of more than 560 federally recognized tribes. The Indian health system includes 46 hospitals, 324 health centers, 309 health stations and Alaska Native village clinics, and 34 urban Indian health programs. Established: 1921 (mission transferred from the Interior Department in 1955).

Health Resources and Services Administration (HRSA)—HRSA provides access to essential healthcare services for people who are low income, are uninsured, or live in rural areas or urban neighborhoods where health care is scarce. The agency maintains the National Health Service Corps and helps build the healthcare workforce through training and education programs. It administers a variety of programs to improve the health of mothers and children and serves people living with HIV/AIDS through the Ryan White CARE Act programs. HRSA also oversees the nation's organ transplantation system. Established: 1982.

Substance Abuse and Mental Health Services Administration (SAMHSA)—SAMHSA works to improve the quality and availability of substance abuse prevention, addiction treatment, and mental health services. It provides funding through block grants to states to support substance abuse and mental health services, including treatment for Americans with serious substance abuse problems or mental health problems. It improves substance abuse prevention and treatment services through the identification and dissemination of best practices. HRSA monitors prevalence and incidence of substance abuse. Established: 1992. (A predecessor agency, the Alcohol, Drug Abuse and Mental Health Administration, was established in 1974.)

Agency for Healthcare Research and Quality (AHRQ)—AHRQ supports research on healthcare systems, healthcare quality and cost issues, access to health care, and effectiveness of medical treatments. It also provides evidence-based information on healthcare outcomes and quality of care. Established: 1989.

Centers for Medicare & Medicaid Services (CMS)—CMS administers the Medicare and Medicaid programs, which provide health care to almost one in three Americans. Medicare provides health insurance for more than 44.6 million elderly and disabled Americans. Medicaid, a joint federal-state program, provides health coverage for some 50 million low-income persons, including 24 million children, and nursing home coverage for low-income elderly. CMS also administers the State Children's Health Insurance Program, which covers more than 4.4 million children. Established: 1965 by legislation; name changed to CMS in 1977.

Administration for Children and Families (ACF)—ACF is responsible for some 60 programs that promote the economic and

BOX 17-4   (CONTINUED)

social well-being of children, families, and communities. It administers the state-federal welfare program, Temporary Assistance for Needy Families, providing assistance to an estimated 4 million persons, including 3 million children. ACF administers the national child support enforcement system. It administers the Head Start program, serving nearly 895,000 preschool children, provides funds to assist low-income families in paying for child care, and supports state programs to support foster care and provide adoption assistance. ACF funds programs to prevent child abuse and domestic violence. Established: 1991, bringing together several already-existing programs.

Administration on Aging (AOA)—AOA supports a nationwide aging network, providing services to the elderly, especially to enable

them to remain independent. It supports some 240 million meals for the elderly each year, including the home-delivered Meals on Wheels. AOA helps provide transportation and at-home services, supports ombudsman services for the elderly, and provides policy leadership on aging issues. Established: 1965, located with HHS in Washington, DC.

THE U.S. PUBLIC HEALTH SERVICE COMMISSIONED CORPS is a uniformed service of more than 6,000 health professionals who serve in many HHS and other federal agencies. The surgeon general is head of the Commissioned Corps.

Source: Summarized from U.S. Department of Health and Human Services. (2015). Retrieved from http://www.hhs.gov/about/foa/index.html

EXAMPLES OF NONGOVERNMENTAL INITIATIVES   Another indication of interest in healthcare quality is not a governmental example but rather one that focuses on the purchasers of care in the private sector. The Leapfrog Group, a consortium of private and public healthcare purchasers of healthcare benefits, has developed a clear interest in healthcare quality (Leapfrog Group, 2014). The group's mission as an employer-based coalition is to examine and support effective changes in improved transparency, quality, and safety in hospitals. There is no doubt that businesses want value for the money they spend on health care, and employers are the major purchasers of care because they provide healthcare coverage for their employees. The development of this type of organization indicates growing interest in collaboration to improve care and control costs by multiple stakeholders. Through the Leapfrog searchable database, consumers can find out more information about hospitals that they might use for healthcare services.

Healthcare professional organizations and accrediting organizations have also developed an increased interest in healthcare quality. The Joint Commission is directly involved with quality issues and has become more concerned with safety due to the recent IOM reports. In 2002 the Joint Commission initiated the Speak Up™ program (Joint Commission, 2014). This initiative urges patients to do the following to help prevent healthcare errors, or to "Speak Up":

- **S**peak up if you have questions or concerns, and if you don't understand, ask again. It's your body, and you have a right to know.
- **P**ay attention to the care you are receiving. Make sure you're getting the right treatments and medications by the right healthcare professionals. Don't assume anything.
- **E**ducate yourself about your diagnosis, the medical tests you are undergoing, and your treatment plan.
- **A**sk a trusted family member or friend to be your advocate.
- **K**now what medications you take and why you take them. Medication errors are the most common healthcare errors.
- **U**se a hospital, clinic, surgery center, or other type of healthcare organization that has undergone a rigorous on-site evaluation against established state-of-the-art quality and safety standards, such as those provided by the Joint Commission.
- **P**articipate in all decisions about your treatment. You are the center of the healthcare team (Joint Commission, 2014, p. 1).

This initiative has expanded into several others that include brochures such as "Help Prevent Errors in Your Care," "Help Avoid Mistakes With Your Medicine," "Five Things You Can Do to Prevent Infection," "Help Prevent Medical Test Mistakes," and others. These brochures are written for patients and are available for use by healthcare providers. There are other formats for this information such as posters, animated videos (e.g., on YouTube), and infographics. Looking at the titles, there is a definite trend toward emphasizing patient-centered, quality care. This approach draws the patient and family into the QI process, as discussed in Chapter 11.

The Joint Commission also now identifies annual National Patient Safety Goals based on data obtained from its accreditation surveys, highlighting areas that need improvement. The goals have focused on issues such as hand hygiene, infection, patient identification, medication administration, falls, and many other issues that can lead to poor quality care. The Joint Commission accredited hospitals are expected to meet these safety goals. There are also specific goals for ambulatory health care, behavioral health care, hospitals, laboratory, critical access hospitals, long-term care, Medicare/Medicaid long-term care, home care, and office-based surgery. Current goals are posted on the Joint Commission website.

The National Quality Forum (NQF) is a not-for-profit, nonpartisan, membership-based organization that serves as a catalyst to improve health care (National Quality Forum, 2014). The NQF is based on the same framework and recommendations as noted by the IOM. Its projects emphasize the need for standardized performance measurement related to structure, process, and outcomes. It has worked to develop collaborations, such as the National Priorities Partnership (NPP), which is a partnership of 52 major national organizations that are involved in improving health care. Nursing is active in NQF and in NPP (Kennedy, Murphy, & Roberts, 2013). Additional information about NQF can be found on its website.

Healthcare quality is a topic frequently found in the media today—television, newspapers, other print media, and the Internet. Stories are presented about complications patients experience due to errors, interventions, or inappropriate care. Examples of this type of media can be found at the local, state, and national levels. Consumers hear these stories and worry about the care they receive; this increases interest in healthcare quality. The Obama administration's initiative to reform health care through the passage of ACA in 2010 led to an increase in media stories about the quality of care and consumerism.

Nursing education is also involved, although not as much as it should be (Finkelman & Kenner, 2012). The Quality and Safety Education for Nurses (QSEN) Institute, funded by the Robert Wood Johnson Foundation to improve nursing care, provides resources and strategies to facilitate learning focused on competency concerns. QSEN focuses on core competencies that are directly related to the IOM five core competencies for health professions (Institute of Medicine, 2003a). However, QSEN increased the number of competencies from five to six and uses slightly different terminology and definitions, which focus on nursing rather than on the interprofessional approach suggested by the IOM (Quality and Safety Education for Nurses, 2014).

- Patient-centered care (IOM: Provide patient-centered care)
- Teamwork and collaboration (IOM: Work on interdisciplinary/interprofessional teams)
- Evidence-based practice (IOM: Employ evidence-based practice)
- Quality improvement (IOM: Apply quality improvement)
- Safety (IOM: Apply quality improvement)
- Informatics (IOM: Utilize informatics)

Figure 17-3 describes the relationship of the IOM core competencies to the major IOM reports.

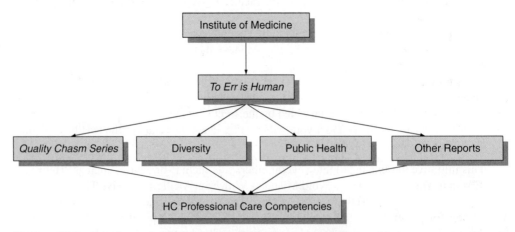

Figure 17-3   Development of the IOM healthcare core competencies

Source: From *Teaching IOM: Implications of Institute of Medicine Reports For Nursing Education* by Anita Finkelman, Carole Kenner. Copyright © 2012 by American Nurses Association. Reprinted with permission. All rights reserved.

QUALITY IMPROVEMENT: A GROWING, COMPLEX PROCESS

The NAM frequently comments on healthcare complexity and views this complexity as a barrier to understanding safety and quality and improving healthcare delivery. To improve, healthcare providers first need to understand the problems and use this understanding to develop strategies and identify outcomes. Without this understanding, it is not possible to know when or how something has changed, and this limits effective policy (Institute of Medicine, 2003c). Why is health care so complex? Health care is different from other businesses that might have one product or a series of highly related products such as manufacturing. Healthcare products are determined by the medical problem, patient, patient prognosis, setting, clinical staff expertise, treatment options, current research, reimbursement, health policy, and legislation. Even geographic location can make a difference in healthcare delivery, as there are practice pattern variations from one part of the country to another or rural versus urban areas. Specialty areas such as obstetrics, psychiatry, emergency care, intensive care, home health care, behavioral/mental health, and long-term care offer varied services that are influenced by their healthcare providers, interventions, roles of the patient and family, patient education needs, prognosis and outcomes, and so on. Patients are very diverse in needs, diagnoses, ethnic and cultural backgrounds, and overall health status. They are also influenced by history and assessment, experiences with health care, genetic background, socioeconomic factors, patient preferences for health care, community differences, and healthcare coverage/reimbursement concerns. The latter is particularly important when people lose their jobs and consequently their healthcare coverage. The ACA addresses this problem for many people who are not employed and has an impact on healthcare economics. For example, if patients put off elective surgery, there is less surgery to schedule. This leads to financial issues for hospitals that may lead to a change in services or elimination of services that are too expensive to offer; however, now with more people covered, there is more need for services.

It is costly to develop and maintain an effective quality improvement program, but CQI programs can lead to improved healthcare quality and, in the long run, save money when complications or extended treatment is avoided. Healthcare organizations want to reduce costs and ensure effective treatment to meet positive patient outcomes. Developing a CQI program that addresses monitoring and improving healthcare quality is in itself a complex process and should include the IOM guidelines, as discussed earlier. There is greater ability today to use informatics for data collection and analysis. Healthcare organizations are dependent on informatics in the CQI monitoring process. (See Chapter 19.) Using evidence-based practice (EBP) and finding new approaches that are better than current care interventions, health care can be improved. (See Chapter 16.) An effective CQI program includes the following (Institute of Medicine, 2001b):

- Continually understand and measure quality of care in terms of structure or the inputs into the system, such as patients, staff, and environments; process, or the interactions between clinicians and patients; and outcomes, or evidence about changes in patients' health status in relation to patient and community needs.
- Assess current practices and compare them with relevant better practices elsewhere as a means of identifying opportunities for improvement.
- Design and test interventions to change the process of care and improve quality.
- Identify errors and hazards in care; understand and implement basic safety design principles, such as standardization and simplification and human factors training.
- Act as both an effective member of an interprofessional team, and improve the quality of one's own performance through self-assessment and personal change (Institute of Medicine, 2003a, p. 59).

Bodenheimer (1999) described several key issues related to quality that were then reemphasized later in the IOM reports. These issues are as follows:

1. Health care is not a single product.
2. Different interventions require different measurements.
3. Different groups focus on different issues when considering quality.

4. Overuse, underuse, and misuse are critical in determining quality.
5. Organizations need a culture of quality to improve.
6. Assessment of quality is expensive to do, and this cost is shifted to purchasers and consumers.
7. Patient satisfaction is a questionable measure of the quality of care (Bodenheimer, 1999).

Another complex issue is patient satisfaction. It is usually tracked by HCOs; however, it is not clear how patient satisfaction affects quality or even what it means. For example, if a patient describes quality of care by saying the staff were friendly yet expected outcomes were not met (e.g., patient is not able to self-administer insulin), did the patient receive quality care? The patient may say "yes" while the healthcare provider would say "no." Patients often do not complete surveys, but if they do and provide negative feedback, is there follow-up with the patient? For example, a patient had surgery and experienced several near misses with medication errors. The patient, a physician, commented on his experiences in the patient survey he received after discharge. No one ever contacted him to ask about these experiences. This is an example that actually occurred, and there are many more examples similar to this one. HCOs and healthcare professionals need to evaluate the effectiveness of the patient satisfaction process in improving care.

Definition of Quality

Can **quality care** be defined? This has been a recurring healthcare question for a long time, and there is no universally accepted definition. The IOM (2001a) defines quality as "the degree to which health services for individuals and populations increase the likelihood of desired health outcomes and are consistent with current professional knowledge" (Chassin & Galvin, 1998, p. 1000). This definition is based on three elements that are usually included in a discussion about quality care and monitoring care (Donabedian, 1980). The three generally accepted elements of quality are *structure*, the environment in which services are provided; *process*, the manner in which services are provided; and *outcome*, the result of services, described in Figure 17-4. These elements serve as the framework for the assessment of care.

Measuring and Improving Quality: A Challenge

If quality care can be defined (even though it is complex), measured, and problems identified, can care be improved? Can improvement be achieved for patients at a cost that society can afford?

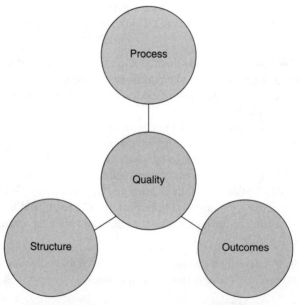

Figure 17-4 Three elements of quality

Honest appraisal of the scientific facts suggests that health care can be improved by closing the wide gaps between prevailing practices and the best-known approaches to care and by inventing new forms of care. A recommended model for improvement suggested by Berwick and Nolan (1998), which is now part of quality improvement, describes the following questions that are important for nurse leaders and managers to consider:

1. What is the organization trying to accomplish?
2. How will the organization know whether a change is an improvement?
3. What change can the organization try that it believes will result in improvement?

These questions aim to arrive at a description of what the HCO considers to be quality care. New nurses soon hear about CQI when they begin their first jobs. Healthcare organizations typically have staff who work exclusively on CQI, and often they are nurses. Committees that focus on CQI typically include nurses, physicians, social workers, medical records staff, laboratory staff, and other staff. Every nurse, regardless of position, has a responsibility to improve patient care. The American Nurses Association (ANA) standards of professional performance include content about the need for registered nurses to provide quality care and participate in quality improvement initiatives (American Nurses Association, 2010).

Insurers are concerned about value or function of both quality and cost of health care. Both are critical to an insurer's financial survival. Key questions on quality in the healthcare reimbursement environment should focus on the needs of the customer or the purchaser of the care and the consumer/patient. The customer, typically the employer or government who purchases insurance for employees, wants the best value, affordable care, healthy employees, and no hassle. The consumer or patient wants services, access, choice, and affordability. Sometimes the customer's and the consumer's viewpoints collide. Chapter 18 discusses CQI measurement in more detail.

MEDICARE AND QUALITY   The Quality Improvement Organization (QIO) is the federal program that monitors medical necessity and quality for Medicare and Medicaid and their respective payment systems. What do QIOs do? "By law, the mission of the QIO Program is to improve the effectiveness, efficiency, economy, and quality of services delivered to Medicare beneficiaries" (Centers for Medicare & Medicaid Services, 2014). Based on this statutory requirement and the CMS program experience, the core functions of the QIO Program are as follows:

- Improving quality of care for beneficiaries.
- Protecting the integrity of the Medicare Trust Fund by ensuring that Medicare pays only for services and goods that are reasonable and necessary and that are provided in the most appropriate setting.
- Protecting beneficiaries by expeditiously addressing individual complaints, such as beneficiary complaints, provider-based notice appeals, violations of the Emergency Medical Treatment and Active Labor Act (EMTALA), and other related responsibilities as articulated in QIO-related law.

The CMS relies on the QIO program, which is required by law, as an important resource in its effort to improve quality and efficiency of care for Medicare beneficiaries. Throughout its history, the Medicare program has been instrumental in advancing national efforts to motivate providers in improving quality and in measuring and improving outcomes of quality (Centers for Medicare & Medicaid Services, 2014).

In the fall of 2008, the CMS made a major change in the Medicare program (Centers for Medicare & Medicaid Services, 2008). The CMS no longer pays for specific complications (reasonably preventable medical complications that result in serious consequences for patients that occur in the hospital and could have been prevented). These events are referred to as hospital-acquired complications (HACs). As discussed in Chapter 5, this change has had an impact on quality care and on healthcare financial concerns for CMS services and for healthcare providers. Table 17-1 provides some data on HACs. Government data are often several years behind the current year, as is true for the HAC data reported here. The HAC initiative has expanded to Medicaid, and now many third-party payers also use a similar system (Galewitz, 2011). Current lists of CMS HACs, which change annually, are available at the CMS website.

Table 17-1	IMPROVEMENT IN HOSPITAL-ACQUIRED CONDITIONS, 2010–2012	
Measure Focus	**Baseline Rate**	**Most Recent Rate**
Incidence of Hospital-Acquired Conditions	145 HACs per 1,000 discharges in 2010[1]	132 HACs per 1,000 discharges in 2012[2]

[1] Agency for Healthcare Research and Quality (AHRQ), Centers for Disease Control and Prevention (CDC), and Centers for Medicare & Medicaid Services (CMS), 2010.

[2] Preliminary data from AHRQ, CDC, and CMS, 2012. See Eldridge, N., (2014). Methods Used to Estimate the Annual Partnership for Patients National Hospital-Acquired Condition (HAC) Rate. Retrieved from http://www.ahrq.gov/professionals/quality-patient-safety/index.html

The total 2010 baseline number of HACs is 4,745,000. The 2012 preliminary estimate is 4,316,000 HACs.

Source: U.S. Department of Health & Human Services. (2014). New HHS data shows major strides made in patient safety, leading to improved care and savings. Retrieved from http://www.innovation.cms.gov/Files/reports/patient-safety-results.pdf

CMS has also been focusing on reducing readmissions. This initiative is demonstrating that it can have an impact along with the HACs initiative. "Preliminary data show an overall nine percent decrease in hospital acquired conditions nationally during 2011 and 2012. National reductions in adverse drug events, falls, infections, and other forms of hospital-induced harm are estimated to have prevented nearly 15,000 deaths in hospitals, avoided 560,000 patient injuries, and approximately $4 billion in health spending over the same period" (U.S. Department of Health and Human Services, 2014c). The Medicare readmission rate was 19% between 2007 and 2011, and it was 18.5% in 2012 and 17.5% in 2013. Continued improvement is expected. Chapter 18 includes more information on these topics.

THE ROLE OF THE HEALTH RESOURCES AND SERVICES ADMINISTRATION IN QUALITY IMPROVEMENT   The Health Resources and Services Administration (HRSA), an HHS agency, is involved in quality improvement and, through its activities, also supports the recommendations of the IOM *Quality Chasm* reports. Examples of some of HRSA's quality improvement tools and resources, which can be accessed at the HRSA website, are as follows:

- Health Disparities Collaboration: A national effort to eliminate disparities and improve the care provided by HRSA-supported healthcare providers, such as health centers, and partners. Includes clinical, financial, and operational quality improvement.
- Patient Safety and Clinical Pharmacy Services Collaborative: A national program to improve care delivered by HRSA grantees and other healthcare providers serving poor, uninsured, and underserved people by replicating leading practices in patient safety and clinical pharmacy services.
- HIV/AIDS Program Quality Care: Ryan White HIV/AIDS Program grantees implement quality management programs that target clinical, administrative, and supportive services.

HRSA developed an extensive quality toolkit that is made available to healthcare providers:

a wide range of practical, convenient, and useful tools were contributed and compiled from several HRSA organizations, where members have proven their usefulness in current CQI healthcare delivery initiatives. The tools and resources were used for implementing data collection and performance measurement techniques, and the organizations that integrated their use into CQI programs effectively improved their deliveries of care. These resources are adaptable and may be used to facilitate the implementation of a new CQI program or fine tune an existing one. (Health Resources and Services Administration, 2014)

The resources apply to all types of healthcare providers and HCOs. Modules are provided on general CQI content and on specific quality measures such as health screening, control of conditions, and other clinical measures. This toolkit is an example of resources that provide valuable information developed by experts, based on EBP and supported by government resources.

Development of such materials that are accessible on the Internet is an example of how the drive to improve care that began with the IOM reports beginning in 1999 has had broad impact. Not only is there need to monitor care and analyze results to identify problems and determine best solutions, but there is also great need to have resources to train staff and provide effective educational materials for healthcare professions students and for staff. Chapter 20 discusses staff education, a critical component of meeting the NAM five core competencies for health professions.

HIGH-RELIABILITY ORGANIZATIONS   Recognizing the need for CQI, there is now greater emphasis on the need to develop **high-reliability organizations** (HROs) within the healthcare delivery system. CQI is not new to health care, but deep, long-lasting change to improve care has not been achieved (Chassin & Loeb, 2011). Some examples include the development of Medicare, which increased access, but at the time, this change did little to improve care other than to impact access. Utilization review and peer review organizations, methods that were developed to improve care, were not as effective as hoped and focused more on costs. The development of clinical guidelines and expansion of the AHRQ seemed to be heading in the right direction with efforts to base the guidelines on best evidence; however, more recent IOM reports on using EBP and on clinical guidelines, as discussed in Chapter 16, indicate that continued improvement is needed. During the Clinton administration the Advisory Commission on Consumer Protection and Quality in the Healthcare Industry (Agency for Healthcare Research and Quality, 1998) opened the door to invite the IOM to begin the extended examination of healthcare quality, leading to the publication of its numerous reports, as discussed earlier in this chapter. However, by 2011, there were some areas of improvement but not enough, and there was greater risk of problems with new equipment, technology, drugs, more acute patients in the hospital, and so on. This all led to recognition that there was great need for consistent performance and use of a collective mindfulness so everyone involved in an HCO is tuned in to need for quality care and preventing errors (Chassin & Loeb, 2011). However, it is critical to note that HROs are not the miracle cure to solving the QI problems, just one approach.

The following are key HRO concepts that help the organization achieve their safety, quality, and efficiency goals, increasing chance of improvement, and are described in Figure 17-5.

- **Sensitivity to operations.** Preserving constant awareness by leaders and staff of the state of the systems and processes that affect patient care. This awareness is key to noting risks and preventing them.
- **Reluctance to simplify.** Simple processes are good, but simplistic explanations for why things work or fail are risky. Avoiding overly simple explanations of failure (unqualified staff, inadequate training, communication failure, etc.) is essential in order to understand the true reasons patients are placed at risk.
- **Preoccupation with failure.** When near-misses occur, these are viewed as evidence of systems that should be improved to reduce potential harm to patients. Rather than viewing near-misses as proof that the system has effective safeguards, they are viewed as symptomatic of areas in need of more attention.

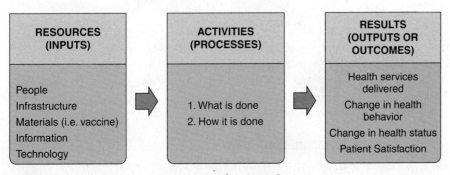

Figure 17-5 Inputs/structure, processes, and outputs/outcomes

Source: Health Resources Services Administration. (2014). Quality improvement. Retrieved from http://www.hrsa.gov/quality/toolbox/methodology/qualityimprovement/

- **Deference to expertise.** If leaders and supervisors are not willing to listen and respond to the insights of staff who know how processes really work and the risks patients really face, you will not have a culture in which high reliability is possible.
- **Resilience.** Leaders and staff need to be trained and prepared to know how to respond when system failures do occur (Agency for Healthcare Research and Quality, 2008, p. 1).

Nursing should be involved in all of these issues within the HCO. With this greater emphasis on developing HROs in health care, there is also increased consumer awareness of medical errors and quality, greater use of health information technology to monitor care, and an increased number of quality improvement methodologies. To develop an HRO, the organization, its leaders, and its staff must do the following:

- Change and respond to the external and internal environments [see Chapter 3].
- Plan and implement improvement initiatives that consider processes, people, and resources [see Chapters 3 and 18].
- Examine approaches to doing the work such as simplifying work process, daily check-ins, rounds, safety huddles, and performance management [see the IOM report *Keeping Patients Safe* and Chapter 18].
- Examine approaches to measuring progress such as measuring fewer things better, simplifying, and using high-performance standards [see Chapter 18].
- Develop and implement improvement initiatives [see Chapters 18 and 19].
- Spread improvements to other units and facilities, for example as demonstrated in the Transforming Care at the Bedside initiative [see Chapter 18] (Agency for Healthcare Research and Quality, 2008, p. 11).

THE NATIONAL QUALITY STRATEGY

The National Quality Strategy (NQS) was developed as a result of the work done by the IOM and the passage of the ACA. The NQS, originally titled the National Strategy for Quality Improvement in Health Care, began operations in 2011 as "the catalyst and compass for a nationwide focus on quality improvement efforts and approach to measuring quality" (Agency for Healthcare Research and Quality, 2014). This federal initiative is directed by the HHS through the AHRQ. Figure 17-6 identifies the NQS aims, and Figure 17-7 explains the six priorities with

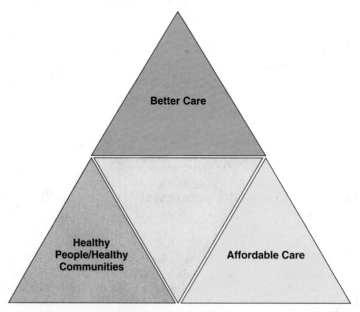

Figure 17-6 National quality strategy: Three aims

Source: U.S. Department of Health and Human Services. Agency for Health Quality and Research. (January 2014), National Quality Strategy: Overview. Retrieved from http://www.ahrq.gov/workingforquality/about.htm

PRIORITIES		LONG-TERM GOALS
	Making care safer by reducing harm caused in the delivery of care	• Reduce preventable hospital admissions and readmissions. • Reduce the incidence of adverse health care-associated conditions. • Reduce harm from inappropriate or unnecessary care.
	Ensuring that each person and family is engaged as partners in their care	• Improve patient, family, and caregiver experience of care related to quality, safety, and access across settings. • In partnership with patients, families, and caregivers—and using a shared decisionmaking process—develop culturally sensitive and understandable care plans. • Enable patients and their families and caregivers to navigate, coordinate, and manage their care appropriately and effectively.
	Promoting effective communication and coordination of care	• Improve the quality of care transitions and communications across care settings. • Improve the quality of life for patients with chronic illness and disability by following a current care plan that anticipates and addresses pain and symptom management, psychosocial needs, and functional status. • Establish shared accountability and integration of communities and health care systems to improve quality of care and reduce health disparities.
	Promoting the most effective prevention and treatment practices for the leading causes of mortality, starting with cardiovascular disease	• Promote cardiovascular health through community interventions that result in improvement of social, economic, and environmental factors. • Promote cardiovascular health through interventions that result in adoption of the most important healthy lifestyle behaviors across the lifespan. • Promote cardiovascular health through receipt of effective clinical preventive services across the lifespan in clinical and community settings.
	Working with communities to promote wide use of best practices to enable healthy living	• Promote healthy living and well-being through community interventions that result in improvement of social, economic, and environmental factors. • Promote healthy living and well-being through interventions that result in adoption of the most important healthy lifestyle behaviors across the lifespan. • Promote healthy living and well-being through receipt of effective clinical preventive services across the lifespan in clinical and community settings.
	Making quality care more affordable for individuals, families, employers, and governments by developing and spreading new health care delivery models	• Ensure affordable and accessible high-quality health care for people, families, employers, and governments. • Support and enable communities to ensure accessible, high-quality care while reducing waste and fraud.

Figure 17-7 National strategies for quality improvement: Six priorities and associated long-term goals

Source: U.S. Department of Health and Human Services. Agency for Health Quality and Research. (July 2013). 2013 annual progress report to congress: National strategy for quality improvement. Retrieved from http://www.ahrq.gov/workingforquality/nqs/nqs2013annlrpt.htm#fig4

associated long-term goals. The initiative is a collaborative effort asking stakeholders to adopt the CQI three aims and the six priorities and to apply at least one of the nine levers:

- **Measurement and Feedback:** Provide performance feedback to plans and providers to improve care
- **Public Reporting:** Compare treatment results, costs, and patient experience for consumers
- **Learning and Technical Assistance:** Foster learning environments that offer training, resources, tools, and guidance to help organizations achieve quality improvement goals
- **Certification, Accreditation, and Regulation:** Adopt or adhere to approaches to meet safety and quality standards
- **Consumer Incentives and Benefit Designs:** Help consumers adopt healthy behaviors and make informed decisions

- **Payment:** Reward and incentivize providers to deliver high-quality, patient-centered care
- **Health Information Technology:** Improve communication, transparency, and efficiency for better coordinated health and health care
- **Innovation and Diffusion:** Foster innovation in healthcare quality improvement, and facilitate rapid adoption within and across organizations and communities
- **Workforce Development:** Investing in people to prepare the next generation of healthcare professionals and support lifelong learning for providers

Figure 17-8 identifies the National Quality Strategy Levers.

Table 17-2 provides a comparison of the NQS and the CMS quality strategy goals and objectives and demonstrates how various government approaches to improving health care are interrelated.

Lever	Icon	Design	Example
Payment		Reward and incentivize providers to deliver high-quality, patient-centered care.	Join a regional coalition of purchasers that are pursuing value-based purchasing.
Public Reporting		Compare treatment results, costs, and patient experience for consumers.	A regional collaborative may ask member hospitals and medical practices to align public reports to the National Quality Strategy aims or priorities.
Learning and Technical Assistance		Foster learning environments that offer training, resources, tools, and guidance to help organizations achieve quality improvement goals.	A Quality Improvement Organization may disseminate evidence-based best practices in quality improvement with physicians, hospitals, nursing homes, and home health agencies.
Certification, Accreditation, and Regulation		Adopt or adhere to approaches to meet safety and quality standards.	The National Quality Strategy aims and priorities may be incorporated into continuing education requirements or certification maintenance.
Consumer Incentives and Benefit Designs		Help consumers adopt healthy behaviors and make informed decisions.	Employers may implement workforce wellness programs that promote prevention and provide incentives for employees to improve their health.
Measurement and Feedback		Provide performance feedback to plans and providers to improve care.	A long-term care provider may implement a strategy that includes the use of Quality Assurance and Performance Improvement data to populate measurement dashboards for purposes of identifying and addressing areas requiring quality improvement.
Health Information Technology		Improve communication, transparency, and efficiency for better coordinated health and health care.	A hospital or medical practice may adopt an electronic health record system to improve communication and care coordination.
Workforce Development		Investing in people to prepare the next generation of health care professionals and support lifelong learning for providers.	A medical leadership institution may incorporate quality improvement principles in their training.
Innovation and Diffusion		Foster innovation in health care quality improvement, and facilitate rapid adoption within and across organizations and communities.	Center for Medicare & Medicaid Innovation tests various payment and service delivery models and shares successful models across the Nation.

Figure 17-8 National quality strategy levers

Source: Agency for Healthcare Research and Quality. (2014). National Quality Strategy: Using levers to achieve improved health and healthcare. Retrieved from http://www.ahrq.gov/workingforquality/reports/nqsleverfactsheet.htm

Table 17-2	COMPARISON OF THE NATIONAL QUALITY STRATEGY PRIORITIES AND CMS QUALITY STRATEGY	
National Quality Strategy Priorities	**CMS Quality Strategy Goals and Objectives**	**Measure Domains (Abbreviated)**
1. Making care safer by reducing the harm caused in the delivery of care	Goal 1: Make care safer by reducing harm caused in the delivery of care • Improve support for a culture of safety • Reduce inappropriate and unnecessary care • Prevent or minimize harm in all settings	Patient Safety (Safety)
2. Ensuring that each person and family are engaged as partners in their care	Goal 2: Strengthen person and family engagement as partners in their care • Ensure all care delivery incorporates patient and caregiver preferences • Improve experience of care for patients, caregivers, and families • Promote patient self-management	Patient and Family Engagement (Patient Engagement)
3. Promoting effective communication and coordination of care	Goal 3: Promote effective communication and coordination of care • Reduce admissions and readmissions • Embed best practices to manage transitions to all practice settings • Enable effective healthcare system navigation	Care Coordination (Care Coordination)
4. Promoting the most effective prevention and treatment practices for the leading causes of mortality, starting with cardiovascular disease	Goal 4: Promote effective prevention and treatment of chronic disease • Increase appropriate use of screening and prevention services • Strengthen interventions to prevent heart attacks and strokes • Improve quality of care for patients with multiple chronic conditions • Improve behavioral health access and quality care • Improve perinatal outcomes	Clinical Process/ Effectiveness (Effective Treatment)
5. Working with communities to promote wide use of best practices to enable healthy living	Goal 5: Work with communities to promote best practices of healthy living • Partner with and support federal, state, and local public health improvement efforts • Improve access within communities to best practices of healthy living • Promote evidence-based community interventions to prevent and treat chronic disease • Increase use of community-based social services support	Population/ Public Health (Healthy Communities)
6. Making quality care affordable for individuals, families, employers, and governments by developing and spreading new healthcare delivery models (Affordable Care)	Goal 6: Make care affordable • Develop and implement payment systems that reward value over volume • Use cost analysis data to inform payment policies	Efficient Use of Healthcare Resources (Affordable Care)

Source: U.S. Department of Health and Human Services, Centers for Medicare & Medicaid Services. (2014). 2015 national impact assessment of the Centers for Medicare & Medicaid Services (CMS) quality measures report. Retrieved from http://www.cms.gov/Medicare/Quality-Initiatives-Patient-Assessment-Instruments/QualityMeasures/downloads/2015-National-Impact-Assessment-Report.pdf

APPLYING LEADERSHIP AND MANAGEMENT

My Hospital Unit: An Evolving Case Experience

Visit the unit you created. Consider the following: What would be an effective approach to integrate the five NAM core competencies into your unit's CQI program? Compose your thoughts in a table with a column for each core competency. Clearly describe how the competency would be integrated into the unit's CQI initiatives, care delivery, your management, and staff education. Review the content in this chapter and some of the HHS and AHRQ resources online to guide you.

BSN and *Master's Essentials:* Application to Content

BSN Essentials (American Association of Colleges of Nursing, 2008) as Applied to this Chapter:

 V. Healthcare Policy, Finance, and Regulatory Environments
VI. Interprofessional Communication and Collaboration for Improving Patient Health Outcomes

Master's Essentials (American Association of Colleges of Nursing, 2011) as Applied to this Chapter:

 III. Quality Improvement and Safety
 VI. Health Policy and Advocacy
VII. Interprofessional Collaboration for Improving Patient Care Outcomes

Applying AONE Competencies

Identify which of the AONE competencies found in Appendix A apply to the content of this chapter.

Engaging in the Content: Critical Thinking and Clinical Reasoning and Judgment

Discussion Questions

1. What are two examples that demonstrate the increasing interest in the quality of care?
2. What does "quality" mean to you? How would you apply the concepts of structure, process, and outcomes to your description? (Online Application Option)
3. How might you apply the continuous quality improvement framework to your practice?
4. Compare and contrast the two IOM nursing reports.

5. What is the role of the HHS and the AHRQ related to quality health care? Provide examples.
6. How do the three questions asked by Berwick and Nolan (1998) relate to the three elements of quality? How would you apply this information if you were a nurse manager? (Online Application Option)
7. What is a high-reliability organization, and why is it important?

Application Exercises

1. Select one of the IOM *Quality Chasm* reports, and go to the NAM website to review the report. The Executive Summary provides an overview of the report. What have you learned from the report? You can divide the reports up and discuss them in teams. What is the key message of the report? Discuss the report's recommendations. How does the report content relate to nursing practice and to nursing management? (Online Application Option)
2. Find out how a clinical site you have used for clinical experiences monitors its care. Interview staff (may or may not be registered nurses) involved in monitoring care to learn more about the healthcare organization's quality improvement program.

3. Interview two registered nurses about their views of quality improvement. Before the interview, prepare five questions to ask them. Summarize the results in a table format, and share your results with a team of students, comparing and contrasting results. (Online Application Option)
4. In teams, analyze the National Quality Strategy and describe how it can be applied to nursing practice. Refer to related content in this chapter and on the Internet (AHRQ website). (Online Application Option)
5. Using two debate teams, discuss the value of the National Quality Strategy.

References

Agency for Healthcare Research and Quality. (1998). The president's advisory commission on consumer protection and quality in the health care industry. Retrieved from http://archive.ahrq.gov/hcqual/

Agency for Healthcare Research and Quality. (2008). Becoming a high reliability organization. Operational advice for hospital leaders. AHRQ Publication No. 08-0022. Retrieved from http://archive.ahrq.gov/professionals/quality-patient-safety/quality-resources/tools/hroadvice/hroadvice.pdf

Agency for Healthcare Research and Quality. (2014). The national quality strategy (NQS). Retrieved from http://www.ahrq.gov/workingforquality/

American Association of Colleges of Nursing. (2008). *The essentials of baccalaureate education for professional nursing practice.* Washington, DC: Author.

American Association of Colleges of Nursing. (2011). *The essentials of master's education in nursing.* Washington, DC: Author.

American Hospital Association. (1999). *Hospital statistics.* Chicago, IL: Author.

American Nurses Association. (2010). *Nursing: Scope and standards of practice.* Silver Spring, MD: Author.

Benner, P., Sutphen, M., Leonard, V., & Day, L. (2010). *Educating nurses. A call for radical transformation.* San Francisco, CA: Jossey-Bass.

Berwick, D., & Nolan, T. (1998). Physicians as leaders improving healthcare. *Annals of Internal Medicine, 128*(4), 289–292.

Bodenheimer, T. (1999). The American healthcare system: The movement for improved quality in healthcare. *New England Journal of Medicine, 340*(6), 488–492.

Centers for Medicare & Medicaid Services. (2008). Medicare and Medicaid move aggressively to encourage greater patient safety in hospitals and reduce never events. Retrieved from http://www.cms.gov/Newsroom/MediaReleaseDatabase/Press-Releases/2008-Press-Releases-Items/2008-07-313.html

Centers for Medicare & Medicaid Services. (2014). Quality improvement organizations. Retrieved from http://www.cms.gov/Medicare/Quality-Initiatives-Patient-Assessment-Instruments/QualityImprovementOrgs/index.html?redirect=/qualityimprovementorgs/

Chassin, M., & Galvin, R. (1998). The urgent need to improve healthcare quality. *Journal of the American Medical Association, 280*(2), 1000–1005.

Chassin, M., & Loeb, J. (2011). The ongoing quality improvement journey: Next stop, high reliability. *Health Affairs, 30*(4), 559–568.

Donabedian, A. (1980). *Explorations in quality assessment and monitoring* (Vol. 1). Ann Arbor, MI: Health Administration Press.

Fineberg, H. (2012). A successful and sustainable health system: How to get there from here. *New England Journal of Medicine, 366*, 1020–1027.

Finkelman, A., & Kenner, C. (2012). *Teaching IOM: Implications of the Institute of Medicine reports for nursing education* (3rd ed.). Silver Spring, MD: American Nurses Association.

Galewitz, P. (2011). Medicaid to stop paying for hospital mistakes. Retrieved from http://kaiser-healthnews.org/news/medicaid-hospital-medical-error-payment-short-take/

Health Resources and Services Administration. (2014). Introduction & overview. The HRSA quality toolkit. Retrieved from http://www.hrsa.gov/quality/toolbox/introduction/

Institute of Medicine. (1999). *To err is human: Building a safer health system.* Washington, DC: National Academies Press.

Institute of Medicine. (2001a). Excerpt from *Crossing the Quality Chasm: A New Health System for the 21st Century.* Washington, DC: National Academies Press.

Institute of Medicine. (2001b). *Envisioning the national health care quality report.* Washington, DC: National Academies Press.

Institute of Medicine. (2003a). *Health professions education.* Washington, DC: National Academies Press.

Institute of Medicine. (2003b). *Leadership by example: Coordinating government roles in improving health care quality.* Washington, DC: National Academies Press.

Institute of Medicine. (2003c). *Priority areas for national action: Transforming health care quality.* Washington, DC: National Academies Press.

Institute of Medicine. (2004). *Keeping patients safe: Transforming the work environment of nurses.* Washington, DC: National Academies Press.

Institute of Medicine. (2011). *The future of nursing: Leading change, advancing health.* Washington, DC: National Academies Press.

Joint Commission. (2014). Facts about Speak Up™ initiatives. Retrieved from http://www.jointcommission.org/assets/1/6/Facts_Speak_Up.pdf

Kaiser Health News. (2014, August 18). Medicare to begin paying physicians to coordinate care for patients with chronic illnesses. Retrieved from http://www.kaiser-healthnews.org/Daily-Reports/2014/August/18/medicare-pay-policy-change.aspx

Kennedy, R., Murphy, J., & Roberts, D. (2013, September 30). An overview of the national quality strategy: Where do nurses fit in? *OJIN: The Online Journal of Issues in Nursing, 18*(3). Retrieved from http://www.nursingworld.org/MainMenuCategories/ANAMarketplace/ANAPeriodicals/OJIN/TableofContents/Vol-18-2013/No3-Sept-2013/National-Quality-Strategy.html

Leapfrog Group. (2014). Who we are. Retrieved from http://www.leapfroggroup.org/

National Quality Forum. (2014). About us. Retrieved from http://www.qualityforum.org/story/About_Us.aspx

President's Advisory Commission on Consumer Protection and Quality in the Health Care Industry. (1998). *Quality first: Better health care for all Americans.* Washington, DC: U.S. Government Printing Office.

Quality and Safety Education for Nurses. (2014). QSEN Institute. Retrieved from http://qsen.org/

Soergel, A. (2014). Report: Veterans neglected in Phoenix VA health care system. Retrieved from http://www.usnews.com/news/newsgram/articles/2014/05/28/inspector-generals-report-finds-veterans-left-off-va-waiting-list-in-phoenix

Subcommittee on Primary Health and Aging, U.S. Senate. (2014). More than 1,000 preventable deaths a day is too many: The need to improve patient safety: Hearing before the Subcommittee on Primary Health and Aging, 113th Cong (2014) (testimony of John James, PhD; Ashish Jha, MD, MPH; Tejal Gandhi, MD, MPH; Peter Pronovost, MD, PhD; Joanne Disch, PhD, RN; Lisa McGiffert). Retrieved from http://www.psnet.ahrq.gov/resource.aspx?resourceID=27773

U.S. Department of Defense. (2014). Military health system review: Final report. Retrieved from http://www.defense.gov/home/features/2014/0614_healthreview/docs/Military_Health_System_Review_EXSUM.pdf

U.S. Department of Health and Human Services. (2014a). *Healthy people 2020*. Retrieved from http://www.healthypeople.gov/2020/default.aspx

U.S. Department of Health and Human Services. (2014b). New HHS data show quality improvements saved 15,000 lives and $4 billion in health spending. Retrieved from http://www.hhs.gov/news/press/2014pres/05/20140507a.html

U.S. Department of Health and Human Services. (2014c). Press release: Efforts to improve patient safety result in 1.3 million fewer patient harms, 50,000 lives saved and $12 billion in health spending avoided. Retrieved from http://www.hhs.gov/news/press/2014pres/12/20141202a.html

18 Implementing Healthcare Quality Improvement

⬤ LEARNING OUTCOMES

Before you begin, take a moment to familiarize yourself with the learning outcomes for this chapter.

> Describe the science of improvement and implications for healthcare quality and culture of safety.
> Discuss examples of critical healthcare quality issues.
> Examine workplace safety as a critical aspect of quality improvement.
> Compare two methods used to measure and improve care and their relationship to structure, process, or outcomes.
> Describe Joint Commission accreditation and its relevance to quality improvement.
> Discuss the role of nurses in continuous quality improvement and nursing initiatives to improve care.
> Discuss the need for collaborative interprofessional quality improvement initiatives.
> Examine the role of nursing leadership in quality improvement and need for changes to improve nursing leadership.

WHAT'S AHEAD

This chapter continues the discussion of quality health care by focusing on the measurement initiatives and strategies to improve patient care. Healthcare quality has long been a concern of healthcare providers, but it is clear that the efforts for improvement have not yet met the outcomes required. Each nurse plays a daily role in ensuring quality care while providing care but also is responsible for participating in organizational continuous quality improvement (CQI) efforts—to meet the key aims discussed in Chapter 17—safe, effective, patient-centered, efficient, and equitable care (Institute of Medicine, 2001). All healthcare organizations (HCOs) such as hospitals, ambulatory care, home health care, long-term care, and so on should have CQI programs. An understanding of healthcare quality policy as found in Chapter 17 is necessary to fully understand implementation of CQI. Other chapters examine factors related to CQI such as leadership and management, financial concerns, staffing, change and planning, evidence-based practice, informatics, and staff education.

KEY TERMS

- access to care
- accreditation
- adverse event
- authorization
- benchmarking
- failure modes and effects analysis (FMEA)
- failure to rescue (FTR)
- handoff
- Joint Commission
- measure
- National Database of Nursing Quality Indicators (NDNQI)
- outcomes
- quality report card
- rapid response team (RRT)
- risk management (RM)
- root cause analysis
- sentinel event
- standards
- threshold
- utilization review/ management (UR/UM)
- variance data
- workaround

SCIENCE OF IMPROVEMENT

The science of improvement is "an applied science that emphasizes innovation, rapid-cycle testing in the field, and spread in order to generate learning about what changes, in which contexts, produce improvements. It is characterized by the combination of expert subject knowledge with improvement methods and tools. It is multidisciplinary—drawing on clinical science, systems theory, psychology, statistics, and other fields" (Institute for Healthcare Improvement, 2014c). This approach focuses on three questions:

1. What are we trying to accomplish?
2. How will we know that a change is an improvement?
3. What changes can we make that will result in improvement?

These questions may sound simple, but as other content in previous chapters indicate, quality care and quality improvement are complex. Effective CQI requires a structured approach and includes planning and change—effective planning such as use of the Plan-Do-Study-Act (PDSA) process. Typically CQI focuses on aggregate data; however, each patient's experience is critical and provides the data for aggregate review of a provider's performance.

Along with this more structured approach, Dr. Berwick, a leading expert in healthcare quality, noted that evidence in healthcare improvement should not just be viewed from the perspective of results from studies that use the traditional experimental research design (2008). Using a traditional research approach does not work well when trying to determine best practice for improved care. Other methodologies are needed. This is a controversial issue among scientists and experts in CQI. What constitutes effective evaluation of CQI systems and practice?

> Healthcare researchers who believe that their main role is to ride the brakes on change—to weigh evidence with impoverished tools, ill-fit for use—are not being as helpful as they need to be. 'Where is the randomized trial?' is, for many purposes, the right question, but for many others it is the wrong question, a myopic one. A better one is broader: 'What is everyone learning?' Asking the question this way will help clinicians and researchers see further in navigating toward improvement. (Berwick, 2008, p. 1184)

A nurse, Dr. Kathleen Stevens, developed the Improvement Science Research Network (ISRN). This network is an example of nursing leadership in this area but also nursing leadership that focuses on interprofessional approaches. "The ISRN is the only National Institutes of Health (NIH)-supported improvement research network. The ISRN's primary mission is to accelerate interprofessional improvement science in a systems context across multiple sites" (Improvement Science Research Network, 2014). Its work focuses on system effects on healthcare delivery, which is the critical element today in CQI. The network also provides resources such as *Building Successful Research Collaboratives for Healthcare Improvement*, which is an evidence-based guide about research collaborative investigative teams (2012). Additional information about ISRN projects can be found on the ISRN website.

A critical aspect of the Science of Improvement and current approaches to CQI is the need to change the approach to quality performance. HCOs have typically handled errors by identifying the staff member who made the error and asking staff to report errors by completing incident reports to describe the error. An example of this occurred with a nurse who had good performance history and was involved in a medication error that led to the death of an infant. Even though the nurse worked in a hospital that described itself as having a culture of safety, the nurse was sent home, and there were other disciplinary steps taken after this action. Staff may have major reactions when errors such as this one occur and the HCO response is negative. Several months later, the nurse committed suicide (Aleccia, 2011). HCOs need to be aware of the impact on healthcare professionals who enter health care to care for people, not to cause harm, and how involvement in errors can lead to stress and even more serious problems. If the nurse continues to work without support, these reactions do have an impact on care.

Over time, the healthcare delivery system punitive approach expanded, but it was not effective in reducing errors and improving care. Not all errors were reported in all HCOs or if reported and if analysis was done, the focus was on individual staff. Most errors are much more complex than just an error made by an individual, a viewpoint supported by the Institute of Medicine (IOM) reports. One of the major early experts in errors noted that the key question should not be

APPLYING EVIDENCE-BASED PRACTICE

Evidence for Effective Leadership and Management

CITATION: Wachter, R., & Pronovost, P. (2009). Balancing the "no blame" with accountability for patient safety. *New England Journal of Medicine, 361*(14), 1401–1406.

OVERVIEW: This article takes the opportunity to reflect back on the 10 years since the publication of the Institute of Medicine report *To Err Is Human* (1999), and its recommendation to move away from the "no blame" environment to reduce errors. The authors discuss the "no blame" approach and the continued need for accountability.

APPLICATION: How does "no blame" impact care and healthcare professionals?

Questions:

1. Why is enforcement of safety standards so weak?
2. How can we find a workable balance between "no blame" and individual accountability for patient safety?
3. Review the examples in the article. What do you think about them, and how would they relate to nurse managers and nursing staff?
4. What is your personal opinion of the "no blame" approach?

one of "Who is at fault?" but rather "Why did our defenses fail?" (Reason, 2000). There are too many people and processes involved in health care, and the healthcare system is too complex to think that one individual is always the reason for an error. As nurses work with multiple healthcare providers and teams, it becomes important to understand that errors are more commonly due to system issues. The IOM (1999) reported that the healthcare system focused on the "blame game" rather than examining causes to improve, and there were limited efforts focused on a culture of safety. The IOM reports used the work done by Reason to understand errors in the healthcare environment. Staff members are anxious or afraid to report errors, which may prevent them from doing so. Near misses, or errors that are caught before they can cause damage, are also important to monitor, but this is not done routinely. However, there is now greater movement to change from a blame culture to a culture of safety, but as noted in the earlier example describing the nurse's response, HCOs have to really engage in a culture of safety—making it an integral part of the organization and not just a thing people say. A culture of safety approach sets the stage for increased communication about errors and near misses to improve care. Understanding errors requires an acceptance that people will make mistakes; the healthcare environment will never be totally error free (Reason, 2000).

There are three perspectives that can be used by nurses and other staff to better understand errors (Henneman & Gawlinski, 2004). A *technical failure* is a system failure, for example, equipment does not work or the nurse does not have the supplies needed. An *organizational failure* also focuses on system failure, and examples of factors that impact these failures include staff education, procedures, clinical pathways, and organizational culture. The third type of failure is *human failure* that relates to skills/competencies, rules, and knowledge. Nurse managers and team leaders set the tone for the safety culture on each unit, communicating how errors are handled on a daily basis, but they must understand how errors occur and their impact. These types of failures are associated with structure, process, and outcomes, which is the most common framework currently applied to CQI. None of this excludes individual staff accountability; however, excluding system factors does not support an effective CQI program.

CRITICAL HEALTHCARE QUALITY ISSUES

Safety is a component of CQI, though some consider it to be separate from quality. Clearly there are many quality issues in health care; some relate specifically to patients, and others to staff. Some examples of critical patient issues are medication administration, use of restraints, violence (violence can lead to injuries for the patient, other patients, family members/visitors, and staff), nosocomial infections, and the wrong patient receiving treatment or a patient receiving the wrong treatment. Each one of these is a complex issue. There are standards related to these safety issues (for example, use of restraints) and the critical steps of medication administration (e.g., right patient, right drug, right dose, right time, and right route). Medication administration, as noted in *To Err Is Human* (Institute of Medicine, 1999), has a high rate of errors. Some of the factors that impact medication errors are time constraints, fatigue, understaffing, lack of knowledge about the drug and/or the patient, interruptions, inadequate documentation, and system failures. Documentation is important in sharing information about patients and their current status, whether this is done with nonelectronic or electronic methods. Nurses and others need to follow standardized requirements to ensure consistency, timeliness, and accuracy as documentation is a critical factor in ensuring quality care. Additional information about electronic methods is found in Chapter 19.

In HCOs, particularly hospitals, nurses represent the greater percentage of the staff. They hold positions in practice, administration, staff education, CQI, evidence-based practice, research, and other areas of the organization. What should be nursing's role in the CQI effort? To be successful in any CQI role, nurses need to understand the problems and circumstances related to errors. Contributory factors are important in the analysis of errors or situations when errors could have occurred or in which quality care is at risk. These factors can be categorized in the following manner:

- **Institutional:** regulatory context, medicolegal environment
- **Organization and management:** financial resources and constraints, policy standards and goals, safety culture and priorities
- **Work environment:** staffing levels and mix; patterns of workload and shift; physical design, availability and maintenance of equipment; administrative and managerial support
- **Team:** verbal and written communication, supervision and willingness to seek help, team leadership
- **Individual staff member:** knowledge and skills, motivation and attitude, physical and mental health
- **Task:** availability and use of protocols, availability and accuracy of test results
- **Patient:** complexity and seriousness of condition, language and communication, personality and social factors (Vincent, 2003, p. 1050)

It is also important to collect data about possible errors (near misses) and share the data and its analysis so prevention strategies can be developed. As the IOM reports indicate, nurses need to recognize that the focus should not be on individual nurses who make errors but rather on system characteristics in which errors can occur. Even with the increased focus on system causes of errors, this does not mean that there is no individual accountability. As an example, if a nurse does not follow a procedure or lacks knowledge and does not ask for help and an error occurs, the nurse is accountable for the actions that led to the error.

Nursing staff-to-patient ratios can impact staff fatigue, consistent numbers of staff and required staff expertise, communication, teamwork, efficiency, and staff turnover, all of which can lead to increased errors (American Nurses Association, 2006a, 2006b; Benner, Malloch, & Sheets, 2010; Christmas, 2008; Hendrich, Chow, Skierczynski, & Zhenqiang, 2008). The *To Err Is Human* report (Institute of Medicine, 1999) identified five principles that might be helpful in designing safe healthcare systems: (1) providing leadership, (2) respecting human limits in the design process, (3) promoting effective team functioning, (4) anticipating the unexpected, and (5) creating a learning environment. These principles apply to nursing care and staff and are related to what has been discussed in this text about leadership and management. They provide a guide to nurse managers as they develop, implement, and maintain CQI initiatives at the unit, departmental/service, or organizational level. Chapter 8 includes additional information on staffing.

The following are examples of situations that increase risk of errors and, as a result, reduce quality care. (AHRQ Patient Safety Network and the Institute of Health Improvement [IHI] websites provide additional information on these topics.)

- **Failure to Rescue (FTR):** FTR focuses on the failure to recognize when a patient is developing problems within a healthcare setting and the problem is not addressed with needed interventions, in other words, a complication of an underlying illness (e.g., cardiac arrest in a patient with acute myocardial infarction) or a complication of medical care (e.g., major hemorrhage after thrombolysis for acute myocardial infarction) (Agency for Healthcare Research and Quality, Patient Safety Network, 2014a; Clarke & Aiken, 2003). Surveillance or structured monitoring of patient status is key to recognizing that a potential FTR may be occurring (Institute of Medicine, 2004). To prevent failure to rescue, once it is recognized, many hospitals now use **rapid response teams** (**RRTs**). These are teams of critical care experts that come to the bedside of patients who are not in intensive care to make rapid decisions when a patient is experiencing life-threatening complications. RRTs are specially trained within hospitals to provide this service. This team and its process require effective interprofessional team communication, coordination, and collaboration. These topics are discussed in Chapters 12 and 13.

- **Handoffs:**

  Discontinuity is an unfortunate but necessary reality of hospital care. No provider can stay in the hospital around the clock, so patients will inevitably be cared for by many different providers during hospitalization. Nurses change shift every 8 to 12 hours, and, particularly at teaching institutions, multiple physicians may be responsible for a patient's care at different times of the day. This discontinuity creates opportunities for error when clinical information is not accurately transferred between providers. (Agency for Healthcare Reseach and Quality, Patient Safety Network, 2014b)

  Handoffs are times in the care process when the patient is moved from one setting to another or from one healthcare provider or service to another. Examples are transfers from emergency care to inpatient; from one inpatient unit to another unit; from an inpatient unit to an operating room; from an inpatient unit to radiology; and from hospital to home or long-term care. These transfers may be for short-term or long-term care and also include transfers from one staff member to another. Handoffs are times of high risk for errors due to decreased sharing of information or confusing communication. Of particular concern are incomplete handoffs and insufficient communication that may lead to adverse events. Richter, McAlearney, and Pennell (2014a) reviewed AHRQ data and concluded that certain organizational factors influence handoffs, including teamwork across units, perceptions of staffing adequacy, and management support for patient safety efforts. Hospital leadership such as nursing leadership is very important in preventing issues that act as barriers to effective handoffs. Handoffs represent a system concern, as they are highly complex, involving multiple staff from different areas, different policies and procedures, and different healthcare environments. Even individual units within the same HCO are different. All of this impacts effective handoffs.

- **Workarounds:** Work is usually organized around functions; however, it is not always clear who does what, when, and how, and this leads to problems.

  From the perspective of frontline personnel trying to accomplish their work, the design of equipment or the policies governing work tasks can seem counterproductive. When frontline personnel adopt consistent patterns of work or ways of bypassing safety features of medical equipment, these patterns and actions are referred to as workarounds. Although workarounds "fix the problem," the system remains unaltered and thus continues to present potential safety hazards for future patients. (Agency for Healthcare Research and Quality, Patient Safety Network, 2014c)

  When there is a breakdown or problem, staff members often figure out ways to get the work done without really analyzing what is going on. This results in a **workaround**. Staff may think this saves time, but it often does not, particularly if a problem occurs. This is often a time of increased risk for errors, and staff and the HCO are not able to learn from the experience, as the errors are not communicated.

  What does matter is that the motivation for a workaround lies in getting work done, not laziness or whim. Thus, the appropriate response by managers to the existence of a workaround should not consist of reflexively reminding staff about the policy and restating the importance of following it. Rather, workarounds should trigger assessment of workflow and the various competing demands for the time of frontline personnel. In busy clinical areas where efficiency is paramount, managers can expect workarounds to arise whenever policies create added tasks for frontline personnel, especially when the extra work is out of proportion to the perceived importance of the safety goal. (Agency for Healthcare Research and Quality, Patient Safety Network, 2014c)

- **Failure Modes and Effects Analysis (FMEA):** FMEA is a method that focuses on safety in systems and prevention of accidents, moving away from the individual focus. This is a systematic proactive method to help identify where a process may fail, why this might occur, and what are the possible consequences. FMEA is a useful method to analyze potential failures in processes (Agency for Healthcare Research and Quality, 2013; Institute for Healthcare Improvement, 2014b). The Institute for Healthcare Improvement (IHI) website provides additional information on FMEA and a tool that can be used to proactively use FMEA.

WORKPLACE SAFETY

Workplace safety has an impact on overall healthcare quality, staff satisfaction, and staff retention.

Examples of Common Workplace Safety Issues

Some of the key safety issues for staff include needlesticks, ergonomic safety, violence, latex allergies, chemical exposure, stress, and infections, such as what occurred with SARS, H1N1, Ebola, and other viruses such as the flu that may be local, regional, national, or global. Ergonomic safety has been a concern of nursing for some time as it is a common problem for nurses in lifting patients and helping patients with mobility. The American Nurses Association (ANA), collaborating with other healthcare experts, such as occupational and physical therapists, risk management experts, and safety and ergonomic experts, developed a set of standards, *Patient Handling and Mobility: Interprofessional National Standards* (2013). Preparing nursing students to practice safe ergonomics is critical, and now many schools of nursing use simulation to prepare students with prevention measures. Nursing management must continue with this initiative, including it in staff education. Staff injuries are expensive and can also lead to patient injuries.

Violence in the Workplace

Violence in the workplace is also a concern in health care, particularly in emergency departments, psychiatric/substance abuse services, and long-term care. Staff members need to learn how to protect themselves and others without harming the patient who may be violent. For example, what are the signs of escalation, and how can the staff respond to reduce escalation? Concern also exists about the emotional response that follows after staff experience these incidents.

OSHA and NIOSH

Staff safety is complex and requires staff who are educated about prevention and interventions to respond when needed, and organizations need to provide support and prevention services as required. The Occupational Safety and Health Administration (OSHA) is the federal agency that is responsible for monitoring safe workplaces. The National Institute for Occupational Safety and Health (NIOSH), a division of the Centers for Disease Control and Prevention (CDC), also provides information and training about healthcare workplace safety (2014). Healthcare workers have the highest level of nonfatal occupational injuries and illnesses of any other industry. Nurse managers need to consider workplace safety in their planning, staff orientation and training, and staff retention and morale and consider the impact it has on staff performance and patient care quality. The OSHA and NIOSH websites provide additional current information on staff safety. The ANA website provides position statements on workplace safety that are of particular interest to nurses.

QUALITY CARE: MEASUREMENT AND IMPROVEMENT

Improvement of care requires measurement of the status of care delivery both for individual patients and in the aggregate (groups of patients, for example, unit, HCO, statewide, national, and so on), and there are some aspects that cannot be measured. It is not easy to measure quality, and HCOs struggle to arrive at the best methods. What are some examples of the difficulty of measuring quality? Measuring the quality of the nurse-patient or the physician-patient relationship quantitatively is not easy as there are many variables and subjective components involved. Effective communication and teamwork are also complex factors that support care improvement but, if not performed well, can become barriers. If knowledge about a specific illness is incomplete, it is difficult to measure quality care for that particular disorder. More research is required before standards and guidelines can be developed to describe the best treatment for many illnesses through the evidence-based practice (EBP) process. Patient satisfaction is complex, and reliable measurement is difficult. Quality is affected by so many factors and with significant differences from one experience to another; however, this does not mean that efforts should not be made to develop strategies and methods to improve care.

As discussed in Chapter 17, the IOM uses the following definition of "quality" in its reports: "the degree to which health services for individuals and populations increase the likelihood of desired health outcomes and are consistent with current professional knowledge" (Chassin & Galvin, 1998, p. 1000). Measuring care to determine quality and developing and implementing strategies to improve patient care are critical processes in all types of healthcare delivery systems, and nurses need to be involved in all aspects of quality improvement.

As healthcare providers and organizations have become more experienced in assessing quality, they have turned more to performance-based quality care evaluation, which has been strongly supported by the Joint Commission. The critical question in assessing care is discovering if the patient benefited from the care received. If so, how? If not, why? Quality really cannot be measured until quality is defined and outcomes are identified. These questions are critical to the development of **outcomes**. When outcomes are assessed, there are several aspects to include.

Understanding Measurement

A **measure** is a measurable dimension of quality, specifying patient care activities and event occurrences for outcomes that can be monitored. Measures must also include a quantity element or **threshold**. This preestablished level indicates the need for more intensive assessment and can emphasize relative rate or trends that need further investigation. For example, an initial, preoperative, and postoperative pain assessment might include localization of pain, type of pain, duration of pain, time of onset, factors associated with pain, and interventions taken and the outcomes, with a threshold of 92%. The threshold indicates when further evaluation needs to be done. If more than 8% of the patient assessments do not meet this measure, further investigation is required. An example of another important measure is one that focuses on sentinel events or events that always require investigation (e.g., suicide attempt, cardiac arrest in labor and delivery, lack of referral to specialist, and patient death). A list highlighting the typical components of quality measures that are discussed in multiple IOM healthcare quality reports appears in Box 18-1.

Measures focus on one or more of the three quality elements: process, structure, and outcomes. The process element includes actual activities done by healthcare providers, and the structure element is concerned with such factors as facilities, equipment, staff, and finances. The outcome focus (short-term and long-term results, complications, health status, and functioning) has become more important. Examples of some outcomes are mortality rates, length of stay, adverse incidents, complications, readmission rates, patient/family satisfaction, referrals to specialists, patient adherence to the discharge plan or treatment plan, and prevention adherence (e.g., mammogram, Pap smear, immunizations).

Overview of Quality Improvement Metrics

Many measurement metrics are used in the CQI process. Some are used for data collection, while others are used to analyze data or guide healthcare improvement. The Department of Health and

---

BOX 18-1	COMPONENTS OF QUALITY MEASURES

- Accessibility
- Appropriateness
- Continuity
- Effectiveness
- Efficacy
- Efficiency
- Patient perspective issues
- Safety of care environment
- Timeliness

Human Services (HHS) provides a Measure Inventory, which is a repository of measures currently used by the HHS agencies for quality measurement, improvement, and reporting. Review of the matrix, found on the AHRQ website, indicates that there are a large number of varied measures that are used by HCOs and the government (Agency for Healthcare Research and Quality, National Quality Measures Clearinghouse, 2014). Measurement has expanded since 1999 and become more complex. Managers and staff need to know about this information and use it effectively when appropriate.

The following content describes examples of some key metrics that focus on structure, process, outcomes, access, and/or patient experiences. Structure, process, and outcomes are the three key components of quality discussed earlier. Access and patient experiences have become more important since the IOM began its extensive examination of healthcare quality including examination of disparities in health care. Disparities may have a negative impact on patient outcomes. Multiple measurement metrics are required to arrive at a clear perspective of the status of healthcare quality.

MONITORING ADVERSE EVENTS: APPLICATION OF OUTCOME METRIC   The IOM report *To Err Is Human* (1999) clearly states that there is no single answer to solving the healthcare safety problem. This report defines "safety" as "freedom from accidental injury" and defines "error" as "the failure of a planned action to be completed as intended or the use of a wrong plan to achieve an aim" (Institute of Medicine, 1999, p. 3). Errors are directly related to outcomes, which is a significant concern in CQI efforts. There are two major types of errors: errors of planning and errors of execution. Errors harm the patient, and some errors that harm the patient may have been preventable adverse events.

Adverse events are now monitored by HCOs to better assess the status of care provided. An adverse event results in an injury from something that was done to the patient or not done as needed (Institute of Medicine, 1999). Not all adverse events are due to errors, and not all are preventable. Analysis is required to determine the relationship of an error to an adverse event. Root cause analysis is used by many HCOs today to better understand these events and improve care. Nurses also participate in the root cause analysis process. An example of an error that has been discussed both in professional literature and in public media is wrong site surgery. Efforts have been made to prevent this adverse event, such as use of checklists and structured communication methods. However, data from 2011 indicates that there still is a problem with wrong site surgery; it is estimated to occur 40 times a week in the United States (Boodman, 2011). There are many other types of adverse events as noted in Table 18-1.

POLICIES AND PROCEDURES: APPLICATION OF PROCESS METRIC   An HCO or insurer provides set standards, policies, and procedures that guide clinical and administrative decisions to support greater consistency and use of an EBP approach. These efforts can help to improve care. Policies and procedures should not conflict with regulatory issues within each state, such as the Nurse Practice Act, and should be in agreement with professional standards. Policies and procedures need to be readily available to staff for review when needed. Many HCOs have made their policies and procedures accessible via their computer systems, reducing the need for hard copy policy and procedure manuals and making it easier to access the information when needed. EBP resources need to be used to develop, review, and update policies and procedures, as discussed in Chapters 6 and 16.

STANDARDS OF CARE: APPLICATION OF PROCESS METRIC   **Standards** of care provide minimum descriptions of accepted actions expected from an HCO or professional with specific skills and knowledge levels. They are important in establishing expectations. Standards are developed by professional organizations, legal sources such as nurse practice acts and federal and state laws, regulatory agencies such as accreditation bodies and federal and state agencies, and HCOs and should be supported by scientific literature [EBP and evidence-based management (EBM)]. Two examples include the American Nurse's Association's *Nursing Administration: Scope and Practice* (2009) and *Nursing Scope of Standards of Practice* (2010). Specialty organizations also develop standards such as the *American Society of Clinical Oncology (ASCO) & Oncology Nurses Society (ONS) Standards for Safe Chemotherapy Administration* (2013) and *Perioperative Standards and Recommended Practices* (Association of Perioperative Registered Nurses, 2014).

Table 18-1	LIST OF SERIOUS REPORTABLE EVENTS

Event	Additional specifications
1. Surgical events	
A. Surgery performed on the wrong body part	Defined as any surgery performed on a body part that is not consistent with the documented informed consent for that patient.
	Excludes emergent situations that occur in the course of surgery and/or whose exigency precludes obtaining informed consent.
B. Surgery performed on the wrong patient	Defined as any surgery on a patient that is not consistent with the documented informed consent for that patient.
C. Wrong surgical procedure performed on a patient	Defined as any procedure performed on a patient that is not consistent with the documented informed consent for that patient.
	Excludes emergent situations that occur in the course of surgery and/or whose exigency precludes obtaining informed consent.
	Surgery includes endoscopies and other invasive procedures.
D. Retention of a foreign object in a patient after surgery or other procedure	Excludes objects intentionally implanted as part of a planned intervention and objects present prior to surgery that were intentionally retained.
E. Intraoperative or immediately post-operative death in an ASA Class I patient	Includes all ASA Class I patient deaths in situations where anesthesia was administered; the planned surgical procedure may or may not have been carried out. Immediately post-operative means within 24 hours after induction of anesthesia (if surgery not completed), surgery, or other invasive procedure was completed.
2. Product or device events	
A. Patient death or serious disability associated with the use of contaminated drugs, devices, or biologics provided by the health care facility	Includes generally detectable contaminants in drugs, devices, or biologics regardless of the source of contamination and/or product.
B. Patient death or serious disability associated with the use or function of a device in patient care, in which the device is used for functions other than as intended	Includes, but is not limited to, catheters, drains and other specialized tubes, infusion pumps, and ventilators.
C. Patient death or serious disability associated with intravascular air embolism that occurs while being cared for in a health care facility	Excludes deaths associated with neurosurgical procedures known to be a high risk of intravascular air embolism.

(continued)

| Table 18-1 | LIST OF SERIOUS REPORTABLE EVENTS (CONTINUED) |

Event	Additional specifications
3. Patient protection events	
A. Infant discharged to the wrong person	
B. Patient death or serious disability associated with patient elopement (disappearance) for more than four hours	Excludes events involving competent adults.
C. Patient suicide, or attempted suicide resulting in serious disability, while being cared for in a health care facility	Defined as events that result from patient actions after admission to a health care facility.
	Excludes deaths resulting from self-inflicted injuries that were the reason for admission to the health care facility.
4. Care management events	
A. Patient death or serious disability associated with a medication error (e.g., errors involving the wrong drug, wrong dose, wrong patient, wrong time, wrong rate, wrong preparation, or wrong route of administration)	Excludes reasonable differences in clinical judgment on drug selection and dose.
B. Patient death or serious disability associated with a hemolytic reaction due to the administration of ABO-incompatible blood or blood products	
C. Maternal death or serious disability associated with labor or delivery in a low-risk pregnancy while being cared for in a health care facility	Includes events that occur within 42 days post-delivery.
	Excludes deaths from pulmonary or amniotic fluid embolism, acute fatty liver of pregnancy or cardiomyopathy.
D. Patient death or serious disability associated with hypoglycemia, the onset of which occurs while the patient is being cared for in a health care facility	
E. Death or serious disability (kernicterus) associated with failure to identify and treat hyperbilirubinimia in neonates	Hyperbilirubinimia is defined as bilirubin levels >30 mg/dl.
	Neonates refers to the first 28 days of life.
F. Stage 3 or 4 pressure ulcers acquired after admission to a health care facility	Excludes progression from Stage 2 to Stage 3 if Stage 2 was recognized upon admission.
G. Patient death or serious disability due to spinal manipulative therapy	

Table 18-1	(CONTINUED)

Event	Additional specifications
5. *Environmental events*	
A. Patient death or serious disability associated with an electric shock while being cared for in a health care facility	Excludes events involving planned treatments such as electric countershock.
B. Any incident in which a line designated for oxygen or other gas to be delivered to a patient contains the wrong gas or is contaminated by toxic substances	
C. Patient death or serious disability associated with a burn incurred from any source while being cared for in a health care facility	
D. Patient death associated with a fall while being cared for in a health care facility	
E. Patient death or serious disability associated with the use of restraints or bedrails while being cared for in a health care facility	
6. *Criminal events*	
A. Any instance of care ordered by or provided by someone impersonating a physician, nurse, pharmacist, or other licensed health care provider	
B. Abduction of a patient of any age	
C. Sexual assault on a patient within or on the grounds of the health care facility	
D. Death or significant injury of a patient or staff member resulting from a physical assault (i.e., battery) that occurs within or on the grounds of the health care facility	

SOURCE: Serious Reportable Adverse Events in Health Care. *Advances in Patient Safety: From Research to Implementation* (Volume 4: Programs, Tools, and Products). Henriksen K., Battles J.B., Marks E.S., et al., editors. Rockville (MD): Agency for Healthcare Research and Quality (US); 2005 Feb. Publication No.: 05-0021-4. NCBI Bookshelf. A service of the National Library of Medicine, National Institutes of Health.

LICENSURE, CREDENTIALING, AND CERTIFICATION: APPLICATION OF STRUCTURE METRIC
Professional licensure verification is an important activity in all HCOs. A license means the person has met expected minimal standards set by the state practice act. State laws require that certain healthcare providers have licenses. Allowing someone to practice without a license means the HCO and the individual are breaking the law. Credentialing is different from checking licensure. It is a more in-depth review process that includes evaluation of licenses, certification if required in a specialty area, evidence of malpractice insurance as required, history of involvement in malpractice suits, and education. Credentialing is not done for all healthcare staff, but rather it is primarily used for physicians who practice or admit patients to an HCO. Credentialing may also be required for certified nurse-midwives (CNMs), certified registered nurse anesthetists (CRNAs), and advanced practice registered nurses (APRNs). Specialty certification has also become more important. Licensure and credentialing information is kept on file by human resources and is part of the recruitment and hiring process. These records may be reviewed during Joint Commission surveys or by other accreditors.

OUTCOME AND ASSESSMENT INFORMATION SET (OASIS): APPLICATION OF OUTCOME METRIC   Some HCOs such as home care agencies and insurers use national evaluation methods that are not sponsored by the Joint Commission. Home care agencies use a specific outcome-based approach to CQI called Outcome and Assessment Information Set (OASIS). The HHS and the CMS developed OASIS in the 1990s. This is a standardized, computerized patient-level assessment with items related to the patient's physical and emotional states. The focus is on whether or not the patient benefited from the care—outcomes and performance, which should be the focus of care in all types of settings (Centers for Medicare & Medicaid Services, 2012). Further information is available on the CMS website.

UTILIZATION REVIEW/MANAGEMENT: APPLICATION OF OUTCOME METRIC   **Utilization review/management (UR/UM)** is the process of evaluating necessity, appropriateness, and efficiency of healthcare services for specific patients or patient populations. UR/UM has been used in acute care settings for a long time; however, it is also very important to third-party payers or insurers. It is, however, controversial as healthcare providers, particularly physicians, are concerned about interference in clinical decisions, and this in turn can upset patients.

To reduce costs, it is necessary to assess appropriateness of care and timeliness and to influence decisions that are made by providers. "Appropriateness" ties UR/UM to CQI. UR/UM is not just looking at numbers such as how many days of treatment. It also focuses on what is appropriate care for the patient's problem. Typically UR/UM focuses on length of stay or treatment, use of services, complications, readmission rates, number of transfers, number and types of prescriptions, number of referrals to specialists, number of procedures, and so forth. **Authorization**, the major method used in UR/UM, is the approval by the third-party payer for a healthcare provider to provide specific care and receive reimbursement for the services. The payer or insurer identifies what services or benefits require authorization. This is done at the time the plan is purchased. To be truly effective in controlling costs, an insurer must be able to influence provider utilization behavior. For example, if an insurer cannot find a way to decrease a provider's number of hospital admissions or the number of referrals to specialists, costs will continue to be a problem. Insurers are particularly active in controlling authorization. The purchaser of the plan, the employer, does not want its healthcare costs to increase and may decide to drop the insurer and contract with another, more cost-effective insurer.

Nurses have the necessary competencies to participate in UR/UM: clinical knowledge and experience; understanding of HCOs, use of the nursing process, communication and collaboration within interprofessional teams, and understanding of documentation. This function also requires that the nurse is knowledgeable about healthcare reimbursement, provider options, benefits, and costs. Nurses can then assist in determining the necessity, appropriateness, and timeliness of services based on protocols established by the HCO or the insurer. Case managers are also very involved in UR/UM and authorization of services. How does UR/UM affect nursing care? It impacts care as it influences which patients are admitted, patient acuity status, length of stay, and treatment that may be approved for reimbursement. Any factor that influences reimbursement also influences HCO budgets, which in turn has a direct impact on the nursing budget (e.g., number of staff, salaries and benefits, and so on).

Utilization review and discharge planning are two functions in hospitals that are interconnected. In some cases the two functions may be combined. It is becoming common for UR/UM to be more important than discharge planning. Why is this so? Many of the UR/UM and discharge planning activities are the same such as admission review, continued stay review, and assessment of readiness for discharge. There are, however, some critical components associated with discharge planning that should not be ignored. Some of these are routine monitoring of changes in the plan, counseling the patient and family about the discharge plan, and effective patient/family education. Today, with higher patient acuity and variable staffing levels, nurses have less and less time to prepare patients for discharge. When patients and their families are not involved in the discharge planning process, there are more likely to be problems in the next level of care, or readmission may be required. This is costly for all concerned.

CLINICAL GUIDELINES AND CLINICAL PATHWAYS APPLICATION OF STRUCTURE, PROCESS, AND OUTCOMES METRICS   Clinical guidelines and clinical pathways are methods or tools that focus on improvement of care. *Clinical Practice Guidelines We Can Trust* (Institute of Medicine, 2011a) is the report from the IOM that resulted from its examination of the best methods used for developing clinical practice guidelines. "To properly evaluate the effects of the standards on clinical practice guidelines development and healthcare quality and outcomes, the IOM encourages the AHRQ to pilot-test the standards and assess their reliability and validity. While there always will be uncertainty in clinical practice, ensuring that clinicians have trustworthy guidelines will bring more evidence to bear on clinician and patient decision-making" (Institute of Medicine, 2011a, p. 11). This is another example of the integration with the National Academy of Medicine (NAM), government entities such as AHRQ as part of HHS, academic researchers, policy makers, and clinicians from multiple healthcare professions.

The AHRQ is an important governmental agency that focuses on healthcare quality issues. Its mission "is to produce evidence to make healthcare safer, higher quality, more accessible, equitable, and affordable and to work within the U.S. Department of Health and Human Services and with other partners to make sure that the evidence is understood and used" (Agency for Healthcare Research and Quality, 2014a). AHRQ has developed quality measures for inpatient care, safety, and prevention. The National Guideline Clearinghouse provides examples of guidelines that are evidence based (Agency for Healthcare Research and Quality, National Guideline Clearinghouse, 2014). The evidence-based guidelines available through the clearinghouse are not necessarily developed by AHRQ, but rather represent a collection of reviewed guidelines from a variety of sources such as universities, clinical organizations, healthcare professional organizations, and others. The guidelines focus on many specialties and problems encountered in health care and must meet AHRQ requirements.

Since guidelines and pathways identify outcomes and support best practices, they can be useful in measuring quality and cost of health care. For example: Was the pathway or the guideline followed? What were the outcomes? Data can help to identify quality problems, particularly problems related to underuse, overuse, or ineffective provision of care. Greater understanding of how patients respond to care for particular problems can help to prevent problems. Patient outcomes and patient satisfaction are important variables to consider as guidelines are implemented and data collected. This should all lead to a more complete view of care required for specific problems and improvement of care guidelines. The promotion of appropriate use of resources in a timely manner is an important component of each guideline/pathway, and this promotes cost effectiveness. HCOs use these tools to orient staff to their care requirements, setting standards. How do guidelines and pathways enhance the quality of care? They provide a consistent approach to care and thus can have a positive impact on the quality of care. However, when a guideline or a pathway is used, it needs to be assessed to determine how it applies to a specific patient so patient-centered care is provided and care is individualized.

When guideline or pathway outcomes are not met, the **variance data** can be analyzed to determine causes and actions that need to be taken to prevent further problems. This information also provides data that can be used to improve care for other patients who might have similar problems.

BENCHMARKING: APPLICATION OF PROCESS AND OUTCOMES METRICS   **Benchmarking** is a systematic method for collecting data, analyzing it, and using the results for comparison with other similar situations and HCOs. It is also a tool that links standards of care, guidelines, documentation, quality improvement programs, and clinical guidelines or pathways. Benchmarking allows organizations to compare their performance both within the HCO and with other HCOs.

It requires that staff use data-driven decision-making processes and, in so doing, makes the HCO and its staff aware of options and focuses on improvement. Benchmarking begins by identifying the areas of greatest need and those for which there is comparable performance data; however, the process needs to be continuous to be effective over time. HCOs should not waste time on correcting problems that will not have an impact or for which it is difficult to obtain data. Methods used to collect and analyze data should consider these factors.

A key component of benchmarking is sharing, and this has not always been easy for HCOs. If information is shared, it will benefit others, but this requires some trust. Any HCO or insurer that participates in benchmarking will undoubtedly want its legal advisers to review policies and procedures related to this project. Competition has not disappeared; in fact, it has increased. Acknowledging competition and also participating in benchmarking can be a complex endeavor.

There are a number of accepted formal methods for collecting data, analyzing it, and sharing results. One of the popular benchmarking approaches is Six Sigma, which is a service that provides a systematic method to collect and analyze data with a focus on performance (Six Sigma, 2014).

QUALITY REPORT CARDS: APPLICATION OF STRUCTURE, PROCESS, AND OUTCOME METRICS

Quality report cards provide specific performance data about an HCO. Data that might be found in an HCO report card include number of admissions and diagnoses, length of stay per admitting diagnosis, mortality rates per diagnosis, procedures, surgical procedures, qualifications of medical staff, patient satisfaction, and so on. The HCO may then compare these data with data from other similar HCOs using benchmarking. The goal is to provide information that is helpful to the purchaser of healthcare services, the consumer of healthcare services, and health plans. Employers are primarily interested in differences in quality related to the costs of plans. Patients or consumers are interested in quality comparison among plans and their providers. Health plans also want performance information for marketing purposes.

Report cards have become more common, and healthcare professionals and HCOs, consumers, and customers are reviewing them more, particularly since more of them are accessible via the Internet. Changes in report card formats and content rapidly occur as needs change and problems are discovered in the report cards. Third-party payers are interested in data about financial performance, operating performance, membership, changes in service, and the services. Report cards, however, are not perfect, and their existence does not necessarily ensure quality care, as they are only a method for reporting data and analysis of results. They are costly to develop and maintain from the perspective of data collection, analysis, and sharing. A report card may indicate improvement in measures used, but there is no assurance that this affects other aspects of care. If a report card indicates that an HCO has problems, the HCO may not want this information shared. There is, however, no guarantee that releasing this information affects quality or the employer's and the consumer's choices. Patients often seek information and guidance from family members and friends, who have their own personal views and values that may not be based on facts, and may base their decisions on information they get from people they know.

RISK MANAGEMENT: APPLICATION OF OUTCOME METRIC

Risk management (RM) focuses on limiting an HCO's financial risk associated with the delivery of care, particularly related to lawsuits, preferably before incidents occur. HCOs maintain insurance coverage to protect themselves from financial loss when there are the inevitable situations that put them at risk, such as initiation of lawsuits. Strategies that HCOs use include incident report system, investigation of incidents and use of root cause analysis, staff education about risk and need for effective, timely documentation, data collection to identify and track potential problems, and development of methods to prevent problems.

Risk management staff work closely with CQI staff as their responsibilities are interrelated. The key source of information is the HCO's occurrence or incident reporting system. Nurses participate in this process by completing the required forms when involved in an incident and following policies and procedures related to incident reporting and analysis. However, if the HCO does not have a culture of safety, there is less chance staff will report errors and near misses (Richter, McAlearney, & Pennell, 2014b). Most incidents, however, do not result in a lawsuit.

Nurses participate in risk management every day when they ensure quality care. Typical areas of high risk include medication administration, falls, overall patient safety, use of technology and equipment (for example, ensuring that equipment is working correctly before using it in the operating room), assessment and communication of allergies, and any action or intervention or lack of action that might harm the patient. Healthcare organizations must also consider the risks to anyone who enters the HCO such as visitors, community members, family members, and so on (e.g., a visitor falls in the hallway). HCOs and providers retain legal services to assist them with risk management. Often nurse attorneys are used because they have both the legal and clinical experience to understand the complex problems that arise. These preventive efforts are expensive; however, they are not as costly as malpractice suits. Attorneys provide counsel about documentation and actions to be taken if an incident occurs that might put the organization at financial risk. Malpractice and nurses are discussed in Chapter 2.

EVIDENCE-BASED PRACTICE AND EVIDENCE-BASED MANAGEMENT: APPLICATION OF STRUCTURE, PROCESS, AND OUTCOME METRICS   EBP and EBM assist in identifying and assessing high-quality, clinically relevant research that can be applied to clinical practice or administration (Institute of Medicine, 2008). EBP and EBM are viewed as methods to improve the care, emphasizing the need to base clinical and management decisions on evidence to better ensure that the care needs are met in an effective, efficient manner. Both EBP and EBM should be part of policies and procedures, standards, and other aspects that are critical to effective organizational functioning. Chapter 16 includes more detailed information about EBP and EBM.

ACCESS TO HEALTH CARE METRIC: APPLICATION OF OUTCOME METRIC   Access to care is a critical issue in today's healthcare environment and an integral component of patient-centered care. The IOM describes **access to care** as the consumer's ability to access personal health services needed to reach the best outcomes in a timely manner (Institute of Medicine, 1993). The major focus today is on accessible primary care, particularly in relation to continuity, time, and provider type. Measurement of access integrates structure, process, and outcome and is an important measure of the quality of care. Decreased access may result in poorer patient outcomes and can be costly if the patient's condition worsens because the patient was not able to access the right care when needed. How easy is it for a patient to receive care (structure)? Economic factors, transportation, and availability of appropriate healthcare providers may make it difficult for the patient to receive care when it is needed (structure and outcome). Access has been greatly affected by the diverse healthcare delivery and financial arrangements present in the healthcare environment (structure, process, and outcome). There is also an ethical issue interwoven in any discussion of access. Is health care a right (process and outcome)? This issue has not been resolved as there is no state or federal law that says it is a right. The United States spends more money on health than any other country, yet not all citizens receive care and the quality is not at the level it should be (Fineberg, 2012). If barriers to coverage and proximity are removed, will this result in equitable access (outcome)? This is unknown, though it is hoped that the Affordable Care Act of 2010 will make a significant difference. The following is a summary of examples of the many elements of access to health care:

1. Ability to get to an appointment (e.g., hours of service for appointments, transportation, time off from work, child care, and so on)
2. Ability to get specialty care or referral required
3. Ability to pay for care
4. Ability to know when care is needed and to seek it
5. Ability to understand healthcare information and use it
6. Ability to access healthcare facility (e.g., disability access, parking)
7. Ability to choose healthcare providers
8. Ability to get exams and tests in a timely manner
9. Ability to better ensure patient-centered care
10. Ability to implement evidence-based practice

Access is more than just initial entry into the healthcare system; it also includes how services are received within the system and the outcomes of that care. As the healthcare delivery system has changed, greater strain has been put on safety net providers (for example, free-care clinics, public and teaching hospitals, and other healthcare facilities that provide care to those with limited funds or insurance coverage). These providers are less able to provide uncompensated care without sustaining major financial hardships. In addition, the strain and overload on the healthcare delivery system affects the quality of the services provided. Given these facts, the improvement of care requires that these problems be addressed to make care more accessible to all who need care. Other factors that are important when considering access are convenience; timeliness, handicap provisions, accommodations for language differences or sight loss (health literacy), hours of operation, provider choice, waiting time for urgent and routine care, and timeliness of laboratory tests. Each of these factors can be used to measure accessibility of care and thus assist in the evaluation of the quality of care.

Access for special populations or vulnerable populations has been a major concern. The National Healthcare Disparities Report (NHDR) discussed in Chapters 10 and 17 is a critical addition to the nation's perspective of health care and provides data about access (Agency for Healthcare Research and Quality, 2014e). *Healthy People 2010* included access as a critical need for all types of healthcare needs, and this is also now part of the *Healthy People 2020* goals (U.S. Department of Health and Human Services, 2014). When a patient does not have access, then the patient's health status is at risk and further complications may occur. Vulnerable populations that often have limited access are people with low incomes, children and adolescents, minorities, homeless, mentally ill, uninsured, disabled, elderly veterans, immigrants, and prisoners. These populations are often less "attractive" to providers and the community. Efforts have been made to resolve some of these concerns, and some of these efforts have been more successful than others. The ACA should gradually have some impact on decreasing this problem.

PATIENT EXPERIENCES: APPLICATION OF OUTCOME METRICS The patient experience is now a critical aspect of most HCOs' CQI programs. As discussed in Chapter 11, it is not easy to collect and analyze data about patient experiences. Healthcare provider and consumer/patient/family perspectives may be very different. There are some surveys that have been tested and are now used routinely by some HCOs, such as the Press Ganey® patient survey (Press Ganey®, 2014a). Collecting and analyzing data are only one part of the puzzle. What is done with this information to improve care is a required component, and if not done or done ineffectively, this means the time and money spent on the first part of the puzzle will be wasted.

THE ACCREDITATION PROCESS

Accreditation of organizations is important to many different types of organizations. For example, universities and schools of nursing are accredited, meaning they receive some type of official approval or accreditation of their services, which in the case of schools of nursing are courses toward a nursing degree. Hospitals and other types of HCOs and third-party payer/insurer organizations may also be accredited. Evaluation is a fact of life; however, it is not simple and can have major ramifications for an HCO—costs, staff time and energy, and public relations. It may require that the HCO change or, in extreme cases, stop providing services. The following discussion offers some information about healthcare accreditation, which serves as a critical measurement and improvement process.

What Is Healthcare Accreditation?

Accreditation is the process by which HCOs are evaluated on their quality, based on established minimum standards and performance. HCOs have been accredited for a long time, but the process still has its critics. An important criticism is whether or not quality can be defined, and this impacts how it might be measured. Previous discussion in this chapter and Chapter 17 provides a recognized definition for "quality of care," although there are many other definitions that have been proposed by a number of authorities. Accreditation focuses on quality, and thus the definition of "quality" is necessary to ensure all who are involved are assessing the same concern, which is quality care. Accreditation has undergone many changes in the past 15 years as it adjusted to the healthcare environment and to changes in perspectives of quality care. The most important changes have been the increased focus on CQI, or ongoing efforts to improve care, focusing on systems rather than just on healthcare provider performance, and avoiding blame. Accreditation is something that all nurses experience, but the level of that experience varies depending on the nurse's position. Today, when hospitals are surveyed for accreditation, all staff are expected to be prepared and participate in the process. The goal is to include more direct care providers rather than just management staff. Accreditation is not perfect, and the designation of an accredited HCO does not necessarily mean that care provided in the HCO meets all quality requirements all the time.

The Joint Commission

The major organization that accredits HCOs is the **Joint Commission** (Joint Commission, 2014). It is a nonprofit organization that accredits more than 17,000 HCOs, including hospitals, long-term care organizations, home care agencies, clinical laboratories, ambulatory care organizations, behavioral health organizations, critical access hospitals, disease-specific care organizations, healthcare staffing services, and office-based surgery practices. Accreditation has changed over time and now focuses on continuous improvement and performance based on minimum standards, requiring understanding and participation from nurses that this is a job that is never really completed. The accreditation process is complex, time consuming, and costly. This is the most important healthcare accrediting organization in the United States. Its purpose is to improve the quality of care provided to the public by assessing performance based on the Joint Commission standards. The Joint Commission establishes minimum standards and benchmarks for HCOs to use as they assess and improve their services, emphasizing quality. HCOs go through a survey every three years, but the Joint Commission may also conduct unscheduled surveys. HCOs voluntarily request this accreditation; however, for HCOs that offer medical training programs, provide clinical experiences for nursing students, and receive federal funding (e.g., Medicare and Medicaid reimbursement, federal grants), this accreditation is required. It is therefore difficult to view accreditation as truly voluntary. Periodic performance review is also required with submission of specific reports, and failure to meet certain outcomes may trigger the need for additional reporting and assessment. The required survey and updated, required, periodic reports that accredited HCOs must submit to the Joint Commission are done to meet the goal of finding out if the patients are achieving expected outcomes, and if not, why they are not meeting positive outcomes. Examples of some outcomes that the Joint Commission assesses are mortality rates, length of stay, adverse incidents, complications, readmission rates, patient/family satisfaction, referrals to specialists, patient adherence to the discharge or treatment plan, and prevention adherence (e.g., mammogram, Pap smear, immunizations). All of these outcomes are also of interest to insurers. The Joint Commission standards typically cover major concerns of healthcare delivery such as documentation, medication management, patient care interventions, quality improvement, safety goals, human resources, healthcare environment, patient confidentiality and rights, and leadership. Nursing services is a major focus for accreditation surveys. Additional information about current accreditation can be found on the Joint Commission website.

The Joint Commission requires its accredited organizations to have active CQI programs. For example, the CQI program should identify and address **sentinel events**, which are unexpected events that lead to risk of or actual experience of serious complication (physical or psychological) or death. A **root cause analysis** or a systematic review of the event is conducted. The key is to assess the process with a system approach, not just focus on the individual staff who were involved and blame them; prevention of further events is the goal. This supports the recommendations from the IOM reports.

The CQI approach was a major change in the accreditation process. Prior to the change to focus on CQI, Joint Commission accreditation required extensive data collection that attempted to cover all areas of concern, and there was a tendency to take a punitive approach. This was a burdensome method, and as noted earlier, quality of care did not sufficiently improve. HCOs felt that once they met a certain Joint Commission requirement, there was nothing else that needed to be done until the next survey. An analogy would be the student who makes an A on the first exam and thinks there is nothing else to learn and no risk of the grade going down. HCOs often did not consistently look for ways to improve but rather just focused on problems during the survey period. This has now changed as QI has become more acceptable, expected, and continuous, and there are focused areas of concern that change rather than trying to cover everything an HCO does or should do.

Related to the change to CQI and a more focused approach, the Joint Commission developed a core measure initiative so HCOs will focus on what matters. These measures should determine if patients are getting the care they should receive, and the data should provide benchmarks. The Joint Commission has developed specific rules for collecting and reporting data to ensure better comparison of data from one HCO to another. Hospitals must develop strategies to improve care for the core areas, and all of these core areas are highly dependent on nursing care. Within HCOs, nurses need to be directly involved in the core measure initiative. Current core measures are found on the Joint Commission website.

Nurses and the Joint Commission

All nurses eventually encounter the Joint Commission—through application of its standards, preparation for surveys, and participation in surveys and other follow-up reports that might be required. Nurses assume leadership roles in all of these phases within HCOs, serve as Joint Commission surveyors, and serve as staff members at the Joint Commission. Quality improvement should be continuous with no end. As problems are resolved and care improved, HCOs then focus on new concerns and review past problem areas to determine if improvement continues. Every HCO needs to develop plans to ensure that care is assessed and that problems are addressed. The Joint Commission survey should not be the major focus, although it usually is; rather, the focus should be on continuous improvement. What usually happens is the survey preparation and process become all consuming. Key steps that organizations complete to meet the improvement goal and be prepared for Joint Commission surveys are as follows:

1. Make sure that staff understand the Joint Commission standards.
2. Develop a plan (includes units, services, departments, and the entire organization) and engage staff.
3. Implement the plan.
4. Collect and analyze the data.
5. Develop reports that summarize the data and analysis so it can be useful in decision making.

CASE STUDY

How Do We Address Poor QI Data?

Four team leaders on a medical unit are meeting with the nurse manager to review CQI data for the last quarter. The data concerns medication errors, falls, and nosocomial infections. The QI Department provided data in the form of a graph. The nurse manager expresses concern about the changes in the data compared to the previous quarter. They discuss the impact these changes may have in light of the new CMS hospital-acquired complications (HACs) policy. One of the team leaders says that she thinks the problem is staff not taking this seriously and all of the team leaders need to identify individual staff who make all the errors. Another team leader argues with her, saying that this is too narrow a view of the problems and focuses on blame. The other two team leaders did not say anything, but they also are confused about how staff respond to errors. Most of the team leaders feel it is their job to focus on individual errors. The nurse manager says that the staff need to come up with a plan to address the changes in unit CQI data. She also says, "I think we really need to address our culture of safety."

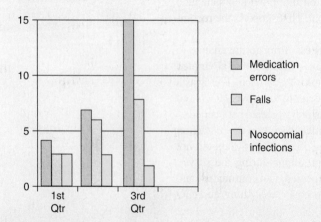

Medication errors

Falls

Nosocomial infections

Questions:

1. Review the data provided in the graph. What does the data tell you?
2. Develop a plan to focus on the problems in the next quarter by identifying goal(s), interventions, and methods to evaluate outcomes. Use the Food and Drug Administration (FDA) Safe Use Initiative information that focuses on collaborating to reduce preventable harm from medications to develop the implementation plan to reduce drug errors and the four stages of the drug system identified by the FDA. (See FDA website.)
3. How would you address the culture of safety on the unit?

6. Share data and analysis with staff, and ask for staff feedback about them.
7. With staff input, develop and implement corrective actions for identified problems.
8. Begin again—with more assessment and engagement of staff, communicating that CQI does not begin and end with the accreditation survey.

Nursing leadership and staff should be involved in all of these steps. As the Joint Commission survey time approaches, organizations begin to prepare for the survey. The staff need education about the CQI program, the Joint Commission, and the survey process. Tension usually increases at the time of a survey. Losing accreditation, although this rarely occurs, is extremely serious. The HCO may be required to make changes and report these changes by specific deadlines, which may require additional surveys. All of this is costly and affects the HCO's public image; thus, HCOs want to avoid negative Joint Commission results.

EXAMPLES OF NURSING QUALITY INITIATIVES

Transforming Care at the Bedside (TCAB)

The IHI was formed after the IOM began its examination of healthcare quality, and it is influenced by the IOM work. The IHI supports projects and develops resources that focus on safety, effectiveness, patient-centeredness, timeliness, efficiency, and equity, all of which are emphasized in the IOM *Quality Chasm* series (Institute for Healthcare Improvement, 2014a). One of the IHI's collaborative projects with the Robert Wood Johnson Foundation (RWJF), nursing, and HCOs is Transforming Care at the Bedside (TCAB). The initiative focuses on a structured approach to engage nursing staff in a process to create projects at the unit level that examine need for change and improvement, with emphasis on safety and reliability, care team vitality, patient centeredness, and increased value (Agency for Healthcare Research and Quality, 2011; Rutherford, Lee, & Greiner, 2004). Examples of projects are transition of patients with heart failure to their homes, reducing patient injuries from falls, and optimizing communication and teamwork (Institute for Healthcare Improvement, 2014d). The IHI website describes examples of TCAB pilots, their methods, and their results.

Taxonomy of Error, Root Cause Analysis, and Practice Responsibility (TERCAP)

Another initiative that was also influenced by the IOM work is Taxonomy of Error, Root Cause Analysis, and Practice Responsibility (TERCAP) led by the National Council of State Boards of Nursing (NCSBN) (2014). TERCAP is a tool that describes nursing practice breakdown. It focuses on (Benner et al., 2010; National Council of State Boards of Nursing, 2014):

1. safe medication administration.
2. documentation.
3. attentiveness/surveillance (patient monitoring).
4. clinical reasoning.
5. prevention.
6. intervention.
7. interpretation of authorized provider orders.
8. professional responsibility/patient advocacy.

TERCAP bases its work on the NAM core competencies and the critical IOM report *Keeping Patients Safe: Transforming the Work Environment of Nurses* (2004). This IOM report examined problematic work environments that impact nurses and can lead to errors due to many factors such as staffing levels, working overtime, interruptions, lack of effective use of informatics, and high pressure for efficiency and productivity. Examining practice breakdown is necessary for the nursing profession to assess patient safety and how errors are reported. Applying TERCAP should support the development and implementation of more effective approaches to interventions to prevent quality care problems and to intervene to improve care (Benner et al., 2010). There is need for shared responsibility from all in the profession to deal with practice breakdown. Using TERCAP, state boards of nursing voluntarily submit data from HCOs about errors reported to state boards after the boards have completed their review process. This then provides a database that can be used to meet the goals of the initiative. The NCSBN website includes more information about TERCAP.

COLLABORATIVE INITIATIVES: A GREAT NEED

Nurses are affected by and have valuable opinions about the quality of care; however, the profession can benefit from collaborating with other healthcare providers such as physicians who have similar views. It is also important to interact with healthcare professionals who may have different views to gain broader collaboration and arrive at the best solutions. A collaborative effort has a greater impact on changing the healthcare delivery system to improve care; however, collaborative initiatives have not been the norm. To reach the goal of improved care, collaboration is needed within individual HCOs and with individual nurses, interprofessional teams, and healthcare professional organizations—all joining together in true collaborative efforts to achieve interprofessional quality improvement. Collaboration is considered to be part of the nursing professional standards (American Nurses Association, 2010) and also is part of the nurse executive competencies described by the American Organization of Nurse Executives (AONE) (2005). (See Appendix A.) The following are examples of some collaborative initiatives led by the federal government.

Comprehensive Unit-Based Safety Program (CUSP)

This is a collaborative effort with AHRQ and quality and safety experts. Figure 18-1 provides a visual of the CUSP framework. CUSP supports the following (Agency for Healthcare Research and Quality, 2014d):

- A wide range of safety tools and approaches
- An understanding that all culture is local and that work to improve culture must be owned at the unit level
- A belief that harm is not an acceptable "cost of doing business"
- Safety measures can be applied by anyone, anywhere

Teams, teamwork, and communication as well as HCO leadership are very important. Effective application requires an understanding of the science of safety and the influence of the system on safety. Examples of factors in the system are patient characteristics, tasks, individual providers, team factors, work environment, departmental factors, and organization factors. Engagement of staff as well as engagement of patient and families are integrated into CUSP. This supports the NAM focus on patient-centered care. A system is complex, and it is important to understand its parts to appreciate the whole. CUSP also emphasizes the need for sensemaking, which includes the following (Agency for Healthcare Research and Quality, 2014d):

- Initiate a conversation among members of an organization involved in an event/issue.
- The purpose is to reduce the ambiguity about the event/issue—literally to make sense of it.
- Each person brings his or her experience of that event/issue to the discussion.
- The conversation is the mechanism that combines that knowledge into a new, more understandable form for the members.
- Members develop a similar representation in their minds that allows for action that can be implemented and understood by all who have participated in the conversation.

Learning from defects should focus on four questions:

1. What happened?
2. Why did it happen?
3. What will you do to reduce risk of recurrence?
4. How will you know the risk is reduced?

CUSP was developed with consideration of sound change theory, particularly Kotter's eight steps of change (Kotter & Rathgeber, 2006). It also aligns and supports other quality and safety tools such as Plan-Do-Study-Act, root cause analysis, FMEA, Six Sigma, and TeamSTEPPS® (Agency for Healthcare Research and Quality, Department of Defense, 2014). CUSP is an example of integration rather than an isolated approach. It includes information about the important role of

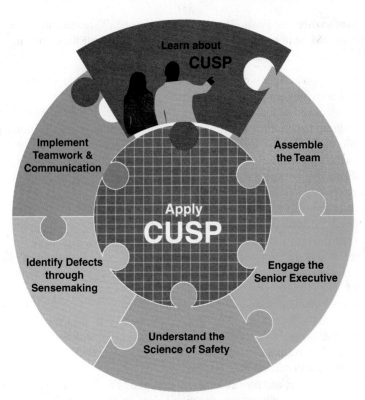

Figure 18-1 Comprehensive Unit-Based Safety Program (CUSP)

Source: Agency for Healthcare Research and Quality. (2014). http://www.ahrq.gov/professionals/
education/curriculum-tools/cusptoolkit/modules/learn/sllearncusp.html#slide1

the nurse manager as leader and manager of operations at the unit level, the center of care improvement (Agency for Healthcare Research and Quality, 2014f). The nurse manager manages operations, acts as mentor and coach, encourages professional staff development, and is directly involved in work alignment to ensure work is based on standards of care and HCO goals.

The AHRQ developed a toolkit that provides staff resources to address safety issues by combining the science of safety and clinical best practice (2014b). It also has several videos on YouTube that provide additional information about CUSP, TeamSTEPPS®, and other patient safety concerns and initiatives.

Healthcare Cost and Utilization Project (HCUP)

The Healthcare Cost and Utilization Project (HCUP) is a "collection of databases and related software tools and products developed through a federal-state-industry partnership, sponsored by the AHRQ. HCUP databases are derived from administrative data and contain encounter-level, clinical and nonclinical information including all listed diagnoses and procedures, discharge status, patient demographics, and charges for all patients, regardless of payer (e.g., Medicare, Medicaid, private insurance, uninsured)" (Agency for Healthcare Research and Quality, 2014c). The databases provide data that can be used to better understand a variety of healthcare policy issues such as cost and quality of health services, medical practice patterns, access to healthcare programs, and outcomes of treatments at the national, state, and local levels. Examples and access to the databases can be found at the AHRQ HCUP website (e.g., databases that focus on inpatient, emergency care, ambulatory surgery, pediatric inpatient, and so on).

PROGRAM EVALUATION

Healthcare programs or services need to be evaluated on a regular basis, preferably annually. This evaluation should include a review of the vision and mission statements, goals, and objectives. The organizational chart describes the staff resources and how they relate to one another, which is important to meet the goals. The budget is reviewed. Were outcomes met? Documentation should be reviewed. Staff records are reviewed. Examples of questions that might be included in a program evaluation are as follows:

- What are the mission and goals of the program? Is revision needed to maintain a current view?
- What specific activities are performed by staff?
- How do managers and staff distribute their time among specific activities and interventions?
- Does the program have sufficient resources: financial, staff, physical facility, equipment, supplies, informatics, and so on?
- Whom does the program serve? Which patients? The community?
- Are the patients appropriately selected? Does the program target the patients in greatest need of services?
- Is the intensity or level of care received by patients appropriate?
- Is the staffing level appropriate for needs? Does staff expertise meet position requirements?
- What does recruitment and retention data indicate?
- Are staff engaged in decision making, and if so, how?
- Have staff and managers received sufficient education and training to optimally do their work?
- Is the program meeting the stated programmatic goals?
- Is the program cost effective?
- Are patients discharged from services when clinically appropriate? Referred to appropriate follow-up care? What are the outcomes?
- What does patient satisfaction data indicate?
- Is care patient centered, and how is it patient centered? Family centered?
- How does the interprofessional team function? How do other teams such as the management team or the nursing team function? What are the staff and team satisfaction levels?
- How is informatics used? How effective are the methods?
- What does the risk management and utilization review data indicate?
- Is there a clear, effective continuous quality improvement plan that is updated as needed?
- What does the quality data indicate—analysis of data and results and implications for improvement? Consider impact of change and outcomes.
- How are evidence-based practice and evidence-based management used? How effective is this?
- How are staff competencies maintained?
- If the program includes health professions students, how is the educational program functioning? Include feedback from students, faculty, and staff.

All position descriptions should be reviewed to ensure that they describe the work that is done. Policies and procedures, clinical guidelines, clinical pathways, standards, and so on should be reviewed to ensure that they are evidence based, current, clear, effective, and applicable. Getting feedback from all stakeholders better ensures a more comprehensive program review. Health information technology (HIT) is now a critical part of CQI. Chapter 19 examines HIT in more detail, but it needs to be recognized here for its roles in CQI such as effective documentation describing care provided and outcomes, data collection, and data analysis. HIT helps to prevent errors for example by providing alerts for allergies when orders are inputted into the electronic medical record and using bar codes for patient identification. It can also be used as a method to better ensure rapid written communication about patient care that is then easily accessible.

NURSING LEADERSHIP IN CONTINUOUS QUALITY IMPROVEMENT

Other chapters, such as Chapter 7, include information about the impact of nursing on care, including impact of staffing levels and degrees. The IOM reports, as noted in Chapter 17, are a major driving influence pushing the need for improvement; however, nurses provide much of the care in HCOs and need to be more involved in the CQI process.

National Database of Nursing Quality Indicators (NDNQI)

Since the mid-1990s, nursing has moved more toward using quality reports that provide data about nursing care. In 1994 the ANA initiated an investigation of the impact of workforce restructuring and redesign on patient care quality in acute care settings. The purpose of this report was to gather information about the relationship between nursing care and patient outcomes as there was limited data to support the relationship (Pollard, Mitra, & Mendelson, 1996). The result provided a framework for educating nurses, consumers, and policy makers about nursing's contributions within the acute care setting. The project tracked the quality of nursing care provided in acute care settings and considered the current efforts hospitals and healthcare systems used to track measures of hospital performance with linkages to nursing services (American Nurses Association, 1996).

This was a major step forward for the nursing profession. To ensure quality data, nurses needed to develop standardized data reporting processes. There continues to be a need to identify objective measures to assess performance of healthcare providers, including nurses. Increased insurer influence on outcomes of care through managed care approaches has made this even more important as consumers and providers have become more concerned about quality care and provider performance. All of this also impacts costs. Identifying nurse-sensitive quality measures was critical in the 1994 ANA report; however, it must be recognized that outcome measurement in health care is still a relatively new area. There is much to learn about it. In general, concern exists that databases and report cards that focus on measuring quality have not included nursing-specific quality measures.

Three types of measures (indicators) are used in the NDNQI report, which are the three critical elements discussed earlier in the chapter and in Chapter 17, but here they are applied to nursing: structure of care, process of care, and patient-focused care. The NDNQI structure of care focuses on nurse staffing patterns; process measures focus on care delivery; and outcome measures focus on how patients and their conditions are affected by their interaction with nursing staff (nursing interventions). The initial study developed by the NDNQI identified two types of process measures: (1) how nurses perceive and discharge their roles or nursing satisfaction, and (2) the nature, amount, and quality of care nurses provide to patients. The development of these nursing measures is part of the ANA's nationwide Nursing Safety and Quality Initiative, a multiphase effort to investigate the impact of healthcare restructuring on the quality of patient care and on the nursing profession (Dunton & Montalvo, 2009; Montalvo & Dunton, 2007). The National Center for Nursing Quality (NCNQ) provides additional information on the ANA website (American Nurses Association, 2015). Evidence-based methods were used to identify the acute care measures and used to develop the community-based, non–acute care measures.

Based on the work described, in 1998 the ANA established the **National Database of Nursing Quality Indicators (NDNQI)** (Montalvo & Dunton, 2007). The database includes a large number of hospitals, increasing the pool of evaluation data. It is the only nursing quality database that provides measures for national, regional, and state norms; however, participation is voluntary, which means not all hospitals are participating. This needs to be considered when NDNQI data are used to describe the current state of nursing care.

The database measures are changed based on needs and current data. The NDNQI focuses on collecting and analyzing unit-level data rather than a hospital-wide approach, considering patient acuity and activity, patient care goals, clinical tasks, role expectations, team relations, and social milieu (Press Ganey®, 2014b). The data collected from patients and nurses are then aggregated per unit, allowing units to identify their particular needs for improvement and to develop unit-specific intervention programs and take into account individual unit differences as even units in the same hospital can be quite different from one another. This initiative is important for the nursing profession and allows nurses to demonstrate their impact on patient outcomes. In 2014 Press Ganey® acquired NDNQI from the ANA (Health IT Outcomes, 2014). Additional information about NDNQI can be found at the Press Ganey® website.

Nursing Leadership in Quality Improvement: Changes Needed

This chapter focuses on implementation of quality improvement, emphasizing that nurses need to be involved in the process. Generally nurses have not been prepared enough to be active in CQI or to take leadership in CQI. One study illustrates some of the problems. The study examines data from a 2004–2005 RN survey. Thirty-eight percent of the 436 responding new nurses thought they were "poorly" or "very poorly" prepared about CQI or had "never heard of" CQI (Kovner, Brewer, Yingrengreung, & Fairchild, 2010). This then leads to increased burden on HCOs to prepare staff to engage in CQI. This problem continues as nursing education also needs to focus more on CQI to prepare nurses at all levels to understand and apply CQI and serve as CQI leaders (Institute of Medicine, 2011b).

> Yet hospitals confront challenges with regard to nursing involvement, including: scarcity of nursing resources; difficulty engaging nurses at all levels—from bedside to management; growing demands to participate in more, often duplicative, quality improvement activities; the burdensome nature of data collection and reporting; and shortcomings of traditional nursing education in preparing nurses for their evolving role in today's contemporary hospital setting. Because nurses are the key caregivers in hospitals, they can significantly influence the quality of care provided and, ultimately, treatment and patient outcomes. (Draper, Felland, Liebhaber, & Melichar, 2008)

Despite these challenges, HCOs need to ensure that nursing staff are prepared to assist with CQI and to reduce barriers that might interfere with staff engagement in CQI. HCOs also need to encourage nursing education to increase CQI content and learning experiences in all nursing programs.

The IOM report *The Future of Nursing: Leading Change, Advancing Health* (2011b) also comments on the need for more nursing involvement in CQI. The report's second recommendation pertains to CQI:

> **Expand opportunities for nurses to lead and diffuse collaborative improvement efforts** Private and public funders, healthcare organizations, nursing education programs, and nursing associations should expand opportunities for nurses to lead and manage collaborative efforts with physicians and other members of the healthcare team to conduct research and to redesign and improve practice environments and health systems. These entities should also provide opportunities for nurses to diffuse successful practices. (Institute of Medicine, 2011b, p. S-9)

This report is directly connected to the IOM quality initiative supporting the need for improvement in care focusing on quality, access, and value. Patient-centered care is highlighted as well as primary care; seamless, coordinated care; need to develop new roles for nurses such as coaches and innovators; and interprofessional collaboration. The key question is: Are nurses ready for this? Studies indicate nurses are not prepared enough, and there is need for greater emphasis on CQI as well as leadership in nursing programs, undergraduate and graduate. The lack of knowledge acts as a barrier to CQI success and to engagement of nurses in the CQI process. Changes are required.

> Nurses must remodel the way they practice and make clinical decisions. They must rethink the ways in which they teach nurses how to care for people. They must rise to the challenge of providing leadership in rapidly changing care settings and in an evolving healthcare system. In short, nurses must expand their vision of what it means to be a nursing professional. At the same time, society must amend outdated regulations, attitudes, policies, and habits that unnecessarily restrict the innovative contributions the nursing profession can bring to healthcare. (Institute for Medicine, 2011b, p. 2-19)

Connecting leadership and management to collaborative interprofessional quality improvement is a challenge, but for care to improve, this is required.

Communication is a critical part of all CQI activities. Nurses need to understand the health policy implications of quality as described in Chapters 2 and 17. There are many different roles that nurses may get involved in as they participate in CQI in an HCO. Examples include providing feedback on performance, participating in their own performance appraisals, collecting data, developing awareness of errors and applying this to their practice, assisting with analysis of data, and using conclusions from quality analysis to improve their practice. Some nurses hold formal positions that focus on CQI activities. All nurse managers are directly involved in ensuring quality care and need to be aware of the impact on outcomes. To be effective, nurses need an understanding of change and how to plan and implement change, access to current literature and critiques of literature, and an understanding of data collection and analysis (typically staff with statistical expertise are used as a resource to assist with analysis) and CQI methods, and ability to work with a team. Most of the competencies discussed in this text apply to CQI responsibilities, including coordination, collaboration, communication, teamwork, and planning.

The nurse's role in CQI is included in nursing professional standards (American Nurses Association, 2010), and it is part of the nurse executive competencies described by the American Organization of Nurse Executives (2005), as described in Appendix A. Chapter 20 discusses staff education, which is a critical part of preparing nurses for engagement in CQI activities at all levels in the HCO. As discussed in Chapter 17, in addition to the critical importance of the NAM core competencies for health professions, the Quality and Safety Education for Nurses (QSEN) initiative has adapted the NAM core competencies (QSEN Institute, 2014).

What does a nurse manager need to do to participate in the improvement process? The following are steps that should be taken:

1. Develop an understanding of quality improvement, measurement, and analysis.
2. Ensure that the staff understand quality improvement, measurement, and analysis.
3. Ensure that CQI responsibilities are included in position descriptions and in performance reviews.
4. Develop awareness of CQI initiatives (nongovernmental and governmental) and strategies used to prevent errors and improve care; determine how these may or may not be applied to the current situation.
5. Engage staff at all levels of the CQI process—make this a requirement, for example, participation in CQI committees, task forces, and staff meetings at unit and higher levels.
6. Use an interprofessional team approach to CQI and in management and practice.
7. Listen to staff as they are at the direct care level and can identify CQI needs and make suggestions for improvement.
8. Recognize staff for their efforts.
9. Monitor CQI data routinely, and work with CQI staff.
10. Engage patients and families in the CQI effort by letting them know their comments are important and they should speak up if there are questions or concerns about the care.
11. Develop realistic interventions to prevent errors and improve care that consider barriers such as time, staffing, expertise, patient acuity, communication, and staff engagement.
12. Integrate CQI reporting into meetings and other methods of communication to keep the topic up front.
13. Assume an active role in CQI at the overall organization level.

An Exemplar: Interdisciplinary Nursing Quality Research Initiative (INQRI)

The INQRI was created by the Robert Wood Johnson Foundation (RWJF) in 2005. RWJF is a strong supporter of the nursing profession and provides a variety of opportunities to expand the profession. INQRI is one of these opportunities: The goal is

> to address this gap in knowledge and identify the ways in which nurses affect the quality of care patients receive and the ways in which they can improve patient care and outcomes, for example, INQRI projects have produced evidence that better nursing improves quality of care by reducing medical errors and identifying measures, processes and protocols that help health systems and health professionals ensure the best patient outcomes possible. (Interdisciplinary Nursing Quality Research Initiative, 2014)

It is important for nurse executives and managers to access this information so it can be applied to improve care. In addition, this initiative is interprofessional/interdisciplinary, supporting the IOM recommendation for interprofessional teams—in practice, research, and EBP. INQRI funding is directed at this type of study, allowing INQRI to have an impact on system changes and on strategies to improve care. The INQRI website provides resources that address quality improvement, providing evidence-based recommendations.

APPLYING LEADERSHIP AND MANAGEMENT

My Hospital Unit: An Evolving Case Experience

You are planning a meeting with your staff to discuss the implementation of the six quality improvement aims that have been identified by the Institute of Medicine. These aims are identified in Chapter 17 and in Figure 17-1, and are important to apply in practice.

What will you tell the staff about the aims? How will you get them involved in integrating the six aims in the unit and patient care? Provide specific examples for the staff to get the discussion on track. Consider the content found in this chapter on implementing CQI aims.

BSN and *Master's Essentials:* Application to Content

BSN Essentials (American Association of Colleges of Nursing, 2008) as Applied to this Chapter:

V. Healthcare Policy, Finance, and Regulatory Environments

VI. Interprofessional Communication and Collaboration for Improving Patient Health Outcomes

Master's Essentials (American Association of Colleges of Nursing, 2011) as Applied to this Chapter:

III. Quality Improvement and Safety

VI. Health Policy and Advocacy

VII. Interprofessional Collaboration for Improving Patient Care Outcomes

Applying AONE Competencies

Identify which of the AONE competencies found in Appendix A apply to the content of this chapter.

Engaging in the Content: Critical Thinking and Clinical Reasoning and Judgment

Discussion Questions

1. Compare and contrast the blame culture with the culture of safety. (Online Application Option)
2. How are structure, process, and outcomes related to the assessment of care and accreditation?
3. Why is accreditation important?
4. What is the value of quality report cards and benchmarking?
5. Do you think nurses can make an impact on the quality of care? If so, how would this occur (provide examples)? How do nurse managers and team leaders impact quality care? (Online Application Option)

Application Exercises

1. Interview a nurse who works in CQI focusing on specific methods used to prevent errors and improve care. Develop your interview questions from the chapter content. Share your information with your learning team or class. (Online Application Option)
2. Identify a safety issue you have concerns about in clinical. Describe the issue and data you can obtain; then analyze the data and plan to improve care related to the issue. Share your information in class. This may be done in teams with different team members assuming different tasks after planning the team's work process. (Online Application Option)
3. Interview five staff nurses, and ask them how they know when quality care has been provided. Summarize the data and compare with data your classmates collected. What are the trends? Differences? Develop a table to describe the data. (Online Application Option)
4. Interview a nurse manager and find out what the manager does to improve care on the manager's assigned unit/service.
5. Go to the Institute for Healthcare Improvement website, and learn more about FMEA, FTR, RRT, handoffs, and workarounds. How might these methods apply to the healthcare organizations where you are for clinical? You might do this as a team and work out sharing of information. (Online Application Option)
6. Discuss the use of root cause analysis in a team discussion. What is your opinion of this process? How do you think it could be used by nurses and by the interprofessional team? Would using this process impact care and how? Search for more information on this topic. (Online Application Option)
7. Search the literature to learn more about the impact of the IOM report *The Future of Nursing: Leading Change, Advancing Health* (2011b). Discuss in small teams how this report relates to content in this textbook. The full report can be found online at the National Academy of Medicine (NAM) website. (Online Application Option)

References

Agency for Healthcare Research and Quality. (2011). The transforming care at the bedside how-to guide: Creating an ideal transition home for patients with heart failure. Retrieved from https://innovations.ahrq.gov/qualitytools/transforming-care-bedside-how-guide-creating-ideal-transition-home-patients-heart

Agency for Healthcare Research and Quality. (2013). Failure mode and effects analysis. Retrieved from http://healthit.ahrq.gov/health-it-tools-and-resources/workflow-assessment-health-it-toolkit/all-workflow-tools/fmea-analysis

Agency for Healthcare Research and Quality. (2014a). About AHRQ. Retrieved from http://www.ahrq.gov/cpi/about/index.html

Agency for Healthcare Research and Quality. (2014b). CUSP toolkit. Retrieved from http://www.ahrq.gov/professionals/education/curriculum-tools/cusptoolkit/index.html

Agency for Healthcare Research and Quality. (2014c). Healthcare cost and utilization project (HCUP). Retrieved from http://www.ahrq.gov/research/data/hcup/index.html

Agency for Healthcare Research and Quality. (2014d). Identify defects through sensemaking. Retrieved from http://www.ahrq.gov/professionals/education/curriculum-tools/cusptoolkit/modules/identify/index.html

Agency for Healthcare Research and Quality. (2014e). *National healthcare disparities report, 2013.* Retrieved from http://www.ahrq.gov/research/findings/nhqrdr/nhdr13/2013nhdr.pdf

Agency for Healthcare Research and Quality. (2014f). The role of the nurse manager. Retrieved from http://www.ahrq.gov/professionals/education/curriculum-tools/cusptoolkit/modules/nursing/index.html

Agency for Healthcare Research and Quality, Department of Defense. (2014). TeamSTEPPS 2.0. Retrieved from http://www.ahrq.gov/teamsteppstools/instructor/index.html

Agency for Healthcare Research and Quality, National Guideline Clearinghouse. (2014). Guideline summary. Retrieved from http://www.guideline.gov/content.aspx?id=36681

Agency for Healthcare Research and Quality, National Quality Measures Clearinghouse. (2014). Measures matrix. Retrieved from http://www.qualitymeasures.ahrq.gov/hhs/matrix.aspx

Agency for Healthcare Research and Quality, Patient Safety Network. (2014a). Failure to rescue. Retrieved from http://www.psnet.ahrq.gov/popup_glossary.aspx?name=failuretorescue

Agency for Healthcare Research and Quality, Patient Safety Network. (2014b). Handoffs and signouts. Retrieved from http://psnet.ahrq.gov/primer.aspx?primerID=9

Agency for Healthcare Research and Quality, Patient Safety Network. (2014c). Workaround. Retrieved from http://psnet.ahrq.gov/popup_glossary.aspx?name=workaround

Aleccia, J. (2011). Nurse's suicide highlights twin tragedies of medical errors. Retrieved from http://www.msnbc.msn.com/id43529641/ns/health-health_care/#.Tm0By09A8j8

American Association of Colleges of Nursing. (2008). *The essentials of baccalaureate education for professional nursing practice.* Washington, DC: Author.

American Association of Colleges of Nursing. (2011). *The essentials of master's education in nursing.* Washington, DC: Author.

American Nurses Association. (1996). *Nursing quality indicators.* Washington, DC: American Nurses Publishing.

American Nurses Association. (2006a). *Assuring patient safety: The employers' role in promoting healthy nursing work hours for registered nurses in all roles and settings.* Silver Spring, MD: Author.

American Nurses Association. (2006b). *Assuring patient safety: Registered nurses' responsibility in all roles and setting to guard against working when fatigued.* Silver Spring, MD: Author.

American Nurses Association. (2009). *Nursing administration: Scope and standards of practice.* Silver Spring, MD: Author.

American Nurses Association. (2010). *Nursing scope and standards of practice.* Silver Spring, MD: Author.

American Nurses Association. (2013). *Patient handling and mobility: Interprofessional national standards.* Silver Spring, MD: Author.

American Nurses Association. (2015). National Center for Nursing Quality. Retrieved from http://www.nursingworld.org/ncnq

American Organization of Nurse Executives. (2005). Nurse executive competencies. Retrieved from http://www.aone.org/resources/leadership%20tools/nursecomp.shtml

American Society of Clinical Oncology & Oncology Nurses Society. (2013). ASCO-ONS standards for safe chemotherapy administration. Retrieved from http://www.asco.org/quality-guidelines/asco-ons-standards-safe-chemotherapy-administration

Association of Perioperative Registered Nurses. (2014). *Perioperative standards and recommended practices.* Denver, CO: Author.

Benner, P., Malloch, K., & Sheets, V. (2010). National Council of State Boards of Nursing Expert Panel on Practice Breakdown. *Nursing pathways for patient safety.* St. Louis, MO: Mosby Elsevier.

Berwick, D. (2008). The science of improvement. *JAMA, 299*(10), 1182–1184.

Boodman, S. (2011). Effort to end surgeries on wrong patient or body part falters. Retrieved from http://kaiserhealthnews.org/news/wrong-site-surgery-errors/

Centers for Disease Control and Prevention. (2014). Healthcare workers. Retrieved from http://www.cdc.gov/niosh/topics/healthcare/

Centers for Medicare & Medicaid Services. (2012). Background. Retrieved from http://www.cms.gov/Medicare/Quality-Initiatives-Patient-Assessment-Instruments/OASIS/Background.html

Chassin, M., & Galvin, R. (1998). The urgent need to improve healthcare quality. *Journal of the American Medical Association, 280*(2), 1000–1005.

Christmas, K. (2008). How work environment impacts retention. *Nursing Economics, 26*(5), 316–318.

Clarke, S., & Aiken, L. (2003). Failure to rescue. *American Journal of Nursing, 103*(1), 42–48.

Draper, D., Felland, L., Liebhaber, A., & Melichar, L. (2008, March). The role of nurses in hospital quality improvement. Retrieved from http://www.hschange.org/ CONTENT/972/?words=Draper

Dunton, N., & Montalvo, I. (2009). *Sustained improvements in nursing quality hospital performance on NDNQI indicators—2008.* Silver Spring, MD: American Nurses Association.

Fineberg, H. (2012). A successful and sustainable health system—how to get there from here. *New England Journal of Medicine, 366*, 1020–1027.

Hendrich, A., Chow, M., Skierczynski, B., & Zhenqiang, L. (2008). A 36-hospital time and motion study. How do medical-surgical nurses spend their time? *Permanente Journal, 12*(3).

Henneman, E., & Gawlinski, A. (2004). A "near-miss" model for describing the nurse's role in the recovery of medical errors. *Journal of Professional Nursing, 20*(3), 196–201.

Health IT Outcomes. (2014). Press Ganey® acquires national database of nursing quality indicators (NDNQI). http://www.healthitout comes.com/doc/press-ganey- acquires-national-database-nursing- quality-indicators-ndnqi-0001

Improvement Science Research Network. (2012). *Building successful research collaboratives for health- care improvement.* Retrieved from http://www.isrn.net/Research CollaborativeGuide

Improvement Science Research Network. (2014). What is the Improve- ment Science Research Network? Retrieved from http://www.isrn. net/about/what_is_isrn.asp

Institute for Healthcare Improvement. (2014a). About us. Retrieved from http://www.ihi.org/about/Pages/ default.aspx

Institute for Healthcare Improvement. (2014b). Failure modes and effects analysis (FMEA) tool. Retrieved from http://www.ihi. org/resources/Pages/Tools/ FailureModesandEffects AnalysisTool.aspx

Institute for Healthcare Improvement. (2014c). Science of improvement. Retrieved from http://www.ihi.org/ about/Pages/Scienceof Improvement.aspx

Institute for Healthcare Improvement. (2014d). TCAB projects. Retrieved from http://www.ihi.org/ search/pages/results.aspx?k=trans forming+care+at+bedside

Institute of Medicine. (1993). *Access to healthcare in America.* Washing- ton, DC: National Academies Press.

Institute of Medicine. (1999). *To err is human: Building a safer health system.* Washington, DC: National Academies Press.

Institute of Medicine. (2001). *Crossing the quality chasm. A new health sys- tem for the 21st century.* Washing- ton, DC: National Academies Press.

Institute of Medicine. (2004). *Keeping patients safe: Transforming the work environment of nurses.* Washington, DC: National Acad- emies Press.

Institute of Medicine. (2008). *Knowing what works in healthcare: A road- map for the nation.* Washington, DC: National Academies Press.

Institute of Medicine. (2011a). *Clinical practice guidelines we can trust.* Washington, DC: National Acad- emies Press.

Institute of Medicine. (2011b). *The future of nursing: Leading change, advancing health.* Wash- ington, DC: National Academies Press.

Interdisciplinary Nursing Quality Research Initiative. (2014). Pro- gram overview. Retrieved from http://www.inqri.org/about-inqri/ program-overview

Joint Commission. (2014). About the Joint Commission. Retrieved from http://www.jointcommission.org/ about_us/about_the_joint_com- mission_main.aspx

Kotter, J., & Rathgeber, H. (2006). *Our iceberg is melting: Changing and succeeding under any conditions.* New York, NY: St. Martin's Press.

Kovner, C., Brewer, C., Yingrengreung, S., & Fairchild, S. (2010). New nurses views of quality improve- ment. *Joint Commission Journal on Quality and Patient Safety, 36*, 29–35.

Montalvo, I., & Dunton, N. (2007). *Transforming nursing data into quality care: Profiles of quality improvement in U.S. healthcare facilities.* Silver Spring, MD: American Nurses Association.

National Council of State Boards of Nursing. (2014). Practice error and risk factors (TERCAP). Retrieved from https://www.ncsbn.org/113. htm

Pollard, P., Mitra, K., & Mendelson, D. (1996). *Nursing report card for acute care.* Silver Spring, MD: American Nurses Association.

Press Ganey®. (2014a). NDNQI. http:// www.pressganey.com/resources/ ndnqi

Press Ganey®. (2014b). Turn nursing quality into improved patient experiences. http://pressganey. com/ourSolutions/performance- and-advanced-analytics/clinical- business-performance/ nursing-quality-ndnqi

QSEN Institute. (2014). Quality and Safety Education for Nurses (QSEN). Retrieved from http:// qsen.org/

Reason, J. (2000). Human error: Mod- els and management. *British Med- ical Journal, 320*(7237), 768–770.

Richter, J., McAlearney, A., & Pennell, M. (2014a, July–September). The influence of organizational factors on patient safety: Examining suc- cessful handoffs in healthcare. *Healthcare Management Review, 3.*

Richter, J., McAlearney, A., & Pennell, M. (2014b, July 28). Evaluating the effect of safety culture on error reporting: A comparison of mana- gerial and staff perspectives. *American Journal of Medical Quality, 25*(4).

Rutherford, P., Lee, B., & Greiner, A. (2004). *Transforming Care at the Bedside.* IHI Innovation Series white paper. Boston, MA: Institute for Healthcare Improvement. Retrieved from http://www.ihi.org/ resources/Pages/IHIWhitePapers/ TransformingCareattheBedside- WhitePaper.aspx

Six Sigma. (2014). What is Six Sigma? Retrieved from http://www.isix- sigma.com/new-to-six-sigma/ getting-started/what-six-sigma/

U.S. Department of Health and Human Services. (2014). *Healthy People 2020.* Retrieved http://www. healthypeople.gov

Vincent, C. (2003). Understanding and responding to adverse events. *New England Journal of Medicine, 348*(11), 1051–1056.

19 Healthcare Informatics and Technology

⬛ LEARNING OUTCOMES

Before you begin, take a moment to familiarize yourself with the learning outcomes for this chapter.

> Discuss current issues related to and influencing health informatics.
> Discuss the impact of informatics and technology on caring.
> Examine critical issues related to privacy and confidentiality in informatics.
> Examine meaningful use and its relationship to health informatics.
> Analyze the current status of the electronic medical record and other associated health information technology methods and the role of the nurse informaticist.
> Critique the implications of health informatics and medical technology to nursing practice and health care focusing on practice, management, nursing education, patient education, nursing research, quality improvement, and reimbursement.
> Examine current governmental initiatives to improve health informatics.

KEY TERMS

- algorithms
- emeasurement
- meaningful use
- protocols
- telehealth
- telenursing

WHAT'S AHEAD

The continued expansion of health information technology (HIT) offers important opportunities for nursing education, practice, research, and management. For nurses to participate in the technology revolution, whether as a staff nurse or in a management position, they need to be knowledgeable about HIT, appreciate the implications of its use, develop the required skills and competencies, and apply them to practice and management. This chapter discusses critical technology issues and their implications for healthcare practice and management.

IMPORTANCE OF INFORMATION AND CLINICAL TECHNOLOGY

The explosion of information and technology has brought the healthcare delivery system into a new era, which has allowed health care to expand into new areas and to improve others. Information and technology have affected clinical practice, communication, structure of organizations, consumers, workforce issues, quality care issues and outcomes, costs and reimbursement, and ethical and legal concerns.

Important Initiatives and Issues Related to Healthcare Informatics and Technology

The Institute of Medicine (IOM) reports about the healthcare system recognize the critical role that HIT has in the healthcare delivery system and will have in the future. The clearest indication of its importance is the inclusion of HIT in the five core competencies for healthcare professions. This competency is described as "Utilize informatics to communicate, manage knowledge, mitigate error, and support decision making using information technology" (2003, p. 4). Every healthcare professional should meet the following requirements:

- Employ word processing, presentation, and data analysis software.
- Search, retrieve, manage, and make decisions using electronic data from internal information databases and external online databases and the Internet.
- Communicate using email, instant messaging, listservs, and file transfers.
- Understand security protections such as access control, data security, and data encryption, and directly address ethical and legal issues related to the use of information technology in practice.
- Enhance education and access to reliable health information for patients (Institute of Medicine, 2003, p. 63).

The report discusses the use of informatics to reduce errors and thus improve care. Some of the methods used to do this are discussed later in this chapter. Healthcare providers can more easily manage knowledge and information needed to provide evidence-based practice (EBP), allowing them to access professional literature. Computerized databases provide greater collection and analysis of data and lead to more effective use of data in practice and research. The IOM also notes that computerized decision-making support systems are effective in improving care. Clearly communication can be more effective and timely by using email, accessing electronic medical/health records (EMRs/EHRs), healthcare organization (HCO) Internet sites, the Internet in general, and by other electronic means of communication (Institute of Medicine, 2003).

The Affordable Care Act of 2010 (ACA) includes provisions about health informatics. For example, there is increased support for and recognition that care delivery needs to improve. Data collection, analysis, and maintaining data over time are critical aspects of improving care. The increased focus on patient-centered care means information needs to be available to patients. The drive to increase community-based care and interprofessional teams indicates there is need for greater efficiency and sharing accurate patient and other healthcare delivery information (e.g., accountable care organizations). The establishment of the Patient-Centered Outcomes Research Institute (PCORI) with its focus on quality improvement and need to provide evidence to support effective care outcomes requires use of informatics. Even citizens who are enrolling in the new healthcare insurance plans are enrolling via the Internet. The law requires that the insurance comparison information is available to consumers online. The ACA also has provisions related to healthcare fraud, and to meet the need to decrease fraud, informatics will be used to track data and problems. The EMR/EHR now makes it easier to track patient information.

In 2002 the American Nurses Association (ANA) held a conference that focused on technology innovation in health care, emphasizing the need for nursing to become engaged in the changes that were quickly altering many aspects of health care. Since that time, information technology has greatly expanded in all sectors, including health care. There is much known and unknown about the implications of a technologically driven environment. At the same time that technology and information are surging forward, there is concern about healthcare quality. In 2010 the ACA was passed, which has had an impact on access to care via improved reimbursement for many who did not have healthcare insurance in the past. Health information technology might be viewed as a possible method for helping to cope with the staff shortage, such as using more effective documentation methods to reduce staff time needed for documentation. Many examples that may make a difference or at least make healthcare delivery more efficient and effective are described in this chapter. Technology may be one of these factors.

In 2001 the ANA published the first nursing informatics standards, indicating that this specialty was now officially part of the nursing profession. Nursing informatics is the "science and practice [that] integrates nursing science, computer science, and information science to manage and communicate data, information, knowledge, and wisdom in nursing practice" (American Nurses Association, 2014, p. 1).

Since 2004, the Healthcare Information and Management Systems Society (HIMSS) has surveyed nurses who hold informatics positions. The 2014 Nursing Informatics Workforce Survey indicates the following (Healthcare Information and Management Systems Society, 2014):

- Nurses are involved in development, implementation, and optimization of clinical applications including nursing clinical documentation, computerized practitioner order entry (CPOE), and electronic medical/health records (EMRs/EHRs).
- Compared to 2011, the 2014 survey indicated that there was an increase of 19% of nurses with a postgraduate degree in any field, and a 24% increase in the number of nurses with postgraduate degrees working in informatics.
- Forty-three percent of the nurses in the survey planned on continuing their education in informatics.
- More than half indicated they would pursue certification in informatics within the next year.
- There was only a 2% increase in salaries from 2011 to 2014, whereas from 2007 to 2011, there had been a 17% increase.
- The top barriers to success for nurse informaticists were lack of administrative support and lack of staffing resources.

The Future of Nursing report (Institute of Medicine, 2011) has had an impact on many aspects of healthcare delivery and healthcare policy. The HIMSS issued a position statement that focused on this IOM nursing report (2011). The HIMSS integrates the IOM nursing report key concerns of leadership, education, and practice in the HIMSS recommendations:

- Partner with nurse executives to lead technology changes that advance health and the delivery of health care.
- Support the development of informatics departments.
- Foster the evolution of the chief nursing informatics (NI) role.
- Transform nursing education to include informatics competencies and demonstrable behaviors at all levels of academic preparation.
- Promote the continuing education of all levels of nursing, particularly in the areas of electronic health records and HIT.
- Ensure that data, information, knowledge, and wisdom form the basis of 21st-century nursing practice by incorporating informatics competencies into practice standards in all healthcare settings.
- Facilitate the collection and analysis of interprofessional healthcare workforce data by ensuring data can be collected from existing IT systems.

Technology and Caring

Even though there are many positive aspects of information technology, some drawbacks exist that need to be considered as healthcare organizations (HCOs) incorporate more IT. It is particularly important for healthcare providers to consider the total impact of technology on practice and organizations and connecting with others. Emotional intelligence leadership, which was discussed in Chapter 1, has become more important in HCOs with staff members tuning in more to their emotions and reactions, how these emotions and reactions affect others, and making changes in behavior to improve relationships and communications. Technology may interfere with this process. Talking through "machines" limits real observations and emotional connections. Does it increase isolation? Does it prevent honest communication? If it does, then it is important to try to figure out ways to prevent these problems. Advancement of technologies is not going away, so it is important to use it effectively. Staff experience this at work and in their personal lives.

Patients need providers who are connected to them, understand the emotional side of health care, and use the power of human interaction. The goal should not be to throw out or ignore information technology but rather to be aware of potential problems and build in methods to maintain personal connection with patients. It is also important to note that this feeling of isolationism can occur with staff. Despite these concerns, health care requires the use of IT. Information technology cannot be separated from knowledge expansion. With so much increasing knowledge, how can one keep up? Healthcare organizations now need clinical decision support tools and information systems more than ever. This is very costly for HCOs to maintain HIT and care technology and invest in their improvement to ensure that the HCO is current and provides best practice. In addition, insurers and accrediting organizations demand more and more data to demonstrate outcomes. The nursing profession needs to appreciate the importance of data and how best to use data. HIT provides much data about health care, including nursing, and tapping in to the data to better understand both the impact of nursing care on patient outcomes and the cost of care can benefit nursing.

Informatics: Terminology and Standardized Language

Computer literacy, or the knowledge and skills needed to use basic computer applications and computer technology, is a required competency today. For most people, this is not a major issue anymore since so many people have integrated computers and other associated technology into their daily lives. Information literacy is the ability to recognize when information is needed and to locate, evaluate, and effectively use that information (American Nurses Association, 2014). Nurses do need more information and experience doing this. With the explosion of information—data, literature, research results, EBP—information literacy is critical. Some of the informatic terms that may be new to nurses are as follows:

- *Data*: Discrete entities described objectively without interpretation.
- *Databank*: A large store of information; may include several databases.
- *Database*: Systematically arranged data in a computer; can be retrieved and manipulated often for analysis purposes.
- *Data Mining*: Locating and identifying unknown patterns and relationships within data.
- *Data Analysis Software*: Computer software that can analyze data.
- *Software*: Computer programs and applications.
- *Security protections* (access control, data security, and data encryption): Methods used to ensure that information is not read or taken by persons not authorized to access the information.
- *Clinical Information System (CIS)*: Clinical information systems support the acquisition, storage, manipulation, and distribution of clinical information throughout an HCO with a focus on electronic communication, for example, electronic medical records, clinical data repositories, decision support programs (such as application of clinical guidelines and drug interaction checking), handheld devices for collecting data and viewing reference material, imaging modalities, and communication tools such as electronic messaging systems.
- *Clinical Data Repository*: This type of system stores longitudinal clinical data, collecting data from multiple clinical information systems, including patient demographic data. Data can be used to improve patient care, in research, for education purposes, and to assist with clinical decision making.
- *Decision Support Systems*: Computer applications designed to facilitate human decision making. Decision support systems are typically rules based. They use a knowledge base and a set of rules to analyze data and information and provide recommendations (American Nurses Association, 2014).

Standardized language is a collection of terms with definitions for use in informational systems databases. This enables comparisons to be made because the same term is used to denote the same condition. Standardized language is necessary for documentation in electronic health records (American Nurses Association, 2014). This is a difficult issue today as healthcare providers often use terminology that is specific to their professions. Nursing has persisted in doing this with the emphasis on the North America Nursing Diagnosis Association (NANDA®), Nursing Intervention Classification (NIC®), and Nursing Outcome Classification (NOC®), which are terminology systems that focus on nursing diagnoses, interventions, and outcomes. They are commonly used in nursing education, yet there is not widespread use in clinical practice. This is confusing for nursing students who might learn this terminology then enter a workplace where it may or may not be used. When it is used in practice, other healthcare professionals, particularly physicians, have no idea what it means. "Creating a common language is no small task. Developing and adhering to distinct profession-specific terms may be a manifestation of professionals' desire to preserve identity, status or control" (Institute of Medicine, 2003, p. 123). All of the National Academy of Medicine (NAM) core competencies are related to communication, and if there is a problem such as with terminology, then patient care is affected. The IOM recommended that an interprofessional group, created by the Department of Health and Human Services (HHS), develop a common language across health disciplines "on a core set of competencies that includes patient-centered care, interprofessional teams, evidence-based practice, quality improvement, and informatics" (2003, p. 124). This will not be easy to achieve and to this date has not been done. It requires compromises among healthcare providers. This also has an impact on EMR/EHR use; standardized terminology is required. There has been movement on the state level, though slow, to make these changes. In April 2014 Minnesota's e-health initiative recommended the use of the ANA's approved standardized nursing terminologies in the EMRs/EHRs for all healthcare settings (American Medical Informatics Association, 2014). Minnesota has long been supportive of nursing terminologies; for example, it uses the Omaha System in community-based settings in almost all counties.

A minimum data set is the fewest categories of data with uniform definitions and categories concerning a specific aspect or dimension of the healthcare system that meets the basic needs of multiple data users. Examples are the nursing minimum data set (NMDS) and the Nursing Management Minimum Data Set (NMMDS) (University of Minnesota Center for Nursing Informatics, 2015). The NMMDS describes patient problems across healthcare settings, different populations, geographic areas, and time. These clinical data also assist in identifying nursing diagnoses, nursing interventions, and nurse-sensitive patient outcomes. This is also useful in assessing resources used in the provision of nursing care. The goal is to be able to link data among HCOs and providers. Data can also be used for research and healthcare policy. The NMMDS focuses on nursing administrative data elements in all types of settings.

There are some other data sets. The International Classification of Nursing Practice (ICNP®) is a unified nursing language system applicable to all types of nursing care. It includes nursing diagnoses, nursing interventions, and nursing outcomes (International Council of Nurses, 2015). The Omaha System is a comprehensive and standardized taxonomy designed to improve practice, documentation, and information management in home health care and community and public health (Omaha System, 2005). The Perioperative Nursing Data Set (PNDS) is a standardized nursing vocabulary that addresses the perioperative patient experience from preadmission until discharge, including nursing diagnoses, interventions, and outcomes (Association of Perioperative Registered Nurses, 2008). There are some terminology systems that cross multiple healthcare professions, such as the Systematic Nomenclature of Medicine Clinical Terms (SNOMED CT®). More of these systems are needed in the future. SNOMED CT® is a comprehensive clinical terminology recognized by the federal government systems for the electronic exchange of clinical health information (U.S. National Library of Medicine, 2008).

Information Technology: Challenges

Given the age of technology and immense amount of available information, staff members want information that is essential to them, thus several issues become important, particularly privacy and confidentiality, nursing informatics specialty, and nursing administration and informatics.

PRIVACY AND CONFIDENTIALITY   The 1996 Health Insurance Portability and Accountability Act (HIPAA) has had major effects on HIT. First, the law mandates that there be a standardized method for insurance companies and physicians to reduce overhead and increase the payment time for patient care, but this must be done in a manner that ensures patient privacy. Privacy and confidentiality have long been issues in health care, and HIT developed with little control of privacy and confidentiality. This law, however, has had an effect on HIT. Chapter 2 contains additional content about this law and recent changes. This law requires HCOs of all types to meet certain requirements to better ensure patient privacy and confidentiality. Table 19-1 identifies critical patient identifiers related to HIPAA.

MEANINGFUL USE   As part of the ACA legislation, the Office of the National Coordinator for Health Information Technology and CMS issued new rules identifying criteria that HCOs and eligible providers must meet to be considered meaningful users of health IT (U.S. Department of Health and Human Services, Centers for Medicare & Medicaid Services, 2010). What is meaningful use? **Meaningful use** involves using certified electronic health record technology for the following purposes. The

Table 19-1	HEALTH INSURANCE PORTABILITY AND ACCOUNTABILITY ACT (HIPAA) 18 PATIENT IDENTIFIERS

1) Names
2) All geographic subdivisions smaller than a state, except for the initial 3 digits of the ZIP code if the geographic unit formed by combining all ZIP codes with the same initial 3 digits contains more than 20,000 people
3) All elements of dates, except year, and all ages over 89 or elements indicative of such age
4) Telephone numbers
5) Fax numbers
6) Email addresses
7) Social Security numbers
8) Medical record numbers
9) Health plan beneficiary numbers
10) Account numbers
11) Certificate or license numbers
12) Vehicle identifiers and license plate numbers
13) Device identifiers and serial numbers
14) URLs
15) IP addresses
16) Biometric identifiers
17) Full-face photographs and any comparable images
18) Any other unique, identifying characteristic or code, except as permitted for reidentification in the Privacy Rule

Source: Adapted from the U.S. Department of Health and Human Services. (2015). Health information privacy. Retrieved from http://www.hhs.gov/ocr/privacy/hipaa/understanding/coveredentities/De-identification/guidance.html

following are identified as the three components of meaningful use (U.S. Department of Health and Human Services, Centers for Medicare & Medicaid Services, 2014):

- Use of certified EMR/EHR in a meaningful manner (e.g., e-prescribing)
- Use of certified EMR/EHR technology for electronic exchange of health information to improve quality of health care
- Use of certified EMR/EHR technology to submit clinical quality measures (CQM) and other such measures selected by the secretary of HHS

Why is it important to have meaningful use rules? The purposes of the federal government meaningful rules are:

1. to improve quality, safety, and efficiency and to reduce health disparities.
2. to engage patients and their families (through electronic communication).
3. to improve care coordination.
4. to ensure adequate privacy and security protection for personal health information.
5. to improve the health of the population as well as public health through data collection and analysis of data.

HCOs and eligible providers may not receive federal funding (CMS reimbursement) related to the EMR/EHR initiative unless they meet the meaningful use requirements. Most hospitals receive

CMS reimbursement as Medicare patients represent a significant proportion of the inpatient population. Nurse leaders and managers need to understand the meaningful use criteria and participate in their application.

DEVELOPMENT, IMPLEMENTATION, AND EVALUATION OF THE CLINICAL INFORMATION SYSTEM   It is difficult to find an HCO that is not using or evaluating for use some type of clinical information system. Some systems have been more effective than others. Making decisions about these clinical information systems is a complex process requiring input from many staff throughout an HCO. Selecting the right system is not easy. It is also a very costly decision. After the selection, staff require training and time to adjust.

As these issues are considered, the HCO needs to review such factors as the role of nurses. Will nurses be able to access the HIT system for documentation, to obtain clinical resource information, email, and so on? Will physician orders be covered by the system, which has an impact on nursing? Will the HIT system become integral to all aspects of the HCO? How will staff have input into the design of the system? These are only a few of the considerations that have an impact on healthcare HIT systems.

Nursing Informatics Specialty

There is a nursing specialty that focuses on HIT.

> Nursing informatics (NI) is a specialty that integrates nursing science, computer science, and information science to manage and communicate data, information, knowledge, and wisdom in nursing practice. NI supports consumers, patients, nurses, and other providers in their decision making in all roles and settings. This support is accomplished through the use of information structures, information processes, and information technology. The goal of NI is to improve the health of populations, communities, families, and individuals by optimizing information management and communication. (American Nurses Association, 2014)

It is important for all nurses to understand the importance of data collection and data analysis then know how to apply data and knowledge to improve patient care. NI specialty certification is available through the American Nurses Credentialing Center (ANCC). These nurses hold positions in clinical practice, education, consultation, research, administration, and informatic businesses. They also provide guidance and leadership in the development, implementation, and evaluation of HIT and assist in staff education about HIT.

Certification is available for nursing informatics from the ANCC (2014). The ANCC website provides details about the requirements. Nurses who apply must be registered nurses, have practiced for equivalent of two years full time, hold a baccalaureate or higher degree in nursing or in another relevant field, have completed 30 hours of continuing education within the past three years, and meet the practice requirements noted on the ANCC website. After successful completion of the certification exam, the RN is certified in nurse informatics for a specified period of time. Nurse leaders who want to establish nurse informatics positions should include the requirement of an academic degree in informatics and certification.

Nursing Management and Informatics

All levels of nursing administration need to play a major role in all aspects of HIT within a healthcare organization. The American Organization of Nurse Executives (AONE) states, "Technology is recognized as a key lever within the system of healthcare delivery. It has the unique capacity to either reduce or increase workload demand. Creating appropriate balance and/or impact is a critical role for leadership" (2009, p. 1). The chief nurse executive (CNE) must assume leadership, along with other leaders in the HCO, in the process to select and implement information systems for the healthcare organization. It is not easy to acquire information systems (American Organization of Nurse Executives, 2007). If nursing leadership is not actively involved, the result can have a very negative impact on patient care and nurses. Nurse managers are directly involved daily in HIT, particularly in HCOs that use an EMR/EHR. Active nurse participation in reviewing EMR/EHR systems, evaluation of process and implementation, staff training, and long-term evaluation of the EMR/EHR is critical to successful transition to the EMR/EHR. A transition to an EMR/EHR will inevitably encounter some problems. If nurses are not actively involved, the problems will be greater. In addition, as noted in the chapter on change, staff who are involved in the change process will have more buy-in, and the change will be more effective. Figure 19-1 provides information about the impact of information technology on nursing practice challenges.

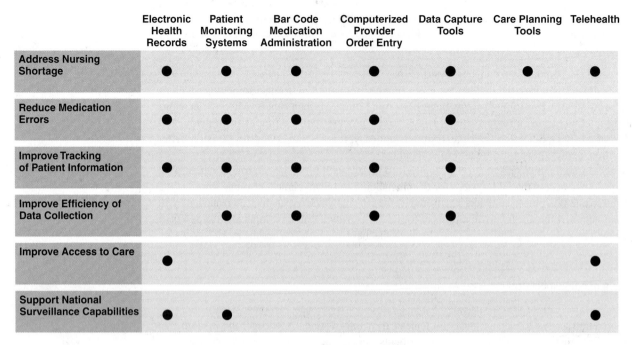

Figure 19-1 Information technology to address nursing practice challenges

Source: National Advisory Council on Nurse Education and Practice. U.S. Department of Health and Human Services. (2009). *Challenges facing the nurse workforce in a changing environment. Part II: Information technology in nursing education and practice*. Washington, DC: Author.

INFORMATICS AND MEDICAL TECHNOLOGY: IMPLICATIONS ON HEALTHCARE DELIVERY

Technology is more than just HIT. It also includes medical technology that can be applied in clinical care, education, and research. The following discussion provides some information about the impact that technology has had and will continue to have on various aspects of healthcare delivery.

Virtual Health: Telehealth

Telehealth is the use of telecommunications equipment and communications networks for transferring healthcare information among participants at different locations. This technology offers opportunities to provide care when face-to-face interaction is impossible. Telehealth applies telecommunication and computer technologies to the broad spectrum of public health and medicine. In addition, it provides many opportunities for consumer health informatics. (See Chapter 10.) The future holds more opportunity for telehealth due to the following ongoing changes in healthcare delivery:

- A shift from a predominately rural focus to the provision of home health care and school-based health care in the inner city
- The movement from a preoccupation with acquisition and transport of information to an emphasis on the quality of the information being transmitted
- A switch from a practitioner-based healthcare system to a patient-empowered and preventive healthcare system, and in turn, from a patient-based system to a consumer-oriented system (Dakins, 2002, p. 14)

The most successful telehealth systems employ a variety of telecommunication modalities including two-way interactive video consultations, teleradiology, and telepathology that link primary care providers in rural areas or inner city clinics to experts in large, tertiary centers. Virtual environments for healthcare delivery and education have been made possible by the same advances in technology that have given us lifelike, computerized video games, and military robotic medics. (Predko, 2001)

The critical factor with effective telehealth is the ability of healthcare providers such as the nurse to envision innovative and practical ways to apply the technology to clinical practice and healthcare management. When it is applied, safety and quality must always be addressed and monitored.

Standards have been developed for most nursing specialties, and telehealth nursing is no exception. The American Academy of Ambulatory Care Nursing (AAACN) developed some of these standards because "Telehealth nursing has been identified as one of the new and exciting areas of interest and specialty in ambulatory care nursing" (American Academy of Ambulatory Care Nursing, Telehealth Nursing Practice Task Force, 2001, p. 7). The AAACN recognized that telehealth nursing is an evolving specialty that requires standards. As has been stated by many experts, this area of health care directly affects consumers/patients and the organization's effectiveness. The AAACN definition of telehealth nursing practice describes it as "Nursing practice using the nursing process to provide care for individual patients or defined patient populations through telecommunications media. Telehealth nursing practice occurs in many different healthcare settings" (American Academy of Ambulatory Care Nursing, Telehealth Nursing Practice Task Force, 2001, p. 1). Critical criteria for telehealth nursing practice include the following:

- Using protocols, algorithms, or guidelines to systematically assess and address patient needs.
- Prioritizing the urgency of patient needs.
- Developing a collaborative plan of care with the patient and the patient's support systems. The plan of care may include wellness promotion, prevention education, advice for care counseling, disease state management, and care coordination.
- Evaluating outcomes of practice and care.

Prioritizing, developing plans of care, and outcome evaluation are typical concerns for nurses. The nurse who provides **telenursing** uses a variety of tools such as protocols, algorithms, and guidelines to guide clinical decisions (American Academy of Ambulatory Care Nursing, Telehealth Nursing Practice Task Force, 2001). For example, patients who call a nurse telephone advice line that is offered to insurance plan members would consult specific protocols, algorithms, or guidelines for questions regarding cardiac, diabetic, or obstetrical concerns. All of these represent standards related to providing care by using technology. **Protocols** define the ongoing care or management of a broad problem or issue in six areas:

1. Assessment/data collection/caller interview process
2. Classification/determination of acuity
3. Nature/type/degree of advice/intervention/direction to the caller
4. Information/education of the caller
5. Validation of patient understanding/verbal contracting
6. Evaluation/follow-up/effectiveness of advice or intervention

A protocol directs the advice/triage/education/counseling process, assisting in the organization of large amounts of significant information in priority order. It helps show the interrelationship of data, forcing consideration of all possible or likely decision choices and directs decision making based on data. **Algorithms** are written clinical questions using branch chain logic (flowchart). An algorithm prescribes what steps to take given particular circumstances or characteristics. Some algorithms also include designated points in the decision-making process where healthcare providers such as the nurse need to discuss patient's preferences for particular options. Algorithms rely on the nurse's ability to analyze and interpret patient responses to clinical questions. Guidelines are typically a more narrative description of assessment steps that includes education and counseling text to support the nurse during the call.

Costs need to be considered for all changes in health care, and the use of technology is no exception. There needs to be careful cost-benefit analysis when decisions are made to use technology. Telehealth is less costly than more traditional methods of practice if one considers staffing and time required, and it can be a cost-effective means of delivering health care. It is clear that there needs to be more research about this topic. Individual healthcare providers (e.g., physician offices, clinics, hospitals, home health care agencies, and long-term care facilities) should do their own cost-benefit analyses before decisions are made about using information technology and telehealth technologies. It is important to avoid jumping on the bandwagon when a strategy appears new and exciting. It may offer much to patient care, but this needs careful analysis. If there is to be effective use of technology, barriers need to be assessed. The most critical barrier is a lack of reimbursement or limited reimbursement for these services. The inclusion of this content in nursing education, continuing education, and nursing research focused on this area of practice would help to lower the barriers and increase understanding of its use.

Mobile Technology and Communication

Many HCOs and healthcare providers use mobile technology today for communication with each other and with patients. This type of technology provides rapid access and in some cases can be a burden if too many calls and messages come in. Individuals need to determine what can be handled and set limits. For example, is it more efficient to return messages/calls as they come in or establish a time during the day to do this activity? Nurse managers can be overwhelmed. When smartphones are used, emails and text messages are also used, increasing the demand to respond quickly. As is true with any method of communication, HIPAA regulations need to be considered to ensure privacy and confidentiality. Nurse managers need to consider the situations when person-to-person communication is best. Even though mobile technology might seem a faster form of communication, it is not always the best method.

Social Media: Risks and HIPAA

With the growth of multiple social media methods such as Facebook®, LinkedIn®, and many others, it is important to remind all staff that care must be taken in what is shared to maintain confidentiality and patient privacy. Information that should not be shared includes details about patients, information about the HCO and its activities, details that would include other staff names, and so on. This also includes photographs. Some of the information may seem innocent—such as posting photographs of a staff birthday—but not when that staff person does not want her photograph or details about her birthday posted. Today it is very easy for people to assume that most information may be shared. If healthcare profession students use the HCO for clinical experiences, they need to also be reminded of the limits.

HIT and Medical Technology: Implications for Clinical Practice

The following are examples of clinical applications of new technology.

Automated medication administration: With increased data indicating that medication errors are an important factor in patient complications and deaths, there is more interest in medication administration methods that might decrease this risk (Institute of Medicine, 1999). Bar coding is also useful in collecting data about medication administration that can be used to improve care. The Institute for Safe Medication Practices (ISMP) strongly supports bar coding, and the FDA proposed legislation that required bar codes (Roark, 2004).

Unit-dose systems: This system provides individual prepackaged doses. This improves patient care by allowing the nurse to safely identify dose and medication without using multiple dose systems. The medication is prepared in single doses for the patient. When this is combined with the bar coding system, the nurse can check the bar code on the unit dose with the nurse's name and the patient's identification. As with any system, for it to work effectively, the nurse needs to follow the required procedure.

Point-of-care clinical documentation systems: This system brings documentation to the patient where care is provided, reducing errors and increasing timely documentation, and is directly connected to patient-centered care. There is less chance that the nurse will forget to document an activity or will document it incompletely. Using an EMR/EHR with point-of-care capability also saves time and improves coordination of care.

Professional order entry system (POES): This type of system is often found in HCOs today. Physicians and other healthcare professionals who write patient care orders enter their orders into the computer rather than on a hard copy of the medical record. This has much to offer patient care and nurses. Orders are legible, which helps, as illegibility is a major problem with medical records. Most computer systems alert providers to errors, conflicts such as drug incompatibilities, and allergies. Providers can be notified when orders need to be reviewed or renewed. This also decreases the need for the nurse to be the "policeman" and remind providers about orders. How does this help nurses? Time is saved when less time is spent following up on orders and setting up possible interprofessional conflicts. Nurses can feel more confident that the orders are correct. Errors can be decreased—physician errors when orders are incorrect and nurse errors when orders are not transcribed correctly as is required in a paper record and when orders are followed incorrectly because the orders were not clear and so on. The medical records become interactive due to these alerts, communicating when something might be wrong or something needs to be done.

Electronic medical record (EMR/EHR): With use of EMRs/EHRs, data are available when needed with less dependence on memory, which improves clinical decision making. This type of documentation reduces dependence on paper and storage needs and decreases documentation time. The record is easier to read. Staff access to the record can occur with more ease. The problem of lost records will be a thing of the past; however, when a computer system goes down, this is a major crisis. EMRs/EHRs require backup systems. It also requires expert support services to maintain the system, respond to problems, and train staff. The software and hardware need to be kept up to date, and this is costly for the HCO.

Clinical decision support: Clinical decision support (CDS) provides clinicians, staff, patients or other individuals with knowledge and person-specific information, intelligently filtered or presented at appropriate times, to enhance health and healthcare. CDS encompasses a variety of tools to enhance decision-making in the clinical workflow. These tools include computerized alerts and reminders to care providers and patients; clinical guidelines; condition-specific order sets; focused patient data reports and summaries; documentation templates; diagnostic support, and contextually relevant reference information, among other tools. (HealthIT.gov, 2014b)

Nurses are very involved in CDS if it is integrated into the EMR/EHR. This support should assist in increasing quality of care, meeting outcomes, decreasing errors and adverse events, improving efficiency, controlling costs, and improving provider and patient satisfaction.

Accelerated health information exchange: Accelerated health information exchange (HIE) is an important part of the U.S. Department of Health and Human Services effort to change healthcare delivery into a patient-centered and value-based system. This is supported by the extensive IOM reports on health care and the ACA. "Critical to the success of these programs and the ultimate goal of a transformed healthcare system is real-time interoperable health information exchange (HIE) among a variety of healthcare stakeholders: clinicians, lab, hospital, pharmacy, health plans, payers and patient. Greater access to patient-level health information is integral to improving the quality, efficiency, and safety of healthcare delivery" (HealthIT.gov, 2014a). This will not be easy to accomplish. For example, interoperability includes two steps: (1) the ability to *exchange* information and (2) the ability to *use* the information that has been exchanged. This is also connected to meaningful use.

"Smart" administration pump: This technology offers a method to administer fluids and medications and at the same time monitor the patient at the bedside for errors (Kerfoot & Simpson, 2002). As time is always important in direct care, it is critical that the equipment maintenance and repair are monitored to ensure safe care.

Pharmacy system: This system provides computerized pharmacy orders, checking, and dispensing, as well as online documentation. (Bar coding may be part of the system.) Online reference systems are also often included in this type of system, allowing for application of evidence-based knowledge (Kerfoot & Simpson, 2002).

Remote telemetry monitoring: This technology allows nurses to receive pages or provides a page alarm that notifies the nurse of the patient's identification and heart rate and provides a readout of the patient's rhythm (Reilly & Humbrecht, 2015). The nurse can then evaluate the patient's condition and take appropriate action. Some examples where it might be used are ECG monitoring and fetal monitoring.

Medical email: Physicians, other healthcare providers, and HCOs are using email more and more to communicate with their patients. This requires the patient's approval and information about the patient's email address. However, careful attention has to be paid to patient privacy issues. Advanced practice registered nurses may also find this to be a useful communication tool. There may, however, be concern that some patients may abuse this communication method, and they may also expect providers to respond quickly. In reality this concern does not seem to be an actual problem. Some providers are using this method for select patients who send the provider daily, weekly, or monthly monitoring data so the provider can get a better picture of a problem. Messages need to be clear as misinterpretation or misunderstandings are risks. Email does offer a paper trail, documenting what has been told to patients, which can be helpful and decreases communication confusion. Whether or not the system has a Web-based, secure message system is of critical concern, and this should be noted on all messages. Since some people in a family share the same email address, this has a direct implication for confidentiality.

Handheld communication systems: There is more and more software for handheld devices such as tablets and smartphones that allow staff to get information quickly when they need it. Now some of this is available through smartphones so the person has to carry only one device. Staff can document and search for medical information, search for information about current drugs or lab tests, communicate with others, monitor patient information, and make work-planning notes. These systems are gradually replacing note pads. Some systems have photograph options, which could be used to document visual data; however, HIPAA is critical and staff must be careful about taking photographs. At this time, some of these systems can be expensive, although prices are decreasing. Most organizations do not provide them for their staff, but some are doing this as they see value in improving communication and access to information when needed by staff. These devices are also helpful to patients, providing options to improve self-management. For example, apps have been developed to monitor exercise, diet, and so on, providing easy monitoring options for individuals on their smartphones and tablets, even on a watch.

Internet prescription: A patient can now go on the Internet and obtain prescribed drugs. There are great safety and legal risks with this practice. "People get deals on shoes, travel, and appliances online. Why not prescription drugs? You can find lower prices and convenience through mail-order or online pharmacies. Just be careful. 'Rogue' pharmacies use the Internet to market counterfeit drugs. You could end up with something that doesn't treat your condition and could harm your health" (Robinson, 2012). The National Board of Pharmacies conducted a review of 8,000 online pharmacies and found that only 4% met its safety standards. Consumers need to get their drugs through reliable Internet sites and consider if the pharmacy has a U.S. location and license, is a verified Internet pharmacy practice site (VIPPS), requires a prescription, and has real people on the telephone (Robinson, 2012).

Home health and HIT and medical technology: What is happening in this healthcare setting? Web-based programs for patient monitoring and interactive video-based programs are expanding. Congestive heart disease, diabetes, and coronary disease are the three conditions that have been focused on when these services have been developed. They are chronic illnesses that, if managed well, can reduce healthcare costs with positive patient outcomes. Many personal monitoring devices related to chronic diseases are either available or in development. Examples of these devices include "a monitor in the bathroom shower that scans for signs of melanoma; a wristwatch-like device that constantly checks pulse, respiration, and temperature; computerized eyeglasses that jog a failing memory with whispered cues; and a 'smart badge' that senses a developing infection and identifies the antibiotic need" (Predko, 2001, p. 79). There has been an expansion of disease management for chronic illnesses, and with this comes the need for greater patient education, self-management, and monitoring methods. Telehealth offers many options to meet these requirements. Home health also is increasing its use of IT for documentation, with many agencies providing nurses with computers that can be used in the home and on the road. Cellular telephones are clearly a major benefit to home health nurses to keep in touch with patients, with home office, and for emergencies.

Informatics: Implications for Nursing Education

Information technology and telehealth certainly have implications for nursing education. Students expect greater use of IT as they use it more in their personal lives. Tools such as Facebook® and Twitter®, and mobile telephones can provide instant information and can also be very interactive. These methods can be used to increase student-faculty communication and have the potential to provide different methods for student-faculty supervision in the clinical area. This is particularly true in areas such as community health when students are in multiple sites with faculty moving from site to site to see students. This whole area is changing the face of learning and education at all levels. Teaching is moving more and more to facilitation of learning. This movement can be seen in the rapid and solid growth of online courses and degree programs, ebooks, increased use of the Web to post course documents, use of email to communicate with students, and video access via university websites. IT also means that there are more and more opportunities for

CASE STUDY

EMR/EHR: Can It Improve Care and Work?

Your hospital implemented an electronic medical record (EMR/EHR) six months ago. An interprofessional task force has been formed including representatives and management from nursing, medicine, informatics, hospital administration, finance, quality improvement, admissions, case management, and the policy and procedure committee. The purpose of the task force is to assess the current status of the project and to determine interventions that might be needed at this point. A nursing staff survey indicates that 60% are satisfied, and a physician survey indicates that 48% are satisfied. These percentages need to increase. CQI reports indicate that documentation is still not complete, the alert systems are not always effective, staff are keeping backup hard copies with no oversight on these copies, and there are an insufficient number of computers on some units. The nursing staff, physicians, and other staff do not feel that they are prepared to use the system. The "talk" in the hallways is that this project will fail.

Questions:

1. What are the problems?
2. Is more information needed to fully understand the problems? If so, what information?
3. What needs to be done to resolve the problems?
4. What could have been done to prevent these problems when the project was initially planned and implemented?
5. How would you plan further evaluation (including timeline)?

learning to be a continuous, lifelong process, as more and more nurses can easily access it; however, quality education is still the major concern.

Distance education, or education provided in such a way that the student and instructor are separated by either time or physical distance, has become an important method for providing continuing education, additional academic degrees, and certification. Benefits of this method are flexibility for the student; decreased cost for students such as less travel, parking, and so on; fewer campus buildings needed at schools; increased opportunity to include faculty, such as experts for short-term teaching; broader mix of students from different geographic areas with different perspectives; opportunity to develop different and innovative teaching strategies; and flexibility for faculty who can travel and work from home while teaching. It is not clear if all content and learning experiences can be effectively offered through technology, but over time more will be known about this issue. Technology can also be used to bring courses to staff within HCOs and allow these organizations with multiple sites to conduct education and training programs and meetings without staff travel by using computers, videoconferencing, and other new technology.

HIT and Medical Technology: Implications for Patient Education

Ehealth is now commonplace in many HCOs. Consumers use the Internet to find health information, store personal health information, communicate with healthcare providers, and in many other ways. This allows the patient or consumer to be in more control of his or her health. This technology is not perfect, and there are concerns about the quality of health material posted on the Web. Much of the information, however, is of good quality and helpful to healthcare providers and patients/consumers. Connectivity is one of the key factors in today's personal and work environment, which includes the healthcare environment. Consumers and providers expect more and more information to be quickly available, but they also want credible information. Consumers also want to be able to get to their healthcare information quickly and easily. Many are also interested in communicating with their healthcare providers via many of the possible technologies (for example, email and voice mail mentioned earlier).

Many HCOs have developed their own websites. A key purpose of these sites is marketing and public relations. HCO nursing needs to be featured on these sites. For acute care sites, the answer is simple. Nurses provide most of the care in hospitals, and consumers should see nursing featured on these sites. Nursing leadership in HCOs need to step up and insist that nurses are featured on the website, and nurses also need to be involved in developing the site, with nurse leaders involved in major decisions related to ehealth. These websites can also assist with the HCO's recruitment and retention (advertising jobs, recognizing expertise, sharing what nurses are contributing), patient education and consumer guidelines, nursing continuing education, linking the nursing staff with resources via the Web, communication of nursing activities such as committees, and so on. Some of this information must be available via personal identification number (PIN) or some sort of privacy system, and other parts should be open to the public. The following are some consumer- or patient-oriented materials that could help nurses in the management of care if they were made available to patients on the organization's website:

- Preoperative instructions
- Patient education guides for common problems (for example, diabetes, cardiac, and so on)
- Description of postoperative experience
- Description of admission process
- Description of discharge process
- Description of discharge planning and role of the patient
- Family visiting guidelines
- Patient rights
- Intensive care guidelines for family members
- Helping your child with hospitalization
- Hospital diets
- Helping your child cope with a parent/grandparent in the hospital
- Appropriate flowers and plants to send to ensure safety
- Reimbursement issues and procedures
- Talking with your doctor
- Talking with your nurse
- Staff photos and profiles
- Patient satisfaction and patient advocacy

These are only a few examples. Any educational content and information also needs to be individualized when patients receive care, and patients would then need to have contact with staff for questions and discussion.

HIT and Medical Technology: Implications for Nursing Research

Informatics has had and will continue to have an effect on nursing research. This effect is felt in the use of informatics both as a tool to facilitate research and as a focus of research—application in the clinical practice and administration. There is a greater need to understand informatics and its implications for the profession. Many HCOs, with their increasing ability to access technology, will probably increase their research activity. There is greater ability to communicate across organizations and to seek information and consultation. Databases can maintain data for use in research, and through various searching capabilities, data can be mined to get a clearer picture of an issue. Nurse researchers need to understand the possibilities and work with IT experts. It is easier now to apply statistics with the various computer-based statistical software packages.

HIT and Medical Technology and Quality Improvement

> There is a perception that [HIT] will lead to fewer errors than strategies that focus on staff performance; however, technology may in some circumstances lead to more errors. This is particularly true when the technology fails to take into account end users, increases staff time, replicates an already bad process, or is implemented with insufficient training. The best approach is not always clear, and most approaches have advantages and disadvantages. (Finkelman & Kenner, 2012, p. 192)

Patient-centered care requires collaboration and coordination, and interprofessional care is part of this process (Institute of Medicine, 2001, 2003). Information is critical to this process.

The way in which information is communicated and maintained impacts the quality of care and control of errors. The ideal system is one that can share information from HCOs to individual providers and vice versa. The United States does not have this type of electronic health system, and to get it will be very expensive and difficult. There is recognition that more must be done to achieve it, but it will take time. Most HCOs do not have the same EMR/EHR systems, making sharing very difficult. Many HCOs have had problems with their EMRs/EHRs, and this has led to problems—and costly ones. There has, however, been a movement to use of EMRs/EHRs, in HCOs. With the passage of healthcare reform legislation, there is hope that there will be improvement. The ACA includes a provision that health plans must implement uniform standards for electronic exchange of health information to reduce paperwork and administrative costs. Table 19-2 identifies some barriers related to staff concerns about use of EMRs/EHRs.

The role of health IT in emeasurement and quality care has become increasingly more important in recent years (Dykes & Collins, 2013). As discussed frequently in this text, healthcare quality is of concern and a key topic in healthcare delivery and policy. **Emeasurement** is the

Table 19-2	OVERCOMING BARRIERS RELATED TO STAFF CONCERNS
EHR Implementation Barrier	**Possible Solutions**
Staff members are against EHR because of inexperience with computers.	• Explain the many benefits new computer skills can bring to them personally (e.g., "will help you connect with your grandkids in new ways"). • Arrange support from other staff members. • Encourage enrollment in classes at a community college. • Invest in a good voice recognition program for those with special needs.
Staff does not want to accept redesigned workflow because they are "set in their ways."	• Involve staff in documenting the existing workflow and creating the new one.
Staff thinks entering data will interfere with patient care and patients may complain.	• Situate the screen so that the clinician looks at patient while using it, or provide tablet-type devices. • Set up the EHR to minimize typing (use tapping, mouse clicks). • Choose an EHR with an intuitive interface (eyes up, less visual searching).
Staff worry about lost productivity.	• Factor lost productivity into budget and implementation plans (fewer appointments during transition; arrange to use temporary employees, administrative interns, or clinician interns). • Work with grant-making organization to adjust productivity requirements temporarily (if applicable).
Staff fear job loss (e.g., records management workers).	• Reassure staff members that they are valued. Train them for other roles.

Source: U.S. Department of Health and Human Services. (2014). Overcoming barriers related to staff concerns. Retrieved from http://www.hrsa.gov/healthit/toolbox/healthitimplementation/implementationtopics/buildworkforce/buildworkforce_5.html

secondary use of electronic data to populate standardized performance measures (National Quality Forum, 2013). The National Quality Forum (NQF) is developing emeasures to make sure data used for clinical documentation can be reused to measure patient outcomes. The federal government has taken leadership in improving how data are collected, analyzed, and maintained so this information can be used to make decisions about healthcare quality. HCOs do this routinely, but there is greater need for sharing of this information. The National Healthcare Quality Report, the National Healthcare Disparities Report, and *Healthy People 2020* depend on electronic data and measures. The AHRQ is very active in the area of emeasurement and provides futher information on its website.

HIT and Medical Technology: Healthcare Reimbursement

With the rapid growth of information technology, the management and provision of health care have been radically changed. Information is available today via many different types of HIT, giving healthcare providers the opportunity to track patient information across healthcare settings and virtually anywhere in the world to analyze the data effectively. In addition, new medical technology requires reimbursement.

Insurers are finding that telephone patient advice is an excellent triage method that allows patients to speak directly with a healthcare professional, who is often a nurse. Questions can be answered, which may prevent the need for an office visit. Patients can also be assessed and referred to the best resource for service. Patient education and guidance can also be provided. Assessment over the phone requires a highly skilled practitioner who can identify critical information that may be communicated in subtle ways. Nurses, with their assessment skills and ability to collaborate with physicians, are particularly effective in this role. Patient advice systems via telephone require clear documentation policies and guidelines that include content related to whom is called, when, for what reason, and required assessment data and interventions. Follow-up is a critical topic as it should be part of the services and the documentation of those services. This form of communication between nurses and patients must take into consideration the importance of trust, the value of establishing a good relationship, and the need to individualize care. The last factor is important because many HCOs and insurers that use patient advice systems follow very specific protocols, algorithms, and guidelines. If, however, this care is not individualized, it could have serious consequences. "Cookbook" care must be avoided. The assessment is the key to successful telephone nursing—providing the interventions for needs that should be addressed, which may or may not be found in the guidelines. Patients may be given advice or advised to

APPLYING EVIDENCE-BASED PRACTICE

Evidence for Effective Leadership and Management

CITATION: Agency for Healthcare Research and Quality. (2012, June). Enabling patient-centered care through health information technology. Executive Summary. Evidence Report/Technology Assessment Number 206. Retrieved from http://www.effective-healthcare.ahrq.gov/ehc/products/451/1158/EvidenceReport206_Patient-Centered-Care_ExecutiveSummary_20120614.pdf

OVERVIEW: This federal government report examines the implications and connections between health information technology and patient-centered care.

APPLICATION: Using EMRs/EHRs is now highly recommended, though as these researchers note, there is limited research to date on its impact. Decision making about EMRs/EHRs and implementing them are not simple processes. Much needs to be factored in, and

we do not know enough to always make the best decisions. Nurses who use EMRs/EHRs often describe their frustrations with this new documentation and technology. "While the healthcare community widely recognizes the potential of health information technology in enabling patient-centered care (PCC), we have yet to see an evidence-based comprehensive analysis of its impact on quality of care. In addition, there does not yet exist a systematic review of barriers and facilitators for health IT-enabled PCC" (p. 1).

Questions:

1. What are the key questions asked in this report?
2. Why is this report considered to be a systematic review?
3. What are the results?
4. Identify two implications for nursing management.

see a healthcare provider. Day surgery unit/ambulatory staff might call patients before surgery to discuss preoperative requirements and after discharge to determine their status and whether they are following discharge advice. Many healthcare providers are using the telephone to contact patients and remind them of appointments to decrease the number of patients who do not show up for appointments. Missed appointments are expensive for providers because this time could have been used to see other patients. Healthcare providers, particularly hospitals, are using the telephone to obtain initial intake information and thus reduce admission time while simultaneously providing the patient with pertinent information. Patients may be called for satisfaction data.

The telephone is certainly not new; however, healthcare providers are now using this technology to their advantage. The use of the telephone for these purposes does take staff time, which affects costs; however, it usually is less time than would be required for an in-person encounter, which saves time for the provider and the patient. Staff members who make the calls need training, policies, and guidelines related to the purposes of the calls, privacy issues, whom to call and what to say, and documentation.

IMPROVEMENT IN HEALTH INFORMATICS

The Progress Report on the Federal Health IT Strategic Plan highlights resources and services the federal government implemented to guide nationwide adoption and use of HIT to support better health and health care for Americans. This strategic plan notes the following.

Federal investments in a wide array of programs and activities, including the Meaningful Use EMR/EHR Incentive Program, have impacted the HIT marketplace, allowing the health care system to improve health and health care.

- As of April 2013, 74% of eligible professionals and 87% of eligible hospitals have registered to participate in the Meaningful Use EMR/EHR Incentive Program
- Hospital EMR/EHR adoption more than tripled since 2009, from 12% in 2009 to 44% in 2012; Office-based provider adoption increased by 86% from 2009 to 2011, from 21% to 39%
- Higher levels of health information exchange, such as e-prescribing (33% of providers had e-prescribing capabilities in 2009, compared with 73% in 2012)
- Health IT use for clinical quality measurement and clinical decision support to improve quality of care
- Success in improving health outcomes in communities across the U.S.
- Updated privacy and security guidelines to address new technologies and uses of health IT
- Greater consumer access to health information through eHealth tools, such as patient portals
- Collaboration between private and public sector on innovative approaches, using health IT to solve health care problems (U.S. Department of Health and Human Services, Office of the National Coordinator of Health Information Technology, 2013).

Goal I from the Federal Health IT Strategic Plan focuses "on increasing adoption of electronic health/medical records (EMR/EHRs) and electronic exchange of health information. The Centers for Medicare & Medicaid Services (CMS) and ONC established a regulatory framework for financial incentives under the Medicare and Medicaid EHR Incentive Programs" (U.S. Department of Health and Human Services, Office of the National Coordinator of Health Information Technology, 2013). These federal investments and regulations have led to rapid increases in the rate of EMR/EHR adoption and electronic information exchange in the healthcare marketplace. While much work to date focused on assisting eligible professionals and hospitals, HHS is exploring methods to encourage ineligible providers to adopt and use health IT. As noted earlier in the chapter, meaningful use of EMRs/EHRs requires structured data capture and advanced clinical processes including health information exchange, eprescribing, lab results, electronic transmission of patient care summaries across multiple settings, and greater patient access to data. Box 19-1 describes additional goals from the federal strategic plan.

	Goal	Objective
Collect	**Goal 1:** Expand Adoption of Health IT	• **Objective A:** Increase the adoption and effective use of health IT products, systems, and services • **Objective B:** Increase user and market confidence in the safety and safe use of health IT products, systems, and services • **Objective C:** Advance a national communications infrastructure that supports health, safety, and care delivery
Share	**Goal 2:** Advance Secure and Interoperable Health Information	• **Objective A:** Enable individuals, providers, and public health entities to securely send, receive, find, and use electronic health information • **Objective B:** Identify, prioritize, and advance technical standards to support secure and interoperable health information • **Objective C:** Protect the privacy and security of health information
Use	**Goal 3:** Strengthen Health Care Delivery	• **Objective A:** Improve health care quality, access, and experience through safe, timely, effective, efficient, equitable, and person-centered care • **Objective B:** Support the delivery of high-value health care • **Objective C:** Improve clinical and community services and population health
	Goal 4: Advance the Health and Well-Being of Individuals and Communities	• **Objective A:** Empower individual, family, and caregiver health management and engagement • **Objective B:** Protect and promote public health and healthy, resilient communities
	Goal 5: Advance Research, Scientific Knowledge, and Innovation	• **Objective A:** Increase access to and usability of high-quality electronic health information and services • **Objective B:** Accelerate the development and commercialization of innovative technologies and solutions • **Objective C:** Invest, disseminate, and translate research on how health IT can improve health and care delivery

BOX 19-1 FEDERAL HEALTH IT STRATEGIC PLAN 2015–2020

Source: The Office of the National Coordinator for Health Information Technology (ONC). Office of the Secretary, United States Department of Health and Human Services (July 2015). Federal health IT strategic plan. p. 8. Retrieved from http://www.healthit.gov/policy-researchers-implementers/health-it-strategic-planning. Draft for approval.

APPLYING LEADERSHIP AND MANAGEMENT

My Hospital Unit: An Evolving Case Experience

Your hospital is implementing an EMR/EHR system. To be proactive, each nurse manager is required to identify issues and problems that might occur on the manager's unit during the change to the EMR/EHR system. You need to consider your unit, patients, staff, documentation issues that might be unique to the needs of your unit and its patients, ability of staff to respond to change, educational needs regarding documentation and EMR/EHR and HIT, and so on. You are sitting down at your office desk to begin this huge task. How will you demonstrate your response? In narrative form, table, or some other format? You want to be clear to your director. Prepare the response that you will send to the director. It should be specific to your unit, and past decisions you have made in other chapters about your unit need to be considered.

BSN and *Master's Essentials:* Application to Content

BSN Essentials (American Association of Colleges of Nursing, 2008) as Applied to this Chapter:

II. Basic Organizational and Systems Leadership for Quality Care and Patient Safety
IV. Information Management and Application of Patient Care Technology
IX. Baccalaureate Generalist Nursing Practice

Master's Essentials (American Association of Colleges of Nursing, 2011) as Applied to this Chapter:

II. Organizational and Systems Leadership
V. Informatics and Healthcare Technology
IX. Master's-Level Nursing Practice

Applying AONE Competencies

Identify which of the AONE competencies found in Appendix A apply to the content of this chapter.

Engaging in the Content: Critical Thinking and Clinical Reasoning and Judgment

Discussion Questions

1. How do you think increasing use of technology in health care for both medical and nursing interventions and communication has impacted the caring part of nursing? Discuss this question with your classmates. (Online Application Option)
2. Define "meaningful use" and explain its importance.
3. What might be the nurse's role in telehealth, and how might it be used?
4. What are three examples of using health informatics in clinical practice and three examples of its use in nursing management? (Online Application Option)
5. Why is patient privacy and confidentiality associated with health informatics? (Online Application Option)
6. How have informatics and technology impacted nursing practice? What have you experienced? (Online Application Option)

Application Exercises

1. Use of technology in health care varies from community to community. You have probably noticed that some healthcare organizations use technology more than others. Use of the computer has become very common, although some HCOs still have a long way to go in how the computer is used. What is used in your community? The class might want to develop a list of HCOs and a survey that would include the common types of technology that might be used today. Then find out what is used in the healthcare organizations: What type of technology is used, by whom, and why? What is the patient population? What is the value of its use? Ask nurses in some of the healthcare organizations what they think about the HCO's computer documentation system (if they have one). What do they see as the pros and cons to using it? You might also ask fellow students to rate different computer documentation systems that they have used in different healthcare settings. Your responses will depend on your local HCOs, but it will probably include use of computers, technology in treatment such as in surgery and other specialties, telephone, videoconferencing, telehealth, and other methods. Criteria that might be used to assess effectiveness would be initial cost, maintenance cost, training costs, error rate, safety issues, need for backup systems, staff reaction, and so on. (Online Application Option)
2. Working in teams, develop a list of potential problems that might lead to errors when using an EMR/EHR. Identify strategies that might be implemented to prevent these problems. (Online Application Option)
3. Working in teams, discuss how telehealth might be used in the future—use your imagination.
4. Search on the Internet for information about the nursing informatics specialty, and search for possible ads for positions. What do you think about this specialty?
5. Your class could ask a nurse who is involved in health informatics to speak to the class. Prepare questions for the presenter. After the presentation, divide into teams, summarize the information gathered, and reflect on the content. Share with other teams.

References

American Academy of Ambulatory Care Nursing, Telehealth Nursing Practice Task Force. (2001). *AAACN telehealth nursing practice administration and practice standards.* Pittman, NJ: Author.

American Association of Colleges of Nursing. (2008). *The essentials of baccalaureate education for professional nursing practice.* Washington, DC: Author.

American Association of Colleges of Nursing. (2011). *The essentials of master's education in nursing.* Washington, DC: Author.

American Medical Informatics Association. (2014, April). AMIA nursing informatics working group member news. Retrieved from http://www.amia.org/sites/amia.

org/files/Minnesota-approved-standardized-nursing-terminologies-in-EHR.pdf

American Nurses Association. (2014). *Nursing informatics: Scope and standards of practice.* (2nd ed.). Washington, DC: Author.

American Nurses Credentialing Center. (2014). Informatics nursing. Retrieved from http://www.nursecredentialing.org/InformaticsNursing

American Organization of Nurse Executives. (2007). *AONE guiding principles: For defining the role of the nurse executive in technology acquisition and implementation.* Chicago, IL: Author.

American Organization of Nurse Executives. (2009). *AONE guiding principles: For the nurse executive to enhance clinical outcomes by leveraging technology.* Chicago, IL: Author.

Association of Perioperative Registered Nurses. (2008). *Perioperative nursing data set.* Denver, CO: Author.

Dakins, D. (2002). Home is where the healthcare is. *Telemedicine Today, 9*(2), 18–21.

Dykes, P., & Collins, S. (2013). Building linkages between nursing care and improved patient outcomes: The role of health information technology. *Online Journal of Issues in Nursing, 18*(3). Retrieved from http://www.nursingworld.org/MainMenuCategories/ANA-Marketplace/ANAPeriodicals/OJIN/TableofContents/Vol-18-2013/No3-Sept-2013/Nursing-Care-and-Improved-Outcomes.html

Finkelman, A., & Kenner, C. (2012). *Teaching IOM* (3rd ed.). Silver Spring, MD: American Nurses Association Publishing.

Healthcare Information and Management Systems Society. (2014). 2014 nursing informatics workforce survey executive summary. Retrieved from http://www.himss.org/ResourceLibrary/genResourceDetailPDF.aspx?ItemNumber=28237

HealthIT.gov. (2014a). Accelerating health information exchange (HIE). Retrieved from http://www.healthit.gov/policy-researchers-implementers/accelerating-health-information-exchange-hie

HealthIT.gov. (2014b). Clinical decision support (CDS). Retrieved from http://www.healthit.gov/policy-researchers-implementers/clinical-decision-support-cds

Institute of Medicine. (1999). *To err is human.* Washington, DC: National Academies Press.

Institute of Medicine. (2001). *Crossing the quality chasm.* Washington, DC: National Academies Press.

Institute of Medicine. (2003). *Health professions education.* Washington, DC: National Academies Press.

Institute of Medicine. (2011). *The future of nursing: Leading change, advancing health.* Washington, DC: National Academies Press.

International Council of Nurses. (2015). ICNP® definition. Retrieved from http://www.icn.ch/what-we-do/definition-a-elements-of-icnpr/

Kerfoot, K., & Simpson, R. (2002). Knowledge-driven care: Powerful medicine. *Reflections on Nursing LEADERSHIP* (third quarter), 22–24, 44.

National Quality Forum. (2013). Electronic quality measures (emeasures). Retrieved from http://www.qualityforum.org/Projects/e-g/eMeasures/Electronic_Quality_Measures.aspx

Omaha System. (2005). The Omaha System: Solving the clinical data-information puzzle. Retrieved from http://www.omahasystem.org/

Predko, J. (2001). Use of distance technology for education, practice, and research. In J. Dochterman & H. Grace (Eds.), *Current issues in nursing* (6th ed.) (pp. 75–81). St. Louis, MO: Mosby.

Reilly, T., & Humbrecht, D. (2015). Fostering synergy: A nurse-managed remote telemetry model. *Critical Care Nurse, 27*(3), 22–33.

Roark, D. (2004). Bar codes & drug administration. *AJN, 104*(1), 63–66.

Robinson, K. (2012). Online and mail-order medicine: How to buy safely. Retrieved from http://www.webmd.com/healthy-aging/features/beyond-the-pharmacy-online-and-mail-order-prescription-drugs

U.S. Department of Health and Human Services, Centers for Medicare & Medicaid Services. (2010). CMS and ONC final regulations define meaningful use and set standards for electronic health record incentive program. Retrieved from http://www.cms.gov/Newsroom/MediaReleaseDatabase/Fact-sheets/2010-Fact-sheets-items/2010-07-13.html

U.S. Department of Health and Human Services, Centers for Medicare & Medicaid Services. (2014). 2014 definition stage 1 of meaningful use. Retrieved from http://www.cms.gov/Regulations-and-Guidance/Legislation/EHRIncentivePrograms/Meaningful_Use.html

U.S. Department of Health and Human Services, Office of the National Coordinator of Health Information Technology. (2013). Federal health IT strategic plan progress report. Retrieved from http://www.healthit.gov/sites/default/files/federal-health-it-strategic-plan-progress-report-0613.paper_version.v2.pdf

U.S. National Library of Medicine. (2008). SNOMED Clinical Terms® (CT®). Retrieved March 12, 2008, from http://www.nlm.nih.gov/research/umls/Snomed/snomed_main.html

University of Minnesota Center for Nursing Informatics. (2015). Minimum data sets. Retrieved from http://www.nursing.umn.edu/icnp/center-projects/minimum-data-sets/

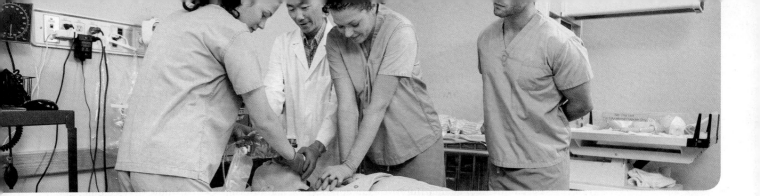

20 Staff Education to Meet Health Professions Core Competencies and Improve Care

⬤ LEARNING OUTCOMES

Before you begin, take a moment to familiarize yourself with the learning outcomes for this chapter.

> Discuss the impact of the Institute of Medicine reports on nursing staff education.
> Examine the impact of staff education on quality health care.
> Examine the nursing professional staff development standards.
> Describe how staff development services might be organized and used within a health-care organization.
> Describe the staff development process.
> Explain the need for effective staff orientation.
> Describe current trends in continuing education.
> Discuss the expansion of interprofessional education.
> Discuss the advantages of offering nurse residency programs.

KEY TERMS

- **continuing education**
- **nurse residency**
- **orientation**

WHAT'S AHEAD

This chapter addresses the critical issue of staff education. Nurse leaders and managers must be aware of the impact of staff preparation, for both incoming staff and maintaining competencies during employment. Staff education is an integral component of an effective healthcare organization (HCO), but to ensure that it is effective, administration at all levels must work to plan, implement, and evaluate staff education on an ongoing basis. Staff education also has an impact on the HCO budget, requiring funds to maintain staff education; however, many HCOs struggle with maintaining sufficient funding for staff education. Nurse leaders must be very involved in staff education and advocate for its continued presence in the HCO in a manner that meets competency needs and supports improved care. This chapter describes some of the key concerns that nurse leaders and managers need to consider.

IMPORTANCE OF STAFF PREPARATION AND QUALITY CARE

The Institute of Medicine (IOM) recognized early in its assessment process of healthcare quality that a critical factor in improving health care is the competency of individual healthcare providers. In response to this concern, the IOM published the report *Health Professions Education* (2003). In this report health professions education is viewed as a bridge to quality care, and the report's content flows from previous IOM reports as described in Chapter 17, Figure 17-3 on page 406.

The IOM discussion does not just focus on nursing education, but rather on the need to have qualified, competent healthcare staff from all healthcare professional groups to improve health care. The report indicates that health professions' education is in need of change to meet the growing demands of the healthcare system today. "All health professionals should be educated to deliver patient-centered care as members of an interprofessional team, emphasizing evidence-based practice, quality improvement approaches, and informatics" (Institute of Medicine, 2003, p. 3). The five core competencies for all healthcare professionals (nurses, physicians, pharmacists, healthcare administrators, allied health, and so on) are as follows:

- Provide patient-centered care.
- Work in interprofessional teams.
- Employ evidence-based practice.
- Apply quality improvement.
- Utilize informatics.

All of these critical areas have been discussed in this text because they are relevant to nurses, nursing care, and nursing leadership and management. In October 2008 the American Association of Colleges of Nursing (AACN) published a new edition of *The Essentials of Baccalaureate Education for Professional Nursing Practice*, which mentions the five core competencies in the first paragraph. The document specifies the essential content areas and competencies for baccalaureate programs. *Essential II, Basic Organizational and Systems Leadership for Quality Care and Patient Safety*, focuses on knowledge and skills in leadership, quality improvement, and patient safety necessary to provide high-quality health care (American Association of Colleges of Nursing, 2008), which are not only important in academic nursing programs but also in staff education. *The Future of Nursing: Leading Change, Advancing Health* (2011), includes recommendations about nursing education, noting that

> major changes in the U.S. healthcare system and practice environments will require equally profound changes in the education of nurses both before and after they receive their licenses. . . . The primary goals of nursing education remain the same: nurses must be prepared to meet diverse patients' needs; function as leaders; and advance science that benefits patients and the capacity of health professionals to deliver safe, quality patient care. (p. 4-1)

This report strongly supports the need for quality education at all levels, which correlates with the earlier IOM report on health professions education (2003).

Staff Development Standards and Model

In 2010 the American Nurses Association (ANA) revised its *Nursing Professional Development: Scope and Standards of Practice* to ensure that these standards reflect current staff education issues (American Nurses Association & National Nursing Staff Development Organization, 2010). The standards should be used to guide nursing staff development activities to improve staff competencies, influence performance, and consequently to impact quality care. Figure 20-1 provides a model of nursing professional development specialist practice that is found in the ANA standards. The model highlights at its end point the importance of protection of the public and provision of quality care, and thus must be considered in the staff development process, connecting the process with continuous quality improvement (CQI). The standards are identified in Box 20-1.

DESCRIPTION OF STAFF DEVELOPMENT

The major goal for staff development is to provide quality educational opportunities to maintain and improve staff competencies and ensure new staff are oriented. Staff development as a department should identify its vision, mission, goals, and objectives and review these annually along with its strategic and operational plans. In addition, these should not conflict with those of the HCO.

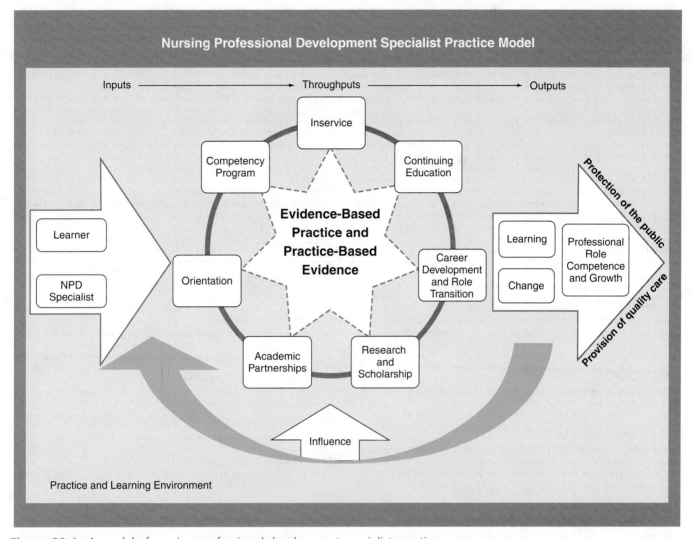

Figure 20-1 A model of nursing professional development specialist practice

Source: From *Nursing Professional Development: Scope and Standards of Practice*. Copyright © 2010 by American Nurses Association. Reprinted with permission. All rights reserved.

(Planning is discussed in Chapter 2.) Staff development is no different than any other department or service; it must meet the same management requirements. Budget is critical and typically is part of the nursing budget and requires the HCO nursing leader to advocate for sufficient funds. When budgets are tight, it is not unusual for staff development to be one of the first areas to be cut.

Organization and Staff Development Personnel

The organization of staff development services in an HCO varies, and this variation is dependent on a number of factors. The size and type of the HCO (types of patients, ages, typical diagnoses, and services) impacts the level of staff development required and clinical focus. For example, a 100-bed hospital requires a smaller staff than a 500-bed medical center and thus requires less staff education resources. If the 100-bed hospital is a psychiatric/mental health center, then the focus is on care of this population, and staff education becomes more focused. The organizational structure of the HCO in general impacts how staff development is organized. Some of the possibilities are:

- a staff development department is centralized and provides education for all staff, though nursing staff usually is the largest group.
- a staff development service within the nursing department centralizes staff education for nursing staff.

BOX 20-1 AMERICAN NURSES ASSOCIATION AND NATIONAL NURSING STAFF DEVELOPMENT ORGANIZATION STANDARDS OF NURSING PROFESSIONAL DEVELOPMENT

STANDARD 1. ASSESSMENT

The nursing professional development specialist collects data and information related to educational needs and other pertinent situations.

STANDARD 2. IDENTIFICATION OF ISSUES AND TRENDS

The nursing professional development specialist analyzes issues, trends, and supporting data to determine the needs of individuals, organizations, and communities.

STANDARD 3. OUTCOMES IDENTIFICATION

The nursing professional development specialist identifies desired outcomes.

STANDARD 4. PLANNING

The nursing professional development specialist establishes a plan that prescribes strategies, alternatives, and resources to achieve expected outcomes.

STANDARD 5. IMPLEMENTATION

The nursing professional development specialist implements the identified plan.

STANDARD 5A. COORDINATION

The nursing professional development specialist coordinates educational initiatives and activities.

STANDARD 5B. LEARNING AND PRACTICE ENVIRONMENT

The nursing professional development specialist employs strategies and techniques to promote positive learning and practice environments.

STANDARD 5C. CONSULTATION

The nursing professional development specialist provides consultation to influence plans, enhance the abilities of others, and effect change.

STANDARD 6. EVALUATION

The nursing professional development specialist evaluates progress toward attainment of outcomes.

STANDARD 7. QUALITY OF NURSING PROFESSIONAL DEVELOPMENT PRACTICE

The nursing professional development specialist systematically enhances the quality and effectiveness of nursing professional development practice.

STANDARD 8. EDUCATION

The nursing professional development specialist maintains current knowledge and competency in nursing and professional development practice.

STANDARD 9. PROFESSIONAL PRACTICE EVALUATION

The nursing professional development specialist evaluates his/her own practice in relation to professional practice standards and guidelines, and relevant statutes, rules, and regulations.

STANDARD 10. COLLEGIALITY

The nursing professional development specialist establishes collegial partnerships contributing to the professional development of peers, students, colleagues, and others.

STANDARD 11. COLLABORATION

The nursing professional development specialist collaborates with interprofessional teams, leaders, stakeholders, and others to facilitate nursing practice and positive outcomes for consumers.

STANDARD 12. ETHICS

The nursing professional development specialist integrates ethics in all areas of practice.

STANDARD 13. ADVOCACY

The nursing professional development specialist advocates for the protection and rights of individuals, families, communities, populations, healthcare providers, nursing, and other professions, institutions, and organizations.

STANDARD 14. RESEARCH

The nursing professional development specialist integrates research findings into practice.

STANDARD 15. RESOURCE UTILIZATION

The nursing professional development specialist considers factors related to safety, effectiveness, and cost in regard to professional development activities and expected outcomes.

STANDARD 16. LEADERSHIP

The nursing professional development specialist provides leadership in the professional practice setting and the profession. The ten Standards of Professional Performance describe a competent level of behavior in the nursing professional development role, including activities related to quality of practice, education, professional practice evaluation, collegiality, collaboration, ethics, advocacy, research, resource utilization, and leadership. All registered nurses are expected to engage in professional role activities, including leadership and advocacy, appropriate to their education and position. Registered nurses are accountable for their professional actions to themselves, their patients, their peers, and ultimately to society.

- a decentralized staff development service requires clinical units and divisions to have designated staff who manage the unit's or division's staff development. The unit/division staff development specialist may report to the unit/division manager and to a small, centralized staff development department. The centralized service includes a director and other staff who provide guidance to units/divisions and provide overall staff development that applies to all staff, for example general orientation.

The HCO high-level administrators decide how staff development will be organized. Often the structure is similar to other support services in the HCO. In addition, the nurse leader (e.g., chief nurse executive) is critical in this decision and should advocate for the most effective organizational design to meet staff education needs efficiently and effectively.

Staff development specialist positions also vary. Typically someone is designated as the lead or to serve as director. Preferably this person should have at a minimum a master's degree, though in smaller HCOs, this may not be possible. The master's degree might be in nursing education or may be focused on the roles of clinical nurse specialist, clinical nurse leader, or other type of graduate specialty. Advanced practice registered nurses typically are not in the director position as their preparation is not oriented toward this type of administration or education. Staff who serve as specialists per unit or division may also have similar preparation as the director and should at the minimum have a baccalaureate degree. All staff educators need to have not only clinical expertise but also knowledge about education particularly focused on staff education. Different specialists in the HCO or external to the HCO may be used for focused educational programs such as quality improvement, pharmacy, pain management, health informatics, and so on. Instructors or presenters for courses or presentations about leadership and management should demonstrate this type of expertise. In addition, staff development requires support staff to assist with daily administrative tasks and technology support. The key questions to consider in organizing staff development and in evaluating its functioning are the following:

- To whom does the director (title may vary) report?
- To whom do the staff development specialists report (e.g., do they have dual reporting, for example, to a nurse manager and to a director)?
- How does the director relate to all levels of the staff?
- How do staff development specialists relate to all levels of staff?
- What type of accountability and responsibility do staff development specialists have toward the patient?
- How does the director relate to academic education programs, such as nursing, that may use the HCO for clinical experiences?

The type of organizational model selected impacts effective functioning and presents challenges. An example is the decentralized approach with no centralized feature. This can lead to a chaotic service with limited consistency across units and divisions. There are certainly individual learning needs per unit or division, and at this level it is easier to evaluate individual staff learning needs and follow them. However, there are many needs that cross all or most units and divisions. A totally decentralized model means that the same learning experiences may be repeated for multiple groups of staff when it could be done more efficiently and with more consistent content, better ensuring that the staff have the same learning experiences for specific topics, for example, fall prevention, medication administration and safety, communication with patients and families, CQI, and teamwork. All these topics have some variation depending on the practice setting and specialty, but there is key content per topic that relates to all staff. This may be handled in a decentralized method or even by identifying variations in a centralized presentation (e.g., asking staff from specific units or divisions to divide into groups to discuss differences that apply to their work area). Orientation, as discussed later in this chapter, is an important example of the need for a centralized and decentralized approach. Each HCO needs to find the organizational model that correlates with the HCO and nursing visions and meets staff learning needs in the most effective and efficient manner. HCOs differ and this is why there is variation in how an HCO develops its staff development.

As staff development is organized, other needs are also important. Administrative work and learning activities require space such as classrooms, conference rooms, and so on, and storage of supplies (e.g., office, clinical supplies for demonstration and practice, and so on). Simulation is discussed later in this chapter, and if it is used, it requires space and equipment as well. Along with the need for planning and a budget, staff development must follow HCO and nursing policies and procedures, but there also need to be policies and procedures that apply specifically to staff development. These policies and procedures may focus on staff development functions; documentation; implementation of services (presentations, programs, and so on); evaluation; and use of the HCO services such as informatics, purchasing for supplies, and so on.

Staff Development Budget

The staff development budget should include:

- salaries and benefits.
- office and clinical supplies (required for educational programs).
- technology equipment and support.
- access to professional literature.
- print materials for educational offerings.
- other special needs, such as staff development specialists attending conferences.

In addition, the nurse executive and the director of staff education need to consider how staff are supported to attend educational activities outside the HCO, such as conferences. Some HCOs provide this benefit to staff, though this is highly variable. The HCO needs clear policies identifying who may apply for this benefit, amount of coverage, and so on. Policies and procedures need to be developed so staff understand the options. Some HCOs provide tuition reimbursement for academic courses, and this, too, requires policies and procedures that should be developed collaboratively with human resources. When staff are approved for these benefits, consideration needs to be given to their requirements on return from external educational events (e.g., if a staff member attends a conference, is the staff member therefore required to present to the staff or share the information in some manner)? The staff need to be encouraged to submit conference abstracts, present at conferences, and publish in peer-reviewed journals. Staff development specialists can help with this process and provide support. These activities not only serve as positive public relations for the HCO but also represent staff scholarly activities as they learn from these experiences, adding to their career development. Staff development needs to collaborate with the staff who are involved in evidence-based practice (EBP) and research so this can also be integrated into staff education.

APPLYING EVIDENCE-BASED PRACTICE

Evidence for Effective Leadership and Management

CITATION: Kovner, C., Brewer, C., Yingrengreung, S., & Fairchild, S. (2010). The new nurses' views of quality improvement education. *The Joint Commission Journal on Quality and Safety, 36*(1), 29–35.

OVERVIEW: With the growing concern about continuous quality improvement (CQI), there is recognition that staff need to be prepared, particularly nursing staff, to participate actively in the continuous quality improvement process. However, if nurses lack sufficient knowledge, concepts, and tools required for CQI, then they would not be able to participate in an effective manner. This study used data from an eight-page survey of new nurses who graduated between August 1, 2004, and July 31, 2005. There were 436 respondents (69.4% response rate) to the mailed survey. "Overall, 159 (38.6%) of new nurses thought that they were 'poorly' or 'very poorly' prepared about or had 'never heard of' CQI" (p. 29). The final conclusion from the study is that both academic nursing programs and healthcare organizations need to

work to better prepare nurses to assume active roles in quality improvement and leadership.

APPLICATION: Staff development needs to be aware of current issues, particularly research in a variety of areas, but particularly when it focuses on nursing education. In addition, with greater emphasis on CQI, staff development needs to be very active in developing staff competencies related to CQI.

Questions:

1. After reviewing this study, describe how it was designed.
2. If you were director of staff development, how would you use the results of this study?
3. What is a major limitation of this study that you might want to address as you assess the need for greater QI staff education in your HCO?
4. What might you do to better understand new staff QI knowledge and competencies?

Staff development should demonstrate how it impacts the HCO, and the best way to do this is to show its impact on continuous quality improvement (CQI). It is clear that the IOM recognizes education and its impact on quality improvement; in fact, the IOM has repeatedly included this in various report recommendations. HCOs can develop policies, procedures, and standards and meet accreditation requirements. However, if staff are not prepared at the prelicensure phase and thereafter to practice safely and provide quality care to reach needed outcomes, then CQI will not be effective and care will continue to be poor.

Staff Development Functions

Communication and documentation of staff development activities are key aspects of effective, efficient staff development services. The following are important to develop and maintain as records:

- Staff development vision, mission, goals, and objectives
- Organizational chart
- Staff development position descriptions
- Staff development staff meeting minutes
- Staff development policies and procedures
- Monthly report of staff development activities
- Lesson plans
- Attendance records that include title of offering, date, length, participant names, credentials, and unit/division/position
- Correspondence
- Continuing education records if the program is approved to offer continuing education (CE) credit
- Participant evaluation data and analysis of data
- Budget and monthly budget records
- List of equipment and supplies on hand
- Performance evaluation records per staff development staff

Communication is complex as staff who work in staff development must relate to many different staff, patients/families, and also members of the community. Collaboration and negotiation are part of daily routine. The director needs to collaborate with nursing administrators and managers to identify the best schedule for staff development offerings, identify needs and assess outcomes, and work through issues. It is easy for staff development to become the "dump" when there are issues such as CQI problems. This often happens before the problem is analyzed—neglecting to use root cause analysis and assuming that training will solve the problem. It may not be needed or may be needed in conjunction with other changes, but assuming this without analysis is not effective or efficient. The director must listen and find ways to communicate with others that staff development is not trying to avoid its responsibilities but rather wants a clear perspective of the problem before education is developed and provided.

The staff development service often assumes a major role as change agent. Changes frequently require staff education, and staff development needs to be involved in the change process and decision making from the beginning. Probably one of the major examples of this today is when the HCO transitions to an electronic medical/health record (EMR/EHR) or makes changes in the EMR/EHR. (See Chapter 19.) This is an administrative decision but requires staff education and extremely effective collaboration to get the training to all the staff who need it—working with administration and all the major services such as nursing, staff development, nurse managers, medical records, medical staff, informatics, and others; developing the learning outcomes and content; scheduling staff; developing and implementing evaluation of the educational experience; arranging use of space and technology; and possibly collaboration with an external vendor for the EMR/EHR. This requires careful planning and communication that is clear, with responsibilities identified. Changes in clinical equipment or adding new equipment are other common examples of changes requiring an active staff development role so the staff is prepared to use the equipment effectively and safely—safely for staff and patients. Staff development needs to be very aware of the change process and its implications. (See Chapter 3.) Supervision should be provided by staff in supervisory positions, not staff development specialists, who are typically not supervisors, though they do need supervisory evaluation feedback about education outcomes to assess orientation and education programs.

A staff development advisory committee can be very helpful in providing information about educational needs and engaging staff in the staff development process. This committee can also assist in the ongoing evaluation of staff development activities. The committee, with nurse manager and staff nurse representatives, should meet regularly and keep minutes. The director of staff development and other staff development personnel, as needed, should attend the meetings. The staff development director typically serves as the chair. The committee also assists with maintaining routine communication between staff development and staff within the HCO.

THE STAFF EDUCATION PROCESS: DEVELOPMENT, IMPLEMENTATION, AND EVALUATION OF STAFF EDUCATION LEARNING ACTIVITIES

Staff education needs to be based on adult education principles. Staff are not students in the traditional sense. They are adults who need to be engaged in the entire learning process, from assessment of learning needs to evaluation within the work setting. They also come to learning situations with experience: clinical, management, and life experiences. Nursing staff are typically more focused on learning when it applies to what they do, and they want to know how something can be applied—not in the future but now. Is it relevant to me? The process to get to the most effective and efficient staff development experiences includes the following.

Learning Needs Analysis

Development of the annual plan of topics and learning experiences requires careful assessment. Analysis of learning needs provides critical information to plan effective educational options that meet the demands of the HCO and its patients and staff. Information is gathered routinely and analyzed as to its relevance to staff education and also to prioritize needs. It is important to include the learner in this assessment as this engages the learner from the beginning and provides information about the learner's assessment of learning needs. Sources of this information may come from the following:

- Staff requests
- Staff and management questionnaires
- Staff development advisory committee
- Management suggestions
- Changes within the HCO (e.g., clinical, administrative, types of patients and services, equipment, informatics)
- CQI data and analysis
- Evaluation from past educational offerings
- Trends in nursing and health care in general
- Observations of practice
- Patient satisfaction data and analysis

Based on the needs analysis, staff development identifies topics and learning experiences that should be offered on a routine basis and additional topics. Critical topics that need to be part of staff education on a routine basis are the following:

- Orientation
- Patient care management and interventions
- Pharmacology
- Continuous quality improvement
- Teamwork: Intraprofessional and interprofessional
- Communication
- Coordination and collaboration
- Patient-centered/family-centered care
- Health informatics, such as EMR/EHR and other electronic methods used in care

- Ethical decision making
- End-of-life care and palliative care
- Care management to improve and prevent errors and problems, such as skin care, fall prevention, and medication administration
- Pain management
- Hospital-acquired complications
- Incivility and conflict management
- Safety culture
- Participation in change and planning
- Cultural competence
- Evidence-based practice

Leadership and management content and related learning experiences should be a part of staff education. This content is typically focused on staff in management positions; however, some of this content also needs to be available to staff who are interested in career advancement or may need to develop these competencies for their current positions. Some HCOs refer staff to external sources for this training; some combine external and internal experiences; and some just rely on internal learning experiences. Whatever approach is used, it needs to be tailored to individual needs based on staff assessment and goals. Managers require ongoing learning experiences to maintain their leadership and management competencies. Content and experiences need to be based on requirements for effective management and centered on typical management functions as noted in this textbook. New managers should work with mentors to further develop their competencies and provide a resource for discussion and guidance. Staff also need to be counseled about continuing their academic education (e.g., RN-BSN or graduate degree). Along with staff supervisors, staff development specialists often are involved in working with staff on their degree planning. *The Future of Nursing* report includes the RN-BSN in its recommendations:

Recommendation 4: Increase the proportion of nurses with a baccalaureate degree to 80 percent by 2020. *Academic nurse leaders across all schools of nursing should work together to increase the proportion of nurses with a baccalaureate degree from 50 to 80 percent by 2020. These leaders should partner with education accrediting bodies, private and public funders, and employers to ensure funding, monitor progress, and increase the diversity of students to create a workforce prepared to meet the demands of diverse populations across the lifespan.*

- The Commission on Collegiate Nursing Education, working in collaboration with the National League for Nursing Accrediting Commission, should require all nursing schools to offer defined academic pathways, beyond articulation agreements, that promote seamless access for nurses to higher levels of education.
- Health care organizations should encourage nurses with associate's and diploma degrees to enter baccalaureate nursing programs within 5 years of graduation by offering tuition reimbursement, creating a culture that fosters continuing education, and providing a salary differential and promotion.
- Private and public funders should collaborate, and when possible pool funds, to expand baccalaureate programs to enroll more students by offering scholarships and loan forgiveness, hiring more faculty, expanding clinical instruction through new clinical partnerships, and using technology to augment instruction. These efforts should take into consideration strategies to increase the diversity of the nursing workforce in terms of race/ethnicity, gender, and geographic distribution.
- The U.S. Secretary of Education, other federal agencies including the Health Resources and Services Administration, and state and private funders should expand loans and grants for second-degree nursing students.
- Schools of nursing, in collaboration with other health professional schools, should design and implement early and continuous interprofessional collaboration through joint classroom and clinical training opportunities.
- Academic nurse leaders should partner with health care organizations, leaders from primary and secondary school systems, and other community organizations to recruit and advance diverse nursing students (Institute of Medicine, 2011, pp. S-10–S-11).

The report also recommends that the number of nurses with doctoral degrees (PhD and Doctor of Nursing Practice) double by 2020. Nurses who are qualified for this degree should be encouraged to pursue it as part of career development.

Other staff education content may be related to changes in the HCO such as new services, different types of patients and treatment, technology, pharmacology, and changes in healthcare policy that can impact care such as increased use of home care referral after discharge; changes in clinic services; increased number of patients who are immigrants or have language differences requiring greater knowledge about health literacy; and CQI data and analysis as well as government and accreditation requirements. For example, the Joint Commission identifies annual safety goals, and these need to be part of the annual staff development plan. Identification of the annual topics should include not only staff needs analysis but also input from management. Even with a plan, issues arise during the year that necessitate additions and/or changes in the list of topics, requiring flexibility on the part of staff development personnel. An example is the Ebola epidemic in West Africa that spread to the U.S. requiring hospitals to train staff in assessment of potential patients with Ebola, staff and patient safety, the need to respond immediately if potential patients were identified, and how to care for these patients. Experience demonstrated that this preparation was not done as early as it should have been done. This is a good example of the need for staff education to be aware of current care concerns and to plan ahead whenever possible.

Planning and Teaching/Learning Strategies

Planning specific educational offerings should include stakeholders and be based on adult learning principles. The plan should be written and include the following information:

- Title
- Learning outcomes
- Number of expected participants and type
- Length of the program
- CE offered or not (if so, who is the CE provider[s])
- Instructor(s) (records of instructor qualifications should be maintained)
- Outline of content
- Teaching/learning strategies
- Equipment, supplies, space required
- Evaluation method(s)

Methods used in staff development programs can vary depending on the topic, targeted participants, and learning outcomes. The typical method is lecture or presentation, although if it does not include methods to engage the audience such as cases, questions and answers, and team/group work, this may not always be the best method. The size of the audience can vary, but smaller audiences provide greater opportunity for participant engagement. Demonstration may be included for clinical topics, and participants may be asked to practice and demonstrate in the session. Some topics are covered in one session, and others require multiple sessions. Use of the Internet is growing, including elearning formats for staff, which can be useful to reach more staff and reduce scheduling challenges. This method requires expertise in developing the content and technology support; however, there are also many resources that the HCO can use to get elearning materials developed by an external source. Staff development needs to review these resources carefully to ensure that the content meets required needs and is current, easy to use, and designed so staff can meet learning outcomes. Cost is also a factor as well as how participants access the course and how the results of participation are tracked. HCO informatics staff may be helpful in assessing the technological aspects of the elearning resource. The Advisory Committee on Interdisciplinary, Community-Based Linkages identifies several common elearning methods such as multimedia (audio, visual, computer animation), virtual patients simulating real-life scenarios; Web-based learning that is instructor led or self-paced; and video or Web conferences (2011).

Simulation is also more common, although it requires special space, equipment, and instructors with simulation training. Some large medical centers develop their own simulation centers. Others share simulation space and resources, for example, with a college of nursing. The instructional staff who guide simulated experiences need specialized training in the effective use of the equipment and integration of learning experiences that meet the required learning outcomes, including use of debriefing so staff can better appreciate the learning experience. Simulation experiences are expensive and require instructional staff to develop learning activities (and their training), setup before and breakdown after simulation, staff to attend and debrief, availability of equipment and supplies, maintenance of equipment, and space. Simulation focuses on smaller teams, requiring repetition if a large number of staff need the experience, which increases its cost. Simulation is also an effective method for developing interprofessional teamwork and addressing CQI concerns. Some advantages of using simulation include:

- repetitive practice opportunities that do not include patient risk.
- structured experiences that enhance specific areas of care.
- learner engagement.
- building on prior knowledge and experiences.
- teamwork: practice, debrief, and analyze team interactions.
- improving confidence: Individual and team.
- improving critical thinking and clinical reasoning and judgment.
- preprogrammed rare events.
- offering varying difficulty levels of scenarios and actions required.
- observing different outcomes of a situation and discuss impact of actions taken.
- emergency response.
- setting priorities.
- practice assessment and determine healthcare problem and action taken.

Implementation of Staff Education Experiences

Implementation can be complex due to the number of staff and the 24/7 nature of most HCOs. Scheduling is always a challenge, and it requires close collaboration with managers and staff. For many educational offerings, repetitive scheduling is required so staff can easily attend. This also means that the schedules for staff development specialists or unit-based staff development specialists must include flexible hours. Since space is often limited, particularly if staff development does not have designated classroom and conference room space, arranging space for education often requires negotiation and collaboration. Staff development ensures that needed equipment and supplies are maintained so there is no last-minute rush to find information, equipment, supplies, and so on. If computers are used for training, this, too, can be difficult as typically the number of computers that can be used for a training session is limited. Audiovisual equipment must be maintained so it is accessible and operational. Setting up for a program and ending a program can take time, depending on the nature of the program. There should be a policy and procedure regarding attendance records that correlates with human resources and information required by management. If CE is provided, then staff development must complete all documentation required as a CE provider, or the CE program may need to be approved by an external organization; required documentation must be completed and submitted in a timely manner so CE can be offered. Marketing is also a significant factor to inform staff in a timely manner about educational opportunities. Multiple methods such as the HCO website, email, print flyers on bulletin boards, announcements at meetings, and so on are used for marketing.

Evaluation

Evaluation is part of planning and implementation of education offerings. It should not be an afterthought. Typically at the completion of an educational offering, participants are asked to complete a brief evaluation questionnaire. Other methods include asking individual participants or nurse managers via interviews or surveys to assess changes in practice that relate to learning outcomes. For some programs, quizzes may be used, though adult learners do not like this type of evaluation; return demonstration may be a better method to determine if learning outcomes have been met. Group feedback may be requested at the end of a program. Evaluation should include assessment of the content and learning outcomes, instructor, learning environment and schedule, and impact on practice. CQI data and analysis may be used during evaluation of educational experiences, but it is difficult to assess the impact of staff development on practice as many factors affect the quality of care. Evaluation is also a good opportunity to ask participants about additional educational needs. Analysis of evaluation data is part of the process. Staff development specialists should participate in this analysis. Any other stakeholders who might provide an important perspective, such as nurse managers and the staff development advisory

CASE STUDY

Improving Care Through Staff Education

You are the director of staff development focused on nursing services for a 600-bed acute care hospital. In this position you attend the weekly chief nurse executive (CNE) meeting with the nurse managers. As you enter the room, you scan the agenda, which you did not have time to review prior to the meeting. You know this was a mistake, and sure enough, there is a surprise item on the agenda: Discuss staff development plan to address increase in hospital-acquired complications (HACs). You review in your head past meetings and scan

the last meeting's minutes, which you brought with you on your tablet. You see no information or discussion about HACs. You sit there and get frustrated. The item comes up in the meeting.

You know this is a complicated issue and has "political" aspects. Your immediate supervisor, the CNE, is at the meeting along with all the nurse managers who do not want responsibility for the problem.

Questions:

1. How should you handle this?
2. What should be your tone? Describe what you propose as next steps.

---

committee, should be included as well. This information then can be used for improvement where needed.

ORIENTATION

Orientation provides a structured method to get all new staff members ready to do the job they were hired to do, and it is important for staff retention. As mentioned later in this chapter, organized postgraduate residencies can be helpful to new graduates, but first they need to complete orientation. The **nurse residency** provides them with more intensive support, guided experience, and further education. Orientation has two major focus areas: General orientation and specific position and unit/service orientation.

A work contract or commitment is established during orientation as new staff gain a greater understanding of the HCO and its expectations. New staff should get the sense of respect given to staff and the importance of staff input and become engaged in the HCO culture. Along with orientation, staff development and continuing education are important tools in not only staff retention but also recruitment. A strong program that ensures staff competency will be noticed by candidates for positions and may have an impact on candidate decisions. Staff candidates should ask about orientation prior to accepting a position—length of orientation, its organization (classroom and clinical), curriculum, and support services such as use of preceptors.

What is an effective orientation program? First, it must be organized, and orientee feedback needs to be used to evaluate orientation and improve the experience. Orientation should include up-to-date general information about the organization. Typical content includes the HCO's vision, mission, goals, objectives, structure, shared governance (if applicable), human resources or personnel policies and procedures, benefits, communication, labor union (if applicable), staff education/development, and career advancement. Orientation specific to the worksite or unit including its relevant goals, structure, communication, and policies and procedures must also be provided. Typically HCOs provide a general orientation covering content that all staff need to know and a more specific orientation related to unit/division and position. Preceptors or mentors should be assigned to orientees to assist with their orientation. The best preceptors are those who volunteer and can be available to the new staff. Preceptors help new staff, particularly recent graduates, develop self-confidence, gain understanding of the workplace culture, improve competencies when needed, and provide a collegial relationship to discuss concerns and get some advice in a situation that is not supervisory. Preceptors should receive orientation to the role, and nurse managers and staff development should work with preceptors routinely to ensure that they are providing effective support to new staff. This should include getting feedback from new staff about their preceptor experiences. This experience has a strong impact on staff retention.

Orientation is often viewed as boring and approached with dread. Orientation programs that try to make orientation an interactive experience, allowing new employees time to get to know one another as well as other staff, are more effective. The experience should provide new employees with the information and tools they need to begin a new position in the organization.

Orientation is also important for employees who are changing positions, transferring from one area to another or through a promotion; however, this orientation is often neglected. Orientation for staff changing positions needs to be specific to the new position. When new positions are considered, nurses should ask about preceptors and their use in orientation to a new position. Potential employees should ask what is provided to staff when staff change positions or are promoted within the organization as this will demonstrate how the organization values career advancement and change.

Orientation content for nursing staff typically includes the following:

- HCO and nursing visions, missions, goals, and objectives
- HCO organization
- Introduction of key leaders
- Policies and procedures
- Human resources and personnel issues
- CQI
- Physical layout and tour
- Nursing service vision, mission, goals, objectives, and organization
- Types of patients and services
- Relationship with the community
- Staff development and continuing education
- Intraprofessional and interprofessional teams
- Patient-centered/family-centered care
- Staff roles and responsibilities; position descriptions
- Delegation
- Performance appraisal requirements and process
- Pharmacy and medication administration
- Communication
- Documentation, including EMR/EHR, if used
- Incivility and conflict management
- Evidenced-based practice

CONTINUING EDUCATION

Continuing education is different from staff development. CE is focused on individual health professionals and their educational needs chosen by the individual professional. Some states require CE for relicensure, or if the nurse is certified, he or she will need to maintain a level of CE activity. Staff development is focused on employer needs for staff education. What do staff need to know to perform at the expected level for the HCO? The IOM report *Redesigning Continuing Education in the Health Professions* (2009) is an important report that continues the conversation about health profession education. The IOM report *Health Professions Education* (2003) focused primarily on prelicensure education and key core competencies for all health professions, and the 2009 report examined continuing education for health professions. The purpose of CE is to provide opportunity for health professionals to keep their knowledge and skills up to date, which should help to improve performance and quality care. The report criticizes current CE efforts for all health professions as inadequate in how CE is implemented, financed, regulated, and evaluated. There is too much focus on regulatory requirements and not enough on individual performance improvement. CE does not use a coordinated approach that would lead to continued competency. Nursing has its own CE provider system, just as do other health professionals, complicating the process and outcomes. The American Nurses Credentialing Center (ANCC), which is part of the ANA, accredits Continuing Nursing Education providers. A recent change provides an option for joint approval and participation in interprofessional continuing education, as described on the ANCC website. The IOM suggests that improvement is needed, and there should be more collaborative interprofessional CE. The report recommends that there should be a system of continuing professional development (CPD), and the U.S. Department of Health and Human Services (HHS) should plan how this system would be designed and implemented, including data collection, development of national standards for regulation of CPD, funding, research about professional development, and evaluation methods (Institute of Medicine, 2009). The ANA now uses the term CPD on its website about CE. The 2011 report *Core Competencies for Interprofessional Collaborative Practice* emphasizes that "healthcare professionals must recognize the limits of their professional expertise within our nation's complex healthcare system, and collaborate with other healthcare professionals to provide quality patient-centered care. This patient-centered and team-based care is enhanced by participating in CPD and demonstrating the five IOM core competencies in practice" (Advisory Committee on Interdisciplinary, Community-Based Linkages, 2011, p. 11). The secretary of HHS made this report to the U.S. Congress. In this report the Advisory Committee on Interdisciplinary, Community-Based Linkages (ACICBL) recommends the following:

1. Congress and Health Resources and Services Administration (HRSA) should expand support for continuing professional development and lifelong learning activities within Title VII, Part D programs through activities such as collaborative partnerships with foundations and other agencies.
2. HRSA should initiate efforts to identify a mechanism, by the end of fiscal year 2013, that will build capacity in Title VII, Part D programs to increase faculty members' knowledge and abilities in the application of distance learning and e-learning technologies. These technologies can be utilized in the ongoing development of interprofessional education, training, and continuing professional development program.
3. HRSA should convene public-private partners, representative leadership of Title VII, Part D programs, and other stakeholders by no later than the end of fiscal year 2014, to develop recommendations and an action plan for the evaluation of interprofessional competencies attained through continuing professional development and lifelong learning, including the collection, development, refinement, standardization, implementation, and dissemination of innovative methods for evaluation (2011, pp. 14, 15, 17).

The ACICBL also recommends that the critical first step is to incorporate the healthcare professions five core competencies into CPD and lifelong learning. "Effective CE, CPD, and lifelong learning must utilize technology-based educational tools, such as e-learning, to disseminate evidence-based knowledge in real time and to accommodate the varying schedules and settings of today's healthcare professional" (Advisory Committee on Interdisciplinary, Community-Based Linkages, 2011, p. 19).

INTERPROFESSIONAL EDUCATION

Interprofessional education (IPE) is a weak component of prelicensure health profession programs, staff development, and continuing education. Some content may be included, but clear designation of competencies has been missing. The nursing profession is now a strong supporter of IPE (Barnsteiner, Disch, Hall, Mayer, & Moore, 2007; Ladden, Bednash, Stevens, & Moore, 2006; Mitchell et al., 2006).

Work in interprofessional teams is one of the healthcare professions five core competencies, as discussed in this chapter and earlier in the text. This requirement relates to other initiatives supporting interprofessional healthcare teamwork. The World Health Organization (WHO) states that IPE "occurs when two or more professionals learn about, from, and with each other to enable effective collaboration and improve health outcomes" (2010, p. 13). Figures 20-2 and 20-3 provide common perspectives of interprofessional teams and IPE. Various terms are used to describe the meaning of "interprofessional," and it can be confusing, but "interprofessional" is the preferred term. The following are key definitions to compare:

- **Interdisciplinary:** In an interdisciplinary representation there is interaction between professions but little, if any, sharing of values or knowledge. Interdisciplinary education lacks a clear process and coordination of education of the disciplines since, although the disciplines practice together, they are not truly collaborative and integrated with priority focus on the patient.

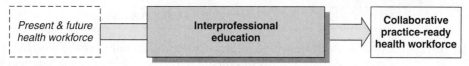

Figure 20-2 Interprofessional education

Source: From *Framework for Action on Interprofessional Education & Collaborative Practice*. Copyright © 2010 by World Health Organisation.

- **Multidisciplinary:** Multidisciplinary implies a coexistence of several disciplines where participants work side-by-side but separately and without substantial interaction. Differing emphases within a multidisciplinary approach may be an impediment to practice or teaching effectiveness. There is no sharing between disciplines in multidisciplinary practice. Disciplines are interacting with the patient but not with one another.
- **Interprofessional:** IPE implies shared goals, a common learning process, coordination of teaching efforts, and shared decision-making and accountability. In the representation of IPE, discipline circles are interlocked, including an interlocking with the patient circle (Olenick, Allen, & Smego, 2010, p. 78).

Chapters 12, 13, and 14 discuss teams in more detail.

Planning IPE experiences should include a clear vision of individual professional competencies, for example, specific to nursing; the five core competencies for health professions; and the interprofessional teamwork competencies. The focus areas of interprofessional teamwork competencies that are included in IPE include:

- **Values/Ethics for Interprofessional Practice:** Work with individuals of other professions to maintain a climate of mutual respect and shared values.
- **Roles and Responsibilities:** Use the knowledge of one's own role and those of other professions to appropriately assess and address the healthcare needs of the patients and populations served.
- **Interprofessional Communication:** Communicate with patients, families, communities, and other health professionals in a responsive and responsible manner that supports a team approach to the maintenance of health and the treatment of disease.
- **Teams and Teamwork:** Apply relationship-building values and the principles of team dynamics to perform effectively in different team roles to plan and deliver patient/population-centered care that is safe, timely, efficient, effective, and equitable (Interprofessional Education Collaborative, 2011, pp. 19, 21, 23).

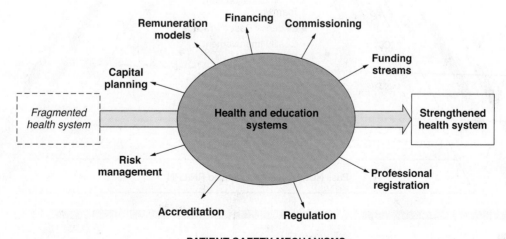

PATIENT SAFETY MECHANISMS

Figure 20-3 Examples of influences that affect interprofessional education and collaborative practice at the system level

Source: From *Framework for Action on Interprofessional Education & Collaborative Practice*. Copyright © 2010 by World Health Organisation.

NURSE RESIDENCY PROGRAMS

Concern about transition to practice has increased over the past few years. The National Council of State Boards of Nursing (NCSBN) describes the problem by highlighting the following (2014):

- **The Problem:** New nurses care for sicker patients in increasingly complex health settings.
  The Impact: More than 40% report making medication errors.
- **The Problem:** New nurses feel increased stress levels.
  The Impact: Stress is a risk factor for patient safety and practice errors.
- **The Problem:** Approximately 25% of new nurses leave a position within their first year of practice.
  The Impact: Increased turnover negatively influences patient safety and healthcare outcomes.

Figure 20-4 describes the NCSBN transition-to-practice model that ties together education, regulation, and practice. The NCSBN website provides additional information that can be used to prepare new graduates for effective practice.

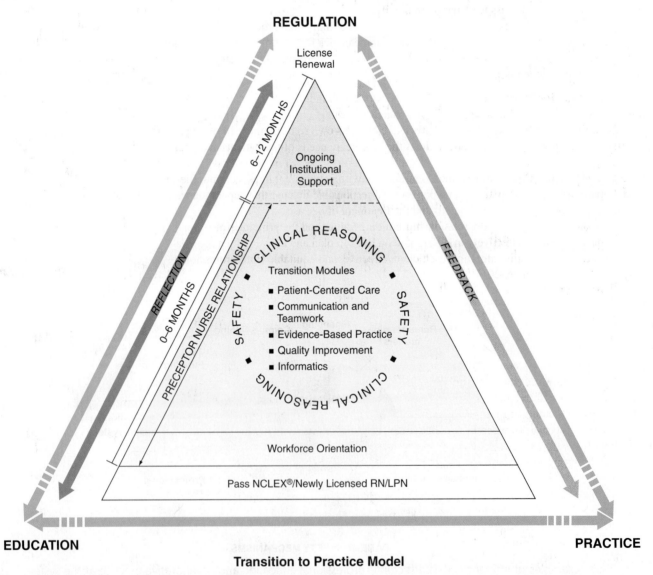

Transition to Practice Model

Figure 20-4 Transition-to-practice model

Source: From *A Transition to Practice Regulatory Model: Changing the Nursing Paradigm.* Copyright © 2009 by National Council of State Boards of Nursing.

The Future of Nursing report also includes information about nurse residencies in its recommendations:

> **Recommendation 3: Implement nurse residency programs.** *State boards of nursing, accrediting bodies, the federal government, and healthcare organizations should take actions to support nurses' completion of a transition-to-practice program (nurse residency) after they have completed a pre-licensure or advanced practice degree program or when they are transitioning into new clinical practice areas.* (Institute of Medicine, 2011, pp. S-9–S-10)

According to this report, the following actions should be taken to implement and support nurse residency programs:

- State boards of nursing, in collaboration with accrediting bodies, such as the Joint Commission and the Community Health Accreditation Program, should support nurses' completion of a residency program after they have completed a pre-licensure or advanced practice degree program or when they are transitioning into new clinical practice areas.
- The Secretary of Health and Human Services should redirect all graduate medical education funding from diploma nursing programs to support the implementation of nurse residency programs in rural and critical access areas.
- Healthcare organizations, the Health Resources and Services Administration and Centers for Medicare and Medicaid Services, and philanthropic organizations should fund the development and implementation of nurse residency programs across all practice settings.
- Healthcare organizations that offer nurse residency programs and foundations should evaluate the effectiveness of the residency programs in improving the retention of nurses, expanding competencies, and improving patient outcomes (Institute of Medicine, 2011, pp. 7-10–7-11).

To address the problem of new graduate transition to practice, there should be an increase in the development of nurse residency programs to provide more options for new graduates. Nurse residencies also impact recruitment and retention of staff. (See Chapter 8.) The staff development service often is connected to these programs or may even administrate the nurse residency program. The American Association of Colleges of Nursing (AACN) through its accrediting organization, the Commission on Collegiate Nursing Education (CCNE), offers accreditation opportunity for post-baccalaureate nurse residency programs that are offered in collaboration with an HCO and an academic nursing program, as described on its website. Standards for this accreditation are available and focus on (1) Program quality: Institutional commitment and resources, (2) Program quality: Curriculum, and (3) Program effectiveness (Commission on Collegiate Nursing Education, 2008). The CCNE identifies the following as factors that have had an impact on the development of nurse residency programs:

1. Research demonstrates improved outcomes for patients when care is provided by a baccalaureate prepared nurse. The American Organization of Nurse Executives and the American Hospital Association released a statement supporting that the educational preparation of the nurse of the future should be at the baccalaureate level. This education will prepare the nurse of the future to function as a collaborator and manager of the complex patient care journey.
2. The complexity of patient care today requires highly competent nurses who use research and other forms of evidence to guide practice to ensure patient safety and quality care. New baccalaureate graduates must develop skills to apply valid, current, and emerging evidence to improve outcomes for their patients. Education, training, and support for new nurses are necessary to fully develop professional practice and skills critical to patient safety and quality of care. Many acute care hospitals provide extended orientation and/or residency programs to support new graduates in the transition into practice.
3. An aging nursing workforce, combined with diverse career opportunities and an increased societal need, are driving the demand for professional nurses. The support and education provided in the post-baccalaureate nurse residency programs are designed to improve retention and job satisfaction for new graduates, and to strengthen their life-long commitment to professional nursing (2008, p. 6).

The purposes of the residency experience are:

1. Transition from entry-level, advanced beginner nurse to competent professional nurse who provides safe, quality care.
2. Develop effective decision-making skills related to clinical judgment and performance.

3. Develop strategies to incorporate research-based and other evidence into practice.
4. Develop clinical leadership skills at the point of patient care.
5. Formulate an individual career plan that promotes a life-long commitment to professional nursing (Commission on Collegiate Nursing Education, 2008, p. 7).

Residency programs are expensive to develop and implement. They require a strong commitment from HCO administration so there is not a drain on other staff development activities when the residency program requirements use resources.

Residency is not a replacement for orientation. New graduates should complete the HCO orientation then enter the residency program. Content and learning experiences in the residency program vary depending on the specialty focus (e.g., intensive care, emergency department, medical nursing, and so on). Listed below are examples of core content and experiences that should be included in nurse residency programs:

- Critical thinking and clinical reasoning and judgment
- Care planning and priorities
- Delegation
- Ethical decision making
- Teamwork: Intraprofessional and interprofessional
- Communication
- Coordination and collaboration
- Leadership
- Professional role
- CQI
- Evidence-based practice
- Career development
- Lifelong learning
- Stress management
- Resource management

The CCNE standards describe many content areas that should be included in the residency curriculum. Typical teaching/learning strategies include lectures, discussions, case analysis, practice and demonstration, simulation, resident projects and presentations, elearning, and other similar types of strategies that would be used to engage the adult learner. Preceptors are assigned to residents to provide a long-term, one-to-one professional experience for each resident. Preceptors need to be prepared for this role and understand the nurse residency program.

Some HCOs offer residency opportunities to staff who are changing specialties, though this is not common. When this type of residency is offered, it is more individualized, based on the nurse's previous experiences and learning needs. The typical residency is one year in length.

APPLYING LEADERSHIP AND MANAGEMENT

My Hospital Unit: An Evolving Case Experience

This is your last visit to your hospital unit as its nurse manager. It is critical that units function effectively and deliver quality care that meets the patients' needs and that staff feel confident about their performance. You now must meet your nurse manager responsibility focused on staff development for your unit. You are in a hospital that uses a decentralized approach, but there is a director of staff development and several staff development specialists who assist the units as needed with staff development unit-based activities. How will you organize the unit's staff development? Who will be involved? What impact does this have on the unit's budget? How will you apply the staff development process and develop your plan? In the plan include a list of content that is specific to your unit that you want covered in the first year. Since this is the unit you have developed throughout this textbook, you need to consider decisions made in the past and characteristics of the unit and staff that you have described.

BSN and *Master's Essentials:* Application to Content

(All *Essentials* apply to this chapter content, but more critical *Essentials* are identified.)
***BSN Essentials* (American Association of Colleges of Nursing, 2008) as Applied to this Chapter:**

VIII. Professionalism and Professional Values
  IX. Baccalaureate Generalist Nursing Practice

***Master's Essentials* (American Association of Colleges of Nursing, 2011) as Applied to this Chapter:**

  IX. Master's-Level Nursing Practice

Applying AONE Competencies

Identify which of the AONE competencies found in Appendix A apply to the content of this chapter.

Engaging in the Content: Critical Thinking and Clinical Reasoning and Judgment

Discussion Questions

1. Why is staff education important? (Online Application Option)
2. What are the key aspects of providing effective staff education?
3. Why is interprofessional education important? (Online Application Option)
4. What are the five healthcare professions core competencies, and how do they compare with interprofessional education competencies?
5. Why is staff orientation important? What do you think should be included in an effective staff orientation program for you?

Application Exercises

1. Search the Internet for examples of nurse residency programs. How are they designed, and what is included in the residency curricula and experiences? Is there a program that appeals to you and why?
2. Interview a nurse who works in staff development. Prior to the interview, develop key questions you will ask. Summarize your responses. (Online Application Option)
3. Working in teams, each team should prepare a list of leadership and management topics that they would want offered to them if they were in a nurse manager position. Other teams should also identify leadership and management content but for a nurse in a staff nurse position. Share results and compare and contrast in discussion, noting similar topics and how the content might be described differently for the nurse manager and for the staff nurse. Consider position descriptions in this discussion. (Online Application Option)
4. Attend a staff development program in an HCO or a CE program offered locally. Summarize your experience and identify the presenter and qualifications, learning outcomes and if they were met, key points from the content, and your evaluation of the experience. (Online Application Option)
5. Review a healthcare organization's listing of staff development/education offerings for one year. What do you find on the list? Does any topic surprise you and why? Are topics repeated? Which topics and why do you think they are repeated?

References

Advisory Committee on Interdisciplinary, Community-Based Linkages. (2011). *Continuing education, professional development, and lifelong learning for the 21st century health care workforce.* Retrieved from http://www.hrsa.gov/advisorycommittees/bhpradvisory/acicbl/reports/eleventhreport.pdf

American Association of Colleges of Nursing. (2008). *The essentials of baccalaureate education for profession nursing practice.* Washington, DC: Author.

American Association of Colleges of Nursing. (2011). *The essentials of master's education in nursing.* Washington, DC: Author.

American Nurses Association & National Nursing Staff Development Organization. (2010). *Nursing professional development: Scope and standards of practice.* Silver Spring, MD: Author.

Barnsteiner, J., Disch, J., Hall, L., Mayer, D., & Moore, S. (2007). Promoting interprofessional education. *Nursing Outlook, 55*(3), 144–150.

Commission on Collegiate Nursing Education. (2008). Excerpt from *Standards for Accreditation of Post-Baccalaureate Nurse Residency Programs.* Washington, DC: Author.

Institute of Medicine. (2003). *Health professions education: A bridge to quality.* Washington, DC: National Academies Press.

Institute of Medicine. (2009). *Redesigning continuing education in the health professions.* Washington, DC: National Academies Press.

Institute of Medicine. (2011). *The future of nursing: Leading change, advancing health*. Washington, DC: National Academies Press.

Interprofessional Education Collaborative. (2011). *Core competencies for interprofessional collaborative practice: Report of an expert panel*. Washington, DC: Author. Retrieved from http://www.aacn.nche.edu/education/pdf/IPECReport.pdf

Ladden, M., Bednash, G., Stevens, D., & Moore, G. (2006). Educating interprofessional learners for quality, safety, and systems improvement. *Journal of Interprofessional Care, 20*(5), 497–505.

Mitchell, P., Belza, B., Schaad, D., Robins, L., Gianola, F., Odegard, P., . . . Ballweg, R. (2006). Working across boundaries of health professions disciplines in education, research, and service: The University of Washington experience. *Academy of Medicine, 81*, 891–896.

National Council of State Boards of Nursing. (2015). Transition to practice. Retrieved from https://www.ncsbn.org/transition-to-practice.htm

Olenick, M., Allen, L., & Smego, R. (2010). Interprofessional education: A concept. *Advances in Medical Education and Practice*, November, 75–84.

World Health Organization. (2010). *Framework for action on interprofessional education & collaborative practice*. Retrieved from http://whqlibdoc.who.int/hq/2010/WHO_HRH_HPN_10.3_eng.pdf

Nurse Executive Competencies

I. Communication and Relationship-Building

a. Effective Communication
- Make oral presentations to diverse audiences on nursing, health care, and organizational issues
- Produce cogent and persuasive written materials to address nursing, health care, and organizational issues appropriate to the audience
- Resolve and manage conflict

b. Relationship Management
- Build trusting, collaborative relationships with
  - Staff
  - Peers
  - Other disciplines and ancillary services
  - Physicians
  - Vendors
  - Community leaders
  - Legislators
  - Nursing and other educational programs
- Deliver "bad news" in such a way as to maintain credibility
- Follow through on promises and concerns
- Provide service recovery to dissatisfied customers
- Care about people as individuals and demonstrate empathy and concern while ensuring that organizational goals and objectives are met
- Accomplish objectives through persuasion, celebrate successes and accomplishments, and communicate a shared vision
- Assert views in non-threatening, non-judgmental ways

c. Influencing Behaviors
- Create and communicate a shared vision
- Reward appropriate behaviors and confront and manage inappropriate behaviors
- Develop, communicate and monitor behavior expectations

d. Diversity
- Create an environment, which recognizes and values differences in staff, physicians, patients, and communities
- Assess current environment and establish indicators of progress toward cultural competency
- Define diversity in terms of gender, race, religion, ethnicity, sexual orientation, age, etc.
- Analyze population data to identify cultural clusters
- Define cultural competency and permeate principles throughout the organization

- Confront inappropriate behaviors and attitudes toward diverse group
- Develop processes to incorporate cultural beliefs into care

e. Shared Decision Making
- Engage staff and others in decision-making
- Promote decisions that are patient-centered
- Provide an environment conducive to opinion sharing

f. Community Involvement
- Represent the organization to non–health care constituents within the community
- Provide consultation to community and business leaders regarding nursing and health care
- Be an effective board member for community and/or professional organizations

g. Medical Staff Relationships
- Build credibility with physicians as a champion for patient care, quality, and nursing professionalism
- Confront and address inappropriate behavior towards patients and staff
- Represent nursing at medical executive committee and other medical staff committees
- Collaborate with medical staff leaders in determining needed patient care services
- Collaborate with physicians to develop patient care protocols, policies, and procedures
- Collaborate with physicians to determine patient care equipment and facility needs
- Utilize medical staff mechanisms to address physician clinical performance issues
- Facilitate disputes involving physicians and nurses or other disciplines

h. Academic Relationships
- Determine current and future supply and demand for nursing care
- Identify educational needs of existing and potential nursing staff
- Collaborate with nursing programs to provide required resources
- Collaborate with nursing programs in evaluating quality of graduating clinicians and develop mechanisms to enhance this quality
- Serve on academic advisory councils
- Collaborate with nursing faculty in nursing research and incorporate nursing research into practice

II. Knowledge of the Health Care Environment

a. Clinical Practice Knowledge
- Maintain knowledge of current nursing practice and the roles and functions of patient care team members
- Articulate patient care standards as published by JCAHO [Joint Commission], CMS, and professional nursing literature
- Understand, articulate, and ensure compliance with the State Nurse Practice Act, State Board of Nursing regulations, regulatory agency standards, and policies of the organization
- Ensure that written organization clinical policies and procedures are reviewed and updated in accordance with evidence-based practice
- Role model lifelong learning, including clinical subjects such as disease processes, pharmaceuticals, and clinical technology

b. Delivery Models/Work Design
- Maintain current knowledge of patient care delivery systems and innovations
- Articulate various delivery systems and patient care models and the advantages/disadvantages of each
- Serve as change agent when patient care work/workflow is redesigned
- Determine when new delivery models are appropriate, and then envision and develop them

c. Health Care Economics
- Articulate federal and state payment systems and regulations, as well as private insurance issues, which affect organization's finances
- Understand and articulate individual organization's payer mix, CMI, and benchmark database

d. Health Care Policy
  - Articulate federal and state laws and regulations that affect the provision of patient care, e.g., tort reform, malpractice/negligence, reimbursement
  - Participate in the legislative process concerning health care through membership in professional organization and personal contact with public officials
  - Educate patient care team members on the legislative and regulatory processes and methods for influencing both
  - Interpret impact of state and federal legislation on nursing and health care organizations

e. Governance
  - Articulate the role of the governing body of the organization in the following areas:
    - Fiduciary responsibilities
    - Credentialing
    - Performance management
  - Represent patient care issues to the governing body
  - Participate in strategic planning and quality initiatives with the governing body
  - Interact with and educate the organization's board members regarding health care and the value of nursing care
  - Represent nursing at the organization's board meetings

f. Evidence-Based Practice/Outcome Measurement
  - Interpret information from research
  - Utilize research findings for the establishment of standards, practices, and patient care models in the organization
  - Disseminate research findings to patient care team members
  - Participate in studies that provide outcome measurements
  - Allocate nursing resources based on measurement of patient acuity/care needed

g. Patient Safety
  - Support the development and implementation of an organization-wide patient safety program
  - Design safe clinical systems, processes, policies, and procedures
  - Monitor clinical activities to identify both expected and unexpected risks
  - Support a non-punitive reporting environment and a reward system for reporting unsafe practices
  - Support safety surveys, responding and acting on safety recommendations
  - Ensure staff is clinically competent and trained on their role in patient safety
  - Articulate and take action to support the JCAHO National Patient Safety Goals

h. Utilization/Case Management
  - Articulate organization for the criteria model adopted by the organization
  - Communicate key points of the model to a variety of audiences (nursing, financial, medical staff)
  - Involve physicians in on-going utilization management practices
  - Design continuum of care options for managing patient throughput (long term care units, urgent care centers, admission/discharge units, etc.)

i. Quality Improvement/Metrics
  - Articulate the organization's QI program and goals
  - Determine patient care quality improvement goals and objectives
  - Define metrics as related to process improvement
  - Explain and utilize metrics as a unit of measure for any process
  - Articulate the link between metrics and goals
  - Articulate the link between organization metrics and national quality initiatives/metrics
  - Target outcomes that are evidence-based (comparison data benchmarking)
  - Define quality metrics by
    - Identifying the problem/process
    - Measuring success at improving specific areas of patient care
    - Analyzing the root causes or variation from quality standards
    - Improving the process with the evidence
    - Controlling solutions and sustaining success

j. Risk Management
  - Identify areas of risk/liability
  - Ensure staff is educated on risk management and compliance issues
  - Develop systems which encourage/require prompt reporting of potential liability by staff at all levels
  - Envision and take action to correct identified areas of potential liability

III. Leadership

a. Foundational Thinking Skills
  - Address ideas, beliefs, or viewpoints that should be given serious consideration
  - Recognize one's own method of decision making and the role of beliefs, values, and inferences
  - Critically analyze organizational issues after a review of the evidence
  - Maintain curiosity and an eagerness to explore new knowledge and ideas
  - Promote nursing leadership as both a science and an art
  - Demonstrate reflective leadership and an understanding that all leadership begins from within
  - Provide visionary thinking on issues that impact the health care organization
b. Personal Journey Disciplines
  - Value and act on feedback that is provided about one's own strengths and weaknesses
  - Demonstrate the value of lifelong learning through one's own example
  - Learn from setbacks and failures as well as successes
  - Assess one's personal, professional, and career goals and undertake career planning
  - Seek mentorship from respected colleagues
c. Systems Thinking
  - Promote systems thinking as a value in the nursing organization
  - Consider the impact of nursing decisions on the health care organization as a whole
  - Provide leadership in building loyalty and commitment throughout the organization
  - Synthesize and integrate divergent viewpoints for the good of the organization
d. Succession Planning
  - Promote nursing management as a desirable specialty
  - Conduct periodic organizational assessments to identify succession planning issues and establish action plans
  - Serve as a professional role model and mentor to future nursing leaders
  - Establish mechanisms that provide for early identification and mentoring of staff with leadership potential
  - Develop a succession plan for one's own position
e. Change Management
  - Utilize change theory to plan for the implementation of organizational changes
  - Serve as a change agent, assisting others in understanding the importance, necessity, impact, and process of change
  - Support staff during times of difficult transitions
  - Recognize one's own reaction to change and strive to remain open to new ideas and approaches
  - Adapt leadership style to situational needs

IV. Professionalism

a. Personal and Professional Accountability
  - Create an environment that facilitates the team to initiate actions that produce results
  - Hold self and others accountable for actions and outcomes
  - Create an environment in which others are setting expectations and holding each other accountable
  - Answer for the results of one's own behaviors and actions

b. Career Planning
  - Develop own career plan and measure progress according to that plan
  - Coach others in developing their own career plans
  - Create an environment in which professional and personal growth is an expectation

c. Ethics
  - Articulate the application of ethical principles to operations
  - Integrate high ethical standards and core values into everyday work activities
  - Create an environment that has a reputation for high ethical standards

d. Evidence-Based Clinical and Management Practice
  - Advocate use of documented best practices
  - Teach and mentor others to routinely utilize evidence based data and research

e. Advocacy
  - Role model the perspective that patient care is the core of the organization's work
  - Assure that the clinical perspective is included in organizational decisions
  - Ensure that nurses are actively involved in decisions that affect their practice

f. Active Membership in Professional Organizations
  - Participate in at least one professional organization
  - Support and encourage others to participate in a professional organization

V. Business Skills

a. Financial Management
  - Articulate business models for health care organizations and fundamental concepts of economics
  - Describe general accounting principles and define basic accounting terms
  - Analyze financial statements
  - Manage financial resources by developing business plans
  - Establish procedures to assure accurate charging mechanisms
  - Educate patient care team members on financial implications of patient care decisions

b. Human Resource Management
  - Participate in workforce planning and employment decisions
  - Champion a diverse workforce
  - Use corrective discipline to mitigate workplace behavior problems
  - Interpret and evaluate employee satisfaction/quality of work surveys
  - Create opportunities for employees to be involved in decision-making
  - Reward and recognize exemplary performance
  - Formulate programs to enhance work-life balance
  - Interpret legal and regulatory guidelines
  - Manage collective bargaining environments or implement programs to avoid the need [sic]
  - Identify and eliminate sexual harassment, workplace violence, and verbal and physical abuse
  - Implement ergonomically sound work environments to prevent worker injury and fatigue
  - Develop and implement bioterrorism, biohazard, and disaster readiness plans
  - Identify clinical and leadership skills necessary for performing job-related tasks
  - Select top talent, matching organizational needs with appropriate skill sets (assess job candidate skills sets)
  - Manage performance through rewards, recognition, counseling, and disciplinary action
  - Provide mentorship and career counseling to aspiring clinicians and leaders so they may develop required skill sets (succession planning)
  - Identify future skill sets needed to remain competitive
  - Analyze market data in relation to supply and demand and manage resources to ensure appropriate compensation
  - Develop and implement recruitment and retention strategies

c. Strategic Management
   - Analyze the situation and identify strategic direction
   - Conduct SWOT and gap analyses
   - Formulate objectives, goals, and specific strategies related to mission and vision
   - Understand what organizations should measure in order to "balance" the financial perspective
   - Measure and analyze performance from the learning and growth, business process, customer, and financial perspectives

d. Marketing
   - Analyze marketing opportunities
   - Develop marketing strategies
   - Integrate marketing and communications strategies
   - Use public relations and media outlets to promote your organization

e. Information Management and Technology
   - Demonstrate basic competency in e-mail, common word processing, spreadsheet, and Internet programs
   - Recognize the relevance of nursing data for improving practice
   - Recognize limitations of computer applications
   - Use telecommunication devices
   - Utilize hospital database management, decision support, and expert system programs to access information and analyze data from disparate sources for use in planning for patient care processes and systems
   - Participate in system change processes and utility analysis
   - Participate in the evaluation of information systems in practice settings
   - Evaluate and revise patient care processes and systems
   - Use computerized management systems to record administrative data (billing data, quality assurance data, workload data, etc.)
   - Use applications for structured data entry (classification systems, acuity level, etc.)
   - Recognize the utility of nursing involvement in the planning, design, choice and implementation of information systems in the practice environment
   - Demonstrate awareness of societal and technological trends, issues and new developments as they apply to nursing
   - Demonstrate proficient awareness of legal and ethical issues related to client data, information, and confidentiality
   - Read and interpret benchmarking, financial, and occupancy data

Source: From *The AONE Nurse Executive Competencies*. Copyright © 2011 by American Organization of Nurse Executives. Used by permission of American Organization of Nurse Executives. Address reprint permission requests to aone@aha.org.

B Health Care Reform Legislation 2010

On March 30, 2010, President Obama signed the Health Care and Education Reconciliation Act of 2010 (Public Law No. 111-152), which made some changes in the Patient Protection and Affordable Care Act (PPAC) (Public Law No. 111-148) and reconciled these two critical bills. President Obama signed the PPAC March 23, 2010. This legislation is expected to provide health coverage for an additional 32 million people when it is fully implemented in 2019. The following is a description of some of the provisions in this significant healthcare legislation. This summary does not represent all of its provisions.

EFFECTIVE 2010

Provision	Healthcare Delivery and Possible Nursing Implications
Lifetime limits on benefits and restrictive annual limits will be prohibited.	This provision will provide greater coverage for insured.
Seniors will get a $250 rebate to help fill the "doughnut hole" in Medicare prescription drug coverage, which falls between the $2,700 initial limit and when catastrophic coverage kicks in at $6,154.	This provision will increase the opportunity for seniors to receive the medications they need. Nurses can better assist seniors to continue to take medications they need.
Insurers will be barred from imposing exclusions on children with preexisting conditions. Pools will cover those with preexisting health conditions until healthcare coverage exchanges are operational.	Eliminating preexisting conditions for children provides more coverage to children. This will increase the number of children who come in for services and also give the opportunity to provide more effective services for children who have need of care.
New plans must provide coverage for preventive services without copays. All plans must comply by 2018.	This provision will improve health status, offer opportunities for nurses to provide more preventive services, and allow better use of prevention in community health.
Young adults may receive coverage from their parents' insurance until their 27th birthday.	This will provide coverage for a large group of the population who typically do not have insurance.
Businesses with fewer than 50 employees will get tax credits covering 35% of their healthcare premiums, increasing to 50% by 2014.	This provision will expand insurance coverage for many people who did not have access to coverage and expand the number of people coming in for health services.
Establish a nonprofit Patient-Centered Outcomes Research Institute to support comparative effectiveness research.	This provision focuses on evidence-based practice and implications for application. Nurses use EBP, and this provides greater opportunities for nurses in EBP.

(continued)

EFFECTIVE 2010 (CONTINUED)

Provision	Healthcare Delivery and Possible Nursing Implications
Improve care coordination for dual eligibles (Medicare and Medicaid) to improve access and quality.	Care coordination is an important part of care and nursing care, emphasized in the Institute of Medicine priority areas of care.
Establish a Prevention and Public Health Fund for prevention, wellness, and public health activities such as prevention research health screenings and immunization programs.	Nurses are directly involved in preventive services and are very active in public health practice, which will increase.
Establish a grant program to support delivery of evidence-based and community-based prevention and wellness services to improve prevention activities, reduce chronic disease, and address health disparities, especially in rural and frontier areas. Funding is appropriated for five years.	This provision provides greater emphasis on evidence-based practice in community health.
Establish the National Prevention, Health Promotion, and Public Health Council. Purpose: to coordinate federal prevention, wellness, and public health activities; develop a national strategy to improve the nation's health; and disseminate evidence-based recommendations.	This provision provides a more structured approach to health prevention and promotion.
Medicaid to cover tobacco cessation programs for pregnant women.	This provision is important for nurses who work in women's health and obstetrics.
Qualified health plans must cover a minimum coverage without cost sharing for preventive services rated A or B by the U.S. Preventive Services Task Force; recommended immunizations; preventive care for infants, children, and adolescents; and additional preventive care and screenings for women.	This is another provision on prevention particularly focused on pediatrics and women's health; important for nurses who work in these specialties.
Provide new options for home and community-based services through Medicaid.	This provision applies to nurses who work in home health and the community and offers additional opportunities for new innovative approaches to care.
Establish a commissioned Regular Corps and Ready Reserve Corps for assistance during national emergencies.	This provision provides an opportunity for nurses to be prepared to assist in emergency situations.
Establish a multistakeholder National Healthcare Workforce Commission to develop a healthcare workforce strategy.	With the growing nursing shortage and shortage of other healthcare professionals, it is important to better understand the shortage and develop a national plan to address it.
Support development of training programs that focus on primary care models (e.g., medical homes, team management of chronic illness, integration of physical and mental health services).	This provision provides for new approaches and models; nurses should be involved in the development and implementation.
Temporary funding ($5 billion) will be assigned for a national high-risk insurance pool for coverage of individuals with preexisting medical conditions who have been uninsured for at least six months.	This is an important provision to assist patients who need care with coverage.
Nonprofit hospitals must conduct a community needs assessment every three years and adopt an implementation plan based on this assessment.	Nurses who work in hospitals should be involved in this type of assessment and planning. Community health nurses should be active also.

EFFECTIVE 2010 (CONTINUED)

Provision	Healthcare Delivery and Possible Nursing Implications
Improve access to care by increasing funding by $11 billion for school-based health centers (effective 2010), nurse-managed health clinics (effective 2010), and community health centers and National Health Service Corps (over five years—effective 2011).	This provision provides opportunities for nurses to expand practice into new areas or improve areas already active.
Insurance plans may not place lifetime limits on benefits and restrictive annual limits.	This provision is important for all insured to limit costs.
Insurers may not rescind policies to avoid paying medical bills when a person becomes ill.	This provision protects patients to ensure payment of medical bills covered by the patient's insurance plan.

EFFECTIVE 2011

Provision	Healthcare Delivery and Possible Nursing Implications
A 50% discount will be provided on brand-name drugs for Prescription Drug Plan or Medicare Advantage enrollees. Additional discounts on brand-name and generic drugs will be phased in to completely close the "doughnut hole" by 2020.	This provision addresses further the problems with Medicare Part D Prescription coverage.
Cover only proven preventive services and eliminate cost sharing for preventive services in Medicare and Medicaid.	This provision further addresses preventive services and also emphasizes need for evidence-based preventive services.
The Medicare payroll tax will increase from 1.45% to 2.35% for individuals earning more than $200,000 and married filing jointly above $250,000.	This type of provision impacts Medicare beneficiaries in that some employees will have to contribute more to the Medicare fund, based on income levels.
States can offer home- and community-based services to the disabled through Medicaid rather than institutional care beginning October 1.	This provision impacts home care and other community-based services, impacting nurses and nursing care for disabled and providing more services outside of institutions.
Medicare will provide free annual wellness visits and personalized prevention plans. New plans will be required to cover preventive services with no copay.	This provision further supports wellness and prevention. Nurses may be involved in providing these services and developing programs.
Pharmaceutical companies will provide a 50% discount on brand-name prescription drugs for seniors; additional discounts will be phased in over the next 10 years.	This provision reduces costs of prescriptions for seniors, increasing use of prescribed medications.
A plan to provide a vehicle for small businesses to offer tax-free benefits will be created. This would ease the small employer's administrative burden of sponsoring a cafeteria plan.	This provision increases insurance coverage to employees who often do not get an insurance coverage option.
Develop a national quality improvement strategy to improve delivery of healthcare services, patient health outcomes, and population health with multiple stakeholders, including measures. The national strategy needs to be submitted to Congress by January 1, 2011.	This provision is directly related to the Institute of Medicine reports on health quality. Nurses should be involved in this initiative. The National Quality Strategy is discussed in Chapter 17 of this textbook.

(continued)

EFFECTIVE 2011 (CONTINUED)

Provision	Healthcare Delivery and Possible Nursing Implications
Community Living Assistance Services and Supports (CLASS), a voluntary long-term care program, will be created. When employees contribute to the program for five years, they will be entitled to a $50 per day cash benefit to pay for long-term care. CLASS does not cover all long-term care expenses. This is the first national government-run long-term care insurance program, primarily offered through employers.	This provision is a significant step toward addressing the needs of the people who require long-term care. This will impact nurses and nursing in long-term care.
Develop a Medicaid plan option for enrollees with at least two chronic illnesses, one condition and risk of developing another, or at least one serious and persistent mental health conditions to designate a provider as a health home.	This provision relates to information in the Institute of Medicine reports on the need for better care for people with chronic illness. Nurses are involved daily in caring for these patients. The focus here is on better care planning.
Develop the Community-Based Collaborative Care Network Program, which would provide support to consortiums of healthcare providers to coordinate and integrate health services targeted at low-income uninsured and underinsured. Funds for this are appropriated for five years beginning fiscal year 2011.	This provision relates to the Institute of Medicine recommendations to better coordinate care. Nurses who work in community health will need to be involved in this program.
Provide access to comprehensive health risk assessment and a personalized prevention plan for Medicare beneficiaries. Health risk assessment model to be developed with 18 months after law's effective date.	This provision relates to nursing, increasing the emphasis on health risk assessment and a personalized prevention plan, which could be done by nurses.
Provide incentives to Medicare and Medicaid beneficiaries to complete behavior modification programs (criteria need to be developed).	There is need to increase effective completion of behavior modification programs for problems such as substance abuse, obesity, smoking, and other similar problems. Nurses frequently direct these programs and also refer patients to these programs.
Five-year grants provided to small employers that establish wellness programs.	Nurses in occupational health may be involved in developing and implementing these programs.
Establish a new trauma center program to increase emergency capacity; fund research; develop demonstration programs to design, implement, and evaluate innovative emergency care models.	This provision is relevant to nurses who work in emergency and trauma care. Nurses should be involved in all aspects of this provision. This is an opportunity to address emergency nursing care issues. More effective emergency services also impacts acute care in that capacity or ability to admit patients should be improved.
Provide resources to evaluate employer-based wellness programs and conduct a national worksite survey to assess employer-based health policies and programs. (Study to be completed by 2012.)	Nurses in occupational health may be involved in developing and implementing these programs.
Chain restaurants and food vending machines must disclose nutritional content of each item.	This provision is relevant to nurses who work in community health.
Establish a Community First Choice Option for Medicaid beneficiaries with disabilities to receive community-based attendant services and supports rather than institutional care.	This is a new program that improves care for patients with disabilities and has implications for nurses who work in home health care.

EFFECTIVE 2011 (CONTINUED)

Provision	Healthcare Delivery and Possible Nursing Implications
Address the nursing shortage and retention of nurses: increase capacity for education, support training programs, provide loan repayment and retention grants, and create a career ladder to nursing.	This provision is important for all nurses and has a direct impact on the quality of nursing care.
Provide grants (up to three years) to employ and provide training for family nurse practitioners who provide primary care in federally qualified health centers and nurse-managed health clinics. (See http://www.cms.hhs.gov/MLNProducts/downloads/fqhcfactsheet.pdf for information on federally qualified health centers.)	This provision focuses on nurses and advanced practice nurses. It recognizes the important role nurses have in these delivery services.

EFFECTIVE 2012

Provision	Healthcare Delivery and Possible Nursing Implications
Create the Independence in Home demonstration program, providing primary care services in the home for high-need Medicare beneficiaries with the goal of reducing preventable hospitalizations and readmissions, improving health outcomes, improving efficiency of care, reducing costs, and achieving patient satisfaction.	This provision emphasizes need for greater in home services, an area that has strong nursing presence.
Improve collection and reporting of data on race, ethnicity, sex, primary language, disability status, and underserved rural and frontier populations, including data on access and treatment for people with disabilities. Data should be analyzed to identify trends in disparities.	The Institute of Medicine reports on disparities are reflected in this provision. The annual disparities report is one method for collecting data. Data need to be analyzed and results applied to improve care. This has a direct impact on nurses and nursing care, and nurses should be involved in this initiative.
Required mental health parity, which means deductibles, copayments, and limits on the number of visits or days of coverage for mental health and substance abuse treatment must be no more restrictive than for medical and surgical needs.	This provision has implications for nurses who work in mental health. This is an area of care that has struggled with parity problems and discrimination.
Establish more training for behavioral health professionals.	This provision should provide more funding for training, for example for advanced practice nurses or nurse clinical specialists in mental health.
Develop nongovernmental research centers to investigate effective treatment for mental illness.	This provision may provide greater opportunity for nurse researchers in the area of mental health.

EFFECTIVE 2013

Provision	Healthcare Delivery and Possible Nursing Implications
Health plans must implement uniform standards for electronic exchange of health information to reduce paperwork and administrative costs.	This provision is an important one in setting standards for electronic information and to reduce costs.
Increase Medicaid payments for fee-for-service and managed care primary care services provided by primary care physicians (family medicine, general internal medicine, or pediatric medicine).	This provision will provide greater access to providers for Medicaid beneficiaries who are often limited in providers who will accept Medicaid payment rates.

EFFECTIVE 2014

Provision	Healthcare Delivery and Possible Nursing Implications
Citizens will be required to have acceptable coverage or pay a penalty of $95 in 2014, $325 in 2015, $695 (or up to 2.5% of income) in 2016. Families will pay half the amount for children, up to a cap of $2,250 per family. After 2016, penalties are indexed to Consumer Price Index.	This provision is a major change. It requires people to have healthcare insurance, and if they do not, fees must be paid. This will pressure people to get coverage, increasing patients and increasing need for more staff.
Companies with 50 or more employees must offer coverage to employees or pay a $2,000 penalty per employee after their first 30 if at least one of their employees receives a tax credit. Waiting periods before insurance takes effect are limited to 90 days. Employers who offer coverage but whose employees receive tax credits will pay $3,000 for each worker receiving a tax credit.	This increases coverage to people who in the past may have not had an offer of insurance coverage. It leads to more patients and the need for more staff.
Health plans will be prohibited from imposing annual limits on coverage.	This provision provides for greater coverage since limits are decreased and reduces costs for enrollees.
Insurers can no longer refuse to sell or renew policies because of an individual's health status. Health plans can no longer exclude coverage for preexisting conditions. Insurers can't charge higher rates because of health status, gender, or other factors.	This eliminates exclusions and discrimination in healthcare coverage.
Health insurance exchanges will open in each state to individuals and small employers to comparison shop for standardized health packages.	This provision will provide more information to allow consumers to make informed decisions about healthcare coverage.
Medicaid eligibility will increase to 133% of federal poverty level for all nonelderly individuals to ensure people obtain affordable health care in the most efficient and appropriate manner. States will receive increased federal funding to cover these new populations.	This provision will increase the number of insured people, requiring more staff at a time of shortage.

Sources: Health Care and Education Reconciliation Act of 2010 (P.L. 111-152) http://www.gpo.gov/fdsys/pkg/PLAW-111publ152/pdf/PLAW-111publ152.pdf; White House Health Reform http://www.whitehouse.gov/healthreform; The Henry J. Kaiser Family Foundation http://www.kff.org; *New York Times* (March 24, 2010). How people will be affected by the overhaul, p. A18; Wolf, R., & Young, A. (March 23, 2010). Bill spreads the pain, benefits. *USA Today*, pp. 4A–3A; Span, P. (March 30, 2010). Options expand for affordable long-term care. *New York Times*, p. D5.

Photo Credits

Index

Note: Page numbers in italics indicate tables or figures

AACN. *See* American Association of Colleges of Nursing
ACA. *See* Affordable Care Act
Accelerating Change and Transformation in Organizations and Networks (ACTION), 381
Access to care, 397, 433–434
Accountability
  defined, 111
  delegation, 362–363
  in knowledge management theory, 11
  in shared governance, 115
Accountable care organizations (ACOs)
  coordinated patient care, 46
  defined, 115
Accounts receivable, 146
Accreditation, 434–437
  CQI and, 435–436
  defined, 434
  hospital, 159
  Joint Commission, 435–437
  process, 434–437
ACF (Administration for Children and Families), 404–405
ACICBL (Advisory Committee on Interdisciplinary, Community-Based Linkages), 476, 480
ACTION network, 381
Active listening, 349–350
Actual figures, 146
Acute care delivery. *See also* Hospitals
  alternative/complementary therapies, 176
  ambulatory surgery and procedures, 175
  continuum of care, 176
  discharges and, 175
  emergency services, 173–174
  examples of changes, 172–177
  leadership in, 177–180
  line of sight (LOS), 178–179
  nurse roles in, 175–176
  patient access to services, 174
  patient education, 174–175
  primary care providers, 177
Acute care organization and governance, 157–158
ADA (Americans with Disabilities Act), 208
Adaptation, organization, 98
ADEA (Age Discrimination in Employment Act of 1967), 210

Administration, 160
Administration for Children and Families (ACF), 404–405
Administration on Aging (AOA), 405
Admissions, 160
Advanced practice registered nurse (APRN)
  in acute care, 175–176
  defined, 106–107
  disease management programs and, 252
  leadership competencies, 15
  scope of practice, 52, 68
Advancing Effective Communication, Cultural Competence, and Patient- and Family-Centered Care: A Roadmap for Hospitals, 264
Adverse events, 426
Advisory Committee on Interdisciplinary, Community-Based Linkages (ACICBL), 476, 480
Advocacy
  components of, 295
  as continuum, 295
  nurse role of, 295–296
  in Synergy model, 114
Affirmative action, 209
Affordable Care Act (ACA), 42–46, 493–498
  access to affordable care, 43–44, 45, 46
  ANA support of, 46
  change and, 66
  consumer protections, 43, 45
  defined, 42
  enrollment, 31
  goals, 42
  health disparities provisions, 269
  health promotion and prevention, 191
  health system structure changes, 46
  healthcare informatics, 448
  healthcare quality and, 402–403
  HHS Disparities Action Plan and, 268–269
  impact on nursing, 3
  improving quality and lowering costs, 43, 44–46
  insurance companies accountability, 44
  key features by year, 43–46
  Medicaid and, 136–137
  overview, 43, 130
  provisions effective 2010, 493–494
  provisions effective 2011, 495–496
  provisions effective 2012, 496–497
  provisions effective 2013, 497

  provisions effective 2014, 497–498
  provisions related to nursing, 42
  reimbursement provisions, 131–132
  staffing provisions, 236
Affordable Insurance Exchanges, 136
Against medical advice (AMA), 81
Age Discrimination in Employment Act of 1967 (ADEA), 210
Agency for Healthcare Policy and Research (AHCPR), 381
Agency for Healthcare Research and Quality (AHRQ), 32, 380–381, 398, 404, 431
Aggressive behavior, 329
Algorithms, 455
Allow-natural-death (AND) directive, 51
Alternative/complementary therapies, 176
AMA (against medical advice), 81
Ambulatory care/outpatient services, 160
Ambulatory surgery and procedures, 175
American Academy of Nursing (AAN), 20
American Assembly for Men in Nursing (AAMN), 22
American Association of Colleges of Nursing (AACN)
  CDC partnership, 186
  development resources, 20
  Essentials II, Basic Organizational Systems Leadership for Quality Care and Patient Safety, 468
  Essentials of Baccalaureate Education for Professional Nursing Practice, 69, 186, 268, 468
  Essentials of Master's Education in Nursing, 69, 186
  Hallmarks of the Professional Nursing Environment, 180
  leadership development, 23–24
  nursing shortage and, 234
  political action, 40
  public health nursing, 187
  The Role of the Clinical Nurse Leader, 23
American Association of Critical-Care Nurses, 114, 318
American Association of Retired Persons, 290
American Diabetes Association, 290
American Health Insurance Plans (AHIP), 122
American Nurses Association (ANA)

  ACA and, 46, 115
  Code for Nurses, 51, 54, 59, 61, 237
  on collaboration, 7, 317, 318
  competency definition, 224
  Core Competencies for Interprofessional Collaborative Practice, 480
  development resources, 20
  lobbying efforts, 39
  membership, 20
  Nursing Administration Scope and Standards of Practice, 321
  Nursing Informatics: Scope and Standards of Practice, 295
  nursing informatics standards, 448–449
  nursing professional development, 470
  Nursing Professional Development: Scope and Standards of Practice, 468
  Nursing Safety Initiative, 441
  policy development process, 40
  Principles of Delegation, 361, 368
  staffing, 235–236
  standards, 20, 409
  technology innovation, 448
American Nurses Credentialing Center (ANCC), 453, 479
American Organization of Nurse Executives (AONE)
  development resources, 21
  function of, 23
  guiding principles, *16*
  Guiding Principles for Excellence in Nurse-Physician Relationships, 332, 333–334
  on nurse executive competencies, 11
  patient care delivery assumptions, 111
  political action, 40
  strategic plan, 384
American Public Health Association (APHA), 190
Americans with Disabilities Act (ADA), 208, 277
ANA. *See* American Nurses Association
ANCC (American Nurses Credentialing Center), 453, 479
Annual limits, 127–128
Anticipation of needs, 281, 396
AOA (Administration on Aging), 405
AONE. *See* American Organization of Nurse Executives
APHA (American Public Health Association), 190
Application formats, 213
Applied research, 373

Appraisals. *See* Performance appraisal
Appraisers, 225–226, 228
Arthritis Foundation, 290
Assault, 49
Assessment
of communication effectiveness, 343–348
of motivational climate, 307–308
organizational challenges and opportunities, 110
of organizational culture, 275–276
Assets, 146
Assignment, 367–368
Assisted suicide, 51
Authoritarian decision making, 79
Authority
in classical theory, 96
delegation, 358, 363
obedience relationship, 10
staff, 99
Authorization, 430
Autocratic leadership, 8, 9
Automated medication administration, 456
Autonomy, 53

Baby boomers, 279
Baccalaureate Education for Professional Nursing Practice, 186
Background check, 218–219
Bad debt, 147
Balance sheet, 147
Balanced Budget Act of 1997, 130
Basic research, 373
Battery, 49
Benchmark Benefit Plans, 137–139
Benchmarking, 431–432
Beneficence, 53
Benefit plan, 128
Berwick, D., 409
Best Care at Lower Costs, 120
Bill of Rights for Registered Nurses, 220
"Blame game," 421
Bodenheimer, T., 407–408
Body language, 342
Budgeted figures, 147
Budgets
capital, 148–149
components, 150–151
development process, 148–151
expense categories, 151
management functions, 149
as nurse leader competency, 200–201
operational, 148
salary and wage, 148
staff development, 472–473
staff role in development, 150
Building Successful Research Collaboratives for Healthcare Improvement, 420
Bureaucracy, 97, *97*
Bureaucratic leadership, 8, 9
Business skills, 491–492

CAHPS (Consumer Assessment of Healthcare Providers and Systems), 291
Capital budget, 148–149
Capitation, 126
Care. *See also* Patient-centered care
accessing, 273, 433–434
based on continuous healing relationships, 281, 395
collaborative, 319
coordination, 246, 397
delivery, discharges impact on, 175
direct activities, 368
effectiveness of, 397
indirect activities, 368
patient-engagement in, 246
superb access to, 246
team, 246
Care and service team models, 113
Care management events, *428*
Career ladders, 23
Caring practices, 114
Case management model, 113
Case studies
budget development, 150
change, 91
changing healthcare delivery systems, 176
communication, 348
conflict resolution, 331
consumer satisfaction, 294
delegation, 369
developing excellence, 383
disaster preparedness, 200
EMR/EHR, 459
leadership style, 13
nursing model, 115
organizational culture, 276
patient-centered care, 248
performance appraisal, 227
policy development, 400
poor QI data, 436
risky staff performance, 56
staff education, 478
team leader, 303
Cause-and-effect diagrams, *87*
CCNE (Commission on Collegiate Nursing Education), 483, 484
CDS (clinical decision support), 457
Center for Champion Nursing, 6
Center for Health Design, 283
Center for Medicare and Medicaid Innovation, 401
Center to Champion Nursing in America (CCNA), 66
Centers for Disease Control (CDC)
AACN partnership, 186
Community Health Assessment and Group Evaluation (CHANGE), 190
defined, 404
Centers for Medicare and Medicaid Services (CMS)
chronic illness decision, 394
defined, 40, 404
fraud and abuse and, 58, 60

HACs (hospital-acquired conditions) and, 409
National Quality Strategy comparison, 414, *415*
Planetree Designation and, 263
QIO program, 409
readmission reduction and, 410
Centralization, 96
Centralized organizational structure, 100
CEO (chief executive officer), 157
CER (comparative effectiveness research), 381–382
Certification
process, 214
as QI metric, 430
Certified nurse midwife (CNM), 107, 175–176
Certified registered nurse anesthetist (CRNA), 107, 175–176
Chain of command, 96
Chain of command authority, 99
CHAMPUS (Civilian Health and Medical Program of the Uniform Services), 60, 129, 139
Change
acceleration, sustaining, 73
acceptance of, 72, 77
barrier removal, 73
case study, 91
coalition building, 72–73
concept of, 70–79
defined, 70
facilitators, 74
factors affecting, 70
financial issues, 77
five "Rs" in, 66–70
force-field model of, 71, *72*
instituting, 73–74
internal and external policies and, 76
leading during, 66
organization, 76–77
organizational responsiveness to, 109
participation in, 75
process of, 72–79
Quinn's theory of, 71–72
readiness for, 74–75
reengineering/redesigning/ restructuring the organization, 66–67
regulations and, 76
reregulating professional practice, 68
resistance to, 72, 75–77
restructuring nursing education, 69–70
rightsizing the workforce, 68–69
short-term wins, 73
urgency and, 72
vision and, 73
volunteer army, 73
where to begin when confronted with, 77
work redesign, 67–68
CHANGE (Community Health Assessment and Group Evaluation), 190

Change agent, 78–79
Change coach, 78–79
Change theory, 71–72
Charge nurse, teams and, 310–311
Chief executive officer (CEO), 15, 16, 157
Chief nurse executive (CNE), 15, 157
Chief nursing officer (CNO). *See* Director of nursing
Chief operating officer (COO), 15, 16
Children's Health Insurance Program (CHIP), 135
Chiropractors, 108
Chronic care model, 250–251, *250*
Chronic illness
chronic care model and, 250–251, *250*
as key healthcare concern, 249–251
statistics, 249
Civil law, 48
Civil Rights Act of 1964, 208–209, 277
Civilian Health and Medical Program of the Uniform Services (CHAMPUS), 60, 129, 139
Classical theory, 96
Clinical decision support (CDS), 457
Clinical guidelines, 431
Clinical information system, 453
Clinical injury, 114
Clinical judgment
in patient-centered care, 247
in Synergy model, 114
use of, 82
Clinical laboratory, 160
Clinical nurse leaders (CNLs)
in acute care, 175–176
defined, 106
leadership competencies, 15
Clinical nurse specialists (CNSs)
in acute care, 175–176
defined, 106–107
Clinical pathways. *See also* Patient-centered care
advantages/disadvantages of using, 253
characteristics of, 253
common elements, 253
comorbidities and, 258
content, 255
defined, 253
development process, 254–257
drafts of, 257
evaluation, 259–260
evolution of, 254
implementation of, 257–259
key indicators, 256
nurse practitioners and, 262
preexisting, use of, 257
problems interfering with implementation, 258
purpose of, 252–254
in quality improvement, 431
staff resistance to using, 258–259
standard format, 255
target population identification, 256
variances, 259–260

Clinical practice guidelines
  defined, 261
  development and implementation
    of, 261–262
  evaluation, 262
  insurer interest in, 261
  nonadherence to, 261–262
  purpose of, 261
  use of, 260
*Clinical Practice Guidelines We Can
  Trust*, 376–377, 431
Clinical practice, technology and,
  456–458
Clinical reasoning, 82, 247
Clinical research, 376
Clinical respiratory services, 161
Clinics, 193
Closed formulary, 142
Closed systems, *97*
CNE (chief nurse executive), 157
CNLs. *See* Clinical nurse leaders
CNM (certified nurse midwife), 107,
  175–176
CNSs. *See* Clinical nurse specialists
Cochrane Center and Collaboration,
  377
Code for Nurses, 51, 54, 59, 61, 237
"Code Pink," 231
Coercive power, 327
Collaboration. *See also* Teamwork
  ANA and, 7, 317, 318
  application of, 320
  barriers to, 318–319
  competencies and strategies for,
    319–320
  coordination versus, 321
  in decision-making process, 84
  defined, 317
  effective, 318–320
  in healthcare policy, 40
  interactive process, 318–319
  interprofessional relationships
    and, 320
  key definitions related to, 318
  overview of, 317–318
  as positive experience, 318
  skills requirement, 319
  in Synergy model, 114
Collaborative care, 319
Collaborative initiatives, 438–439
Collaborative leadership, 13
Collaborative planning, 319–320
Commercialization of health care,
  32–33
Commission on Collegiate Nursing
  Education (CCNE), 483, 484
Committees
  ad hoc, 163
  chairperson role, 168
  characteristics of, 162–163
  member roles, 168–169
  nursing roles, 163
  policy and procedure, 167–168
  standing, 162
Common law, 48
Communication, 337–356
  active listening and, 349–350
  assessment of effectiveness,
    343–348

assessment questions and methods,
    343–345
  barriers to, 345–346
  case studies, 348
  in collaboration, 319
  competency, *354*
  confidentiality and, 343–344
  context, 341
  defined, 338
  delegation and, 366
  diagonal, 339–340
  documentation and, 344
  downward, 338–339
  effective, 349
  email, 344, 351–352
  face-to-face, 344, 349–350
  feedback, 341, 345, 346–347
  grapevine, 347–348
  improving, 353–354
  information overload and, 346
  information technology and,
    350–353
  interprofessional, 481
  lateral (horizontal), 339
  lines of, 338–340
  medical records and, 344
  medium, 341
  methods, 348–353
  mobile technology and
    communication, 456
  mutual trust and, 344
  nonverbal, 342
  as nurse executive competency,
    487–488
  overview, 337
  patterns, 109
  policies and procedures, 171–172
  problems, resolving, 353–354
  questioning and, 350
  receiver, 341
  secrecy and, 346
  sender, 341
  sensitive, 345
  social networking, 352–353
  staff development and, 473
  staff-to-staff, 343
  storytelling, 350
  systems thinking, 338–340
  teamwork and, 338
  telephone, 344, 350–351
  upward, 339
  verbal, 342
  videoconferencing, 352
  websites, 352
  written, 348–349
Communication process
  components, 342
  defined, 340
  elements, 341
  illustrated, *340*
  steps in, 340–341
Communities
  healthy, 190
  nursing leadership in, 199–202
  policies and procedures and, 165
  staffing task forces, 236–238
Community Health Assessment and
  Group Evaluation (CHANGE),
  190

Compacts, 68
Comparative effectiveness research
  (CER), 381–382
Compensation. *See also*
  Reimbursement
  annual limits, 127–128
  capitation, 126
  covered services and employee
    benefits, 128–129
  discounted fee-for-service, 126
  employee contributions to
    coverage, 126–127
  for health services, 125–128
  per diem rate, 126
Competence
  cultural, 268, 280–281
  defined, 224
  demonstration of, 224–225
Competencies. *See also* Core
  competencies
  for collaboration, 319–320
  communication, *354*
  for coordination, 322
  in creating positive environment,
    311
  delegatee, 358
  gets results, *324*
  nurse leader, 15, 200–202
  nursing executive, 11, 487–491
  teamwork, 481
Competency-based performance
  appraisal, 224–225
Complaints, to board of nursing, 55
Complementary models, 113
Complexity, 114
Complexity leadership, 13
Comprehensive Unit-based Safety
  Program (CUSP), 438–439, *439*
Conflict resolution, 323–334. *See
  also* Teamwork
  aggressive and passive-aggressive
    behavior and, 329
  case study, 331
  defined, 323
  gender issues and, 330
  individual staff members and,
    329–330
  issues and strategies, 327–332
  key definitions related to, 323–324
  mediation in, 334
  negotiation in, 332–334
  nurse-physician relationships and,
    330–332
  overview, 323
  powerlessness and empowerment
    and, 327–329
Conflicts
  causes of, 325
  defined, 323
  felt, 326
  individual, 323
  intergroup/organizational, 323
  interpersonal, 323
  latent, 325–326
  manifest, 326
  occurrence of, 325
  perceived, 326
  positive view of, 325
  predictors of, 325

prevention of, 326
  staff coping with, 329–330
  stages of, 325–326, *326*
  verbal abuse and, 331
Connective leadership theory, 10
Consensus, 318
Consent emergency exception, 50
Consent implied by law, 50
Consolidated Omnibus Budget
  Reconciliation Act of
  1985, 130
Consonant culture, 274, 275
Consumer Assessment of Healthcare
  Providers and Systems
  (CAHPS), 291
Consumer Health Informatics, 292
Consumerism, 288–289
Consumers, 287–297
  assessment of healthcare providers
    and systems, 291
  costs and, 291
  focus on, 287
  healthcare policy and, 33
  information resources and, 292
  lack of choice, 56
  macroconsumer, 288
  microconsumer, 288
  perspective, 289
  protections, ACA, 43, 45
  public policy and, 289–291
  quality care and, 292, 293–294
  rights of, 290–291
  role in healthcare reform, 289
  special reports and initiatives and,
    291–292
Context, communication, 341
Contingency theory, 10
Continuing education, 479–480
Continuous decrease in waste,
  281, 396
Continuous quality improvement
  (CQI), 419–446
  in accreditation process,
    435–436
  barriers to success, 442
  defined, 202
  disease management programs
    and, 251
  effective, 420
  evaluation, 420
  health information technology
    (HIT), 440
  initiatives, 422
  leadership, 442
  nurse's role in, 422, 443
  nursing leadership in, 440–443
  outcome-based approach, 430
  science of improvement, 420–421
Continuous quality improvement
  (CQI) programs
  development of, 407
  elements of, 407
  evaluation, 439–440
  Joint Commission requirement,
    435
  staff education about, 436–437
Continuum of care, 176
Cooperation, among clinicians,
  281, 396

Coordination. *See also* Teamwork
  application of, 322–323
  barriers to, 321–322
  care, 397
  collaboration versus, 321
  competencies and strategies for, 322
  defined, 321
  effective, 321–322
  examples of changes, 321
  key definitions related to, 321
  overview of, 320–321
  skills requirement, 322
Copayments/coinsurance, 127
Core competencies
  defined, 243
  evidence-based practice, 372–389
  healthcare informatics, 447–467
  interprofessional teams, 372–389
  IOM development, *406*
  patient-centered care, 100, 244–266
  quality improvement (QI), 390, 419–446
Core Competencies for Interprofessional Collaborative Practice, 480
Corporate culture, 108
Cost center, 147
Cost containment, 152–153
Cost-benefit analysis, 35, 85, *88*
Costs
  addressing, 120
  change and, 77
  consumers and, 291
  direct, 147
  disability, 211
  fixed, 147
  healthcare policy and, 30–31
  hospitalization, factors that decrease, 122
  indirect, 147
  per unit of service, 147
  telehealth, 455–456
  total, 147
  turnover, 221
  variable, 148
Country club leadership, 10
Court decisions, 165
Covered services and employee benefits, 128–129
CQI. *See* Continuous quality improvement
Credentialing, 157, 430
Criminal events, *429*
Criminal law, 48
Critical thinking, 82
CRNA (certified registered nurse anesthetist), 107, 175–176
Cross-training, 113
Cultural competence
  defined, 268
  demonstration examples, 281
  toolkit, 280–281
Culture
  barriers, 277
  in communication, 342
  consonant, 274, 275
  dissonant, 274, 275
  filters, 277

  organizational, 274–276
  perspective, 280
  staff and, 278
CUSP (Comprehensive Unit-based Safety Program), 438–439, *439*
Customers, 124

DAMA (discharge against medical advice), 174
Data
  making sense of, *87–90*
  variance, 431
Data collection
  common methods, 86
  in decision-making process, 84
Decentralized organization structure, 100
Decision making, 79–90
  alternatives, selecting, 84
  authoritarian, 79
  barriers to, 83–84
  conditions, 83
  cost-benefit analysis in, 85
  critical thinking in, 82
  data collection in, 84
  decentralized, 116
  deep dive process in, 86
  evidence-based, 281, 396
  five "Rs" in, 66–70
  gap analysis in, 85
  implementation in, 84–85
  individual, 79
  intuitive, 80
  need for, 82–83
  participation in, 114
  patterns, 109
  PDSA cycle in, 86
  process, 81–85, *81*, *385*
  processes, tools, and methods, 85–90
  procrastination in, 85
  results, evaluating, 85
  shared, 72–79
  styles of, 79–81
  systematic, 80
  team, 80–81
  unilateral, 79
  workarounds, avoiding, 85
Decisions
  delegation, 365
  effective, 81
  nonprogrammed, 81
  programmed, 81
  styles of, 79–81
  types of, 81
Decoding, 341
Deductibles, 127
Deep Dive, 67, 86
Delegatees, 358
Delegation, 357–371
  accountability and, 362–363
  assignment and, 367–368
  authority and, 363
  barriers to, 366–367
  benefits of, 358
  case study, 369
  characteristics of, 358, 365–366
  communication and, 366
  as cylindrical process, 364

  decision, 365
  decision tree for, *359–361*
  defined, 357
  effective, 365–369
  five rights of, 364
  issues, 362
  lack of knowledge about, 366
  legal issues related to, 358–363
  malpractice and, 362
  NCSBN guidelines, 364–365
  process, 364–365
  registered nurses (RNs), 357, 361, 362
  relationships and, 367
  responsibility and, 363
  self-confidence and, 367
  staff relationship with, 366
  standards of practice, 361
  state law and, 361–362
  supervision and, 367
  unlicensed assistive personnel (UAP), 358, 362, 368
Delegators, 358
Deming's theory, 8
Demographics, 270–271
Department of Health and Human Services (HHS)
  Action Plan to Reduce Racial and Ethnic Health Disparities, 268
  agencies, 404–405
  chart, 33, *34*
  CMS, 40, 58
  defined, 404
  in disaster preparedness, 196–197
  HCFA, 132
  Healthy People 2020, 185, 187–190, 403
  HHS in the 21st Century: Charting a New Course for a Healthier America, 187
  Insurance Exchanges, 122
  overview of, 404
  priority conditions, 395
  rule enforcement, 60
Departmentalization, 100
Depreciation, 147
Diagnosis-related groups (DRGs)
  assignment, 133
  defined, 132, 133
  elements affecting rates, 133
  severity of illness and, 133
Diagnostic procedures, 161
Diagonal communication, 339–340
Dichotomous thinking, 82
Dietetic services, 161
Direct costs, 147
Direct patient care activities, 368
Director of nursing (DON), 15, 157
Director of nursing practice (DNP), 107
Disaster preparedness, 195–198
  case study, 200
  issues, 197
  leadership in disasters and, 198
  National Health Security Strategy (NHSS) and, 195–196, *196*
  planning, 196–198
Discharge against medical advice (DAMA), 174

Discharges, impact on care delivery, 175
Discounted fee-for-service, 126
Disease management programs
  defined, 251
  development, 252
  disease examples, 252
  provider response to, 252
  purpose of, 251–252
Disparities, 31–32, 267–270
Dissonant culture, 274, 275
Diverse Communities, Common Concerns: Assessing Healthcare Quality for Minority Americans, 271
Diversity, 267–286
  culture and climate and, 274–276
  demographics, 270–271
  health disparities and, 267–270
  health literacy and, 268
  healthcare literacy and, 272–274
  management and, 278
  patient population, 270–272
  response to, 114
  strategies that facilitate, 280–283
  team members and, 310
  workforce, 277–283
Division of labor, 96
DNP (doctor of nursing practice), 107
Doctrine of *res ipsa loquitor*, 49
Documentation
  in communication, 344
  as HCO concern, 238
  legal issues and, 46–48
DON (director of nursing), 15, 157
Do-not-resuscitate (DNR) directive, 50, 51
Downward communication, 338–339
Drucker, P., 8, 11
Drucker's theory, 8–9
Durable power of attorney, 51

EAP (Employee Assistance Program), 228
EBP. *See* Evidence-based practice
Educating Nurses: A Call for Radical Transformation, 69
Education. *See* Nursing education; Patient education
EEOC (Equal Employment Opportunity Commission), 208, 210
Effective care
  framework for, 163–172
  policies and procedures, 163–172
  standards, 163
Effective leadership, 47–48, 110
Effectiveness
  of care, 397
  workforce, 202
Efficiency, 98, 397
Electronic medical/health records (EMRs/EHRs), 92, 448, 452, 453, 457, 459, 463
Email, 344, 351–352, 457–458
Emeasurement, 461–462

Emergency Medical Treatment and Active Labor Act of 1986 (EMTALA), 174
Emergency services, 173–174
Emotional intelligence theory, 10–11
Empathy, 74
Employee Assistance Program (EAP), 228
Employees
  contributions to coverage, 126–127
  in performance appraisal, 227
  problems with, 228–229
Employment process
  application formats, 213
  background check, 218–219
  certification process, 214
  evaluation criteria, 218
  interview process, 214–218
  licensure, 214
  references, 214
  résumés, 213–214
  screening, 213
  selection process, 218
Empowerment
  boundaries/limits and, 328
  in conflict management, 328–329
  defined, 73, 328
  in leadership, 14
  shared governance and, 115–116
  team, 308
EMR/EHR Incentive Program, 463
EMRs/EHRs (electronic medical/health records), 92, 448, 452, 453, 457, 459
EMTALA (Emergency Medical Treatment and Active Labor Act of 1986), 174
Encoding, 340
Environment
  healing, 282–283
  healthcare, 7, *124*, 299–301, 394, 488–490
  physical, 283
  work, 19–20
Environmental events, *429*
Envisioning the National Health Care Quality report, 397
Equal Employment Opportunity Commission (EEOC), 208, 210
Equal Pay Act of 1963, 211
Equity theory, 307
Errors, 393
To Err Is Human, 340, 390, 391, 392–393, 422
Essentials II, Basic Organizational Systems Leadership for Quality Care and Patient Safety, 468
Essentials of Baccalaureate Education for Professional Nursing Practice, 69, 268, 468
Essentials of Master's Education in Nursing, 69, 186
Ethical decision making, 53–54, *53*
Ethics
  code of, 54
  complaints to board of nursing and, 55
  critical issues related to, 30
  defined, 48

ethical dilemmas, 61
fraud and abuse, 57–60
healthcare rationing, 57
healthcare reimbursement and, 55–57
impact on decision making, 52–61
organizational, 60–61
professional, 54–55
research and, 374–375
standards for insurers, 56–57
Evaluation
  clinical practice guidelines, 262
  collaborative planning, 320
  CQI systems, 420
  pathway, 259–260
  in performance appraisal, 223
  self, 225
  staff education, 477–478
  360-degree, 225
Evidence-based decision making, 281
Evidence-based management (EBM), 384–387
  barriers to, 385–386
  decision-making process, *385*
  defined, 384
  evidence application, 385
  evidence presentation, 385
  principles of, 384
  process, 384–385
  QI linkage, *387*
  quality assessment, 385
  in quality care, 433
  question formulation, 384
  research evidence acquisition, 384
  strategies, 386–387
  system incorporation of, 12
Evidence-based practice (EBP), 372–389
  active use of, 377
  advantages of, 379
  applying, 14, 47–48, 78, 110, 152, 158, 186, 222, 264, 272, 293, 309, 322, 353, 386, 402, 421, 462, 472
  barriers to, 379–380
  communication gap, 380
  databases, 378
  defined, 377
  description of, 376–383
  evidence types, 377
  evidence use in practice, 382–383
  evidence-based management (EBM) and, 384–387
  federal government and, 380–382
  incorporation into organization, 382
  information availability, 378
  IOM reports on, 376–377
  lack of knowledge about, 380
  lack of resources, 380
  lack of technological skills, 380
  nursing leadership in, 382–383
  organization not embracing, 380
  patient education and, 383
  policies and procedures, 165
  process, 377
  in quality care, 433
  quality improvement (QI) and, 387
  question, 377–378

research and, 372–376
research not valued barrier, 380
resistance to change barrier, 380
results synthesis, 378
systematic reviews, 377, 378
time barrier, 379
Exclusions, 129
Expenditures
  defined, 147
  Medicare, 130
  national healthcare, 120–123, *121*
Expenses
  categories of, 151
  defined, 147
Expert power, 327
Extended care, 194–195

Face-to-face communication, 344, 349–350
Facilitators, 74
Failure modes and effects analysis (FMEA), 424
Failure to rescue (FTR), 422–423
Faith-based hospitals, 159
False Claims Act (FCA), 58
Family and Medical Leave Act (FMLA), 209
FDA (Food and Drug Administration), 404
Federal Drug-Free Workplace Act, 210
Federal Employees Health Benefit (FEHB) Program, 129, 139
Federal Health IT Strategic Plan, 464
Federal legislation, 40–41
Feedback
  in communication effectiveness, 345
  defined, 341
  giving and receiving, 346–347
  importance of, 346–347
  improving, 347
  methods for increasing, 347
  staff education, 477
FEHB (Federal Employees Health Benefit) Program, 129, 139
Felt conflict, 326
Fiedler, F., 10
Finance and budget department, 161
Financial activities, 146
Financial issues
  budgeting process, 148–151
  cost containment, 152–153
  expenditures, 120–123, *121*
  government health benefit programs, 129–140
  macro level, 120–129
  microlevel, 145–153
  productivity, 151–152
  reimbursement, 123–129
Financial management terminology, 146–148
Finding What Works in Health Care: Standards for Systematic Reviews, 377
Fiscal year, 147
"Five Things You Can Do to Prevent Infection," 405
Fixed costs, 147

"Float" staff, 237
Flowcharts, *89*
FMEA (failure modes and effects analysis), 424
FMLA (Family and Medical Leave Act), 209
Followers, 303
Followership, 303–304
Food and Drug Administration (FDA), 404
Force-field model of change, 71, *72*
Formal teams, 300
Forming, 305
Formularies, 142–143
For-profit organizations, 103–104, 159
Framework for effective care, 163–172
Fraud and abuse, whistle-blowing, 58–59
FTR (failure to rescue), 422–423
Full-time equivalents (FTEs), 67, 151, 233
Functional nursing, 112
Future of Nursing Campaign for Action, 6
The Future of Nursing: Leading Change, Advancing Health, 4–6
  change stimulated by, 66
  collaboration, 318
  on CQI, 442
  defined, 4
  EBP support, 383
  emphasis, 181
  healthcare delivery concerns, 4
  leadership development, 18
  nursing education, 468
  nursing research priorities, 5–6, 25
  on nursing shortage, 234–235
  overview, 200
  recommendations from, 5
  response to, 6
  scope of practice, 52
  transformational models, 115

Gap analysis, 85
Gender issues
  in conflict management, 330
  team leader, 302–303
Generation X, 279–280
Generation Y, 280
Generational issues
  baby boomers, 279
  effects on organizational culture, 278–280
  Generation X, 279–280
  Generation Y, 280
  traditional generation, 279
Global health care, 198
Goals
  alignment across subsystems, 109
  four Ps of, 105
  Healthy People 2020, 187, *188*
  marketing, 104
  National Quality Strategy (NQS), *413*
  quality improvement (QI), 394
Goleman, D., 10

Government departments and agencies, 34
Government health benefit programs. *See* Medicaid; Medicare
Government hospitals, 159
The grapevine, 347–348
Graphs, *89*
Groupthink, 309–310
Guidance for the National Healthcare Disparities Report, 185
Guide to the Code of Ethics for Nurses with Interpretive Statements, 52
Guiding Principles for Excellence in Nurse-Physician Relationships, 332, 333–334

HACs (hospital-acquired conditions), 143, *143*, 409, *410*
Hallmarks of the Professional Nursing Environment, 180
Handheld communication systems, 458
Handoffs, 423
HCFA (Health Care Financing Administration), 132
HCFAC (Health Care Fraud and Abuse Control Program), 57
HCOs. *See* Healthcare organizations
HCUP (Healthcare Cost and Utilization Project), 439
Healing environment, 282–283
Health care
  commercialization of, 32–33
  financing of, 31
  increasing cost of, 30–31
Health Care Financing Administration (HCFA), 132
Health Care Fraud and Abuse Control Program (HCFAC), 57
Health delivery services
  compensation for, 125–128
  covered, 128–129
Health disparities
  ACA and, 269
  defined, 268
  diversity and, 267–270
  impact on quality and cost, 271–272
  NHDR and, 272, 273
Health education
  as nurse leader competency, 201
  professions, 399–400
Health equity, 268
Health inequity, 268
Health information exchange (HIE), 457
Health information technology (HIT). *See also* Healthcare informatics
  challenges, 451–453
  clinical information system, 453
  clinical practice and, 456–458
  in CQI, 440
  expansion of, 447
  federal strategic plan goals, 464
  implications on healthcare delivery, 454–463
  initiatives and issues, 448–449
  meaningful use, 451–453

mobile technology and communication, 456
nursing education and, 458–459
in nursing practice challenges, *454*
nursing specialty, 453
patient education and, 459–460
privacy and confidentiality, 451
quality improvement (QI) and, 460–462
reimbursement and, 462–463
research and, 460
social media, 456
telehealth, 454–456
Health insurance
  annual limits, 127–128
  copayments/coinsurance, 127
  covered services, 128–129
  deductibles, 127
  defined, 124
  exclusions, 129
  government health benefit programs, 129–140
  process, 125
  state programs, 140
Health Insurance Portability and Accountability Act of 1996 (HIPAA), 52, 57, 246, 451, 452
Health literacy
  defined, 268
  impact of, 272
  improving, 201
Health Literacy: A Prescription to End Confusion, 185, 185–187
Health maintenance organizations (HMOs), reimbursement, 55
Health Professions Education, 69, 186, 224, 467–468, 479–480
Health promotion and prevention, 191–193
Health Resources and Services Administration (HRSA)
  continuing professional development and, 480
  functions of, 404
  grant funding, 39
  online educational resources, 271
  quality improvement (QI) and, 410–411
Health system infrastructure, 397
Healthcare and Education Reconciliation Act of 2010, 130
Healthcare consumers. *See* Consumers
Healthcare Cost and Utilization Project (HCUP), 439
Healthcare delivery services, reimbursement for, 123–129
Healthcare delivery systems
  change implications, 6–7
  changing, 176
  disparity in, 31–32
  ethics in, 52–61
  healthcare policy in, 29–41
  legal issues in, 46–52
  multiprovider, 156
  organizations important to, 35
  for-profit and not-for-profit, 103–104
  purposes of, 102
Healthcare diversity. *See* Diversity

Healthcare environment
  changing, 7
  key players in, *124*
  knowledge of health care environment, 488–490
  quality improvement (QI) in, 394
Healthcare expenditures, 120–123, *121*
Healthcare fraud and abuse
  current status of, 58
  Operation Restore Trust, 60
  overview of, 57–58
  in psychiatric hospitals, 59–60
Healthcare informatics, 447–467
  caring and, 449–450
  clinical practice and, 456–458
  implications on healthcare delivery, 454–463
  importance of, 447–449
  improvement in, 463–464
  initiatives and issues, 448–449
  mobile technology and communication, 456
  nursing education and, 458–459
  nursing management and, 453
  nursing specialty, 453
  patient education and, 459–460
  quality improvement (QI) and, 460–462
  reimbursement and, 462–463
  research and, 460
  social media, 456
  telehealth, 454–456
  terminology and standardized language, 450–451
Healthcare Information and Management Systems Society (HIMSS), 449
Healthcare organizations (HCOs)
  career ladders, 23
  change and, 70
  community view of, 157
  consumer-based approach, 289
  culture of safety, 59
  documentation and, 238
  ethical dilemmas, 61
  factors impacting structure, 103
  framework for effective care, 163–172
  leadership characteristics, 5
  marketing, 104–106
  not-for-profit, 104, 159
  nurse leader positions in, 15–18
  organizational analysis, 108–110
  political component, 61
  for-profit, 103–104, 159
  self-scheduling, 233–234
  service levels, 101–102
  structure history, 95
  in work redesign, 67–68
Healthcare policy, 29–41
  collaboration in, 40
  commercialization of health care, 32–33
  consumers, 33
  critical issues related to, 30
  defined, 35

disparity in healthcare delivery, 31–32
increasing cost of health care, 30–31
key issues, 29–33
legislation, 40–46
nursing and, 37–40
overview, 29
policy-making process, 35–37
political process and, 37
private, 33–35
public, 33–35
purpose of, 35
relevance to nurses, *29*
understanding, 39
Healthcare providers. *See* Providers
Healthcare quality, 390–418. *See also* Quality improvement (QI)
  changing view of, 401
  critical issues related to, 421–424
  current reports on, 392
  envisioning national report on, 396–398
  indicators of increased interest in, 402–406
  IOM reports on, 391–401
  key measurement areas, 397
  National Quality Strategy (NQS), 412–414, *412*, *413*, *414*, *415*
  priority areas, 398
  six aims for improvement, *394*
Healthcare rationing, 57
Healthcare reimbursement. *See* Reimbursement
Healthcare settings, 102
Healthy People 2010, 434
Healthy People 2020, 187–190
  access as critical need, 434
  communities, 190
  consumers and, 291–292
  defined, 185, 187
  goals, 187, *188*
  health measures, 188
  healthcare quality and, 403
  national trends, 189
  vision, 187
"Help Avoid Mistakes With Your Medicine," 405
"Help Prevent Errors in Your Care," 405
"Help Prevent Medical Test Mistakes," 405
Herzberg's two-factor theory, 307
HHS. *See* Department of Health and Human Services
HHS in the 21st Century: Charting a New Course for a Healthier America, 187
HIE (health information exchange), 457
High-reliability organizations (HROs)
  defined, 411
  development requirements, 412
  inputs/structure, processes and outputs/outcomes, *411*
  key concepts, 411–412
HIMSS (Healthcare Information and Management Systems Society), 449

HIPAA (Health Insurance Portability and Accountability Act of 1996), 52, 57, 246, 451, 452
Histograms, *89*
HIT. *See* Health information technology
HMOs (health maintenance organizations), 55
Home health, 194, 458
Horizontal structure, 99
Hospice and palliative care, 194
Hospital Acquired Complications (HACs) Initiative, 402
Hospital systems, 156, 160
Hospital-acquired conditions (HACs), 143, *143*, 409, *410*
Hospitals. *See also* Healthcare organizations (HCOs)
  accreditation, 159
  acute care organization and governance, 157–158
  administration, 160
  admissions, 160
  ambulatory care/outpatient services, 160
  classification of, 158–160
  clinical laboratory, 160
  clinical respiratory services, 161
  defined, 156
  departments, 160–162
  development of, 156–163
  diagnostic procedures, 161
  dietetic services, 161
  discharge process, 145
  faith-based, 159
  finance and budget, 161
  framework for effective care, 163–172
  government, 159
  housekeeping/environment service, 161
  infection control program, 161
  information management, 161
  infusion therapy services, 161
  length-of-stay, 142, 159
  material/resource management, 161
  medical equipment management, 161
  medical records, 161
  not-for-profit, 159
  number of beds, 159
  nursing roles on committees, 163
  nursing service/patient care, 161
  occupational therapy services, 161
  organizations and committees, 162–163
  ownership, 159
  perspectives, 156
  pharmacy/pharmaceutical care services, 161–162
  physical therapy services, 162
  policies and procedures, 163–172
  for-profit, 159
  public access, 158–159
  quality improvement (QI), 162
  radiology, 162
  readmission reduction program, 143

respiratory care services, 162
social work services, 162
staff development/education, 162
standards, 163
teaching, 160
Housekeeping/environment service, 161
HROs. *See* High-reliability organizations
HRSA. *See* Health Resources and Services Administration
Human failure, 421
Human resources
  defined, 207
  functions and activities, 207
  legal issues, 208–211
  policies and procedures, 207–208
  use of, 110

ICN (International Council of Nurses), 199
ICNP (International Classification of Nursing Practice), 451
ICRC (International Committee of the Red Cross), 199
IHS (Indian Health Service), 404
Illness management, 273
Immigration Reform and Control Act of 1986, 211
Implied consent, 49
Impoverished leadership, 10
Incentive formulary, 142
Incivility, 231–232
Income statement, 147, 148
Indian Health Service (IHS), 404
Indigent care, 41
Indirect costs, 147
Indirect overhead, 147
Indirect patient care activities, 368
Individual conflict, 323
Individual decision making, 79
Infection control program, 161
Influence, 14
Informal teams, 300
Information management, 161
Informational power, 328
Informed consent, 49, 50, 373–375
Infusion therapy services, 161
INQRI (Interdisciplinary Nursing Quality Research Initiative), 443
Institute of Medicine (IOM). *See also The Future of Nursing: Leading Change, Advancing Health*
  Best Care at Lower Costs, 120
  care delivery rules, 395–396
  Clinical Practice Guidelines We Can Trust, 376–377, 431
  core competencies development, *406*
  defined, 4
  effective programs, 248
  To Err Is Human, 340, 390, 391, 392–393, 422
  Finding What Works in Health Care: Standards for Systematic Reviews, 377

The Future of the Public's Health in the 21st Century, 185–187
Guidance for the National Healthcare Disparities Report, 185
Health Literacy: A Prescription to End Confusion, 185
Health Professions Education, 69, 186, 224, 467–468
  initiatives, 4
Keeping Patients Safe: Transforming the Work Environment of Nurses, 4, 400, 437
Knowing What Works in Health Care: A Roadmap for the Nation, 376
Leadership by Example, 14
  patient-centered care, 245, 287
Priority Areas for National Action, 398
Quality Chasm, 28, 95, 281, 391, 396, 398, 410
  quality initiative, 442
Redesigning Continuing Education in the Health Professions, 479–480
  reports on quality care, 292
  staffing issues, 232
  on teams, 299
Unequal Treatment: Confronting Racial and Ethnic Disparities in Healthcare, 32, 185, 271
Who Will Keep the Public Healthy, 185
Institutional review boards (IRBs), 374–375
Insurers
  managed care and, 140–143
  reimbursement, 140–143
Interdisciplinary Nursing Quality Research Initiative (INQRI), 443
Interdisciplinary representation, 480
Intergroup/organizational conflict, 323
International Centre for Nurse Migration, 278
International Classification of Nursing Practice (ICNP), 451
International Committee of the Red Cross (ICRC), 199
International Council of Nurses (ICN), 199
Internet prescription, 458
Interpersonal conflict, 323
Interprofessional communication, 481
Interprofessional education (IPE)
  defined, 480, 481
  examples of influences that affect, *481*
  illustrated, *481*
  teamwork competencies, 481
  WHO and, 480
Interprofessional practice model, 113–114
Interprofessional teams
  advantages, 301
  defined, 300

Interviews
  as data collection method, 86
  guidelines, 214–218
  job candidate and, 218
  performance appraisal, 226–227
  planning for (interviewer), 214
  process, 214
  structured, 215
  suggested questions for, 216–217
  unstructured, 215
Intuitive decision making, 80
IPE. *See* Interprofessional education (IPE)
IRBs (institutional review boards), 374–375

Joanna Briggs Institute Evidence-Based Practice, 377
Job analysis, 212
Job screening, 213
Job sharing, 237
Johnson, Lyndon B., 209
Joint Commission
  accreditation, 435–436
  Advancing Effective Communication, Cultural Competence, and Patient- and Family-Centered Care: A Roadmap for Hospitals, 264
  defined, 435
  nurses and, 436–437
  as policy and procedure resource, 164
  quality issues, 405
  Sentinel Event Alert, 231
  survey preparation, 436–437
Justice, 54

Keeping Patients Safe: Transforming the Work Environment of Nurses, 4, 400, 437
Knowing What Works in Health Care: A Roadmap for the Nation, 376
Knowledge management theory, 11–12
Knowledge workers, 11–12

Laissez-faire leadership, 9
Latent conflict, 325–326
Lateral (horizontal) communication, 339
Law
  civil, 48
  common, 48
  consent implied by, 50
  criminal, 48
  defined, 48
Leaders
  competencies in public/community health, 200–202
  core competencies, *19*
  in HCOs, 15–18
  increasing, 22–25
  influence, 14
  manager similarities, 16–18
  power, 14
  preparation and development of, 18–20

role in clinical research, 376
roles of, 17
team, 301–303
traits, 8
transformational, 14
values, 14
vision of, 13
Leadership
authority-obedience, 10
autocratic, 8, 9
bureaucratic, 8, 9
collaborative, 13
complexity, 13
conceptual base for, 2–27
country club, 10
in CQI, 440–443
development, 23–24
in disasters, 198
effective, 47–48, 110
in evidence-based practice, 382–383
by example, 398–399
healthcare delivery changes and, 6–7
historical perspective of, 8–15
impoverished, 10
laissez-faire, 9
mentoring and, 23
new approaches, 8
as nurse executive competency, 490
organizational "man," 10
presence of, 21–22
proactive, 92
in quality improvement (QI), 441–443
servant, 13
situational, 10
stressed aspects of, 3
team, 10
transformational, 13–15
Leadership 2.0, 12
Leadership by Example, 14
Leadership theories and styles, 7–15
connective theory, 10
contingency theory, 10
decision, 13
Deming's theory, 8
development stages, 8
Drucker's theory, 8–9
emotional intelligence theory, 10–11
historical perspective of, 8–15
knowledge management theory, 11–12
Leadership 2.0, 12
management grid theory, 10
Leapfrog Group, 405
Learning
facilitation of, 114
needs analysis, 474–476
strategies, 476–477
Legal issues, 46–52
critical, 30
delegation, 358–363
documentation and, 46–48
importance of understanding, 48
patient privacy, 52
red flag areas, 51
scope of practice, 52

Legal terminology, 48–51
Legislation. *See also* Affordable Care
Act (ACA); *specific legislation*
federal level, 40–41
healthcare quality, 402
impact on delivery and policy, 40–41
major, 42–46
Medicaid-related, 135
Medicare-related, 130
policies and procedures, 164–165
state level, 41
understanding history of, 40–41
Legitimate power, 327
Length-of-stay
in hospital classification, 159
management, 142
Liabilities, 147
Licensed practical/vocational nurses
(LPNsLVNs), 67, 107
Licensure, 159–160, 214, 430
Line authority, 99
Line of sight (LOS), 178–179
Lines of communication, 338–340
Living wills, 50
Lobbyists, 39
Long-term care, 194–195
LPNs/LVNs (licensed practical/
vocational nurses), 67, 107

Mackoff, B., 178
Macroconsumer, 288
Macrosystem, 77, 98
Magnet recognition, 237
Malpractice, 48, 362
Managed care
impact on health insurers, 140–143
provider panels, 141
Management
budget functions, 149
conceptual base for, 2–27
diversity and, 278
effective, 47–48
functions, 11
healthcare informatics and, 453
impact of decision making in, 46–52
length-of-stay, 142
in patient-centered care, 245–247
theories and styles, 7–15
Management grid theory, 10
Managers
as change agent/coach, 78–79
core competencies, 18–19
employee barrier prevention
strategies, 228
key functions, 17
leader similarities, 16–18
malpractice claim avoidance, 51
preparation and development of, 18–20
in QI process, 443
role in clinical research, 376
staff care, 19–20
work environment and, 19–20
Mandatory overtime, 237
Manifest conflict, 326

Marketing
elements of, 104
goals, 104
HCO, 104–106
plan, 105–106
Maslow's theory, 307
Material/resource management, 161
Matrix organization structure, 100
McClelland, D., 307
Meaningful use, 451–453
Measurement
quality, key areas, 397
understanding, 425
Measures, 425, 435
Mediation, 334
Medicaid
ACA and, 136–137
Benchmark Benefit Plans, 137–139
benefits, 138–139
changes, 135–136
funding, 135
legislative and regulatory issues, 135–139
mandatory benefits, 138
optional benefits, 138
overview, 129–134
for people with chronic/disabling
illnesses, 138
poverty guidelines and, *136–137*
uninsured and, 138
Medical email, 457–458
Medical equipment management, 161
Medical model, 190–191
Medical power of attorney, 51
Medical records, 161, 344
Medical-industrial complex, 32
Medicare
benefits, 134
diagnosis-related groups (DRGs), 132–134
eligibility, 133
expenditures, 130
fraud and abuse, 58, 60
legislative and regulatory issues, 130–134
overview, 129–134
Part A, 134
Part B, 134
Part C, 134
Part D, 134
Medicare Catastrophic Coverage Act
of 1988, 130
Medicare Prescription Drug
Improvement And
Modernization Act of 2003, 130
Medicare Trust Fund, 129
Medium, communication, 341
Mentoring, 23
Mesosystem, 77, 98
Messages, 338
Metrics, QI
access to care, 433–434
adverse events, 426
benchmarking, 431–432
clinical guidelines and pathways, 431
EBP and EBM, 433
licensure, credentialing, and
certification, 430

OASIS, 430
overview, 425–434
patient experiences, 434
policies and procedures, 426
quality report cards, 431–432
risk management, 432–433
standards of care, 426
UR/UM, 430–431
Microconsumer, 288
Microsystem, 77, 98
Microsystems, 301
Military health care, 139
Mission statements, 13, 101
Misuse, 393
Mobile technology and
communication, 456
Moncrief, Michael J., 59
Motivation
climate assessment, 307–308
defined, 307
strategies to improve, 308
in teams, 307–308
theories, 307
Multidisciplinary approach, 481
Multidisciplinary teams, 300
Mutual recognition, 68
Mutual trust, 344

NANDA (North America Nursing
Diagnosis Association),
450
National Academy of Medicine
(NAM)
core competencies, 12, 111, 178,
235, 243, 450–451
costs and, 120
defined, 4
HCO visions/goals and, 100
healthcare quality reports, 392
IOM reports accessible through,
391, 392, 393
patient-centered care, 100
National Alliance for the Mentally Ill,
290
National Clinical Guidelines, 377
National Council of State Boards of
Nursing (NCSBN)
decision tree for delegation,
359–361
delegation guidelines, 364–365
on regulating professional practice,
68
transition-to-practice model, *482*
as umbrella organization, 361
on workforce diversity, 277
National Database of Nursing Quality
Indicators (NDNQI), 441
National Guidelines Clearinghouse,
381, 431
National Health Care Anti-Fraud
Association (NHCAA), 57
National Health Security Strategy
(NHSS), 195–196, *196*
National Healthcare Disparities
Report (NHDR), 32, 272, 273,
397
National Healthcare Quality Report
(NHQR), 272, 393, 397, 398,
434

National Institute for Occupational Safety and Health (NIOSH), 424
National Institute of Health (NIH), 404
National Institute of Nursing Research (NINR), 373
National League for Nursing (NLN), 21, 40, 120
National Prevention Strategy (NPS), 191
National Priorities Partnership (NPP), 406
National Quality Forum (NQF), 406, 462
National Quality Strategy (NQS)
   aims, *412*
   CMS quality strategy comparison, 414, *415*
   defined, 412
   levers, 413–414, *414*
   priorities and long-term goals, *413*
National Student Nurses Association (NSNA), 23
NCSBN (National Council of State Boards of Nursing), 68, 277
NDNQI (National Database of Nursing Quality Indicators), 441
Needs analysis, learning, 474–476
Negligence, 48–49
Negotiation
   in conflict resolution, 332–334
   defined, 332
   mediation and, 334
   strategies, 332–334
Networks, 156
Newly licensed registered nurses (NLRNs), 221
Nexters, 280
NHCAA (National Health Care Anti-Fraud Association), 57
NHDR (National Healthcare Disparities Report), 272, 273, 397
NHQR (National Healthcare Quality Report), 272, 393, 397, 398, 434
NHSS (National Health Security Strategy), 195–196, *196*
Nightingale, Florence, 282
NIH (National Institute of Health), 404
NINR (National Institute of Nursing Research), 373
NIOSH (National Institute for Occupational Safety and Health), 424
NIOSH model, 229, *229*
NLN (National League for Nursing), 21, 40, 120
NMEP (Nurse Manager Engagement Project), 177–178
NMHC (Nurse-Managed Health Clinic), 115
NMMDS (Nursing Management Minimum Data Set), 451
NOC (Nursing Outcome Classification), 450
Nolan, T., 409
Nonmalfeasance, 61
Nonprogrammed decisions, 81

Nontraditional healthcare providers, 108
Nonverbal communication, 342
Norming, 306
North America Nursing Diagnosis Association (NANDA), 450
Not-for-profit organizations, 104, 159
NPP (National Priorities Partnership), 406
NPS (National Prevention Strategy), 191
NQF (National Quality Forum), 406, 462
NQS. *See* National Quality Strategy
NSNA (National Student Nurses Association), 23
Number of beds, 159
Nurse executive competencies
   AONE work on, 11
   business skills, 491
   communication and relationship building, 487–488
   knowledge of health care environment, 488–490
   leadership, 490
   professionalism, 490–491
Nurse leader competencies. *See also* Leaders
   budget, 200–201
   continuous quality improvement (CQI), 202
   health education, 201
   health literacy improvement, 201
   planning, 201
   political and advocacy strategies, 201
   in public health, 200–202
   staffing, 201–202
   workforce effectiveness, 202
Nurse Manager Engagement Project (NMEP), 24, 177–178
Nurse managers. *See* Managers
Nurse residency programs, 482–484
   core content and experiences, 484
   development factors, 483
   implementation and support of, 483
   orientation and, 478
   purpose of, 483–484
   transition-to-practice model and, *482*
Nurse-managed health centers (NMHCs)
   ACA and, 194
   coordinated patient care, 46
   defined, 115
   as public/community health service, 194
Nurse-physician relationships, 330–332
Nurses. *See also specific kinds of nurses*
   acute care hospital changes and, 177
   code of ethics for, 54
   consumers and, 287–297
   expanding opportunities to lead, 401
   Joint Commission and, 436–437

key issues facing, 3
as patient advocates, 295–296
policy issues affecting, 39
political process and, 37
reimbursement impact on, 144–145
Nursing
   defined, 110
   functional, 112
   generations in, 278
   healthcare delivery changes and, 6–7
   healthcare policy and, 37–40
   image of, 21–22, 237
   men and women statistics, 22
   primary, 112–113
   team, 112
   views of, 21–22
Nursing Administration Scope and Standards of Practice, 321
Nursing education
   entrepreneurial professional development, 401
   focus, 18
   informatics and, 458–459
   IOM recommendations, 468
   restructuring, 69–70
   videoconferencing, 459
Nursing leadership. *See* Leadership
Nursing management. *See* Management
Nursing Management Minimum Data Set (NMMDS), 451
Nursing models
   ACA, 114–115
   care and service team, 113
   case management, 113
   complementary, 113
   defined, 111
   examples of, 113–115
   functional nursing, 112
   historical perspective of, 112–113
   interprofessional practice, 113–114
   nursing practice within, 110–116
   patient navigation, 114–115
   primary nursing, 112–113
   shared governance, 115–116
   Synergy, 114
   team nursing, 112
   total patient care/case method, 112
Nursing Outcome Classification (NOC), 450
Nursing Professional Development: Scope and Standards of Practice, 468
Nursing quality initiatives, 437–438
Nursing Reinvestment Act, 235
Nursing Safety Initiative, 441
Nursing service/patient care, 161
Nursing shortage, 234–235
Nursing teams, 300

OASIS (Outcome and Assessment Information Set), 430
Obama, President, 399
Observation, 86
Occupational health, 195
Occupational Safety and Health Administration (OSHA), 424
Occupational therapists (OTs), 107

Occupational therapy services, 161
Omaha System, 451
Open formulary, 142
Open systems, *97*
Operation Restore Trust, 60
Operational budget, 148
Operational planning, 91–92
Oregon, rationing system, 57
Organizational analysis, 108–110
Organizational culture
   assessment of, 275–276
   case study, 276
   consonant, 274
   defined, 274
   dissonant, 274
   generational issues, 278–280
   historical review, 274
   theoretical view of, 274–275
Organizational ethics, 60–61
Organizational failure, 421
Organizational "man" leadership, 10
Organizational process, 100–101
Organizational readiness, 110
Organizational responsiveness, 109
Organizational theories, 96–101. *See also* Healthcare organizations (HCOs)
   bureaucratic organizations, 97, *97*
   classical theory, 96
   macrosystem, 98
   mesosystem, 98
   microsystem, 98
   process and, 100–101
   service-line organization, 98
   structure and, 99–100
   systems theory, 97–98
Organizations, 101–110. *See also* Healthcare organizations (HCOs); *specific organizations*
   adaption, 98
   autocratic, 8
   bureaucratic, 8, 97, *97*
   efficiency, 98
   high-reliability (HROs), 411–412
   mission statement, 101
   service-line, 98
   structural design of, 108–109
   vision, 100
Orientation
   content, 479
   defined, 478
   in staff education, 478–479
   staff retention and, 223
OSHA (Occupational Safety and Health Administration), 424
OTs (occupational therapists), 107
Outcome and Assessment Information Set (OASIS), 430
Outcomes research, 373
Overhead, 147
Overuse, 393
Ownership, hospital, 159

Paramedical technologists, 108
Pareto charts, *87*
Participation in care, 114
Participation in decision making, 114
Passive-aggressive behavior, 329

Patient-centered care, 244–266
  activation model, 248, *248*
  attributes of, 246–247
  care planning in, 247
  chronic illness and, 249–251
  clinical judgment in, 247
  clinical pathways, 252–260
  clinical practice guidelines, 260–262
  clinical reasoning in, 247
  critical issues related to, 263
  current approaches to, 262–264
  defined, 245
  disease management programs, 251–252
  education in, 247
  elements of, 245
  in HCO visions and goals, 100
  key elements of, 264
  management in, 245–247
  management tools, 251–262
  myths, 263
  Planetree Designation, 263
  self-management and, 247–248
Patient centeredness, 397
Patient-Centered Outcomes Research Institute (PCORI), 382
Patient classification systems (PCSs), 235
Patient education
  in acute care, 174–175
  EBP and, 383
  HIT and medical technology implications, 459–460
  in patient-centered care, 247
Patient experiences, 434
Patient Handling and Mobility: Interprofessional National Standards, 424
Patient navigation, 114–115
Patient protection events, *428*
Patient rights, 165
Patient safety, 397, 400
Patient Safety and Quality Improvement Act of 2005, 403
Patient satisfaction, 288, 293–294, 408
Patient Self-Determination Act of 1990, 49, 50, 290
Patients
  access to services, 174
  justice in treatment, 54
  as source of control, 281, 395
Patton, Rebecca M., 46
Pay-per performance, 236
PCSs (patient classification systems), 235
PD (patient day), 147
PDSA (plan-do-study-act) cycle, 86
Peer appraisal, 225
Per diem rate, 126
Per diem reimbursement, 147
Perceived conflict, 326
Performance
  delegation, 358
  provider, 141
  standards, 163, 224
Performance appraisal, 223–229
  appraiser's role, 225–226

case study, 227
competency-based, 224–225
defined, 223
employee's role, 227
interview, 226–227
legal and regulatory issues, 225
process, 224, 225–227
Performing, 306–307
Perioperative Nursing Data Set (PNDS), 451
Personal Responsibility and Work Opportunity Reconciliation Act of 1996, 135
Persuasive power, 328
Peter Principle, 17
Pharmacists, 108
Pharmacy system, 457
Pharmacy/pharmaceutical care services, 161–162
Physical environment, 283
Physical therapists (PTs), 108
Physical therapy services, 162
Physician care models, 102–103
Physicians
  nurse relationships, 330–332
  overview, 107
  perspective, 331
PICO question, 377–378
Pie charts, *88*
Plan-do-study-act (PDSA) cycle, 86
Planetree Designation, 263
Planetree Model, 263, 282–283
Planning
  collaborative, 319–320
  concerns, 92
  defined, 91
  in disaster preparedness, 196–198
  educational offerings, 476–477
  financial, 109
  information infrastructure, 109
  as nurse leader competency, 201
  operational, 91–92
  overview, 91
  project, 92
  reasons for, *80*
  strategic, 91
  team, 92
  TeamSTEPPS®, 313
PNDS (Perioperative Nursing Data Set), 451
Point-of-care clinical documentation systems, 456
Policies and procedures, 163–172
  approval, 171
  committee, 167–168
  community and, 165
  content development, 170
  court decisions, 165
  defined, 164
  development process, 169–172
  evaluation and revision, 172
  evaluation indication, 169–170
  evidence-based practice (EBP), 165
  first steps in development, 165–166
  formats, 167
  functions of, 163–164
  human resources (HR), 207–208
  implementation and communication, 171–172

  influences on, 164–165
  Joint Commission and, 164
  key issues in development of, *166*
  need identification, 169–170
  objectives, 166
  patient rights, 165
  professional standards and, 164
  quality improvement (QI), 426
  reimbursement, 165
  role of committee chairperson, 168
  role of committee members, 168–169
  role of nursing administration/ management, 168
  state and federal legislation, 164–165
Policy-making process, 35–37
  applying, *38*
  criteria, 36
  defined, 36
  illustrated, 37
Political process, 37
Population health, 190–191
Porter-O-Grady, T., 6, 24
Position description, 212, 224
Poverty guidelines, *136–137*
Power
  coercive, 327
  in conflict management, 327–329
  expert, 327
  informational, 328
  in leadership, 14
  legitimate, 327
  persuasive, 328
  referent, 327
  reward, 327
  team, 308
  types of, 328
Powerlessness, 334
PPS (prospective payment system), 125
Predictability, 114
Premium rate setting, 126–127
President's Advisory Commission on Consumer Protection and Quality in the Healthcare Industry, 391
Prevention, 191–193
  of conflicts, 326
  helping patients understand need for, 296
  job stress, 230–231, *230*
  primary, 192
  secondary, 192
  tertiary, 192
  turnover, 221
Primary care
  defined, 101
  as public/community health service, 193–194
Primary care providers, 177
Primary nursing, 112–113
Primary prevention, 192
Principles of Delegation 361, 368
Priority Areas for National Action, 398
Priority populations, 397

Private policy, 35
Privileging, 157
Proactive leadership, 92
Procedures. *See* Policies and procedures
Process, organizational, 100–101
Product or device events, *427*
Productivity
  defined, 151
  input and output, 152
  issues, 151
  workplace, 275
Professional ethics, 54–55
Professional order entry system (POES), 456–457
Professional standards, 164
Professionalism, 490–491
Programmed decisions, 81
Project planning, 92
Prospective payment, 125
Prospective payment system (PPS), 125
Prospective reimbursement, 147
Protocols, 455
Provider panels, 141
Providers, 106–108. *See also specific types of providers*
  defined, 124
  nontraditional, 108
  performance, 141
  primary care, 177
Psychiatric hospitals, 59–60
PTs (physical therapists), 108
Public access hospitals, 158–159
Public health
  core functions, 189, *191*
  defined, 185
  disaster preparedness, 195–198
  health promotion and prevention, 191–193
  Healthy People 2020 and, 185, 187–190
  nurse leader competencies in, 200–202
  nursing leadership in, 199–202
  population health versus medical model, 190–191
  at state level, 41
Public Health Act of 1944, 41
Public policy
  categorization, 35
  consumers and, 289–291
  defined, 35
  types of, *36*
Public/community health services
  clinics, 193
  description of, 193
  extended and long-term care, 194–195
  home health, 194
  hospice and palliative care, 194
  occupational health, 195
  primary care, 193–194
  public health/government departments/agencies, 193
  rehabilitation, 194
  school health, 195
  types of, 193–195
Purchase care, 41

QI. *See* Quality improvement
Quality, as a value, 109
Quality and Safety Education for
    Nurses (QSEN) Institute, 5, 406
Quality care, 424–434. *See also*
    Quality improvement (QI)
    access to care, 433–434
    benchmarking, 431–432
    clinical guidelines and pathways,
        431
    collaborative initiatives, 438–439
    defined, 408
    elements of, 408, *408*
    evidence-based management
        (EBM), 433
    evidence-based practice
        (EBP), 433
    IOM reports on, 292
    licensure, credentialing, and
        certification, 430
    measurement, 424–434
    nursing initiatives, 437–438
    OASIS, 430
    outcome, 408
    patient experiences, 434
    process, 408
    program evaluation, 439–440
    quality report cards, 431–432
    risk management, 432–433
    structure, 408
    UR/UM, 430–431
Quality Chasm, 28, 95, 391, 396,
    398, 410
*Quality First: Better Health Care for
    all Americans*, 391
Quality Improvement Organization
    (QIO), 409
Quality improvement (QI), 419–446.
    See also Continuous quality
    improvement (CQI)
    adverse events and, 426
    aims for, *395*
    environmental impact on, 4
    evidence-based practice (EBP)
        and, 387
    goals, 394
    as growing, complex process,
        407–412
    in healthcare environment, 394
    HIT and medical technology
        implications, 460–462
    hospital department, 162
    manager participation in, 443
    metrics, 425–434
    nursing leadership in, 441–443
    policies and procedures, 426
    policy and programs, 402–403
    standards of care, 426
Quality report cards, 432
Questioning, 350
Questionnaires/surveys, 86
Quinn's theory of change, 71–72

Radiology, 162
Rapid response teams (RRTs),
    236, 423
RDs (registered dieticians), 107
Readiness for change, 74–75
Readmission reduction program, 143

Reality shock, 231
Reciprocity, 68
Recruitment, 212–220. *See also*
    Staffing
    defined, 212
    employment process, 213–220
    process, *212*
*Redesigning Continuing Education in
    the Health Professions*, 479–480
Redesigning the workforce, 67–68
Reengineering, 66–67
References, 214
Referent power, 327
Registered dieticians (RDs), 107
Registered nurses (RNs)
    in acute care, 175–176
    Bill of Rights, 220
    delegation, 357, 361, 362
    educational routes, 106
    newly licensed, 221
    in work redesign, 67
Regulation, state legislation, 41
Regulations, 76
Rehabilitation, as public/community
    health service, 194
Reimbursement. *See also*
    Compensation
    ACA provisions, 131–132
    customer, 125
    ethics and, 55–57
    healthcare delivery services,
        123–129
    HIT and medical technology
        implications, 462–463
    impact on nurses, 144–145
    insurer, 140–143
    issues, 144–145
    key players in process, 124, *124*
    per diem, 147
    policies and procedures, 165
    prospective, 147
    prospective versus retrospective
        payment, 125
    provider, 125
    retrospective, 147
    third-party payer, 125
Relationship-building, 487–488
Relationship-management cluster, 11
Remainder systems, 387
Remote telemetry monitoring, 457
Reportable events, *427–429*
    care management, *428*
    criminal, *429*
    environmental, *429*
    patient protection, *428*
    product or device, *427*
    surgical, *427*
Reregulating professional
    practice, 68
Research, 372–376
    applied, 373
    barriers, 375
    basic, 373
    clinical, 376
    comparative effectiveness (CER),
        381–382
    defined, 373
    description of, 372–374
    ethics and, 374–375

HIT and medical technology
    implications, 460
informed consent and, 373–375
institutional review boards (IRBs)
    and, 374–375
outcomes, 373
priorities, 383
strategies, 375
Resiliency, 114
Resistance to change. *See also*
    Change
    concerns, 75
    coping with, 76
    defined, 72
    loss in, 75
    response to, 76–77
    value in, 75–76
Resource allocation
    as healthcare rationing, 57
    state legislation, 41
Resources
    availability, 114
    consumers and, 292
Respiratory care services, 162
Respiratory therapists (RTs), 108
Respondeat superior, 49
Responsibility
    in classical theory, 96
    defined, 111
    delegation, 363
    in shared governance, 115
Restraining forces, 71
Restructuring nursing education,
    69–70
Résumés, 213–214
Retention, staff
    importance of understanding,
        220–223
    long-term, 206
    losing staff and, 222–223
    orientation and, 223
    staff role in development, 222
    turnover and, 221
Retrospective payment, 125
Retrospective reimbursement, 147
Reward power, 327
Rightsizing the workforce,
    68–69
Risk management (RM), 432–433
RNs. *See* Registered nurses
Robert Wood Johnson Foundation
    forums, 180–181
    Future of Nursing initiative, 66
    INQRI, 443
    Nurse Manager Engagement
        Project (NMEP), 24
    poll, 21–22
*The Role of the Clinical Nurse
    Leader*, 23
Root cause analysis, 435
RRTs (rapid response teams), 423
RTs (respiratory therapists), 108

Safety
    defined, 393
    patient, 397, 400
    as system property, 281, 396
    as a value, 109
    workplace, 424

Salary and wage budget, 148
SAMHSA (Substance Abuse and
    Mental Health Services
    Administration), 404
Schein, E., 274
School health, 195
Scope of practice, 52
Screening, job, 213
Secondary care, 101
Secondary prevention, 192
Secrecy, 346
Selection process, 218–219
Self-management
    cluster, 10
    support, 247–248
Self-scheduling, 233–234
Sender, 341
Sensitive communication, 345
Sentinel Event Alert, 231
Sentinel events, 435
Servant leadership, 13
Service-line organization, 98
Sexual harassment, 209–210
Shared decision making, 72–79
Shared governance, 115–116
Shared knowledge, 281, 396
Shift manager, teams and, 310–311
Sigma Theta Tau International
    (STTI), 199, 377
Simulation training, 476–477
Situational leadership, 10
Skinner's theory, 307
"Smart" administration pump, 457
SNOMED CT (Systematic
    Nomenclature of Medicine
    Clinical Terms), 451
Social media, 456
Social networking, 352–353
Social Security Act of 1935, 41
Social Security Act of 1965,
    130, 135
Social work services, 162
Social workers (SWs), 107
Social-awareness cluster, 11
Solution analysis grid, *90*
Span of control, 100
Speech-language pathologists, 108
Stability, 114
Staff
    authority, 99
    communication, 343–345
    coping with conflict, 329–330
    coping with inadequate staffing,
        237
    culture and, 278
    "float," 237
    losing, 222–223
    in pathway evaluation, 260
    resistance to clinical pathways,
        258–259
    role in retention, 222
    termination, 222
Staff development. *See also* Staff
    education
    budget, 472–473
    department, 162
    functions, 473–474
    model, *469*
    personnel, 469–472

services organization, 469
specialist positions, 471
Staff education, 467–486
  case study, 478
  continuing education, 479–480
  department, 162
  development description,
    468–474
  evaluation, 477–478
  experiences, implementation of, 477
  group feedback, 477
  interprofessional education,
    480–481
  learning needs analysis, 474–476
  nurse residency programs, 478,
    482–484
  orientation, 478–479
  planning and teaching/learning
    strategies, 476–477
  process, 474–478
Staffing, 206–241
  ACA provisions, 236
  basics, 232–234
  as critical issue, 232–238
  defined, 233
  human resources (HR) and, 207–211
  mandatory, 236
  mix, 233
  as nurse leader competency,
    201–202
  nursing shortage, 234–235
  performance appraisal and,
    223–229
  problem strategies, 235–238
  recruitment and, 212–220, 212
  retention and, 206, 220–223
  self-scheduling, 233–234
  strategies, 236–238
  stress, 229–232
  terms and issues, 233
Standard of practice, 361
Standards
  hospital, 163
  performance, 224
  professional, 164
  of professional nursing practice, 163
  of professional performance, 163
Standards of care, 426
Standards of practice, 361
State insurance programs, 140
State legislation, 40–41, 361–362
State Nurse Practice Acts, 52
Stevens, Kathleen, 420
Storming, 305–306
Storytelling, 350
Strategic planning, 91
Stress, job
  defined, 229
  factors impacting, 229
  incivility and, 231–232
  individuals and, 229–231
  new graduates and, 231
  NIOSH model, 229, 229
  prevention, 230–231, 230
  reasons for, 230
  response to, 231
Structure, organizational,
  99–100
Structured interviews, 215

STTI (Sigma Theta Tau
  International), 199, 377
Substance Abuse and Mental Health
  Services Administration
  (SAMHSA), 404
Sullivan Commission report, 277
Supervision, 367
Surgical events, 427
Susan G. Komen Breast Cancer
  Foundation, 290
SWOT analysis, 92, 105
SWs (social workers), 107
Synergy, 298
Synergy Model, 114, 318
Systematic decision making, 80
Systematic Nomenclature of
  Medicine Clinical Terms
  (SNOMED CT), 451
Systematic reviews, 377
Systems, 390
Systems thinking, 114

Taft-Hartley Act of 1948, 211
Tax Equity and Fiscal Responsibility
  Act of 1982, 130
Taxonomy of Error, Root Cause
  Analysis, and Practice
  Responsibility (TERCAP),
  437–438
TCAB (Transforming Care at the
  Bedside), 67, 437
Teaching hospitals, 160
Team care, 246
Team decision making, 80–81
Team leader
  case study, 303
  characteristics, 301–302
  defined, 301
  followership, 303–304
  gender issues, 302–303
  leadership, 10, 302–303
  tasks and responsibilities, 302
Team leadership, 10, 302–303
Team nursing, 112
Team planning, 92
Teams, 298–316
  barriers to success, 308–310
  building of, 306
  charge nurse and, 310–311
  competency and, 311
  composition of, 305
  defined, 299
  development stages, 305–307
  diversity and, 310
  effective, 305–310
  formal, 300
  forming, 305
  groupthink and, 309–310
  in healthcare environment, 299–301
  informal, 300
  interprofessional, 300–301
  as microsystems, 301
  motivation and success, 307–308
  multidisciplinary, 300
  nursing, 300
  organized approach to, 312–314
  performing, 306–307
  power, 308
  shift manager and, 310–311

  size of, 305
  spirit, 308
  storming, 305–306
  structure, 304–305
  tasks and functions of, 304–305
  types of, 300
  unproductive, 309
  workload distribution, 310
TeamSTEPPS®
  delivery system phases, 312
  implementation, 313
  overview, 312
  planning, 313
  site assessment, 312–313
  sustaining a intervention, 313–314
  training, 313
Teamwork
  collaboration, 317–320
  communication and, 338
  conflict resolution, 323–334
  coordination, 320–323
  defined, 299
  improving, 317–336
  IPE competencies, 481
  as learning priority, 299–300
Technical failure, 421
Technology. See also Health
  information technology (HIT)
  caring and, 449–450
  innovation, 448
  mobile, 456
Telehealth, 454–456
Telenursing, 455
Telephone communication, 344,
  350–351
TERCAP (Taxonomy of Error, Root
  Cause Analysis, and Practice
  Responsibility), 437–438
Termination, 222
Tertiary care, 102
Tertiary prevention, 192
Theory X and Theory Y, 307
Third-party payer, 124
360-degree evaluation, 225
Timeliness, 397
Total costs, 147
Total patient care/case method, 112
Training. See also Staff education
  simulation, 476–477
  TeamSTEPPS®, 313
Transformational leadership
  defined, 13
  development of, 14
  qualities and characteristics of, 14
Transforming Care at the Bedside
  (TCAB), 67, 437
Transition-to-practice model, 482
Transparency, 281, 396
TRICARE, 129, 139
Trust, techniques to promote, 349
Turnover, 221

UAP. See Unlicensed assistive
  personnel
Underuse, 393
Unequal Treatment: Confronting
  Racial and Ethnic Disparities in
  Healthcare, 32, 185, 271
Unilateral decision making, 79

Uninsured, 138
Unit cost, 147
Unit of services, 147
Unit-dose systems, 456
Unity of direction, 96
Unlicensed assistive personnel (UAP)
  delegation, 358, 362, 368
  education and training, 237
  overview, 107
  in work redesign, 67
Unstructured interviews, 215
Upward communication, 339
UR/UM (utilization review/
  management), 430–431
U.S. Preventative Services Task
  Force, 193, 290
U.S. Public Health Service
  Commissioned Corps, 405
Utilization review/management (UR/
  UM), 430–431

Values, 14
Variable costs, 148
Variance data, 431
Veracity, 54
Verbal abuse, 331
Verbal communication, 342
Verified Internet pharmacy practice
  site (VIPPS), 458
Vertical structure, 99
Veterans Affairs hospitals, 399
Veterans Health Administration, 60
Vicarious liability, 49, 362
Videoconferencing, 352, 459
Violence, in the workplace, 424
Vision
  change, 73
  integration in structure, 108
  leadership, 13
  organization, 100
Voice mail, 351
Vulnerability, 114

Wagner Act of 1935, 211
Websites, 352
Whistle-blowers, 58–59
WHO (World Health Organization),
  191, 199, 480
Who Will Keep the Public Healthy,
  185
Work environment, 19–20
Work redesign, 67–68
Workarounds
  avoiding, 85
  defined, 85
  problems with, 423
Workers' compensation, 210–211
Workforce
  diversity, 277–283
  effectiveness, 202
  redesigning, 67–68
  rightsizing, 68–69
Workplace safety, 424
World Health Organization (WHO),
  191, 199, 480
WOTS-up, 90
Written communication, 348–349

Zander, Karen, 254